Rhodesia

Last Outpost
of the British Empire
1890 - 1980

Peter Baxter was born in Kenya in 1962. His father was an agriculturalist and tea planter within the British Colonial Service who moved his family south ahead of the tide of indigenisation that displaced many colonial civil servants. He accepted an offer to join the Rhodesian parastatal TILCOR which saw the family settled in the border town of Umtali adjacent to the beautiful and productive tea estates of the Eastern Highlands.

Peter was schooled in Umtali and left Zimbabwe at independence and embarked on an extended bout of world travel that has never ended. He entered the travel industry on his return to Africa in the late 1980s and remains a committed traveller, conservationist, mountaineer and guide within the region. His enduring interest in African history, particularly the history of the country where he grew up, gave him the opportunity to write this first complete history of colonial Rhodesia.

Rhodesia

Last Outpost
of the British Empire
1890 - 1980

Peter Baxter

GALAGO

GALAGO BOOKS

Galago Books are published by Galago Publishing (1999) (Pty) Ltd
PO Box 404, Alberton, 1450, Republic of South Africa
web site: www.galago.co.za

Galago Books are distributed by Lemur Books CC
PO Box 1645, Alberton, 1450, Republic of South Africa
Tel (Int +2711 — local 011) 907-2029. Fax 869-0890
Email: lemur@mweb.co.za

Rhodesia: Last Outpost of the British Empire: 1890 - 1980

Peter Baxter has asserted his moral right to be
identified as the author of this work

First edition (hardback limited to 150 copies) published, April 2010
ISBN 978-1-919854-39-7
Second edition (trade softcover) published, April 2010
ISBN 978-1-919854-28-1

Typeset by Galago in 11 point Times New Roman
Photographic layouts, colour corrections and cover design
by Madelain Davies

Printed and bound by CTP Printers, Cape

Dedicated to the memory of Jeff Gregory Baxter

Do not talk to me of gold,
the element that brings more dissension, misfortune
and unexpected plagues in its trail than benefits.

Paul Kruger.

The Matabele had previously led a better life, if it is good for anyone
to live the life of a magnificent brigand.

Robert Tredgold

Behold, my son, the wheel-scarr'd road!
Be shamed, and be afraid,
For we, the first, were greater men
Than those for whom we made.
We wrought in death and hunger,
We fought the veld? we few!
Behold this effort of our hands,
This road we built for you.

Kingsley Fairbridge

Acknowledgements

Mum, Rachel and Stevie Sparx for hours, nay days, in the mountains listening to endless repetitions of the same story.

Particular thanks to Peter Stiff for his inexhaustible patience, encyclopaedic knowledge and exacting narrative standards without which this book could not have been written.

Credits for Photographs and Illustrations

Peter Baxter collection, the late Ron Blackmore, the late W Ellerton Fray, Duff Fraser, Imperial War Museum, London, Museum of Military History, Johannesburg, RSA, National Archives of Rhodesia, National Archives of Zimbabwe, Peter Stiff collection, Rhodesia Herald, Rhodesian Ministry of Information, Majorie Todd and the Alistair Webb collection. The copyright of a few photographs are not acknowledged, although the publishers have made every effort ro establish authorship which has been lost in the mists of time or by the winds of change that blew away the Federation of the Rhodesias and Nyasaland and changed Rhodesia into Zimbabwe.

Contents

Name changes since Rhodesia became Zimbabwe

Old Name	New Name
Balla Balla	Mbalabala
Belingwe	Mberengwa
Chipinga	Chipinge
Chibi	Chivi
Dett	Dete
Enkeldoorn	Chivu
Fort Victoria	Masvingo
Gatooma	Kadoma
Gwelo	Gweru
Hartley	Chegutu
Inyanga	Nyanga
Inyanzura	Nyazura
Mangula	Mhangura
Mashaba	Mashava
Marandellas	Marondera
Melsetter	Mandidzudzure
Mrewa	Murewa
Mtorashanga	Mutoroshanga
Mutoko	Mutoko
Nkai	Nkayi
Nuanetsi	Mwenezi
Que Que	Kwekkwe
Salisbury	Harare
Selukwe	Shurugwi
Shabani	Zvishavani
Sinoia	Chinhoyi
Sipolilo	Chipuriro
Somabula	Somabhula
Tjolotjo	Tsholotsho
Umtali	Mutare
Vila Salazar	Sango
Wankie	Hwange

Foreword

This is the first complete history of Rhodesia, the country founded by Empire builder, Cecil John Rhodes. It tells how Rhodes' men engaged Lobengula, the Matabele king, in lengthy discussions while at the same time seeking a Royal Charter and the right for white pioneers to occupy Mashonaland. It tells of the Pioneer Column and the occupation in 1890, the Matabele War, the Matabele and Mashona Rebellions, Rhodesian military involvement in the Anglo-Boer War and World War-I when Rhodesians fought for King and country in SW Africa, East Africa and on the Western Front. Baxter explains the granting of self government by Britain in 1923 and the rapid development that took place between the wars, including the realisation of the tobacco dream. He writes about Rhodesian involvement in World War-II when conscription was introduced as a necessity to halt a flood of volunteers that had become so great that if it had not been stopped it would have damaged the economy of the country. Men and women were detached to British and South African units to avoid the savage casualties of World War-I when volunteers had fought in purely Rhodesian units. In this way the Rhodesians fought in every theatre of war, on land, sea and in the air. Baxter details the tide of white immigration after the war, the establishment and breakup of the Federation of Southern and Northern Rhodesia and Nyasaland and the rising political awareness of the black populace. The bid for full independence from Britain and finally UDI when Rhodesians went alone despite comprehensive UN sanctions. He details the rising tide of the Bush War waged by black nationalists, sustained by the military support of the Soviet Bloc and Red China, and finally the Lancaster House talks that led to a 'free and fair' British-and Commonwealth-supervised elections which led to the black demagogue Robert Mugabe coming to power. Throughout this historical tapestry the author has skilfully threaded in the many often larger-than-life personalities who shaped Rhodesia's destiny from the early historical characters like Cecil John Rhodes, Leander Starr Jameson, Frank Johnson, King Lobengula, Archibald Colquhoun and many others, to the later ones like Godfrey Huggins, Sir Edgar Whitehead, Garfield Todd, Joshua Nkomo, Robert Mugabe Ian Smith and a host of others.

Map of Southern Africa (1600-1667)
Shows Empire of Monomotapa

1

Explorations and exploitations

Portugal and the Mwane Mutapa

D r David Livingstone, celebrated Scottish missionary and explorer, is most widely credited with the 'discovery' of the Victoria Falls. Although exploration of the Zambezi River in the early 1850s was not the most rigorous venture in African travel, it was certainly one of the most iconic. Resulting from it — apart from locating the Falls themselves — much of the south central interior, the virtual entirety of the Zambezi Valley, the Shire River and its tributaries, and the last of the great lake formations of Africa, were all brought into the realm of European ken. In memory of these enormous achievements, a large and heroic bronze statue of the Doctor stands adjacent to the Devil's Cataract in Zimbabwe. From there, with a proprietary air, Livingstone surveys the hinterland that he dared hope would one day come under the sway of British Christianity and commerce.

However, Livingstone's were not the first cobbled boots to tread the dust of the great Zambezi Valley. Many others preceded him, but their names will probably never be celebrated, for they were Portuguese, not British, and often they were people of colour. Frequently too their objectives were nefarious and secretive. By the time of Livingstone's arrival on the Zambezi, the territory of Portuguese East Africa was experiencing an economic resurgence based on the Indian Ocean slave trade. Many Portuguese explorers courted anonymity, but even if they had not, it was the British who were largely writing the history of Africa in those days. And to the British, as events in the region would prove time and again, coming second did not always mean losing the race.

If Livingstone ever felt that there was any irregularity in the claims of primus inter pares[*] he might have fortified himself with the thought that the Portuguese were by then a spent force on the global stage, and had no business leading an enlightened world in geographic discovery. With their greatest glories behind them, and wallowing in moral decay and the infamy of the human trade, he dismissed them as 'an utterly effete, worn-out, used-up syphilitic race.'[1]

Whatever the moral consequences of Portuguese involvement in Africa, and as poor a record as they tended to have as civilisers and colonisers, it is nonetheless a tragedy that so many of their early explorations of the interior went unrecorded. A century or more before the kindling of European enlightenment began to glow, it was Portuguese mariners who were testing the East African wind and peering with curiosity into the dark and forbidding interior of Africa. Simple and often illiterate men — the scrapings of Lisbon's slums and gaols — spread out from coastal settlements and moved inland to map out the trade networks that would later establish Portuguese mercantile dominance.

In an attempt to vindicate Portuguese claims to much of the African interior — then being so imperiously tramped by Livingstone –scholar Dr José de Lacerda produced extensive documentation asserting that all of the discoveries attributed to Livingstone by his peers had in fact been previously explored by the Portuguese. Livingstone was by then well on the way to completing the first recorded crossing of the continent from west to east — a feat that had apparently already been accomplished half a century earlier by two Portuguese mulattos, Pedro João Baptista and Amaro José. Livingstone would soon afterwards proceed north to Lake Nyasa where the Portuguese had already explored.

However none of this was taken particularly seriously anywhere other than in Lisbon. The pioneering accomplishments of Livingstone — and accomplishments they undoubtedly were — were hailed throughout Britain and the English-speaking world…and thus the record of achievement largely remains Livingstone's to this day.

The Portuguese chapter of the East African story began in 1488 with one of a long sequence of great maritime achievements — in this case the arrival at the Cape of Good Hope of a small flotilla of ships under the command of Bartolomeu Dias. Nine years later this expedition was followed by a second, under the command of Vasco da Gama, who then continued around the Cape to become the first European to log a successful sea voyage to India.

As da Gama journeyed home along the East African coast, he was intrigued to observe a bustle of commercial activity under the broad control of Arab merchant mariners and their local Swahili surrogates. Mombasa, Malindi and Zanzibar — the trade capitals — dominated a network of settlements with a distinctly Islamic flavour. Although the merchant fleet posed no particular threat, da Gama brought his cannon to bear in order to enjoy a little plunder. As he did he happened upon the celebrated Arab navigator and cartographer Ibn Majid, who swept his arm up the length of the coast and extolled its riches and beauty. Beauty was of little account to da Gama although riches were of the most profound interest.

In the harbour of Zanzibar da Gama discovered an established trading centre founded originally by ancient Assyrians, centuries before the birth of Christ. The islands saw the first arrivals of Arab traders in about the 1st century AD. Seasonal trade winds linked this most southerly outpost with the rest of East Africa, the Middle East, India, Southeast Asia and China. Zanzibar Island itself was originally held to have no particular value other than as a sheltered harbour from which traders were ideally positioned to interact with the mainland. By the 12th century the main port settlement of Zanzibar Town had been established, and a local hierarchy heavily tinted by Islamic culture and religion had evolved. As da Gama's flotilla drifted into port that day in 1499 his ships would have been jostled by ranks of groaning dhows being serviced by black slaves of widely diverse origins.

Alert to any maritime gossip, da Gama soon began to hear tales of an empire of gold in the adjacent interior. It had been the gold of conquered kingdoms in the new world that had catapulted Spain to global prominence, and da Gama was tempted to speculate that this might be Portugal's moment of opportunity. He hurried home with the news and a mere eight years later, the first permanent Portuguese settlement on the East African coast was established. The site was known as Sofala, an Arab trading village not far from the present day city of Beira, a settlement probably founded sometime in the 9th century. The Portuguese flag was hoisted, and a certain Francisco d'Almeida was appointed the first official resident.

> The Portuguese found here a large quantity of pure drinking water. Flasks of very good perfume are exported from here and a large quantity of glass of all types and all kinds of cotton piece-goods, incense, resin, gold, silver, and pearls.[2]

In 1505 Fort San Caetano was constructed of stone shipped from Portugal block by block. In the meanwhile d'Almeida assembled and dispatched an expedition into the interior to search for the expected cities of gold. Thus began the silent glories of the Portuguese infiltration into the East African interior. What was reported back some months later, when a weary and thoroughly depleted party of men returned, must have seemed almost too incredible for d'Almeida to believe. The daily evidence of his eyes betrayed a slothful and indolent population of local natives, often weighed down by parasites and disease, and increasingly tormented by the slave trade. To an observer there was nothing about them that alluded to greatness. Yet d'Almeida's men returned with excited accounts of an entirely different kind of native. The Resident was tempted to assume, as many others have done since, that what his men had discovered was the progeny of a biblical migration, now settled on a landscape of fabulous wealth. Surely here was salvation for the long guttering flame of Portuguese imperial dignity.

In a way, d'Almeida and others, who ascribed the achievements of the interior peoples to foreign influence, were right. Although he had failed to discover King Solomon's Mines, the Kingdom of Prester John and the palace of the Queen of Sheba, d'Almeida did indeed stumble on a society born out of a vast migration — a migration that laid the bedrock of southern African native society as it is perceived today. Anthropologists and archaeologists today refer to this phenomenon as the 'Bantu Migration'.

* * *

The word Bantu is an umbrella term that broadly defines the indigenous races of Africa that make up the bulk of its modern population. The word is a variant of abaNtu, meaning 'people' or 'the people', as an expression of humanness or simply being human. In this context the name was first coined by German linguist Wilhelm Bleek in his 1862 study *A Comparative Grammar of South African Languages*, from where it has since entered the established lexicon of African anthropological study. Although the principle of the Bantu Migration is simple, it remains a contested theory rather than an established historical fact.

Africa, the cradle of mankind, exported primitive man to the rest of the globe, but speculation persists that later and more modern variants of Homo sapiens re-entered the continent down the conduit of the Nile Valley. However the currently accepted theory of the dispersal of the Bantu race across most of sub-Saharan Africa places its origins near the southwestern border between Nigeria and Cameroon.

Precisely when the development of agriculture and ironwork among the Bantu began to permit more aggressive expansion is not known. What is known is that the movement south of Bantu speakers caused the gradual displacement of an older, Neolithic population well established south of the equator. By the beginning of the second millennium AD the Bantu Migration had reached and begun to cross the Zambezi River into the subject area of this narrative. With the arrival of the Bantu the slumbering Eden of southern Africa stirred against the first breezes of the tempest that was to follow.

The first to be buffeted by these winds were the loose-knit Neolithic communities of hunter-gatherers known as the San, who until then had enjoyed unchallenged mastery of their universe. Other branches of this non-aggressive and spiritual group were to be found scattered over much of the region. In due course they became known to white settlers as the Bushmen. The San lived in unique harmony with the landscape, and initially tried to foster the same relationship with the incoming Bantu. Before long, however, the superior organisation and technology of the immigrants succeeded in driving the San to the very extremities of viable existence. By the time of white occupation, these — the oldest inhabitants of the southern African landscape — had effectively disappeared from the habitable areas of the central watershed and emigrated to the high mountains and deserts.

Today the only tangible remains of the ancient San legacy are cave and rock paintings scattered throughout south and central Africa. For a combination of reasons, both spiritual and temporal, the San recorded an opus of these sweeping mural compositions. It is mainly from this that archaeologists have been able to surmise the history of the San, as well as the approximate dates of the first Bantu arrivals. It is noteworthy too that a certain sequence of paintings, discovered in present day Zimbabwe documents the first appearance of a horse-riding European. The artist who painted this scene must have been one of the very last of his kind to remain at liberty in the country of his ancestors.

By the time of their appearance on the central plateau, and in contrast to the San, the Bantu had evolved strong community, social and political structures. Several branches among those who crossed the Zambezi found on this agreeable landscape the raw materials of an ideal home. In due course a static and loosely confederated society began to form. Meanwhile the majority continued further south to test the boundaries of infinity.

The momentum of the migration was sustained primarily by pastoralism and a system of shifting cultivation that was premised on a limitless resource of land. In such a state of grace, Bantu society displayed little of the aggression and violence that would come to characterise it in later years. As one generation settled, another would pass by and press on. So long as nothing impeded this incremental movement, pressures on land and resources were never felt. The first arrivals were able to consolidate their society without major challenge, as the greater movement continued on without being harried.

By the 11th century AD a more modern social organisation had begun to take root on the central plateau. Evidence of trade is widespread in the form of recovered artefacts of Arab, Indian and Chinese manufacture.[3] Agronomy developed to support interdependent communities that as yet had not bonded into strong and chauvinistic affiliations. Confined between the two great rivers the Zambezi and the Limpopo — and hemmed in on the western side by the Kalahari Desert, and in the east by mountains, the raw materials of a unique culture were there to exploit. Over the ensuing centuries this is precisely what happened.

The first to settle in the area were the twin groups of Tonga and Tavara. The next were the Rozvi who settled in the southeast of the plateau. Behind them came the more numerous and dominant Karanga. It is thought that the vital pillar of Karanga ascendancy was their adherence to the cult, or religion, of Mwari. It has been suggested, probably fancifully, that this belief structure emerged from Semitic origins, since the direct translation of Mwari is 'thou who art', which is similar to Yahweh or Jehovah. To his devotees Mwari was, and remains, the one god concerned with human welfare and piety — and who, in certain instances, is available for consultation and prayer. Mwari was, and again still is, aided in his day-to-day ministry by ancestral spirits who serve in roles not dissimilar to saints and angels. He enjoys earthly support from various theocracies that live by and perpetuate the cult.

As has been common throughout history, God and King might at times have merged, while underpinning religious and cult activity would always have been affairs of state and matters of law and civil administration. The power and significance of Mwari is evident in the longevity of the credo, for even in recent times, when being sworn in at a court of law, blacks always swore to Mwari as the deity. It was the Karanga who are widely considered to be responsible for introducing this powerful binding agent into a dispersed population. This in turn sowed the seeds of commonality and subsequently a gradual blossoming of political and social renaissance. In time the scattered whole would be fused into a single, close-knit and almost common identity.

The prehistory of the area now defined as Zimbabwe — that is the central plateau lying between the Limpopo and Zambezi Rivers — remains speculative except for certain broad hypotheses. Moreover modern politics has not infrequently interceded to uplift or diminish the national reputation. Life, however, was known to have centred around the chief shrine to Mwari, set up on a rocky hill close to the Zambezi River. Here the huts of the Mambo, or Divine King, were situated. The place became known as Zimbabwe, and as successive Mambos made their individual mark the name Zimbabwe came to apply to the Mambo's court, and thus anywhere the Mambo chose to settle.

There are a number of theories as to the origin of the name Zimbabwe, which of course achieved increased historic significance with the relatively recent birth of the nation-state bearing that name.

In the year 1531 the captain of the Sofala garrison, Vicente Pegado, wrote of a fortress in the interior, built of stones of marvellous size, with a tower of more than 12 fathoms. This he called Symbaoe, presumably according to his interpretation of the name that he was given by the natives.[4] Pegado was very possibly describing what is now known as the Great Zimbabwe Ruins, a stone city of exceptional architectural achievement, the bulk of which is still identifiable. The Great Zimbabwe monument visible today covers approximately seven square kilometres.

Zimbabwe has been described as meaning the 'burial place of kings', but more likely it was derived from the Karanga *ziimba remabwe*, or *ziimba rebwe*, meaning the 'Great House of Stone'. This interpretation would certainly describe a place that is in itself a strong evidentiary symbol of local social and political accomplishment, serving as the central shrine and capital of the emerging tribal confederation, from the 11th century onwards. Its construction was conceived by visionary architects and was built over a period of about 400 years.

It represented an advance on Mapungubwe, the first of the city-state units of social organisation that enjoyed extensive trade arteries as far eastward as the coast. Mapungubwe, situated on the southern boundary between present day Zimbabwe and South Africa, lent much influence to the later development of Great Zimbabwe as a cultural centre, and to the powerful polities on the central plateau that followed.

The ruling Mambo drew his power partly from a general acceptance of his divinity, and was supported in this position by the potent religious theocracy. The closed structure of priests and mediums provided a conduit for the common people to the Mambo, and thus to Mwari himself. This fraternity assumed an additional secular function as royal messengers and advisors to the king, which in effect made them bureaucrats, spies and informers. Spirit mediums were usually drawn from the common run of village folk, who by some means had been possessed by the spirits of the clan elders.

Much of the ability of the various Bantu groups to survive and proliferate had to do with their talent for mining and forging iron, copper and gold. This played a large part in the subsequent rise of trade and export, augmenting an existing trade in ivory, beeswax and skins. The introduction by the Portuguese of food-crops such as maize and sweet potatoes also added to the agricultural potential of the landscape, and consequently a sharp rise in the numbers of people that could be supported. It was gold, of course, that played the largest part in trade, and in attracting the Portuguese into the hinterland.

As we have observed, the Portuguese were the latecomers to the gold trade. By the time they arrived on the scene, the Arabs were well established and had already exported an enormous amount of wealth. The natives of the interior too had become a prosperous people by any standards. However, in the period prior to significant European influence, the loose confederation of tribes spread across the central plateau had yet to consolidate into a unified polity. Likewise the Mambo, seen primarily as a medium and prelate, remained somewhat less than a paramount leader.

With such a vast amount of wealth circulating in a closed economy, and with a political identity still needing its rite of fire, it was perhaps inevitable that war would follow. The pretext for this turned out to be neither gold nor territory, but the more humble and primitive currency of salt.

In certain places and at certain times, salt was more valuable than gold simply because of its scarcity. Salt was usually drawn from burned animal droppings and grass. Popular myth has it that a mid-15th century Mambo — a certain Mutota, or Nyatsimba Mutota — upon receiving word that the Arabs had begun trading salt up the Zambezi Valley remarked to his people that henceforth 'they could stop eating shit'.

The people of the highveld duly took up arms and fell on the tribes of the Zambezi Valley. These submitted easily and with apparent good grace to conquest, after which they pondered with admiration the vigour that inhabited their neighbours from the south. While this war hardly entered history as Africa's bloodiest, it was significant insofar as the Mambo for the first time asserted himself as a military leader, and did so under the aegis of an established political entity. Salt consequently became just one commodity among many that began to be traded back and forth from the hinterland to the coast.

The event also incidentally gave the fledgling empire its name. The Tonga and Tavara were so awed by the cyclonic power that had overwhelmed them that they gave Mutota the title of 'Lord of Conquered Lands', or Mwane Mutapa. Many variations of this title, including the ubiquitous Monomotapa, have over the centuries been ascribed to the heirs of Mutota; but currently the former is the accepted version.

Mutota was duly impressed by the grand tribute accorded him, and in this he was not alone. In due course his new title would resonate around the known world as a symbol of native African authority and accomplishment. Meanwhile, the kingdom of the Mambos, now the kingdom of the Mwane Mutapa, emerged from a long period of history cloaked by the obscurity of Africa. Its discovery inevitably excited the interest of the Portuguese who began to pay close attention and report their findings in some detail.

By the death of Matope, Mutota's son and heir, the Mwane Mutapa dominion extended over the entire north and north-west three quarters of present day Zimbabwe, as well as over a significant stretch of the coastal belt of what is now Mozambique. Such rapid expansion required a correspondingly rapid decentralisation, and astute administrative placements at regional government level helped to maintain a cohesive structure of vassal states under the suzerainty of the Mambo. With no comparable opposing power to necessitate a full military state, and with a surfeit of natural bounty, the kingdom of Mwane Mutapa was able to evolve peacefully towards a high level of administration and culture. Predictably, however, as the empire grew, the seeds of its own destruction were sown.

According to, among others, the 19th century South African historian George McCall Theal — whose prolific research was inspired to some degree by Rhodesian founder Cecil John Rhodes — during the Matope period Changa, the illegitimate son of the Mambo and a certain slave woman, was given the governorship of a district occupied by a large and powerful clan. Changa cultivated a power base of his own from where he and his successors waited for the right moment to act against Karanga supremacy.

It is worth noting that the emergence of the Mwane Mutapa Empire was remarkable not just for its wealth and geographical expansion, but also for the ability of the Karanga and vassal societies to liberate themselves from an oppressive orthodoxy that had long been central to Bantu life. It seems that ideas circulated freely that would — perhaps even today — shock the sensibilities of mainstream Bantu society. At about the same time as the English King John was being forced to sign the Magna Carta, some measure of individual human rights had become enshrined in a centralised doctrine between the Limpopo and Zambezi rivers. It is possible that Theal overstated this position, but unlikely that he was entirely misled. The weakness of the system, of course, was that no written language existed to preserve it; it survived only as a state of mind and as such it could endure only so long as peace and plenty prevailed.

As the phenomenon grew, the gifts and abilities of the individual were recognised and fostered. This served to release whole strata of society from the constraints of uniformity. The idea of private property added to this general emancipation, and the right to trade and retain this property over successive generations, created accumulated wealth beyond the usual aggregation of women, children and livestock.

To appreciate the extent of this liberalisation it helps to look at even relatively recent Bantu attitudes to property. Within the mainstream of Bantu society, a conspicuous accumulation of wealth on the part of any person or organisation not directly related to the central leadership will inevitably lead to disaster. At the very least, a plethora of dependants will appear to stake a claim to charity that by its nature ensures the smoothing out of inequalities. More likely, however, accusations of witchcraft born of jealousy or political paranoia will with tragic certainty return the upstart to the common fold with a bump.

This principle, one assumes, would have served to protect the governed classes of Bantu society from the jealousy and discontent that runs alongside basic human inequality. The regions under the sway of Mwane Mutapa, however, chose for a brief season to accept human inequality and to work with it. By doing so they triggered an explosion of individual achievement in arts, religion and commerce. It was indeed a glorious if tenuous moment in African history — a period of self-sustained greatness that has arguably yet to be repeated.

It was this unexpected sophistication in a land of otherwise diseased and oppressed natives that so captivated early Portuguese explorers. The finesse of religious practice, the practicality and effectiveness of political administration, the pleasantness of language and general deportment, were subjects of Portuguese praise. Since those times, archaeologists have unearthed ample evidence to support such early impressions. Imported items from across the Middle and Far East appeared in the form of fine ceramics from Asia and Persian rugs from the Gulf as well as glass beads and porcelain from Gujarat and China.

The royal household was run on lavish lines. A ruler moved through his day to day affairs with as many as 60 attendants and a seraglio of anything up to 3 000 wives. Militarily the Mwane Mutapa, at the peak of the dynasty, could field upwards of 100 000 men for a single campaign. This was greater than even the accumulated military might of the Zulus, that would explode onto the African landscape a little over a century later.

However, by the close of the 15th century, as the Portuguese were poised to step onto the stage, the usual indications of end of empire had begun to find a way into the stitch of the imperial cloth. The most damaging of these was the customary rot of a disputed succession alongside a growing and general complacency. The diminishing of gold reserves, the depletion of elephant on the plateau, and a curious reluctance on the part of the dominant groups to capitalise on the rich trade in slaves, all contributed to a decline. A slow degeneration gathered pace as a succession of weak Mwane Mutapa ascended and were then toppled from the throne. In themeantime the Changa centre of power aligned with the Rozvi in the south and created an opposing power known as Urozvi. Changa kings, who were by then using the addition of the Arab title Emir, ruled the Urozvi. Changamire in due course became arguably a more potent dynastic title than Mwane Mutapa itself.

The seat of the Mwane Mutapa was weakened, but not destroyed. Each side glared at the other over a parapet of mutual hostility with neither caring to acknowledge the truth of their mutual decline. This was the condition of native society on the central plateau that allowed for the first effective Portuguese penetration. While it is true that the great days had passed, the power of the Mwane Mutapa was by no means exhausted. All the trappings of centuries of monarchy were still evident, and these were, of course, deeply attractive to outsiders seeking gold, opportunity and prestige.

When word of all this reached Lisbon the attention of a famished monarchy was immediately captured. With the arrival of the Portuguese in Brazil in 1 500, Portugal staked its claim to a large mass of the Americas, but there the easy pickings of Central America were absent. Apart from the Arabs, no other foreign nation had made any claim to East Africa, and if judiciously exploited, this could be the opportunity the poor man of Europe needed to realise his destiny.

The Church was quicker to react than the State, for Africa could be relied upon to be as rich in pagan souls as it was in gold and silver. A Jesuit priest by the name of Father Dom Gonzalo da Silveira followed the scent of paradise and arrived at the Port of Inhambane some years in advance of the first official expedition. In his wake he brought not only the gospel, but also the echoes of cannon and musketry. His were undoubtedly the first substantive steps towards the eventual and overwhelming domination of the region by European powers.

Gonzalo da Silveira was the first Christian missionary to approach the seat of the Mwane Mutapa, and in 1561 he actually did succeed in baptising the incumbent Mambo. His success was perhaps less a triumph of the message than the result of a desire to please on the part of a young monarch — and very likely a brief lapse in vigilance on the part of the attendant Arab traders. But it was not long before a combination of suspicion, superstition and Moslem intrigue brought about Silveira's end. He was murdered, and his body dumped in the Musengezi River, which it was hoped would carry away both his corpse and his Christian legacy. This was not to be. In a devout Catholic nation news of the martyrdom of Father da Silveira provided precisely the casus belli needed to motivate the secular authorities in Lisbon to act.

Within a very short time of the news becoming known the Portuguese nation was galvanised into frenzied demands for a Christian crusade. Obviously the common perception of the Mwane Mutapa was vague at best, and tailored largely to appeal to a slavishly religious population. Contemporary etchings of Silveira's martyrdom place the setting in fields of classical architecture with men of medieval cut garrotting a faithful Christian prelate. The incident stirred a visceral reaction that transcended mere commercial adventure; among the morally superior if materially disadvantaged Portuguese, the matter soon became one of national prestige, and calls for revenge grew shrill.

An ad hoc expedition was hastily authorised to sail from the Algarve in search of national satisfaction. The expedition was passionately hailed but predictably sluggish. It finally took to the water only in 1569, a full eight years after the death of da Silveira. Thereafter it proceeded with no clear objective towards a barely understood battlefield on the farthest reaches of the known world. After blundering on the high seas for over a year, the ships landed on the east coast, and by the end of 1571 the expedition had established itself at the settlement of Senna at the mouth of the Zambezi River. After a devastating wet season during which malaria claimed the lives of a great many men, a lacklustre attack was finally directed towards the interior.

It must have been a very curious sight for the tribes of the Zambezi to behold a body of sweating and feverish white men marching resolutely up the rugged valley in their polished mail and armour, and in their midst, lumbering artillery pieces and streaming standards born aloft to display the symbols of Empire and Christendom. Although relatively few in number, these armed men clearly marched with aggressive intent. The natives duly formed up into their traditional battle lines, but were quickly cut down in droves by concentrated musket and cannon fire. After a short and one-sided battle, the tribes melted away into the forests of the valley floor, leaving the Portuguese free to occupy the chief kraals and consolidate their conquest.

Despite being heavily outnumbered the Portuguese suffered minimal losses and were able quickly to quickly turn both their guns and attention south towards the heartland of the Mwane Mutapa Empire. But the attack was never mounted. The expedition was succumbing rapidly to enemies against which it had no defence. Malaria, blackwater fever and other unnamed scourges where killing off men at a rate that could not be sustained. In due course it became evident to all that they were dying at an unbearable rate. The survivors were faced with no choice other than to retreat rapidly back towards the hardly less malodorous Zambezi mouth.

It must have come as a considerable relief then, for the commanders to be met in Senna by a delegation from the Mwane Mutapa anxious to discuss terms of peace. However, any advantage gained was only measured submission on the part of the Mwane Mutapa, and was overridden by the silent killers of Africa. Malaria was to the Portuguese invasion force what the Russian winter would be to Napoleon. The expeditionary force was decimated by waves of fever, and internal dissent and poor leadership ran what remained to ground no less than this.

In due course a more ordered and peaceful settlement came about, under which ventures into the interior took on a significantly less aggressive tone. A veteran of the Zambezi incursion, a certain Fernandes Homen, decided to abandon the gateway of the Zambezi and approach the central plateau directly east from Sofala. By this route he was not long in reaching the clean embraces of the escarpment and the feverless high country beyond. There, by a combination of threat and treaty, he was instrumental in prying one or two vassal groups away from their loyalty to the Mwane Mutapa.

While this expedition lacked the forlorn pageantry of its predecessors, it did mark a trend that in future would far exceed the bounty achieved by military conquest. This was the establishment of a network of trade treaties and contracts with tribal groupings all along the fringe of the Mwane Mutapa Empire. These were often groups that only nominally owed allegiance to the centre and were thus easily persuaded to ally themselves with the new and exciting power finding its feet on the coast. Trade was brisk and wealth began to circulate, until in due course Portuguese pirate diplomacy permeated like an infarction to the very heart of the crumbling Mwane Mutapa kingdom.

These positive events in East Africa, meanwhile, were soon to be compromised by the greatest Portuguese national embarrassment of all time. In 1578 a youthful King Sebastian led a military campaign to seize Morocco, and was so completely defeated that it is conceivable that Portugal never recovered. Apart from the king's own death or capture this catastrophic reversal ensured that the days of grand intervention overseas were abruptly brought to an end. Just when dividends might have been expected to flow from the lives and revenue so far invested, Portuguese power in east and central Africa crumbled. Impetus for exploration and exploitation was taken out of the hands of agents of the Crown and largely given over to a new class of colonialist known as Prazieros.

These Praziero were a breed of independent trader barons that had grown out of the network of earlier treaty gatherers who built the economic empire, some of whom evolved into freebooters of great personal means and consequence while others simply lapsed into assimilation and evolved mulatto chieftainships barely distinguishable from the native chieftainships themselves. By the beginning of the 19th century some Prazieros governed vast and almost entirely autonomous fiefdoms. They proliferated mainly in the Zambezi Valley and owed no significant allegiance to either the colonial or the national government.

As the Prazieros proliferated, some acquired a grim reputation. These were mainly working class men or criminals who were given 'leases' over immense territorial concessions and charged with the task of creating enterprise. Usually this enterprise consisted of harvesting the readily available manpower and selling it off on the Indian Ocean slave market. After the abolition of the slave trade, this practice shifted only slightly into a system of centrally traded bonded labour.

While the Portuguese presence fell short of a decisive occupation, their gradual insinuation into the community resulted in an ever-growing dependence on them by the Mwane Mutapa. Among other services the Portuguese provided armed assistance during the monarch's many wrangles with wayward vassals. In exchange the Praziero were permitted to charge their own taxes, take over the operations of mines, raise their own armed levies and live in almost every respect as native chiefs.

The Portuguese also held regular trade markets where trade goods were bought, sold and dispatched. It is estimated that by 1596 upwards of 500 Portuguese Prazieros and traders were active in the Mwane Mutapa Kingdom, the largest and most established centre of which was Dambarare, situated just north of modern day Mazoe in central Zimbabwe. It might be added that the gathering empire of the Urozvi suffered little if any intrusion by the Portuguese, for although substantial gold deposits existed in the southeast, this fact remained unknown to the Portuguese until it was too late for them to be fully exploited.

By the reign of the indolent and corrupt Mwane Mutapa sovereign Gatsi Ruseri between 1589 and 1623, the stage had more or less been set for the end of the empire. The Portuguese had already loosened the bond of hegemony that for 200 years or more had held the subject groups to the core of the Mwane Mutapa. In no small measure this helped to undermine the structure of local society. The Urozvi, sensing a decline in Mwane Mutapa fortunes, intensified its pressure. Gatsi Ruseri, recognising that his situation had become too perilous to be sustained, handed himself, his office and his entire domain to the Portuguese in exchange for their protection.

In 1610 a limited rebellion broke out against the Portuguese, mainly fomented by the Urozvi. In the face of this insurrection the Portuguese temporarily retreated from the country. Most took brief refuge in the settled areas at the mouth of the Zambezi River, but it was not long before they returned. A substantial Portuguese counter-attack routed small rebel units and re-imposed general control. The Portuguese then installed a puppet Mwane Mutapa in the traditional seat of Chitake. Although they regaled him with European honours, he was confined under arms and allowed to rule and move freely only in a small area.

Meanwhile new and elaborate plans began to be formulated in Portugal for the effective colonisation of the central plateau. Initial economic enterprise had proved lucrative, while the ministrations of the Catholic Church pioneered the proselytizing of the natives. In the end, however, these plans were illusory. Global events and the profound reverses suffered in Portugal cut the ground out from under the feet of those early and stalwart colonists. Resources were gradually diverted from East Africa to such diverse locations as India and Brazil. In Portuguese East Africa, as the territory came to be known, activities of the colonists were confined to the port cities and the immediate hinterland. The greatest Portuguese contribution to Africa turned out to be the humble imports of sweet potatoes and maize from South America. It was thanks to these two important food staples that the massive population explosion of the colonial period was made possible.

The Portuguese, meanwhile, watched in disappointment as, in 1652, a Hollander by the name of Jan van Riebeck landed a small flotilla at the Cape of Good Hope. The regions of the Cape and Natal had until then vaguely figured in Portuguese plans for the future, but with the arrival of the Dutch the moment was lost. Van Riebeeck's arrival, of course, began the long process of Anglo/Dutch domination of southern Africa.

By the time the Portuguese withdrew entirely from the central plateau, the ancient kingdom of the Mwane Mutapa had itself withered to a shadow of its former glory. The value of trade from the interior to the Indian Ocean diminished as the reserves of gold and ivory were depleted. But this was not the only reason. As we have seen, the rulers of the central plateau also curiously failed to move towards exploitation of the Indian Ocean slave trade — a major economic factor to the north and east. The economic decline precipitated a social decline and the influence of the local Portuguese authority diminished. Although not wholly dissipated, little of the past magnificence remained.

The seat of authority lingered for many years — with the last of the Mwane Mutapas dying out only in 1902. But by the time of the arrival of the next wave of European colonists, there were almost no visible traces remaining on the landscape of what had once been a great empire. It was as if a curtain had fallen at the end of a three-act play — as the audience drifted out of the auditorium, the actors packed up and left the stage. After the withdrawal of the Portuguese, another century passed before events of any consequence shed new light on the life of the central plateau. By then the social and moral advances of Mwane Mutapa had been forgotten, and Bantu life had returned to the great and moderating orthodoxy of old.

As the years slipped by, the heirs of Mwane Mutapa lost all power and aspiration to rule, and were gradually subjected to the Rozvi. With neither challenge nor contest, the powers of the Rozvi also atrophied, and in due course they too became a ruling caste of indolent and effete aristocrats. They existed mainly on the impotence of their subjects and by a mystical and increasingly arcane claim to cult ascendancy. To this no significant challenge appears to have been mounted, and the population of the central plateau simply waited in a state of nervous suspension for the next great chapter of change to overtake their history.

2

Genesis of the Matabele

Almost at the moment that the Bantu Migration reached its conclusion, an age of great suffering replaced the relative peace of centuries past. Unsurprisingly the day came when the great movement was halted, setting in motion upheaval and change. In due course this brought about the Mfecane, one of the first of the great humanitarian tragedies to blight the region in the modern age.

The agency that arrested the Bantu Migration was not, as one might suppose, the end of the African land mass itself, but the boundaries of white expansion that — following the Dutch landings of 1652 — had pushed steadily forward, eventually reaching some considerable distance north of the Cape itself. At first the Dutch occupied the Cape peninsular for the sole purpose of victualing passing ships of the Dutch East India Company. By 1770, however, Dutch and Huguenot religious exiles had succeeded in pushing the occupation beyond the hinterland of Cape Town, and certainly beyond the direct interest or control of the Dutch East India Company.

Independent minded settlers, styling themselves Boers — meaning 'farmers' but with a certain added nationalistic flavour — fortified by gunpowder and Calvinism, succeeded in expanding their land holdings all the way to the south bank of the Great Fish River. There they confronted the vanguard of the Bantu Migration, which they looked upon as something of a biblical plague. Bible doctrine had taught them that blacks were the Sons of Ham — the pagan Canaanites whom the people of Israel had been given licence by God to vanquish. To the Boer this was their promised land, and the symbolic parallels thereafter are hardly difficult to divine.

Historians describing the effect of this collision between two equally conservative cultures have often drawn on the simple analogy of a breaking wave, which is a convenient way to simplify a highly complex human, mercantile and natural collision. Channelled by the Drakensberg Mountains, the human wave quickened its pace down the narrow coastal plain of Natal until it broke against a sea wall of white occupation. The wave then turned back on itself, fermenting a process of rapid political and social crystallisation among a people of otherwise borderless and free-roaming sensibility. Independent family and clan units merged into tribal confederations in order to mount credible defences against other similarly forming coalition. As populations burgeoned, complex pressures created a violent backwash and tensions mounted steadily. Ever more desperate bickering and jostling created the alchemy of a firestorm that needed only a spark of strong leadership to ignite it.

That spark came in the form of the young bastard child of an insignificant chieftain, a black Caesar who rose to create a martial cult with perhaps no parallel in African history. The story of Shaka and the Zulu nation is long, convoluted and fascinating, but unfortunately it falls outside the scope of this narrative; it is important only insofar as it affected political events north of the Limpopo some half a century later.

Shaka Zulu — sometimes Chaka or Tshaka — was born into a society galvanised by the events described above. He possessed the common personality defects of tyrannical leadership whereby he tolerated no moderation and foreswore all humanity in his rise to power. Cruelty, paranoia and great personal authority combined with charisma and vast intelligence to create a despot both dreadful and magnificent. Whatever else he might have been, Shaka was moulded in perfect symmetry to his times, and was constituted in mind and body perfectly to forge and shape the destiny of a nervous land.

What was probably most remarkable about Shaka was his development and use of almost revolutionary military tactics. Refining a somewhat haphazard system of indigenous warfare, he introduced Romanic concepts of assault weaponry, disciplined manoeuvre and tactics. Against this kind of advanced military philosophy there was at that time and in that place little effective defence. Thus began a process of natural selection that to this day has left a legacy of stern, intractable and courageous people.

Shaka instituted a reign of terror on the littoral of Natal that in due course spilled over to consume the Basutho tribes of the interior. Conquest and counter conquest, relocation and dislocation, all combined in a conflagration that raged across the sub-region and became known as the Mfecane, or the Burning.

The significance of Shaka and the impact of his vision long outlived the political eminence of the Zulu people themselves. The effects of the Mfecane and the predations of the Zulu military creed created waves of traumatised refugees who to a large extent reversed the flow of the Bantu Migration. This time, however, the moving tribes found not empty and inviting lands, but country already occupied. The skills of Zulu warfare, learned often by default, then became applied in a cycle of ongoing slaughter and expulsion. The domino effect of relocation and dislocation spread across the highveld like a firestorm, leaving utter desolation in its wake.

Of the three main Bantu groups formed by the violent permutations occurring on the littoral of Natal, it was the Matabele, or Ndebele under Mzilikazi that would most profoundly affect the political direction of the trans-Limpopo territory. The other two were the Angoni under Zwangendaba and the Shangaan, or Gaza, under Shoshangane. In fleeing the Zulu these latter two groups moved north through Swaziland, the Shangaan eventually to settle uneasily in the Gaza region of southern Mozambique, and the Angoni in the lakes region of Nyasaland much further to the north.

Mzilikazi was the most potent, the most poetic and the most charismatic of the three refugee empire builders. His career had begun as a favoured general in Shaka's military within which he commanded the regiments and the people of the Kumalo clan. He was personally acquainted with Shaka and had been an astute student of his methods. In return he was favoured with a rare degree of paternalism from the royal kraal. The rupture came when Mzilikazi, on returning from a particular campaign, decided to not relinquish captured cattle to Shaka as was required by law and protocol. With due regard to Mzilikazi's favoured status the King sent a group of emissaries to enquire politely after the oversight. The messengers were shorn of their ceremonial accoutrements and sent back to the king empty handed. Shaka is said to have lamented:

'Ho! My child has voided his diarrhoea on me!'

Mzilikazi had no choice but to evacuate his clan as quickly as possible before the inevitable bloody storm overtook him. He led the Kumalo clan northwest by a circuitous route into the vicinity of present-day Gauteng, where they settled for a short while. With a degree of ruthlessness and cruelty that would come in time to characterise him, Mzilikazi carved his own path of blood through the already devastated countryside. As he did so, he assimilated numbers of related Swazi and Basutho tribesmen who began to form the nucleus of a new nation. In time the Matabele grew to become a major force in southern Africa.

For the time being, however, they remained a fugitive people. Shaka, and more importantly his successor Dingane, could not be seen to sanction secession. Therefore the Zulus made a number of attempts to bring the Matabele to heel and to punish Mzilikazi personally. Although ultimately unsuccessful, tough campaigns were fought between the two fraternal groups that served to keep the Matabele in a semi-nomadic state. A second factor that frustrated Mzilikazi and his people, as they searched for a permanent home, was the sudden intrusion of migrating Boers arriving from the south. The Great Trek was then reaching its climax, and under its aegis a steady stream of Boer malcontents were moving up from the Cape in search of land beyond the reach of the British.

To the Boers these bruising encounters with the Matabele were the first and only real obstacle to their epic migration north. For both the Zulu and the Matabele, however, the effects were a great deal more humbling. It was the first time since the Portuguese campaign of two centuries earlier that native armies had been challenged by mechanised warfare, and certainly the first exposure to powder and lead suffered by the two warrior castes.

The back country whites who made up the Boer vanguard, on the other hand, were rugged individualist and frontier people well adapted to survival beyond the pale. They had perfected the tactic of drawing their wagons into the protective circle of a laager and using the open country of the highveld to direct withering fusillades of fire outward. Against this courage and iron discipline supported by spears and shields could have little impact. Battles were fierce and terrifying, but with a handful of brutal exceptions, they were steeply one sided.

The Matabele people were driven across the Limpopo River and arrived in the present-day Matabeleland South Province of Zimbabwe around 1838/9. Here they found the manna of their dreams in a deceptively fine and unpopulated realm. But it was hardly unpopulated, of course, for the orphans of the Mwane Mutapa — soon to be styled Mashona — a name given after the Matabele word itshonalanga, or 'where the sun sets' — were still to be found living in their pleasant land. The Mashona were regarded by the Matabele as being in every respect irrelevant, as indeed they appeared to be. Neither were the Matabele the first to intrude on the century-long slumber of the Mashona, for indeed very bad things had recently been happening to the hapless natives of the plateau.

The long decline of the pervious century had ended one day, both brutally and abruptly. The runaway cult of militarism that had gripped the south broke over the horizon and arrived on the central plateau towing horror and catastrophe in its wake. With a degree of force and violence never before known, the population of the watershed was attacked and decimated. First it was Zwangendaba, with his now swollen and confident army of Angoni warriors, who surged up the Sabi Valley from Gaza, looking for new spoils to pillage and new people to kill. Here they found plenty of both. Later the Shangaan would follow and do precisely the same. Thus when the Matabele made their appearance, the Mashona had been softened up and were ripe for a regime of systematic abuse and exploitation. While his two predecessors played small and sporadic roles in the future of what would become Zimbabwe, Mzilikazi and his Matabele remained to scar and shape the country up to this day and beyond.

The relationship between the Matabele and the Mashona has throughout its duration been circumspect and replete with suspicion and violence. When Mzilikazi formalised his occupation of Matabeleland, he found that no war of conquest was necessary. With the general exception of the religious hierarchy he subjected the population to the most consistently brutal usage any African tyrant had so far devised.

Mzilikazi has been variously described as an awful despot of matchless cruelty and a man of subtle wit and deep sensitivity, with an occasional tendency towards both humour and kindness. Such dichotomies are not unusual in great leaders. In terms of his qualities of both ruthlessness and humanity, Mzilikazi can only be judged against the rigours of his times. Then, as now, empires that are formed and sustained by the force of an individual personality burn bright but briefly. Rarely is there time for statutes or traditions of government to develop, and even less for them to be passed on, sanctified or recorded.

Despite this the Matabele did develop an effective system of administration based on the predominance of the military. Under this code large areas of land were ceded to the control of generals — or indunas — centred on a military garrison occupied by a particular regiment. While decentralisation allowed for better government of remote areas, it also exposed the centre to the risk of localised loyalties coalescing against it. Mzilikazi responded to this by deploying his extensive household of wives to various outlying centres where they were able to test the wind for traces of insurrection. It goes without saying that for any instance treason, real or perceived, punishment was swift and severe.

Thus Mzilikazi established the real and social boundaries of his new kingdom. It was buttressed in the west by the Kalahari, to the north by the Zambezi River, to the south by the Limpopo River, and in the east by the Portuguese and an uneasy accommodation with Shoshangane. Mzilikazi then worked to solve a basic problem that many others like him have experienced throughout history. He had bonded together a cohesive nation under exodus and many wars of accumulation and survival, but at peace he found that he could not maintain a large standing army in idleness. It is exactly here that the Mashona found their relevance in the new order of life on the central plateau. With the arrival of the Matabele, the Mashona were handed the role of spear fodder for Mzilikazi's impis, and for the next 60 years they lived at the sharp end of the assegai.

Contemporary observations give us a fairly clear idea of how the subjugation of the Mashona took place. The Matabele economy was simple — it was based on the husbandry of cattle and the parallel husbandry of any unfortunate neighbours less warlike than themselves. The striking difference between the two systems of stock management was that cattle were nurtured and humanely treated while human prey were used and butchered in the most cynical and inhumane manner imaginable.

Winter on the central plateau was the raiding season. The twin reasons for this were that the weather was cool and dry and conducive to the movement of manpower across country; and also that the Mashona would by then have brought in their annual harvest and grain reserves would be conveniently stored in standing granaries scattered around the countryside. The King, at the annual Festival of the First Fruits, would hurl a spear in a predetermined direction, and thus launch on the Mashona settlements thereabouts a tornado of death and destruction.

While the raids appeared haphazard and uncontrolled, this was not in fact the case. Annually only particular areas were selected for raiding, leaving others to enjoy a measure of peace. Many Mashona groups were able to settle beneath the Matabele shadow under terms of tribute, but many others could not. It must be added that there were also those that did not submit to Matabele tyranny in any way, and for extensive periods lived unmolested on the fringes of central influence. On the whole, however, few were the inhabitants of the plateau who did not in some way feel the weight of the Matabele arrival.

A sustainable programme of support evolved allowing the Matabele to maintain their military establishment and yet still grow fat on the land. Studies of the Matabele put this point as the moment of their decline, where without a viable enemy against which to maintain a high level of military preparedness they began to lose the potent edge that they had hitherto enjoyed. The Mashona were largely kept on the back foot, able at the very most to maintain a broken up national unity, with their wider social cohesion almost completely destroyed.

Of course in most cases direct defence against the Matabele assaults and raids was unimaginable. The only way the Mashona could hope to survive was to maintain their village structure amid the cover of broken hill country from where a close vigil on all the leading approaches could be kept. Nevertheless Matabele attacks were usually swift, silent and unexpected, and mostly, though not always, successful. In the customary manner all men of productive age and the elderly were slaughtered, while young women and children were carried off in the first instance to porter home the booty of war, and later to be murdered or claimed as booty. Numerous reports from missionaries, travellers and prospectors who witnessed acts of unnecessary torture and barbarity inflicted against the Mashona suggest a gratuitous attitude to violence coupled with a systematic application of terror as a tool of political repression. In due course, the Mashona inductees into Matabele society grew to occupy a huge lower class of slaves known as amaHoli that before long came to outnumber the higher and older classes of Nguni and Basutho.

Thus it was that by a process of brutality and attrition, the Mashona in many places were reduced to a remnant of the great culture they had once been. But it would be wrong to assume that the Matabele scourge was universally felt over the highveld. There were large areas of Mashonaland that felt no impact — or at least very little — from Matabele raids. However for many others, the regime was relentless, predatory and murderously brutal.

It seems also from contemporary accounts that the necessities of survival bred out any shreds of nobility from the Mashona and replaced them with traits of guile, evasiveness, cunning and dishonesty. This further inspired in the Matabele a bitter contempt for their neighbours, whom they referred to at times as amaTswina, or loosely as filth, or shit. The London press of the day lionised the Matabele as the greatest but most cruel power in Africa. Conversely Victorian observers described the Mashona in terms both unflattering and unfair. Such opinions stood in stark contrast to the enthusiastic references made about the Mashona by the Portuguese some 200 years earlier. Time and circumstance had so reduced them that it seemed absolutely nothing of their past remained to mitigate their current circumstances.

Meanwhile Mzilikazi's primary foreign policy was to keep white expansion south of the Limpopo River. In this he was largely successful, although there were a few notable exceptions. Robert Moffat, white missionary, explorer and sometime diplomat, became a close and personal friend to Mzilikazi. In one of the stranger anomalies of the times, it seems that the Matabele king had a great and genuine affection for the salty old missionary, whom he had first met during his occupation of the region of the trans-Vaal region. His relationship with Moffat was historically important, and would have a bearing on white relations with his court for some time to come.

Besides his dealings with Moffat, Mzilikazi conducted a certain amount of carefully controlled trade in ivory and gold. He even allowed one or two prospectors and hunters access to roam the country at will, albeit accompanied at all times by an induna escort. On the whole, however, Mzilikazi was not welcoming to the white man. As he grew older and subsided into alcoholism, dropsy and melancholia, he found it ever harder to ward off the insistent attentions pressed on him. Andries Potgieter, a Boer commando and trek leader, who had in the past scouted some of the lands north of the Limpopo, even launched a raid. The raid achieved nothing in military terms, but made it clear to Mzilikazi that the white man would not go away, and would one day want more from the Matabele than his people would be willing to give.

Mzilikazi was fortunate in a way. He was the last of his kind. His life and the great permutations of white interest underway in Africa did not fatally overlap. It was to his son and heir, Lobengula, that the ghastly responsibility of confronting white encroachment would fall. Some years would pass before that day came, but come it would.

3

Rise of the Diamond King

Arrival of Cecil John Rhodes

The death of David Livingstone in 1873 marked the end of one glorious phase of British Empire building and the birth of another. By and large the great geographical questions of the age had been answered and for the most part the continent was mapped and understood. The British had led this effort, so naturally it was to them that the lion's share of Africa would fall. South Africa was arguably the choicest of these territories, mainly by dint of the fact that it had a climate conductive to long-term white settlement. The riches, such as they were, that flooded into the coffers of Liverpool and Whitehall at that time were drawn largely from the Gold Coast and the Slave Coasts — the 'white man's grave' region of West Africa. Here no sane man other than a missionary, a criminal or an appointee would realistically consider settling. South Africa, on the other hand, lay in the temperate zones and as a consequence its white population far exceeded that of any other territory in sub-Saharan Africa. Thanks to this fact it enjoyed the advantage of a relatively organised and modern society.

South Africa was not without problems, however, which existed mainly as a consequence of two factors. Firstly, separate British colonial and local Dutch administrations shared the government of the region uneasily; and secondly the region as a whole appeared to have very little in the way of short-term economic potential. The latter condition changed dramatically, however, with the chance discovery in 1866 of a rough crystal in the dust of Griqualand West. This stone fixed South Africa firmly on the global economic map, where it has remained ever since. The then Colonial Secretary, Lord Kimberley, weighed the celebrated diamond in his hand and predicted to the Cape Parliament that upon it the future success of South Africa would be built.[1]

Lord Kimberley was quite right, of course. That first diamond set in motion changes that catapulted South Africa from an impoverished colonial backwater to the main theatre of capital adventure — and war — in the British Empire. A clash of arms between Briton and Boer, that had once seemed likely, suddenly became inevitable. The diamond fields were manoeuvred into British territory by creative boundary delineation. Later though, more lucrative gold discoveries were made in the heartland of the Boer territory — the Transvaal Republic.

The Afrikaners, however, did not necessarily welcome either the gold or the diamonds. They recognised both meant change, and to the *volk* — the people — change was undesirable. Within the next few years the soil of South Africa would yield not just impressive deposits, but the world's highest concentrations of both gold and diamonds. Men and capital flooded into the Witwatersrand and Kimberley, and within a short time both had permeated throughout the region. No matter how much the Boers might resist it, this precipitated a flood of men and capital into the Witwatersrand and Kimberley, bringing economic development and progress. It brought everything, in fact, that the Afrikaners had crossed their hearts and sworn never to countenance. Most bitterly resented was

British social and economic predominance.

Into this cauldron of change, on a cool September morning in 1870, stepped an unremarkable immigrant by the name of Cecil John Rhodes. In the company of many other arrivals, Rhodes stood on the docks, looked around at the shabby little port town of Durban and pondered an uncertain future. Little did he, or anybody else attending to their business that day, realise that this particular anonymous arrival would set in motion one of the most colourful chapters of British imperial history.

Cecil John Rhodes was born in July 1853 to the growing family of an unremarkable English country parson — the fifth, in fact, of 11 children. By then the British Empire was approaching its zenith and Rhodes grew up as one of its typical sons. With its vast markets and huge reservoirs of raw materials, the Empire played a vital role in the explosion of industrial development, which in turn became the engine that drove the new age of enlightenment.

Enlightenment to the English masses usually amounted to jingoistic celebrations of global power, but to those of the upper and middle classes such as the Rhodes family, it meant much more. It represented human liberty in a world of huge scientific, philosophical and artistic advances. It meant vast global reach, which brought with it equal global responsibility. The British Empire placed the English-speaking peoples at the very pinnacle of human achievement. Victoria, Imperator Regina, sat virtually at the left hand of God, from where heaven and earth were governed accordingly.

As Cecil Rhodes grew up he would have taken all this for granted. Barge traffic on the River Stort, which flowed quietly at the bottom of the Rhodes family garden, fascinated the young boy. From his vantage point across the towpath he could picture this little transport artery branching out through southern England and then spreading beyond into the wider world, into the great Pax Britannia that defined the British Empire. For all intents and purposes, Pax Britannia was the world.

Cecil Rhodes, however, never expected to personally see or play much of a part in the growth of the Empire. As a child his health was poor, which combined unfavourably with the fact that, academically, he was the least promising of the Rhodes boys. The Victorian credo that a family should deliver up one son to the army, another to the Empire and a third to the church, left Francis Rhodes with a few sons to spare — and one in particular whom he deemed perfect for the clergy. Cecil himself was ambivalent about this map of his future. He had thought briefly about a career in law, but his lack of education and his apparent predestination made this course unlikely. Therefore he drifted relatively easily towards his father's preference.

Francis Rhodes had very adroitly stretched the means of his large family by resolutely sending all but one of his sons to public school. Cecil was generally deemed to be a poor investment, so he attended the local grammar school. However, at age 16, persistent ill health seemed to moot even that humble avenue, and in due course he was taken out of school altogether. First he was diagnosed as suffering from consumption, but later he would suffer many heart attacks too, strongly suggesting a weak heart as well as tubercular lungs. He would live under the shadow of both of these ailments for the remainder of his life.

As his teens progressed and his life expectancy declined, the family doctor rather despairingly suggested a sea journey to help fortify his lungs. His elder brother Herbert had already emigrated to the new British colony of Natal where he secured title to 200 acres, upon which he was attempting to succeed as a cotton farmer. Since Herbert was already abroad, the easiest solution was for Cecil to go out and join him. Nothing was planned for the youngster beyond this, since the doctor held the opinion that Cecil Rhodes would not live to see his 19th birthday.

So it was then that the 17-year-old set off alone on a sea journey that would in a few months deposit him on the shores of Natal. By way of capital he carried the very respectable sum of £2000 lent to him by his Aunt Sophie. She alone, to her credit, seemed prepared to gamble that there was more than mediocrity and an early death in store for Cecil John Rhodes.

Herbert Rhodes was a drifter and a disappointment to his father. He forswore the trinity of imperial vocations and never laboured at any particular venture for very long. Despite this, he was the Rhodes sibling with potentially the most to gain from the Pax Britannia. The opportunities were limitless for Englishmen of wit and guile in the colonies, but Herbert, gifted with an abundance of charm, had neither wit nor guile in any discernable quantity. He was a thoughtful man of independent temper. He was the kind of rugged frontiersman and gentleman philosopher without which no adventure story of the period would ever be complete, and needless to say he was Cecil Rhodes' favourite brother.

When the two were reunited in Natal, Cecil was somewhat disappointed be told frankly that farming in the colony was a waste of time and that Herbert was off to try his luck on the diamond fields. Having delivered this news Herbert then lost no time in packing up and joining the steady stream of privateers making their way west. Cecil, now all alone in the African wilderness, was left with his older brother's best wishes and an ill conceived and half constructed cotton farm. Attached to it were a few listless black labourers who had long been accustomed to erratic wages and a general life of ease.

Cecil then made one of the most telling decisions of his life. He could have gone home, found a job in Petermaritzburg, or even followed his brother to Kimberley. Yet he determined to stay on the farm and make it pay. He had come to South Africa with the intention of growing cotton, and grow cotton he would.

He was not without a pragmatic streak, however, and this would be as vital to his survival on the frontier as his nerve and temerity. When the time came to concede that the land would more likely be the fortune of future generations he cut his losses and swiftly abandoned the farm. Above all else he had an innate understanding of the importance of capital, which no one — perhaps with the exception of Aunt Sophie — seemed to have noticed. Although he lost money in his first year, the experience taught him how to manage his money, and this he did with the instincts and caution of a born usurer. Incidentally, and no less importantly, it put him in the way of managing black labour, which was a skill that one could scarce get by without in the African colonies of that time.

Thus his first year in Africa had fortified his health and revealed in Rhodes two important qualities. The third vital element necessary for survival was personal courage, and here Rhodes too showed no deficit. When he arrived at the decision to abandon the farm he packed a wagon and set off to follow the steady stream of fortune hunters making their way to the diamond pipes of Kimberley.

* * *

The journey took Rhodes four months to complete — arguably the most important months of his short life. The trek was in the main a solitary undertaking, although he did travel in the anonymous company of a few wagon boys. Once adrift on the open veld his mind was soon cleared of disorder and he set about the business of thinking things out.

With no one to talk to or to anchor his imagination, his thoughts soared in unaccustomed space. His passage became the pilgrimage of a boy journeying towards both manhood and a destiny that he could sense, but scarcely imagine. History has been filled with men who by chance and timing have found providence. He was as gifted as a blade of grass seeded under a dripping tap. Tossed by fate into circumstances that would both nourish and guide him towards explosive growth. A gamut of sentiments and talents, some due to the indoctrination of his society and others stitched together by happenstance, would see Cecil Rhodes move towards a brilliant future. It just so happened that Kimberley, South Africa, and indeed the entire Anglo/Saxon empire was poised and waiting for a man with his peculiar symmetry of idealism, pragmatism and grit to open the door to a new and luminous age.

The South Africa Highveld was as soulful then in its silence as it was beautiful. From time to time Rhodes might have encountered a Boer family in the deep isolation that they preferred. He might have mused over coffee with a Dutch patriarch suspicious of the advancing world, and perhaps dreaming of another Great Trek north. He walked in the same faith as every man of his generation. He had been conditioned to believe that only Britain and a population of English speaking settlers could release from an empty landscape — such as this — the full fruits of its potential.

As he travelled deeper into the interior Rhodes saw around him an empty country. He was not the first to see it, but he was one of few to view it in the context of its potential. This was his first glimpse into the vast hinterland of the British Empire; the rich land that lay waiting for the hand of English creativity and courage. It lent him his first insight into what Empire actually meant in real, practical terms. He understood the concept clearly and instinctively, seeing in sharp focus the God-given undertaking of his, the gifted generation of mankind.

Underscoring this lofty view of the world would always be a curious core of practicality. Back in Natal he had left behind men much older than he who had been forced back on their wits by his candour and ripened perceptions. There were few among his acquaintances at that time who had been unimpressed by the breadth of his musings, his blunt sincerity and his grasp of practical necessity. Unlike his brother Herbert he was hardly the kind of young man that a Victorian woman would fall in love with, but without doubt he was the type that she would conspire to marry.

Cecil Rhodes thought hard about the empty landscape and the Boers who claimed it. He mulled over future British advancement in southern Africa, but above all he thought about money. It was said of Rhodes that his weakness was size. He contemplated nothing less than a United States of Africa stretching from the Cape to Cairo, and he saw it in the essential context of money. Capital. And the power the money offered. In the young mind of Rhodes, money had come to mean the engine of every quest of value. He knew this with the instinct of a pigeon on its homeward flight. If he dared to dream, as many did, he knew that his dreams would be realised only after the amassing of power and a great deal of money.

It was almost incidental that a year on the farm had repaired Rhodes' health. Far from dying, his skin had darkened and his arms sprouted muscles. This was just as well, for as he entered the outskirts of the outlandish profusion of digger life called Kimberley, it was obvious that he would need strong arms and a stiff back. He fell into the company of tough men without fear, and became tough himself.

Not surprisingly, after a month or two, there proved to be a lot more to Cecil Rhodes the digger than just the blisters on his hands. While he wanted to make money and was willing to work for it, he knew that work in itself would not be enough. Digging was one thing, and dig he did, but even with outrageous fortune there was a limit to what digging could achieve. Most diggers were content with a few lucky finds to recover their grubstake before moving on. On the other hand Rhodes and a few other young men played entrepreneur. They began to speculate on the sidelines by buying and selling defunct claims. It was Rhodes, however, who led the way in forming an early mining business that sought to use accumulated capital in markets more productive than grog and women. One or two observations of Rhodes at that time have survived. Biographers paint a picture of him as an earnest young man, tall and rather loosely formed, fiercely territorial, fastidious in the crude business at hand, and alert always for a lucrative opportunity. A letter to his mother talks of him averaging £100 a week, which, by Victorian standards, already had him in the league of successful businessmen.

Early on he formed a partnership with another young man by the name of Charles Rudd. Rudd was as hard working as he, although of somewhat lesser intellect. In due course he became Rhodes' right hand man and fixer. The two drifted into such sidelines as making ice for the diggings and taking contracts to pump the mines. They took substantial risks, but also at times seemed to be able to conjure money out of thin air. Rhodes in particular developed a blunt and persuasive nature that caused him to become known as a man impossible to divert. He made few friends, but gained considerable respect, the latter carrying more weight for him than the former. Before long he began to drift beyond the threshold of moderate returns and towards the acquisition of substantial wealth.

With his business thriving Rhodes turned his attention to the other great quest of his early years. This was his curious but equally unalterable desire to earn a degree from Oxford University. His preoccupation with practical virtues had taught him that money would open many doors, but would not in itself offer access to the governing classes. There was also a less easily definable sentiment that drew Rhodes to Oxford. He had always been in awe of the institution, but lately it had become more to him than just a matter of education and acceptance. Perhaps it was the exclusivity of study or the blue-blood credo, that time and again he sought to identify with and failed.

Oxford did not willingly reciprocate his love while he lived, but he was like Macbeth — drawn ever to the witches, and wanting to know more, but never truly learning. Before he could give the matter much attention, however, he suffered the first of his many heart attacks. He was shocked by the experience and physically weakened. Herbert persuaded him to take time off and trek with him to investigate other diggings that were opening up on the Rand and in the Eastern Transvaal. Herbert's motivation was not entirely his brother's health. He also sought to persuade his brother to look into possible alternative investments elsewhere in the country. Cecil agreed. He had a hankering for fresh air and pleasant company. Months of ponderous travel and long conversations with his brother were precisely what he needed to order his thoughts and restore his health. During this trip he began the delivery of an idea that had been gestating in his mind for many months — indeed since he first arrived in South Africa.

It was then that Rhodes began to reveal both to himself and his brother a hint of his unfolding vision. Still only 19 years old, he was already moderately wealthy and somewhat over-impressed by his own abilities. He had also lately become something of an amateur student of politics and in this field, as in everything, he held very definite opinions. He now sensed that the seemingly endless territory of their journey was one of the last great unclaimed landmasses of the world. At that time the territory of South Africa was broken up into a handful of limping colonies and half-nations shared unequally and uneasily between two unhappy partners. Rhodes dreamed of a federation under the British flag, where the English-speaking peoples and their surplus millions could settle and proliferate.

His first will and testament — written soon after this journey with the images of the South African backcountry still fresh in his mind — vividly portrays the world as it appeared to the young Cecil John Rhodes. He appoints as executor the then Colonial Secretary Lord Carnarvon and instructs him — with the help of a fortune as yet unmade — to pursue the following quest on his behalf:

> ... the establishment, promotion and development of a Secret Society, the true aim and object whereof shall be the extension of British rule throughout the world, the colonisation by British subjects of all land where the means of livelihood are available by energy, labour and enterprise, and especially the occupation by British settlers of the entire continent of Africa, the Holy Land, the Valley of the Euphrates, the islands of Cypress and Candia, the whole of South America, the islands of the Pacific not hitherto possessed by Great Britain, the whole of the Malay Archipelago, the seaboard of China and Japan, the ultimate recovery of the United States of America as an integral part of the British Empire, the consolidation of the whole Empire, the inauguration of a system of Colonial Representation in the Imperial Parliament which may tend to weld together the disjointed members of the Empire, and finally the foundation of so great a power as to hereafter render wars impossible and promote the best interests of humanity.

By this means Rhodes proposed to end all wars. He would introduce as a global standard the tenets and mores of European, English-speaking civilisation. It was no small ambition for the son of a Hertfordshire country parson. This vision further reinforced his belief that for him and his schemes to be taken seriously he needed the social vehicle of a university degree. He left his business in the hands of Charles Rudd and sailed back to England to try his luck at the world's most eminent seat of learning.

Rhodes' weakness was size...

Rhodes did not impress the Master of Oxford University College who declined to accept him as a student. He did, however, offer Rhodes an introduction to the Provost of Oriel College where standards were thought to be more flexible. Rhodes was accepted into this, the college that had finished Walter Raleigh, master empire builder of the Americas. Rhodes would cultivate a lifelong attachment to Oriel.[2] On his death Rhodes left the college an endowment of £100 000.

During his early life in England and South Africa, Rhodes might have felt that his intellectual power was worth something above the average — primarily because he had hitherto been mingling with men of a practical cut. Oxford, on the other hand, brought him into contact, not only with his intellectual equals, but also many who were significantly more accomplished than he. It was against these that Rhodes needed to sharpen his arguments and polish his opinions. He was swimming in advanced notions of Empire, world government and globe-dominating illuminati, all of which once again served to illustrate the fact that Cecil Rhodes was uniquely in step with his times.

Beginning a series of lectures, at this time, was the great Victorian thinker and social philosopher John Ruskin. The inadequacy of Rhodes' own philosophical vision was swept away and usurped by Ruskin who also spoke for his age, articulating and proclaiming everything that Rhodes believed in, and would later create.

> A destiny is now possible to us, the highest ever to be set before a nation to be accepted or refused. Will you the youths of England make your country again a royal throne of kings, a sceptered isle, for all the world a source of light, a centre of peace...? This is what England must do or perish. She must found colonies as fast and as far as she is able, formed of the most energetic and worthiest of men; seizing any piece of fruitful waste ground she can get her foot on, and there teaching her colonists that their chief virtue is to be fidelity to their country, and that their first aim is to be to advance the power of England by land and by sea.[3]

Rhodes added to this thesis his own variant when he composed a document — a kind of article of faith — which later he sent to his friend and publisher W.T. Stead. In it he pondered the meaning of life, and at the age of 24, he found the meaning profound.

> I contend that we are the first race in the world, and the more of the world we inhabit, the better it is for the human race. I contend that every acre we add to our territory provides for the birth of more of the English race, who otherwise would not be brought into existence. Added to which the absorption of the greater portion of the world under our rule simply means the end of all wars.[4]

How clear and tantalising such a vision must have seemed to a man who, from his power base in Kimberley, could look north and see nothing but empty space. Empty space? Of course, it was not entirely empty. The native inhabitants of these lands had only to submit themselves to the theft of both their country and their identity in exchange for the right of some future generation to call themselves

British. Nowadays such ideas only survive in the extreme right of British nationalist politics, but in Victorian England, Rhodes would have found, and been part of, a wide and approving audience. In fact, it was a core of idealists akin to such men as he who created the latter form of the British Empire; by 1921, the creeping red stain on the global map touched every continent from Southeast Asia and the Indian sub-continent to Arabia through 16 territories in Africa, plus British Guyana, Honduras and Canada. The mightiest Empire that the world had ever seen was English in origin, and they were Englishmen of Rhodes' intellectual caste who were its principal architects.

During that period the natives of these lands were generally not sophisticated and had no voice of consequence. From the Polynesians to the East Indians to the native Americans, indigenous peoples were credulous and easy to overawe. Neither was it entirely a mercantile philosophy. It was Rhodes' quaintly termed principal of philanthropy plus 5%. In this regard it was a vague principle defined by many to suit many purposes.

When Rhodes was later forced to contemplate the role of indigenous people in his schemes, his solution was as simple as it was obvious. It had already been proved that the bulk of the globe occupied by backward natives would and could not be left unaltered. Rhodes let it be known to the Cape Parliament: 'I believe that the natives are bound gradually to come under the control of Europeans.' A native society could after all ask no more of life than to join and participate in the Pax Britannia.

Rhodes' second term at Oxford was interrupted when he contracted a chill. For a while he was seriously ill and his doctor's prognosis was dire. In private notes that Rhodes happened to see, the doctor gave his patient no more than six months to live. As a consequence Rhodes took fright and temporarily quit Oxford, returning for a while to Africa where he immediately began to grow stronger. It would be two years before he could return to England. However, in that time his achievements would be startling.

4

This is Rhodes' land

Rhodes the enigma

Cecil Rhodes was by now steeped in politics and forming a concrete opinion of how South Africa could be repaired. The initial diamond rush in Kimberley had slowed to the point where most of the freebooters had abandoned the diggings for rumours of gold and diamonds elsewhere. This left young Rhodes and a few others in control of a steady production of diamonds. Although Rhodes, neither then nor ever, exhibited any overt sexuality, he had in a subtle way he had fallen in love.

Few of his biographers have been prepared to step into the realm of Rhodes' emotional attachments. It would be naive to suppose from this that he felt no natural yearnings, and yet practical to imagine that any he did feel would be suppressed. Oscar Wilde was already beginning to raise eyebrows in Victorian society, and in 1895 prove that the world was unprepared for powerful men to admit to homosexuality — possibly not even to themselves.

Whatever the fact, Rhodes' intimate behaviour was curious. He habitually and conspicuously surrounded himself with men. This fact was widely observed by contemporary biographers, but always commented on without innuendo or suggestion. Modern biographers have tended to over-compensate for this with ridiculous allusions to buggery and flagrant indiscretion that carry even less weight than earlier denials. In a professional context, Rhodes' preoccupation with men might not have been altogether unusual, but it was a noticeably different pattern of behaviour from men such as his brother Frank, who was a lothario, and particularly brilliant in the company of women.

Conversely there is no evidence at all to suggest that Rhodes had any sexual interest in women. Since he himself had absolutely nothing to say on the matter, it will remain a mystery. He did, however, share a cottage in Kimberley with another unhealthy youth by the name of Neville Pickering.

> Pickering is endowed with a lank blond fringe which he flicks to good effect at the sexually tormented Cecil. And when Pickering finally goes down with septicaemia, Rhodes announces that he's not having 'any damn fool woman' in there and will nurse the dying man himself.[1]

Despite assiduous personal nursing by Rhodes, the illness did indeed prove fatal. For Rhodes the bereavement was devastating. The intensity of his grief surprised even his closest friends. He would never replicate that depth of attachment with anyone ever again, and would never truly recover from the shock.

In one of Rhodes' numerous last testaments he had bequeathed his worldly goods to Pickering, at a time when his assets were considerable. He beseeched his friend to spend the money in the pursuit of his imperial dream. But although Rhodes himself would die at a comparatively young age, he outlived his friend by a considerable margin.

Pickering's death, meanwhile, only briefly interrupted the aggressive campaign Rhodes had begun to conduct. His objective was to amalgamate the fragmented Kimberley diamond diggings. The logic was simple. With a disunited body of mine owners all competing with one another, the world diamond market was flooded, and prices permanently depressed. Since the bulk of the world's diamonds at that time originated from Kimberley Rhodes surmised that if one company could gain a monopoly on production, prices could be artificially inflated and maintained by a controlled release of stones.

Rhodes succeeded by shrewd and ongoing acquisition and the adroit manipulation of shares and claims. His only real competition came in the form of a Jewish trader of uncertain lineage who called himself Barney Barnarto. Barnarto had arrived penniless in Kimberley a year or two earlier, but had rapidly created a financial empire as illustrious as even that of Rhodes.

It was thanks to his signature persistence and an incredible persuasive ability that Rhodes eventually triumph over Barnarto. The latter was heard to lament some years later:

> The worst of Rhodes is that when you have been with him for half an hour, you not only agree with him, but you come to believe that you have always held this opinion.[2]

Barnarto was compensated with a life governorship of Rhodes' consolidated interests and membership of the Kimberley Club, which hitherto — and largely at Rhodes' instigation — had been denied to him. Such membership was a mark of arrival and acceptance in the inner sanctum of Kimberley's buccaneer business fraternity. Barnarto joined Alfred Beit, another Jewish financier, and also one of Rhodes' many disciples, under the dominating shadow of the colossus.

Alfred Beit originated from Hamburg, Germany and emigrated to the Cape in 1875, from where he was drawn into the diamond rush. He quickly became one of the key early financiers instrumental in incorporating the diamond business into a few powerful hands. Beit provided much silent impetus towards Rhodes' conspicuous financial successes, just as he would feature in and support Rhodes in many of his failures. Rhodes himself retained practical control of the resulting company. De Beers Consolidated was registered in 1888 with a capital of £200 000.

* * *

By 1881 Rhodes had, after erratic attendance, graduated from Oriel College, founded the De Beers Company, and entered the Cape Parliament as member for Barkly West. All this he achieved at age 28 and after less than a decade of endeavour. It was at this point that he finally felt ready to begin the great work that would dominate his life from then on.

The political landscape of South Africa was no less splintered then than it had been a decade earlier. The country was still broadly divided into four separate political cantons, and the wealth that had been generated in the years since the gold and diamond strikes had done nothing to ease the suspicions between Briton and Boer. These sub-divisions were the original Cape Colony, that existed under a degree of self-government, the Colony of Natal, and the independent Boer Republics of the Transvaal and the Orange Free State. The diamond mines at Kimberley fell under the territorial control of the Cape Colony, while the main gold producing areas were principally in the Transvaal. It was, however, the goldfields that became — and remained — the open sore of South African politics. Less obviously, the Boer suffered from a gamut of lingering animosities towards the British as a result of a century or more of misunderstanding, mistrust and incompatible political and social objectives.

Boer policy was still based on an early and cherished aim of establishing a homeland in the wilderness particular to their needs. The *Volk* — the Boer peoples — desired to live in the open country, free from any outside intrusion, and with a native population no greater than needed to fill their labour requirements. Working to this ideal they established an almost exclusively agrarian system of farming fiefdoms premised on the absolute independence of the individual. Central government was haphazard and ineffective, and the lifestyle of the Boer virtually untaxable. As a consequence the republics — and particularly the Orange Free State — tended to exist in a perpetual state of economic stagnation.

In the case of the Transvaal, however, gold discoveries changed this state of affairs promptly and radically. Mining provided the treasury with a steady stream of revenue from taxation, which mainly affected the Uitlander (Foreigner) class. The Uitlanders, as their name implies, were typically English speaking and of mixed European and colonial origin. They were the diggers, the mine owners and the entrepreneurs of the gold fields. They lived alongside the Boers in a state of mutual suspicion, and were heavily taxed with no commensurate political representation. This situation placed the government of the Transvaal in a unique quandary. As long as taxes were collected and franchise denied, resentment bred and conditions for unrest were ever present. Yet if the authorities afforded the Uitlanders access to government, their superior numbers and generally superior abilities would marginalise the Afrikaner electorate immediately. Not only was this situation tenuous internally, but it also provided an ongoing pretext for agitation on the part of the Transvaal's English-speaking neighbours to the east and south.

An additional complication arose when the Germans annexed Damaraland. This territory, later to be German South West Africa, and later still Namibia, provided a conduit for, arguably, the only friendly international relation that the Transvaal enjoyed at that time. The Germans exercised their own complex antipathy towards Britain by threatening to close the divide between German South West Africa and the Transvaal, which would have effectively blocked the passage for British expansion north. The Germans would then have been able to effect a measured embrace of all of south central Africa between Damaraland and German East Africa without fear of running foul of anyone. President Kruger of the Transvaal saw this as a likely precursor to his own people crossing the Limpopo into present day Zimbabwe and claiming it as another independent homeland. In the interests of British expansion, these were ambitions that Rhodes urgently needed to contain.

This was the view of things that Rhodes pondered from the Cape Parliament as he took his seat for the first time. His immediate goal was the amalgamation of all the units of South Africa into a single federation under the British flag. After this the unclaimed vastness of the central African interior would be closed to the Germans. All that was necessary was to direct and focus the political will and capital of those around him towards that one vital objective. The irresistible force…

One way or another the free natives of the interior were doomed to follow the fate of their dispossessed neighbours to the south. The fair lands north of the Limpopo lay directly in the path of European progress, poising the last of the indigenous rulers of Africa to topple like so many dominos. It would be a race on the part of the great powers to secure the unclaimed and strategic portions of the African map. Lobengula, successor to the Matabele throne, felt this fact more acutely every day.

Lobengula was the unhappy heir to a nation in crisis. The Matabele needed only to consider the recent fate of their mother tribe to predict the shape of their own future. The Anglo-Zulu war of 1879 had been provoked by the Natal Administration and pressed on the Zulu people as part of a general drive to pacify the colony. The Zulus, as we know, were a highly mobile, disciplined and motivated warrior nation whose short but bloody history was rich with conquest and territorial gain. In a series of dramatic battles, however, the Zulu regiments were fought to a standstill by a modern army equipped with firearms and supported by the limitless means of empire. Thereafter they had no choice but to succumb to British rule.

Added to this, a steady stream of white concession seekers had begun to appear in the capital to harass the Matabele monarch with all the spurious devices of European diplomacy. Each maligned the other and agreed only that the nature of progress was such that the King had no choice but to select his imperial ally from among them.

Lobengula had only the vaguest idea of what these men were talking about, and his advisors could not help. For a generation the Matabele had maintained an isolationist stance against European encroachment, and following the philosophy of Mzilikazi, they remained determined to deny all they preferred not to acknowledge. Now, though, the future was now upon them, and on Lobengula in particular, it had become a complex gamble with no winning formula for either himself or his people. The best that he could hope to achieve was to negotiate his nation's slide into irrelevance at the hands of the least disreputable of his many petitioners.

What the Matabele were unable to understand was that the political face of Africa had changed irrevocably, and most particularly since the 1884/5 Berlin Conference. There the rules of engagement between opposing European powers over the question of Africa had been fixed. It had been agreed, among other things, that viable occupation of any new territory needed to be proved before annexation would be generally acknowledged. This set in motion a phenomenon that became known as the Scramble for Africa, a massive land grab that saw the last native controlled areas of the continent swallowed up by one or another of the old world powers. The plight of the Matabele was therefore not unique, but was echoed in similar attacks on hundreds, if not thousands of indigenous societies across the length of the continent.

Portugal had been the first of the European powers to show any interest in southern Africa, and she had throughout maintained the idle notion that the interior fell under her sphere of influence. Although the Berlin Conference had stirred her into some desultory action, by the late 19th century there was little she could do in the face of wealthier and more aggressive powers than to complain poignantly from the sidelines.

The Germans, in the meanwhile, had annexed both South West Africa and the territory of Tanganyika. Bismarck dreamed of unifying these two by claiming all the territory in between. Britain already held sway over huge areas of Africa, including Sudan, Kenya, Uganda, Nigeria, Gold Coast (later Ghana), Sierra Leone, and, of course, the two opposing points of Egypt and the Cape of Good Hope. The French and British had partitioned West Africa more or less between them, while France claimed most of the north-facing Mediterranean shore. Smaller European interests included an ineffectual Italian presence in the Horn of Africa and in Libya, and an irregular personal claim on the great Congo basin by Belgian King Leopold.

For Rhodes to annexe central Africa on behalf of the British Crown, it was imperative that he act to somehow frustrate the further ambitions of all these potential suitors. He therefore saw it as his duty to seize Matabeleland and its vassal territories as quickly as possible.

Lobengula might have preferred to dream that all of this was not happening, but so long as Cecil John Rhodes dreamed to the contrary, he would know no peace. It might have come as some small consolation to the Matabele king to appreciate that the British were known to be more conscientious in their colonial practices than many others. Were it not for Rhodes the destiny of the Matabele might easily have fallen into the hands of Portuguese, French or Belgian colonisers. Of these powers Lobengula had no experience, but he had noticed that a neighbouring chief, Kgosi Khama III who ruled over the BaNgwato people of central Bechuanaland, had accepted the protection of the British Crown and now seemed none the worse for it. Lobengula had often thought about doing the same.

Lobengula appeared often, justly or unjustly, to be a weak and indecisive man. Unlike Rhodes, he was not ideally suited to his role. He was torn between pressure from the whites in his court and a complete rejection of reality by the rank and file of his nation. In addition his generals and advisors consistently pressured him to order the slaughter all the white men in Matabeleland. A few advised caution, but most had very little interest in talk of compromise. The Matabele, like their forefathers now resting in noble graves, knew and understood war and little else. While Lobengula's rule might have been less determined than his father's, what he lacked in fire and passion he made up for with superior powers of diplomacy. And while he might have lacked the iron fist of his father he was no less the undisputed lord of his people. As a consequence his personal indecision quickly became the mood of his nation. For better or for worse the white men were allowed to stay, and in due course Lobengula made a faltering choice on the matter of granting to one of them a concession.

It so happened that Lobengula, who had during the course of his life enjoyed a number of cordial relationships with whites, was on amicable terms with an Afrikaner trader by the name of Piet Grobler. Grobler was a fluent Zulu speaker and regular visitor to kwaBuluwayo, the royal kraal of the Matabele, situated slightly north of the present day city of Bulawayo. On behalf of the government of the Transvaal, Grobler succeeded in persuading Lobengula to submit his mark to a treaty of friendship and amity with the Transvaal Republic. The facts surrounding this event were somewhat obscured when Grobler was murdered under mysterious circumstances on his return to the Transvaal. Despite this, news of the treaty's existence soon reached the ears of Cecil John Rhodes. Malignant suggestions have been made that Rhodes' hand was somehow behind Grobler's murder, but logistically this would have been very difficult, even if Rhodes had ever contemplated behaviour of that sort. In all likelihood Grobler fell victim to common banditry. The value of the episode to history is mainly that it spurred Rhodes to enter the race for the annexation of Matabeleland before the chance was lost.

Through his earlier efforts to have the territory of Bechuanaland annexed for the Crown, Rhodes had come to realise that the British Government needed considerable persuasion to act. Cabinet was reluctant as usual to draw upon the treasury, and while Rhodes might fairly have accused his government of lacking vision, they might just as easily have accused him of parochialism. In the event he decided to fall back on his faith in capital and to proceed by way of a Royal Charter.

The idea of private capital taking on the role of government in claiming and exploiting colonies was not unique. Since the loss of the United States in the late 18th century, Whitehall had tended to prefer defining a territory as a sphere of influence rather than claiming it as a colony. If it should happen that a territory proved viable and a colony emerged, then all well and good. In principal, the treasury would absorb any economic benefit that might accrue while any political liability could be ignored. This was the case with a number of territories in Africa and many others worldwide. The most famous British foreign possession to be privately governed was India under the East India Company.

In Africa the Great Lakes region as well as east and central Africa were being opened up and exploited primarily by publicly subscribed companies. A Royal Charter empowered the directors to undertake all kinds of civil administration as well as to conduct exploration, defence and justice on behalf of both settler communities and indigenous societies. The great advantage that chartered companies held for the British Government and others was that they removed the expense of opening up new territory using the resources of central treasuries and instead placed the burden on the shoulders of private enterprise.

As with his peers in the business of privatising the colonies, for Rhodes to obtain a Royal Charter it would be necessary for him to approach the Crown with some proof of acquiescence on the part of the ruling native authority. In instances where no, or very little native government was evident, this was relatively simple. However, in the case of Matabeleland and most of Mashonaland, it was quite clear that a central government of not insignificant authority was incumbent.

Rhodes' immediate course of action was to enlist the help of his friend Sir Sidney Shippard who was at that time Assistant High Commissioner for Bechuanaland. Together the two men made an approach to the High Commissioner to the Cape Colony, Sir Hercules Robinson. Like Shippard, Robinson was a friend and admirer of Cecil Rhodes, and as the highest representative of the Crown in southern Africa, his support in the matter was vital.

Sir Hercules was enjoying the Grahamstown races on the Christmas Eve of 1887 when he was unexpectedly visited by the duo of Rhodes and Shippard. After the briefest of civilities Rhodes cited the matter of Piet Grobler's treaty, pleaded that the territory was about to be lost, and urged Robinson to immediately declare Matabeleland a protectorate. As partisan as Sir Hercules might have been, he was unwilling to take such a definite step on his own authority. As a short-term alternative, he suggested that Lobengula might be persuaded to sign a treaty of friendship with Her Majesty's Government to supersede that of Pieter Grobler. This would buy time so that the means to obtain a Royal Charter could be more carefully prepared. This compromise did not entirely satisfy Rhodes, but it was the best that the High Commissioner could offer at such short notice and it would have to do. The ideal man for the job happened, coincidentally, to be in Bulawayo at the time and needed only to be alerted by dispatch. Thus John Moffat entered the stage of Rhodes' frontier diplomacy.

Using one of Her Majesty's agents was to obtain a Royal Charter — a strictly private objective — was the first of many favours that Rhodes would wring from his friends in public office by means of subtle duplicity. For the moment this was a simple case of back scratching, but in time Rhodes lost sight of the remit of public officials, and lured many to compromise themselves in exchange for patronage. It is interesting that both Robinson and Shippard benefited materially from their involvement with Rhodes.

Rhodes was very fortunate to have a man like John Moffat of the British Bechuanaland Colonial Service to act as his ambassador in Bulawayo. Moffat had been exposed to the Matabele from a very early age through his father Robert's relationship with Mzilikazi, and the two younger sons had themselves been friends for some time. In 1859 young Moffat had been among the pioneers of the London Missionary Society's first mission in Matabeleland. Although retired from missionary service since 1879, Moffat had maintained a cordial and familiar relationship with Lobengula. While his personal regard for the Matabele King was probably genuine, Moffat — like most missionaries who tried to sow the seeds of Christ in the hard soil of Matabeleland — had no love for the regime itself and was eager to work for its collapse.

By the end of January 1888, less than a month after Shippard, Rhodes and Robinson had met to decide on a course of action, Moffat received his instructions. Conceivably, he felt gratified that the first missiles to be hurled at the pagan walls of Matabeleland would come from his own hand. Rhodes was still unknown to him, and besides, held no official position other than as a parliamentarian. So for the moment Moffat would be acting on the instructions of the High Commissioner. Later, when it became clear to him what was underway, and Rhodes' reputation in all its variety had matured, he would rise in indignation to write to the London Missionary Society about the occupation of Mashonaland:

I feel bound to tell you that I look on the whole plan as detestable, whether viewed in the light of policy or morality…when Lobengula finds it all out, as he is sure to do sooner or later, what faith will he have in you?

This was all in the future however, and for the moment Lobengula responded well to Moffat's overtures. In fact he seemed grateful at last to be able to place his confidence in a man he knew and trusted. He was receptive to the proposition of a treaty of friendship between he and the British Queen Victoria, although he chose to interpret this as a tender of Crown protection along the same lines as that enjoyed by his neighbouring Chief Khama.

Despite this apparently accommodation, Moffat still fought an uphill battle to get Lobengula to actually append his mark to a supporting document. Lobengula — apart from his natural tendency to prevaricate — was under the most stringent pressure from his assembly of indunas to submit no verbal agreement to paper. The reason for this was both wise and simple. No Matabele at the capital of Bulawayo was able to read or write, so none could verify the content of any treaty signed. It was a sensible position that Moffat certainly understood, but he was able to overcome it with some difficulty. On 11 February 1888 Lobengula put his mark and affixed his seal to the following document.

The Chief Lobengula, ruler of the tribe known as Amandebele, together with the Mashona and Makalaka tributaries of the same, hereby agrees to the following articles and conditions:

That peace and amity will continue forever between Her Britannic Majesty, her subjects and the Amandebele people; and the contracting Chief, Lobengula, engages to use his utmost endeavours to prevent any rupture of the same, to cause the strict observance of this treaty, and so to carry out the treaty of friendship which was entered into by his late father, the Chief Umsiligaas, with the Governor of the Cape of Good Hope, in the year of our Lord 1836.

It is hereby further agreed by Lobengula, Chief in and over the Amandebele country, with the dependencies as aforesaid, on behalf of himself and people, that he will refrain from entering into any correspondence or treat with any foreign state or power to sell, alienate or cede or permit or countenance any sale, alienation or cession of the whole or any part of the said Amandebele country under his chieftainship, or upon any other subject without the previous knowledge and sanction of Her Majesty's High Commissioner for South Africa.

In faith of which I, Lobengula, on my part have hereto set my hands at Gubulawayo, Amandabeleland, this eleventh day of February, and of Her Majesties reign the 51st year.

Lobengula: His X Mark.

Witnesses: W. Graham & GB van Wyk.

Before me, J.S. Moffat.
Assistant Commissioner.

The content of the treaty of February 1888 seems innocuous, and it was. There is nothing particularly definitive or substantive in the text except perhaps that Rhodes had achieved some form of negative option on the country. In truth the treaty carried no more weight than had Grobler's before it, the only difference being that Rhodes was generally perceived to enjoy the full backing of the British Empire. This, of course, was not entirely so — not yet anyway.

After the signing of the Moffat treaty, a period of nervous calm settled over the Bulawayo community, although it was not long before intrigue was generated anew. Lobengula had made his decision and for all intents and purposes the British were in the ascendancy. The King felt that he might now expect some dignity under their protection as well as restraint from opposing powers, but nothing could have been further from the truth. The whites at court agitated against Rhodes, swore to Lobengula that he had been duped and offered themselves as the only solution. For Lobengula the promised peace of mind never came.

5

End of the Matabele road

The Rudd Concession

Rhodes was very conscious of the limitations of Whitehall when it came to territorial expansion. As aggressive as the British Empire often appeared to be it was in reality always curiously reluctant to accept new responsibility. Extra territory did not always mean extra wealth, but often simply new wars and new expenses.

There were two distinct facets to the surge of imperial acquisition in the 19th century. The first of these was official in the form of planners, diplomats and administrators; the second involved the privateers and capitalists who had the means, and often the vision and the will, to provoke filibuster. In the absence of obvious global-strategic advantage, it was frequently they who had to drag the body politic along with them. In the light of a further advance into central Africa there was certainly strategic advantage in the annexation of the trans-Limpopo territories. At that time, however, Rhodes was among very few British imperial administrators and agents who preached Africa as a priority.

A large part of British Prime Minister Lord Salisbury's legacy remains the partition of Africa — and in fact specifically the creation of Rhodesia. However his preoccupation was mainly with overseeing the balance of power in Europe and upgrading the Royal Navy to a strength at least equivalent to that of France and Russia combined. In the midst of this, Rhodes often drifted close to being a severe irritant to the British Prime Minister, and on occasions even suffered direct rebuke. It was only with difficulty that Rhodes was able to bring the Lord Salisbury along with the movement north from the Cape. In fairness, though, the prime Minister had a world to worry about, while Rhodes had only a region.

Another factor complicating Rhodes' plans was the fact that Matabeleland was not an empty landscape searching for the direction of a greater power, but a domain, effectively governed by an established monarchy. The Moffat Treaty, as satisfying as it was, fell short of a plea from Lobengula for annexation or protection. Until such a plea, or some reasonable facsimile of it, could be presented to the Imperial Government, the Colonial Office would baulk at any heavy-handed and potentially costly action.

In the aftermath of the Moffat Treaty, Rhodes concluded that he would have to revisit Lobengula in order to clarify the terms of a concession and press for specific leave to exploit and settle the country. He knew this was unlikely to be a simple matter and was at first uncertain how to proceed. In the event, his hand was forced by a duo of London businessmen by the names of Gifford and Cawston who, at about this time, announced their own commercial interest in the trans-Limpopo territory.

Maurice Gifford was an aristocrat with a chequered background enlivened by many colonial wars.

His adventurous spirit eventually drew him to Africa where he saw action during the Anglo/Zulu war. It was during this period that he first gave thought to the commercial exploitation of Matabeleland, and perhaps even Mashonaland. He persuaded prominent London stockbroker George Cawston to join him in forming the Bechuanaland Exploration Company. The company was formed primarily to exploit the Bechuanaland Protectorate, but the two were candid in their plans to gain control of Matabeleland as well.

Meanwhile, early in 1888, Rhodes visited London and discreetly inquired here and there about the possibility of establishing his Chartered Company. Later that same year a charter would be granted to the Imperial East Africa Company for the exploitation of territories that would later become Kenya and Uganda; two years earlier a similar Charter had been granted to the Royal Niger Company for the region that would later become Nigeria. So while Rhodes was not pursuing anything unprecedented, it was confirmed to him that he was lacking the single most important requirement — a binding contract with the Matabele.

Early in May of that year George Cawston put pen to paper and outlined his company's plans to the Colonial Secretary. In a letter to Lord Knutsford he asked for approval for a representative of the Bechuanaland Exploration Company to travel to Bulawayo in order to secure a mining concession from Lobengula. Knutsford, fortunately for Rhodes, demurred until such time as he had consulted with the relevant authorities on the ground. Since Rhodes was one of those authorities, Shippard another, and Sir Hercules Robinson perhaps the most important, Rhodes was alerted in sufficient time to act. Despite this he was caught somewhat on the back foot when an agent for Gifford & Cawston, Edward Maund, arrived in Cape Town in June of 1888.

Maund wasted no time and set off for Matabeleland some weeks in advance of any preparations that Rhodes was able to make to head him off. This in itself did not unduly disturb Rhodes, for he was confident by then of the loyalty of Robinson and Shippard, both of whom could help delay Maund long enough for him to be beaten to Bulawayo. Shippard, as Her Majesty's most senior representative in the Bechuanaland Protectorate, could — and did — bring to bear any number of frustrations to hinder the unfortunate Maund.

Rhodes then selected an interesting triumvirate of men to journey north on his behalf. Principal among these was the phlegmatic Charles Dunell Rudd. Rudd was an austere man of limited vision but who could be counted upon to be solidly trustworthy, loyal and reliable.

The second group member was an old friend, Rochfort Maguire, a barrister by profession. Handsome, dapper and cultivated, Maguire would seem at first to have been an unlikely candidate. He was a Fellow of All Souls whom Rhodes had met at Oxford and with whom he shared a common conviction regarding home rule for Ireland. As a lawyer, Maguire would ensure that any business transacted by Rudd would be suitably committed to contract.

Lastly Rhodes chose a very skittish and unpredictable character called Francis Thompson — better known as Matabele Thompson — to make up the trio. Thompson had a reputation as a native expert due mainly to the fact that he was fluent in a number of local native dialects, and also because he had organised a compound system for De Beers to limit the theft of diamonds by members of the black labour force. Thompson's role was to advise on the Matabele, and deal directly with them, but one wonders how well he was suited to this. Because he had witnessed his father's murder during a native revolt, he was hampered by a deep distrust of the native temper. Thompson senior had suffered a rifle ramrod pushed down his throat until it came out of his back. The sight of this had understandably scarred his son and certainly it influenced his conduct when in contact with arguably the most ruthless society yet seen on the continent.

With his negotiating trio assembled, Rhodes prevailed on Sir Hercules to endorse the mission by providing an introductory letter on behalf of Queen Victoria. The letter was of ostentatious size and replete with gilt devices. Furthermore it was stamped with Sir Hercules' official seal in order that Lobengula, despite being illiterate, might be suitably impressed by its imperial substance.

The three-man delegation set out from Kimberley on 15 August 1888 and made their way directly to Bulawayo. Apart from the letter and the colossal sum of £1000 Sterling in gold sovereigns, they carried with them the usual consignment of hard liquor of which Lobengula was fond. After ten weeks of hot and dusty travel they arrived without mishap on the borders of Matabele territory.

At that point progress was halted by a Matabele border guard that informed Rudd of a royal decree forbidding any white man from proceeding into Matabeleland without the prior and express consent of the King. Naturally any incoming petitioner would be expected to adhere to this by dint of basic courtesy, if not self-preservation. Rudd and his companions, however, effectively ignored it. While a runner was dispatched to Bulawayo to announce their arrival, the party continued on. They met the runner on his return with Lobengula's denial of permission to enter the country. With absolute indifference to this royal edict the party pressed on, arriving in Bulawayo close to noon on 20 September.

It was perhaps only thanks to their profound audacity that the three were not murdered on the spot, for indeed that was the fate of the troops who permitted Rudd and his companions to enter Matabeleland in breach of royal command. Instead the three were met by John Moffat who was urged by the businesslike Rudd to press the King for an immediate audience. A few hours later an audience was granted, but it was brief since the King refused to discuss business. Instead he left the three petitioners with nothing for it but to retire to the fringes of the capital where they set up camp.

By late September the dry but pleasant winter months in Matabeleland were making way for the 'suicide months' of October and November. During this time the ubiquitous dust, smell and heat were bound to make life very uncomfortable. Maguire in particular found conditions under canvas, the lack of creature comforts, or any kind of privacy from curious natives very difficult. Colonial life had been an unpleasant enough shock for this cultivated Oxford fellow, but he now found the Matabele idea of court life a aberration, and the fly-blown capital of Bulawayo no better than a medieval sewer.

Bulawayo was indeed primitive, but it was not without some primal grandeur. The King's enclosure itself was a large and imposing structure covering several acres. It consisted of three separate, circular kraals. The first was the outside wall, fenced with tightly laced wooden poles. The second formed an inner enclosure containing the huts of the King's wives, his councillors and other personages of importance. Finally, contained within — but separated by its own wooden fence — was the private enclosure of the King himself.

Beyond the walls of the royal kraal sprawled a closely packed assortment of tribute settlements among which most of the various foreign camps were situated. To Maguire this greater capital was no more than a haphazard sprawl of huts, villages, cattle and goat kraals, and every other factor of native life packed into a huge and stinking miscellany. He described the King himself as a tall, overweight, unwashed and indolent savage. Lobengula was attended by wives who themselves existed in various degrees of degradation, and in common with all the other bipeds living in or alongside the royal enclosure, they stank magnificently and appeared to think a great deal more of themselves than their circumstances justified.

If conditions for the three were generally malodorous, they were also not without danger. Francis Thompson in particular winced at the sight of the armed and hostile men who were in constant attendance, for it was widely known that a white skin was protected from brutal execution in Matabeleland by nothing more than the pleasure of the King.

Despite this Sword of Damocles the trio were by no means the only whites sojourning on the fringes of the royal kraal. Apart from missionaries, a handful of whom lived in the district of Bulawayo, rival concession seekers clung to their individual camps and rarely socialised. Rudd and his two companions sat in the shade of their wagons, observed the disorder of daily life around them, occasionally strolled in the bush, and otherwise occupied themselves smoking, playing whist or backgammon and drinking copious amounts of black tea.

Principal among their rivals for Lobengula's stamp — the 'Foreign Legion' as they were known — was a formidable gentleman by the unlikely name of E.R. Renny-Tailyour. Renny-Tailyour represented a group of German banks headed by a certain Edward A Lippert. Lippert would later be of indirect assistance to Rhodes, but in the Meanwhile he maintained an implacable rivalry. As his agent Renny-Tailyour sustained a similarly hostile posture. Throughout the period of uncertainty that marked the expedition, both did their utmost to thwart the efforts of Rudd and his companions.

Less hostile was the Rev Charles D. Helm of the London Missionary Society. Helm had assisted in the interpretation of the Moffat Treaty — a role he would duplicate on Rudd's behalf. Lobengula seems to have taken a dislike to Matabele Thompson who appeared to do little to advance matters, so the party was in need of an alternative more or less from the onset. Moffat, of course, was in constant attendance, as was the sanguine Dr Knight-Bruce, Bishop of Bloemfontein. Knight-Bruce was engaged with a friend on a tour of inspection of the missionary establishments thereabouts and spent a lot of time engaged in idle conversation with Rudd and Maguire.

All in all Lobengula hosted a variety of white chancers, ne'er-do-wells, desperados, liars and thieves who, for reasons close to their own hearts, saw value in keeping themselves beyond the reach of British justice, and had no interest in seeing Rudd or any other succeed. As a consequence, a ferment of lying, backstabbing and intrigue accompanied every act of diplomacy undertaken in the King's presence.

Without any historical catalogue or records of his own, Lobengula has tended to be regarded in this episode only insofar as he related to his enemies. His state of mind during that period is therefore a matter of conjecture. His delay in attending to Rudd and his associated probably had less to do with discourtesy or anger than fear. His situation was manifestly impossible, for although he could not have directly viewed it as such, he was running out of space and time to act. Surrounded and advised by sycophants no better informed than he, he was walking blind on a veritable minefield of awful possibilities.

To try and get to the bottom of matters he held a daily council with his senior indunas, including on occasions one or other of the Europeans. His indunas had nothing to offer, and of course any white man would have advised him strictly according to his own agenda. The missionaries, who probably meant well, had no love for the regime and at no time did Lobengula feel that he could fully trust any of them. The only thing that he could be fairly certain about was that Rudd was of a different cut to the others. His arrogance when entering Matabele territory and the confidence with which he negotiated, suggested that he was backed by something more than idle verbiage. Lobengula had heard of Rhodes and the British Empire, so presumably he at least knew that Rudd represented a formidable force. Precisely what form this force might take, however, he could not be expected to understand.

Among Lobengula's generals and fighting men there remained a restless enthusiasm for blood. The Matabele had developed over the course of their brief history just one response to crisis, and that was storm force and slaughter. There is no doubt that the Matabele impis could with ease have swept the country clean of whites in a single afternoon. There were many close to him who urged Lobengula to do this, but the King was in no doubt that such an action would bring down on him and his nation the full weight of the British Empire.

All this competed in Lobengula's mind with the realisation that he was personally a weaker man than his father had been. By comparison to Mzilikazi, Lobengula was a wavering dauphin who was palpably doomed no matter what route he chose. He was a pawn in the game of history. Indecision was his enemy, and yet indecision was in his nature. In the end he chose the line of least resistance and delegated as much of the decision as he could to his council of indunas. In particular he was reliant on his chief advisor Lotje.

Like Lobengula, Lotje was a shrewd and intelligent man, but he had the courage to say what Lobengula had been unable to. Lotje advocated the only possible route available to the Matabele at that point. It was neither a safe nor easy route, but if the declining fortunes of the native peoples of Africa could not be arrested in that generation then nothing but it remained.

The sons of the Nguni had no choice but to negotiate surrender with the most powerful of their enemies.

This simple wisdom was of course not easily digested, but Rudd and his lieutenants were omnipresent in court and applied steady pressure. Lobengula held back as Lotje fought for some consensus in the council. The King conferred with Helm, but the missionary was not with him. Helm's faith was in God and the British — and he advocated the cause of both. On hearing this, Lobengula called a full meeting of his Council of indunas to which he invited Rudd and his confederates for something of a final showdown.

A spontaneous display of native anger followed. The council turned a deaf ear to what was said to them, but heckled and jibed the Englishmen, forcing them back on their wits. This did not mean that the council rejected reality or failed to recognise the facts, but simply that they wanted to vent their frustration and go down with the dignity of a fight. It also did not mean that a concession was immediately forthcoming.

Underhand promises of personal gifts to certain individual indunas, including Lotje, affected the pace of negotiations. Ultimately, however, it was a pledge of firearms that sealed the bargain. Obviously guns would be difficult to deliver, but they were just the kind of inducement that appealed to a weak dictator.

The offer of guns also gave Francis Thompson the opportunity to make a relevant point: if Rhodes' intent was hostile, then why would he arm the very people he intended to attack? Thompson would not be the only one who would ask that question in the months ahead.

Meanwhile, waiting on the borders of Matabeleland and ostensibly investigating the murder of Piet Grobler, was Sir Sidney Shippard. Shippard made himself available as Her Majesty's representative to be summoned as necessary. It was anticipated that his presence would add the right measure of implied imperial weight to Rhodes' petition. Lobengula agreed to meet with Shippard before any final decision was made. The latter duly paused in his investigations and spurred his horse towards Bulawayo, arriving on 16 October 1888, just two days behind the hapless Edward Maund.

A plump, balding and rather portentous man, Shippard did not present a particularly vigorous symbol of the Empire. He did, however, impress Lobengula by becoming the first man ever to approach him in a standing posture. Not even Rudd had so far chanced that degree of familiarity. Thereafter heartfelt endorsements of Rhodes, mingled with subtle allusions to the destruction of the Zulu, conveyed a very clear message to Lobengula.

By the time Shippard left Bulawayo two days later, the status quo had dramatically changed. Deflated and worn to the quick, his indunas sullen but compliant, his army restive, Lobengula surrendered to pressure and consented to affix his seal to a concession.

It is necessary here to consider the negotiated terms of the Rudd Concession and how they were later represented on paper. The terms were simple. The Matabele were offered 1 000 Martini-Henri rifles, 100 000 rounds of ammunition and a gunboat on the Zambezi River, although Lobengula could waive the latter in exchange for £500 if he chose. In addition to this Lobengula himself, his dependents and his heirs, would receive £100 per month for the remainder of their lives. In exchange Rudd hoped to secure the right to prospect over all the territory under Lobengula's control, which, according to both parties, included much, if not all of Mashonaland. With this right came absolute assurances from Rudd that no actual land was desired from the Matabele, and that very few whites would in reality come into the country.

The text of the concession as Maguire prepared it contained all the specific rights conceded to Rhodes, and yet was conspicuously thin on reference to the Matabele stipulations. Lobengula had specifically stated that no more than ten white men were to enter the country for the purpose of mining. Rudd agreed to this, but it did not appear in the subsequent text. The written document was also deliberately vague about the extent of operations proposed, and in fact imposed no limitations on itself at all.

The unlikely villain in this piece was none other than the Rev Charles D Helm. Playing very heavily on Lobengula's trust, he committed a blatant and unconscionable deception. Despite the obvious omissions to the text Helm added his signature to it stating that it represented exactly the words and intent that had been agreed upon by the two parties. Much later he admitted the deception in a letter to the London Missionary Society.

> [Rudd & Co] …had promised that they would not bring more than ten white men to work in his [Lobengula's] country, that they would not dig anywhere near towns etc and that they and their people would abide by the laws of his country and in fact be as his people. But these promises were not put in the concession.[1]

There was only one possible explanation for this. Helm, like Rhodes and others, felt a misplaced sense that, while the native may rebel against the imposition of outside standards, and squirm under the unaccustomed light of civilisation, it would ultimately be to his advantage to stand up and perceive his nakedness. While questionable tactics might have been used to bring him under British control, he would be happy and forgiving when he arrived.

There was, of course, some truth in this. Men of sensitive disposition like Helm, Knight-Bruce and Moffat must have been revolted by the oppression and violence that characterised the Matabele regime. Lobengula was conspicuously less cruel and violent than his father had been, but nonetheless the Matabele people lived daily under a spectre of arbitrary and at times extreme brutality. Any means to lift the natives out of their current condition could not but be blessed in the eyes of God.

While the gist of the concession was the right to mine, Rhodes had only an academic interest in what might be discovered. He had passed beyond the simple quest for money. His principal desire was now to create a society where Englishmen of character and industry could build a homeland and thrive. He wanted to drive the influence of the British Empire deep into the interior of Africa. There he would confront the interests of his rivals, and try to claim the entirety of the sub-equatorial landmass for the British Crown. Gold and diamonds was simply to attract necessary capital subscription.

This was the enigma of Cecil John Rhodes. He was one of the richest men in the world by then, an artist whose canvas was painted with money. His highest objectives were above reproach, but they were consistently sullied by sharp practice, and in this the Rudd Concession was no different.

So while Lobengula dared to hope for the narrowest possible definition, Rhodes was already thinking ahead. The next phase of his quest would begin with a Royal Charter. As Charles Rudd made his way south with the precious document, Rhodes had already begun to prepare the groundwork for his submission to Imperial Government.

In his African works, meanwhile, he stirred a great deal of speculation in the press. Both those for and against the Rudd Concession agreed on one thing at least: that Lobengula had fallen into the net. He had given away, if not all, then at least a significant part of his country.

The Matabele Embassy

Lobengula had plenty of time in the aftermath of the signing to reflect on events, and of course there was no shortage of sceptics to stir up his fears.

Rudd left Bulawayo with the signed concession. He left behind his two associates, which was certainly a mistake. Neither Maguire nor Thompson was a forceful man, and the vacuum gave Lobengula and his counsellors much opportunity to ruminate on bad advice. As word of how the Rudd Concession was being viewed abroad began to filter through to Matabeleland, Lobengula set about trying to understand exactly what he had done. He summoned a meeting of all the whites in Bulawayo, and they naturally fed him a banquet of contradictory propaganda. Lobengula justifiably felt trapped, deceived and in imminent peril of invasion.

An interesting result of this gathering was a later meeting held between Maund, Renny-Tailyour and a few others where all decided to form a united if temporary front against Rhodes. They convinced Lobengula that Rhodes had not been acting with the authority of the Crown, and put it to him that only a direct appeal to the Queen would expose him as a fraud. It was further proposed that Lobengula appoint an ambassador to travel to London to explain his position directly to the Queen.

Lobengula was delighted with the suggestion, although it goes without saying that the proposal had not been made with any benefit to him in mind. Lobengula was by necessity hopeful, and that he placed any real faith in the scheme was simply a measure of his desperation.

The King selected two members of his inner circle — Indunas Mtshete and Babayane — to undertake the mission to London. They took with them at least one letter, although there could have been two; the existence of the second has never been established for certain. It is very likely, of course, that neither letter represented what Lobengula actually wished to say.

The first asserted Lobengula's territorial claims with regard to the Portuguese in Mashonaland and was really no more than a plea for assistance under the terms of protection of the Moffat Treaty. The second, less credibly, questioned the very existence of a Great White Queen and announced that Lobengula was sending his indunas to investigate the matter. To this the King apparently added that concession seekers were odiously troubling him, and that he could not find any among the whites whom he could trust. He asked that Victoria send an emissary of her own.

The Matabele Embassy set off from Bulawayo in the company of Edward Maund in late November of 1888. Initially Maund chose a route that carried the three by a combination of road and rail through the Transvaal, hoping by this means to avoid any interference from Rhodes. Just how enthusiastic Kruger and his government were to help in discrediting Rhodes is indicated by the fact that Mtshete and Babayane were permitted to travel on the inside of a mail coach — probably the first natives ever to do so in the Transvaal.

Despite the precautions, Rhodes inevitably intercepted Maund and his party when they finally reached the railhead at Kimberley. Rhodes tried alternately to bribe and threaten Maund, but could not persuade him to share the letter or letters that he was carrying. Maund then continued south to Cape Town leaving Rhodes both anxious and enraged. In Cape Town the travelling party was delayed considerably thanks to Sir Hercules Robinson as Rhodes frantically sought some solution to the crisis.

As his emissaries proceeded south, Lobengula's mind still churned over the issue of the Rudd Concession. In response to ongoing newspaper coverage, he decided to compose his own statement and submit it to the press. On 18 January 1889 he dictated a letter in which he stated:

> I hear it published in newspapers that I have granted a concession of the minerals in all my country to Charles Dunell Rudd, Rochfort Maguire and Francis Thompson.
>
> As there is a great misunderstanding about this, all action in terms of the said Concession is hereby suspended pending an investigation to be made by me in my country.

Lobengula sent this communiqué south, but it was not picked up and published until the following month when it appeared in the limited circulation Bechuanaland News. By that time Maund and his companions, as well as Rhodes himself, were on their way to London to do battle over the Royal Charter.

For the two Indunas the sea voyage must have been the climax of an odyssey that had already taken on a surreal dimension. It is not difficult to imagine what effect the gathering pace of industrialisation must have had on them with every mile they travelled. Tales they might have been told about the white man and his abilities would by then have crystallised in their minds completely. They would have realised with sinking hearts that their little empire was insignificant indeed.

Besides this, the tide in London had already begun to move against them. Lord Knutsford had advised Lord Gifford to consider an amalgamation with Rhodes, to which Gifford agreed. Rhodes had once again squared his rivals, and although the marriage would not be consummated for some time, it rendered the Matabele Embassy irrelevant before the two indunas had made landfall.

Nevertheless Edward Maund did not falter. By the time the ship came within sight of Southampton docks the Matabele Embassy had assumed a ceremonial function, and the press where there to greet them as such. The two were received at Windsor Castle where some time later they met and briefly exchanged pleasantries with the Queen. Misunderstanding the monarch's constitutional role, they were anxious to discuss the business at hand, but conversations were deliberately kept general and they were not given the chance. It was only later that they would met and handed their communiqué over to Lord Knutsford, and later still that they received his reply.

Meanwhile the two visited all the major sights of London. They attended a number of banquets and met a variety of notable personalities. They were taken to the naval base at Portsmouth where they were treated to a tour of naval installations... and conducted to Aldershot where they reviewed military manoeuvres, observed mock cavalry attacks and were shown an artillery and machinegun demonstration. These last two visits, of course, were designed to impress the pair with Britain's military might and demonstrate the utter futility of their own position.

In early April, after events had entirely overtaken the purpose of their mission, the envoys — now an entirely irrelevant pair of African gentlemen — embarked at Southampton docks, still in the company of Maund, for the long sea voyage home.

As a sad epilogue to this particular little tragedy, the two indunas took home with them a plethora of impressions that must have stunned the King and those in council. Few could embrace the wonders that their fellows had seen. Lobengula and many others in Matabeleland were given to wonder once again what the future held for them. Where once they had thought that their military prowess alone kept the white man respectful in court, they now realised this was not the case. Clearly, if it wished to do so, Britannia could crush the Matabele like an insect.

Rhodes: Man of destiny
The British Prime Minister Lord Salisbury was fond neither of Rhodes nor men like him. However, beset by domestic issues, he was reconciled to allow aggressive private capital to lay the new stepping-stones of empire. It is also worth remembering that Rhodes and his peers enjoyed a great deal of public recognition at that time. The closing decades of the 19th century saw the Victorian public enthralled by great events overseas, embodied by men such as Rhodes and captured in verse and prose by others such as Rudyard Kipling and Alfred Austin. With the huge wealth of empire to draw upon, and great strides being made in literacy, science and industry, the era of global colonial expansion was arching towards its zenith. It was an energetic and exciting period for Britain, offset and spoiled only somewhat by the ghastly backwash of the slave trade.

The Dark Continent in particular held great fascination for the British public. They stood firmly behind the men of vision and vigour — the heroes who were willing on their own account to take to the field for the wealth and glory of Britannia. By then Livingstone had explored much of the southern interior. Burton, Speke and others had extensively mapped the Great Lakes. Henry Morton Stanley had journeyed down the Congo River and seen for the first time the snow-capped peaks of the fabled Mountains of the Moon. Africa was indeed the growing frontier of the British Empire.

The English-speaking race did not forget the great and civilising aspect of this mission. Wide–ranging exploration had brought to British attention just how much of the world, particularly in Africa, was excluded from progress by its primitive and untutored condition. It became a significant part of the Empire objective to see this situation changed. The world needed to — in fact, it deserved to — bask in the cleansing light of Anglo-Saxon civilisation.

This notwithstanding it would be naive to suppose that all the efforts at global expansion on the part of the European powers were philanthropic. It was, however, a manifest feeling of having the power to uplift the downtrodden that enabled men like Rhodes, with their more complex objectives, to proceed at pace.

Rhodes was travelling a few weeks behind Maund and his two Matabele charges as they arrived at Southampton docks for their British tour. He was girding his loins to do battle with some very powerful enemies in London that spring. Still only 36 years old, he was both rich and influential, and although many supposed that he would enter British politics, he had no such intention. He was confident that he had done what could be done in Bulawayo to secure his charter, and now what remained was to win the support of the British establishment. He was moreover so satisfied in this that he could both rely on his supporters to support him to the hilt, and that those that did not support him could be paid off or won over. His enemies back in Bulawayo had also not been idle. Lobengula's letter of 18 January 1889 — by which he tried to suspend the Rudd Concession pending an investigation by himself — appeared in a small newspaper on February 14. A month earlier Sir Hercules Robinson had dispatched a copy of the much criticised Rudd Concession to his superiors at home, accompanied by a report, the language of which rather betrayed his awe.

> The effect of the concession to a gentleman of character and financial standing will be to check the inroad of adventurers as well as to secure the cautious development of the country with proper consideration for the feelings and prejudices of the natives.

The contents of Lobengula's rebuff might not confirm Rhodes in anyone's mind as a gentleman of character, but no one could deny that he was a man of financial standing. He was also an individual of tested ability, and ultimately it would be this that would serve him most effectively. The two Matabele Indunas were told by Sir Foxwell Buxton, chairman of the Aboriginal Protection Society, that before long Englishmen and Matabele would meet in the valleys of the Limpopo as happily as they did that day in Westminster. Cecil Rhodes set about the serious business of ensuring that this rather naïve? (diarasis) hope would never come to be.

Rhodes' first and most important trophy had been the partnership of Lord Gifford and George Cawston. By April of 1889 differences between the two parties had been largely bridged. Gifford appealed to the Colonial Secretary on behalf of the Exploring Company for a charter to develop Bechuanaland and the countries to the north. He was assisted in this by a letter signed by Rhodes and Alfred Beit on behalf of Goldfields of South Africa.

In parenthesis it would seem likely that Maund — at that moment on the high seas with Mtshete and Babayane — would automatically move to support Rhodes. As events would reveal, it did not turn out quite that way. On 26 March Lord Knutsford had dictated his reply to Lobengula's dispatch. In the circumstances it was curiously worded, and in no way helpful to the cause of the Charter. It warned Lobengula that Rhodes had not operated under the authority of the Queen, and added that the King might exercise caution in any future dealing with Englishmen seeking concessions. In the pivotal paragraph he remarked:

> It is not wise to put too much power in the hands of the men who come first, and to exclude other deserving men. A king gives a stranger an ox, not his whole herd of cattle, otherwise what would other strangers have to eat? [2]

It is difficult to understand exactly why Lord Knutsford should have chosen this approach, but it is conceivable that it emerged from a personal dislike of Rhodes. This dispatch — together with another from the Aboriginal Protection Society which was no less denigrating of the Rudd Concession — were now in the hands of Maund, and despite much pressure from Rhodes he would not consider relinquishing either. The letters were not delivered until the following August, and caused more embarrassment than actual harm. However the incident did cause Rhodes later to have much of a disparaging nature to say about Maund, and arguably his career was fatally damaged by a momentary adherence to principal.

While Rhodes, with relative ease and considerable expenditure, was disposing of rival claims both genuine and fraudulent, he was having more difficulty squaring those whose motivations in opposing him were not financial. The London Chamber of Commerce, for example, complained that the Rudd Concession represented a monopoly, in terms of which Rhodes and his associates would have sole access to the mineral wealth of an entire country. This, it was argued, was against the principals of free trade. Rhodes had little interest in such arguments since his entire fortune had been constructed pursuant to the monopolisation of the Kimberley diamond output. Others, like the South African Committee — with a membership including such social luminaries as Albert Grey, soon to succeed to the title of the 4th Earl Grey — suspected that Rhodes intended the mass appropriation of native lands. The Colonial Office, ever sensitive to pressures on the purse, predicted that a war would be inevitable. Missionary societies and Afro-paternalists opposed the charter for reasons ranging from land rights to the counter-intuitive policy of supplying the Matabele with firearms. Rhodes reacted to all these with his customary composure, either disposing of the objections or ignoring them.

Of greater concern to Rhodes was the fact that his charter would not under any circumstances see the light of day without the support of the aristocracy. This fact more than any other must have cut to the quick of his personal dilemma. His acceptance by the governing classes could not depend on money alone, nor for that matter on a second-class degree from Oxford. It would depend on the indulgence of those he both venerated and despised. To be told, and instinctively to realise, that he needed the endorsement of a group who would fundamentally never accept him as their equal must have been a hard pill to swallow.

Despite this, Rhodes applied the considerable force of his personality to the task of winning friends amongst the nobility. The extent to which he succeeded is illustrated by directors of the British South Africa Company that was floated for the purpose of exploiting the anticipated charter. The first was Lord Cecil, who, as the prime Minister's son, Rhodes hoped, would positively influence his father. Other illustrious names on the list were the Duke of Abercorn, the Duke of Fife, and the future Earl Grey.

Having co-opted the aristocracy Rhodes turned his attention to the press. Until then he had been less than the darling of the newspapers which portrayed him not only as an uppity colonial but also as a deceitful pirate motivated by greed. One of his most vociferous detractors was W.T. Stead, a society commentator and charismatic publisher of the popular Pall Mall Gazette. Famously, Rhodes won

Stead and converted him to a staunch and powerful ally during a lunch party that the two attended in April of 1889. Stead was followed in close formation by *The Times* correspondents Scott Keltie and Flora Shaw. All three thereafter never deviated from a slavish devotion to Rhodes and his vision. The powers of persuasion of the Colossus were never more impressive than this.

These dramatic conversions marked a turning point in the popular perception of Rhodes. Eulogies began to flow from such prestigious publications as *The Times*, the *Pall Mall Gazette*, the *St. James Gazette*, *The Fortnightly Review* and *The Nineteenth Century*. In May 1889 even the Royal Geographical Society endorsed the concept of commercial associations as the best means of disseminating civilisation throughout central Africa.

Under the surface of Rhodes' tour de force, a little of his dubious methodology went largely unnoticed. As shares and options in the Chartered Company were being allocated, the public and the directors believed that the British South Africa Company owned the Rudd Concession. This was not so. In fact the Rudd Concession was owned by a shadowy entity formed at more or less the same time and known as the Central Search Association. The principal directors of the Central Search Association were Rhodes, Alfred Beit, Gifford, Cawston and Charles Rudd.

The essence of the deception was an agreement among them to allow the British South Africa Company use of the Rudd Concession in exchange for half its profits. In July of the following year the Central Search Association reinvented itself as the United Concessions Company with a capital of four million £1 shares. These were founded on its claim to the British South Africa Company's profits. Thereafter the BSA Company bought out the United Concessions Company for one million specially created shares. These shares stood at between £3 and £4 apiece, but the expectation was that they would inflate substantially, thus allowing for immense profit taking on the part of the principal directors. It was a very cunning piece of corporate engineering indeed.

Here again lies the great tragedy of Cecil Rhodes. While he was able to inspire such devotion in a diverse following, somehow an element of villainy would always stain the linen. This would come to characterise the work of the great man more and more, and the older he got the worse it became.

Despite awkward questions raised in the House of Commons about the less than glorious contribution of the Rev Charles Helm and about the inappropriate use of Her Majesty's representatives, and opposition from the paternal element of British society and reservations expressed by the establishment, elements of the press and even by the great hunter-explorer Frederick Courtney Selous, Rhodes' petition for a Charter was debated and approved. Queen Victoria signed it into being on 29 October 1889.

Soon after the departure of the Matabele Embassy from London and as Lobengula restlessly anticipated their return, the King was moved once more to put pen to paper. On 23 April 1889 he composed a sad missive to the Great White Queen in which he lamented:

> Some time ago a party of men came into my country, the principal one appearing to be a man named Rudd. They asked me for a place to dig for gold, and said they would give me certain things for the right to do so. I told them to bring what they would give and I would show them what I would give.
>
> A document was written and presented to me for signature. I asked what it contained and was told that in it were my words and the words of those men. I put my hand to it.
>
> About three months afterwards I heard from other sources that I had given by that document the right to all the minerals in my country.
>
> I called a meeting of my Indunas and also of the white men, and demanded a copy of that document. It was proved to me that I had signed away the mineral rights for my whole country to Rudd and his friends.

I have since had a meeting of my Indunas, and they will not recognise the paper as it contains neither my words nor the words of those who got it.

After the meeting I demanded that the original document be returned to me; it has not come yet, although it is two months since, and they promised to bring it back soon.

The men of the party who were in the country at the time were told to remain until the document was brought back. One of them, Maguire, has now left without my knowledge and against my orders.

I write to you that you may know the truth about this thing, and may not be deceived.[3]

6

Doctor Jim

Before Rhodes and his associates could proceed much further the most important feat of diplomacy was yet to be achieved. This was, of course, to persuade Lobengula to take delivery of the first consignment of the promised firearms. The moment that he did so the Rudd Concession could be considered fully ratified. Thereafter Lobengula could hardly gripe to the world about ill usage, with British South Africa Company weapons in his hands.

Rhodes, meanwhile, was soon to travel to London to begin negotiations for the Charter, and these regular and plaintive denunciations of the Rudd Concession emanating from Bulawayo were not helping him at all. Lobengula needed to be satisfied or silenced: either way this was a task beyond the powers of Rochfort Maguire or Francis Thompson. Rhodes required a very particular type of man for this job, and while the colonies were brimming with such good men, it so happened that he found just the candidate in his own circle.

Until that moment it seemed that Leander Starr Jameson had been content to play the role of country doctor in the cash-happy atmosphere of Kimberley. While he and Rhodes had been friends for some time and had shared a town house in Kimberley, Jameson had successfully resisted any temptation — and indeed a number of casual invitations — to involve himself in one or other of Rhodes' complex affairs. He was both a credible doctor and a charismatic man about town. A crisp and occasionally derisive sense of humour had made him many friends, most of whom were patients and all of whom had at one time or another observed a devious tendency at the bridge table. His bedside manner was a widely prescribed tonic, and in general he was confident, expansive and witty.

On the surface Jameson could not have been a less likely candidate for frontier diplomacy, but Rhodes, unfailing as always in matters of character judgement, had sensed differently. He had surmised quite correctly that Jameson was a terrier — short, aggressive, charming, gifted and with deep reserves of courage, tenacity and cunning.

Jameson might, after years of study, have safely stuck with the medical profession. However, as Rhodes the cotton farmer had discovered, the colonies were a cauldron of opportunity and like Rhodes, Jameson was at heart an opportunist. Equally important, Rhodes was a consummate manipulator, and Jameson was ripe for manipulation. He recognised his friend's determination, and furthermore knew from old the moment Rhodes made up his mind was the moment the matter was decided.

Soon thereafter Jameson set off for Bulawayo in the company of Rhodes' principal secretary, Dr. Frederick Rutherfoord Harris, and a transport contractor whose job it was to haul a consignment of half the firearms promised to Bulawayo. Rhodes, meanwhile, set off for London feeling much easier in his mind. Jameson had been thoroughly briefed, and, as Rhodes had anticipated, the two men understood one another perfectly. Jameson had made it absolutely clear to Rhodes that this would be his one and only intercession, but Rhodes gave no thought to this at all. He was confident that from then on Jameson would do precisely what was expected of him.

On his first visit Jameson spent only ten days in Bulawayo. He met Lobengula and bettered both Rudd and Shippard in uncommon familiarity, approaching the King directly and pausing only at the threshold of shaking his hand. By then Lobengula was becoming accustomed to this sort of thing and took Jameson at face value, in return for which Jameson unleashed his customary arsenal of charm. Gone was the down-talking, imperious and arrogant white man, nor was there sign of the snivelling missionary or the sycophantic trader. Jameson was the first white man in whose company Lobengula felt at ease. What is more, Lobengula was ailing with the gout for which Jameson prescribed morphine. The drug obliterated the pain and eased Lobengula's mind considerably, but despite this he would not, under any circumstances, consider accepting delivery of the Martini-Henri rifles.

Jameson took this apparent setback in his stride, sensing that he had achieved a better result in winning Lobengula's trust and affection. On 12 April he and Rutherfoord Harris set off on the return journey to Kimberley. Rochfort Maguire, feeling that he had endured as much of Bulawayo as he could stomach, abandoned his post at the last minute and joined them. Francis Thompson's incessant paranoia and unending predictions of a horrible death had worn him out. This left Thompson alone in Bulawayo, which was not only ill advised, but cruelly unfair too.

By August Rhodes was back in South Africa having satisfactorily disposed of his business in London. The Matabele Embassy had returned, and Lobengula had been briefed. Lord Knutsford's reply had been read to the Council and the intelligence widely circulated. On the 10th of that month yet another plea was sent on Lobengula's behalf to Queen Victoria, and this time the note of hopelessness was unmistakable.

> … the white people are troubling me much about gold. If the Queen hears that I have given away the whole country, it is not so. I do not understand where the dispute is because I have no knowledge of writing.

Lobengula had meanwhile, summoned a meeting of his indunas and, during a stormy debate, a senior councillor called Hlesingane, who was one of few Matabele to have actually visited Kimberley, openly admonished him. Hlesingane put it to the King and his council that it would be impossible for just ten whites to mine gold, for mining required land and how would these men be able to mine and not need land? What about producing food, he argued, and firewood, and labour? Would all this not take land? Others clamoured in agreement. In due course Lobengula directed his eyes at his erstwhile councillor Lotje and saw that this hapless man, with his loyalty and good intentions, must be sacrificed. Within a few minutes of being indicted Lotje was escorted beyond the royal enclosure and executed along with his family, dependents and livestock.

Francis Thompson was briefed on the slaughter while returning home in a four-horse cart from a visit to Charles Helm's Hope Fountain mission station. A Matabele woman whom he knew called across to him that further killings were being planned. Already weighed down by paranoia and neurosis Thompson promptly untethered the fastest horse from the team and fled the scene in a blind panic. From Mafeking he cabled Rhodes with the news and nervously waited on events.

Rhodes was horrified by this dereliction of duty and promptly approached Jameson to fill the vacuum. The good doctor set off immediately for Bulawayo by way of Mafeking where he collected a sullen and reluctant Thompson. The two continued north and arrived in Bulawayo on 17 October, a little less than a fortnight before Queen Victoria would sign the Royal Charter into existence.

On his arrival, Jameson was gratified to be welcomed in the Royal Kraal as an old friend. However nothing had changed. Lobengula still resolutely refused to accept the guns waiting in storage, and was insistent now that Rhodes present himself in Bulawayo in person. Ilodzi, as Rhodes was known in Matabeleland, had by then assumed almost mythical stature, and Jameson rightly supposed that it would hardly do to hang upon this legend the mortal flesh of a sickly man. Besides, Rhodes was always too busy and as a consequence, he and Lobengula were never to meet. Jameson continued to work valiantly, but could make no impression on Lobengula and the validity of the Rudd Concession remained in question.

As the year progressed and the rains came and went, Jameson settled reasonably comfortably into the court life of Bulawayo, attending to Lobengula's ailments, reading to him, entertaining him, and with infinite patience and cunning wearing him down. As a sign of the King's personal regard, Jameson was made an honorary induna in council and charged with certain ceremonial duties — which he undertook dressed as a Matabele. All the while he badgered Lobengula for permission to travel inland with a party of miners, and after some time was given limited authority for a small group to work on an old and abandoned concession at Tati. This mine had lain deserted for years, but Jameson quickly sent word back to Kimberley and arranged for a group of 'miners' to occupy it and appear to be working.

Towards the end of January 1890, after Jameson had been in Bulawayo for almost three months, a party of Royal Horse Guards arrived in the capital, and in full regalia trotted into the Royal Kraal. Their purpose was threefold: to return the visit of the indunas to London, to present Lobengula with gifts and to make formal notification of the Royal Charter. This had been Rhodes' idea; by then he was at the height of his powers and if he felt inclined to wave the Union Jack as if it was his own, he could hardly be blamed. With the formal notification came a royal despatch address to Lobengula, and written by Lord Knutsford in words carefully chosen to impress the King with the gravity of the Charter. Jameson, however, took no chances and substituted the letter for a forgery of his own which relayed unqualified support for the Rudd Concession. He also added sober warnings of Boer and Portuguese plans for an invasion of Matabeleland.[1]

Once the Horse Guards had left and the dust had settled, Lobengula was struck with a sense of hopelessness and quickly lapsed into depression. Jameson's importunity also seemed now to be wearing on him at last, and to Jameson's complaints that the miners at Tati had unearthed no gold, Lobengula — in an apparently offhand remark — suggested that they ought to consider looking elsewhere.

A second version of this story states that the troop of Horse Guards were invited to take part in a Great Dance — which put the King in such high humour that Jameson won his concession by the perfect timing of his request.

Either way Jameson was astonished, but immediately seized on the remark, airing the thought that the miners might go east into Mashonaland. To this Lobengula did not demur. Even as Jameson traced a few possibilities out on a map, Lobengula maintained a posture of tragic indifference. Jameson then ventured further still and secured an undertaking from Lobengula to provide labour to cut the road east, to which Lobengula applied only one pre-condition: that at all times Jameson accompany the party himself. After that Lobengula fell silent, and Jameson pressed him no further.

7

Birth of a colony

The Pioneer Column

Back in Kimberley Rhodes now began to give serious thought to the practicalities of occupying Mashonaland. He had invited the opinion of General Sir Frederick Carrington, at that time commanding officer of the Bechuanaland Border Police, who estimated that at least 2500 troops would be needed to occupy Mashonaland at a probable minimum cost of £1 million. Rhodes was horrified, for although he was a man of very significant means, his wealth was not limitless.

The story then goes that Rhodes happened one morning to be sharing a breakfast table at the Kimberley Club with a young man by the name of Frank Johnson. During the conversation Rhodes mulled over some of his plans, and in particular the problem of mounting a viable expedition into Mashonaland. Johnson, although only 24 years old at the time and between employments, suggested that Carrington was being over cautious, and that given pen and paper and a quiet corner he, Johnson, would within an hour or two come up with a much more reasonable figure.

Rhodes might have smiled and dismissed Johnson as a young opportunist, but the Colossus had once been a young opportunist himself, and since then had made quite a few others very rich men. He was also rarely mistaken over questions of character — besides which he had been impressed by Johnson, who had gained something of a reputation in his short career in Africa.

Thus stepped onto the stage one of the principal characters of Rhodes' imperial adventure. Frank Johnson, the quintessential colonial fortune hunter, would later be described by an acquaintance of both he and Rhodes as 'a short, thickset, furtive eyed, dark man, with lungs of the bulls of Bashan, and the knack of handling men and hustling things. It was precisely those lungs, and this knack, and the talents Rhodes had divined in him that would carry him through.

Young as he was, Johnson had indeed already amassed some worthwhile experience. At 16 he had left his native Norfolk to come to South Africa where he enlisted in the Bechuanaland Border Police. There he saw active service on the Warren Expedition, the British response to Boer and German ambition in southern Bechuanaland. At 18 he formed a high-sounding syndicate called the Great Northern Trade and Gold Exploration Company, which was established with the usual objective of obtaining mining concessions from Khama and Lobengula. He had also spent a long time in Bulawayo jostling for attention, but in the end fell foul of Lobengula and withdrew. He later became managing director of the Gifford & Cawston organisation in Bechuanaland, but ironically was dropped without compensation on the eve of the amalgamation with Rhodes.

Johnson and a few friends then formed the Selous Exploration Syndicate with the hunter and explorer, Frederick Courtney Selous. This equally high-sounding company was founded on the principal that concessions could be negotiated with individual Mashona chiefs, but not with the

Matabele. In due course Johnson found himself at odds with Selous and in this end the syndicate was stillborn. Selous then set off on further travels, cutting adrift his young partner to fall across the path of Cecil Rhodes.

Popular myth suggests that Johnson initially proposed to Rhodes that a lightning raid, utilising just 500 trained men, should strike into Matabeleland with the purpose of killing or taking Lobengula hostage. The political ramifications of this approach would obviously have been explosive. Also, in terms of practicalities, a commando of that size without extensive logistical support would probably not have survived for long in Matabeleland. The chances were that it would either be annihilated or require a hugely expensive rescue. Johnson contends that Rhodes initially gave serious consideration to the proposal and was only dissuaded later by Sidney Shippard, and by an expression of horror from the then High Commissioner for South Africa, Sir Henry Loch who, it was said, did not particularly care for Rhodes.

It was hunter-explorer Frederick Courtney Selous who later advised Rhodes to plan prudently and not underestimate any military threat from the Matabele. Even assuming a peaceful occupation, the main problem would remain Lobengula's expectation that any party entering the country would follow the road that, by dint of geography and protocol, led through his capital. The Matabele would then see for themselves that they had been lied to. Selous therefore proposed forging a new route that would enter the country to the southeast and give the Matabele heartland a wide berth. This plan was agreed to by all and duly adopted. It was, nonetheless, still probable that the expedition would see at least some action en route, so exhaustive military precautions were still needed.

Frank Johnson did his arithmetic and, as promised, presented Rhodes with a tender that pleased him very much indeed. For the sum of £87 000, 80 000 acres of land and 20 gold claims, Johnson proposed to construct a road from Palapaye to Mount Hampden, and to lead there a body of 200 pioneers. Johnson later claimed to have made £20 000 out of the deal, which presumably did not include his land and mining claims. He later remarked that he had found just enough gold in the country to make a wedding ring for his bride, but that is almost certainly a wild understatement of what he eventually took away from the country.

Some 2 000 such men in the Johnson mould applied to join the expedition. This allowed Rhodes to turn his mind to planning the future white demographics of the country that would bear his name — and it must be said that he had very particular ideas on this matter. Clearly the successful applicants needed to be able to ride and shoot, but the various trades and professions that would be necessary to built a country also had to be considered. Central to this was the need for English-speaking men of a certain caste — what Rhodes often termed 'young men of good family'. By this he meant the disinherited younger sons of the British aristocracy who could be relied upon to use their education and higher sensibilities not only to raise the general standard of the population, but to make their fortunes too. There was the added advantage that parents of influence might pressure the Imperial Government to weigh in for their rescue if the need ever arose.

The 2 000 applicants were whittled down to an eventual 196. These were what author and administrator Hugh Marshal Hole later described as a Corp d'elite of farmers, artisans, miners, doctors, lawyers, engineers, builders, bakers, soldiers, sailors, cadets of good family with no particular occupation, cricketers, three parsons and a Jesuit.

Since no one could be certain how the mood of the Matabele would play out, Johnson tried to plan for every eventuality. With this in mind the pioneers were obliged by their contracts to submit to military discipline. Each was equipped with a Martini-Henri rifle and a six-shot .45 Webley revolver, plus a uniform consisting of trousers and tunic of brown corduroy with yellow leggings and regulation army boots. On their heads they wore brown soft felt hats known widely as the Buffalo Bill. A trooper's pay was 7s 6d a day with the promise of 3 000 acres of Mashonaland and 15 gold claims.

Officers, of course, earned a little more.[1]

After kit distribution the men were divided into three troops. Troops A and B were mounted infantry commanded respectively by Maurice Heany and an American ex-sea captain by the name of Skipper Hoste. An Irishman named Jack Roach commanded C Troop. The latter was an artillery detachment equipped with two seven pounders, two machine guns — a Maxim and a Nordenfeldt — and two 24 pound rocket launchers. A unique addition was a 10 000 candle power searchlight powered by a mobile steam engine.

While Rhodes was satisfied with these arrangements, he reluctantly agreed at the insistence of Sir Henry Loch to recruit an additional 500-man police force for garrison duty and extra defence capacity. This force was placed under the regular military command of Lt. Colonel E. G. Pennefather of the Inniskilling Dragoons. It later became the genesis of the famed British South Africa Police (BSAP) that would serve Rhodesia well until 1980.

Military uncertainties were not the only imponderables. Rhodes chose veteran colonial administrator Archibald Colquhoun as administrator designate. This was an eccentric choice and evidence that Rhodes had no better idea than anyone else of knowing precisely what to expect in Mashonaland. Colquhoun was a well-meaning and very able character, but often misunderstood. He was a typical sahib of the Colonial Service who pictured himself in a kind of viceregal role with all the accoutrements of Imperial governorship. For the journey he packed a consignment of 1 000 best and 1 000 ordinary Havana cigars, and these he augmented with cases of whisky and champagne, as well as a vast selection of light delicacies purchased on his behalf from Fortnum & Mason.[2]

In the fullness of time, Colquhoun distinguished himself more as a traveller and chronicler than as a colonial administrator. By the time of his death he had published 13 books on travel, including *Overland to China* (1901) and *Greater America* (1904). Mainly for reasons of poor company, Mashonaland — even from a distance — could not have been a brilliant proposal for him. He was not, however, in a position to be choosy. A long career in colonial administration — including Burma, India, China and Central and South America — had been beggared by the kind of howler that PG Wodehouse could scarcely have composed.

As a civil servant in Burma, Colquhoun was attending to his correspondence one day when he accidentally slipped two letters into a single envelope. The first was a response to criticism from his administrative superiors and was composed of suitably restrained language. The second was a richly worded attack on government policy in general and his own department in particular, which was addressed to *The Times* of London. He had carefully post-scripted the letter, urging that the contents be not traceable back to him. The envelope was stamped and accidentally sent on to the head of his department. Not surprisingly word came down in due course that he might find work in the private sector more to his taste.

Jameson, of course, missed no opportunity to embellish and circulate this tale — which helped in setting up Colquhoun as an early object of ridicule. His corpulent, bespectacled and rather beakish appearance did nothing to ameliorate this, nor make him appear or feel any less out of place.

This was just one of many factions that soon formed within the Pioneer Column. Very unwisely Rhodes had given Jameson a loosely defined power of attorney over the whole expedition, a fact which he neglected to communicate officially to Colquhoun and one which Jameson went out of his way to make known. In fact Colquhoun was only to take up his duties upon arrival, and so he could assume no authority over the expedition itself. This oversight planted the seeds of a very damaging feud between the two men, and one that would reverberate for years into the future.

A quarrel had also broken out between Johnson and Pennefather over the question of who was in actual command of the expedition. In the end it was agreed that Pennefather would take command of the police, and Johnson the pioneers — which included anybody who was not officially defined as a police detail. One of the few relationships between the senior men that seemed to be on an even keel was that between Johnson and Jameson. Both got on very well and remained friends into the future.

Rhodes appointed Frederick Courtney Selous to the expedition as ordinance officer, guide and road builder. Their personal feelings for one another had to be put aside for the sake of the expedition. Rhodes had often been scalded by bitter public criticism from Selous, who was a respected figure both in South Africa and Britain, and was seen to be a champion of fair play and equality in Africa. His opinions carried weight, and although in later life he professed support for the imperial ethos, rarely did these opinions support Rhodes. Certainly the two men were extremely unlikely bedfellows in the upcoming dismemberment of the Matabele and Mashona nations.

Frank Johnson shared with Rhodes a deep antipathy towards Selous that in his case probably had its roots in the difficulties of their earlier business partnership. This hostility was not eased in the slightest by Selous' tendency to upstage Johnson and unconsciously undermine his brash and sometimes maverick overconfidence. Selous was seldom ruffled and as a rule he ignored the tension, tending to rely on his own company and his own quiet but consummate professionalism.

Selous was indeed one of the principal characters and a curiosity of British Africa. In popular mythology he was a hunter and frontiersman, a man's man to the core and yet also a gentleman, a scholar and a philosopher. He might easily be pictured reading Wordsworth or Keats as he balanced the heavy elephant gun on his knee, and might periodically glance up from his musings to direct a line of porters singing in native harmony as they hauled his ivory to the coast. More than any other, he defined the popular image of a great white hunter, and as such he inspired H. Rider Haggard in the creation of his popular hero Allan Quartermain.

* * *

As preparations for the departure of the column were being finalised, problems of a broader political nature persisted. The expansionists within the Transvaal Republic had begun to sense that their opportunity to claim Mashonaland as a third Boer republic was slipping away. Word found its way to Rhodes that a private trek (journey by Boers) was being assembled in the Transvaal and was ready to move on the territory. This fact coincided with Lobengula reaching the conclusion that something significantly more than an assembly of ten miners was preparing to march on his country. As futile as it might have been, he lamented his observation as loudly as he could, and threatened to deny passage to all whites through his domains.

Rhodes met the Transvaal president Paul Kruger on 12 March 1890 and put it to him that his Boer colony had little in the way of legal empowerment to interfere with the British occupation of Mashonaland, to which Kruger was forced to agree. This was the first meeting between the two and it set the tone for a future of unmitigated mutual antipathy. Kruger was later heard to retort that he feared only four men: 'God, the Devil, General de la Rey and that damned Englishman Cecil Rhodes.'

To pacify Lobengula, meanwhile, it was once again Dr Jameson whom Rhodes sent on a flying visit to Bulawayo. Lobengula, of course, was as unimpressed by events as Kruger, but he was no less outmanoeuvred.

Jameson left Kimberley for Bulawayo on 11 April 1890 and arrived at the capital a fortnight later. Lobengula greeted him with friendship, but demanded once again that Rhodes himself come to Bulawayo to settle matters. Rhodes was by then the Premier of the Cape Colony, so a visit to Bulawayo was obviously out of the question. Besides, Jameson's visit on this occasion was intended more to mollify Lobengula than to threaten him. Friendship of old was exposed as a sham when Jameson let it be known that if Lobengula refused to grant permission for the expedition to proceed, armed confrontation would follow.

Lobengula retreated. He had always known that this day would come. He replied that the only road he was willing to permit into Mashonaland was through Bulawayo, for he wanted to see with his own eyes the miners who were entering his country.

'The King told me that I might make the road', Jameson coldly insisted. 'Did the King lie?'

Lobengula paused and pondered his antagonist for a long time before at last he whispered: 'The King never lies!'

Jameson departed Bulawayo on 2 May, never to see Lobengula again. Four days later the Pioneer Column lumbered out of Kimberley with its 117 wagons, some thousands of draught oxen, almost a thousand men and countless native and coloured retainers. A month later it arrived at its formal staging point on the Motlutsi River, where it was formally dispatched by perhaps the most bizarre valediction so far rendered in British colonial history. Major-General Methuen, Deputy Adjutant-General in South Africa, addressed the assembled officers of the BSA Company Police as follows:

Methuen: Gentlemen, have you got maps?
Officers: Yes Sir.
Methuen: And pencils?
Officers: Yes Sir.
Methuen: Well, Gentlemen your destiny is Mount Hampden. You go to a place called Siboutsie. I do not know whether Siboutsie is a man or a mountain. Mr Selous is of the opinion that it is a man; but we will pass that by. Then you get to Mount Hampden. Mr Selous is of the opinion that Mount Hampden is placed ten miles too far to the west. You had better correct that; but perhaps on second thoughts, better not — because you might be placing it ten miles too far to the east. Now good morning, gentlemen.

On that facetious and somewhat addled speech the full weight of the British South Africa Company Pioneer Column moved off to take its place in southern African history.

8

Occupation of Mashonaland

With the Pioneer Column poised on his border, it was possible for the first time for Lobengula to see the entire sham laid out unabashed before him. Indeed the facts were at last there for the whole world to see — if anyone would only consent to notice. In fact no one did. With the controversy of the Rudd Concession and the Royal Charter superseded by this new and most glorious enterprise, Lobengula's voice was easily lost in the jingoism and excitement. For a moment he believed that if he could alert the Queen, then she would see at last the truth of his words. For this he chose a veteran of the earlier London Embassy. Mtshete was instructed to travel to Cape Town, this time to plead with Sir Henry Loch.

Loch interviewed Mtshete, emphasised Her Majesty's and his own unqualified support for the Chartered Company, and moreover introduced Rhodes himself into the meeting. As Cape Prime Minister, it might be said that Rhodes was one of those who commanded Sir Henry's loyalty. Loch addressed a letter to Lobengula reassuring him and adding that the armed members of the group were no more than friends who desired only his good.[1]

On receiving this letter and the report of his ambassador, Lobengula could do little more than address a sarcastic yet feeble communication to Jameson. On 30 June 1890, while the column was camped between the Motlutsi and Shashi Rivers, Jameson received the following brief:

> Why so many warriors at Macloutsie (sic)? Had the King committed any fault, or had any white man been killed, or had the white man lost anything that they were looking for?[2]

Jameson replied that the soldiery were meant merely for the protection of the column and would not harass the King or his people. Thereafter he ignored the gloom and protestations seeping through from Bulawayo and pressed on resolutely with the business at hand.

Under Selous' direction and with the labour of 250 BaNgwato tribesmen recruited in Bechuanaland, a road was cleared through the bush ahead. Everybody, including the whites, laboured at the heavy work on a diet of maize meal, fresh or canned beef, coffee, sugar, tea, pepper, salt, dried and split peas, compressed vegetables and ship's biscuits. The column was spread out over a distance of two to three miles and 16 oxen spanned in eight pairs hauled each wagon. Each averaged a distance of about 12 miles a day and typically travelled from dawn until early evening. It was Selous who usually selected the site for a laager. Trees were cut left and right so that in an emergency the wagons could mobilise in either direction. The laager was formed with the leading wagons marking the north side. The front wheel of the incoming wagon was placed just past the back wheel of the wagon ahead. Cattle and oxen were tethered outside the laager while the horses were picketed inside. Four men slept under each wagon four to a wagon and a roving watch was always alert to sudden attack. A steam engine chugged all night as the spotlight beam crept backwards and forwards through the bush.

Little was seen or heard of the Matabele until, on 6 August when the column was between the Lundi and Tokwe Rivers. Johann Colenbrander — a British South Africa Company agent — arrived in camp directly from Bulawayo carrying an ominous message from Lobengula.

> Who are you and where are you going? What do you want, and by whose orders are you here? Where are you leading your young men to like so many sheep and do you think they will get back to their homes again? Go back at once, or I will not be answerable for the consequence. Do you not think that white blood can flow as well as black? [3]

Such news had not been unexpected, but it was unnerving nonetheless. Lobengula added for the benefit of his two least favourite white men that Johnson and Selous could look forward to being skinned alive if the column was overrun and destroyed. Pennefather took it upon himself to reply.

> I am an officer of the Queen of England, and my orders are to go to Mashonaland, and there I am going. We do not want to fight, we only want to dig for gold, and are taking this road to avoid your young men; but if they attack us, we know how to defend ourselves. [3]

Four days later scouts sighted an impi of upwards of 2 000 warriors. The movements of the impi were observed from a discreet distance and it was determined that it was moving broadly parallel to the column. It seemed that the Matabele were waiting either for an advantageous opportunity to attack or for reinforcements. Sufficient firepower was concentrated in camp to hold off an attack by 2 000 men, but it was to be expected that the sighting was the vanguard of a much larger force. A few days later scouts were able to report that the impi had abruptly disappeared. Nerves remained stretched, however, as reports persisted among villagers questioned that the Matabele were in the vicinity and still intending to fight.

During those tense weeks elaborate security precautions were followed every night. Wagons were arranged in a wedge with a seven pounder or a Maxim at each corner. The searchlight continued to illuminate the night, and perhaps its supernatural aura more than anything else kept the Matabele at bay. Men stayed awake, alert to any signs of movement, but the expected attack never came. Each morning the laager would cautiously disengage to continue gingerly forward.

Despite his warnings, Lobengula was in the end clearly able to restrain his army. The wary Pioneer Column continued north through Matabeleland without incident. Why Lobengula resisted what must have been extraordinary pressure to act is uncertain. It could not have been because he was weak, since the Matabele command and control structure would not have been held intact by weakness.

From Selous' point of view, Lobengula '... had a very difficult part to play, and it is wonderful that he managed to restrain his people as he did'.

Hugh Marshall Hole was less charitable, speculating that Lobengula had '... met the difficulty by talking in a bellicose manner and doing nothing'.

Whatever the truth, it was certainly with tremendous relief that the column cleared Matabeleland and reached the highveld on 17 August 1890. From the beginning one of the main anticipated difficulties had been the feasibility moving vast significant herds of livestock and huge quantities of equipment off the sandveld and up onto the central plateau. It was at this point that the column would free itself of the heat of the lowveld, the horse sickness, the tsetse fly and perhaps the immediate threat of attack. This would also be the moment that Frank Johnson's oft-repeated assertions of Selous' incompetence would be proved true or false. Could he find a safe and practicable route for the extended column with all its manpower, stock and equipment to negotiate?

Johnson was to be disappointed if he hoped for a spectacular failure. Selous chose his route so well that it seemed provided by a higher power, or at least that was how it was seen during those tense days. The passage was named Providential Pass, and thus it remained. Today the national road between Beit Bridge and Harare still follows the same route. The head of the pass camp was pitched and the first cricket match held in the country was played in the atmosphere of a village fair. The site was named Fort Victoria and garrisoned by a company of BSA Company Police in order to protect and guard the line of communication. This was the point at which it could be said that the country had been effectively occupied.

A hundred miles further north, Fort Charter was similarly founded. On 10 September Pennefather and Captain Ted Burnett, the Chief Scout, rode on ahead and crossed the rather insignificant Makabusi River. They then pegged a suitable site at what they believed was Mount Hampden. In fact the actual site of Mount Hampden lay a few miles to the north.

On 12 September 1890 the Pioneer Column arrived at its destination in the territory of Chief Harari. The following day Lieutenant Tyndale-Biscoe ran the Union jack up a temporary flagpole dug into the empty veld, at a spot they called Fort Salisbury. Prayers were led by the Rev Canon Balfour, after which a 21-gun salute was fired. The Pioneer Corps stood on parade and cheered the occupation before they were released by Frank Johnson to take up their claims. Rhodes' great colonial experiment was underway.

A land bridge to the ocean

Rhodes had at last gained his toehold in the interior. His thoughts, however, were already running far in advance of this, and his agents had already begun to penetrate the country north of the Zambezi. All were under commission to gather concessions and treaties across the territory in order to lay the groundwork for a second British South Africa Company territory extending as far north and east as borders of the Congo Freestate and German East Africa. But even this was not the limit of Rhodes' ambition, for he desired to push the British Empire forward in every direction. For the time being, however, he was forced to pause in his march and consider the practical communications difficulties affecting Mashonaland as well as the inconvenient occupation of the coastal littoral by the Portuguese.

Occupying Mashonaland as a grand political gesture had been one thing, but rendering it humanly habitable was another. An isolated body of white men stranded over a thousand miles from the Kimberley railhead would not survive for very long. Fort Salisbury could be sustained in the short term with highly inflated imports from the south, but the frustrating lack of direct access to the Indian Ocean tempted Rhodes to wonder how he could seize a sizable portion of east coast from the grip of the Portuguese.

Politically, and in the light of the rules defined in Berlin in 1885, Portugal had failed to occupy or prove claim to the territories on the fringes of Mashonaland — and indeed many other parts of the region she claimed as her own. This did not stop the Portuguese Crown persisting with its claim — and no small claim was it. Portugal felt that she was owed the entirety of the south central African interior. Rhodes had simply ignored this fact and marched his column directly into Mashonaland, tearing through the fragile fabric of Portuguese imperial dignity as he went. It now appeared that he was intent on doing the same with the lands that abutted on legitimately held Portuguese territory to the east.

The question of Manicaland — a belt of highland and mountains lying between Mashonaland and the coastal plain, but geographically distinct from both — was potentially both the Portuguese bridge into the interior and Rhodes' land route to the sea. Neither party was in actual occupation of the area, so according to the rules of global imperialism, it was open to seizure by either.

Before the advance into Mashonaland, Rhodes had issued written instructions to Archibald

Colquhoun to proceed as early as possible to visit a certain Chief Mutasa, who was the ostensible ruler of the disputed Manica territory, and from him to secure the usual concession for mineral and prospecting rights. This in theory should have secured occupation and cut the ground from beneath the feet of the Portuguese. In further, secret instructions, Rhodes added that Colquhoun should endeavour to secure a 'right of communication' with the eastern seaboard, which, if at all possible, should include seizure of the port of Beira.

This rather improbable command set the stage for a variety of diplomatic skirmishes, a handful of extraordinary personal adventures and a military clash or two along an ill-defined frontier. In the end very little was achieved and the natural frontier of high mountains prevailed by dint of both geography and diplomatic agreement.

What did emerge from the contretemps was the laying of a unique foundation of heroism and bravado that would set in motion the long and colourful mythology of white Rhodesian history.

Ten days before the Pioneer Column arrived at the future site of Fort Salisbury, Archibald Colquhoun left the expedition and slipped away on a journey east in the company of Dr. Jameson and Frederick Selous. Selous had resigned his commission as chief of the intelligence department for in his view he had guided the column over the worst of its journey, and as far as he was concerned Pennefather, Jameson, Colquhoun and Johnson could bicker as they pleased over the rest of the way. It was the American Captain Burnett, who assumed his position and cautiously guided the column on the last leg to Mount Hamden.

Frank Johnson was delighted that Selous had removed himself from the expedition. He had reached the conclusion that Selous was a fraud, and even 50 years later, when Johnson came to record his memoirs, his dislike of the charismatic hunter-guide had not diminished at all. 'Frankly', he wrote, 'I was glad to see Selous gone. He knew no more about the country we had come through than anyone else; he was not amenable to discipline, and he wasted a great deal of his time uselessly with a compass in the veldt.'[4]

For his part Selous was naturally also happy to put it all behind him for a few weeks at least, and to ride out onto the open veld in the more congenial company of Colquhoun and Jameson. Colquhoun's personal secretary Harrison and a handful of mounted police accompanied the three. Unfortunately the experience for all was overshadowed by the barbed exchanges traded incessantly between Jameson and the overly serious but ever comedic Colquhoun.

Rhodes had issued his instruction to Colquhoun and not Jameson. Colquhoun was therefore determined to see the business through without Jameson's help. Jameson, on the other hand, emboldened by his diplomatic victory over Lobengula — which incidentally was reinforced by the fact that Lobengula had not ordered the destruction of the column — felt otherwise. In his view Colquhoun, should mind his manners, enjoy his champagne and his Havanas, and leave the real work to men of wit and action such as he. Jameson, it must be remembered, enjoyed a bond with Rhodes that some would have said made him Rhodes' alter ego. Rhodes had given him a verbal carte blanche to pursue the silent charter of underhand territorial seizure, and this he was to do whatever the superficial diplomatic landscape might otherwise suggest.

The conflict at the upper echelon of the expedition was Rhodes' failure, of course, for he often left the distinction of whose job was what and who was in charge of whom, unclear. But that was in the nature of Rhodes' ambiguity and it happened to suit Jameson. The latter felt that Colquhoun's officious and ponderous devotion to protocol would eventually frustrate the venture, and he was right. Time would also prove the correctness of Colquhoun's oft spoken conviction that Jameson's arrogance and over-confidence would one day be his ruin.

Meanwhile the party found itself travelling over arguably the loveliest quarter of the new country during its most flattering time of year. An American trooper in the escort wrote later that the landscape reminded him of the prairie grasses of Kansas with here and there a few trees. It was the season when the ubiquitous msasa trees open their buds and show tannin leaves to the world, and is without doubt the moment of rarest beauty on the highveld. The plains were laced with clear streams and hirsute with grassland that spoke to all of future fields, homesteads and pastures. The air was clean and cool, with the blue line of mountains opaque in the distance. This was the fairer face of the land they had come to conquer, and it was just this magnificence of nature that would for the next 90 years define to white Rhodesians the inimitability of the land they fought so hard to tame.

Colquhoun thought it some of the most charming scenery imaginable. He detached himself from his squabble with Jameson to appreciate for a moment the fates that had brought him there. The ongoing power struggle was abruptly diffused, however, when — to Colquhoun's inexpressible delight — Jameson, responding to a wager, jumped his horse over a fallen tree, took a tumble, and broke two ribs. His determination not to be usurped saw him weather another a few days, but eventually he was forced to turn around and set off back towards the column. He was mortified, of course, and as he trudged back he determined that somehow he would get his own back on the pompous and now insufferably self-satisfied Colquhoun.

Colquhoun and Selous then set off with the remainder of the party and arrived in the vicinity of Mutasa's kraal a day after the column reached Fort Salisbury. There they found a native chief both wretched and timorous. Mutasa was reputed to be continually drunk on Portuguese brandy, and this fact the party could easily confirm with their eyes. He was also eccentrically coutured to greet them in a naval hat and tunic and a leopard skin cape.

It was Mutasa's misfortune to find himself squeezed between the escalating tension between Cecil Rhodes and the Portuguese colonial government. To his guests Mutasa did not appear to be an impressive man, and like him his people seemed both cowed and apathetic. He had until then enjoyed a relatively easy entente with the Portuguese, who fed him alcohol in exchange for loose trading rights and periodic confirmations of allegiance. Otherwise they remained largely at the coast and left Mutasa to his own devices.

Further south a more powerful neighbour, in the form of Chief Guganyana of the Gaza (Shangaan) people, maintained his seat of government. A reasonably longstanding diplomatic peace was in existence between he and the Manica, which allowed Mutasa to enjoy all the benefits and suffer few of the hazards of his precarious political situation. Manifestly, however, this comfortable balance was about to change.

Mutasa was eager to assure Colquhoun that he had no political obligations towards either the Portuguese or the Shangaan — which obviously was untrue. As far as the Portuguese were concerned, political enforcement with the tribes of the interior was customarily left in the hands of Prazieros, and in Mutasa's case the Praziero was Manuel Antonio da Sousa, who went by the nom de guerre of Gouveia. Gouveia had for many years ruled his own private trading empire centred on the isolated mountain of Gorongoza. Whilst the hinterland had been empty, and there had been no political pressure, the relationship between he and Mutasa had been easy. Now Mutasa found that he had to consider which of the forces pressing him for allegiance was the most dangerous.

From Gouveia he certainly had much to fear, for the Praziero was a notorious cutthroat with a reputation for wanton savagery — and this Mutasa was naturally reluctant to rouse. In comparison, Colquhoun's rather paternal appearance inspired no terror. However Mutasa was shrewd enough to know that Britain was ultimately the greater power, and making a quick decision, he pleaded for Crown protection against Gouveia and the Portuguese, grandiosely swearing his undying allegiance to Britannia.

Colquhoun had arrived expecting a protracted stay and the usual procrastinations, so this turn of events delighted him. After less than a week he made his way triumphantly back to Fort Salisbury where he waved his concession under the disjointed nose of Jameson. He also shrewdly sent back one of Colonel Pennefather's senior officers, Major Patrick Forbes, with a small detachment of 16 men to keep an eye on Mutasa and events in his kraal.

It was just as well that he did, for no sooner had the dust settled than Mutasa received a visit from Gouveia and a certain Colonel Joachim Paiva D'Andrada, supported by a detachment of 300 Angolan levies.[5] Mutasa had in the meantime been tormented by doubt at his swing towards the British, so at first sight of the two irate Portuguese officials he fell prostrate and begged their forgiveness. The Union Jack was summarily torn down and replaced by the Portuguese flag — after which Mutasa was severely and publicly chastised.

Forbes observed all this, but laid low in the surrounding countryside and waited for reinforcements. These arrived just in time for a 15 November summit organised by D'Andrada to include Mutasa and all of his local clan chiefs. Clearly expecting nothing untoward, D'Andrada and Gouveia hosted the meeting, leaving the bulk of the Angolan militia stood down and camped some distance away. Forbes seized the advantage, stormed the camp and with just 40 men, successfully routed a numerically far superior force. He then marched on Mutasa's kraal and dramatically arrested both D'Andrada and Gouveia. The popular version of the story suggests that Gouveia, notwithstanding a fearsome reputation for violence and cruelty, fell on his knees and begged for mercy. It is unlikely that Forbes would have treated either man too harshly. With both in irons, his mind turned immediately towards pressing home his advantage with an even more daring escapade.

For the time being Forbes held the local balance of power, and in theory nothing now stood between him and Beira. He was confident that Rhodes would support him if he pushed for the port town, since Rhodes had made it clear time and again that the Imperial Government was on his side. Lord Salisbury might register some shock and complaint, but he would accept a fait accompli if Rhodes dropped one in his lap. Forbes as a regular and disciplined soldier could be relied on to do precisely as he was ordered — and these, after all, were Rhodes' standing orders.

Having left a small detachment of men to garrison the fort at Macequece and with another sent to escort the two Portuguese captives to Salisbury, Forbes was left with a force of only six men. Beira was well garrisoned with white Portuguese troops, so even taking into account the perceived inferiority of the Portuguese, it is hard to imagine how he thought he would storm the settlement. He set off immediately, however, and marched his men the 150 miles or so to the banks of the Pungwe River. From there they set off downstream in a handful of requisitioned native canoes.

* * *

Coincidentally, Dr. Jameson and Frank Johnson had narrowly preceded Forbes down the same river, in an expedition to test its viability as a river route to the sea. Jameson, convalescing in Fort Salisbury, was still ruminating bitterly over Colquhoun's coup and the fact that he had neither been invited to command nor even to accompany Forbes on his journey east to enforce the recently signed treaty. He and Johnson had formed something of a confederacy out of their mutual aversion to Colquhoun and agreed to sail down the Pungwe River in a collapsible boat that Johnson, with his keen eye for detail, had included in the stores for just such an eventuality.

One of the region's principal waterways, the Pungwe flows for a little over 300 miles, the last 100 of which sees it dispersed through an area of wetlands and swamps about which very little was then known. The chronicles of the few hunters and explorers who had visited the flats reported a suicidal incidence of malaria and a plague of man-eating lions. Howard C Hillegas, 19th century hunter, author and chronicler, offered this brief opinion of the valley:

Notwithstanding the fact that almost every South African claims to have slain a lion at one time or another, those beasts continue to exist in large numbers in the Pungwe region … nowhere in the world is there anything comparable with this territory and its wild animals. Hunters who have been in the game districts of southern Asia, Australia, and the Western Hemisphere say that those fields are of insignificant value beside those of the east coast.[6]

Although the region was, and remains to this day, an area of extraordinary natural beauty, it was conceived by nature to be as hostile to the European temper as any place on earth. In fact, the entire coastal plain of Mozambique was an area of such poor health that early Portuguese convict-pioneers could hope to survive for perhaps a year before dying either of disease or depredation.

The Pungwe is the intestinal tract of both the escarpment and the adjacent coastal plain, and few men of average constitution could have hoped to survive a journey down its length without contracting and dying of either malaria or blackwater fever. Circumstances happened to arrest Forbes' progress, but Johnson and Jameson took the river to its mouth and did indeed survive. If nothing else, this proved to those who did not already know it that neither man suffered from an average constitution. While their minor exploration has never held great status in the history of the period, by all rights it should have.

By the beginning of October Jameson felt well enough to travel, and so on the 4th he and Johnson set off eastwards on horseback. A fortnight or so earlier a bullock cart had been sent ahead with the boat and whatever kit and stores were needed. Colquhoun had not noticed the arrangements being made and was astonished when he heard that the two had left Fort Salisbury without notification or permission. As the travelling party approached the banks of the Odzi River, it was overtaken by a trooper who saluted and rather abashedly reported that he had orders from Colquhoun to arrest the principals and escort them back to Salisbury.

Jameson tore up the letter and threw it away, muttering that it had been he after all who had secured the damned fool his job. As far as he was concerned Colquhoun could go to hell and take his arrest warrant with him. The trooper was sent back with this message while the two men and the bullock cart forded the river and continued on their way.

Their first stop in Portuguese territory was at the residence of the Governor General of the Manica Province, where they lodged their horses before plunging into the adjacent swamps on foot. They spent two ghastly days struggling through the heat of October, with the boat on their heads, and blind expanses of pampas grass and bamboo cutting their clothes and flesh to ribbons. Finally the pair located the main channel where they assembled and launched the boat.

Once afloat their journey progressed reasonably smoothly — at least until one night, when sharing a grass hut lent to them by local natives, Johnson knocked over a candle and started a fire that quickly engulfed the hut and those around it. He and Jameson managed to escape the blaze, but they emerged dressed only in their underwear. According to one account they salvaged a part from a seven-pound tin of icing sugar. Johnson's own later recollections — never wholly reliable it must be said — record that he had worn his bandolier and a belt containing £90 in gold. He listed other salvaged items thus:

3 singlets.
1 blanket, partially burnt.
1 odd dress slipper.
1 revolver without cartridges.
1 7lb tin of Morton's icing sugar.
4 oars.
2 masts.

1 rifle and bandolier.
1 sheath knife.
26 Gibbs-Metford .450 cartridges.
1 empty leather writing case
My wife's photograph partly burnt
1 sovereign belt containing about £90 [7]

The situation for the two had suddenly taken a very grave turn. A little amateur exploration had turned overnight into a desperate bid for survival. Neither man was entirely certain where they were or where the nearest European settlement was. Although the natives were well meaning, they were primitive and unhelpful. The two had one pair of boots between them and a single dress slipper that happened to be the property of Jameson. All of their money had been burned.

There was not much else to do but try and find humour in their situation, and as they launched their craft and set off down river in their underwear they unleashed a gale of gay but undeniably strained laughter.

Soon the pain of sunburn and the unrelenting attentions of mosquitoes began to wear the humour very thin — and even thinner when in due course they drifted into lion country. As Howard C. Hillegas had noted, the report of rifle fire in this region was so rare that lions were curious and not in the least fearful of man. The waters too were infested with hippopotamus and crocodile that made the thought of either making landfall or staying adrift equally unappealing.

Despite all this the makeshift river craft arrived safely in the Pungwe estuary. The two adventurers were weak, starved and desperate.

Before their departure Johnson had arranged to have a ship wait for them at the mouth of the river. Although it was evening before the first ocean breakers were sighted, the lights of a vessel were visible beyond the first line of surf. Seeing this the two men were speechless with relief

The small boat, however, was invisible from the deck, and before the two could fix a bearing and strike out into open water the ship's lights were extinguished. Thereupon they were left floundering in darkness and heavy surf with nothing but the icing sugar tin to use as a bailer. It was by sheer luck that they noticed the masthead against a moonless sky, and paddled desperately towards it. Having attracted the attention of the crew they gratefully clambered aboard the *Lady Wood*. It was sober pair who were told as they dried off that they had come within minutes of missing the boat. The captain was at that moment preparing to cast off on the assumption that the two had not survived.

The technical findings of the trip were inconclusive and worth little. The Pungwe was deemed navigable for small craft along some of its length, but it would prove to be unreliable and dangerous, and five years later it would be superseded by the construction of a railway line.

As Dr. Jameson and Frank Johnson sailed south in renewed comfort, sipping port and claret on the decks of the *Lady Wood* and very likely engaging the officers on board with exaggerated tales of pluck and daring, Major Forbes was busy preparing his own expedition to the coast.

* * *

Forbes had remained in occupation of the Portuguese fort at Macequece until 22 November when he set off with his six troopers towards the banks of the Pungwe. A correspondent of the London *Times* who had made his way to Macequece to report on the international intrigues, attached himself to the expedition in anticipation of excellent copy. Sadly he was attacked by one of the famed man-eating lions and devoured, ending a fantastic tale that was digested and deposited somewhere deep in the African bushveld. Forbes, meanwhile, had neither Jameson's luck nor Johnson's bravado. He was an officer of the regular British Army, so when an order from Colquhoun caught up with him forbidding him to continue he had no option but to obey.

Colquhoun had by then come to the wise conclusion that his future did not lie with the British South Africa Company. He knew that if the scheme went wrong — as it was bound to — it would be he alone who would carry the blame. Rhodes could be relied on to disown his secret instructions, after which Colquhoun would probably never work again. As it was his, the decision to recall the raiding party cost him dear, for he brought upon himself part, if not all the blame for Rhodesia never gaining her vital seaport. Soon he would find himself tossed into the dustbin of Rhodesian history never to raise his head again.

The abandonment of Forbes' expedition did not mark the end of Rhodes' efforts to inveigle a slice of the eastern seaboard. A second potential avenue was through an additional treaty negotiation with the Shangaan chief Guganyana. For this, Rhodes had engaged Dutch hunter and explorer Dr Aurel Shultz to travel to Gazaland with the customary mandate to secure a concession. Shultz was perhaps best known for his journeys of exploration along the Chobe River and his discovery of the Okavango Delta.

Guganyana's territory straddled the disputed escarpment and spread east to include most of present day Maputo and Gaza provinces of Mozambique. What was of particular interest to Rhodes was that nominally his domain included the main Portuguese port of Delagoa Bay. Guganyana was sharper than Mutasa, and although no less fond of alcohol, he was not intimidated by either the Portuguese or the British. He therefore proved to be a much tougher nut to crack than his malleable northern neighbour.

In Shultz, Rhodes had made another excellent choice. The doctor was slow but persistent, and if he lacked Jameson's mercurial brilliance, he also lacked his unpredictability and regular lapses of conscience. Patient, thorough and not in the least self-serving, Shultz laboured steadily over Guganyana's changing demands, forgetfulness and persistent insobriety. Once again it proved to be the offer of firearms that won the day, despite the obvious risks that running weapons into disputed territory would carry.

In the meantime Jameson had arrived back from his perambulations and was again in residence in Fort Salisbury. His journey had taken him to the Cape and then on to Kimberley where he briefly met up with Rhodes. He was gratified to find that in his absence he had become wealthy and moderately famous. Men sought his company, bought him drinks and solicited his favours — and behind his back remarked that there was now very little trace to be found of the old Jameson.

He had travelled a long way in a short time, and in a self-congratulatory frame of mind he was anxious to let it be known that he could achieve so much more. He was now even deeper in Rhodes' confidence, and empowered to take greater control of affairs at the cutting edge of the empire.

Rhodes was also bolstered by more confidence and optimism than perhaps was warranted. With his vast wealth and his sweeping power he was apt to feel unassailable, perhaps even omnipotent.

The first thing that Jameson did when he arrived back in Fort Salisbury was to enquire how Schultz was progressing in Gaza. On hearing reports of slow progress, he thought he might join his fellow doctor and hurry things up a bit. Colquhoun was still rankling over the business of the flouted arrest warrant, but was now fully aware of the fact that Jameson had won the battle. Whilst both men maintained a cordial diffidence, Jameson felt the atmosphere in the settlement uncomfortably strained. Since Colquhoun was not of a disposition to leave the fort, it took little persuasion for Jameson to plan an expedition to Gazaland despite the fact that the wet and feverish summer season had commenced.

Jameson set off early in the new year of 1891 with a poorly provisioned expedition consisting of horses, a handful of wagons and two white companions. The first of these was a young Scottish prospector by the name of Dunbar Moodie, who would later find fame as organiser of the first column of wagons to occupy Gazaland. The other was the rugged young adventurer Denis Doyle, who was fluent in the local languages and so engaged as an interpreter.

The expedition proceeded relatively easily — as far as the Sabi River, swollen by torrential rain to more than a mile wide and flowing swiftly. To most men it would have presented an insurmountable barrier, but Jameson and his companions were made of sterner stuff. They found a canoe that must have belonged to local tribesmen, and with great difficulty ferried over essential supplies in repeated trips. The wagons and horses, of course, could not cross and were abandoned on the west bank.

The opposite shore was no less of a challenge. In a journey of truly Jamesonesque proportions they struggled on in mud, waist deep at times, and at others swimming through feverish swamp and flood water. All three men succumbed to malaria with Doyle being the worst affected. Near death, he had to be manhandled forward by the other two who were only slightly less incapacitated than he. It seemed this time that Jameson in his impetuousness and inexperience had bitten off more than he could chew. But the critically weak and desperate doctor cajoled, dragged and willed his companions on. It was an altogether unnecessary and ill-planned expedition that mutated into a feat of sheer grit and survival. It was truly the stuff of Victorian comic book and legend, and absolutely vintage Jameson.

* * *

While the three adventurers battled nature in the trackless wilds, Rhodes received word from Shultz that an agreement with Guganyana had been reached. The promised consignment of firearms was to be shipped as soon as possible and conveyed under the care of Rhodes' principal secretary Frederick Rutherfoord Harris. Harris duly set off on his own enthralling journey by sea and river steamer, that took him up the Limpopo River to within portage distance of Guganyana's capital.

Word of this British intrigue and disregard of protocol naturally reached the ears of the Portuguese administration, and in due course a riverboat patrol made its way upriver to investigate.

Shultz and Rutherfoord Harris concluded the exchange and were about to begin the journey back when word reached them of a trio of desperate white men making their way through the sodden bush to meet them. Both were utterly astonished then to witness Jameson and his companions — skeletal, feverish, barefoot and reduced to rags — emerging like spectres out of the rain-washed landscape.

After greetings and the ministration of whisky and quinine, Jameson's wit was quickly revived. Suspecting that the Portuguese would not take gun running in their territory lightly, he predicted that a detachment of police would be waiting at the steamer with warrants of arrest. He took possession of the treaty document and entrusted it to one of his companions, probably Doyle, to carry it overland to the coast.

Portuguese officials were indeed waiting for them when the party arrived back at the steamer. A thorough search was conducted, but of course no trace of any treaty document was found. The four whites were arrested and transported back to the coast where they were roughly if briefly imprisoned. Once Rhodes had negotiated their release, Jameson intercepted the document, and on his return to Kimberley presented it to Rhodes. Shultz, who had done the hard work, was given little credit, and like Colquhoun he disappeared soon afterwards into relative obscurity.

* * *

Meanwhile the dust in Manicaland that had settled somewhat since the Forbes incident, was about to be raised up afresh. Forbes returned to Fort Salisbury leaving behind the Macequece garrison under the command of a young captain by the name of Herman Melville Heyman. Heyman was a man of good character of the type of whom Rhodes was fond and who in due course would sit on the local legislature and inherit the title of Lord Melville. For the time being, however, he and his men sat in occupation of the fort from which he was ordered to keep an eye on events in Manicaland. Trouble was certainly afoot for Captain Heyman, but this time it was brewing a long way away from Manicaland.

News of the arrest and the return to Portugal of Colonel Joachim Paiva D'Andrada had stirred up a hornet's nest of public outrage. Such an insult touched the raw nerves of a people whose national prestige had for centuries been in steady decline. Portugal had already been forced to back down over the matter of the disputed area of Lake Nyasaland and the Shire Highlands by British gunboat diplomacy, and this simply exacerbated a humiliating national condition. The government fell, the British consulate was stoned, and members of the British community in Oporto were forced indoors against insults, missiles and sometimes violence.

For the second time a body of outraged Portuguese citizens assembled an army to avenge perceived slights to national pride and challenges to colonial conquest in East Africa. The riverboat incident that saw Jameson, Shultz and Rutherfoord Harris flouting international law and protocol would prove to be the last straw. Portuguese anger was public and very animated. A subscription list was set up for the purchase of a battleship while a volunteer expedition was assembled. Students jostled to enlist until, by the beginning of 1891, it seemed possible that Britain and Portugal might find themselves at war.

In late February the student militia in their ageing battleship arrived on the shores of Portuguese East Africa and, despite diminishing ardour, they mobilised on the littoral and prepared to advance inland. In the interest of international relations, the Portuguese Government kept the student army at arms length, and so it remained the unofficial expedition as it had started. While the diplomatic ramifications were not as severe as they could have been, Rhodes came under immense pressure from Whitehall to curb his military adventurism and leave his boundary dispute to the politicians.

Nonetheless on 3 May reports reached Heyman's garrison that the Portuguese irregulars were on their way. Heyman withdrew some distance to Mutasa's kraal where he settled in to observe events. Three days later a demoralised and much diminished force of students arrived at Macequece, and were relieved to take occupation of the fort without a fight. At that point they numbered about 500 men, 100 students and 400 native levies, all under the command of a certain Colonel Ferreira. Captain Heyman then positioned himself in the hill country overlooking the fort of Macequece and prepared his 50 troopers for engagement. Ferreira issued an ultimatum that Heyman ignored, and the following day the attack commenced.

By the clever subterfuge of relaying false flag signals to imaginary reinforcements, Heyman threw the enemy into confusion. Uncertain from where the attack would come, the Portuguese lacked direction, cohesion and enthusiasm. They had been armed with a brace of superbly modern quick-firing artillery pieces but had left these at the fort lest they hinder the planned lightning advance. Without them they were absurdly vulnerable and cut down decisively by well-directed fire from Heyman and his men.

With the help of a few canisters from the British 7-pounder, the Portuguese and their levies were soon put to flight. They retired on the fort where they quickly re-commissioned their 11-pounders, and a minor artillery duel commenced. The BSA Company artillery destroyed the Fort with well-aimed fire but was put out of action itself by a lucky round. By then, however, the Portuguese advance was already in a shambles and was soon in swift retreat back towards the coast. Heyman and his men were jubilant and joined the growing list of Company men who reaped the peculiar laurels of Rhodesian heroism. It had been a spectacular victory achieved with neither loss of British life nor serious injury. In addition several new artillery pieces were captured.

Sensitive once again to Rhodes' plea for territory, Heyman dispatched a patrol under Lieutenant Eustace Fiennes to complete the rout, and try his luck at seizing Beira. Anticipating this, Sir Henry Loch sent his military secretary, Major Sapte, to intercept the raid and order it back. Fiennes, junior in rank and probably overawed, felt that he had no alternative but to withdraw and report back to Heyman.

When he heard the news Rhodes was furious. This was the second squandering of an apparently ideal opportunity to seize Beira. As a consequence Rhodes never forgave Fiennes and asked him later why he had not simply slapped Major Sapte in irons and reported that he was drunk. Jameson would have done just that, he declared, which was almost certainly true. Jameson might very well have succeeded in sequestering the port, but that was Jameson and few could match him.

* * *

Thus ended the first eventful year in the life of the new colony, and along with it Rhodes' efforts to obtain a portion of the eastern seaboard. Archibald Colquhoun would survive no more than a year in the employment of the British South Africa Company, after which he was to occupy a particularly maligned place in the folklore of the colony. The contest against Jameson defined in acute ways the emerging political struggle of Rhodesia. As Jameson was mercurial and often brilliantly impulsive, Colquhoun was tutored, accomplished and utterly orthodox. Jameson was by then becoming accustomed to the success of daring methods, while at the same time cultivating a dangerous contempt for orthodox authority. Colquhoun would later complain to Rhodes that Jameson: "instead of acting with me as colleague and friend, has worked all the mischief which his ingenious and busy brain can devise."[8] He ought not to have bothered. By then Jameson and Rhodes had become such inseparable confederates that nothing would have induced one to criticise or to accept criticism of the other.

9

Conquest, settlement and subjugation

Settlers and the Company

William Ernest Fairbridge made his timely arrival in one-year-old Fort Salisbury in the summer of 1891. It was a timely event because Fairbridge was a newspaperman and the infant community desperately needed a vehicle of public expression to air and diffuse growing political tension. The Pioneer Corps had by then dispersed and its individual members — those at least who had stayed the course so far — were busy laying the foundations of a working colony. But as a sign of things to come, however, a rich crop of disaffection was already emerging from the mottled soil of Company rule. Everyone except Company officials — and in fact even some of them — had something to say about the deficits of the British South Africa Company, and each welcomed a medium through which to be heard.

Ordinary Pioneers had been promised 3 000 acres of land and 15 gold claims each. However to be regarded as a bona fide land claimant, a Pioneer was required to be in actual occupation of his land; and unless his 15 claims happened to be on the same land as his farm, it was often either one or the other. Most Pioneers had signed on principally to get rich quick, and in the first instance most forgot about the land and concentrated on the gold. In the end many ended up with neither, since gold proved elusive and the land truculent, unyielding and unhealthy. At around this time a good many packed up and left the colony.

Fort Salisbury had begun life in two camps. Johnson, Heany and Borrow had identified a small outcrop that came to be known as the 'Kopje', and there they pitched their tents and began to assemble a community that included a majority of the settlers. The reminder put up around the police camp in the vicinity of the original flagpole. Most structures other than the administrative headquarters and the police barracks were crudely built and temporary. The reason for this was that the Company had given no indication of where the capital would be established, so anyone venturing to build a more substantial structure risked losing it should the capital be re-sited.

In due course the settlers took the attitude of 'to hell with the Company' and the streets of a town began to emerge from the dust with no formal plan or any particular civic signature. Colquhoun and Jameson were at each other's throats so the administration was in paralysis. The shrewder among the business community suspected that the prime site would be the Kopje, so the tussle for land in that quarter was brisk. A commercial centre formed around the first rough thoroughfare leading to the Kopje and appropriately it became known as Pioneer Street.

The Kopje dwellers were proved to be on the money, and soon a survey of the area was underway. The value of stands already claimed shot up, and many made early profits trading a dusty acre or two to unsuspecting newcomers. In a short time substantial buildings began to replace huts, until on either side of Pioneer Street a welter of bars, restaurants, attorneys, traders and a washerman set up shop.[1]

About a year later the administration did indeed change its mind. It was then decided that a new site would be surveyed on the far side of the vlei that became known as the Causeway. Pressure was put on those already clustered around the Kopje to move, but a certain partisanship was developing. The Kopje dwellers held back unless the Company paid substantial damages — which of course it refused to do. The settlers then muttered darkly among themselves and the Kopje remained occupied.

The administrative headquarters moved to the Causeway, and Salisbury duly separated into three separate cantons. The third of these was the Fort, which was more a police barracks than a canton. It was there, however, that the first public square was marked out along the lines of the Union Jack. The amenity was named Cecil Square after the son of Lord Salisbury and director of the BSA Company.

The ebb and flow of pioneers leaving the territory in disgust, or arriving in optimism, meant a steady turnover of new faces. All were men because Rhodes — in keeping with his dislike and general distrust of women — had issued an edict that due to the rigors of pioneer life, neither women nor children were to be allowed into the colony during the early stages. This did not discourage a fallen French aristocrat by the name of Edmond, Vicomte de la Panouse, who thought he would try his luck with Mashonaland gold.

The Vicomte contrived to smuggle in his consort, Englishwoman Fanny Pearson, disguised as a man and calling herself Billie. The woman was soon unmasked and attained the distinction of being the first woman in Rhodesia. Neither was ordered to leave, but nor did they find any gold. The pair subsequently bought Avondale Farm and pioneered the settlement that in due course would become one of the capital's most pleasant suburbs.

Countess Billie was followed a little later by Mrs Pascoe, wife of Major Pascoe, founder of the local Salvation Army — and shortly after that by a brace of Dominican Sisters. It was these ladies who founded the first hospital and school. Mrs Pascoe incidentally became a patient as the first white woman to give birth in the colony.

In the first year of its life, administration was the mainstay of the Fort Salisbury economy, and it was to the administrator that W Ernest Fairbridge made his first visit. He found Archibald Colquhoun languishing in his crude 'pole and dagga (mud)' offices from where law, justice and taxation were administered. Colquhoun was in residence but largely inactive, and still brooding over his ongoing quarrel with Jameson. News had recently reached him of Jameson's successful sortie into Gazaland, along with the mixed blessing that he had survived. As we have heard Jameson launched that expedition into the teeth of a particularly violent wet season, the consequences of which also badly affected the poorly prepared body of pioneers. All had spent most of that first season under thatch or canvas, wondering in their abjection why no one had thought to prepare them for the fury of the highveld rains.

Like everybody else, Fairbridge found Colquhoun relieved that the wet season had passed and that the cool, dry and pleasant winter months were upon them. The forced isolation that had come about as a consequence of flooded rivers and impassable roads was over. Communications with the outside were once again open and fresh supplies were getting through. The natives had murdered no one so far, and apart from the usual high rate of mortality from malaria and a general feeling of dissatisfaction, all appeared to be well.

Almost a year had passed since the hoisting of the Union Jack and the colony was open for business. The aspect of Fort Salisbury was perceptibly changing from a horribly isolated group of men camping out in the wilderness to a community in incubation, spreading its roots into the surrounding countryside.

Archibald Colquhoun listened with amused lethargy to his visitor's proposal to start a newspaper in the colony. He supposed after some thoughtful consideration that it could do no harm. Rhodes appeared to be behind the venture, and what interested Rhodes had a habit of coming to fruition.

Colquhoun allocated Fairbridge a hut on the Causeway and allowed him to pick through the remains of a cyclostyle machine that the ever-diligent Frank Johnson had carried up from Kimberley. Fairbridge had no other means of printing a word so he accepted the gift with gratitude.

This began the *Zambesian Times*, which would later evolve into the *Mashonaland Herald*, and finally the *Rhodesia Herald*. As with all things in the new colony — and as Colquhoun had suspected — Rhodes' hand could be traced to the root of it. The arrival of the press in the colony also settled the question of its name. Rhodes had preferred Zambesia, and Jameson Charterland, but Rhodesia became the preferred journalistic nomenclature, and when the name of the *Rhodesia Herald* was settled, so in de facto terms was the name of the colony.2

Fairbridge was an employee of the Argus Group of Newspapers based in Cape Town. The proprietor, Francis Dormer, had been a close friend of Rhodes since 1875 when the two met on board ship. Rhodes was by then an old Africa hand and well on his way to amassing his fortune, while Dormer — more or less the same age as he — was an immigrant on his way to take up a position on the staff of the Educational Institute of Cape Town. The two became friends and before disembarkation Rhodes offered Dormer any help that he could if ever it was needed.

Dormer's career in education was brief, and from the Cape Institute he went on to try his luck in journalism. He temporarily joined the staff of the *Queenstown Representative* before moving on to cover the Anglo-Zulu war for the *Cape Argus*. At the end of that episode he took up the position as a sub-editor on the Argus and in due course was promoted editor. A few years later the owner of the Argus, the famous South African publisher and politician Saul Solomon, retired and put the business up for sale. Recognising his opportunity and remembering Rhodes' offer, Dormer paid the young diamond magnate a visit.

Rhodes was by then campaigning for his seat in the Cape Parliament and obviously was not blind to the potential benefits of an interest in an influential newspaper. He backed Dormer with the capital that enabled his friend to buy the Argus and acquire one of the most enduring and respected publishing names in southern Africa.

Under the wide terms of the Charter, Rhodes was empowered to do almost anything that he wanted north of the Limpopo, which included starting a newspaper. To turn this thought into a reality he approached Dormer and called in the favour. The Argus board took up the question and agreed that the venture would be of benefit to all. Rhodes, in his turn, agreed that the BSA Company would offer facilities to no other applicants. The project was ratified and soon set in motion.

Transporting plant and equipment into Mashonaland at that time proved to be prohibitively expensive. There was as yet no railway link and transport consisted of ox wagons hauled labouriously up from Kimberley or from the Cape. Instead, William Fairbridge was plucked from his position as contributor to the Argus in Kimberley, and with a typically Rhodes-like brief, was sent north into a virtual wilderness to do what he could to set up and publish a newspaper. With him he carried little more than pioneering ingenuity and a will to succeed.

Despite a limited expectation, the founder was gratified to observe that Fairbridge was soon achieving a great deal. He began by examining Frank Johnson's old cyclostyle and managed to master the mechanics fairly quickly. He found later, though, that it had no roller, but by using glue made from animal bones and some imported treacle he moulded a workable alternative inside a cylindrical German sausage tin. He then scrounged paper from whatever source he could and with these simple means began to print his newspaper from a humble pole and dagga structure on a dusty stretch of the Causeway.

Much trial and error went into the publication of the *Herald*, and while the first editions were extremely crude, Fairbridge's early mistakes tended to be less technical than journalistic. One such fundamental error was featuring the Company crest on the front page of his first edition, with its motto of 'Justice, Freedom, Commerce'. As innocent an oversight as this was, it immediately gave settlers the impression that his editorial bias lay in favour of the Company. Although in the early stages at least this was not the case, the impression stuck. Matters were complicated further by the fact that Company staff, who came in for so much public lampooning, tended to believe that the publication was sympathetic to the settlers. This double misconception not only hampered Fairbridge enormously in his early work, but perhaps more importantly it exposed the factionalism that had already begun to take root in the colony. This phenomenon was destined to grow exponentially as the white population bourgeoned and it continued to contaminate the political atmosphere of the country for many years to come.

Nothing could better illustrate this state of polarisation than the events surrounding the first anniversary of the colony. So far the occupation had been a mixed experience for all, but for some it had been worse than others. For those who filtered out into the countryside, the depredations had been appreciable. They were shocked by the severity of the first wet season which immediately shattered Jameson's earlier descriptions of Mashonaland as a happy combination of Canaan, Ophir and the Black Country. The apparently serene countryside was transformed overnight into a landscape of wetlands, swamps and swollen rivers. Mosquitoes and rats — never mentioned in the previous year's promotional advertisements — tormented everyone. Many people subsequently died from malaria and blackwater fever, while rats were such a hazard that a kitten was regarded as the best acquisition a newcomer to the colony could hope for.[3]

The most depressing fact of all was that not a single significant gold strike had so far been recorded. The first public gathering in the capital therefore promised to be a very stormy affair. The occasion was an official banquet on 12 September attended by all the town's prominent citizens. The guest of Honour was intended to be Dr Jameson — who had by then officially superseded Archibald Colquhoun — but Jameson was away in the veld again, so Dr. Rutherfoord Harris took his place. The principal speaker was to be Advocate A.H.S Bird, supported by the settlement's medical expert Dr Rand and a certain Mr F.E Lochner.[4]

Bird began by assuring Rutherfoord Harris that he was not in any way antagonistic towards the BSA Company or any of its officials. Having established that, he immediately launched into a scathing attack on both. The theme that he chose to illustrate Company insensitivity was an interesting one. The BSA Company had forbidden any interference by anyone with the Great Zimbabwe ruins. The site had been rediscovered by Adam Renders in 1867 and reported on by German explorer Karl Mauch in 1871. By 1890 it had still not been explored or properly catalogued, but it was nonetheless being attacked by frustrated settlers who, finding no gold by traditional means, had taken to looting gold artefacts from the ruins and melting them down to sell. The BSA Company published a notice to the effect that persons caught removing relics from the site would be deported from the country immediately.

Bird portrayed this as the autocratic actions of a dictatorship. In the light of the depredations suffered by the settler community, he declared that it was wholly unreasonable to prevent people making a living by any means possible. Bird concluded his attack with much table pounding and indignant applause from his audience. In response a beleaguered Rutherfoord Harris stood up and did his best to reply.

Jameson would have done better. In fact it is debatable whether any such explosion of temper would have occurred at all had he been present. None the less, Fairbridge reported all this and many other speeches besides, and published all the details in his Saturday edition.

A few days later he was visited by the Government Attorney Mr Alfred Caldecott, who notified him that the government would proceed against the *Herald* for libel unless an apology was inserted to correct his erroneous reporting. Fairbridge did not insert an apology, and no action was taken. But sides had been drawn, and often as not both sides saw Fairbridge as the enemy.

A month after this incident, the *Herald* reported Cecil Rhodes' imminent arrival in the territory. It was to be the founder's first visit, and apart from his natural desire to see the territory for himself, he also wanted to assess the situation after the first year of activity. He was not altogether surprised to find the Pioneer Corps in generally poor physical condition and disillusioned almost to a man. He later described the situation to his shareholders:

> I found the position at the time as follows: a discontented population of about 1 500 people and an expenditure of about 250 000 pounds a year upon police. Things looked rather bad, because it was not only the large number of police, but also the feeding of them, which had to be done by carting the food 1 700 miles from the coast. Doctor Jameson and myself have talked matters over, and he said, 'If you will give me 3 000 pounds a month I can pull through.[5]

Rhodes heard complaints about Fairbridge and took sides with his administration against the *Herald*, expressing unhappiness with the apparent independence of the newspaper's editorial policy. Like Caldecott, he felt that Fairbridge's reporting of the delicate balance of public opinion served only to inflame an already difficult situation. Not long after his arrival Rhodes summoned Fairbridge to visit him for a 'chat'.

Fairbridge arrived at Jameson's tent to find Rhodes seated at a table with Jameson standing behind him. Rhodes greeted his visitor courteously before proceeding directly to the point.

'All these things', he told Fairbridge, referring with a sweep of his hand to the discontent of the settlers, 'mean money, and the Company hasn't any.'

Fairbridge replied that the Company's problems were not his.

'Do you know that we can deport you?' Rhodes asked him.

'Oh, yes, I know,' Fairbridge replied.

'Well, what would you do?'

'You would have to give me a first class train fare to the coast and a first class passage to England, and there I would state my case on behalf of the settlers.'

Rhodes turned to Jameson. 'There Jameson', he said, 'I told you so.'[6]

Fairbridge was permitted to remain in the colony and was not interfered with again by Rhodes, the Company or the settlers. He was able to expand and develop his publishing enterprise in peace. This was fortunate, for in the following year events of enormous magnitude would overshadow the mediocre squabbles between administration and settler, and would give Fairbridge a great deal more to report on than an editor in his second year of publication had any right to hope for.

Don't forget the natives

The infighting between the Company and the settlers meant that the question of the natives was largely ignored. No formal debate had yet been heard regarding their place in the new order of things. As the best Mashona land and resources were being claimed by the whites, and since the Matabele were stripped of raiding rights and plunder, the settler community found the status quo to its advantage. A wary surveillance of Matabeleland was maintained, but only because Matabele power remained unbroken. The Mashona might have been ghosts on the landscape for all the thought that was given to their view of current events.

From Lobengula's point of view the situation was moving from bad to worse. His agreement with Jameson that the Company might look 'elsewhere' had largely been premised on the fact that he doubted they would. When they did, he hoped that shadowing the column with a heavy Matabele force would oblige them to turn back. Now, far more than digging a few holes and clearing a bit of land, the whites were consolidating their two settlements at Fort Victoria and Fort Salisbury and at the same time filtering out into an ever-widening belt of countryside.

In an effort to thwart this expansion Lobengula made a melancholy attempt to try and beat Rhodes at his own game. Aware of the competition that still existed between the agents of British and German interests, he concluded that if he could play one off against the other, the two might ultimately cancel out. On the advice of Renny-Tailyour he awarded a second concession to E.A Lippert that theoretically nullified the Rudd Concession.

Among other things, the Lippert Concession granted the holder the right to allocate land in Mashonaland for the next 100 years. This had a limited legal basis since Lobengula had already promised, under the Rudd Concession, to grant no land without the consent of the Chartered Company. Rhodes could have approached the problem in a number of ways — not least of all to ignore it — but typically he opted for the payoff. He offered Lippert £30 000 for his concession — to which Lippert readily agreed. For both it was an excellent arrangement. Lippert walked away with an easy mark while Rhodes gained the right to allocate land throughout Mashonaland for a full century. Lobengula, needless to say, gained nothing. In fact at that moment he lost the future altogether.

The average Mashona tribesman had no clear idea of what was going on. The Matabele raids were suddenly a thing of the past and that at least was a very good thing. However in exchange for this, the whites were rough in their demands and hungry for land. Their assumption seemed to be that having freed the Mashona from the Matabele curse, the Mashona then owed them an eternal dept of gratitude. Some appreciation was due and in a way this was recognised, but gratitude did not run to absolute dispossession. The Matabele had sucked the blood out of the people but they had never laid hands on the one thing that kept the tribes of the Mashona whole: the land.

To the Mashona the question of land ownership was bound to be confusing, since no one actually owned the land. The land was there, there was plenty of it and like the game in the veld, the fruits of the wild or the air they breathed was the common property of all. To the settlers, on the other hand, private ownership was as fundamental as Christianity, and since the Mashona had no identifiable national structure, they were easily absorbed as squatters in a European system of land tenure. Furthermore they appeared to most whites to submit to this renewed bondage with an uncanny aptitude.

However, despite what many thought, no welcome mat had been thrown out in Mashonaland for the white man. The facts were plain. The Mashona were a loosely bonded people with no central leadership to treat with and no army to fight. White attention therefore remained focused on the Matabele, and the Mashona were left largely to make of it all whatever they cared to.

Much later, historians cataloguing oral records of Mashona history unearthed a prophecy of sorts relating to the occupation. It was said that there existed an important spirit medium in the northeast of the country. The northeast, it might be remembered, was the seat of the Mwane Mutapa. The medium had warned the people that an improbable invader would one day arrive and dispossess them of their land.

> There shall come from the sea a race of kneeless white men [The Shona saw the white men in their long trousers as having no knees] who will build white houses throughout the land. They will bring with them a mighty boulder [probably the railway] such as has never been seen before. It will ride with such force that no-one will be able to stop it, or divert it from its course. The kneeless people will rule the land with an iron fist for many years. Be that as it may, the ancestor spirits will restore the land back into the hands of their progeny, not

permitting the foreigners to rule the land forever.[7]

The Mashona, therefore, can be seen to have taken something of a fatalistic view of the occupation. They did at least have protection from the Matabele, and although the whites were ravenous, they were not genocidal. Time was on their side, and for the moment it would be wise to see how things turned out for the Matabele. In the meantime a handful of lesser chiefs and headmen took the opportunity to treat the Matabele insolently. This in turn stimulated powerful voices in Matabeleland urging Lobengula to act.

Thus it became inevitable that Lobengula would begin to flounder in the face of new and irreconcilable demands. Without the power of life and death over the Mashona, the Matabele identity itself was in danger of being lost. In a society such as theirs how could a situation like this be rectified by any means other than war? The Matabele were a small nation and this was the core of their dilemma. Since they could not be relied on to step passively aside in the face of white progress, at some point they would have to be beaten down. Precisely the same dilemma had affected the whites of Natal as they looked across the Tugela River at the unbroken Zulu who, despite treaty and commitment, maintained the potential to do terrible damage. While in the beginning a temporary understanding between Jameson and Lobengula sufficed, both men knew that a more permanent solution would have to be found.

10

Matabele War

There were many reasons why war between the settlers and the Matabele was inevitable, but principally it was because the Matabele knew no other way. It was how they had been wrought, it was how they lived and it would be how they died. It is also a fact that the Matabele had failed to digest the lesson visited upon them by their first encounter with firearms a generation earlier, and that they still believed in the capacity of their army to overrun and drive out a handful of lightly armed whites.

From the Company's point of view — especially before the purchase of the Lippert Concession — a war of conquest would have cut through all the difficult problems associated with the Rudd Concession. Moreover, on 9 May 1891, an Order in Council of the British Parliament declared southern Zambezia to be a British protectorate. The Imperial Government's position was that, while the Company had the right to send men into Mashonaland for the purposes of occupation, it did not possess any judicial or administrative powers over anyone within the colony.

A war of conquest would not only give the victors temporary authority to govern, but it would add lucrative tracts of Matabeleland to the British South Africa Company portfolio. With the weight of modern weaponry and tactics in their favour, there was no fear on the part of Jameson et al that a war would be lost. All that was important was for Rhodes and Jameson to ensure that the victor was the BSA Company and not the Imperial Government. Both recognised that if Her Majesty could claim conquest of Matabeleland, the territory would become a Crown Protectorate, and gone would be Rhodes' operating formula of philanthropy plus 5%.

Not to be forgotten was another factor of equal weight pointing towards war. With the dearth of good financial news coming out of the colony, trade in Company shares on the London Exchange had dwindled. Rhodes attempted to counter this by arranging for society journalist Lord Randolph Churchill to tour the territory on the understanding that he would write optimistic articles. However Churchill played the spoiler and did the opposite. He found Rhodesia to be what he called a dystopia, and lampooned, ridiculed and diminished everybody and everything he saw. He concluded his submissions with the comment that the colony was neither Arcadia nor an Eldorado.[1] With this sort of negative press now adding to the gloom, it became clear to the Company's board that something needed to be done to distract attention. The expenses of the enterprise so far — including the costs of maintaining the forts, construction of the railway, the telegraph and the armed forces — ran to upwards of £700 000. For this there was nothing to show except a yawning deficit and an unhappy population of settlers.

Rhodes sat Jameson down one day and tried to drill economy into him. Of the 3 000 or so settlers who had responded to the call, 650 were police. These men were maintained at a cost of between £150 000 and £200 000 per annum. In response to Rhodes' anxiety over the deficit Jameson took the decision to reduce their numbers down radically to only 150. Later he wrote a musing telegraph to Rutherfoord Harris airing the merits of war on the companies' diminished stock capital and prospects. Later he wrote a musing telegraph to Rutherfoord Harris airing the merits of war on the companies diminished stock capital and prospects.

> Rhodes might consider the advisability of completing the thing. The cash could be found and it could be done pretty cheaply if the Macloutsie Police and the High Commissioner keep out of it. I know Ferreira's terms are 500 mounted Boers to hand over the show, a moderate sum in cash and ammunition supplied, each man to receive a farm and his loot…I suggest the Ferreira trick, as we have an excuse for the row over murdered women and children now and getting Matabeleland open would give us a tremendous lift in shares and everything else. The fact of its being shut up gives it an immense value both here and outside.

It is then hard to understand exactly why Jameson and Rhodes should have agreed to reduce the colony's defences so drastically when every indication of a fight existed. Lobengula was still trying to make a significant point of asserting his rights over the Mashona. On one occasion he sent a small impi as far north as Lomagundi to punish a local chief for a minor infringement. Such serious incursions were rare, and indulged as much as possible by the local legal administration, but since there was no formal border between the two territories, raids and killings along the grey line were frequent.

What liberties the Mashona clans were emboldened to take with the Matabele they took no less with the settlers. Having been beaten down with dreadful cruelty in the past, any relaxing of the regime was an invitation to crime. Stock theft, and indeed any kind of theft, was rampant in the countryside. Such commodities as tools and wire were irresistible, and as the telegraph arrived in the country and nosed its way north through Mashonaland, the lifting of miles of copper wire became routine. On a few occasions Jameson himself dealt only slightly less heavily with miscreant Mashona chiefs than did the Matabele.

In the meantime Lobengula and Jameson reached a working agreement regarding the boundaries of one another's jurisdiction. This was a line following the Tokwe, Shashi and Umniati rivers. In the first season of no raiding since their exodus from the Transvaal, Lobengula occupied his forces by garrisoning this line between respective spheres of influence with regimental units stationed 15 to 30 miles apart. This presented its own peculiar difficulties. To define a border implied open acknowledgment of a neighbouring state, and Lobengula was unable to do that. Instead he did his utmost to try and honour the boundary, and although raids across the Shashi River did occur, they were few, and Jameson for the most part tried to ignore them.

At the core of much of the tension between the Matabele and the Company's administration lay the tendency for the Mashona to make use of the relaxing of their circumstances, to enact mischief in a manner that annoyed both European and Matabele. In the case of the theft of copper wire from the newly strung cable telegraph line, this was more than just an annoyance — it destroyed communications and cost the Company a great deal of money. In order for it to be clearly understood that the practice must cease, fines and other repercussions were harsh. One particular incident was answered by a heavy fine in cattle to be paid with beasts that in fact belonged to the Matabele. The culprits then explained the loss to Lobengula by claiming that the Company had stolen the cattle. Lobengula was initially outraged, and complained bitterly to the High Commissioner in Cape Town using the cable telegraph. However he soon learned the truth and decided to make his irritation felt.

For a month or more nothing happened, then Lobengula unexpectedly deployed north a more aggressive force than had hitherto been seen. His intention was not only to deal with the errant parties but also to set a general example to all the Mashona in the territory, with the additional object of making it known to the whites that the Mashona still laid within his jurisdiction. This was a highly provocative ploy and suggested difficult internal pressures. Probably hoping that Jameson would accept the raid for what it was, Lobengula put his men under fear of death regarding any aggressive action against the whites. In the beginning, Jameson did take the action for what it was, but some loosening of the King's authority was evident in local commanders, exceeding this very restricted rule of engagement. As the raid gathered momentum Jameson was forced to think again.

The Matabele fell on the tribes in the vicinity of Fort Victoria with shocking ferocity. Whites observers were appalled at the degree of violence applied, with wanton and apparently senseless torture of men, women and children. Large numbers of Mashona cattle were appropriated, as well as many head belonging to a white farmer that may or may not have been seized in the belief that they were the property of plundered Mashona villages. Jameson, although still playing the incident down, was no less appalled as he rode into Fort Victoria and saw the evidence of carnage all around. He must have immediately apprehended that if war was not inevitable, then at least a significant turning point had been reached. A very sober Jameson dismounted his horse in the town centre that afternoon of 17 July 1893.

As soon as he had composed himself, Jameson sent for the commander of the impi. An hour or two later he met an induna called Manyau, or Manyewu, who listened politely but denied any knowledge of borders. With the support of a younger and considerably less courteous induna called Umgandan, and with the help of a letter apparently written by Lobengula outlining the objectives of the raid, Manyau maintained his right to proceed as he had been ordered. He also made the demand that all Mashona refugees in Fort Victoria be handed over to the impi. His single concession was that he would not contaminate the drinking water of the town killing them upstream of the river.

Jameson eventually abandoned the discussion and issued a simple ultimatum. He gave Manyau an hour to lead his detachment back across the border (although there is some dispute as to whether this hour was to 'get moving' or to actually be across the border). Failing this he would send out Captain Lendy with an armed patrol to enforce his instructions. In the event he allowed two hours to pass before Lendy was dispatched. Lendy had not advanced far before he came upon a bloody attack in progress against a local village. He took this to be an act of hostility and opened fire. He later maintained that the Matabele fired on his men first but this remains in doubt. Umgandan and an indeterminate number of his men were killed in a sharp exchange of fire before the remainder of the attack force retreated. Whether Lendy executed his orders correctly or not hardly matters. War was inevitable, and thereafter Jameson wasted no time in turning his mind to the practicalities of it — and more importantly how it could be turned to the Company's advantage.

The decision on the part of the Matabele raiders to seize white-owned cattle suggests that the rank and file of the army were themselves keen to provoke a war and were willing to flout a direct order to do so. This raises questions as to the degree of control that Lobengula actually exercised over his troops. Whether Manyau was either unwilling or unable to return cattle claimed by whites, it presented a convenient pretext for war.

As soon as Rhodes received word that war was a reality, the publicity machinery of the Chartered Company swung into action. The financial impact on an otherwise undecided board of directors was eased when Rhodes offered to underwrite the expenses from his own pocket. Any other critics were either silenced or ignored. On 14 August the Victoria Charter was instituted. This afforded each volunteer — not only any 'loot' he could lay his hands on — but also 20 gold claims and a 6 000-acre farm in Matabeleland. The entire Matabele nation had suddenly come up for plunder and the race was on.

During October 1893 Lobengula attempted to send another plea south to Sir Henry Loch. An embassy of two senior indunas and a young relation of the King carried the message on his behalf. Tragically the three were left unattended one night in the settlement of Tati while their white escort went out for a drink. The commander of the garrison, Lieutenant-Colonel Gould-Adams, was ignorant of who they were and attempted to arrest them. A scuffle turned into a shootout and the two indunas were killed. It is not difficult to imagine what Lobengula's interpretation of these events must have been when word reached him.

Sir Henry Loch found himself in a very difficult position. He was not quite as in awe of Rhodes as Hercules Robinson had been, and entertained a preference for state rather than private enterprise. However Matabele justice was obviously incompatible with British administration, and however much he disliked Rhodes, it was clear that the anachronistic rule of Lobengula needed to be brought to an end. He was ambivalent towards the Charter and as a consequence keen to see Her Majesty's forces assume control. Intelligence emerging from Bulawayo was also mixed. The Rev Charles D Helm maintained that the Matabele were not united on a course of war. Conversely British South Africa Company resident Johann Colenbrander assured the High Commissioner that the Matabele were indeed deeply committed to war.

Loch claims to have received reports of minor skirmishes with the Matabele around Bulawayo. Upon this he erred on the side of caution and mobilised the Bechuanaland Border Police under the same Colonel Gould-Adams who had killed the two indunas at Tati. Gould-Adams was authorised to proceed towards Bulawayo and take command of the situation as quickly as possible. At precisely the same time, Jameson and his 200 volunteers spurred their horses and set off at a gallop for the Matabele capital. Jameson at all costs had to beat Gould-Adams to the prize, for if agents of the Crown were seen to have occupied the capital, Company control of Matabeleland would be lost, shares would collapse, and that would probably be the end of it for everyone.

* * *

The character of the Matabele War was brief, bloody and one-sided. The Matabele manifestly failed to make use of their natural advantages. Where they could so easily have formed their superior numbers into highly mobile, flexible and harassing guerrilla units, they instead chose classic battle formations that were vulnerable to orchestrated gunfire. In two major battles impis were driven against volleys of musketry and machine gun fire until losses became patently unsustainable.

The short and brutal campaign ended with Jameson and his volunteers riding into the smoking ruins of Bulawayo on 4 November 1893. Lobengula fled north, leaving his capital in ruins and the remnants of his army scattered. Gould-Adams arrived a day or two later, too late to impose Crown authority on the situation.

The long, long road had finally come to an end and the Matabele nation was no more. Rhodes might well have toasted himself and his settlers with justifiable pride. Had he done so, however, the celebration would have been premature, for the defining episode of the pioneer period was yet to be played out. The Shangani Patrol incident, with all its symbols of human frailty and heroic failure, epitomised in so many ways the fumbling valour of Rhodes' ongoing colonial experiment.

Shangani Patrol, they did not die in vain [2]

As Jameson rode into the smoking ruins of Bulawayo he somewhat naively expected to find Lobengula waiting to surrender formally. This would have crowned an impressive advance with a clean victory and wrapped up the war in favour of the BSA Company with a minimum of dispute. However, with no formal surrender in hand and the King still at large, the game was still wide open.

Technically the threat of an official decree from Sir Henry Loch on behalf of the Imperial Government remained.

Neither Jameson nor Lobengula had expected such a swift advance on Matabeleland, and Lobengula could certainly not have foreseen such a conclusive initial rout. The rapid pace of events, and his hurried departure left him confused and disorientated. He had in fact not been in Bulawayo during the fighting at all, but had retreated seven miles north to the smaller location of Umvutcha Kraal where he received news of the defeat.

Had the unfortunate incident at Tati not occurred, there is every chance that Lobengula would have begun early negotiations, but the apparent murder of his indunas at the hands of Gould-Adams convinced him that he would suffer the same fate if he were to try and make overtures to peace.

Instead the frightened King ordered the muster of four ox wagons and hurriedly assembled a small entourage including his household counsellors, available wives and family members. The group set off northwards towards the lands of the Gwaai and the lower Shangani rivers. Around them were spread the surviving regiments of the army, no single unit of which had yet given any indication of surrender. Despite being sick, demoralised and very probably dying, Lobengula remained the focus of the nation.

For the settler militias to pursue the war any further than the capture of Bulawayo would have necessitated a campaign more on military lines than had hitherto been the case. Jameson was commander-in-chief at that point, and although not a military man, his self-confidence had bloated to the point that he believed himself capable of anything. He was surrounded by a motley collection of adventurers who were equally brash and equally inclined to believe that the capture of Lobengula would be a simple formality.

Principal among these was Major Allan Wilson. Since Wilson was neither an orthodox soldier nor a commissioned officer, 'Major' in his case was something of an arbitrary rank. He had been put in charge of the Victoria contingent of the Mashonaland Volunteers, and as such he was in the fight largely for the plunder and the glory. Wilson was an affable 37-year-old Scotsman who had arrived in South Africa some 15 years earlier and had served in the Cape Mounted Rifles, seeing action during the Anglo-Zulu and first Boer wars. He was a tall powerfully built man of enormous daring and ability, and of a generally amiable and easygoing nature. This made him fairly typical of his command and typical of most if not all the other irregulars. He was also a popular and trusted commander.

As a military man, his fellow major could not have been more different. Patrick Forbes was a thickset, pedestrian and rather humourless man. He was also conspicuously loyal to the old spit and polish school of the British military establishment. Lately he had succeeded to the position of Resident Magistrate for the district of Fort Salisbury. He still commanded wide respect for his earlier actions in Manicaland where he had commanded the Salisbury Volunteers. At age 32 he was the youngest of Jameson's senior officers. Most importantly, however, Forbes was the only one among Jameson's technical subordinates who had any conventional military training. This he had received primarily from Sandhurst Military Academy, then with his first commission in the Inniskilling Dragoons. It goes without saying that as a product of the British Army, he would have found serving under a civilian quite a novelty. But life in the colonies was brimming with novelty and the whole enterprise was nothing if not unorthodox.

The most inscrutable of all the men attending Jameson's strategy meeting that day was the enigmatic bush fighter Pieter Raaff who more than anyone typified the irregular colonial commando rider. He was a butcher/magistrate from Tuli who had joined the expedition as a privateer and raised a body of 250 Transvaal freebooters who called themselves Raaff's Rangers. At 44, Raaff added a considerable weight of experience to the expedition. He and his Transvaal rangers had scouted for the British and been involved in a number of the battles of the Anglo-Zulu War. In stature he was short, standing only five foot four inches, but like Jameson he compensated for this fact with a tremendous ego. He was pampered in appearance, which was deceptive, for Raaff was doubtless the single most competent commander present in Bulawayo on that day.

Perhaps the most dangerously underrated commander in the war, however, was not in Bulawayo at all, but moving rapidly north with the dislocated remains of the Matabele army. His name was Mjaan, or Mtjane, and his immediate objective was to support and protect his King's retreat. Mjaan was a man in his early fifties with a lifetime of military experience behind him. Not least of his battles had been the two recent engagements of Shangani and Bembezi where he and his Mbizo Regiment had faced the settler militia and seen the pride of the Matabele decimated by a combination of trained musketry and machinegun fire. From this he learned that if such tactics were encountered again he would need to quickly revaluate the established procedures of his men and commanders, otherwise their defeat would be absolute.

Jameson's first action, meanwhile, was to send a messenger to Lobengula with a letter inviting him to 'come in'.

> I send this message in order, if possible, to prevent the necessity of any further killing of your people or burning of their kraals. To stop this useless slaughter you must at once come and see me at Bulawayo, when I will guarantee that your life will be saved and that you will be kindly treated. I will allow sufficient time for this message to reach you and return to me and two days more to allow you to reach me in your wagon. Should you not arrive I will at once send out troops to follow you, as I am determined as soon as possible to put the country in a condition where whites and blacks can live in peace and friendliness.[3]

Four days later a rambling and predictably equivocal reply arrived from Lobengula. It offered no definite promise of surrender, and as Jameson suspected, it was probably intended only to buy more time. On 14 November Jameson dispatched a strong mounted force under the command of Major Forbes with orders to scatter the remaining Matabele and intercept and capture the King.

No one could have been more surprised than Allan Wilson when Jameson announced the composition of the force, and Raaff too could scarcely believe his ears. With their age and combined experience, both men felt they were the obvious choice for this command — and of course each was supported in this by his respective unit. It is probable that even the Salisbury Volunteers felt that Forbes would have been better off in support of a man more experienced than he.

Initially Forbes was oblivious to the controversy, and since he was accustomed to accepting orders with a minimum of reflection, this is precisely what he did. However the seeds of his future difficulties were there to be seen had he only thought to look. Not only was he younger than his subordinate officers, but he also had almost no experience of conducting irregular operations. Of course neither Raaff nor Wilson, nor any of their men, were accustomed to the normal military discipline that Forbes would have taken for granted.

Johann Colenbrander, who was an extremely able and versatile company man, attached himself to the column as interpreter. Jameson added the flamboyant American, Major Frederick Russell Burnham, and his only slightly less colourful brother-in-law and compatriot Peter Ingram, as additional scouts.

The first thrust out of Bulawayo proved to be unpromising. Forbes felt that a vigorous push north along the Bubi River would catch Lobengula off guard and bring matters to a speedy conclusion. However, he soon found himself mired in difficulties, the first of which was the sudden breaking of the annual rains that turned the countryside into a slough. The second was the foot-dragging discontent of men who had been hauled away on an uncomfortable mission when most had assumed that the war was over. Forbes responded to this malingering in the customary military manner — by driving his troops on despite obvious resistance and generally plunging morale.

Complaints among his officers became so insistent that to silence them he ordered a general parade and invited all those who were dissatisfied to take one step forward. He was horrified when all but six men did. This flummoxed Forbes, but with little creativity to call upon he simply forced the unhappy column on. On it struggled until Raaff at last managed to persuade Forbes to pause and reconsider.

Numbers of Matabele fighters began to appear among the general throng of refugees, most of whom claimed that they were moving south to surrender. Raaff sensed differently and believed that a hostile mobilisation was underway — a sentiment he made known both widely and frequently. Forbes tried to ignore him — and continued to ignore him until the situation provoked the first of many open and biting exchanges between the two.

Most of the men of the column took Raaff's side in the matter. Forbes had never experienced factionalism in his ranks, and for the first time in his career had no choice but to defer to the opinions of a subordinate. Nevertheless, his capitulation was not total. He would not consider turning back but gave an undertaking to withdraw if things became too difficult. Raaff patiently explained to him that if things became too difficult the column would probably no longer have the option of withdrawal.

Allan Wilson listened to all this but kept his opinions to himself. Like everyone else, however, he was dismayed at Forbes' bulldog attitude and his absolute lack of tact. However if Wilson was content to keep his peace, his junior officers were not. Lendy in particular carped incessantly among his fellow officers about Forbes' treatment of Raaff. He was the most vociferous member of Raaff's informal inner circle that Forbes later referred to as 'Raaff's Staff'. Forbes was eventually forced to concede that the column had been too lightly provisioned to penetrate very far, and so on 23 November he ordered it to fall back on Inyati.

Conditions continued to deteriorate. Forbes was simply unable to grasp the fact that with a force of irregulars, a driving approach would not work. Had Wilson or Raaff been in command, both would have known that men of an individual tendency could be led but never driven. Such a mood of pessimism had taken root in the column that Forbes was eventually obliged to order it back to Shiloh Mission to await fresh orders and re-supply.

At Shiloh the column stood down temporarily while the bickering continued. Raaff protested to Forbes that the military situation had become untenable, and added for the benefit of a fertile audience of troopers that the column was in real danger of annihilation. To many of the Salisbury men, this was all that they needed to hear. They announced that since they were volunteers and could not be forced to go anywhere, they intended to return. Another vote was held and this time Forbes was not particularly surprised to find only 17 out of the 90 men of his Salisbury Column were prepared to stand with him. Of Raaff's rangers only four elected to go on while of the Victoria men all voted to continue. The small Bechuanaland Border Police contingent, being the only regular imperial troops assigned, was not consulted.

In the meantime fresh supplies arrived from Bulawayo along with orders from Jameson to reorganise and re-deploy. The majority of the Salisbury Volunteers turned back, leaving Wilson's Victoria men as the only complete unit. Although they remained part of the column the Victoria contingent stayed firmly loyal to Wilson, leaving Forbes effectively without support. However, the more pressure Forbes found himself under, the more trenchant he became. This lack of adaptability fatally undermined his leadership and placed the remainder of the column under a magnified risk.

Forbes then drew supplies of three quarter food rations per man for 12 days, and on the 25th set off with his remaining 290 men. A little later, when hauling wagons in the wet conditions proved futile, another group returned with the transports, leaving only 160 mounted men and two Maxims.

As the column made its way north, lightly wooded country and rolling savannah began to thicken into forests. This, together with the persistent rain and ever-present mist, caused visibility to diminish considerably. Frayed nerves were stretched even tighter as scouts brought in new reports of a large body of armed Matabele moving parallel to the column. Those they encountered gave the appearance of being demoralised, maintaining that they were moving south to Bulawayo. Raaff and others sensed a bluff, a feeling reinforced by regularly untrue reports that the King was just a short distance ahead.

From Shiloh Mission the column struck directly north, crossing the Bubi River on 1 December. It was later revealed that at this point it came to within a stones throw of Lobengula's retreating entourage. Matabele who were travelling with the King later reported that a small group of scouts moving ahead of the column had actually ridden into a village where Lobengula was taking shelter. The King apparently panicked when this happened and sent a trusted induna back in the general direction of the column with two bags containing 1 000 gold sovereigns and a note that read: 'White men, I am conquered. Take this and go back.'[4] Tragically the induna, nervous of approaching the leading edge of the column, came up from the rear and handed the bag and the note to two troopers. The pair destroyed the note, secreted the gold and mentioned the incident to no one. The fact was only revealed later, and the whereabouts of the gold never discovered. The two troopers were charged with theft, but later their sentences were quashed and they were freed of any culpability for subsequent events.

Of Lobengula's efforts to communicate, nothing was known to either Forbes or any of his officers. Had his letter reached Forbes, Colenbrander or either of Forbes' deputies, it is likely that the King could have been persuaded to surrender In turn this would have meant a guarantee of a safe return for all. In the event, the column arrived in the vicinity of the Shangani River with Lobengula again in retreat and reportedly less than a days march ahead.

By this time Mjaan had gathered together as many of his fighting men as he could and was observing the progress of the flying column as it moved towards the Shangani River. He had decided to use the King as a decoy, hoping that he could lure the column across the Shangani River where he would cut off its means of retreat. From that vantage he could attack and easily overwhelm it from the front and rear. To this end he placed the King's wagons in clear sight of the south bank. A herd boy was meanwhile prepared with false intelligence and positioned where he could be easily detained by roving scouts.

At about 3 o'clock on the afternoon of 3 December the column reached the banks of the Shangani, where it paused to regroup. The young cattle herder was duly detained and brought in by scouts who delivered him to Raaff. Raaff drew the information that the boy had been coached to deliver before handing him over to Colenbrander who also interrogated the boy. Both men were somewhat sceptical. Forbes, perhaps desperate for a conclusion, was inclined to believe the boy and, to verify the facts, he crossed the river with a small escort and rode down towards a collection of huts. There he found fresh evidence of occupation and returned to the column in a high state of excitement. As he alighted from his horse he called a meeting of his two senior officers.

Forbes outlined the situation. According to him the column was in very close proximity to the King. He intended to consolidate defences on the banks of the river and be in a position to mount an attack the following morning. Furthermore, it was his intention to leave both Wilson and Raaff in command while he took a small force to complete the final phase of the operation. Needless to say, both Raaff and Wilson were appalled at this news.

Forbes continued with a short summary of the herd boy's story — at which point Raaff interrupted, reminding him that it had been he, Raaf, who had first interrogated the boy, so he knew exactly what the position was. Upon that he spun on his heel and stalked off. Forbes watched him leave and for a moment stood speechless. In that moment Wilson was thinking fast. Like Raaff he badly wanted to be part of the capture, but unlike Raaff he had some control over his impulses. He needed permission to leave camp so he could operate freely and on his own initiative. By the time Forbes regained his composure, Wilson was ready to offer him an alterative strategy.

Wilson proposed that while sufficient daylight remained, he would mount a brief reconnaissance across the river. With a small detachment of men he would attempt to establish the exact whereabouts of Lobengula's camp. If it were possible to capture the King that night he would do so, although his main object would be to reconnoitre.

There are many reasons why Forbes should have refused this request, or at least seen through it, not least because of waning daylight and heavy rain. Also Forbes could not have been ignorant of the partisanship already rife in his force. With more experience, and certainly in retrospect, he might have seen his folly. However he authorised the patrol with just the vague proviso that if Wilson captured Lobengula he was to bring him back on horseback. Failing this, he should keep him under observation until the main column came up. Finally he made it clear that they were all to return to the column by nightfall. Such ambiguity was manna to Wilson and license for him to do precisely as he pleased.

Wilson wasted no time, and before Forbes could change his mind he selected the 12 best mounted men of his Victoria contingent and made ready to leave. Several officers who were friends of Wilson sought permission from Forbes to accompany the patrol. Forbes consented and added to the group on his own account the two American scouts Burnham and Ingram. Thus 19 mounted men formed up and set off across the vlei towards the river. As he watched the riders fade into the twilight Raaff, was heard to grumble that not one of them would return alive.

The strategy for the King's capture now rode on the simple testimony of a Matabele herd boy, Forbes' wishful observations and the tempers of a trio of feuding egos. Lobengula had been moved on to a safer location a day earlier and a simple trap had been laid, and baited by the tantalising possibility of the King being in close proximity. Raaff might have suspected all this, but when it counted his lips were sealed. Colenbrander was certainly puzzled, but by nothing that he could put his finger on. As a defensive camp was struck that evening, a mood of expectation mingled with uncertainty. Men separated into groups, fires were lit and conversations muted. No one strayed too far from his weapons.

Mjaan was disappointed. He had not expected the column to split up as it did with just a small patrol venturing across the river. As he observed events, he ordered his men not to interfere with the patrol, and it was for this reason that Wilson crossed the river without being engaged and without seeing any obvious signs of a sizeable military force.

The patrol rode on for a mile or so in high spirits. The time was a minute or two past five o'clock, and on a summer evening they might expect another hour and a half of usable daylight. This ought to have allowed plenty of time to intercept the King if the patrol managed to locate him promptly. Each man felt — for a while at least — relieved to be free of the oppressive atmosphere in the column. Also, of course, they were convinced that they were hot on the trail of the King and that the credit for his capture would soon be theirs.

Back in camp, Forbes was also indulging in a moment of comfortable certainty. Content that Wilson would locate the King, he was also satisfied that he would be unable to bring him in alone. Forbes himself would do that in the morning and he would take the credit.

Wilson led his men a few miles upstream before crossing the river and moving in under cover of woodland. They were led further away than Wilson would have liked by a native guide who did not seem particularly knowledgeable. The patrol soon found itself hampered by dwindling daylight, with an uncertain distance yet to cover and separated now from the main column by some miles. They were also coming into increasing contact with Matabele who appeared hostile when Captain Napier called out for directions.

Wilson had by then begun to mull over a fateful strategy. It was becoming clear to him that the patrol would not find or capture the King that evening, but at the same time he was reluctant to give up the advantage that the extra few miles of reconnaissance gave him. The first stars were peering through gaps in the cloud, while in the distance a murmur of thunder promised rain. Under the last light of day, the sails of Lobengula's wagons suddenly came into view, and that was all that Wilson needed to confirm his intentions. He elected to retire to higher ground and under cover of dense woodland make camp for the night.

At that point Wilson had no means of knowing that back in camp Forbes had made a very grim discovery. Soon after the patrol rode out of camp he and Colenbrander questioned the herd boy again, and this time they succeeded in exposing the truth. Now, to his horror, Forbes realised that a mobilisation of several thousand Matabele warriors was underway around them, meaning that the Shangani Patrol was in mortal peril.

Forbes' initial response was to sit on the information and do nothing. As he recalled, he had been quite specific in his instructions that the patrol should return by nightfall. For the time being then, he felt it unnecessary to try and warn or reinforce them. However, as he anxiously paced the ground inside camp, pictures of disaster, recrimination and a ruined career began to pass before his eyes.

Minutes turned into hours. From the edge of camp he peered periodically into the night, but all there was to disturb the pitch darkness were distant flashes of lightning and the low rumble of thunder. Gnawing doubt defeated any attempt to rationalise his position. He should have seen it before... with hindsight it was perfectly obvious. Wilson had manipulated him to seize the advantage and naturally he would not willingly surrender it. He would now be perfectly poised for the coup, and any effort to alert him to his danger would be seen as a ruse to get him back.

Forbes tried to console himself with the thought that the herd boy might have been wrong. If he rode out promptly the next morning with his own force then Wilson's advantage would serve him too. But in the pit of his stomach he knew that the whole edifice he had held together by sheer force of character was about to crumble. There was no doubt in his mind that Wilson intended to lead his Victoria men on a solo dash in the face of all rational strategy and contrary to a direct order. Added to this, Forbes also sensed that an attack on the column itself was probably imminent. There was no other way to look at it. The situation was dire.

As Forbes agonised, on the far side of the river, and deep in the silent bushveld, Wilson was not without grave concerns of his own. The cloud had closed in overhead and the early evening drizzle was thickening into a steady downpour. The woodland surrounding him was saturated and he could hear the waters of the Shangani, that he had crossed so easily an hour or two earlier, beginning to rage. Above the river and the steady beating of the rain, he and his men could hear another sound. It was a soft murmur — a combination of half-heard footfalls and the whispered conversations of many voices. It was clear now that many more enemy fighters were massed in the vicinity than they had at first thought. Although troop morale remained high, confidence was perceptibly waning as the lonely night closed in.

After a brief consultation with his men Wilson elected to send Captain Napier and two troopers back to brief Forbes. He made no definite request for support, perhaps assuming that Forbes would make immediate plans to follow in his direction. But it is also possible that he did not want any support. This would prompt a race for the King's capture that might have either Forbes or Raaff claiming the laurels. To appeal for assistance would also mean admitting that he had swum out of his depth — which would give Forbes the last laugh after almost three weeks of jostling. Moreover, a rapidly rising river would in any case soon render an attempt at reinforcement impossible.

Around o'clock that night Forbes' worst fears were confirmed when Napier and his party arrived to report the news. Napier added on his own initiative that Wilson expected Forbes to mobilise the main column and proceed in support at once. He pointed out, however, that the river was now so high that moving the whole column across that night would be very difficult, although perhaps not yet impossible.

At this point there was absolutely nothing Forbes could have done that would alter the course of events, and nothing that would not be seized upon and used against him by his junior officers. He was dismayed by Wilson's independence of mind, and for the first time at a complete loss. Nothing in his background equipped him for either mobile planning or the vagaries of undisciplined subordinates. He consoled himself with the fleeting hope that the patrol might not be in such tremendous peril after all. Napier and the two troopers had, after all, come through unscathed. For a moment he even allowed himself to contemplate an immediate mobilisation, but about this at least his instincts were true. The mere possibility of a general massacre froze the idea out of his mind.

Mjaan, meanwhile, had been carefully observing movements in and around the camp. He by then was aware that the patrol was separated from the column but he continued to allow movement between the two groups to continue unhindered. He was still hoping that he could draw the main force to move during the night — which would indeed have set the stage for a comprehensive slaughter.

After several hours of indecision, Forbes was eventually persuaded to send Captain Borrow with 20 mounted men in an attempt to reinforce Wilson. In agreeing to this, he made the worst of all possible decisions. He diminished the strength of the main column while at the same time consigning more men to their deaths. Raaff attempted to intervene at this late stage but succeeded only in infuriating Forbes. The two eventually agreed not to weaken the column by sending a machine gun — which prompted Captain Lendy to remark that this seemed ridiculous to him.

Before dawn on 4 December, Captain Borrow and his men slipped quietly out of camp and headed through the darkness towards their stranded comrades. Wilson was horrified when he peered into the dawn light and saw only 20 figures emerging. For most of the night the patrol had heard and sensed the movement of Matabele fighters around them. The hunger for the chase had by then become fear for their own lives, and most had hoped at least to see a Maxim if not the entire column riding to their support.

Wilson then sought the advice of his men. All were pessimistic and pleaded with him to order an immediate retreat, failing which none of them gave much for their chances of survival. Wilson disagreed, vetoing the majority and urging them to move against Lobengula immediately. It says much for Wilson's personal authority and the respect he commanded that even under those dismal circumstances all his men agreed. It may still have been possible for them to get back to the column if they had moved quickly, but from the moment they mounted their horses and cantered off in the direction of Lobengula's camp, they were doomed.

A little later the patrol arrived at the place where they had seen Lobengula's wagons the previous evening. There they were confronted by a body of Matabele fighters emerging out of the dripping dawn and ominously announcing that all the white men would be dead before the day was over.

The first attacks began with a volley of misdirected fire from the direction of the wagons and from tree cover a short distance beyond. One horse was killed and a trooper wounded as the patrol fought a brief rearguard action before falling back and forming a defensive circle around a termite mound. The first rushed attack was beaten back reasonably easily, after which the Matabele retreated and observed the patrol from a short distance.

It was only at this stage that Wilson began to consider a hot retreat. Forming a square, the patrol managed to cover a short distance before it became apparent that they would not escape unless they mounted an aggressive charge. This would mean leaving those on foot as well as the wounded to the mercy of the Matabele. As Ingram later observed, these were not men given to abandoning their friends.[5] Instead it was decided that they would form another defensive circle, dig in, and then send Burnham and Ingram — who had the best chance of getting through — to the column to urge Forbes to send reinforcements.

The two Americans duly mounted up and spurred their horses through a forming body of Matabele warriors. By the time they reached the column, firing could already be heard from the direction of the patrol. The pair struggled across the swollen river and found when they arrived that the column was also engaged in action against a large force of Matabele. It was evident at that point that the patrol had no chance of survival. The column fended off the worst of the attack but there was no possibility that Forbes could consider relieving the patrol.

Mjaan rightly concluded that the column with its riflemen and machine guns was invulnerable and began redirecting his troops across the river and throwing more into the assault against the patrol. Since no white man survived that action, accounts of it are vague and are coloured largely by the views of surviving Matabele fighters.

Whatever may have transpired during those last hours, it is certain that an uncommon meeting of minds occurred between the two sides. The Matabele were a brutal and often crude society. Warfare defined their cultural identity and killing was their supreme expression. Terrible cruelty born of contempt was usually inflicted on inferior persons, but men of calibre — those who fought with courage — heard in death the sincere accolades of their enemy. Men, both white and black, met for a moment in time in an engagement more intimate than any other known to man. It was a rare instance when each side understood the other and met on a plane of equality. Never again in the history of Rhodesia would the black race achieve anything close to a victory of this magnitude over whites. It was the first and the last, and as such it lives in the memory of the Matabele as one of greatest of all their glories.

Legend portrays the event in all its awful magnificence. Initially the usual practice of throwing waves of men armed with assegais into withering rifle fire was employed. As the morning wore on and Matabele losses mounted, the warriors retreated into dense woodland and were content to wear down the doomed patrol by insistent and overwhelming sniper fire.

Mjaan was interviewed some time later and his fragmented account paint a vivid picture of the final moments:

> Shouted demands for surrender met with defiant refusal. I would have spared their lives, for they were brave men. Then from the ranks of the doomed came the suggestion that one should live to tell the tale. Matabele agreed. But I think they could find no-one willing to leave his brothers lest he was accounted a coward among women in after years.[6]
>
> At sunset, Inyamazane, we made an end of it. It was quick. They were finished. There was great rejoicing in our camp that night, for many assegais were wet with the blood of the white man and meat was eaten and beer drunk.[7]
>
> Having assegaied the wounded, who were too weak to fight…'they do not die like Mashonas. They never cry or groan. They are men. No! I will never fight whites again. They are not afraid to die: They are men.'[7]

11

Days of plunder: The Jameson era

White occupation of Matabeleland

T he Shangani Patrol marked the end of the Matabele war. Although no definitive information emerged, it was widely accepted that Lobengula died shortly thereafter from a broken heart and a plethora of physical ailments. It is also possible that he took poison. Soon afterwards Matabeleland was occupied, and behind that the first efforts at native administration began. By necessity these would be experimental, and would reflect more than anything a phase of government characterised by Jameson's own erratic and rather unprofessional standards.

Rhodes' cavalier approach to the creation of Rhodesia was reflected in the subsequent attitudes of both the company administration and settlers. The European minority revealed its estrangement from the native by the blanket assumption that the Matabele had been beaten. This was manifestly not the case. The Matabele had certainly tasted defeat, but they did not regard the death of their king and the loss of their capital as the end of the war. Undercurrents of resistance were very much alive.

With regard to the Mashona the same was largely true. A surface obsequiousness towards the white man and an apparent embrace of servitude were both dangerously deceptive. The thoughtless, indifferent, and at times heavy-handed manner in which the white man marched into the future merely insulated coals of resentment that burned both hot and deep in the belly of the black nation.

* * *

Matabeleland did not enjoy civilian administration in the accepted sense until the end of 1894. It was then that Rhodes replaced the rule of the police, which was composed entirely of whites — what is more of young, disinterested and largely ignorant whites — with native commissioners whose work centred specifically on the issue of blacks and their rights. In practice these men were quite often only marginally more mature and informed than their predecessors, inheriting as they did the same policy of mass land and cattle appropriation. Many observers of the period lamented the poor standards of general administration in Matabeleland — in particular in the field of native administration.

At the end of the war Jameson found himself with a great deal of power concentrated in his hands. The conclusion of hostilities had been achieved with little imperial involvement — which meant that moral sway over the new country lay with him and Rhodes almost exclusively. Jameson was also faced with the fact that after the seizure of Matabeleland, Rhodes was obliged to recognise those who had contributed money and support to the venture. The spoils amounted to an entire country along with its natural resources that were Rhodes' and Jameson's to give away more or less as they chose.

Rhodes had indeed relied on many important people to expedite his route to prominence — not just in terms of his occupation of Rhodesia, but in the usual ways and means of capital and political cronyism. It was now incumbent on him to show generosity. Lavish recognition by way of naming streets, squares, parks, schools and public buildings after peers and capitalists was not enough. Hard assets like land, livestock and mining rights were also expected.

By then Rhodes had reached the apex of his career. At 40 years of age he was not only prime minister of the Cape Colony, but he also controlled a vast and diverse financial empire. Unlike most of the Victorian nouveau riche, he enjoyed if not the embrace of kinship, then at least some fellowship and a great deal of respect from the ruling classes. As a consequence he felt empowered and munificent like never before, and he celebrated his successes with largesse to many of his associates and titled supporters. According to Sir William Milton, one of Jameson's later successors, the 'honourable and military' elements appeared to be everywhere in Rhodesia.

Consequently, before any coherent native policy could be put in place, Jameson distributed lavish quantities of land to largely speculative, absent or unproductive recipients. The solution with regard to the natives was to resettle them in remote and often sterile reserves where few willingly went, preferring to remain as squatters on their original homelands, now owned, often in absentia, by a white man.

Of course it would be wrong to categorise all whites who occupied Matabeleland as villainous, as it would be equally wrong to imply that all native commissioners were imperious, indifferent and self interested. This was not so. The numbers of both who were warned off and who survived the Matabele Rebellion is testimony to the fact that many were on cordial terms with their charges and tenant neighbours. The majority of whites, however, tended to justify in one way or another negative black opinions held of them, just as the blacks themselves often did very little within their cultural pursuits and personal habits to alter negative white opinions. Suspicion, ignorance and chronic misunderstanding bedevilled any number of well-intentioned efforts on both sides to bridge the gap. The dominant view across the racial divide, therefore, remained one of mutual mistrust, dislike and contempt.

Jameson struck at the very pivot of Matabele values when he began the mass expropriation of cattle. There would have been a margin acceptable to both sides under the rules of booty, but Jameson and the BSA Company administration went much further than this. It is to the credit of a few, including Sir Henry Loch, that voices were raised in protest at all, but it is to no one's credit that nothing of substance was done to alter the ruinous process of dismemberment that went on unchecked.

The Matabele inherited from their Nguni blood line a love of cattle and a primitive economy at the core of which lay their herds. It is impossible for a white man to understand fully the bond that the black man had and has with his cattle. A white man confronting a black man over the issue of cattle is as risky as laying a hand on a virgin daughter. Jameson began by claiming the royal herd as a right of conquest. This led to immediate confusion and much criminality. The assumption — viewed by many later observers and historians as an assumption of convenience — that all things can be accounted for by individual ownership led to the supposition that the king had a specific herd of his own — which was not the case.

The king held the national herd, such as it was, in trust — much like a national treasury — and dispensed largess to individuals only by dint of loan, favour or convenience. This misunderstanding, deliberate or not, laid open to plunder upwards of 200 000 head of cattle ostensibly owned by the king. Before any effective control could be put in place, the Matabele national herd had been reduced to just 41 000 beasts. Most of those lost had been claimed as booty on the run, or simply seized and redistributed with no authority or control.

At precisely this time a plague of the cattle disease rinderpest arrived in southern Africa from Somalia, where some years earlier it had broken out. This disease ravaged herds across the region, and it was a bitter harvest for the Matabele to watch the white man enter their reserves and slaughter most of their remaining cattle after having already taken the best for themselves. The Matabele were not to know that this was part of a regional control measure to slow the pace of the disease that was ruining as many white cattlemen as black. Up the length of the Pioneer Road from Vryburg to Fort Salisbury, families were stranded and made destitute as wagons were stalled by dead oxen. Lord Baden Powell recalled counting 200 wagons and 3 200 dead oxen at Palla in Bechuanaland soon after the outbreak of the disease. The Matabele, however, took the event at face value and saw it as spiteful and vindictive — indeed almost genocidal in its impact and implication.

To further alienate the blacks, a coercive regime of hut taxation was put in place that had the dual effect of raising revenue and of forcing a population averse to employment to engage in paid work. If a deep rancour existed in the Matabele nation, it could not have been much eased by men being driven to do women's work for the whites on land stolen from them. Without such labour, the growth of a cash economy would have been impossible, but the Matabele could scarce have given a damn about that.

A native police force was also soon raised for the purpose of assisting native commissioners in their administration. It was naively supposed that a force recruited mainly from the Matabele would be sympathetically received and would be sensitive and effective in dealing with their own people. Many, if not most, of the early white administrators neither spoke the language nor had any fluency in matters of African society and culture. They were therefore genuinely surprised when the native police emerged as yet another source of grievance held against them by the Matabele. It would, of course, have been unreasonable to expect a recent arrival in the country to know anything about the intimate structure of Matabele society. However, many native commissioners in due course became very adept at interpreting Matabele language, culture and society, but in those vital early days ignorance plagued both sides.

Under the cover of officialdom, native police details simply tyrannised their own, usurping their betters and taking advantage of their authority to settle old feuds and grudges. It was said in justification that the ranks of the native police were made up of Lobengula's crack troops; and in criticism that they were of the lower classes (integrated Mashona captures, or *AmaHoli* as they were known). Whatever their composition, the native police were largely free to conduct their own regime of oppression, hidden from white interest, or indeed any oversight at all.

It was in their treatment of women, however, that the native police drew most criticism from the population — as ironically had white police details before them. Frank W Sykes, in his book *With Plumer in Matabeleland* remarked that: 'The conduct of many of the whites towards their black sisters, married or virgin, in Matabeleland, certainly contributed to the causes which have led up to this unfortunate rebellion.'[1]

Although they were tolerated under the laws of conquest — which the Matabele of all people understood — it was the whites themselves who were probably the most discernable source of black discontent. It is true that on a central administrative level a degree of sympathy and a will to succeed drove native policy, but this was only so long as it did not compromise the future of the whites. Inexperience and a disregard for the Matabele's need for strong, consistent and visible leadership tended to see individual administrators rotated frequently, with the result that the natives felt unbalanced. Added to this was the settler element itself that seemed always to conspire by ignorance, greed and artificial superiority to undo whatever positive work the Native Department might, largely by accident, have achieved. This, and all the other instances of confusion, misunderstanding, malice and robbery, combined to convince the Matabele that their best interests were not being served by the white man.

All of these issues helped to cement a mood of rebellion in a society that did not by any means consider itself to be conquered. The occupation of the country proceeded apace without much prior effort to test the political waters or to provide the settlers with adequate security. Miners, storekeepers, missionaries and farmers fanned out, believing that the natives had accepted the new order and were happy to be part of it. Unbeknown to most, though, was the gradual reformation of the old Matabele command structure that was underway around them. The absence of a strong central command temporarily disorientated the rank and file, but it would only be a matter of time before this situation was healed.

Rhodes had shrewdly removed Lobengula's two most likely heirs from the country and enrolled them at school in Cape Town. This created some confusion over the issue of succession and presented an opportunity for a religious figure to step into what had always been a secular role. It is worth noting that a little over a century earlier Mzilikazi had assimilated Mashona religious practice and elevated some of its practitioners to high status. This raised the interesting possibility that general leadership could be assumed by a figure who enjoyed powerful links to both the Matabele and the Mashona.

In Mashonaland the underlying currents were little different from those in Matabeleland. In Mashonaland white complacency was even more marked thanks to the fact that the Mashona had no known history of militancy — or at least not on the scale of the Matabele. Isolated and vulnerable communities of whites gathered where mines or trading posts were situated, often with hundreds of miles of bush between them and the safety of the larger settlements. The Mashona seemed passive and compliant, but this was an illusion. The truth was that they hated the whites no less than the Matabele and wanted to see them banished. They were like a sponge to ideas and talk of sedition spreading through the countryside faster than even the rinderpest. A majority of whites, of course, new nothing of this.

For some time, however, the Matabele languished in indecision and the status quo persisted. White force of arms was too potent a threat to ignore and besides, it was supported by the power of an unimaginable empire. It would take an act of particular lunacy on the part of Jameson to alter this perception. As it happened Archibald Colquhoun's prediction that Jameson would one day grow too big for his boots would come true just at this vital juncture.

12

The Raiders

Even as Rhodes consolidated his power in the Cape Colony, he found himself increasingly drawn into the complexities of Anglo-Boer antagonism. The focus of public attention at that time was the gold rush on the Witwatersrand, and this created powerful political and economic ramifications for both Briton and Boer. As with the diamond discoveries in Griqualand West, the Witwatersrand gold strike emerged as the greatest of its kind in history, and attracted fertile interest from both the City of London and the political hawks of Westminster.

As news of massive gold discoveries filtered out, miners and speculators began to flood into the Transvaal. They were mainly English speakers, but also included a variety of other European and colonial expatriates. These Uitlanders were taxed to such an extent that they began to feel they were owed some political representation. Although the Transvaal government profited handsomely from taxation, it could see no merit in giving outsiders the vote — especially when the Uitlanders began to outnumber the Transvaalers themselves. The formation of the Transvaal Republic had, after all, been a Boer solution to progressive British domination of the Cape, and Kruger had no wish to see that scenario repeated in Pretoria.

Rhodes, in his dual roles as Prime Minister of the Cape Colony and head of both De Beers and Goldfields of South Africa, saw in this an opportunity to draw the Transvaal into the British sphere of influence. He had by then established his myth, and like Jameson in regard to his own, he was finding himself daily more inclined to believe it. Mark Twain, in his journey around the world, noticed the moment he arrived in South Africa that a certain Mr Rhodes was beginning to run ahead of himself. 'In the opinion of many people Mr Rhodes is South Africa.' Twain observed. 'Others think he is only a large part of it.'[1]

Rhodes had no doubt that he was a vital lynchpin in the affairs of South Africa. He had established a country, displaced an imperial power and fought a war. All of this he had achieved by his own force of character and paid for it largely through his own financial genius. There was no reason for him to suppose that he could not do much more.

The problem that Rhodes was beginning to feel more and more acutely was that time was not on his side. His health had always been questionable, and having lived more than 20 years past his lease, he could be forgiven for sensing that his sands were running low. If he was to accomplish even part of what he wished he needed to act fast and cut corners.

As the unrest in the Transvaal Republic continued to ferment, Rhodes and Jameson, as well as others close to both men in Whitehall and the Cape, sensed in the Uitlander discontent the possibility of an uprising. With judicious assistance, this uprising might topple the government of the Transvaal and usher in an administration more sympathetic to a union with the British colonies.

The outcome of this thinking was a muddled plot devised by Rhodes and his secretaries and advisors. The scheme enjoyed to a greater or lesser degree the approval of both Sir Henry Loch and current Colonial Secretary Joseph Chamberlain. Most of the controversy that surrounded the incident in later years revolved around the degree of complicity of these and other highly placed players. Certain facts about the incident, however, were never in dispute.

The Boer population of the Transvaal Republic in 1895 stood at approximately 30 000, while the Uitlander count was roughly double that. Neither Paul Kruger nor his government had any intention of allowing this amorphous body of opportunists to dominate national affairs, so laws were passed to limit their influence. Kruger's initial concession was to make the vote available to the Uitlanders contingent on a period of 14 years of continuous residence. Considering that by its nature the gold rush community was itinerate this was not ungenerous, but under extreme pressure it was modified to five years. However, according to Transvaal Attorney General Jan Smuts, Rhodes wanted not the little finger but the whole hand, and neither was Rhodes a man to let scruple stand in his way.[2]

Rhodes began to support actively and encourage the growth of extreme elements among the Uitlanders. An ad hoc organisation called the Reform Committee was formed on quasi-military lines, while arms were smuggled into Johannesburg and secreted away in preparation for some kind of military action. Jameson would be waiting with an armed force just beyond the Transvaal border in Bechuanaland. The pivotal aspect of the plot was that Jameson would make a spirited dash to Johannesburg and give support and direction to the uprising. This, it was believed, would be sufficient to bring down Kruger's government.

The details of the conspiracy lie beyond the scope of this narrative, other than to observe that arrangements were bungled from the outset and characterised by appalling displays of amateurism and perfidy. Perhaps most critically insufficient account was taken of the nature of the Uitlanders themselves. These were business people after all, who, despite everything, were making money hand over fist; and economic contentment does not usually stimulate revolution. Rhodes had also of late tended to allow the details to be handled by subordinates, principal among these being Rutherfoord Harris.

Harris seems to have been very quickly swept up in the cloak and dagger nature of the planning. The players were 'shareholders', Jameson alternately the 'veterinary surgeon' or the 'contractor', and the whole debacle was codenamed the 'flotation'. Even Rhodes was drawn into the ruse by advising his brother Frank — who held the fort in Johannesburg, to 'keep the market firm' when the Uitlanders appeared to be wavering.[3] The most profound weakness in the scheme, however, was that no one seemed yet to have noticed how dangerously independent Jameson himself had become.

The simple plan was expanded in Johannesburg in November 1895. A meeting of the National Union was to be held to divert the attention of the Boers while the arsenal in Pretoria was seized and a provisional government set up to replace the deposed Kruger. Jameson and his 500 or so men of the Mashonaland Mounted and Bechuanaland Border Police would spur their horses, kick up the shimmering sand and ride gloriously to Johannesburg to settle the matter.

This was just the sort of stuff on which the overgrown schoolboy in Jameson thrived. After Matabeleland his confidence was soaring, and in classic Jameson style, he had told a friend three weeks earlier that 'anyone could take the Transvaal with half a dozen revolvers'.[4] Jameson had a good many more than half a dozen revolvers to hand and strong was his desire to use them — so strong in fact that he purposefully ignored evidence all around him that the plot was flawed and rapidly falling apart.

As zero hour approached and the reality of a war grew near, the 'Reformers' began to get cold feet. Messages arrived at Rhodes' telegraph terminal urging him to delay the 'flotation' indefinitely. Joseph Chamberlain was worrying about the timing and threatening to scupper the plan.

Meanwhile, nervous communications travelling between Whitehall, the Cape and Mafeking naturally leaked to the Boers, who in due course were fully briefed. By 23 December, Jameson, drilling his men in the border town of Pitsani, had received no less than 17 telegraph messages in various tones of urgency begging or advising caution. The plan was variously on, off, on again, postponed or cancelled.

Of all this correspondence though, the one man whose authority Jameson would have respected had signed not a single message. By the time Rhodes did try to pour cold water on the scheme, the telegraph lines had been cut and Jameson and his men had crossed the border into Transvaal. Nothing could be done. They were riding into their particular valley of the shadow of death.

When Rhodes heard that Jameson had launched the raid he was crushed. The possible ramifications that he had ignored in the weeks past suddenly appeared stark and uncensored before him. It was one of those situations, as Julius Caesar might have reminded him, that breaking the law in pursuit of power can only be justified if the endeavour succeeds. It was clear that this ridiculous enterprise had no chance whatsoever of succeeding. 'Old Jameson has upset my apple cart' Rhodes lamented, with a degree of understatement that did no justice to the calamity.

By New Years Day 1896 it had become apparent that the raiders were being shadowed by a Boer commando — a circumstance confirmed by a brief exchange of fire near the first Transvaal border outpost. Even then — and despite being overtaken by advice from both Sir Henry Loch and the British Government's agent in Pretoria to turn back immediately — Jameson pressed on. In Krugersdorp, where he expected to be met by a force of Reformers marching out of Johannesburg, he was welcomed instead by two cyclists carrying no more than hearty messages of solidarity.

Within sight of the mine-heads of Johannesburg, the raiders found the road blocked by a strong Boer contingent of suited men who had hurried away from New Year celebrations and armed themselves to confront the 'invasion'. Skirmishes followed that cost the lives of several raiders and their mounts. That evening Jameson withdrew in order to escape relentless sniper fire and also to try and outflank Boer positions. At dawn he sent a typically droll message to Johannesburg stating that although his raiders had fought one or two 'scrimmages', they were all right and in good spirits. A little help, he suggested, would nonetheless be appreciated, if any could be spared.[5]

The Boers had no difficulty in tracking Jameson's movements overnight and the following day the raiders were confronted by a substantial force stiffened with artillery. By then the raiders had been in the saddle for three days. The men were exhausted, their field gun had run out of shells, and rifle ammunition was running perilously low. A brief battle was fought at the cost of 30 men before Jameson came to the inevitable conclusion that his position was hopeless. He surrendered his force to Piet Cronjé, after which his tired body of shocked and dispirited raiders were marched off in ignominy to a Pretoria gaol.

Rhodes survived the affair, but with much reduced power and prestige. Jameson and his force were fortunate in that Paul Kruger permitted them to be tried in England. Most importantly, however, this took Jameson and virtually the entire military capacity of Rhodesia to London, and away from their area of responsibility. If the white settlers of Matabeleland were so preoccupied with the drama that they did not notice how completely unprotected they were, the Matabele did not. With almost no force of arms remaining to oppose them the Matabele high command deemed that the moment had arrived to act.

13

Rhodes, the rebellion and victory

William Usher was a long-time resident of Matabeleland and, at one time, a confidant and adviser to Lobengula. For some time he had been warning the administration about the imminent danger of native violence. His opinion was supported by a number of native commissioners who were among the few whites in the territory who might be expected to know. In trying to warn his fellow settlers, Usher met with considerable resistance, for with Jameson gone and his replacement trying to pick up the threads, the attention of most whites was not focused on the mood of the natives. Usher's pleas became so persistent that an irritated administration threatened him with arrest if he did not stop behaving like a gadfly and spreading alarm and despondency.[1]

The spirit of revolt had, of course, been alive in Matabele society since the conquest. The royal bloodline had been scattered, and this conspired with the general terms of occupation to make the revival of any kind of central command structure — in accordance with Matabele tradition — very unlikely. The old council of Indunas and other military commanders had never been conditioned to act as a committee, far less to take individual political responsibility. The leadership vacuum was filled by the next most powerful national institution — the cult of Mwari, or Mlimo as it was known in Matabeleland, which Mzilikazi adopted upon occupation of Matabeleland and directed towards his own political ends. In later years Lobengula would become a minor office bearer within the cult.

The internal political machinations of a decapitated Matabele nation gave rise to a powerful Mlimo oracle by the name of M'Quati, or Mkwati. Very little is known about this man, other than he was a captive of a Matabele raid conducted somewhere north of the Zambezi, and began agitating for a renewal of hostilities against the occupation sometime in 1895. He motivated his audience with the prediction that once the Europeans had been removed, a pernicious drought would end. This indeed came about almost the moment that the killing began. Mkwati established his battle headquarters at the cave shrine of Thabas-zi-ka-Mambo in 1896 and began the military organisation of the Matabele impis. His plan was not particularly original, and simply depended on the main force surprising the whites in Bulawayo while the fifth column of servants — represented in almost every household — would respond by universally murdering their individual employers.

The uprising had been mooted to begin on the full moon of 28 March 1896 but was prematurely triggered by an incident a week earlier, in which a group of armed Matabele set upon a native police detachment and murdered a constable. This action squandered the vital advantage of surprise, which in turn proved disastrous for the rebellion. Seven survivors of the police detail made their way to the native commissioner of the district and reported to him what had happened. Meanwhile, another black policeman was murdered in a different district that same night.

The initial reaction in Bulawayo was panic. Evidence that a general uprising had been triggered arrived on 23 March with reports of the murder in Insiza of a group of miners and traders. This was followed by further and ongoing reports of whites in the district surviving, succumbing or being forced to form protective laagers against organised attacks.

The Acting Administrator HAF Duncan, who was standing in for Jameson's replacement, Lord Albert Grey, took command of the situation. Grey himself had been called away to attend to matters related to the Jameson Raid. A council of defence was rapidly appointed to respond to the emergency. It contained three members of the current honourable and military class, General Digby Willoughby and Captains Nicholson and Garden. Their first orders were for the remainder of the Matabeleland Mounted Police, under the command of Inspector Southey, to mount a patrol to Insiza and rescue a group of settlers under siege.

In the meantime the trickle of refugees into Bulawayo rapidly turned into a flood. It was obvious from reports that the uprising had spread and was becoming general. Violence was taking place from Umsingwani to Filabusi, in Insiza and even against the defences of Bulawayo itself. By 30 March it was clear that no settler remained alive in the unfrequented portions of Matabeleland. Between March 23 and 30 numerous patrols went out to search for survivors. This was risky work as all around the capital large groups of warlike Matabele were gathering. Within the town's defences, conditions were growing increasingly cramped and unsanitary for a white population that numbered about 2250, of whom a third or so were women and children.

Duncan held a public meeting to report on the gravity of the situation and to remind the many able-bodied men present that under the terms of their contracts they owed the Company military service. This was hardly necessary since so many gruesome tales were circulating that Duncan was pressed to deal instead with the clamour of citizens urging action. Rather late in the day the native police were disarmed, but not before 200 of their number had absconded with their weapons and were training to support the other side.

On 25 March the accidental discharge of a rifle somewhere in the cramped centre of Bulawayo triggered a frenzied rush for the arsenal. Women and children were chivvied into the hallowed precincts of the newly built Bulawayo Club as men ran to and fro looking for weapons. Those who had them fired randomly, while at the government store men who had never held a rifle were each given a Lee Metford repeater and sent off to the barricades. Numerous, otherwise innocent blacks ran for cover with bullets whistling past their ears, while many others fled the city defences and took refuge with the rebels. Calm was restored after a good while, but not before the few military men in the town realised that some weapons training for civilians was essential.

A laager was built around the town square to prepare for a last stand if that day came. Empty wagons throughout the town were requisitioned and worked into the barricade. Barbed wire was threaded through the gaps and artillery pieces were positioned at each corner. Maxims, Gattlings and a Nordenfeldt were all trained on the leading approaches. The construction of such a morbid defence proved a psychological disadvantage, for at the first suggestion of any threat there was a general rush to the laager. It was too small for everyone and proved if nothing else that the town needed a proper army to defend it. A good measure of the conversation in Bulawayo focused on Jameson and what ought to be done to him if he ever had the gall to reappear in the colony.

By the middle of April the Matabele had abandoned their various sieges in the countryside and begun to gather in large numbers around Bulawayo. By then the many patrols scouring the countryside had rescued or confirmed dead all the known white inhabitants. In other locations strong laagers were built where small white communities banded together. Bulawayo itself was in slightly more buoyant spirit, and by then staunchly fortified and well defended. Initially the Matabele did nothing but observe, although some bold among them crept into town at night and killed herd boys and stole cattle. Occasional shootouts at checkpoints were reported, but on the whole the situation was static.

By then a number of militias had formed in Bulawayo, including the Bulawayo Field Force, Grey's Scouts and a small commando of Afrikaner settlers. Under the command of the few military men in residence these units took more of an offensive stance and began engaging the Matabele in a series of mobile skirmishes. These encounters were usually indecisive, claiming many Matabele lives without materially altering the status quo.

Frederick Selous continued his catalogue of adventures by losing his horse in battle along the Umguza River and being rushed by a large body of jubilant Matabele. None of these warriors would have forgotten Lobengula's decree to skin him alive and would have succeeded had not a certain Lieutenant Windley ridden into the fray and carried him off to safety.

Later examinations of the rebellion identified poor command and decision making on the part of the Matabele for the failure of the initial rising. Surprise, of course, had been lost when the rebellion commenced prematurely. However the failure of the Matabele to storm Bulawayo in force and to cut supply lines to the south have also been deemed blunders. The road to Mafeking through the Mangwe Pass was never threatened and remained open throughout the rebellion. It has been suggested that the reason for this was that the Figtree/Mangwe district fell under the control of a Mlimo priest who did not support the rebellion. Others have suggested that the route was kept open in order for whites to flee — which appeared to be the general expectation of the Matabele. Either way, it was perhaps this fact more than any other that ensured the survival of the colony by allowing for eventual reinforcement.

In the meantime the twin powers of Britain and the BSA Company were hard at work mobilising troops for the relief. Rhodes, like almost everybody else, was caught completely off guard and manoeuvred once again to keep things both as quiet and cheap as possible. He walked a tightrope between avoiding imperial involvement and the shocking financial cost of yet another war. Expenses would largely be borne by the Company and Rhodes himself, while blame for it all would fall on the shoulders of his great friend Jameson.

Rhodes in fact only learned of the rebellion as he was on his way into the country from Beira. He was returning to the Cape from London, having been forced by the effects of the Jameson Raid to resign his office as Cape premier. He had also only very narrowly retained the Charter and his position of managing director of the Company, although in due course he would indeed be forced to resign his position on the board. For the moment, however, he maintained de facto control of the Company, and throughout the remainder of the Matabele Rebellion, was a keen and interested observer.

Paradoxically the situation in the colony came as something of a godsend to Rhodes, providing a distraction at a vital time. He had chosen to visit Rhodesia at that particular moment primarily to avoid the first session of the 1896 Cape parliament — for obvious reasons. The fruit of his life and labours lay in tatters around him. The events of the past few months had worn him down and aged him. He was fortunate to have survived the shambles at all, and he knew it. At that moment he was searching for some sort of absolution. More than anything he needed to confirm to himself and to the world at large that he was still a man of destiny, still an important person — and the rebellion seemed to provide him with just that opportunity.

As Rhodes poured his energy into organising a relief column for Bulawayo, the Matabele remained on the fringes of their erstwhile capital from where they continued to threaten an all-out offensive. Hopes for this, however, began to fade as a steady stream of reinforcements began to arrive in the besieged town. May became a month of consolidation for both sides, but in particular for the settlers for whom every moment and every arrival was heaven-sent.

For the Matabele every passing moment saw the prospect of victory and freedom fade further into despair and hopelessness. As Lobengula had always feared, an attack on the few whites in the country had brought in hundreds, if not thousands more. The design for the rebellion could ultimately never have succeeded, but even in the short term it had floundered critically — not for any lack of fighting courage, but for a lack of iron at the core. The Matabele command, barely a shadow of what it had once been, could now see the folly of leaving a line of communication open to the south.

Rhodes' Salisbury Volunteer Force arrived in Bulawayo on 1 June, a day ahead of the Matabeleland Relief Force under the command of General Sir Frederick Carrington. Supporting Carrington was a staff that included Colonel Robert Baden-Powell and his colleague Major Herbert Plumer. The latter was in direct command of the Matabeleland Relief Force with the local rank of Lieutenant-Colonel. Carrington at that point had at his disposal nearly 2 000 irregular white troops comprised of the Matabeleland Relief Force with a strength of 800 men, Rhodes' Salisbury Volunteer force of 150 men, the Bulawayo Field Force under Colonel Napier with 700 men, and the Gwelo Field Force of 336 men under the command of Captain Gibbs.

Carrington decided to strike immediately, and on 6 June he sent out a large patrol under Major CW Watts that encountered the enemy mobilising in significant numbers not far from Umguza River. The Matabele were easily routed under artillery and machine gun fire with the loss of some 300 warriors.

After this the Matabele were forced to re-evaluate their overall situation. With white troops flooding into the territory, the situation had clearly become hopeless. They abandoned the siege of Bulawayo and retreated to defensive positions in the Matopo hills and the hills of Thabas aMambo north of Insiza. Whatever vague strategy might once have underpinned it, the rebellion quickly evaporated. After the bloody eviction of the defenders of Thabas aMambo, the remainder consolidated in the Matopos. There the impis took refuge with their women and children in the rugged and scattered hill country with no better objective than to fight to the last.

For the BSA Company, the relief of Bulawayo and the victory at Thabas aMambo was only half the battle won. The Matabele had to be beaten soundly and disabused of any hope that their defeat could be reversed. The white man was here to stay, and this fact needed to be wholly appreciated by the natives of the territory.

After a series of inconclusive engagements in the area of the Matopos, Carrington reached the conclusion that the campaign must carry on through to the following season. By then the remaining Matabele forces would be starved out and pacified, and with luck permanently destroyed.

Rhodes, however, realised that this would require an outlay that the British South Africa Company simply could not sustain. And if it could not carry the weight of a siege then the Imperial Government would shoulder the burden, effectively erasing the Company's claim to hegemony over Matabeleland. Clearly another solution had to be found.

It so happened that in Mashonaland an almost identical scenario was playing out. The white residents of Salisbury and its surrounds had fallen victim to precisely the same chain of events as pertained in Matabeleland. The journey south of Rhodes' Salisbury Relief Column left Mashonaland as vulnerable as Matabeleland had lately been. Similar misconceptions regarding the native's state of mind prevailed while no one appeared to have spared a moment of thought to the possibility that the Mashona might rise with equal ferocity.

From the onset the Mashona people had been ignored in favour of the Matabele, and after the general occupation, their fighting and organisational abilities were largely disregarded. Certainly the Matabele would have been happy to receive intelligence of a second front opening up in the north, but no serious attempt was made to link up or unite with the Mashona. It would probably have been too much to expect, but it does seem that a vital opportunity was lost to both.

Hostilities broke out in Mashonaland towards the end of June 1896, when 120 whites in various rural locations were slaughtered out of hand. Again the sudden pace of events sent panic through a denuded and ill-prepared settler population. After an initial frenzy of concurrent but dispersed attacks, several local chiefs rose up and attempted to co-ordinate the rebellion. As in Matabeleland a leading spiritual figure rose to the forefront of the leadership. Spiritual identity then became the symbol and inspiration of revolt and helped to mould a few otherwise isolated incidences into a cohesive pattern.

Gumporeshumba was a powerful personality in the John the Baptist mould of message bearers. He was the medium of a powerful Shona spirit, Kaguvi — or Kagubi — whose name he adopted. Thanks to the dearth of written history, little is actually known about Kaguvi or his equally influential co-conspirator, Mbuya Nehanda. Nehanda was a woman of deep spiritual authority, but unlike Kaguvi she had a temperament both cruel and volatile.

At the time settler interest in these two important individuals amounted to capturing, trying and hanging them. They would soon come to know better, for to future generations of indigenous historians and revolutionary propagandists, the martyred Kaguvi and Mbuya Nehanda have assumed a potent symbolic authority. They soon became icons what was termed the first Chimurenga, (The Struggle), and also of all future resistance, culminating in the defining liberation struggle of the 1970s. Nehanda in particular has been endowed with a mythology far exceeding her actual contribution to the uprising, and has on occasion been unjustifiably compared to British Queen Boudicca, who in AD 60 led a revolt against Roman rule. The very public trial and execution of Nehanda and Kaguvi contributed much to their immortality, and predictably they became significantly more influential dead than alive.

Carrington, however, allowed none of this to divert him from his assault on the Matabele. He permitted the Salisbury Volunteers to return to Mashonaland with the support of a further 100 men of the Matabeleland Relief Force, and also directed a unit of regulars to Salisbury from the Cape via Beira and Umtali. Thereafter he launched a series of attacks on the Matopos beginning with the iconic Matabele stronghold of Thabas-zi-ka-Mambo. After a battle that lasted most of the day of 5 July the Matabele were routed by fierce fighting and fled deeper into the Matopos, leaving most of their supplies and belongings behind them.

Mkwati fled in a different direction. His detractors have hinted that he abandoned the cause of the Matabele the moment it became clear that the rebellion had failed. It is probable that he was never committed to reforming the Matabele nation, but just the eradication of the whites. He took refuge with the Mashona and went on to play a part in prolonging that rebellion.

Carrington, meanwhile, responded to the concentration of Matabele in the Matopos with scorched earth. His forces destroyed cattle, crops and grain reserves, which virtually guaranteed the destruction of the Matabele nation. Rhodes, on the other hand, had built a career on identifying weakness and squaring his enemies, believed that the moment would never be better to open negotiations. Here was his opportunity, and suddenly a glow of the old Rhodes radiance was revived.

Rhodes had until then played an important but less than pivotal role in the campaign. He was mostly to be seen riding in close congress with Carrington's commanders, but always unarmed and uninvolved in the actual fighting. The first hand spectacle of war had a sobering effect on him, and while by modern standards he could hardly be considered a liberal, he was less trenchant than most and was moved by the plight of the Matabele. He had also taken the time to examine first-hand the evidence of what had gone before, and it was impossible for him to ignore the fact that the Matabele had suffered much in his name. He became one of the few prepared to acknowledge that their rebellion might have been justified. Some may say that this epiphany came a bit late, but until then Rhodes had not paid much attention to the details, and unlike Jameson whose hand was visible everywhere, Rhodes was guilty less of commission than omission.

Carrington, meanwhile, arrived at the conclusion that an offensive campaign in the hill country of the Matopos would be prohibitively costly in manpower and very likely fruitless. He maintained his insistence that a war of attrition to starve out the rebels was the only practical strategy. For his part,

Rhodes recognised that this approach would be the end of everything. Even as matters stood, the Royal Charter could be revoked at any time, and not even a quick and cheap end to the affair was guaranteed to save it. If anything at all was to be salvaged out of the whole tragic business, Rhodes had to try and find an alternative solution. He was, after all, the soul and spirit of the new country. He was not a weakling and nor was he a coward. He alone had the stature and moral weight to frame a truce that both the Matabele and the settlers might find acceptable.

The story of Rhodes' negotiations with the Matabele ranks alongside the Shangani Patrol in the heroic tradition of Rhodesian pioneer history. The common picture of Rhodes seated on an anthill, engaging a semi-circle of squatting natives, had the air about it of a vice regal council rather than a desperate compromise. Certainly the former rings clear in white memory, and the episode without doubt contributed much to the popular myth of Rhodes in the future.

As is often the case with imperial myth, behind the efforts of a white man who reaps the laurels, is usually hidden the endeavours of several natives. This was no less true for the great Indaba, or Council, that took place in Matabeleland during August of 1896. In this case it was the courageous and highly skilled advances of native scout John Grootboom that set the stage for the negotiations that followed. Grootboom was by definition a 'Cape boy', although he knew the Matabele intimately. He could mimic an induna so successfully that during countless covert missions he never slipped up or was exposed. As Frank W Sykes, who catalogued the events of the Rebellion in his book, *With Plumer In Matabeleland,* and who met and knew Grootboom, observed:

> Divested of the ordinary garments of civilisation, with clean shaven face and head, tonsured a la Matabele, John has little difficulty in passing for one when occasion requires.[2]

It is impossible to understate the courage of men like Grootboom. He moved alone in the field surrounded by an enemy partial to torture, spied on their movements and strengths, and reported back to Colonel Baden Powell, who he referred to as Colonel Baking Powder. It was to Grootboom, therefore, that Rhodes looked to establish the contacts necessary to facilitate a meeting between himself and the Matabele leadership.

Rhodes was acting as an individual in this matter and initially at least, he proceeded without the support — and occasionally without even the knowledge — of BSA Company administration and the military commanders. When news of his plans leaked the settlers were naturally outraged since most regarded rumours of possible clemency as absolute heresy. Sir Richard Martin, who acted as the imperial representative in Bulawayo, also stood opposed to negotiation, although on the more plausible grounds that he felt it was his prerogative alone to treat with the Matabele.

This might technically have been the case, but the simple fact was that no one in the country had the ghost of a chance of usurping Rhodes. At that moment nothing but charisma and force of character could succeed, and nobody possessed those qualities to the degree that Rhodes did.

The Matabele, in agreeing to a preliminary meeting, did not demand that Rhodes be present. The reason was — in the words of writer and journalist Vere Stent who was a personal friend of Rhodes — that they '…did not venture to summon so great a man as he to them, but if he came he would be welcome.'[3] Likewise, the personal courage necessary to meet the Matabele with neither arms nor escort eliminated many serving on the fringes. There were also few, of course, who had as much at stake in the matter as Rhodes himself. This does not serve to imply that Rhodes approached the affair as a solo performance — far from it; the contribution of several others was just as worthy.

The turning point came early in August when Grootboom discovered a very old native woman who claimed to be a wife of the great king Mzilikazi, and it was through her that initial approaches were made. Before Rhodes and Johann Colenbrander made their first direct contact on 14 August, a great many preliminary meetings were held between Grootboom and a variety of Matabele leaders.

The first formal indaba took place on Friday 21 August. Rhodes' delegation included Colenbrander, Rhodes' friend and colleague Dr Hans Sauer, Vere Stent, and of course John Grootboom. A native interpreter by the name of John Makunga also attended. Rhodes and his party arrived first and waited in the shade of a tree until a group of indunas cautiously stepped down from the hilltops carrying a white flag. The halting procession was watched by thousands of whispering Matabele tribesmen lining the surrounding hills. As the group of indunas slowly descended, Rhodes turned and remarked to another member of the party alongside him: 'This is very exciting. This is one of the incidents in life that make it worth living.'[5]

The indaba began with 44 indunas gathered in a semicircle around Rhodes, who had seated himself halfway up a sizable termite mound. Arranged to his left and right were his associates who listened attentively as he greeted the indunas and initiated the meeting. An august induna by the name of Somabulana introduced himself and his people by way of a lengthy historical discourse that was typical of a Matabele saga. It began with the nation's origins as members of the Zulu group, and then traced the break-up that led to their homicidal march north. He spoke of the death of Mzilikazi and the reign of Lobengula, the coming of the whites, the days and months of anguish, war with the whites, the death of Lobengula and their wretched condition as a conquered nation. Rhodes heard a litany of grievances about their treatment at the hands of the Company's administration. Jameson was named on a number of occasions, and such issues as cattle, land and the native police were underscored by complaints about individual native commissioners and the treatment of Matabele leaders at the hands of men younger and less worldly than themselves.

While Rhodes was sensitive to these issues, and enlightened to a degree, he was careful not to be dragged into an exchange of blame and apology. Instead he pushed the issue to the burning question of war and peace. After some minimal horse-trading and the settling of such matters as the removal of certain individuals from the public service, the disbanding of the native police and the maintenance of routes for the importation of food — peace in broad principal was agreed upon.

A second indaba was held on the following Thursday near the homestead of William Usher. Over 100 armed men in belligerent mood enlivened the encounter. This prompted Rhodes to remark later that the interview had just a sufficient spice of danger to make it interesting. Included in Rhodes' party were Colonel Plumer and a number of members of his staff. Two women, Molly Colenbrander and her sister Mrs Smith, observed the exchanges discreetly. Rhodes appeared to overlook this intrusion by the irksome sex, for Mrs Colenbrander was regarded as an exception. She was bold and deeply interested in the politics and anthropology of the region, and also sufficiently lacking in feminine delicacy to invite Rhodes' scorn.

Initially the atmosphere of the meeting was highly charged as young men talking over their elders and shouting threats constantly disrupted any attempt at discussion. In due course Johann Colenbrander closed the meeting and refused to continue until all weapons had been laid aside. After some time this was achieved but it did not curb the insolence of the younger men present. Rhodes then refused to respond or listen any further, and would not proceed until the induna Dhliso imposed order on his retinue and silenced the younger men. Again it took some time for this to be achieved.

Discussions thereafter were brief and to the point. The indunas were, of course, in favour of peace, but they asked for time to test the opinion of their people. While Rhodes agreed, he warned that continued war would result in starvation and annihilation of the Matabele. Little time remained that season for them to leave the protection of the hills and venture back into the valleys and onto the plains to cultivate their crops.

A third indaba was staged a few days later, this time with some official formality in the form of Sir Richard Martin with an accompaniment of 12 lancers flying the Union Jack. Also present was

Jameson's replacement Earl Grey, his wife, and once again the ubiquitous Molly Colenbrander. In the first instance Earl Grey addressed the combined assembly and articulated most of the points previously covered, and such agreements as had been made. On behalf of Her Majesty he endorsed Rhodes' efforts before making way for Sir Richard Martin, who added little other than the Queen's own endorsement of Rhodes. A general amnesty was approved which would exclude only those who had committed cold-blooded murder. Rhodes then closed the proceedings with an appeal to the Matabele to lay down their arms and come down from the hills — because now, he assured them, they had nothing to fear.

As Vere Stent wrote: 'Throughout the conference, which lasted some hours and was of a deeply interesting nature, past grievances were as far as possible discussed, and the lines of the modus vivendi gone into thoroughly.'[6]

Rhodes remained on hand for some time afterwards to canvass opinion and deal with individual petitions, although initially few indunas visited him. This changed when news spread that not only was tobacco being dispensed as gifts, but also other offerings such as clothes and blankets. In no time Rhodes was besieged by petitioners and soon not only the fact of peace but the spirit of it became a reality.

* * *

Sadly, affairs in Mashonaland were not to be concluded in such a civilised and humane manner. Indeed there were few in the country that felt that the Mashona were worthy of the effort. Such was the poor opinion held of them that it was commonly felt that compromise would only result in back-handed treachery and murder. For the Mashona this was a bitter conclusion to what had been no less a courageous uprising than that of the Matabele.

Mkwati's efforts to sustain the rebellion in Matabeleland failed, as his exhortations began to be viewed in a tribal light. He soon abandoned the apparently lost cause and focused his attentions on efforts still underway in Mashonaland. There too success proved to be limited. The Mashona had not been diplomatically pursued in preceding years since it was widely perceived that they held no particular authority, and would fall into whatever accommodation was reached with the Matabele. The original defeat of the Matabele certainly liberated the vast majority of Mashona, but it also had the effect of rekindling their own political senses. Unfortunately for the execution of their revolt, a number of individually powerful chiefs acted in the general spirit of rebellion, but without any central co-ordination. This meant that there was no discernable leadership that could be consulted with or brought to parley. After the initial rushes on isolated settlements, the Mashona in the main adopted a purely defensive posture that meant individual chieftainships and districts had to be cleared separately as part of an ongoing programme. Rhodes, who was engaged in his indabas in Matabeleland, was not available then to lend his weight to compromise — besides which the imperial authorities were anxious that he did not.

Once the fact of a general uprising in Mashonaland became apparent the authorities were quick to act. Salisbury itself did not come under threat, which allowed the war to be focused on the countryside more effectively. The Salisbury Volunteers easily cleared the road from Bulawayo to Salisbury. Colonel E.A.H Alderson with 480 mounted infantry launched an attack on the influential Chief Makoni. The battle was inconclusive but sufficient to debilitate Makoni, who offered to surrender two weeks later in exchange for amnesty. Rhodes favoured this, as did the Company administration, but Sir Richard Martin demurred and no amnesty was offered. Makoni went back to the countryside and was brutally routed late in August. He was taken into custody and summarily tried and shot on the perimeter of his kraal.

Rhodes arrived in Salisbury late in November and persuaded Sir Richard Martin to relax the military pressure by returning Colonel Alderson and his mounted infantry to the Cape. Matabeleland Relief Force troops had earlier left the territory and Martin reluctantly agreed to follow suit with Alderson's regulars. Rumblings of alarm reached Salisbury from Whitehall but, fortunately for Rhodes, nothing untoward happened. Much of the work had already been completed and all that really remained was extensive mopping up that continued until the end of the year. This was typically achieved by dynamiting the host of caves and rock shelters where the rebels remained hidden. The strategy was highly effective but enormously costly in Mashona lives. In July Martin himself routed Mashiangombe and most of the other rebellion leaders were then either driven into exile or executed.

Kaguvi surrendered in October while Mbuya Nehanda was apprehended after a fight sometime in December. Both were tried for murder and hanged in Salisbury. Before he died Kaguvi, apparently received Catholic rites after accepting baptism at the last minute. Nehanda, on the other hand, was defiant, loquacious and savage to the last. Mkwati's fortunes waned until chiefs wary of the trouble he had caused allegedly disposed of him. He reported to have been killed and dismembered in such a way that he could not reincarnate.

By the end of the year the uprisings were all largely over, and the new colony could at last look beyond its most potent rite of passage.

Birth of Rhodesia
Death of the Colossus

Rhodes makes his peace

The Great Indaba that was held in the shadow of the Matopos — when the Matabele proclaimed Rhodes their father, and believed in him because they had no choice — was Rhodes' finest hour. Even this, however, would be blemished by dishonest brokerage. Rhodes had promised the Matabele the restoration of their traditional lands, and to this promise he was initially true. Two years later, though, the Matabele discovered that Rhodes had struck a second, silent bargain with his new land beneficiaries. With them it was agreed that, after that time, rentals and levies could be charged once again, and these could be claimed either in cash or labour. Either way this meant dispossession for the bulk of the Matabele. Here was the quintessential Rhodes once again, this time, in the words of Sarah Gertrude Millin, perhaps his most sympathetic biographer:

> Yes, it is a new Rhodes, a troubled, divided Rhodes, a Rhodes speaking, as he says, to two audiences: one in London and one in Rhodesia, torn between his settlers and his shareholders, his dreams and his directorate, his beautiful hypothesis and the little ugly facts.[1]

By the time that this particular ugly fact had been revealed, it was too late for the Matabele to protest, for Rhodes had long since left the territory. In his wake the black man tumbled into a pit of obscurity within which he would be ensnared for almost a century. Rhodes to his credit did try to enforce some sort of fair usage of the Matabele, but his efforts lasted only as long as he lived. The smaller figures that remained could not act in quite the way he had, as a levy against the rising floodwater of white ambition. The end of the Matabele Rebellion had confirmed to all — and most notably the Matabele — the white man's conquest of Rhodesia. By the accepted rules of any war, this had won him title to the country.

The whites by then were returning to the countryside, re-establishing their positions and fortifying themselves more thoroughly. A year later the railway line from Mafeking to Bulawayo was completed, allowing for a rapid mobilisation of force at any time. The Matabele were now a broken people, and even more so the Mashona. The whites on the other hand were prepared, energised, increasing in numbers and militant in ways not noticed in the past.

Rhodes left the colony late in 1896, but not before he was forced to attend to the grievances that had long been accumulating. Anger came to a head rapidly after the twin rebellions, and with Rhodes finally among them, many demanded that he must provide answers. Primarily the settlers were aggrieved at the antics of Jameson, who had rubbished the reputation of the colony and almost destroyed it with his hare-brained raid on the Transvaal. Jameson was blamed for the rebellions, and by proxy, so was the BSA Company. The blood of the innocents was on both their hands and Rhodes would have been able to find few honest words to disagree. Knowing this he did not even try, but instead turned once again to his chequebook.

The Colossus silenced the critics with compensation to the tune of £350 000. In 1896, this amounted to a staggering personal intercession — £255 000 went to Matabeleland and £100 000 to Mashonaland. For a small population this was uncommonly generous. The amount was added to the steeply mounting personal cost to Rhodes of protecting the Charter and the Company and of keeping his dream alive. The Jameson Raid and the twin rebellions ultimately cost Rhodes and Alfred Beit nearly £400 000 apiece — hardly small change.

Complaints about Jameson, however, were just the beginning of a litany of grief. Occupation and settlement of the country had been premised on the expectation of huge gold reserves. When these proved illusory the Company still failed to relinquish its restrictive controls over whatever mineral reserves were present. These controls, in essence, required mine operators to write the Company in as an equal partner in any strike, and to share the profits of actual production. Although this had been the bedrock of BSA Company stock flotation, the policy was increasingly implemented to the detriment of the small digger. Capital-rich corporations, on the other hand, flourished. Most were trading on ghost strikes and optimistic share issues, often founded on nothing more than the discovery of old native mine workings.

To keep the capital flowing, the Company waived many clauses and stipulations for the big players that were strictly applied to the small man. Moreover large tracts of land were often appended to big company claims to render them more attractive — which differed sharply from the compromises the bulk of the white population were forced to make. This partly fuelled the groundswell of anger directed against over zealous and clearly cronyistic Company rule. The settlers justifiably felt that the Company had duped them into manning the territory and fighting its wars, only to be locked out of any access to its riches.

Rhodes acknowledged all this and agreed to implement adjustments. For the time being, however, these were minimal. The Company had no choice but to do what was necessary to maintain the loyalty of countless small and large capital investors who kept the Company afloat. Settlers came and settlers went but if the public subscription collapsed the game would quickly be over. Not until after Rhodes' death would mine regulations be relaxed sufficiently to give the small man what could be termed a sporting chance.

Issues related to the cost of living and transport were also high on the agenda. Without any homegrown productivity to speak of, people in the territory subsisted off the land or on inflated imports usually transported and sold by the Company itself. Rhodes' compensation helped, and a little later the situation was further eased by the arrival of the railway. This prompted a general proliferation of commerce and trade in the country, although high transport rates, rail tariffs and related issues would cause considerable dissatisfaction for a very long time.

These issues were economic and relatively easy for Rhodes to address. More difficult was the abstract question of governance, and in particular how appropriate it was for the administration of a growing colony to be conducted by a commercial enterprise. Company rule in the traditional sense was only applied when the white population of a territory was either employed by the company or contracted to it, or where white settlement in general was regarded as impermanent. However with a growing and diverse population of tax paying settlers, each in one way or another trying to put down roots, company administration had clearly become redundant.

With blood still fresh on the ground, settlers were also irritated by criticism flowing from the British press regarding the conduct and causes of the war. Sir Richard Martin conducted an inquiry that served to illuminate much of the ill treatment recently visited against the natives. The paternalists, Afrophiles and Fabians of England all had a great deal to say about matters, much of which appeared out of context as far as the settler community was concerned. To people steeped in the traditions of moderation and fair play and secure under the rule of law, criticism of this nature might have appeared justified. But to those on the frontline it was not. When living beyond the pale, rules of conduct are necessarily less defined. The settlers believed that their sacrifices were for Queen and Empire, and for that they were owed a dept of gratitude, not obloquy and disapprobation. A grain of suspicion against the homeland was dropped into the mix at this point that would never thereafter be entirely expunged.

Rhodes therefore faced two questions. What time limit should apply to British South Africa Company rule? And what degree of representation could the settlers expect in exchange for their contribution to the economy and to the construction of society?

These were indeed interesting questions, for central to Rhodes' philosophy had always been the idea of a permanent white colony, appended to a greater South African union. Rhodesia was fast emerging as a dominion rather than a commercial colony, and in the usual course of events, settlers could expect authority to be shared between a local representative assembly and Whitehall. However Rhodes also had a board of directors to consider. Massive amounts of publicly subscribed capital had been invested in the founding of Rhodesia and so far not one penny had been returned. Rhodesia had to show a profit, and until it did the Company could not relinquish control. No one was happy about it, least of all the Company, but that was the was the way it was.

On 10 November 1896 Rhodes delivered a speech to a selected body of settlers in which he suggested a semi-elective system that would lead eventually to self-government. He proposed that the colony retain an administrator appointed by the BSA Company board. The administrator would lead a legislative assembly comprising himself, five members nominated by the Company and four elected from the community. There would be a de facto colour bar brought about by property and income qualifications that would limit black inclusion on the voters roll. This was in fact aimed less at excluding the natives, who were not at that stage really recognised in terms of their political potential, than to limit the influence of poor whites drifting north from the ruination of the rinderpest and later the Anglo/Boer War.

The imperial factor, as always the cautious moderator, would play a third role. This would be a little anomalous insofar as direct rule was vigorously forsworn — yet a significant degree of guidance, and control over the affairs of the colony, was inescapable. Equally important to the English exchequer was that the new colony should cost no money and cause no trouble. Joseph Milner, current High Commissioner at the Cape, to whom it had fallen to resolve the future constitutional status of Rhodesia, felt this most keenly. He favoured Company rule into the foreseeable future but with close imperial supervision.

To this end the Colonial Office reserved certain crucial powers to itself. Milner had an extremely low opinion of Jameson and believed, like most of the British establishment, that irresponsible administration had been the main contributing factor to the Rebellion. In future, issues related to native affairs would be scrutinised by a Resident Commissioner, who would sit on the legislative assembly and report directly to the High Commissioner. The former would also fill the role of a Commandant-General, to control the police and armed forces. The Company itself also limited any independent manoeuvre by reserving the right to act on fiscal issues without consultation.

These arrangements were contained and formalised in the country's first instrument of government — the Order in Council of 1898. This device represented a compromise between imperial and Company interests while also conceding some formal if nominal involvement to the settlers. For the time being it sufficed, and the settler body was, if not elated, then at least satisfied.

The time had come for Rhodes to leave the territory that bore his name. His next ordeal was to submit to the odious business of a parliamentary enquiry into the Jameson Raid. Before he did, however, he briefly made the acquaintance of the younger cousin of William Ernest Fairbridge. A second branch of the Fairbridge family had recently arrived from South Africa, and it was young Kingsley Fairbridge who best captured the combination of stress and serenity that afflicted Rhodes, in what would turn out to be the closing phases of his life. In his later biography Fairbridge wrote:

> I knew that great trouble had befallen Mr. Rhodes. My Father had told me that his best friend, Dr. Jameson, had been put in jail; that Mr. Rhodes himself had resigned, or was about to resign, his public appointments both in England and South Africa. The 'raid' had left dissentions, and many of Rhodes' old associates at the Cape had turned their backs on him. Finally Groote Schuur, his beautiful house near my old playground of Devils Peak, had burned to the ground, and with it the treasures of old Dutch and Huguenot art which he had spent years in collecting. All this had happened in that one year of 1896, and men said he was greatly changed and that his hair turned white.[2]

A new age

One of the most important effects of the twin rebellions was not only closing the book on the Jameson period, but also the ushering of Rhodesia into the modern era and into the family of settled British colonies. Jameson's immediate replacement had been the 4th Earl Grey, one of Britannia's more enlightened imperialists. He was also one of Rhodes' most respectable conquests. Although he had been one of those who had stood firmly against Rhodes over the acquisition of a Royal Charter, he became not only the most stalwart of Rhodes apologists, but also an investor and director of the British South Africa Company. After Rhodes' death, Grey kept his seat on the Board of Directors of the Company and took a seat as a trustee of the Rhodes Scholarship Fund. He would later serve as Governor General of Canada.

Grey had only really been an emergency stand-in, while Jameson languished in a Transvaal prison. He had arrived in the midst of the rebellions and did little more during that period than contribute much nervous anxiety to the violent excesses associated with the uprising. He thereafter swam very much against the current of public opinion by advocating the industrial education of the Mashona, believing that they possessed the potential to contribute enormously to the future economic health of the colony. To this end he consulted with prominent African American activist Booker T Washington, who he invited to visit Rhodesia and advise on the best ways to 'raise, educate and civilise the black man'. Washington gave careful consideration to this request, but temporised for the apparently genuine reason of overwork at his Tuskegee educational institute in Alabama.[3]

Later Grey made way for a completely different type of man — one hand-picked by Rhodes to put Rhodesia on a proper, organised and legal footing.

William Milton was a year younger than Rhodes, but like the Colossus he was born into the middle classes. He was also a child of the Empire and grew up steeped in the same philosophy of Anglo-Saxon dominance as the founder. Unlike Rhodes, however, his health was excellent, and his voluntary move to the colonies had been made strictly in the furtherance of his career.

Before emigrating to South Africa, Milton had been capped as an England fullback during the 1874/75 rugby season. In South Africa he made his debut as the national team's second cricket captain in the test series of 1891/92. He championed rugby in Rhodesia, and as a consequence founded a pervasive national obsession. No less impressive than his sporting accomplishments were his administrative achievements. Throughout his term as Cape Premier, Rhodes retained Milton as his official secretary before he went on to serve as head of the Prime Minister's department of the

Cape Parliament. He joined the British South Africa Company in July 1897, but not before completing three more first class cricket matches — two for Natal and one for Western Province.

There was, however, a touch of confusion and unpleasantness to be overcome before Milton could fully take up his appointment as Administrator of Rhodesia. The incident in question rather defines the proprietary view that Rhodes held of his colony, and demonstrates how he reserved a comprehensive power of veto. Grey had promised the top position to his former private secretary Arthur Lawley. Lawley was the son of Lord Wenlock and one of the 'Honourable and Military' that Milton felt took up so much space in the colony. Grey made his choice because it was his prerogative to do so, and moreover the decision was made with the approval of the board of directors. This put Rhodes' choice of Milton in jeopardy, and although anxious not to offend Grey or the board, Rhodes was nonetheless determined to uphold his own appointment.

His motivation and instincts in this matter were sound. He happened to share Milton's opinion of the Honourable and Military, and wanted to shake off the criticism of the last year and get matters properly established. He had also been warned by Joseph Chamberlain in the aftermath of the Raid to get his house in order or risk losing the Charter altogether.

An accommodation was eventually reached whereby the colony would temporarily have two administrators, one in Bulawayo — this being Lawley, which actually suited Milton for he despised Bulawayo — and one in Salisbury, which would be Milton himself. After a suitable period of reflection, Arthur Lawley resigned in 1901 to take up the post of Governor of Western Australia and was not replaced.

While he was Rhodes' man, Milton was also deeply critical of Jameson and keen to distance himself from the errors of the past. Among the many changes he introduced was an immediate overhaul of the civil service. Jameson had left things much as they were when he took over from Colquhoun, and in his brief term Lord Grey did almost nothing to advance this. The civil service at that time was composed of the kinds of clerks and bookkeepers that one might find in any other business. Administration remained the primary business of the colony, which caused this clique to view itself as something of an elite — a fact not always reflected in the quality of its work.

In the absence of an army, the British South Africa Company Police dealt with internal security as well as all the usual responsibilities of law enforcement. The latter function was in cooperation with the Southern Rhodesia Constabulary, which was an urban police service confined largely to Bulawayo and Salisbury. This agency eventually merged with what became the British South Africa Police in 1902. To complete the law and order framework was an amateur judiciary arbitrating laws that were largely lifted from Britain and South Africa.

As a sportsman and a professional, Milton happened also to provide something of a paradigm of what a white Rhodesian male would be — a pattern which was stamped first and foremost on the civil service. Writer and policeman, Tony Tanser, reflecting on the Milton period in his 1965 book of memoirs, *A Scantling of Time*, noted:

> Where as previously one had to be a member of the 'la-di-da' class to get a job in the civil service, now you had to beat the hide of a ball.[4]

Milton held the office of Administrator for 17 years during which time he was almost solely responsible for putting in place the administrative and judicial system that would serve the nation long after Company rule. He also presided over the first bona fide Legislative Assembly elections provided for by the Order in Council of October 1898.

The Legislative Assembly was to be composed of four elected members — two from Matabeleland and two from Mashonaland — and five members appointed by the BSA Company board. The results of the first election showed that Dr Hans Sauer and a certain Mr Hutchinson were elected for Matabeleland, and Colonel Grey and Mr Grimmer for Mashonaland. The nominees of the Company were Sir Thomas Scanlen — the de facto Attorney General — Justice Vincent and Messers Castens, Griffin and Orpen. Resident Commissioner was Lt-Col Sir M.J Clarke KCMG. The first meeting of the legislature was held on 15 May 1899 in Salisbury with William Milton presiding.

Until that time, settlers in Rhodesia had been exempt from formal taxation. The required revenues were provided through the treasury of the British South Africa Company. One of the first tenets of an organised government, therefore, was self-sufficiency in matters of finance. Not altogether unpredictably, a motion tabled to introduce taxation was immediately met with a furious rebuttal from the elected members. The Chartered Company members were equally adamant, their argument being that the settlers demanded representation ... well here it was — and naturally, with representation came responsibility.

Following this thought the administration proposed the imposition of customs duties on certain classes of goods imported into the country. Again this was met with howls of dismay from the elected seats. Their counter argument went along the lines that, while there could be no disputing a population's liability to taxation, this should in no way exceed one third of annual expenditure and should exclude the cost of maintaining the police force, since it was thanks to company folly that an armed police force was necessary at all.

Expenditure for the year 1899 was calculated at £739 713. Income, including customs, licensing and royalties, was set down at £381 000. This left the Company with a deficit of £358 713. The cost of maintaining the police was estimated at £285 706. How, the Company asked, was it to recover this amount — which represented just one year's worth of administrative deficit — if taxation was withheld?[5]

The elected members then switched tactics and asked where it was written in the Orders in Council that the government had a right to levy taxes at all? The Company, they maintained, had a much larger stake in the country than the settlers, and therefore it should shoulder the lion's share of expenses. In fact, Article 47 of the Orders stated that no customs duties would be levied that were any more onerous than those imposed between countries of the South African Customs Union. Alfred Milner was called in to mediate and his response was to scoff at any suggestion that the white citizens of Rhodesia were immune to a system of revenue collection that was universally applied. With this the Company went ahead, and on 1 August 1899 imposed the first customs duties on goods entering Rhodesia.

Such was a day in the life of Milton's Rhodesia. If, in the year of 1899 alone the British South Africa Company was expected to absorb a loss of over £350 000, some sense of its dilemma becomes apparent. That the settlers clamoured for participation but balked at assuming any financial burden was also part of that dilemma.

*   *   *

While a sporting life may have been the lot of the territory's civil servants and the capital's business elite, Milton had also to focus his attention on the many who were beating the hide not off a ball but their bare knuckles in a desperate attempt to remain solvent. It was all very well for the Company to sustain the elegant existence of a handful of whites charged with nothing more challenging than governing themselves, but to more practical men the question had become one of survival. One of Milton's primary concerns was to find some means to staunch the exodus of settlers, and this before he could begin to contemplate how he could attract more.

All this was easier said than done. Cured early of gold fever, most of the good men of the colony had already been washed out of the pan. For the few who remained, capital was scarce in an economy where precious little was being earned. Many good men had died on the banks of the Shangani and of those who survived, most had collected their booty, sold their land and their gold claims and left the colony. Some who stayed could not leave due to poverty. A few had independent means and could make the best of it without suffering too much.

Vicomte de la Panouse was one of those who quickly abandoned the search for nuggets and took refuge in the crude shelter of a few rooms on Avondale Farm. After a very narrow escape during the Rebellion, he and Countess Billie, although hardly prospering, at least lived under a roof of sorts, and grew enough food to keep body and soul together. They were among the lucky ones.

Communications were also very difficult, particularly in the countryside. The completion of the combined Mashonaland and Beira Railway at the turn of the century did make things easier. CH Zeederberg established the first mail coach service to Mashonaland in 1891. It ran from Pietersburg in the Transvaal via Fort Victoria and Fort Charter to Salisbury. In 1903 a certain Lt-Col Flint of the Southern Rhodesia Volunteers imported a small herd of camels from India in the hope that they would prove useful for military and other purposes. The animals, however, failed to acclimatise and the experiment was abandoned. Also that year the first motor car, a 1903 6½ HP Gladiator of French manufacture, was imported by Major Charles Duly and sold to engineering contractor George Pauling.

Thereafter motorcars became an increasingly common sight on the dusty streets and bush tracks of the countryside. For a while rickshaws were popular as urban transport. In Umtali a tram system was instituted in 1898. This utilised a mule drawn trolley along a single line up Main Street, a service that continued to operate until 1920. Settlements of tents, huts and shanties rapidly grew into streets of brick and corrugated iron. Supplies were limited, of course, and luxuries rare, but thanks to the Dominican Sisters, Salisbury at least had a school and a hospital. In Bulawayo, the first copy of the *Bulawayo Chronicle* appeared on the streets on Saturday 12 October 1894. A year later the town boasted a roller-skating ring accommodated in the Market Hall.

The opening of Matabeleland renewed some of the old faith in gold, and soon Bulawayo became the main port of entry and trading entrepôt for a new wave of miners and speculators. By the turn of the century, crude standards of construction had given way to avenues of rough brick and corrugated iron, with occasional examples of thoughtful colonial architecture such as the Bulawayo Memorial Hospital, with its domed tower, wide verandas and pointed brickwork. Bulawayo, however, remained the ugly duckling of the colony, but it regarded Salisbury folk as effete, self-satisfied and elitist. The residents of Salisbury, for their part, looked down on Bulawayo as a rather grubby industrial settlement and a magnet for the poor working classes. William Milton, for one, had no particular affection for Bulawayo and rarely visited it. This would persist and in later years the Bulawayo people would sarcastically label Salisbury as *Bamba zonke* (grab it all).

Prospectors fanned out into the Matabeleland countryside while rows of mud brick and corrugated iron buildings began to rise out of the ashes of Bulawayo. The route for goods and equipment from the south was easier via Bulawayo than by sea to Beira and then on by rail to Salisbury. Bulawayo therefore became the main centre for distribution and industry while Salisbury remained the hub of the highveld farming community and the home of the administrative elite.

Besides newspapers, hospitals and schools, other institutions important to Englishmen abroad were quickly established in Rhodesia. As early as February 1893 a body of 18 notable citizens met in the BSAC Police officers' mess in Salisbury and agreed to form the Salisbury Club. Charles White, resident magistrate and third son of the 2nd Baron Annaly, became the first chairman. Cecil Rhodes himself was a founding member, as were Dr Jameson, Alfred Beit, Rutherfoord Harris and Lieutenant Tyndale-Biscoe. Another was the Vicomte de la Panouse whose title compensated somewhat for his general lack of financial substance.

The Salisbury Club seeded the Bulawayo Club and then the Umtali Club. 1909 saw the establishment of the Salisbury Sports Club followed by the Queens Sports Club in Bulawayo. The first authentic cricket tournament in Rhodesia was organised in 1903/4 by South African cricket enthusiast J.D Logan. Lord Martin Hawke, a notable British cricketer and promoter, donated the cup for the event. On that particular occasion the trophy was awarded to Matabeleland.

Many other clubs and associations grew up over the years, particularly those dedicated to sport, but the Salisbury Club always maintained the dignity of its imperial associations. It had reciprocal arrangements with the Rand and Kimberley clubs in South Africa and a variety of gentlemen's clubs in London and throughout the Empire. The Salisbury Club soon became the informal meeting place for all gentlemen of consequence — women, of course, were not accommodated. And since it was situated just across the road from Parliament it also served as the unofficial forum of all the main government and commercial bodies in the country.

Such was life in the capital. In the countryside things were very different. The population of white settlers in the backveld was broken down into miners, storekeepers, farmers and missionaries. For them life was never easy or pleasant, and conditions were often not far removed from those of the natives. The few who were modestly succeeding might reside between walls of mud brick under thatch, bathe in river water carried up in tins, and enjoy pit latrines as a slight improvement over squatting in the bush. Mealie meal and green vegetables became the staple diet of both black and white, with the rare inclusion of cuts of bush meat shot and smoked for the pot.

Victorian traveller and commentator Charlotte Mansfield remarked of early Rhodesia that things would only begin to improve once the tax on whisky had been trebled and gentlewomen encouraged to immigrate. She had noticed an emerging third force of half-caste children proliferating despite fervent denials from every quarter. This phenomenon was usually blamed on the loneliness of isolation, the lack of respectable women and the appalling prevalence of alcoholism.

This then made up the unstable bedrock of white Rhodesia as it stood at the end of the century. Against a steady exodus of disillusioned pioneers, were nonetheless men and women who drifted into the country, and if they would make little or nor impact on the direction of the colony themselves, their sons and daughters certainly would. One such immigrant was Thomas Moodie, who in 1892 led a trek from Bethlehem in the Orange Free State to occupy the Gaza area of the Eastern Highlands. He and his nephew Dunbar Moodie settled and laid the foundations of what would later become the Chipinga District, one of the richest and most pleasant farming areas of Rhodesia. En route, Dunbar married his sweetheart Sarah in Fort Victoria, and the two pioneered honeymooning at the Great Zimbabwe Ruins.

Moodie was followed over the next two years by a further six treks. The leader of the Du Plessis Trek spoke for most when he defined his motivation and ambitions as having enough land once and for all to make a living without debt. From Chipinga some moved on up the Nyhodi River Valley to found new settlements that would later become Melsetter. This group was led by Martinus Martin and included the large Du Plessis family as well as a number of other Afrikaans speaking families. They brought a distinctly Dutch flavour to the area by endowing farms and settlements with such picturesque names as Pietershoek, Groenkop, Hendriksdaal, Moodie's Nek and Tanknek.

Another early immigrant with a mixed destiny was Scotsman Jock Smith who arrived in 1898. He settled in the mining town of Selukwe where he involved himself in trade, mining and farming. He later married Agnes Hodgson, daughter of a local miner, who bore him three children — Phyllis, Joan and Ian, the last better known for becoming the first Rhodesian-born prime minister.

Yet another early arrival was Rhys Fairbridge, cousin to the Argus Publishing Group agent in Salisbury, who in 1896 brought his family up from the Cape to live in Umtali. The Fairbridges were all descended from Dr. James William Fairbridge, who arrived in the Cape as district physician and surgeon in 1824. Rhys Fairbridge was a whimsical man and despite an excellent education, a lesser achiever than his cousin Ernest. In 1891 he began work as a surveyor on the construction of the Beira railway, an endeavour that became one of the epic tales of Rhodesian pioneering achievement.

The Commissioner of Public Works, George Pauling — a huge man who could lift his horse and carry it about — was the contractor for the Beira railway project. As he pushed the line through virgin bush and over febrile flood plain, he lost upwards of 60 percent of his black, white and 'coolie' labour force to malaria, blackwater fever and marauding animals.

Rhys Fairbridge was one of those who survived, and towards the end of the Mashona Rebellion he brought his family north to settle. As a company surveyor he employed his 11 year-old son Kingsley as a beacon builder, introducing the child to the fresh highveld environment that would later nurture the writer. Kingsley Fairbridge grew up to become the first literary commentator and unofficial Poet Laureate of Rhodesia. He was also one of Rhodesia's first Rhodes Scholars, and thereafter a promoter of empire migration. He would remember and be remembered most fondly in Umtali, where he spent his boyhood tramping the hills and countryside that inspired tender, often brutal — and sometimes suicidal poetry and prose.

> Great gangs of boys from Nyungwe and Senna were working on the streets that were to be. Mabandawi and Magorongoza dug side by side, trenching the two streams that flanked the township; the deadly mud, packed with the germs of malaria, was cast up beside the trenches. At that time everybody was too busy to be ill, but they died later. This draining was sound work, however, and the two trenches have since done much to make Umtali healthy; that those who made them died when the harness of endeavour fell from their shoulders is only in keeping with the story of all pioneers.[6]

By committing such youthful observation and experiences to paper Fairbridge anglicised and made accessible for newcomers the imponderable interior of Africa.

> *Inkoos!*
> *Inkoos, we have come back.*
> *By train we came, and very swift the route.*
> *I-jonnisiberg is very full of wealth;*
> *Wilhelm and Winkel drew five pounds apiece,*
> *And every month they drew it. In those mines*
> *They drill deep holes; dumblain* where it is hot.*
> *Good were the captains, and the food was good;*
> *Next year we come again, if thou wilt send.*
> *Now let us seek Matshanga, and the south.*
> *Inkoos!*[7]

In 1897 a retiring young Englishman by the name of Hugh Swynnerton arrived in Salisbury at the suggestion of Sir Guy Marshall, Director of the Imperial Institute of Entomology. In Salisbury, Swynnerton worked first in the Bates and Marshall store on Second Street before moving to Melsetter where he became a manager on Guganyana Farm. Guganyana was situated in a unique area of forest on the flanks of Mount Selinda, the mystique of which inspired Swynnerton to emerge later as the country's leading amateur naturalist. He conducted pioneering work in entomology, ornithology and agriculture. The endemic Swynnerton's Robin is a reminder of the many animal species credited to this self-effacing but pioneering immigrant.

Drifting into the country alongside a stream of other hopefuls came a poor Lithuanian Jew by the name of Welensky. With him he brought his Afrikaner wife with whom he settled in the southern suburbs of Salisbury. The youngest of their 13 children, Roland, was born in Salisbury in 1907. He became a professional boxer, a railwayman and as Sir Roy, second and last prime minister of the Federation of Rhodesia and Nyasaland.

Another thoughtful settler was Ethel Tawse Jollie, widow of the late Archibald Colquhoun, who had since married a Chipinga farmer and entered politics as the country's first female legislator. As a sitting member she was an activist and stalwart of the Responsible Government party. Her reluctant and somewhat misogynist mentor, Charles Coghlan, was an Irishman born in South Africa who later became a prominent Bulawayo lawyer. Coghlan arrived in Rhodesia towards the end of the Anglo/Boer War and would in due course lead the Responsible Government Party to partial independence.

Impoverished aristocrats, wealthy colonials, Jews, Afrikaaners, Scotsmen, Englishmen, Frenchmen, women, men and children — by the turn of the century the white population of the colony was creeping towards 10 000. The railway line was edging north and within a few years it would span the Zambezi and race towards the borders of the Congo Freestate. The towns of Salisbury, Bulawayo, Umtali, Gwelo and Fort Victoria were linked by rail or road and were evolving their identities quite as the nation was establishing its own. Administration, be it native or civil, touched almost every quarter. The law was established, enforced and arbitrated by a police force growing in confidence, and a judiciary growing in reach.

The lying in state

For Rhodes, however, the future seemed at times to be impeded and overwhelmed by men and institutions whose preoccupations were rooted in the past. The repercussions of the Jameson Raid were long and ponderous, as inquiries, discussions, interviews and investigations roved far beyond the Raid, penetrating every aspect of Rhodes' life, his work and his achievements. It was an entanglement of blame and counter-blame, of accusation, denial and evasion. While it never seemed to go anywhere or end anywhere, in one way or another it sucked in almost everybody active on the British political stage.

Jameson and the other conspirators were imprisoned, while threats of execution or worse were made against them. But after a rather inconsequential trial and an equally inconsequential period in Holloway Prison, Jameson's career blossomed. His notoriety seemed to open many more doors than it closed. This anomaly was illustrated by poet Laureate Alfred Austin in his colour-saturated ode to the magnificent event:

> *I suppose we were wrong, were madmen,*
> *Still I think at the Judgment Day,*
> *When God sifts the good from the bad men,*
> *There'll be something more to say.*
> *We were wrong but we aren't half sorry,*
> *And as one of the baffled band,*
> *I would rather have had that foray,*
> *Than the crushings of all the Rand.*

This view might have titillated the jingoists but it was by no means universal. The seasoned critics of Rhodes — in particular who he termed the Fabians and the Liberals — held a different opinion.

Among them was prominent parliamentarian, liberal journalist and writer Henry Labouchere:

> If ever men died with blood on their heads they are the men who fell in this raid, and if ever prisoners of war deserve scant mercy, Jameson and his comrades are those prisoners. They may thank their stars that they have fallen into the hands of men who are not likely to treat them as they themselves treated the Matabele wounded and prisoners.

Rhodes often appeared not to hear criticism, and more frequently not even to care. He had to be shaken from an almost metaphysical reverie to attend to this earthly tedium. He seemed to do this amid thoughts of his own annihilation — thoughts that grew from a strangely removed frame of mind. The emotional torrent of the Raid, the battles of the Rebellion and the extraordinary risk of the indabas, had changed him. He had taken to looking at his country from a mountaintop, finding himself ever more grateful for its consistency and solidity in the face of unpredictable relationships. With his worn copy of Aurelius' Meditations close at hand, he began to find sand and stone comforting in the face of capricious turns of events, and trees of the veld anchored securely against the turbulence buffeting his life. He began to think of Rhodesia as his monument, the indabas as his redemption, and the Matopos — the burial place of kings — as his own future resting place.

Rhodes might have expected many things as he steamed south from Beira, but while his legacy and reputation were being flogged at the post of public expedience in London, he could not have guessed how well things had gone for him in the Cape. There, word of his sorcery in the Matopos had not only impressed the general public, but also most of those who had been appointed by parliament to judge him. The Committee of Inquiry concluded that he had not been party to, nor in approval of the actual act of the Raid, but found him guilty of intent and deeply involved in its conception.

He might not have been surprised at this, and was grateful for leniency, but he hardly expected to be received in the Cape as a hero. Admittedly since his resignation and the alienation of the Afrikaner Bond, the rapture came mainly from those he had derided as jingoists. It was this element that now feted and applauded him in Port Elizabeth, unhorsing his carriage to pull it to the town hall by man-power, and then applauding him all the way to the Cape.

Back in London, however, on 16 February 1897, Rhodes faced a Parliamentary Committee of Inquiry that was less adulatory in tone. The Victorian press rather wryly labelled it: 'The Lying in State in Westminster'. Rhodes was by then an old man of 44, and his great vision somewhat frayed at the edges. He sat through three weeks of intermittent questioning where he frustrated the inquisition by anchoring his thoughts in the abstract. He tried to direct the attention of the select committee away from the facts of the Raid, to the wider political muse of a Union of South Africa, on Anglo/Boer entente, and on the Empire as a whole.

More than a latter-day Ruskin, Rhodes was a man moulded less by theory than reality. He was a builder tarnished by grubby trousers and a profuse sweat, but with authentic monuments that had risen like empires from paper…a man of England who had hoisted the standard higher than any so far, and yet in such an English way that the establishment demanded that he be reduced for his magnificence and ridiculed at all costs.

Rhodes was no fool. He had protected himself from the very beginning by accumulating a weight of evidence proving that Colonial Secretary Joseph Chamberlain, among other notable figures, had been in covert support of the scheme from the very beginning. Like Rhodes these men were largely freed of blame because Jameson had not waited for explicit orders. In fact little serious attempt was made by anybody to get genuinely to the bottom of the issue. Evasion and duplicity appear to have been both widely employed and widely accepted.

For his role in the Raid, Rhodes was not unduly censured, while almost nothing was heard about the administration of the territory by his company. Joseph Chamberlain claimed that Rhodes had done nothing in any respect inconsistent with the character of an honourable man. Of course this obvious bending of the truth could not be allowed to settle entirely without comment. Chamberlain later received a written memorandum from the prosecuting member, Sir William Harcourt — Liberal member for Oxford and an implacable critic of British policy in South Africa — concluding no more accurately that since the Raid, he had come to believe that Rhodes was the evil genius of South Africa.

Thus Rhodes' power and guiding light began to diminish as the great works of his hand were slighted. Yet he seemed strangely energised and closed his reign with unexpected diversions that proved he was far from a spent force.

Late in 1897, Rhodes suffered his third heart attack and, in deference to mortality, began to construct the final monuments to his life. He rebuilt his house at Groote Schuur — not with a view to it ever being his home again, but as the residence for future prime ministers and presidents of a greater South Africa.

The project that Rhodes desired most of all to crown his legacy was his through route from the Cape to Cairo. The railway had by now arrived in Bulawayo amid fanfare and applause. This achievement, which had cost neither the Cape Colony nor England a penny, was poised to edge further north to expand the influence of the British Empire. Two million pounds was all that was needed to advance the line north to Lake Tanganyika; but where once Rhodes needed only to ask, this time his board of directors demurred — as did Her Majesty's government. Rhodes was left to reflect that the two principal objections to the scheme were that it was unusual and that he himself was involved.

Nevertheless he was re-elected to the board of directors of the Chartered Company in 1898, the year of the Order in Council that recognised Rhodesia as a British colony. Even with some part of his prestige restored, his friends still found Rhodes a changed man. He now seemed to be driven by passion rather than resolve, perhaps sensing that his death was near.

He travelled south again and plunged into an election in the Cape that for him seemed to hold no hope. He stumped for the Progressive Party, his jingoists of yore, and with the passion and pleas of a dying man, he advocated a union of South African territories, extolled Rhodesia and begged that she be included in the great nation in incubation. He joked that while he was offering the expanse of Rhodesia to the proposed Union, it was not for any personal gain...the nation would acquire a new province while he would only get a plot measuring six feet by four.

Rhodes carried his seat although his party was defeated. The godchildren of his creation, in their quest for self-government, were not thinking about union at all. A quarter of a century later they would bear testimony to how Rhodes had wasted his last years on another cherished dream of no substance.

Still, this was not the end. In 1899 Rhodes returned to England to try again to raise the money he needed for the Cape to Cairo railway. He failed. Others who advocated the more practical solution of constructing railways inland from East African ports prevailed, and this is the structure of African railways as they are today.

Rhodes' failing heart was enlivened by an honorary Doctorate of Civil Law from Oxford, delivered together with one for Lord Kitchener. But Rhodes was feted and hailed as the Colossus, showered with accolades that Kitchener did not receive.

War broke out in South Africa on 11 October 1899 as racial disharmony between Boer and Briton finally exploded into violence. If he accepted blame for at least some part in inciting this war, it did not alter the pace of his last run. The British lost the initiative in the countryside and withdrew under siege to Kimberley, Mafeking and Ladysmith. Rhodes hurried north to Kimberley on the last train to enter the town, and to the disgust of the military commander, he established himself there for the duration of the war. The Boers felt a particular hatred for Rhodes, and his presence in Kimberley ensured that determined efforts would be made to break it. Rhodes, however, could not give a damn, for it seemed that he had reserved the best of his truculence for such a moment.

Rhodes assumed command and proceeded to irritate the defenders of the town beyond endurance. He had ridden with his irregulars in Matabeleland and had learned a few things, he supposed, about war. Out of a general distrust of military men, he opposed and contradicted the commanders of the garrison at every opportunity. Colonel Methuen, en route to relieve the town, wrote: 'On my entry into Kimberley, Mr Rhodes must make his immediate departure.'[8] In the intervening two months, Rhodes attempted to square the generals Roberts and Kitchener by offering supplies in exchange for authority, but neither was prepared to hand over conduct of the siege to him.

At this point Rhodes was largely without support. Rhodesians — for such they had begun to call themselves — were present further north at the siege of Mafeking, but were absent from Rhodes' side in Kimberley. The Imperial Government had made a specific request for two mounted regiments of Rhodesians to defend the Rhodesian and Bechuanaland borders. These men were mainly recruited by Colonel Robert Baden Powell who was himself made famous largely thanks to his defence of Mafeking. The force was made up of a combination of BSAC Police members and civilian volunteers. The 1500 men involved made up approximately 12.5% of the Rhodesian population as it then stood.

Mafeking was the key centre for the defence of Bechuanaland, and it was there that one regiment was sent, with the second being dispatched to Fort Tuli. An armoured train, fabricated in the Bulawayo railway workshops, was used to run guns for the defence of Mafeking, but it was ambushed at Kraaipan on 13 October 1899 with the death or capture of all the men of the contingent. This was in fact the first act of the Anglo-Boer War.

Rhodesians saw action in various locations in Bechuanaland, and after the relief of Mafeking in May 1900, they fought several actions during the guerrilla phase of the war.

* * *

It was a sick and dying Rhodes who passed the remaining two years of his life restlessly moving between the Cape, Rhodesia and England. His autumn was blighted not only by his own unwillingness to rest but also by that which had always been so noticeably absent throughout his life.

Rhodes enjoyed relationships with women on many levels. His conquests, at least on a companionable level, included such literary luminaries as Flora Shaw and Olive Schreiner, while many other Victorian society ladies contrived to own a few Chartered shares so that they might be in his company from time to time. Yet none of these liaisons was ever observed to be sexual. He neither empathised with women nor seemed to trust them, and there is no convincing evidence that Rhodes ever had a lover from either sex. It is therefore ironic that the closing passages of his life were ruined by the intrusion of a calculating woman.

Princess Radziwill, a middle aged dowager of Polish descent, contrived to meet Rhodes on a sea voyage between Southampton and Cape Town. From then on she aggressively manoeuvred herself into his company, and when he resisted, she began to spread rumours that they were lovers and then soon to be married. Rhodes was scandalised and at first could scarcely believe that this was happening. She forged his name to obtain £29 000, and was duly prosecuted and jailed. But if Rhodes thought that he had pulled her off his skin he was wrong. She persisted, and threatened to sue the Rhodes trustees before committing her memoirs to print in a book about the 'affair'.

The episode ruined Rhodes' last years and certainly hastened his death. On 26 March 1902, two months before the end of the Anglo-Boer War, he expired, fighting for breath through balmy Cape spring days in a modest cottage in the coastal town of Muizenburg.

He was given his six by four portion of Africa. The Colossus was laid to rest atop the Matopos Hills overlooking the view of the world that he had loved so well. A tomb of imperial simplicity was cut into granite, with a slab placed on top with a plain inscription reading: 'Here lie the remains of Cecil John Rhodes.'

The country of Rhodesia that immortalised his name surged forward towards a promising future while, amid the storms and recriminations of war, the Empire crumbled back into the dust of nations. Perhaps Rhodes' most enduring legacy has been the Rhodes Scholarships that were endowed to express his gratitude to Oxford, and to perpetuate his ideal of a young man going forth to create an empire.

15

Fertile industry born

While Rhodes was alive he was the moral authority that governed and guided Rhodesia. It was he who ordered the wide width of Bulawayo's streets and the planting of the trees that shaded them. For his farmers he imported fresh bloodlines of chickens, cattle, sheep and goats. He introduced new strains and cultivars of fruit for future orchards. He decided who went where, who received what and who partnered whom. Out of enterprises that succeeded he took a cut, and towards those that failed he contributed his share. He engineered the character of the early white population and managed their projects. His dream was practical, and as such it gave rise to a practical people in a land of practical achievement. Rhodes was Rhodesia, and Rhodesia was Rhodes. His people were created in his own image and so it remained for as long as he lived.

When he died the character of the landscape changed. The settlers and the British South Africa Company's board of directors were abruptly forced to shake themselves awake, and confront the reality of what Rhodes had left behind. His material legacy was huge, but it was vested in the Company. The Company was bankrupt and so was the country. It was no longer possible to shelter behind the reputation of Rhodes; the Company and its denizens now had to find a way to make the enterprise pay.

A solution, however, was not so easily identified. The directors were understandably aloof and, since many of the early settlers themselves had failed or given up, it would seem unlikely that a clique of remote London-based businessmen would fare any better. As a consequence, the economic situation in Rhodesia stagnated, with the only alternative strategy emanating from the top, seeming to be 'wait and see'. There were, however, a handful of men on the ground who were determined not to fail, and as it turned out, a most unlikely hand sowed the seeds of an economic rebirth.

At the time the rail system was the only bona fide working industry in Rhodesia. The administration of it, and of the colony itself, was in fact the only substantial business being conducted in the country. The railway was a superb infrastructural asset, having been both well and cheaply built. Its purpose in the first instance had been to stamp the fact of white occupation on the landscape, and thereafter to support a mining industry that it was assumed would soon rival that of the Witwatersrand. The original Mafeking to Bulawayo line was pushed through to Salisbury, and in due course eastwards to Beira. When the anticipated gold boom did not materialise, the colony found itself with a wonderful facility but with nothing much to do with it. It was this abstract thought that occupied the mind of the colony's second Administrator, Lord Albert Grey.

Grey happened to be something of a connoisseur of good cigars and, during the Mashona Rebellion, he was given some home-cured shag and a few hand-rolled cigars produced on the Mashonaland farm of a certain C.E Howell. Grey tried some of the shag himself and distributed the rest among the local soldiers to sample. He later commented to Howell that the pipe tobacco had proved too strong for the white troops, but the native contingent had thought well of it. The cigars, he said, were abysmal. Grey had passed a handful of these on to a few friends who he hoped Howell would never have the misfortune of ever meeting.

Such banter was perfectly in character and was not taken seriously by Grey, Howell or any of the other Mashonaland farmers who had recently taken to growing tobacco. Grey, however, did not forget the incident. He went on to introduce the subject at the Salisbury Club, where so much informal policy in the colony was decided, and there the notion provoked a lingering debate. Until then no one had really thought of agriculture as a potential money-spinner since most of those that had tried farming in Rhodesia found it a bloody and thankless business. It was regarded merely as a means to feed the settlers and as subsistence for the farmers themselves while they searched the land for gold.

Grey, however, was convinced that he had stumbled on something. From the moment he took his first draught of Howell's primitive leaf, the idea of cultivating tobacco commercially lingered in his mind. To him the railway seemed more ideally placed to service an agricultural industry than a defunct legacy of mining. It happened also that the railway followed the line of the central watershed — the area of greatest agricultural potential, and the part of the country most attractive to European settlement. Farming as an industry would tend to attract settlers who actually wanted to settle, rather than those transitory fortune seekers of the Uitlander type, who could be here today and gone tomorrow. The timing was also opportune, for the country was full of broken diggers who would soon pack up and leave, taking their experience and capital with them unless something better was offered.

Although not a pioneer of any sort himself, Grey diligently worked the idea on any farmer who showed the slightest interest. The first to really take up the prospect was a young and dynamic Mashonaland agriculturalist by the name of G.W Oldum who took the idea very seriously indeed. As with the majority of Mashonaland landholders, Oldum was primarily a maize producer, and like others he was frustrated with the limitations of a locally consumed food crop. He went home and applied some research to the question of tobacco, and the first conclusion of many he reached was that the practical difficulties of growing tobacco on a commercial scale in central Africa would be huge. Tobacco required a market, and although a sizable market did exist in South Africa, it was dominated by American tobacco, as was virtually the entire world market. Besides this, Oldum had no means other than practical testing to establish the growing potential and no resources to experiment. He concluded that tobacco was not the short-term solution that the country needed, but rather a true pioneering enterprise that would have to be started from scratch.

Despite the obstacles, Oldum grasped the potential and travelled to the United States where for a year he learned what he could about tobacco production. His first discovery was that global trends were shifting away from pipe and cigar tobaccos towards the Virginia type used in the manufacture of cigarettes. His second finding was that the sandy soils of the central watershed region of Rhodesia were in theory perfect for the production of Virginia leaf. As early as 1903, samples of soil were being sent across the Atlantic for analysis and information was being exchanged with American growers.

While Albert Grey moved on to assume his Governorship of Canada, Oldum returned to Rhodesia in 1904 and began experimenting in earnest. The tobacco industry would necessarily have to germinate for a year or two before any signs of sturdy growth could appear. Grey's enthusiasm for the product had been a little ahead of its time because the board was not as yet willing to depart from the hope and expectation that the future of Rhodesia lay in mining. The Company had dropped its demand for a half share of every mine in Rhodesia, which helped to make the business more viable for the small operator, but did not answer the question of how administrative costs were to be recouped and money earned.

Meanwhile, the early experiments in the field of tobacco had created a minor stir in the country that took time to reach the ears of London Wall — but in due course it did. The news did not in itself

(Right) Great
Zimbabwe ruins.
All that remains
of what was once
the home of the
Mambo kings

(Below Left) Robert Moffat established the
important Kuruman Mission in 1825. This
formed a base for all expeditions to the far
north. His relationship with King Mzilikazi
resulted in the establishment of the first mission station in Matabeleland at Inyati.

(Below Right) Thomas Morgan
Thomas was one of the original
missionaries who settled at Inyati. He attended Mzilikazi during
his last illness and witnessed the
coronation of Lobengula.

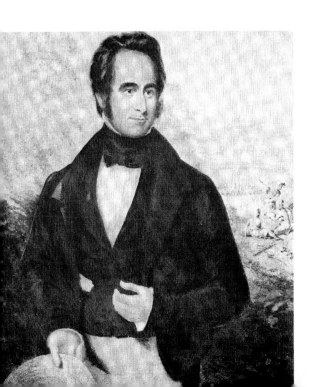

(Left) King Lobengula

(Right) Lobengula holding court outside his Bulawayo residence.

(Left) Bishop Knight-Bruce first visited King Lobengula in 1888. He assisted Rhodes in getting his concession to occupy Mashonaland and afterwards became the Bishop of Mashonaland.

(Right) Rhodes bought and consolidated all the concessions granted by Lobengula and through them gained a Royal Charter from Queen Victoria for his British South Africa Company to occupy Mashonaland. Dr Jameson (right) was the last envoy he sent to the Lobengula.

(Left) A prospector's wagon overturned on the road from Macloutsie to the Shashi in the 'Disputed Territory'.

(Right) Major Frank Johnson was contracted by Rhodes at a bargain price to see the Pioneer Column safely through to Mashonaland.

(left) Frederick Courtney Selous was appointed as the column's guide and Intelligence officer.

(Right) Lt Col E.G. Pennefather (6th Innskilling Dragoons) commanded the British South Africa Company Police during the trek and afterwards until 1991.

(Below) The Pioneer Column in laager south of the Tuli River. Matabele country lies beyond the river in the middle distance.

(Right) Lobengula's envoys with spears and rifles appeared at Tuli and confronted the Pioneer column. 'What', they asked, 'has the white man lost that they are coming into our country?'

(Left) With the column (l to r seated): Dr Jameson, F.A Calquhoun — who was to set up the civil administration, F.C Selous and Harris, the administration's secretary.

(Below) On the road to Mashonaland.

(Above) Officers of the Pioneer Corps (l to r front row seated): Lts W Ellerton Fry, E.C Tyndale-Biscoe, R.Beal and Surgeon Lt J. Brett. (Seated): Capts A.E. Burnett and M. Heany, Major F. Johnson and Capt F.C Selous.. (Standing): Lts E'O.C Farrell and F. Mandy, Surgeon Lt J.W Lichfield, Capts J.J Roach and H.F Hoste, Lts H.J. Borrow, A Campbell and R.G Burnett and the Rev F Surridge

(Right) On route. A group of tribesmen at M'tibi's mountain.

(Left) A Mashona kraal in Chibi's country.

(Right) The Great Zimbabwe ruins

(Left) Part of the camp at Fort Salisbury. The Kopje looms in the background.

(Right) W.E. Fairbridge standing in front of his editorial office. He established the first Rhodesian newspaper. 1891.

(Left) Offices of the Rhodesia Herald, 1892.

(Below)Occupation of Matabeleland. The Battle of Bembesi, 1 November 1893, when Lobengula's crack regiments were routed. Maxim machine guns were used for the first time in battle anywhere and the warriors, brave as they were, were unable to get within 300 metres of the laager.

(Below) The Fort Victoria contingent in the Matabele War comprised 414 whites assisted by 450 blacks. Picture shows them assembling at the onset of the campaign.

(Right) The Matabele regiments, many of whom were armed with fire-arms, proved themselves incapable of beating the whites in open battle. Lobengula ordered the destruction of his royal kraal and fled. The troopers entered the town the next day and raised the Union Jack .They found only a smoking ruin.

(Left) Major Alan Wilson and his 33-man patrol's last stand on the Shangani River against the Matabele regiments on 4 December 1893. Depiction by R Caton Woodville.

(Right) A meeting of the directors of De Beers Consolidated Mines Ltd in 1894. Rhodes is seated in the centre with Jameson on his right.

(Left) The Jameson Raid. Jameson' surrender to the Boers at Doornkop in January 1896. Jameson had foolishly denuded the colony of the BSA Company's police. This left the colony virtually defenceless.

(Right) The Jameson Raid. Jameson (4th from left standing) and his officers.

(Left) After the occupation of Matabeleland, native police were locally recruited to keep order. This company deserted to the rebels, taking their rifles with them, when the Matabele Rebellion broke out in early 1996.

(Right) An artist's impression of the Matabele attack on Cummins Store near Filabusi.

(Left) Officers examine the remains of Assistant Native Commissioner A.M Grahams and four other whites murdered at Inyati on 26 March 1896.

(Right) An artist's impression by Frank Dodd, R.A, of Lt Crewe rescuing a comrade at the Battle of Umguza. 22 April 1896.

(Left) The Bulawayo laager during the rebellion.

(Right) Reports noted the 'plucky' behaviour of women and their unselfish service in the Bulawayo laager's hospital.

(Left) The Afrikander Corps in Bulawayo.

(Right) Base camp in the Matopos under the command of General Carrington.

(Left) A seven pounder mountain gun bombarding rebel targets in the Matopos.

(Right) Base camp in the Matopos. Rhodes, centre, flanked by General Carrington and Mrs Molly Colenbrander.

(Left) The peace indaba in the Matopos, Cecil Rhodes, Captain Colenbrander (right) a Mr Stent — war correspondent at the Cape Times. After five weeks the negotiations ended with the surrender of the chiefs.

(Right) Cecil Rhodes' hand written definition of a civilised man.

My motto is
equal rights for every civilised man
South of the Zambesi
What is a civilised man
a man whether white or black who has
sufficient education to write his name, has some property or works,
in fact is not a loafer C.J.Rhodes

(Left) Courtroom scene at the trial of three Matabele chiefs.

(Right) The Mashona Rebellion, 1896. Scene at Norton Farm after the massacre of the household. The homestead was close to the site of the later Hunyani Dam wall

(Left) Troops on the march in Mashonaland. Wagons near the River Umsawe. An artist's impression by C.E. Fripp.

(Right) A skirmish with rebels during the Mashona Rebellion.

(Left) The surrender of Kagubi and Nyanda in October 1877 signalled the end of the Mashona Rebellion. Nyajnda went to her death on the gallows with courage.

(Right) Departure from Bulawayo of Zeederberg's mail coach, 1896.

(Left) At Figtree 1897. Laying the rails to Bulawayo

generate as much interest in agriculture as an industry, as the potential it offered for the disposal of land at a premium. Under the terms of the Lippert Concession, the Company felt that the vast tracts of land still available for distribution were its own. It began to occur to the directors that the sale of land, in combination with the excellent rail transport system, would be the most likely means of turning a quick profit and paying off the shareholders.

Oldum teamed up with fellow farmer H.E South, and the two began to experiment in tandem with flue-cured leaf on South's property of Warwickshire Farm. The results were mixed but encouraging, and historically significant because this was the first case of yellow Virginia leaf being flue-cured anywhere outside its home belt in the southeast United States. In due course the administration was directed to invest a modest sum in assisting the development of a nascent tobacco industry, with a view to increasing the value of the land. Seed was made available to growers, and trials started at an agricultural experimentation centre founded just outside Salisbury. Many friendly exchanges of advice, information and technical support from the United States followed, that gave powerful impetus to the fledgling industry. In 1905 about 500 000 lbs (pounds weight) of tobacco of different types was produced in Rhodesia and exhibited as far afield as Cape Town. Viability had now been demonstrated, so all that remained for the pioneers of the industry was to establish reliable markets.

Traditional producers naturally tended to maintain the loyalty of their regular buyers, and in the beginning, Rhodesian growers satisfied themselves with a burgeoning local demand. Cigarettes were hand rolled by small manufacturers working in farm outbuildings. Skilled workers were recruited from as far afield as Greece, Turkey and even Russia. The homegrown brands that evolved found local favour and bore such names as Warwickshire Farm's Sublime Brand and Lachie Black's Stapleford Specials. The latter was described as 'Best Tobacco' for the Englishman, 'Boer Tobacco' of an intermediate quality and 'Kaffir Tobacco' that was usually the floor sweepings, was reserved for the blacks.

By 1910 tobacco still made up no more than one percent of total exports — which were still dominated by royalty paying products like gold. However, the establishment of farmer's associations such as the Rhodesian Agricultural Union, formed in 1905, was helping to buttress foundations. At its first annual general meeting, the Agricultural Union recognised tobacco, by recommending the construction of a central tobacco warehouse. This in turn had the effect of stimulating greater interest from South Africa in bulk purchasing, while even the British admiralty began making enquiries into the supply of tobacco for the Royal Navy. Prices of Rhodesian leaf were significantly higher than American leaf, and only the willingness of South Africa to purchase bulk supplies allowed the industry to sustain its first years of growth.

The local industry received an unexpected boost when its Nyasaland (Malawi) counterpart was pitched into disarray in 1905 by a South African decision to impose a punitive duty on agricultural imports from the lakes region. Consequently an exodus of experienced farmers from Nyasaland arrived in Rhodesia to fortify the blood of the fledgling home industry. Nyasaland farmers also brought with them a trained body of native labour that began a lengthy tradition of migrant agricultural labour from the lakes to Southern Rhodesia.

In 1910 the first auction sale of flue-cured tobacco was held. 120 000 lbs of leaf was sold at an average price of 1s 2d per lb. Only three buyers were present and prices were still high compared to the United States. A quarrel between American and British tobacco interests caused the British to accept these uneconomic rates briefly — which in turn tempted Rhodesian growers to ignore otherwise instructive global market trends. As a consequence, 1914 saw an inevitable collapse in prices and the withdrawal of most of the annual crop. The Rhodesian tobacco industry then slumped for a period, with some bitter lessons having being learned by all. War would soon divert attention, however, and briefly relieve colonial commodity producers with a sudden upsurge in demand.

The tableau of white Rhodesia continued to form as immigrants steadily trickled in. By 1907 the white population had crept up to 14 000, and by 1911 that figure had grown to 24 000. This increase might have been even greater had not the administration and the existing settler population pursued something of an elitist policy regarding European immigration. The Boer War and the rinderpest both conspired to produce in South Africa a class of poor urban Afrikaners that the Rhodesian authorities and public went to great lengths to keep out. This was indicative of a wider policy of selective immigration which is best illustrated by the response of the BSA Company when approached by Kingsley Fairbridge with proposals to introduce child migration to Rhodesia.

Fairbridge had by then left the colony, and in 1911 graduated from Oxford under the Rhodes scholarship scheme. While at Oxford he gathered around him a clique of other young colonials interested in fortifying the white blood of the Empire. The concept of child migration was simply that children of disadvantaged circumstances should be transported at a young age to the colonies where they would be educated in specially established farm schools. This would serve to acclimatise them to life in the tropics before the worst characteristics of urbanisation could take root.

Under Fairbridge's direction, a committee of Oxford colonials was formed for the purpose of pushing forward this programme. The young man, however, received a sudden and unexpected disappointment when in 1911 the BSA Company took the view that Rhodesia did not have sufficient infrastructural development to accommodate a child migration programme. Permission to set up facilities was therefore denied. While this reasoning was sound, the real truth lay in the fact that there was simply no place in Rhodesia for a class of white, rural yeomanry.

As a location for permanent white settlement, Rhodesia was fundamentally different from Canada, Australia and New Zealand. The large population of natives — who had proved immune to genocide, alcohol and disease — were physically superior to whites in terms of their ability to labour in tropical conditions. This allowed the white man to tame the African landscape with barely a swing of his own axe or a blister on his hands. What Rhodesia required was not an infusion of white labour, but of men with breeding, capital and expertise. This was Rhodes' fundamental dictum, and it was pursued with vigour long after death.

After this disappointment at the hands of the authorities of his own colony, Kingsley Fairbridge was forced to approach the government of Western Australia whose need for a white working class was much greater. There in January of 1913 he started his first farm school for child immigrants at Pinjarra. He never again returned to Rhodesia, and died in Australia in 1924 at the age of 39.

16

Dream of union

The governance debate

The rise of agriculture in Rhodesia brought in its wake another sample of the fractious internal politics that had only partly been laid to rest by Rhodes' cash payments and his limited political concession. Since land was now the currency of preference, it was not long before it became the new source of dissent and tension. The specific irritant was the Company's assumption that the unalienated land of the country was its own commercial asset. This position was wholly rejected by the elected members of the Legislative Assembly, adding significant grist to a mill that had been steadily grinding out discontent against the Company since 1890.

While it is true that settler dissatisfaction seemed to encompass just about everything, it was above all rooted in the fact that a commercial company was an inappropriate system of government for a settled colony. It had by then become obvious to all — including both the Imperial Government and the Company itself — that an alternative form of administration had to be found. Rhodes had briefly dressed the wound, but he was dead, and his de facto monarchy had evolved into government by committee. Ethel Tawse Jollie adequately defined the mood of the settlers when she remarked that:

> … all British people are born free and have a right to govern themselves; that the taxpayers have a right to a voice in the spending of their own money and that the land of a country should be a national possession.[1]

Central to Rhodes' dream had always been the notion of a greater South Africa. Exactly how great would only be limited by the breadth of vision of his heirs. By 1909 South Africa had achieved political union, but nothing thus far seemed to suggest that the settler community of Rhodesia was interested in joining it. This is strange in retrospect because in many ways union with South Africa would have seemed the obvious choice at the time. If nothing else, the chances of long-term white domination of southern Africa would have been assured. A strong gravitational pull would have developed that might in time have drawn in Northern Rhodesia and Bechuanaland, and perhaps even German South West Africa. A United States of Africa under the Union Jack, that stretched as far north as the equator, would not have been beyond the realms of possibility.

There were, of course, also some sobering aspects of this concept to consider. Dr. Jameson, in a speech delivered to the Salisbury Club shortly before his death, hinted at some of the risks that union with South Africa might pose for Rhodesia.

What is going to happen to this young, vigorous child when it gets into the bed of that large and corpulent mother, the Union? What always happens? In this case at all events all your aspirations are going to be killed, and at the inquest the next morning the verdict will be 'overlaid by the Union'[1]

Although politically united, the Union of South Africa was still socially divided, and in the years since the Anglo-Boer War, racial acrimony between Briton and Boer had not noticeably diminished. The war had inflicted a defeat on the Boers that had finally frozen altogether an already chill attitude towards the British. Despite being magnanimous in victory, British contempt for the Afrikaners was palpable, and was as evident in Rhodesia as it was anywhere in southern Africa. Their language, their rustic and backward-looking mentality and their innate chauvinism unnerved the Rhodesians. No less were they anxious to avoid an invasion of poor Afrikaners into Rhodesia, coupled with a reverse flood of local black labour seeking better pay on the mines of the Witwatersrand.

An alternative to this was amalgamation with Northern Rhodesia — a second British South Africa Company territory, founded on a series of concessions and treaties gathered since 1888 — in pursuit of a viable political and economic body to counterbalance the power of the Union. Failing this it would be a choice between direct rule from Whitehall, rule by the Company into perpetuity, or some sort of local settler government along the lines of the Cape Colony. Since the 25-year term of the Royal Charter was due to expire in October 1914, time for all to decide was fast running out.

The Company steadfastly maintained that its primary assets were the railway system, the mineral rights and the 40 million or so acres of land that remained unclaimed or unoccupied. Of course the settlers saw things differently. There was no dispute yet regarding the railway system, and the question of mineral rights would continue to fester for some time. But when it came to the unalienated land, the majority of settlers were emphatic, maintaining that the land belonged to the territory and was therefore a national asset.

Should the British South Africa Company be forced to concede to this it would find itself in a very difficult position. As of 1904 it carried a deficit of £8 million. Out of its purse had come the railway, the telegraph, and all public buildings and institutions across the country. Added to this was the financial input related to maintaining a police force, a civil service and the governing institutions of a relatively modern country. The Matabele and Mashona Rebellions alone had prejudiced the Company treasury to the tune of more than £2.5 million. In the depressed climate following the Anglo-Boer War, the Company was unable to raise further loans on its own credit, so the commercial venture of Rhodesia was effectively bankrupt. The shareholders, of course, had so far seen no return whatsoever on their investment.

It ought to be added that, despite superficial impressions, the settlers were not entirely without gratitude to the Company, and nor were they universally opposed to it. Many were scathing and unrealistically hostile, but others had a more reasonable and sympathetic view. Farmers, railwaymen and miners usually voiced the loudest criticism, while the imperial men of the middle and upper classes were inclined to be less judgemental. Many, in fact, found no fault with the Company at all, and leading this cohort was the Argus Press, now firmly behind the Company. The editor of the *Rhodesia Herald*, C.D Don, spoke for these in a later article published on the eve of World War-I. In it he remarked:

Whatever the shortcomings of our local administration, whatever the anomalies of our form of government, whatever the mistakes made by the British South Africa Company, the fact remains that the resources and credit of the Charter, plus the pluck and grit of the settlers themselves, have made possible the Rhodesia of today.

While this might have been true, and reflective of the views of the professional and administrative types, it did not offer any solutions. It was Don again who illustrated some of the options available to the settlers:

> The position may be summed up in a brace of alternatives. Either we continue under the Charter, with legislative control, including control of land policy, but without financial responsibility, until such time as we are strong enough to go to the Imperial Government with the request for responsible institutions; or we endeavour to thrust the Charter on one side and take our chance of what may replace it as the governing factor in Rhodesia.

The Company directors turned to city financier Sir George Goldie to suggest a way out of the impasse. Goldie was no fool, and neither was he without considerable relevant experience. He was to the Niger region of West Africa what Rhodes had been to Rhodesia. He could claim credit for the birth of the Royal Niger Company and the subsequent birth of Nigeria as a nation. His work in that region, however, typified exactly the state of affairs that did not exist in Rhodesia. Neither Nigeria, nor the Gold Coast — or Sierra Leone for that matter — ever really hosted a viable white population, and as a consequence never demanded or justified a home-based civil administration. It could be assumed therefore that Goldie did not fully understand the nuances of the situation in Rhodesia. Although he examined the circumstances of the Company in depth, his conclusions were reached with very little understanding of the needs and current mood of the settlers.

Goldie announced his findings in a letter to the elected members of the Legislative Council. In it he reviewed the various calamities that had beset the colony in its brief life. Among these were the rinderpest and other cattle diseases, the native rebellions, the Boer War and the consequent economic depression. All of these could be considered acts of God, but all had contributed to the drain on the Company's treasury — a liability which in turn threatened the country with ruin. Goldie proposed that the people of Southern Rhodesia accept the accumulated deficits as a funded debt of the country, and if this were agreed to, then the Company would undertake to raise a loan of £3 million to be spent on developing agriculture, industry and immigration.

Tom Shillington, director of the *Rhodesia Herald*, responded for the settler majority when he declared:

> The (Goldie) financial proposals show evidence of being launched as a means of tiding over the B.S.A. Company, and not as a serious endeavour to aid Rhodesia. They are first of all to keep going a corporation that is inherently unsound. It seems the height of imprudence to propose that if the loan is raised on a funding debt the Colonists are not to have the administration of it. There is no evidence in the history of the British South Africa Company to justify the belief that such monies would be expended in the direction indicated — they would doubtless be devoted as heretofore to the maintenance of an extravagant Administration.[2]

Although public opinion on the subject was by no means unanimous, Shillington's view was widely supported. It left the BSA Company in no doubt that the Goldie Report had been rejected.

A national conference was held in Salisbury on 9 June 1904, but little was achieved. In a letter read on his behalf Dr Jameson, who was then Prime Minister of the Cape Colony as well as a senior director of the Company, proposed that a settler deputation be assembled to confer directly with the board of directors. The conference lasted two days, but since most settlers present attended as individuals, no agreement could be reached except that a problem existed. However the following resolution was tabled:

This conference records its conviction that Southern Rhodesia can make no true progress as long as the British South Africa Company, as an administrative or commercial body, has control of public affairs, and instructs its delegates to strive for the elimination of the Company as an administrative or commercial body in Southern Rhodesia. Should such delegates find it impossible, with the assistance of the Imperial Government, to bring this about it will be open to them to bring for consideration of Southern Rhodesia any other proposals.[3]

Five delegates from the conference were selected to meet the directors, but this achieved nothing either. The Company refused to consider complete withdrawal from the territory and the settlers rejected a counter-proposal that they could assume financial authority only if the Company kept political control. The only concession by the board was the withdrawal of one nominated member to give the elected members a majority of one. Limitations placed on financial decisions served to render this meaningless too. The *Rhodesia Herald* effectively summed up the mood of the settler population in its leader column of 13 September 1904:

> Such preposterous proposals were never before offered for the acceptance of an enlightened and businesslike people, and it is gratifying to learn that they have been practically flung back into the faces of those who devised them.[4]

Thereafter both sides retreated to their corners to consider their positions. The matter thereupon fell into abeyance for ten years. By 1914, with no new solutions in sight, all parties agreed to maintain the status quo by approving a ten-year supplementary charter that would give the country until 1924 to resolve the governance issue.

Meanwhile, the only immediate result that might have been viewed as positive was that the Company administration reviewed its own procedures and made some effort to become more accessible to the general public. However no solution to its financial woes was in sight, and it continued to struggle to make ends meet.

For the settlers the door had not been shut completely. Provision remained for the Legislative Assembly to petition for responsible government at such time as it achieved an absolute majority, and was able to present some evidence of its financial fitness. No agreement was reached regarding the two vital matters of ownership of the land and the question of responsibility for the Company's past administrative deficits.

The more divisive of these two issues — the question of unalienated land — was put to His Majesty's Government for consideration. The eventual response to this was vague. The Imperial Government took the view that whatever opinion it chose to express would not be legally binding and that the issue could only be decided by a court of law. The following year the same question was asked and the Government again dodged it. There the matter rested, despite the settlers complaining that the status quo stood to the advantage of the Company.

The country's debilitating shortage of capital continued until, in 1905, the Legislative Council, with the support of the Company, passed an ordinance allowing it to contract its own public debt. This measure was vetoed by the Colonial Office as long as the Company remained the owners of all the country's assets and responsible for its administration.

Thus it appeared that the country's political stalemate was destined to continue. Increased settler representation in 1913 allowed for a settler majority of 12 members to six. However, in practice, this meant very little because an Order in Council of 1911 restricted the unofficials from passing any fiscal proposals, or ordinances interfering with the land and other rights of the Company. As Ethel Tawse Jollie remarked, 'it merely carried off some of the smoke without quenching the fire.'[5]

In 1908 a delegation led by prominent Bulawayo lawyer and responsible government activist Charles Coghlan, and including the Administrator William Milton — now Sir William Milton — attended a National Convention held in Durban to discuss the unification of the colonies south of the Limpopo. At the conclusion of the conference they returned home with little enthusiasm for union. While not precluding the possibility in the future, it was agreed that union with South Africa was not a practical consideration at that moment.

Consequently a general mood of depressed acceptance set in until, on the eve of World War-I, the 25-year term of the Charter expired. Thereafter a supplemental charter of ten years duration came into effect. Sir William Milton retired as Company Administrator and was succeeded by Sir Drummond Chaplin.

Like Milton, Chaplin was a contemporary and friend of both Jameson and Rhodes. Of the three, Chaplin was the better placed in the English social hierarchy, and more astute in the field of public relations. Educated at Harrow and Oxford, he maintained the tradition of the Honourable and Military, but deviated somewhat by initially choosing journalism as a career choice. He was managing the Consolidated Goldfields of South Africa when he first came into contact with Rhodes. He later served as the President of the Transvaal Chamber of Mines before joining the Chartered Company in 1914. While Milton had been a reluctant recruit to the Company, Chaplin accepted his commission with vigour. Once in office he resolved to clear up some of the bad blood between the administration and the settlers, that his predecessor had done little to ease.

Chaplin, however, did not deviate far from Milton's orthodox opinions on imperial affairs. He was as irreconciled to the notion of responsible government as he was to union with South Africa. Like most members of the British establishment, he instinctively regarded the Boer as a stump-headed idiot and his natural enemy. He found himself supporting the idea of a greater Rhodesia as a counterpoise to the increasing power of South Africa and the rise of Afrikaner nationalism. He therefore strongly backed Dr Jameson and other members of the board when, in December 1915, the idea of the amalgamation of Southern and Northern Rhodesia was first seriously mooted.

For the Company the advantages of amalgamation were in part economic and in part political. A merger would halve administrative costs and settle the question of the viability of two struggling colonies. It would also positively effect the balance of power in the region should South Africa become a republic under Afrikaner rule. A greater Rhodesia might also in time involve the East African colonies, thereby ensuring a brighter political future for all the British territories in the region. Notwithstanding the probable economic and political benefits of the scheme — which were not as obvious to the south as they might have been with the later discovery of copper in the north — the fly in the ointment remained the parochialism and narrow vision of the two settler communities themselves.

Northern Rhodesia, with its handful of white settlers, feared that it would become a province of Southern Rhodesia. The settler community of Southern Rhodesia held that amalgamation would abruptly increase the ratio of black to white from its current 27:1 to 60:1. This would make it even less likely that the Imperial Government would agree to Southern Rhodesian self-government. The *Rhodesia Herald* leader column of 12 April 1917 betrayed the newspaper's support for amalgamation. It read:

> Sir Charles's [Coghlan] alarm is based on the belief that if the franchise laws of Southern Rhodesia are extended to the North the result will be that the native voters there will swamp the local European electorate and the Legislative Council at Salisbury. To us the argument presents a strong reason for taking advantage of the amalgamation scheme to ensure an early revision of our franchise laws. For if the danger is as great as Sir Charles Coghlan professes

to believe, how many years will it be before the natives of Southern Rhodesia produce a sufficient number of educated adults to dominate or swamp the white electorate? We have yet to learn that the native education in Northern Rhodesia is vastly more advanced than it is in the South.

The Legislative Council approved amalgamation, although the elected members voted against it eight to four. The Company judged the mood of the settlers accordingly and let the matter drop. There the situation remained as the population of both Rhodesias, in common with South Africa and indeed the entire world, found itself preoccupied with the outbreak of war.

17

World War-I

West and East Africa

World War-I was the first major test of the global Anglo-Saxon union. A great deal of diplomacy between Britain and her dominions worked to buttress loyalty in the advent of a world war, but despite mounting belligerence in Europe, many of Britain's colonial administrations were unseemingly reluctant to commit themselves to the defence of the motherland. Canada saw herself as a member of a new sphere of influence where the United States dominated, while Australia and New Zealand were preoccupied with the Japanese threat. South Africa had been a dominion since the union came into being in 1910, but a residual anti-imperial feeling — particularly among the Afrikaans speakers — caused her entry into the war to be by no means a foregone conclusion. Ultimately South Africa would play a unique and very important role in the conflict, but it would not be without profound political consequences, and not without causing deep divisions among the differing white tribes in the country itself.

Despite the general mood of circumspection, any doubts about the patriotism of individual British men and women, was put to rest in the summer of 1914, when thousands from every corner of the British Empire flocked to recruiting stations and signed up for combat in a festival atmosphere. In Rhodesia things were no different. The British South Africa Company watched this rush of white men to the khaki line with mixed feelings. The question that immediately concerned the board was who was going to pay for it all? William Milton was less reserved and on the eve of his retirement cabled London, stating that all Rhodesia was united in its loyalty to the King, and ready to do its duty.[1]

The *Rhodesia Herald* struck a more cautious note, and in a thoughtful editorial warned that Southern Rhodesia ought not to forget the lessons learned during the 1896 rebellions, when the denuding of the colony's manpower had led immediately to a native uprising.

Such warnings had no effect. The settler community put aside its squabbles and flocked to lend its weight to the great war effort. By the end of the conflict, three million fighting men had been drawn from the colonies, with almost a million and a half from India alone. Some 630 000 were recruited in Canada, 420 000 in Australia, 126 000 in New Zealand and 136 000 in South Africa.[2] Among the latter were some 5 500 white and 2 700 black troops from Southern Rhodesia. Bearing in mind that the white population of Southern Rhodesia was a mere 24 000, this was the largest single per capita contribution to the allied war effort from all the colonies.

A point also worth mentioning is the fact that out of the Southern Rhodesian contribution of white men, over 1700 held commissions. This would be noticed again in World War-II, and can be explained largely by the fact that white Rhodesian youth was of a higher calibre than those in other parts of the empire. Significantly also was the fact that most of these young men had acquired experience of command as a result of their early apprenticeship managing large labour forces.

The main contribution of Rhodesian forces to the eventual allied victory, tended to be in localised African campaigns, and primarily in combination with South African forces. Apart from a handful of individuals, who took it upon themselves to travel to Britain to enlist in the British Army, the Southern Rhodesian Volunteers were organised into two divisions, to be mobilised in the event of a general native uprising. Besides this, the opening months of the war saw Rhodesians posted on the Caprivi Strip in order to garrison the area against any possibility that German forces — positioned in South West Africa — might be tempted to launch an invasion of British Central Africa. In the event nothing of this sort happened and the general disgust at such operational inertia saw many more Rhodesians take it upon themselves to enlist as individuals in the main European theatre.

While initially Britain had neither the resources nor the manpower to isolate the German colonies in Africa, both German East and West Africa were considered to be of strategic importance. Ports in both territories were regarded as probable threats to the allied war effort, since a handful were equipped with deep-water harbours that could host submarines and other large naval vessels. Also there was the possibility that the old German ambition — to link East and West Africa through British Central Africa — might be expedited on the back of a global war, allowing Germany to assume control of most of south, central and east Africa. Strategically this would have been a disaster, and would doubtless have precipitated a German victory not only in Europe, but in other pivotal theatres of the war too.

With all this in mind, the British placed a grievous burden on the shoulders of South Africa's Prime Minister Louis Botha. A request was made for South Africa to attend to a locally unpopular campaign to clear neighbouring South West Africa of its German garrison. Germany had morally and materially supported the Boers against the British during the Anglo-Boer War, and to many Afrikaners, Britain — not Germany — was the enemy. While neutrality in the war would have been acceptable to them, the expectation that they actually fight their German neighbours on behalf of the British was more than many could stomach.

Until that point, South Africa had been unwilling to absorb any specific Rhodesian military units into its command. Instead, Rhodesians were offered terms of service as part of a South African invasion force being prepared to attack German West Africa. A local rebellion that erupted in the Cape in October 1914 — when Boer commander Manie Maritz defected to the German side and threatened a counter invasion of the Union — helped to change Botha's mind. The 1st Rhodesia Regiment was quickly formed to assist the Union in what could have been another South African civil war, but fortunately that never happened. The Rhodesians were instead moved from Bloemfontein to the Cape in readiness for deployment to South West Africa. On Boxing Day 1915 the Rhodesian force landed in Walvis Bay as part of the greater South African Expeditionary Force.

Military historians have come to regard the South West Africa Campaign as a pioneering lesson in modern desert warfare. The salient points of South African strategy were adopted, and used by Erwin Rommel some 25 years later in the deserts of North Africa. The Germans had only lightly garrisoned the territory with a force of no more than 8 000 men, believing that the vast Namib Desert that surrounded the western seaboard would effectively prevent any land invasion from the east. They did not reckon on the sheer tenacity of South African forces and the visionary brilliance of 45-year-old Anglo-Boer War general Jan Christiaan Smuts. To a lesser extent the same was also true of General Louis Botha, the overall commander.

Pivotal to the campaign was the advent of mechanised warfare that made motorised transport available for the first time. While the Germans were preoccupied with supporting the Boer rebellion, Smuts was ensuring the availability of water for his troops by drilling a series of boreholes deep into the Namib sands. This allowed him to sustain a rapid motorised advance at a later stage.[3]

The campaign was divided into two zones of command: General Botha took Walvis Bay as his forward operating base and concentrated his column in the north; Smuts assumed his command in Luderitz and directed his assault south. With 45 000 troops he surprised and totally overwhelmed an astonished and hopelessly outnumbered German force. Simultaneously, Botha moved north in a series of rapid mobile engagements. He attacked the Germans at Jakalswater, forcing them back in pitched retreat. Then, without breaking his stride, he took the settlements of Otjimbingwe, Karibib, Friederiksfelde, Wilhelmsthal and Okahanja, before triumphantly entering Windhoek on 12 May 1915. Smuts captured the settlement of Keetmanshoop, and using mobile tactics, drove the Germans north to Windhoek, where they found Botha waiting. Thus ended a brilliantly planned and executed campaign.

In all this drama and glory, the 1st Rhodesia Regiment was used almost exclusively in a garrison role and saw action only once as part of a combined force that dealt with a German stand at Trekkopjies. This battle was brief and offered little more than a distraction from endless guard duty. The Regiment was pulled out of the territory in early July after the surrender of Windhoek, and returned to the Cape. Discontent over its almost complete exclusion from action resulted in successful calls for the regiment to be disbanded so that individuals could be released to enlist in the British Army before it was too late.

With the South African Expeditionary Force released from service in the South West Africa Campaign, attention could be focused on German East Africa. There a more equal and bruising clash of arms had been underway for some time. An anaemic allied force made up largely of local colonials lay under the death grip of a superior German garrison. Although the German force in East Africa was no larger than the Allied, it enjoyed the advantage of a higher quality of command. German General Paul Von Lettow-Vorbeck led a small army of some 2 000 German officers commanding 20 000 local black Askaris. These he used in a series of bold attacks aimed at regional allied targets including the strategically important Kenya/Uganda Railway. While bogged down in Europe there was little that Britain could do, while, with her hands full in South West Africa, South Africa could offer little assistance. But by the second half of 1915, with mopping up in South West Africa complete, an allied campaign in East Africa could at last be seriously mooted.

The command of the East African campaign was offered to Jan Smuts, who at first was reluctant to accept it thanks in part to the negative political effect the recent South African victory over Germany had had in the Union itself. However he finally agreed, and on 10 February 1916 he took command over a polyglot force representing almost the entire gamut of languages and cultures of the British Empire. There were troops from Britain itself, from Kenya, Nyasaland South Africa, the Gold Coast, Nigeria, India, Boer settlers from East Africa, Ugandans, Arabs, Belgians, Portuguese and natives from both Northern and Southern Rhodesia — and ,of course, a significant body of white Rhodesians themselves. This included two companies of BSA Policemen who fought with Norforce as Murray's column — named after their commander, Colonel R E Murray, DCM.

Of the Rhodesians, some moved from the disbanded 1st Rhodesia Regiment to the newly formed 2nd Rhodesian Regiment. With the prospect of genuine fighting ahead, morale in this unit was much higher. In early 1916, the Regiment travelled by train from Salisbury to Beira from where it sailed on to Mombasa on board the *SS Umzumbi*. In Mombasa it disembarked into an atmosphere of gloom.

The Allied force was moribund following an ill-conceived attack on a gap in the impregnable ramparts east of Mount Kilimanjaro that had, until then, blocked allied progress south into Tanganyika.

Ineffective reconnaissance had led South African troops into a virtual massacre that became known as the Salaita Hill Disaster. It was in the aftermath of this that Smuts assumed his command, and on 23 February set up his headquarters in Nairobi. The 2nd Rhodesia Regiment was promptly deployed into the Kilimanjaro operational area in preparation for the first of Smut's major offensives.

Until then Von Lettow-Vorbeck had fought the war somewhat in the style of Lawrence of Arabia, making excellent use of one of the few aspects of German colonial policy that could be viewed as enlightened. This was the recruitment and training of a large native force placed under the effective — and at times excellent — command of white German officers. Tanganyika territory was then a vast area of over 900 000 square kilometres of virtually unmapped territory. To move and mobilise effectively, required intimate local knowledge, and to this end Vorbeck used his black troops as guerrilla and reconnaissance units, able to track and ambush effectively, and otherwise move with complete familiarity through the countryside. With this advantage he succeeded with relative ease in dominating the battlefield — at least until he met his match in Jan Smuts.

Smuts was a master in his own right in the art of commando-style warfare. He could instinctively understand and predict Vorbeck's apparently random mobilisations and deployments. Unlike the static attrition of trench warfare in Europe, the East African campaign was a game of mobility, of chess board manoeuvres, feint and jab, lighting raids on supply lines, march, counter march, skirmish and ambush. Up-to-date intelligence was vital. The two generals matched one another in cunning and both made much use of small and mobile reconnaissance patrols.

Early in 1917 Smuts launched a combined allied assault that was effective in breaking up the cohesion of Vorbeck's force, but at a huge cost in casualties and an almost unimaginable degree of depredation. Transport animals died by the thousands from the bite of tsetse fly while almost unbelievably the ratio of disease to battle casualties stood at 31 to 1.4 Of the 58 000 troops engaged in the early offensives, 50 000 went down with malaria: many of whom died and many others never fully recovered.

With Von Lettow-Vorbeck now on the run, the war quickly degenerated into an exhausting slog of extensive marches, inconclusive contacts and hit-and-run guerrilla tactics. The Germans concluded early that the territory was lost, but maintained their small force of officers to force the allies to commit large numbers of men to what had become to them an enormous waste of resources, time and manpower.

In January 1917, Smuts was recalled in order to represent South Africa at the Imperial Conference. For the 2nd Rhodesia Regiment, the war ended that same month when it was withdrawn from East Africa. It had become so depleted that it could no longer function as a cohesive fighting force. About 150 fresh recruits per month were required to replace the losses, and clearly the small white population of Southern Rhodesia could not sustain this. The devastated regiment arrived back in Salisbury on 14 April 1917, leaving many of its number scattered in graves, hospitals and convalescent homes from Nairobi to the Cape. On 12 October the regiment was formally disbanded. In total, 783 Rhodesians had been killed, plus enormous numbers wounded or debilitated by disease. Two Victoria Crosses and 400 other decorations for conspicuous gallantry were awarded to Rhodesian troops.

Among the dead was the veteran scout, hunter and explorer Frederick Courtney Selous, one of the most august figures in early Rhodesian history. He was shot in the head by a sniper at Beho-Beho in Tanganyika while serving as a captain with the 25th Royal Fusiliers. He died on 4 January 1917 at the age of 65, just a few days before both Smuts and the 2nd Rhodesia Regiment left the stage. Although Selous did not serve with the Rhodesia Regiment, his death was a sad epilogue to the Rhodesian involvement in the campaign. He carried with him to a lonely grave a Distinguished Service Order for conspicuous gallantry and perhaps the most poignant collection of sights, sounds and memories that any white man of Africa could claim.

By late 1917, although Von Lettow-Vorbeck's army had withered beyond repair, he continued to fight with a remnant force of about 1 500 men. His resistance persisted until 18 November when, upon hearing news of the German defeat in Europe, he formally surrendered himself in Kenya and returned to Germany to national acclaim. He later served briefly as a deputy in the Reichstag, and tried to establish a conservative opposition to Hitler before retiring from war and politics in 1930. He lived on for another 34 years and ironically it was Jan Smuts who helped to establish a pension that saved the old general from penury.

As for Smuts himself, his career would continue to rise through many dimensions of higher statesmanship, but for the moment he returned to a very unsettled South Africa that would in turn unbalance the wider region including the two Rhodesias. This, however, is a story for another chapter.

The 2nd Rhodesia Regiment was eventually withdrawn from East Africa because it had suffered so many casualties from tropical diseases. It was decided that the war there could better be fought with Indian and African troops who were more immune to such diseases. Many volunteered for service with South African units on the Western Front, but along with their South African comrades they were virtually decimated during the attack on Wood Lane and during the defence of Delville Wood in the Battle of the Somme in 1916. After this the Kings Royal Rifle Corps actively recruited Rhodesian volunteers for service with its 2nd and 3rd Battalions. So many Rhodesians found their way into the regiment that a Rhodesian platoon was formed. This was later increased to two platoons. Despite heavy casualties both platoons maintained their existence with volunteers arriving regularly from home. The Kings Royal Rifle Corps, together with its Rhodesian element, later fought in Salonika. The Rhodesians maintained their ties with the KRRC and the badge of the Rhodesia Regiments was later based on their black Maltese Cross..

The use of black soldiers in World War-I presented whites in Rhodesia with a conundrum. It occurred to the planners that black troops ought not to be allowed to engage in battle against whites, be they German or otherwise, for reasons primarily symbolic. An unpalatable precedent might be set that could not be allowed to take root in the black man's mind. A less emotive but equally important reason was that the war would demand skilled blacks to serve as drivers, mechanics, clerks and messengers, and people trained to this level tended to be in perpetually short supply at home.

By the closing stages of the war manpower shortages on the front line had become so acute that a modification of policy was required. Drivers and scouts were recruited into the 2nd Southern Rhodesia Regiment, and by mid-1916 it was deemed necessary to raise a specific native regiment for combat deployment in East Africa. Originally the idea had been to recruit a force of 500 Matabele on the assumption that they had a more natural proclivity for war than their Mashona cousins. However this policy was in due course modified to include the Mashona and other smaller tribal groups. While all black men were poorly regarded as fighting material, the Mashona were held in particularly low esteem. When a second battalion of the Rhodesia Native Regiment was raised, recruiters made a point of trying to attract natives from north of the Zambezi, especially from Northern Rhodesia and Nyasaland.

The first 500 recruits were put through a minimal two month training course before being deployed directly to the German East African front. There they were sent into action with pioneer era Martini-Henri single shot carbines, although later they were issued with newer bolt-action Lee Metford rifles. If anybody had hoped that the first black Rhodesian soldiers would distinguish themselves on the battlefield, they were to be disappointed. Managing the men in the field proved difficult. If, for example, a chance sighting of an antelope or other wild animal happened, the marching formation would disintegrate as a wild fusillade was fired. Although this was aimed in the general direction of the wild animal, it usually proved more injurious to the troops themselves.[5]

Desertions were common, as was the looting of bodies and pillaging of local villages. Despite this, a natural feeling for the bush and the landscape did lend some opportunity for black troops to distinguish themselves, and a handful did. Three medals were awarded to the Rhodesia Native

Regiment, including one Distinguished Conduct Medal. The black Rhodesian troops also proved to be far superior to whites in resistance to disease. Moreover their powers of endurance under trying conditions were judged to be excellent.

On the whole the experiment was deemed a success, and in due course the two regiments were combined into a single Rhodesia Native Regiment. This unit became the first regular military formation in Southern Rhodesia. During the East Africa Campaign relatively few natives were killed — perhaps due to their late arrival. A total of 31 died and 116 were wounded

18

Responsible Government

Rhodesia for the Rhodesians

L ouis Botha was aware that his decision to bring South Africa into the war would be poorly received by at least half of the whites in his dominion. The attempted coup of October 1914 was relatively easily suppressed, but it was quickly followed by an armed uprising of nearly 10 000 angry Afrikaner nationalists. Soon afterwards the right-wing National Party was formed by James Barry Munnik Hertzog, who not long afterwards split from the government. He accused Botha of, among other things, working too closely with English speaking mine owners, of not doing enough to advance Dutch/Afrikaans as an official language, and not doing enough to enforce the separate development of blacks. Support for the National Party blossomed in the wake of the war and, under Hertzog, Afrikaner nationalism was quick to find dimension and focus.

Afrikaner nationalism was initially built on a fair foundation. Afrikaans speaking South Africans were undoubtedly discriminated against in a country defined by British money and English values. The Anglo-Boer War and the rinderpest had driven many into the cities, and because English speakers then ran almost all commercial enterprise, Afrikaners often had little success in obtaining jobs, loans or advancement. By the end of World War-I another exclusively Afrikaner organisation had taken root. This was the *Broederbond*, or Brotherhood, which was established by young professionals and clerics who believed that there was a need to protect and celebrate an eclipsed Afrikaans culture. It was this growing nationalism, directed against Anglophile institutions, that mostly unnerved Southern Rhodesians, by then drifting home from the war and giving thought to their own political future. It was also these very pressures that made Jan Smuts and the Union of South Africa such ardent suitors of the potential Rhodesian vote.

Although the war was behind them the anger surrounding it was still fierce, Smuts and Botha's ruling South Africa Party looked north. There they saw a significant block of English speaking voters who could prop up a waning liberal support base in South Africa. A secondary but still powerful influence was Jan Smuts' inherited dream of a union of states stretching north into the equatorial regions. World War-I had brought this dream a step closer by removing Germany from Africa, and bringing the two German territories of South West Africa and Tanganyika under South African and British control respectively.

The red stain of British imperial influence now covered a large swathe of the map of Africa. To the north of the Union of South Africa lay South West Africa — now mandated to South Africa by the League of Nations — Bechuanaland, the two Rhodesias and Nyasaland, Tanganyika, Kenya, Uganda, Sudan and Egypt. All that was lacking was the right brand of leadership to consolidate the units into a single, formidable political amalgamation. Was Smuts the man to do this? As a commander of Her

Majesty's forces, a member of the Imperial War Cabinet and founder of the League of Nations, he certainly had the courage, the intellectual breadth and the gravitas. Yet ironically he was to discover that his most challenging obstacle would be the obstreperous little nation that Rhodes himself had created.

The year 1918 held more for Southern Rhodesia than just the end of the Great War, and the beginning of the devastating world-wide influenza epidemic. It also brought the return of the long awaited Privy Council judgement on the question of land ownership. The closing of this ulcer would mark the final phase of a long squabble over who would rule the country; a country the destiny of which had so far occupied more imperial thought and resource than its net worth seemed at times to justify.

As the day of judgement approached, Jameson repeatedly assured an anxious board of directors that the work of the Privy Council was simply a formality. In his view a verdict would without question be returned in favour of the Company. His optimism was misplaced, however, for while the Council's judgment favoured neither the settlers nor the Company, it came initially as more of a bitter blow to the directors than it did to the settlers. Jameson, however, died on November 26 1917, so he was spared this final disappointment at the end of a sensational life.

What had begun as a dispute between the settlers and the Company had broadened to include the Aboriginal Protection Society on behalf of the natives, and then the Imperial Government on behalf of itself. After a 30-year silence on the matter, the Colonial Office weighed in at the last minute and declared its claim to the land. The Judicial Committee agreed to its claim. While it consented not to meddle in any property previously allocated by the Company, all land that remained unalienated after the date of judgement was to pass to the custodianship of the Crown. The Company was acknowledged only to have conquered and maintained the territory on behalf of the Crown.

Any hope that had been nurtured in the London Wall headquarters of the Company, for an end to this protracted nightmare, were crushed. The only ray of light came with a codicil that the Company could lodge a claim against the Crown for its accumulated administrative deficit. It was a very dim light, however, for the Judicial Committee went on to rule that its own mandate did not extend to naming a figure — which meant the matter had to be decided by other means.

On reflection, it is probable that the board of directors did not feel so hard done by. When all was said and done its land rights in Northern Rhodesia were not affected, neither was the combined railway system, nor the mineral rights for both territories. Clearly the losers in real terms were the settlers themselves — and even more so the natives.

It now became clear to the directors that there was no point in administering the country for any longer than was strictly necessary. The new question was what claim they could make against the Crown. While the Company submitted a bill to Whitehall of £8 million, it fell to Alfred Milner to establish on behalf of the Government what it considered to be a legitimate figure. To determine this, Milner in July 1919 appointed a commission chaired by former lawyer and Conservative Lord Chancellor of the Exchequer, Lord George Cave.

After endless delays the Cave Commission delivered its report in February 1921. Its recommendations came as yet another blow to the Company. Crown liability was fixed at £4.5 million with neither addition nor interest — which was much less than the board had hoped for. The Commission also ruled that from this sum should be deducted the value of land currently under use by the Company, as well as the value of land distributed for considerations other than cash. This last stipulation made it clear that the cronyism of the Jameson era had not been forgotten. The final value of these deductions was left to independent assessment, while the Company's counter claim for the value of public buildings and works was ignored. Finally the Cave Commission recommended that the Company repay £2 million in respect of advances made for expenses relating to the Matabele War.

The net result, minus variables such as Jameson's undocumented allocations of land and what land currently lay under Company use, was disappointing to say the least.

An indication of the how the monies to pay all this were to be raised by the Crown, came when Milner hinted that the Privy Council judgment would place 'further financial responsibilities' on the country itself'. This caused many in Southern Rhodesia to wonder whether they would be made to pay in cash for what they considered to be their own hard-fought rights and national assets.

A Legislative Council election held in 1920 proved to be a litmus test of public opinion in the aftermath of the Judicial Committee findings. The vote, not surprisingly, was a clean sweep by the Responsible Government Party. This gave clear notice — even before the Cave Commission delivered its findings — that the public mood was tilting sharply towards some sort of self-governing status.

Another interesting fact about the 1920 elections was the appearance of Ethel Tawse Jollie, as the first and only female elected representative of the colonial period. Ms Tawse Jollie was herself quick to point out how the fact of her election illustrated the political maturity of the Rhodesian electorate. Considering that the suffragette movement was still quite novel, and that Rhodesia was known for ultra conservatism, this was probably so. While her election certainly was remarkable for the period, she revealed certain personal stresses when she remarked further:

> Only exceptional circumstances justify a woman in entering a career where she sat at such
> a perpetual disadvantage [at the hands of her male peers].[1]

How much more, therefore, should Ethel Tawse Jollie have felt sympathy for the un-franchised native population who were themselves searching for landmarks in a blinding political sandstorm? The verdict of the Judicial Committee was punishing for both the settlers and the Company, but for the natives it had completely obliterated the thin hope that some might have held.

In fairness it ought to be said that the native population, as it stood in 1920, had no real basis upon which to expect political consideration in the abrupt transition to modern political government. They had a right to point out — assuming anyone was listening — that they had not asked for their circumstances to be so radically revolutionised. But revolution had come, and the facts had to be faced as they stood.

It was true also that a new generation of blacks was slowly beginning to emerge into the ostensible light of civilisation. Through the new medium of Christianity — and the often apocalyptic interpretations of it — some were finding a political voice.

The early government of Rhodesia was not as remote from its responsibilities towards the upliftment of the natives as later governments would be. As we have seen, Albert Grey put the matter to Booker T. Washington, betraying the fact that at least some thought was being given to the future of the native. However, so enormous was the black population in relation to the goodwill and resources available, that only a small number could be introduced by degrees to the new order. It would obviously be some time before even their voices were noticed, and a lot longer before any of them were taken seriously.

It is Ethel Tawse Jollie again who illustrates the benevolent, but eerily patronising tone of white-black entente in the 1920s. In her memoirs she describes their picturesque poverty thus:

> They remind one [early Rhodesian farmsteads] of homesteads in some of the states of
> America, only instead of the loose-limbed, soot black, blubber-lipped darkey with his fat
> wife in her turban of red and sloppy white dress, one sees the thin, athletic looking 'northern'
> boy, clad only in a sack with holes for his arms and head, but a far more picturesque figure
> than his American cousin.

If even a champion of extended suffrage such as Ms Tawse Jollie paused at the threshold of considering actual universal suffrage, it must certainly have seemed a very remote prospect indeed to the black man.

Ironically, it was the responsible government faction that enjoyed almost universal support from the educated black, mixed blood and Indian communities. Union with South Africa — with its oppressive race laws and rigid social order — boded ill for those non-whites in Rhodesia who held an opinion. Most were happier to steer clear of Pretoria and take their chances with the British Crown.

The election of 1920 defined the direction in which the white electorate wished to proceed, and the non-whites of the country were thought on the whole to agree. It was the journey towards this solution that defined politics in the post war years. In keeping with this preoccupation it became the first task of the 1920 Council to pass by an absolute majority a resolution to request self-government.

Despite their long-standing mutual antipathy, the population of Southern Rhodesia had become dependent on the deep purse of the Company. Many worried that the country would be unable to sustain itself as an independent economy if the break were made. It was the inability of the country to make money that had reduced the Company to the position that it was in, and before the Imperial Government would contemplate a grant of responsible government, the colony had to show some proof of its financial fitness.

For many settlers who were fearful of union with South Africa and yet pessimistic about responsible government, amalgamation with the north was still an attractive alternative. Unfortunately amalgamation had ceased to be an option for the Company. Since the publication of the Cave Report it had become clear to the board of directors that union with South Africa represented its best and only chance of viable restitution.

Jan Smuts, who had led both the Union and the South Africa Party since Botha's death in 1919, found — as he had feared — that the rise of Afrikaner nationalism had begun to threaten liberal dominance of South Africa. Smuts was determined to bring Southern Rhodesia into the Union, and to this end he launched an offensive not only to win over the British South Africa Company, but also the Southern Rhodesian voters themselves. Naturally the Company proved easy to seduce, but once again the electorate were coy. Smuts had the lavish means of a wealthy country at his disposal, but he also, unfortunately, was given to tough displays of hard line autocracy when dealing with labour dissent at home.

The Labour Party in South Africa, which was formed in 1909 as a counterpoint to Afrikaner militancy, attracted many English speaking mine workers, while the National Party drew in belligerent Afrikaners. The Labour Party gave rise in 1915 to the more extreme International Socialist League of South Africa, that in 1921 emerged as the South African Communist Party. In 1922 the tensions between opposing factions of white labour exploded into an orgy of violence that became known as the Rand Revolt or the 1922 Strike.

The essential cause of these disturbances was a crisis of viability faced by mine owners. White wages were prohibitive and white labour highly organised. To counteract this wages were reduced and the statutory colour bar lifted. The inevitable result was that blacks flooded into industry and whites were pushed out. As protest strikes were organised, militant Afrikaner nationalists assembled commandos and marched on Johannesburg where they barricaded the mines and declared the zone a white worker's republic.

To crush the revolt Smuts deployed force. He mobilised 20 000 troops together with tanks, artillery and even bomber aircraft in a show of strength that resulted in the deaths of 76 strikers. Five thousand arrests were made and four of the main strike leaders were tried, convicted and executed.

This episode not only sent shockwaves through the restive white unions of Rhodesia, but it also gave advocates of responsible government the perfect whip. To both labour and the gentrified middle classes of Rhodesia, the whole business was deplorable, and far removed from the undeniably more civilised politics north of the Limpopo.

But Smuts was also an urbane, persuasive and charismatic man. He was handsome in appearance, flavourful in prose and speech and, unusually among his compatriots, very fond of the British. As a lawyer, a head of state, a British Army general and an international statesman he was perfectly constituted to appeal to a British public. Such qualities were cruelly lacking in Herzog, and in fact in almost every other Afrikaner politician currently visible on the stage.

Smuts was confident that he would eventually strike a deal with the BSA Company, but until he did, he could not approach the settlers on the more delicate question of social compatibility. Discussions between him and the Company took on a cosy outward appearance that alarmed many in the Responsible Government Party. A rumour circulated that the Company was planning to sell the railway system to South Africa. If this was true, it would drag Rhodesia into an economic union whether she liked it or not.

The Responsible Government Association was formed in 1917 for the purpose of highlighting the anti-union and anti-amalgamation lobby. In 1919 Charles Coghlan joined, and in 1920 he led the party to victory in Legislative Assembly elections. In May of that year the Legislative Council sent the required majority resolution requesting home rule to a cautious Alfred Milner. Milner allowed that responsible government would be granted not later than October 1924 — provided that the Legislative Council could still field a majority and show some evidence of financial fitness.

This did not satisfy either Coghlan or the Council, and both replied with a strident request for responsible government immediately. Coghlan ended his speech before the dispatch of this resolution with a call to arms: Liberty in rags, he exhorted, was better than well-fed tutelage.

The Imperial Government's reply did not arrive until January the following year. Although welcoming the principal of responsible government, Whitehall suggested that the matter should remain on the table until the council had completed its current term. This would bring a solution into force no later than 24 October 1924. The Company was no less anxious, now that the Cave Report had settled its rights, for a speedy resolution to the matter. The directors were busy wooing Pretoria and it was rumoured that Smuts had been very generous.

In the interim a young Winston Churchill replaced Joseph Chamberlain as Colonial Secretary. Churchill brought new blood to the office and quickly proposed a commission of inquiry to look into the question of responsible government. The composition of the commission suggested that he already accepted responsible government as a fait accompli and was concerned only with its implementation.

Lord Buxton, a wealthy businessman and prominent politician who knew the people and countryside of Rhodesia well, chaired the commission. He was, incidentally, the grandson of Sir Thomas Buxton who had met the Matabele Embassy in London in the spring of 1889, on behalf of the Aboriginal Protection Society. Buxton was current chairman of the Africa Society and an ex-Governor General of South Africa. He was directed by the Colonial Office to recommend when and with what safeguards responsible government should be granted, and also to propose interim measures for phasing out Company rule, and to advise on the procedure of drafting a new constitution.

Buxton compiled a report that he submitted to the government in April 1921. In it he concluded that all parties — the settlers, the Imperial Government and the Company — had a duty to bring the present anomalous state of affairs to an end. He proposed that a draft constitution be put to a referendum no later than May 1922.

A Rhodesian delegation immediately travelled to London to contribute to a constitutional conference. They managed to steer agreements away from their own clear disadvantage, but much remained about the subsequent draft that did not please them. The terms were published in the press on 19 January 1922 to widespread derision. The *Rhodesia Herald* leader of that day had this to say:

> There is virtually nothing in the draft constitution which is calculated to arouse enthusiasm
> on the part of the public. It is far more remarkable for the reservations it imposes than for any
> privileges that are conferred on the electorate and administration of a self-governing
> Rhodesia.

Most notable in the draft constitution was the clause dealing with native administration. As had been implied from the very beginning, the Imperial Government was not prepared to trust a self-governing colony to attend equitably and fairly to the needs of the black population. The commissioner and all officials of the native department were to be appointed by a Crown governor with the necessary approval of the High Commissioner. Land set aside for native reserves would not be contested except in specific circumstances, and then only in exchange for other suitable land.

By dint of this and other signs of progress even the press now began to accept grudgingly that responsible government was the overriding preference of the day. Alfred Harrington, editor of the *Bulawayo Chronicle*, wrote:

> I believe that if any election was held in Rhodesia today on the straight issue of Responsible
> Government versus Union there would still be a big majority for Responsible Government
> despite General Smut's victory in the Union elections. None the less a large proportion of
> Responsible Government supporters admit that Union is inevitable at some time.

While union appeared not to be the peoples choice, it remained the preference of both the Imperial Government and the British South Africa Company, and as such it could not be ignored. The Company was even less impressed with the findings of the Buxton Commission than it had been with the Cave Commission, since it was now proposed that the Company recoup all its claims from the sale of un-alienated land. It added that although it was the right of the Company to expect as much for the land as possible, it was more importantly the right of the citizens to expect the same to be sold to them as cheaply as possible.

Smuts then entered into the most earnest phase of his diplomatic assault. His task was to convince a sceptical body of responsible government supporters, that union was not only in the best interests of the Company, but also in theirs. He had still not reached a firm agreement with the Company so he could not be specific, and Coghlan and his followers were so gripped by haste that they could not wait.

Smuts did what he could, and in the meantime invited a delegation from Rhodesia of pro- and anti-union delegates to Cape Town for talks. It was unfortunate for Smuts that the visit coincided with the Rand Revolt and its violent labour incidents. The acrimonious parliamentary sessions that followed, left the Rhodesians wondering what home they could find in such a fractured and irreconciled political union as this. Under pressure from Coghlan, Smuts promised that the political terms of union would be published no later than 30 July 1923. Thereafter it was agreed that a referendum would be held on 27 October to test public opinion.

The terms of union were unquestionably generous. Rhodesia was to be given preferred representation in the Union House of Assembly and the Senate, as well as liberal financial incentives. As a new 'province' of South Africa, Southern Rhodesia would have ten representatives — which was more than its economic weight and numbers deserved. This meant that 1200 votes in Rhodesia would have the same value as 2046 in Natal, and 2958 in the Transvaal.

Nevertheless, the fact still remained that ten members in a house of 140 was hardly a formula for influence. Rhodesia would have no independent voice, nor could it guarantee that Smuts would remain in office. Preferential terms of finance were also offered, although the territory would lose control over its largest source of revenue — the land — while having to submit to heavier taxation. Coghlan, and others aspiring to power, would have to forfeit possible cabinet positions for some watered down provincial council office. The most important inducement was a lowering of railway tariffs. This appealed to all Rhodesians, and unquestionably influenced a great many votes.

In essence the arrangement suggested that in the long term white government spread over a large area had a greater chance of survival than small and elitist settler communities surviving alone. It was a message that would reverberate for many years. The Union of South Africa was significantly more economically and socially advanced than Rhodesia, and Rhodesia would be free to take advantage of all that if she chose. Capital would flood in and stimulate growth, but on the other hand, Rhodesia would be drawn into the tense racial potboiler that was South Africa.

Further apparent advantages were the absorption of the civil service by Pretoria, while the vested rights of Rhodesians — whatever these might be — would be guaranteed under law. Black labour would not be recruited into the Union from Rhodesia, although no limitations could be placed on the movement of poor whites migrating north across the Limpopo. While northward migration and the dual language issue touched a raw nerve with Rhodesians, Smuts could hardly have pushed the larger measure through his own parliament without conceding to these.

To the British South Africa Company, Smuts was equally generous. Almost £7 million in cash was offered for administrative deficits, public works and railways, while the Company would retain all its other assets, including mineral, commercial and ranching rights. Indicating its pro-union position, the Colonial Office also offered to drop its rather thin claim of £2 million for war expenses.

Smuts rounded off his campaign by visiting Rhodesia a few weeks before the referendum. He toured extensively on an apparently apolitical programme, but nonetheless took every opportunity to speak in support of union. He endeared himself to many in Rhodesia by his unaffected humour, easy manner and gentle personal charisma.

The referendum was contested under conditions of drought, depression and continuing labour unrest in the south. Campaigning was brisk and cut the nation as evenly down the middle as any pundit could call. 'Family was divided against family, good friends became bitter enemies; never before was a campaign conducted with such vehemence.'[2]

On referendum day, polling was brisk but sombre. 14 856 votes were cast, and on 7 November the results were announced: for responsible government, 8774, for union 5989 and 93 papers spoilt.

Harrington of the *Rhodesia Herald*, like most Unionists, took the result on the chin. He wrote his last sanguine word on the subject in his leader of that day:

> We trust and believe that the 5 989 Rhodesians who voted for Union, assisted by the friendly co-operation of the 8 774 who voted for Responsible Government, will sink their differences and work harmoniously for Rhodesia.

19

First Parliament

In the aftermath of the referendum, both the lingering governance debate in Rhodesia and Rhodes' vision of a union from Cape to Cairo were laid to rest — at least for the time being. Smuts' fears were soon realised and he was swept out of office in the general election of 1924 by Barry Hertzog and his National Party. In due course many of the concerns that had helped win the day for responsible government in Rhodesia came to pass. Afrikaans joined English as an official language, Afrikaner interests were promoted above English, and the institutional isolation of non-whites began in earnest. The Rhodesian establishment had good reason to congratulate itself on a decision well made.

Meanwhile, Southern Rhodesia had its Letters Patent published on 24 September 1923. On 1 October the political transfer took place with the formal annexation of the territory to the crown. The first Governor was Sir John Chancellor. The British South Africa Company Administrator Sir Drummond Chaplin duly handed the administration over to him and left the political stage, bringing the curtain down on 34 years of Company rule.

Much of the BSA Company legacy remained, however, with the new administration taking over most of the structures of the old. The civil service transferred its loyalty with no more than the usual jitters of institutional workers regarding pensions, terms of service and the maintenance of their status. In fact the Company administrative machine, consisting on a local and national level of some 14.5 percent of the white population, was extremely competent and widely respected. This was in large part attributable to the work of Sir William Milton who had perhaps been guilty only of overstaffing the service. Now, not without some justification, civil servants feared for their job security once the public wage bill became the responsibility of a tax supported treasury. A powerful Public Service Association sought to protect their interests, but was noticeably excluded from a commission set up soon after the handover to assess the cost of the civil service to the tax payer — and ominously, to make recommendations.

Provision was made for a single legislature of 30 members, acting on a simple majority from which the Governor could appoint six members for various cabinet responsibilities. The Governor would be the constitutional head of state with powers that would to a large extent depend on the relationship he enjoyed with the new government. Sir John Chancellor appointed Charles Coghlan as interim premier pending Legislative Assembly elections. The franchise was limited to British subjects over 21 who had passed a literacy test and could prove assets worth at least £150 sterling, or an income of £100 per annum. This protected the vote against both poor whites and non-whites — with the exception of a handful of Indians, coloureds and one or two wealthy black farmers.

Coghlan did not stray far from the old BSA Company template in selecting his new cabinet. He chose two past Company treasurers, Percival Donald Fynn and Sir Francis Newton, as current

Treasurer and Colonial Secretary, responsible for Internal Affairs respectively. Major Robert Hudson became both Attorney General and Minister of Defence, William Mutter Leggate, an outspoken Scottish farmer, was given the Ministry of Agriculture. Howard Unwin Moffat, a descendent of the missionary family and former manager of the Bechuanaland Exploration Company, took over the Ministry of Mines and Public Works. Ethel Tawse Jollie, who might have expected a cabinet appointment by dint of hard work and unstinting support for Coghlan, was not rewarded. She did retain her Umtali seat with 404 votes. while Coghlan did the same in Bulawayo North with 830 votes. Coghlan it seems had very little respect for Ms T J whom he found both pushy and abrasive. He also did not care for rumours of her alcoholism — which was somewhat a case of the pot calling the kettle black. In an environment of male chauvinism Ms T J was excluded by her sex from membership of the Salisbury Club, which would probably have caused her to miss a majority of cabinet meetings.

Coghlan went directly to the country, preaching a doctrine of national unity in the interests of strong government. With the experiment in home rule so young and with many predicting — and indeed hoping — for its failure, it was advisable to make certain that old rivalries were deeply buried. In this manner, at least for a little while, the settler tendency to buck all authority was tamed. While he appealed to all sectors of Rhodesian society, Coghlan aimed his message particularly at the ex-unionists and the Argus Press.

Throughout the recent campaign the Argus had stumped for union with an almost obsessive zeal. When the time came for a realignment of national loyalties, the company seemed to suffer a most painful bout of indecision. RH Douglas, Editor of the *Rhodesia Herald*, wrote the following in a private letter to his superior John Martin.

What ought to be the policy of the *Herald* towards the Responsible Government Party?' He wrote. 'As you know, in recent months I have refrained from dwelling on the difficulties that confront Sir Charles Coghlan and the country, especially in matters of State finance...I have decided on a policy of doing or saying nothing needlessly to embarrass the new Ministry or add fuel to the flames of political strife.' He went on, however, to voice a concern that many in the ex-unionist camp shared as they pondered the future under Sir Charles. 'I have among my acquaintances men who have approached the Responsible Government leaders in the most friendly spirit. Without exception they have been shocked to learn that these leaders have not the vaguest notion of how they should, or intend to, proceed, in financial and other matters.

Home rule had indeed begun under grievous financial constraints. In response, Coghlan was able to tap into a well of universal discontent that could positively be relied on to unite the country. Nothing stirred up national feeling in Rhodesia quite like a real or imagined grievance against the British South Africa Company. In the sharing out of liability between the Company and the Imperial Government, Coghlan found just the whip that he needed to stir up a rich broth of anger.

The burden placed on Rhodesia itself was £2.3 million. Of this £300 000 was owed against loan advances made between 1921 and 1922, and the rest was the amount the British Government considered appropriate for the unalienated land plus building projects and other public works undertaken by the Company. It was assumed by Whitehall that the country itself would shoulder this burden.

This deal, fairly typical of Company/Imperial relations, gave notice that Rhodesia would be the only country in the British Empire to actually pay for the privilege of achieving self-government. Coghlan, an Irishman congenitally suited to finding fault with the British, was able to generate respectable momentum over this issue — which in turn prompted the *Rhodesia Herald* to dig him in the ribs with a final and ironic valediction to the old days:

> The necessity for prudence and caution is … [a lesson] that the people of Southern Rhodesia have yet to learn. Hitherto they have been free to clamour for extra expenditure on this scheme or that, often with success. They could do so with all the greater freedom because they knew that if the year closed with a deficit, the shortfall would be transferred to the exchequer of the Chartered Company.

Not much had changed since Rhodes and Beit dug deep into their pockets to quieten the post-Rebellion clamour. Although the landscape was not quite as barren, the mind-set persisted. It was doubtless unnerving for the settlers to face the future without the deep purse of the Company, and the happy prognostications that were floated were nothing more than the airy optimism of amateurs.

The Responsible Government Party, which had never been much more than a pressure group, was in due course dissolved and a new party formed. The Rhodesia Party was successful in attracting a strong membership from across the political spectrum, while a weak Labour Party stood as the only real opposition. Coghlan was careful to cobble together as broad a base of representation for the future Legislative Assembly as he could. In this spirit he tried to include the Labour Party by offering them an effective five seats in the House. He generously undertook not to run Rhodesia Party candidates in those constituencies, but Labour held out for eight seats and the deal collapsed. The country was divided into 15 two-member constituencies and the two parties took their campaigns to the people.

Huggins and the trials of Rhodesian tobacco

Included on the list of Rhodesia Party candidates was the name Godfrey Huggins. Huggins, a local surgeon and something of a m an-about-town, put his name into the hat for the Salisbury North seat with Treasurer Percival as his running partner. Both men were ex-unionists and committed imperialists, with Huggins in particular a debonair and affable character who was widely respected and well liked in the community. He was an obvious candidate for the exclusive civil service constituency that he hoped to represent.

Huggins was initially a reluctant candidate, but once persuaded to stand, his election to the backbenches set in motion a long and extremely important political chain reaction. As we introduce Huggins to the story of Rhodesia, it would perhaps not be overstating the importance of the moment to place him among the principal trio of men who served, guided and governed the country through its brief and troubled history. The first of these men was Cecil John Rhodes, the last would be Ian Douglas Smith, but the middle years of growth, prosperity and leisure belonged to the paternal, engaging and much loved Godfrey Huggins.

Godfrey Huggins arrived in Salisbury on 18 February 1911 after a long and not particularly enjoyable train journey from the Cape. As a new arrival he had found Cape Town surprisingly pleasant, as most newcomers did. He was soon entrained, however, for the long journey north. By the time he and his fellow passengers where drawing into the railhead at Kimberley, the last stop before the great north, Huggins began to wonder if he had not made a terrible mistake. Mafeking was a shock, the endless bushveld of Bechuanaland another, and the grubby little settlement of Bulawayo yet a third depressing encounter. The young surgeon was more than once tempted to turn back towards the Cape before he ventured beyond the point of no return.

However as the train steamed through the lush midlands his spirits were tempted to rise. Here at last was the signature heartland of Rhodesia, and although not quite the Cape, the colours of the landscape were soft, the atmosphere cool and the air sweet and dry. Finally he sensed that here was a place where a white man of cultivated manners and tweedish tastes might make himself at home.

Huggins' history until that point held a lot in common with the early life of Cecil John Rhodes. Huggins was the survivor of a chronic inner ear infection that as a child had been a source of ongoing trauma. It had compromised his early education and made the achievement of his fellowship in the Royal College of Surgeons more difficult than it might otherwise have been. It also, of course, left him with a permanent hearing impairment. Unlike Rhodes, however, it was not his health that brought Huggins to the colonies. Armed only with an unremarkable qualification, as he entered a strictly regulated and highly competitive fraternity, Huggins opted to chance his luck in the colonies simply as a means to get ahead.

So it was that Godfrey Huggins arrived in Rhodesia. He took up his locumship with the medical practice of Appleyard and Cheadle, and viewed his future with the amiable optimism that was so much part of his nature. In his duties he was conscientious, willing often to tramp or cycle the countryside and operate on a butcher's block. Everything he did, he did unfailingly well. He made friends quickly, and since his contracted term of service was only six months, this was fortunate. The pleasant Highveld winter had begun, and to Huggins it seemed that these would be very enjoyable months indeed.

He was soon put up for membership of the Salisbury Club and introduced to the leading political and commercial personalities of the capital. Even as an anonymous Londoner, and a journeyman surgeon to boot, he was gratified to be received in town as something of a celebrity. Indeed, among a population of 3 000 whites, Huggins could count himself among the few hundred civil servants and businessmen who made up the elite of Salisbury society.

By 1911 the capital was still at best a rustic provincial settlement spread over a wide expanse of veld. Roads were unpaved and grass uncut, but beneath the dust, the mud and the generally crude exterior, a certain energy and charm was unmistakable, Here and there the odd flourish of imperial dignity had begun to compete with ubiquitous red brick and corrugated iron. The former was most evident in such edifices as the imposing Town House and the splendid but rather isolated Queen Victoria Memorial Museum and Library that had been opened in 1902. Many of the wealthier private dwellings were situated in the area of the Administrator's residence. The main shopping precinct was Manica Road that offered a post office, a bank, several outfitters, as well as a variety of fancy goods and professional establishments serving a rapidly diversifying population.

Huggins was a highly personable gentleman with a crisp style and a dry sense of humour. The early respect accorded him by the community grew from his light, even-handed and levelheaded perspective on most matters. It therefore came as no surprise to his friends that, before his term of service with Cheadle and Applegate was up, he was offered a partnership. This was as much a personal coup for Huggins as it was an admission that Salisbury was critically short of competent medical doctors. Compliment or otherwise the offer put him in something of a dilemma. Should he return to London as had been his original intention, or throw his lot into a career in Rhodesia?

While doubtless drawn to a profession at the centre of things, Huggins could equally not dismiss the powerful attraction of life in the colonies. Professionally he was routinely performing procedures that would have been denied to him for years in London. He was a big fish in a small pond and there was a great deal to be said for that.

Apart from these practical considerations, a man of Huggins' background could rarely have hoped to replicate in Britain the social and sporting pursuits that he enjoyed in Salisbury. Recently he had purchased a horse and joined the hunt, although equestrian frolics in pursuit of a jackal hardly compared with the real thing. He played polo indifferently, but for his efforts found himself in the company of such local luminaries as Sir William Milton, the Company treasurer Sir Francis Newton, Judge John Watermeyer, Resident Commissioner Colonel Robert Burns-Begg, and many others of the honourable and military set. He also secured a commission in a mounted unit of the Southern Rhodesia Volunteer Regiment.

These and more were the advantages of life for the British middle class in Southern Rhodesia. Then, of course, there was the climate. As Rhodes had once observed in a moment of blatant understatement, 'it was one that a white man could tolerate'. Even the routine colonial race issue was not by any means as acrimonious as it would later become. Huggins saw blacks as part of the mission of a great empire, and still very much in the kindergarten of life. The eventual necessity of an accommodation with them did not mar in the slightest his view of the future.

Needless to say Huggins stayed in Rhodesia. His career included service during World War-I, first in England and then in Malta. Later he laboured through the great flu epidemic of 1918, that seemed to afflict Africa with particular fury. He married, remained a distant observer of politics and, as we have seen, found himself rather unwillingly seconded as a candidate for the Rhodesia Party in the first general election of the self-governing colony.

Thereafter he was drawn into the active life of parliament over many issues such as race, the civil service, immigration and health. Popular myth contends that he was at all times a reluctant politician, but this could not always have been the case. Even in the genteel little world of Rhodesian affairs of state it is unlikely that he could have risen to the highest office — and stuck to it through war and enormous change — without some compulsion to do so. His tools were his wit, charm and unfailing sense of humour. He rarely failed to find the heart of any matter, and if his oratory was always amusing, it was never without substance.

* * *

Huggins' career began as a result of Coghlan's desire to keep the next sitting of the House as bipartisan as possible. The young surgeon had successfully kept clear of the divisive union/responsible government debate, and had friends on both sides of the fence. Initially a prominent local haulier by the name of George Elcombe had targeted Salisbury north, and although a Rhodesia Party member, Elcombe was an unrepentant unionist and no particular friend of Coghlan's. Alarmed at the possibility of Elcombe leading the civil service constituency, Coghlan pondered his options and came to the conclusion that the genial and popular Godfrey Huggins was his man.

As had been expected the country formed up overwhelmingly behind the Rhodesia Party with Labour gaining no seats at all, and the opposition amounting to just four independents. Huggins took his seat on the backbenches while Percival Fynn took his in the cabinet. As Coghlan had hoped, the complexion of the first parliament reflected the composition of the white settler community fairly accurately. There was a clique of the upper management of such industries as the railways, a bloc of retired civil servants, a handful of white farmers, a few established leftists and a sprinkling of smaller businessmen and professionals. These, like Jewish lawyer Max Danziger — and of course Huggins himself — represented the townsmen and club men of their own ilk.

In a Legislative Assembly, uncertain of its role and rather lacking in colour, it fell to Huggins to entertain the members. He employed as usual his canny grasp of the essentials and his airy, deceptively humorous, but always unfailingly accurate oratory. Coghlan, although a shrewd and intuitive politician, could never have been regarded as charismatic. The loyalty he was owed by his party was entirely as a consequence of political necessity, and since Huggins harboured no aspirations to the premiership, he spoke with both candour and honesty. His opinion therefore was sought after, and it came to mark him as the only leader of genuine calibre in the House. He was also inclined to keep himself remote from the political bickering of others, while Coghlan, conversely, seemed to be a constant magnet for all kinds of controversy and unpleasantness.

With limited political experience, Coghlan was apt to be overly sensitive to criticism. When *Rhodesia Herald* editor R.H Douglas slated William Leggate's proposals for the disposal of unalienated land, Coghlan took personal umbrage. He wrote angrily to Argus General Manager John Martin, complaining that Douglas had launched his criticism before the government could adequately explain its proposals. He added darkly that a new daily newspaper might be licensed for the territory. In fairness to his editor, John Martin forwarded a copy of this letter to the *Rhodesia Herald* office.

Douglas was stung. In his view he had been consistently moderate in his criticism of the government, and it was also true that up until then he and Coghlan had been on the most cordial terms possible, bearing in mind their opposing positions on the field. Both were members of the Salisbury Club, and since Coghlan had moved up to Salisbury from Bulawayo, he had been a permanent resident of that establishment. He and Douglas had regularly been seen sharing a lunch table, although it was clear that Douglas was generally the more popular of the two in the gentleman's bar.

The issue came to an ugly head when Coghlan put William Leggate up for membership of the Club, only to find him blackballed by the Douglas faction. Although this was rectified in due course and Leggate welcomed as a member, Coghlan never entirely forgave Douglas that particular piece of villainy.

Like his Company predecessors, Coghlan placed a lot of importance on the question of European immigration. The post-war wave of new arrivals was being supported mainly on generous land grants and a growing agricultural industry. This being the case Northern and Southern Rhodesia, along with Nyasaland, Kenya and Uganda, were keen to promote their agricultural products and the agreeable prospects of their colony. A prime means to achieve this was presented by the British Empire Exhibition held in London between 1924 and 1925. The purpose of this event was to promote the Empire and its products and industries while also exploiting interest in empire migration. It was one of the most important events to occur during Coghlan's premiership.

The newly built Wembley, or Empire Stadium in northwest London, housed a vast array of stalls and displays from all over the Empire. An astonishing 27 million visitors were attracted and the first Royal Mail commemorative stamp was issued to mark the occasion. King George V opened the exhibition on 23 April 1924 to a huge display of British jingoism and flag waving, despite the spring weather being as damp as the domestic economy.

In a harbinger of things to come the event was marred somewhat by an attempted Indian boycott, prompted by the perceived ill treatment of Indian nationals in Kenya. In the event, only Gambia and Gibraltar of all the Empire family did not take part. Fifty-five other dominions, colonies and protectorates were represented and packed the auditoriums with their produce and ruddy-faced colonists. Lord Robert Baden-Powell mustered the largest Boy Scout Jamboree to date including, incidentally, several troops from India. Rhodesia's stall featured primarily her agricultural products including the perennials of cotton, maize and beef, but most importantly on this occasion the Virginia Gold tobacco upon which so much hope was pinned.

Unofficial Rhodesian representative at the event was the loquacious West Country baronet Sir Castel Richard Bourchier Wrey. Wrey was competing for the attention of British ex-servicemen with not only the other African colonies, but also with Australia, New Zealand and Canada. As a conscientious advocate, he was given to colourful exaggeration and more than a little overstatement.

'With luck and a modest reserve to tide over a possible bad season', he declared, 'there is a fortune in either cotton or tobacco growing in Southern Rhodesia. The soil is right, the climate is right, labour is plentiful and cheap, and there is an unlimited market for all we can produce.'

These prognostications were ostensibly backed up by a British tobacco expert who visited the Rhodesian exhibition, and after testing samples of leaf, stated that it would not so much be a question of finding markets for Rhodesian tobacco, but producing enough quality leaf to meet the demand. In

July 1925, the British Government also contributed to a potential boom in the industry by increasing the imperial preference by 50%. This meant that empire leaf was charged only three quarters of the standard import duty paid to the government by American producers.

The Empire Exhibition certainly did succeed in promoting interest in emigration to Southern Rhodesia, and among those attracted, most were interested in farming. Still by no means wholly established, agriculture in Southern Rhodesia was showing definite signs of promise.

Three million lbs of Virginia and 500 000 lbs of Turkish leaf had been produced in the 1921 season. This exceeded pre-war highs and introduced some cautious optimism into a fledgling industry. However, Rhodesian farms still covered only about 250 000 acres of land consisting of slightly over 2000 commercial properties. In 1921 Southern Rhodesian farmers and their dependents made up just 25% of the white population.[1] Cattle, maize and tobacco were emerging as the mainstays, although in 1923 potential was diversified when lowveld pioneer Murray MacDougall commissioned the first commercial irrigation furrow. This project was to take seven years of backbreaking labour to compete, but in 1931 it would reward the visionary Scotsman with the sight of water flowing onto the fields of what would become the mighty Triangle Sugar Estates. With tobacco confidently projected to boom, many sunk their life's savings into a tract of Mashonaland. It was unfortunate for these optimistic pioneers that no sooner had the doors shut on the Empire Exhibition than Rhodesian tobacco began to bear down on its second point of crisis.

This second collapse was due in no small part to unwarranted caution on the part of tobacco growers reacting to earlier disasters. All but a few of the growers had formed up under the umbrella of the Tobacco Warehouse, and as a cooperative body they entered into a three year contract with their main South African purchaser, the United Tobacco Company. The object of this arrangement was to ensure a market for future production at fixed prices according to grades. In theory this would take a lot of the guesswork out of marketing — and would allow farmers to concentrate on production in the sure knowledge that they would be paid a fair price. On paper the whole arrangement was very reasonable. However the onus was on the buyers to determine the grade of the leaf, and it was here that the tobacco producers revealed their naivety.

If it happened that a trace of green leaf could be found in a bale of tobacco, the price could be forced down. Buyers naturally began searching diligently until the merest hint of green was exposed. Thereupon a buyer would decry the grade and prices would duly collapse. There was a time when primary producers might have shrugged off this sort of canny monopolistic behaviour. The British South Africa Company had been a monopoly, and Rhodes' control of mining in Rhodesia had been an early example of this. However, to an elected legislature looking for ways to assert independence, such issues were manna.

It was Godfrey Huggins who first took up the topic, and in his debut speech he condemned price fixing and monopolistic practice by United Tobacco. Coghlan was always receptive to the anger of the common man, and although he was a solicitor and not particularly touched by agricultural issues, he was impressed by Huggins' call to action. He had built up his law practice on challenging the BSA Company and was as sensitive to the scent of exploitation as anybody. He promised to investigate tobacco marketing procedures in the colony and declared that he would pepper the tails of any offenders if it turned out that Huggins was right.

While widespread frustration did exist among growers, South Africa remained Rhodesia's only real market and rocking that particular boat made many a tobacco farmer nervous. Agriculture Minister William Leggate was himself a farmer and likewise sensitive to these concerns. He railed fitfully at the cavalier treatment of local farmers and fired the first shots in a hot war on the issue at a farmers meeting held in Arcturus in April 1924. His speech on the matter was later widely reported in the press.

The time had come, he told his audience of angry farmers, for the tobacco industry to strive to open new markets beyond South Africa. It was in this way alone that the Rhodesian tobacco industry would be able to 'get out of the hands of that monopoly, the United Tobacco Company, which this last few years has been considered by the tobacco growers of this country as a grievous burden'.[2]

This was strong language and United Tobacco was swift to react. Both Leggate and the *Rhodesia Herald* were threatened with legal action if the government's defamatory comments were not withdrawn. Those, of course, were innocent days when ministers of government were bound by the law, and it was therefore expected that Leggate would follow the hasty apology published by the *Rhodesia Herald* with one of his own. However he did no such thing, and instead composed a lengthy letter that the Rhodesia Herald only published with stated reservations. In it, Leggate not only reinforced his point but also drove home some further sobering facts about the state of the tobacco industry.

Prices for Rhodesian tobacco had dropped since the 1917-18 season when the crop fetched 9s 8d. per pound; in 1922-23 it brought only 8s 5d. In 1921 there were about 9 000 acres under Virginia tobacco but this had dropped to only about 6300 by the end of 1924. Clearly, Leggate surmised, tobacco growers were being squeezed out of production by monopolistic trading practices, and as things stood, these were primarily being perpetrated by United Tobacco. He also pointed out that tax-free dividends, paid to UTC shareholders between 1917 and 1923, were at a respectable level of between 25% and 30%, which was a clear indication that good profits were being made on Rhodesian tobacco in Johannesburg. Leggate concluded his barrage with a firm commitment to aid in every possible way the efforts of local producers to open up overseas markets. Clearly he had in mind the British market which remained the Holy Grail.

The result of Leggate's minor campaign was that United Tobacco refrained from any legal action and instead released the Tobacco Warehouse from its contract to the extent that 10% of the crop could be sold in Britain. Samples of Rhodesian leaf were immediately despatched to the United Kingdom where they were well received and fetched prices exceeding those being paid by South African buyers. Again optimistic but untested projections were made that it was not so much a question of finding a market for Rhodesian tobacco, as growing enough to fulfil the future demand.

At that time the United Kingdom was purchasing 94% of her tobacco from the United States with only a nominal supplement sourced from empire producers. Rhodesia had, however, put a foot in the door, and would edge that gap wider over the next few years.

Warnings were issued to South African tobacco buyers that contracts would not be renewed under previous terms. As the letters went out, growers sized up the British market with an ever-increasing sense of optimism. South African manufacturers were spurred into a willingness to pay more, but by then it was too late. Rhodesian farmers had once again begun to tilt dangerously towards the siren call of British marketeers.

Prices increased, immigration increased, and a higher acreage of land was put under tobacco. Tobacco barns became a feature of parts of the Mashonaland landscape where tobacco could never be grown. Each month the ignorant rushed to try their luck on any piece of earth where a plough could be sunk. Opening the Salisbury Agricultural Show of 1927, the Secretary of State for the Dominions — the Right Hon. Colonel LL Amery — chose for his speech the subject of increased British markets for Rhodesian Tobacco. He predicted that a time would come when Rhodesian tobacco producers would be growing more than the United Kingdom could absorb. That day of course lay far in the future and for the time being Britain could take up to ten times as much as local farmers were currently producing. While Amery's speech was clearly little less than delusional, the unworldly tobacco growers cheered the news and carried on with scarcely a backward glance.

It turned out, however, that the bonds of loyalty linking Britain to her traditional suppliers were not so easily broken. It was also true that Rhodesian Virginia leaf could never be authentic since it was not grown in Virginia. Accordingly, for the time being the Rhodesian product was used mainly to blend with American leaf and as such it did not compete in any significant way.

William Leggate followed Amery onto the podium that afternoon and to the beery appreciation of all who listened, added his own sprinkling of hazy facts to the brew. In 1924, he stated, tobacco exports to the United Kingdom amounted to just 700 000 lbs. The current stockpile now sitting in British warehouses was a staggering ten million lbs. What neither Leggate nor his audience appreciated was the vital difference between a product sitting on a warehouse floor and a product sold and paid for.

In the wake of the Empire Exhibition, representatives of the Imperial Tobacco Company, Britain's largest tobacco buyer, visited Rhodesia with a view to establishing a trade relationship, but again only as a counterpoise to American suppliers. In the event Imperial Tobacco over-purchased, which simply added to an already existing stockpile of Rhodesian tobacco. It was estimated that at current rates of usage, British manufacturers were sitting on at least seven years worth of supply. The 1927 crop, of which Leggate was so proud, had in fact been exported to England purely as a matter of speculation.

The Tobacco Warehouse had borrowed money to finance growers against the security of the crop, and at the same time retained agents in the United Kingdom to sell off the leaf. Try as they might, however, the 10 million lbs proved to be unsaleable. The bank was no longer willing to accept the leaf as security and called in the loan. The entire tobacco industry in Rhodesia was for the second time in its short history — and for largely the same reasons — brought to the brink. The bank could sell the huge stocks in London but would gain no significant return. Dumping the tobacco on the market at bankruptcy rates would also set a very poor precedent for Rhodesian tobacco in the future.

The already cash-strapped government of Rhodesia weighed in and assumed the Tobacco Warehouse's liability. The stockpile in London remained the property of the growers, but they collectively owed the government all they had received as an advance. But that was not all. The 1928 crop, estimated at 24 million lbs, was due on the auction floors soon, and by all accounts, it now had no market whatsoever.

The government again stepped in and advanced the Tobacco Warehouse a percentage per pound in the hope that some of this would be returned when the leaf was sold. This did not happen. While foreign speculators went on to make a fortune, Rhodesian growers survived by the slimmest of margins. The Government reeled under an outlay of over £500 000 from an average annual revenue of only £2.5 million.

Such were the trials of Rhodesian agriculture in the roaring twenties. Tobacco farmers, in truth, were the poor relations of an otherwise fairly steady farming economy. Maize and cattle remained the bedrock of a sector that faltered only rarely on its march to general prosperity.

It had, however, been a bold decision on the part of a small treasury to gamble so heavily on a relatively untested industry. This early faith of the Rhodesian Government betrayed great maturity, and would be amply justified in years to come.

20

First steps of black and white

By the standards of the time Charles Coghlan was not racially intolerant, nor was he unaware of how vulnerable and isolated the natives of Southern Rhodesia had been left by recent political events. He did not resent the powers reserved to the Crown regarding native administration, and in fact welcomed these as not only necessary, but for liberating he and his cabinet from any concerns related to the silent majority.

The Native Affairs Department was the body concerned with administering the native reserves, and although Coghlan held that portfolio, under the new administration, as under the old, it remained almost a state within a state. At the handover of government, white Rhodesians were given effective legislative control over internal affairs as they related to themselves, but the management of internal affairs as they related to blacks, was reserved by the Crown. This was operated through a chain of responsibility that ran from the Chief Native Commissioner through the Governor in Council to the High Commissioner in South Africa, and finally the Secretary of State. Coghlan and the cabinet were bypassed entirely.

Policy within the Native Affairs Department required the approval of the Governor, who in turn answered to the High Commissioner. Legislation with a direct bearing on the black population was subject to Imperial Government veto, although in practice this was almost never applied. In fact the British Government tried to remain as aloof as possible from the administration of the colony, and as a consequence, the Chief Native Commissioner found himself in a position of virtual autonomy. He administered law, justice and the collection of taxes in the native reserves, as an area of responsibility separate and distinct from that of the colony.

The obvious potential for abuse within this system was mitigated by the fact that the Native Affairs Department was manned by professional civil servants who took pride in their work. Their standards were high thanks to a colonial service recently invigorated by the humanising effect of World War-I. Individual native commissioners had come to view themselves less as the instruments of colonial repression than as a shield from the worst of its excesses. Their attitude tended to be paternal and their powers in the management and organisation of native affairs were very wide.

At the handover there were two provinces: Mashonaland and Matabeleland, within which were 32 native districts, each the responsibility of a native commissioner who managed several assistants responsible for the various sub-districts. Sub-districts were themselves divided into chiefdoms that comprised headmen's districts and kraals under kraal heads. Chiefs were selected according to what was understood to be local custom, after which they became in effect salaried administrative assistants to the native commissioners. They were invested with the authority of constables, paid an allowance, and were required to notify their commissioner of criminal activity as well as to publicise government orders, and aid in the collection of taxes. Headmen were appointed by the commissioner on the advice of the chiefs, who were assisted by kraal heads. The fundamental mandate of the department was the safeguarding of African interests, which in practice meant maintaining a framework of 'traditional life'.[1]

All this was symptomatic of an Imperial government attempting to evolve a deeper appreciation of the rights of indigenous peoples under British suzerainty. One of the many sea changes in global consciousness brought about by World War-I was a general revision of established colonial administration practices. After the war the colonial service was institutionalised, professionalised, and put largely in the hands of young, educated and socially conscious Britons. These men took overseas with them both training and a determination to create for their children — and the children of the empire as a whole — a better world. For a new generation of blacks gaining modern political acumen, this ought to have been a great comfort, but it many cases it was not. The Native Department structure was by necessity a system of micro-management that controlled every detail of life in the black communities. It was still based on the premise that black people were privates in the Rhodesian economic army — a rank that it was intended they should occupy for some time.

Certain key events in other parts of the region tended to confirm that the white man's view of Africa did not include active black participation at any level of government or administration. One event in particular deserves attention because of the spotlight that it shone on the roots of proto-political organisation in Africa.

On the morning of Sunday 24 January 1915, settlers and the administration of the Nyasaland Protectorate awoke to the astonishing news that a native uprising had taken place the night before, and indeed was still under way. A little known and apparently deranged Baptist cleric by the name of John Chilembwe had launched a rebellion that claimed the lives of three white estate workers, one of whom — William Jervis Livingstone — had been beheaded in the presence of his wife and children by a baying mob of disgruntled natives.

This of course was the official version. Although the mob was hardly baying, there was no denying that Livingstone had lost his head — a trophy that was later found appended to the altar of Chilembwe's Providence Industrial Mission Church. John Chilembwe himself was one of the first international, university-educated blacks of the region to return to his home colony with a vision of inclusive, secular, pan-African government. Deeply influenced by Booker T Washington, he at first adopted co-operation and accommodation as a means of political development, but found himself ignored, derided and frustrated. In due course his influences grew less conciliatory as it became clear to him that violence alone would galvanise the kind of attention that he demanded. He also realised that it was distinctly possible — if not inevitable — that he would be martyred the moment he launched a rebellion.

Significantly Chilembwe chose the church as his medium of political expression. As was the case in the United States, when the folly of the reconstruction period began to dawn on the Negro minority, political activism first took root first within the organisation of the Christian church. Chilembwe was initially influenced by radical Baptist missionary Joseph Booth, who swam against a fierce tide in central Africa by pressing the theme of 'Africa for the Africans'. He promulgated a theory, also subscribed to by Booker T Washington, that excessive book learning for emergent peoples would not serve them as well in the short term as the acquisition of industrial skills. Thus John Chilembwe founded the Providence Industrial Mission in the Chiradzuzlu district of Nyasaland, and from its pulpit preached both Christianity and the politics of majority rule and self-sufficiency.

It was with unseemly satisfaction that the colonial authorities hunted down and killed Chilembwe and most of his followers, and dynamited his church off the face of the earth. This was a lesson that depressed and set back a generation of Malawians as well as other black societies within earshot that were likewise governed from without by an insensitive white bureaucracy.

Black trade unionism in Nyasaland was comparatively advanced in relation to other colonies and protectorates in the region. In 1927, Nyasa trade unionists attempted to form a union among black workers in Southern Rhodesia using the template of the powerful South African Industrial and Commercial Workers Union, but the effort was premature and failed, largely upon the deportation of the two organisers. Rhodesian blacks were tentative, nervous and lacking in education compared to those in both Nyasaland and South Africa. It was a South African, Abraham Twala, who migrated north in 1923 and founded the Bantu Voters Association — the first wholly black political alliance to be formed in Southern Rhodesia.

One important result of the twin rebellions of 1896/7 had been the unequivocal shattering of tribal society in the face of wanted or unwanted European advancement. The Matabele — or Ndebele, as the name was tending more correctly to be used — had enjoyed a negotiated truce that allowed their political structures to remain valid and respected. The Mashona, on the other hand, were given no such privilege and were beaten soundly and thoroughly. Their leadership and political structures were decimated and their sense of cohesion severely undermined. As a result the Ndebele were quicker to recognise the potentialities offered by white society and take up the useful aspects of it, forming as they did the pre-cursors to modern political resistance. Early union organisation, social clubs and proto-political parties all emerged, if not always under Ndebele tutelage, then certainly predominantly in Bulawayo. It was, however, the Mashona who formed the bedrock of educated blacks in those early days, and despite their disadvantages, they quickly overtook the naturally conservative Ndebele in matters of education, religion, commerce and politics.

The fact remained that to acquire material wealth by means of commerce — as was the primary ambition of all — was an avenue tightly shut against the vast majority of blacks both Mashona and Ndebele. Thirty-five years had passed since the settler column had arrived in Mashonaland and the black generation that met it had largely died off. Of the new generation most lived and viewed life in a manner little different from their forefathers, although a few gifted amongst them stood out. They recognised that at the root of white predominance was wealth, and at the root of that wealth sat capital and education.

As was the case with John Chilembwe, the only means by which blacks in Rhodesia could educate themselves in those early days was through the various missionary societies. Christianity had been making quiet but steady progress in the colony and it was this Christian effort that scattered the first and vital seeds of knowledge. As the Reverend Thomson Samkange, one of the first of this new generation of blacks and the founder of an indigenous political dynasty, observed:

> The white man has changed our world … he has aroused in us the stirring of divine discontent. [Yet] it is amazing how little the white man really knows about the stirring of new life in the native peoples living in his midst.[2]

Of the 60 or more path-finding nationalists, active during the liberation struggle of the 1960s and 70s, 48 received at least their early education from missionary schools, and 18 were born to parents who were either black evangelists or missionary schoolteachers. Most were born between the wars and had no recollection of traditional autocracy or the catastrophic changes that had overtaken their patents.

The Portuguese introduced Christianity into central Africa in the 16th century, although modern missionary activity did not really commence until much later. A group of American Methodists arrived not long after the Matabele had entered the future Rhodesia themselves, but their efforts were premature — primarily because Mzilikazi was wary of whites after his early encounters with the Boers. In addition he had very little sympathy for any doctrine that might impose upon or challenge his own. Conditions were primitive and dangerous in Matabeleland at that time and the Methodists predictably fell victim to disease and isolation before withdrawing. All in all very little was achieved.

Mzilikazi had by then established his unlikely relationship with Robert Moffat, and it was to Moffat that he often looked for some explanation of the new and seditious philosophy of equality, forgiveness and mercy. Under the guidance of Moffat, the London Missionary Society's first problematic Matabeleland Mission was born. In its formative years this mission achieved as little as the Methodists of 20 years earlier. It was a thankless enterprise characterised more by continuous internecine squabbling than by any evangelical achievement. Again this was due to conditions of service, but also the frustration caused by the mission's inability to compete with Mzilikazi's centralist cult of monarchy. It was the hope of missionary WA Elliot in 1890 that:

> ... this [BSA] Company will bring about the downfall of this Matabele tyranny and the entrenchment of a more righteous government.'[3] ...and when, after the Matabele war of three years later, this was achieved...now is the grand chance of Christianising the Matabele.[4]

For the 30 years or so that the Matabele Mission at Inyati laboured without success, it did achieve at least one thing. When the invasion of the country by the white man commenced, the cultural shock for both black and white was lessened by the preparatory work done by the mission staff. Even after the first invasion, though, conversions were minimal. It was not until the spirit of the people had been wholly crushed by the unsuccessful rebellions that the population become susceptible to Christianity. Only then did missionary work begin to make significant and rapid inroads and mainly, again, in the field of education.

After the disappearance of the early Portuguese missions the Catholics returned to the country with the founding of Empandeni Mission in 1887. A second Jesuit group followed the Pioneer Column and established the famous Kutama Mission where a young black revolutionary by the name of Robert Gabriel Mugabe would later receive his early education. Missionaries from the South African Dutch Reformed Church opened Morgenster Mission in September 1891, and hardly two months later the Salvation Army began work on a mission in the Mazoe area. The American Board of Commissioners for Foreign Missions established an important station in Mount Selinda in 1893, and another in Chikore in 1895.

Seventh Day Adventists founded Solusi Mission in Matabeleland in 1894. The American Methodist Episcopal Church, under the famous Bishop Hartzell, founded Old Umtali Mission in 1898, while the Brethren in Christ opened the Matopo Mission in 1898. The South African General Mission began the Rusitu Mission north of Chipinga in 1897, and after 1898 a number of others, including the Presbyterian Church of SA, the Church of Sweden, the Swedish Free Church Mission, the Free Methodist Church and the South African Baptist Missionary Society, squeezed in to make their contribution to this burst of evangelical zeal.

One of the largest and most successful missionary schools was the Wesleyan Institute established in the Zvimba Chieftaincy of Lomagundi. The Nenguwo Institute — later renamed the Waddilove Institute — was established primarily to produce black teachers, catechists and evangelists, to widen the reach of education and the gospel. Perhaps the most famous black son of Waddilove was the Rev Thompson Samkange himself. In many ways he epitomised and set the standard for a progression of nationalists and revolutionaries to follow. Samkange, himself a moderate nationalist, was the nation's first substantive spokesman for black Rhodesian political aspiration.

Samkange was born with the name of Mushore in 1893 to a noble family steeped in traditional belief and practice. He his father, Mawodzewa, was a hunter of the Zvimba Chieftaincy, and while he tried to keep his son within the traditions of tribal life, Mushore was drawn — along with many others — to an exciting modern alternative. He was first exposed to literacy and Christianity when in his late teens he left his home area to find work in the cotton settlement of Gatooma. On his return he entered the Nenguwo Institute where he came under the influence of the pioneer Methodist missionary John White, and after baptism assumed the Christian name of Thompson.

Conditions at Nenguwo in the early part of the century were primitive, but also richly infused with liberation theology. Students from all over Rhodesia gathered and mingled in an atmosphere of intellectualism, discussion and debate. In this environment Samkange shone and it did not take long for him to attract attention. Having completed his standard six he became a teacher himself, and then married his spiritual and temporal partner, Grace Mano. Theirs was one of very few monogamous, Christian marriages amongst blacks at that time. In due course Grace Samkange grew into a social activist and political pioneer in her own right.

In 1922 Thompson was posted to the rough and ready mining town of Wankie where he was to conduct pastoral work among the mixed inhabitants of the worker's compounds. There he found life difficult and often degraded. Men from varied backgrounds, usually separated by great distances from their communities and families, laboured and lived for long periods in a state of virtual confinement. At that time he also began to find expression in the internal organisation of the Wesleyan Church, and at the 1922 Wesleyan Evangelists and Teachers Association Convention, Samkange was appointed General Secretary under the presidency of John White.

Emboldened by this, Samkange soon found himself contemplating far-reaching organisational changes in the church, including the founding of a body that would bring together representatives of all the protestant churches of Southern Rhodesia. John White was urged by Samkange to press on his executive the need for an exclusively African conference, and in 1927 the decision was made to appoint a special committee to set up the first African Missionary Conference.

The following year Samkange was accepted as a candidate for the ministry, and in Bulawayo he began the seven-year process of testing and examination. This was an important period for him, both for his rise within the church and for his interaction with urban African society — a society in which the embryo of radical black consciousness was beginning to gestate. In March 1928 the first Missionary Conference of Christian Natives was held with John White as chairman, and crucially with Samkange serving as secretary. The conference was supported by a wide spectrum of missionary societies and was a triumph for both Samkange personally and for the young movement of black intellectual consciousness as a whole.

Such were the successes of the early missionary societies in releasing the potential of a handful of blacks. Samkange and others were introduced to western styles of institutional organisation and administration through the Church. The Church in turn fostered the first quasi-political organisations that would in due course grow into support groups, representative associations, labour unions and eventually political parties.

For its part the British South Africa Company made a fair contribution by welcoming the missionaries into the country and giving them facilities and liberal grants of land. By 1925, upwards of 400 000 acres had been granted to various missionary bodies. The Company was prone to run foul of the settlers on various issues, and it certainly did so here. A majority of settlers felt no sympathy for this kind of work, which it was felt would simply produce a crop of troublesome black intellectuals. Most early colonists believed that educating the black man before he had become accustomed to the concept of work would be counter-productive. Efforts to do so were usually deemed further evidence of the dangerously misguided doctrine of the missions. Bishop Knight Bruce responded to relentless criticism of this nature with characteristic pragmatism:

We prefer to educate them to work by degrees rather that terrifying them with a stick into running about spasmodically for a month, tempting them to take the first opportunity to escape, and to take something of their master's with them.[5]

The missionaries persisted, and in the long term they prevailed. Although successes were few, and the process never easy, it was entirely thanks to the missions that by the turn of the 19th century a programme of regular schooling in the countryside existed at all. Early pupils were apt to reject Christian discipline, often choosing to return to kraal life after very limited exposure. Many expected some sort of material inducement for attending, or encouraging their children to attend, and lost interest very quickly when this was not forthcoming. By 1904 a total of only 180 blacks in the entire country were undergoing what might be termed a proper education.

Popular resistance to education in the villages was often centred on a rejection of Christianity, and this was thanks often to an overly dogmatic approach. As far as most missionary organisations were concerned the education of blacks was undertaken solely with a view to easing the process of conversion. Christian orthodoxy tended to offer very little scope for blacks to enter the faith by degrees, and literacy was offered for the purpose of reading the bible, and that alone.

Conversion was required to be total and to the absolute exclusion of every aspect of previous belief. To achieve this the church demanded much that the blacks were unwilling to give. Polygamy was the first and most obvious target, and yet to remove this most treasured institution was to compromise the core of the domestic economy. Many wives and many children made light work, which allowed the patriarch to claim and enjoy affluence. Drinking also encouraged the wrath of the missionaries, and yet this was as steeped in traditional practice as polygamy itself, and as visceral a pleasure as sex in a life where pleasures were few.

Early missionaries also failed to recognise the extent to which black spiritual practice and tradition influenced daily life. Few outsiders had any opportunity to observe indigenous spiritual practices, besides which the Mashona in particular are not known for visible ritual. This absence of outward worship helped those with an interest in doing so to downplay black standards of civilisation. Impoverished temples do not in themselves imply a diminished faith.

There were some advantages to be gained by the similarity of Christian doctrine to Mashona animism. Mwari is the one God. He is as aloof to mankind as God of the Old Testament — all-powerful, omnipresent and imponderable. If his name is not trumpeted at all times, it is not due to his absence but rather to an acceptance of his inexplicable nature. Below Mwari sits the Chaminuka spirit who occupies a status not dissimilar to that of an archangel, or a tier of the Holy Trinity. Below this are the tribal spirits who communicate through accredited mediums or priests. Under the tribal spirits are stationed more lowly spirits tethered to issues of purely local or family concern.

Christian structure, especially Catholic, lends itself to an easy transition from one set of beliefs to another, and to many blacks one set of beliefs did not necessarily exclude the other. To this day certain aspects of animism remain very important to the black interpretation of Christianity. It is also a fact that those who convert to Christianity with total and exclusive commitment will often revert to animism if it is suspected that they have become a victim of witchcraft or a bad omen.

While the monarchy was in place very few blacks would have been able to contemplate any kind of change from their traditional belief structures, but once the king had fallen, the system fell with him. Mwari did not disappear, but his keepers largely did. The only door open to blacks searching for an alternative system of belief belonged to the Christian Church. The Church offered forgiveness to the sinner and hope to the hopeless. In exchange for this, a convert needed only to drink the blood and eat the flesh of Christ.

When Baba White spoke of Jesus and His power to free one and all from fear and evil spirits, thus making it unnecessary for anyone to carry charms for this, that or the other thing…[and] when they were told that the only thing they were required to do in order to have the aid of Jesus was to repent, ask forgiveness for sins and own Him as their saviour, it seemed a cheap price to pay for an all-powerful and all-purpose charm.[6]

On the back of all this, an official native education policy began eventually to take shape. Despite it being informal for a long time, one or two guiding principals did emerge.

In the first instance the principal of initially encouraging practical skills among the blacks was revived. Again it was determined that this would be best achieved by placing emphasis on industrial training in contrast to the literary education that the missionaries preferred. It was agreed that limited education should be given on a broad front so that large numbers of blacks could be introduced to literacy at a measured pace. This was in marked contrast to the Northern Rhodesian approach of educating to a high level those few that showed particular promise. It was felt in Southern Rhodesia that this strategy would give rise to a superficial intellectualism that might overly impress those who did not have any education at all. Blacks would be given what education they needed to make them useful workers in agriculture and industry. Included in a standard syllabus would naturally be a working proficiency in the English language. It was the opinion of the Chief Native Commissioner of Mashonaland, expressed in his report of 1909, that:

> A purely literary education should not be considered for years to come; the policy should be
> to develop the native's natural proclivities first, on lines least likely to lead to any risk of
> clashing with Europeans.

One gets the impression that the Native Commissioner was not so much defining policy as striking a cautionary note. For black education to survive, it must be compliant with and compatible to its more resource rich cousin of white education.

A certain Sir James Graham conducted an inquiry into native affairs in 1911. Among his suggestions was that one of the principal responsibilities of the dominant race was to impart some measure of its own cultural heritage to the emerging race. This could be done without fear, he added, because the superior quality of white workmanship must always triumph, and in any case, for many years to come the instruction given to Africans would be of a simple and rudimentary nature.[7]

Over and above all this, it was clear that the colony had a lesser need for blacks aspiring to higher education than for a greater number of black teachers on various levels who could lead the majority forth out of ignorance. Clear also was the fact that without a plainly defined policy, the missionary organisations and a few under funded government schools could never satisfy the projected demand for native education.

Before 1924 the Legislative Assembly had given no formal consideration to the question of native education. This situation changed with the advent of Responsible Government, by which time the settler community had begun to engineer some sort of a unique and permanent identity with the country. With this came a realisation that racial dichotomy was going to be a fact of life. Ignoring the blacks might have been justified as the colony fought to establish itself, but by the 1920s it had become clear that a social blueprint would be necessary to effectively map the way forward. Key to this process was that black education had to come under formal government control. This marked the beginning of a period of willingness on the part of the white community to recognise blacks as partners — albeit very junior partners — in the enterprise of nationhood.

The 'native problem' had already to some degree been observed and recognised. Evidence of this can be found in some early aspects of law that clearly reflected white concern at growing black influence. The infamous Land Apportionment and Labour Conciliation Acts of the 1930s had not yet been drafted, but an informal convention dating from self-government divided the land of Southern Rhodesia between European and African.[8] Even in those days, however, the most interesting of the creeping articles of restrictive legislation were those related to sex.

A certain amount of sexual overlap along colour lines was to be expected during the early phases of the colony's development, and for want of respectable white women, the usage of black women was tolerated. It was frowned upon, of course, but so widely practised that it could hardly be effectively legislated against. As more white women arrived in the territory, miscegenation diminished to a fringe activity that typically occurred in the domestic environment. Thus developed a preference among housewives for male house servants in order to keep out of the home the most obvious source of temptation.

Those whites who openly took black wives and parented half-breed children, were never wholly welcomed back into the mainstream of white society. Even such a celebrated man as Frederick Courtney Selous fathered at least one mixed blood child. Selous was naturally very cautious about revealing this fact and it only emerged when his son James John Selous was discovered by the press in the 1960s and revealed to the public.

Until very recently, for a white woman in southern Africa to take a black husband was as unheard of as it was shocking. Ostracisation from the community rendered normal life for such a woman impossible. Such women needed either to seek refuge deep in black culture or simply to leave the territory altogether.

The law was reflective of this anomalous attitude, and in 1903 two important measures on the subject passed through the Legislative Assembly. The first was the Immorality Suppression Act that made extramarital intercourse between a black man and a white woman illegal — the maximum penalty for the man being five years and the woman two. The second was legislation that imposed the death penalty for attempted rape. Actual rape was already a capital offence, but enforcement was complicated by the fact that a white woman could not be reasonably expected to admit to having been raped by a black man. However to accuse a black man of attempting to rape her was much easier and from then on it was deemed sufficient to hang a man.

These laws, as well as a gamut of other less clearly defined racial anomalies, quickly alerted blacks to the lie of the land. The natives were still confined largely to Jameson era reserves and tolerated outside of these only when providing labour for white mining, agriculture and industry. Blacks looked increasingly to the missions and the equalising philosophy of Christ for salvation in the midst of such social ruin.

Mathew Zvimba was one of two brothers born to Chief Chigaga of the Zvimba lineage. As migrant workers in Salisbury in 1900, the two were converted to Christianity. Later Mathew was admitted to the Nenguwo Institute from where he emerged as a widely respected teacher and evangelist. Unlike others who meekly progressed through the lower strata of the church hierarchy, he displayed both an unmanageable pride and a bold and confrontational nature. To his assessors he was excellent material but tending towards the insolent. Such arresting character traits would become his signature, and over the years they would carry him far in his confrontation with the white religious and secular establishment.

In 1909 Mathew Zvimba established a branch of the Wesleyan Methodist Mission at his home kraal in Zvimba. There he committed himself to the work of educating and converting his people. He did so according to his own conscience, and with an independence of mind that brought him increasingly into conflict with the white missionaries under whom he nominally worked.

The Nenguwo Institute encouraged a degree of independence among its black catechists and teachers — but only a degree. A feature of the work of Rev Thompson Samkange was a gradual loosening of the paternal bonds in church society that tended to limit black responsibility. He fought from within the establishment while at all times remaining loyal to it. His confrontations with the white doyens of the Wesleyan church were on occasions sharp, but never permanently damaging. Mathew Zvimba, on the other hand, chose a directly confrontational stance that belonged strictly to another generation.

In 1915, the same year that John Chilembwe displayed the head of William Jervis Livingstone on his church altar, Zvimba openly rebelled in a manner somewhat less violent and established his own independent church. Zvimba's Original Church of the White Bird was reflective of a handful of breakaway denominations adhering loosely to the Ethiopianist principal. This was defined by psalm 68:31 that stated 'Ethiopia shall soon stretch forth its hands unto God.' This psalm, articulated towards the end of the 19th century by radical black emigrationists in the United States — a clique advocating the mass return of American Negroes to Africa — and in particular the founders of the African Methodist Episcopal Church, was a politico/religious rallying call presaging the role that Africa was destined to play in its own liberation and that of the global oppressed. It was adapted further within Africa itself to encompass a homegrown style of liberation theology, that served as a precursor to more orthodox patterns of political organisation. Within its various manifestations the first voices of violent opposition to white rule across colonial African began to be heard.

How much Mathew Zvimba was in tune with the intellectual tenor of this movement is open to question, but his response to white domination of both church and state in the colony was absolutely in keeping with the Ethiopianist spirit. He occupied the existing mission in his home area and chased away the white Wesleyan Methodists who were stationed there. In August of 1915 he applied to the local Native Commissioner for permission to formalise his church. The application was forwarded to the Chief Native Commissioner, who concluded from the evidence that Zvimba was an undesirable character and declined the application.

Zvimba ignored this decision and proceeded to found his church. On two occasions the Native Commissioner warned him that the government would not allow him to preach or teach independently, but he took no notice whatsoever. The commissioner thereupon circulated word throughout the surrounding community that Mathew Zvimba would not be permitted to preach or teach without European supervision. After much official agonising, however, the conclusion was reached that under the law there was very little that could be done and the matter was temporarily dropped.

Tension was increased when Zvimba supplanted the orthodox Christian saints with a list of heroes from the Zvimba district who had fallen during the Mashona rebellion. He listed these as the saints and martyrs of his new church. This act was immediately construed as sedition, which gave the authorities grounds to arrest and briefly detain him.

Author Stanlake Samkange recounts in barely fictional terms one of many myths that grew up around Mathew Zvimba:

> When a Native Commissioner is sent to Sinoia [Chinoyi], the Chief Native Commissioner in Salisbury summons him to his office and personally warns him to be careful how he handles Mathew Zvimba. When the Native Commissioner visited Chikaka to address a meeting, Matewu (Mathew) had his chair placed right next to the Native Commissioner and sat there, next to the Nkosi. They were all to scared to remove him … six men like him in this country would change this land completely.[10]

Mathew Zvimba's Original Church of the White Bird achieved little and was not widely supported, but it was important because it attempted more than just political agitation. It endeavoured to establish a synthesis of foreign and indigenous faiths, and to give the Christian religion its first localised identity. It also attempted to create a style of revolutionary iconography that might have had wider appeal to the depressed senses of a subject people if channels had existed to disseminate it more effectively.

21

Land and the native problem

Whatever intellectual and material constraints the emerging black intelligentsia grappled with, for the simple people of the countryside — and even the black working classes in the towns — it was the emblematic question of land that was at the centre of their sense of dispossession.

After the failure of mining, land had by the 1920s become as pivotal to the white economy as it was to the black. Under the surface of their passivity, the appropriation of the land rankled deeply in black society. Broadly unaware of this, the whites made their claim based on the two simple expedients of conquest and ability. They not only had the means to claim and keep the land, but they also had the skills and the will to manage it productively.

Whites generally held that subsistence agriculture was incompatible with progress and had no place in a modern economy. Apart from the few blacks who adopted modern methods, the majority had no choice but to accept and work around this philosophy. However, whites again had to recognise that the blacks were in their midst, would not go away, and that their status in the division of spoils needed to be established in law.

In 1925 a Land Commission report compiled by Sir Morris Carter was published. The Carter Commission was an impartial enquiry appointed by the Imperial Government to establish whether a need existed to amend the current laws on land tenure. The native reserves as they stood were a hangover from the Jameson era with only superficial adjustments having been made between 1914 and 1917. The assumption had been that as the blacks evolved into a kind of post-industrial-revolution proletariat, the reserves would eventually become irrelevant and disappear. This idea pre-supposed that having decided to leave the reserves, the blacks would automatically achieve the same rights as any other Rhodesian. This might have been the case in theory, inasmuch as no law actually restricted them from doing so, but in reality things were very different.

The blacks tended to cling more tenaciously to their rural heritage than had been expected, and when they did migrate to the cities it was usually temporarily, for the purpose of work. This was so primarily because whites were on the whole unwilling to countenance the long-term settlement of blacks within the predominantly white towns and cities. As a result the native reserves evolved from a short-term into a permanent solution, and as such their inadequacies became evident to all.

Questions were asked about what would happen if blacks did begin to spill out of the reserves and into the apparently neutral areas on the outside. Would they assimilate into suburban neighbourhoods, buy homes and start businesses? Would they be so audacious as to contemplate moving into white farming areas, or buying into and competing in the agricultural and mining sectors? To limit any possibility that they might, the parameters of black aspiration had to be clearly defined for the benefit of all.

The Carter Commission submitted recommendations to the Crown for the division of the country on strictly racial lines. It recommended that out of the 75 million acres of land outside the native reserves, a little over 48 million should be available for purchase by Europeans only, with just under seven million reserved for purchase by blacks only. The remaining 17 or so million would theoretically be available for allocation to either race. State and crown land made up the balance.

Seven million acres was at that time more than enough to accommodate those few blacks in a position to buy land, so this in itself was not where the problem lay. The problem was that white farming areas included almost the entire central watershed region that was not only made up of good, well watered and well drained soils, but also gave easy access to the railway. Maps of land delineations from the period strikingly illustrate this fact.

The second recommendation of the Carter Commission that militated heavily against blacks was the inclusion in white zones of every important urban centre in the country. This effectively meant that, notwithstanding being ushered into the cities to provide labour, blacks would never be able to buy or rent homes or business premises in any urban centre.

Both of these recommendations were couched in terms that might have led a casual observer to suppose that they were aimed mainly at protecting blacks from exploitation by whites. It was suggested that without proper control, capital-rich whites would quickly occupy the entire country to the detriment of poor blacks. Naturally this was not the whole truth, as Sir Robert Tredgold — later to be Federal Minister of Justice and Defence — reported in his memoirs, *The Rhodesia that was my Life*:

> I would concede that the legislation was intended to be in the interests of all the inhabitants, black or white, of the colony, but the Europeans had much more to gain from it than the Africans.[1]

Even this was a rather benign view of what was the first serious article of restrictive legislation contemplated in the country. Strangely, the Imperial Government agreed with the Carter Commission and, with very minor adjustments, the Act was debated in the Legislative Assembly and became law on 1 April 1931. By then Charles Coghlan was dead and had become the last member of the triumvirate of Jameson, Rhodes and he to be buried in the Matopos. It was his successor, H.U Moffat, who suffered the unenviable responsibility of signing into law this disreputable Act.

The Land Apportionment Act was to be followed in 1934 by the equally ambiguous Industrial Conciliation Act that sought to equalise industrial wages. Again this might have superficially suggested a measure of implied protection for black workers, but in reality it rendered them redundant in the workplace. The reason for this was that no white businessman would employ a black artisan for the same wages as a white if the latter was available. Since the vast majority of employers in the territory were white, the effect on the black workforce was obvious.

If, by 1933, educated blacks had any doubts as to the future direction of race relations in Rhodesia, these would soon be dispelled by the manifesto with which Godfrey Huggins wrested power from the Rhodesia Party. The intrigues that saw Huggins assume the premiership of Southern Rhodesia in 1933 are not within the scope of this chapter. For the moment it is his adaptation of the twin pyramid concept of separate development that concerns us.

In Rhodesia the global depression of the 1930s witnessed the rare phenomenon of unemployment among whites. For the first time the colony experienced unskilled and semi-skilled whites resorting to manual labour in a virtual food-for-work programme. Whites lacked the deeply rooted social support network that the blacks could rely on and as a consequence, poverty affected them deeply. This situation was exacerbated by the emergence of literate blacks, who were prepared to accept less pay for blue-collar work. Whites saw this kind of black competition as an infringement on the silent charter that had always guaranteed them better jobs, better pay and better conditions, and they clamoured to see these principals enshrined in something more substantial than a mere understanding. It was to this mood that Huggins responded as the general election of 1933 approached.

By then the Rhodesia Party had all but collapsed, and Huggins led a weak Reform Party along an uncertain road to power. Huggins himself was not a man given to passionate displays or intemperate language, and he articulated his philosophy quietly, allowing those more radical around him to analyse and redefine it as a suitable doctrine.

The concept of a twin pyramid system was no more than a refined version of what became South African apartheid. It was conceived to ensure separate development while, at the same time, allowing for a certain overlap to assist white industry in its need for labour. The theory was illustrated by the depiction of two equal-sized pyramids. The first was a white pyramid with a black base that it was hoped would become entirely white as a result of continued immigration. The second pyramid was black, representing a society pertaining only to blacks. The idea was for two wholly separate societies to exist without interdependence. For a black man pondering this concept, it would not have been difficult to predict what share of resources would accrue to each pyramid.

Huggins, as an intelligent man, could not seriously have imagined that this plan would work. It is indeed likely that he had no intention of ever trying to implement it, especially when it became clear to all that white industry would lose its ability to survive if it lost its supply of cheap black labour. By then the two economies were so deeply interdependent that they could never be cleanly separated — even if the genuine will to do so existed.

It is an indication of how profoundly the race conundrum affected whites that the idea was ever mooted at all. Later, more deeply layered legislation would settle white minds, but the native problem would never entirely be solved. From the safety of retirement Huggins later remarked:

> What it boiled down to was plain apartheid, with a lot of fancy bits to show how fair and realistic it was. The black and white pyramids were illustrated as being the same size: what was never defined was how far up the black pyramid went before the little white dot that represented real power came and sat on it.[2]

22

End of the first Parliament

The success or failure of the Southern Rhodesian agriculture industry was bound up in the fortunes of thousands of isolated individuals. These were the men and women of the British middle classes engaged in the thankless work of committing raw veld to production and primitive blacks to work; and the thin thread of viability that kept these backveld farmers alive was the railway system.

Like the British South Africa Company that owned it, Rhodesia Railways was yet another private monopoly. This was a fact that irritated not only the farmers, who relied on it, but also the settler community at large who usually needed very little persuasion to take issue with the Company. Most felt — with some justification — that something as fundamental as a railway system ought to be an asset of the country itself. In fairness to the BSA Company, the railway system had been built both cheaply and efficiently, thanks mainly to Rhodes' financial genius. So it was not entirely untoward that after the economic disaster the colony had proved to be, that the Company might expect a return on some aspect of its investment. Also, because it was still smarting from the mistreatment of old, the Company was not filled with regret and anxiety about riding the settlers of Southern Rhodesia as hard as it possibly could.

Coghlan came under intense pressure to find a solution to the problem and this was just the sort of fight he loved. The timing was also right because the political unity that he had inspired during his election campaign was beginning to fray, and while he still enjoyed broad support, it was becoming impossible for him to ignore a steady stream of defections. These came from such groups as the white working class, that had begun to find fault with the government's fiscal conservatism, and from farmers, miners and other miscellaneous backveld radicals who depended on transport for their livelihood.

Playing the Company card in a tight corner was almost always a sure winner, but on this particular occasion the lie of the land was decidedly in the Company's favour. The country could not afford to buy the railway system outright, and legally there was little that could be hoped for in an appeal to the Privy Council. Company ownership of the system had been enshrined in Letters Patent and was clearly indisputable.

Coghlan was therefore forced to approach the Company rather than attack it. This was something of a novelty for him and he was gratified to find that his old enemies were for once prepared to be reasonable. In 1926 he, Howard Moffat and John Downie — Leggate's replacement in the Agriculture Ministry — travelled to London and satisfyingly quickly arrived at an agreement with the board of directors.

While responsible government itself was Coghlan's signature achievement, the Railway Bill of 1927 was one of the few successes of his period in office. The Bill proposed the setting up an inter-territorial Railway Commission with representatives from the two Rhodesias and Bechuanaland. The object was to control the lines and limit the Company's dividends to an agreed sum. Godfrey Huggins was deeply involved and campaigned hard when the Bill ran into difficulties in the House. He advocated centralised supervision and stressed the importance of management building up a financial reserve to safeguard its ability to assume new credits. By specifying both maximum and minimum earnings, the bill hoped to strike a fair balance between investors and users. It was also hoped that this would free the Legislative Assembly from seeking Crown consent for minor railway legislation, including for the construction of additional district and branch lines. The bill passed with a majority of 22, and in 1927 became law.

Immigrants on immigration

As he began to grow in confidence, Huggins was among the first in the new Assembly to take up in earnest the perennial issue of white immigration. This was, besides anything to do with the Company, the second most complex issue that defined white Rhodesia. On the back of a surge of post war arrivals, Huggins was one of many who preached caution in selecting the type of white man the country needed. At that time, conditions of entry simply required capital of £50 and the ability to read and write a European language, which for the purpose of the law was defined as including Greek and Yiddish.[1] While Rhodesia was anxious to attract a healthy stream of fresh white blood, there was also a strong sense that not just any blood would do. It was widely felt that a certain exclusivity should be maintained in the interests of preserving standards.

A free passage scheme had been operated by the British Government between 1919 and 1922, and from over 8 000 people who left Britain for the colonies, some 6 000 made their way to South Africa — many of whom then continued north to Southern Rhodesia. As far as many in Rhodesia were concerned, however, most these assisted-passage types were not what was wanted in the country. In the years following World War-I the majority of newcomers to Rhodesia remained the younger sons of wealth and influence along with a strong showing of ex-regimental and naval types.

Many of the leaders of post World War-II Rhodesia entered the country during this period. A young Humphrey Gibbs, gentleman farmer and in due course the last Imperial Governor arrived in 1928. That same year Edgar Whitehead, another gentleman farmer and the man destined to be one of the most controversial prime ministers in Southern Rhodesia's history, came in. They were joined by other men of sinew and character, toughened by the harsh circumstances of war, who also chose to make Rhodesia their home. These were the ones who stuck with the regimen of labouring in the heat and dust, surviving bad seasons and chaotic fluctuations while persevering in building the cornerstones of the colonial economy.

Many others, however, were opportunists, remittance men or stoep farmers. It was these who cultivated their crops from around the bar at the Salisbury Club or the veranda of Meikles Hotel. They habitually drifted away when capital ran dry, or when a season or two of poor production diminished their interest. In the decade from 1921 to 1931, 20 000 immigrants arrived in the country against 14 000 who left.

Huggins led a campaign to discourage the practice of inviting men to immigrate for what he regarded as sentimental reasons — or purely for the sake of a whiter Rhodesia. He could see no sense in encouraging impoverished smallholders with backveld manners and limited capital to flood the country. In his view the future lay not with small producers — and certainly not with the subsistence production of the majority of black farmers — but with big producers who were invariably white men with capital, education and drive. The country needed public school men, men who had been, according to Huggins, fagged and flogged and had learned as a consequence how to command and obey. Black labour was cheap but ineffective, and the future did not depend on either it or a white proletariat, but with the white man of character and his expertise and capital.

In blunt disagreement with Huggins on this basic question was none other than Frank Johnson, who had lately been dusted down and revived as the jaded champion of the Rhodesian working classes. In a 1927 by-election, Johnson, by then a 62-year-old veteran, campaigned for his seat by calling for increased immigration across the board and a generally 'whiter' Rhodesia. He also demanded a dominion that would embrace both Rhodesias and a western port — said to include Walvis Bay in South West Africa. In the House, Johnson bayed on this theme with great humour and the lungs of the Bulls of Bashan, entertaining his fellow members with a rollicking oratory that offended as many of the Honourable & Military as it enlightened. This continued until the attention of the 30 members was abruptly torn away by the sudden death of Charles Coghlan. All matters of policy, no matter how urgent, were duly postponed in deference to the passing of a man of great stature in the brief tableau of white Rhodesian history.

Coghlan had in fact been ailing for some time and so his death did not come as a total surprise to the many who knew him. He had of late been delegating most of his cabinet duties to his personal friend and Minister of Mines, Howard Moffat. Since the heady days of responsible government, Coghlan had been struggling to keep his head above water and was reluctant to confront a decline in his personal popularity. A second political front called the Progressive Party had been formed around the handful of independents and a few Rhodesia Party malcontents, and although this was hardly an unnatural development, it had upset Coghlan deeply.

Time and again Coghlan was guilty of taking political attacks and the intrigues of office too personally. He also worried incessantly about the colony's ability to survive its poor financial health. His own financial circumstances were no better and he wondered how his wife and daughter would survive after his death. He took the unusual step of petitioning the government for pensions for the two — which were granted but did not ultimately cure his anxiety. Alcohol, meanwhile, adversely affected his heart, liver and blood pressure, and as Godfrey Huggins had frequently warned him he would, he collapsed with a cerebral haemorrhage and died on 9 April 1927.

With the utmost reluctance Howard Moffat succeeded Coghlan. Reluctant as it might have been, Moffat's appointment survived a minor controversy caused by the Governor, Sir John Chancellor, who tried to impose on the Cabinet his own choice of premier. Unlike his Northern Rhodesian counterpart, Chancellor wielded no real executive authority, except his power to appoint the premier and, on Coghlan's death, he was determined that he would appoint his sometime deputy, Judge Murray Bisset.

Moffat, a quiet and self-effacing man, was the only member of the cabinet to support the Governor's choice. The majority decision, however, followed Coghlan's wishes and Moffat was obliged to accept the premiership himself. This odd situation provoked a brief standoff between Cabinet and Governor that was of very little consequence other than to confirm the precedence of imperial non-involvement, and it had been naive of John Chancellor to suppose otherwise.

Notwithstanding misgivings about his own ability to govern, Moffat took the oath of office and completed the first Parliament. Thereafter he led the Rhodesia Party in a general election for the second Parliament, and after the vote was counted, he was probably more surprised than any to have lost only four seats to a still largely unconstituted opposition. The old Labour Party gained one seat at the expense of the independents, leaving only one independent in the House. Frank Johnson, despite packing political meetings throughout the capital, lost his seat after which he quit the colony and returned home to retirement in Britain.

The Moffat era

Howard Moffat's premiership was marked by no particular achievement and might easily have slipped into history unnoticed had it not been for the Land Apportionment Act. The spirit of the Act has already been discussed, and although that spirit might have reflected the mood of his administration and the broad Rhodesian attitude to the race question, it did not reflect the character of Howard Moffat.

Moffat thought of himself as an assimilationist and a race liberal, and in this regard his pedigree stood above reproach. He was a grandson of the great egalitarian missionary Robert Moffat, and was born in Kuruman in the northern Cape at one of the earliest and most august of all southern African missionary institutions. Racial division was certainly not the political epitaph that Moffat would have preferred, and not at all what he had hoped for the future of the colony. However, to comment on his premiership is to either not to comment at all or to comment on the defining issue of race.

By the end of the 1920s race had come to occupy a prominent place in the thoughts and attitudes of both white and black Rhodesians. This corresponded with a preoccupation on the part of the Imperial Government as to how a future accommodation between the races could be achieved. The white settlers in British Africa and the British Government looked at the issue from sharply opposing perspectives. Consequently the ramifications of the race question would freeze both in a cold war that would endure right up to the end of the colonial period.

Calls by the likes of Godfrey Huggins and Frank Johnson for a whiter Rhodesia were in many ways deceptive. While there was a strong interest in populating the colony with the correct type of white man, there were other priorities too. Whites were beginning to take note of the fact that a population explosion was underway in black society. Left unchecked, this would see whites so vastly outnumbered that they would soon be overwhelmed. By the 1930s both races had arguably acquired enough knowledge of the other to accept their mutual incompatibility. This led many whites to the conclusion that the status quo would not ultimately be to their advantage.

While most whites at the time would have denied it, those who gave the matter serious thought recognised the inevitability that southern, central and east Africa was one day destined to pass to the stewardship of the black man. Upon this point the Imperial Government was in firm agreement. By that equation, therefore, the white man was to assure his future in the region would be the substance of another half century or more of fertile debate. The Land Apportionment Act was an early attempt by Southern Rhodesian whites to provide an answer to this question, but few truly believed that it could ever be a permanent solution.

One of the main problems bedevilling southern Africa after World War-I was the fact that it was rarely the wise or the prudent who defined race policy. It tended rather to be those who regarded blacks as no more than a cheap labour resource and an ignorant appendage to society. To these the fundamental requirement of a successful race policy would be the physical separation of blacks with the exception of those required as labour by farming and industry. The aspirations, opinions, requirements and future of the blacks themselves rarely seemed to intrude on the debate.

By the beginning of the 1930s, it was unfortunate, but also wholly understandable that, although blacks were beginning to understand the language of modern life, few among them were poised or articulate enough to mount any credible political challenge. Informal labour movements, social clubs and pressure groups were emerging, but they maintained a supplicated view of white rule, believing it to be insuperable, and contenting themselves with trying by what means were available to limit its excesses. Whites broadly took this attitude to mean that tranquillity and a general acceptance of white governance reigned in black society.

The pattern of white immigration that followed World War-I also did nothing to bridge the gulf. Although agriculture attracted a handful of immigrants, the majority moved into the cities and began to form the bedrock of white, urban, middle-class society. New arrivals moved into commerce, industry, trade and the professions while laying the foundations of the pleasant suburban aspects that came so much to characterise Rhodesia. Ensconced thus, they did nothing in spirit or kind to reach out to the many blacks who worked for them or watched them from the sidelines. Almost without exception an immigrant employed a black person or two as gardener, cook, houseboy, office messenger, cleaner, teaboy or nanny. Few newcomers were sufficiently interested to learn the native language and fewer still took the trouble to look at the lives of blacks in the reserves, and certainly not in the burgeoning urban squatter settlements. Most simply tried to replicate their old lives and enjoy the old comforts of home on an African landscape.

Taken from the point of view of the professionals of the Native Affairs Department, the 'native problem' was not a local political question, but rather a broader social conundrum impacting the latter-day British Empire as a whole. The suggestion that a black man might have the capacity to govern on any level would have been as outlandish as proposing that he wear a bowler hat to work and carry *The Times* under his arm. The black man of Rhodesia, like the aborigines of Australia, the natives of New Guinea or the Eskimos of Canada were children of the Empire, for whom the heirs to the British Crown were indefinitely responsible. To even the most sensitive and enlightened of these men, the possibility of majority rule was ludicrous.

Native Affairs officials came no more sensitive than author Kenneth Bradley, who governed a huge district in the Fort Jameson area of Northern Rhodesia. Bradley's view of colonialism was simple. 'All that we can say, with the gift of hindsight, is that we were still handing out democracy in doses as big as we thought the Africans could take instead of giving them the bottle.'[2] By the 1920s, however, blacks were beginning to reach out for the bottle, and even more worrying for the settlers, the Imperial Government was apparently considering giving it to them.

The latest British territorial acquisition in Africa had been the 1919 takeover of German East Africa — or Tanganyika as it became known. After Germany's defeat in World War-I, Britain was granted a mandate by the League of Nations to govern under terms very different from past practice. The new governing mandate was deemed to be a 'sacred trust'. To the settlers of the region this alarming choice of words had an even more disturbing corollary. The premise of these post-war mandates — for Tanganyika was just one of a handful — was to: '…nurture and protect peoples not yet able to stand by themselves under the strenuous conditions of the modern world.'[3]

Policy such as this marked an abrupt turn in a direction that British African settlers did not want to contemplate. The fire was fuelled a little more when, in 1923, Victor Cavendish, the 9th Duke of Devonshire and serving Colonial Secretary, addressed the House of Commons over the status of Indians in Kenya.

In the case of Kenya, Indians had been introduced in large numbers for the purpose of railway construction and general labour. They were active and resourceful and so prospered and multiplied, until by the mid 1920s they far outnumbered whites. Whites, for the usual reasons, claimed an unequal share of government, against which the Indians threatened to rebel. The Imperial Government feared this would exacerbate tensions in an already restive India, and in an effort to reassert imperial responsibility Cavendish had this to say:

> Primarily Kenya is an African territory, and His Majesty's Government think it necessary definitely to record their considered opinion that the interests of the African natives must be paramount, and that if, and when, those interests and the interests of the immigrant races should conflict, the former should prevail. Obviously, the interests of the other communities, European, Indian or Arab, must severally be safeguarded . . . . But in the administration of Kenya His Majesty's Government regard themselves as exercising a trust on behalf of the

African population, and they are unable to delegate or share this trust, the object of which may be defined as the protection and advancement of the native races.[4]

This statement sent a collective shudder down the spine of colonial Africa. The Imperial Government had delivered advance warning that if — and in fact when — the time came for His Majesty's Government to decide between the rights of the natives and the rights of its nationals abroad, its sympathies would ultimately lie with the natives. If acceptable local solutions were not found in the meanwhile, the future for white settlement in Africa lay under black government.

Devonshire's comments set in motion one of many revivals of the question of a general amalgamation, or the formation of a grand union of African colonies under the Union Jack. This time the colonies of east and central Africa were thrown into one another's arms, in contemplation of a marriage deemed necessary, to find safety in numbers. Once again Rhodes' dream flickered into focus, and again the lack of a leader of his stature thwarted it. The British Government remained preoccupied with a multiplicity of minor problems until the Colonial Office did what indecisive British secretariats were wont to do and appointed a Commission of Inquiry.

The Commission was constituted in 1927 under the chairmanship of Privy Councillor and Member for Norwich, Sir Edward Hilton-Young. The Hilton-Young Commission was given reasonably wide terms of reference that exceeded the simple examination of a union of British colonies, and included a comprehensive examination of the implications of imperial trusteeship itself. Serving on the Commission were Sir George Schuster, educationist and financial advisor to the Indian Government, and J.H. Oldham, Secretary of the International Missionary Council.

The Commission did not produce a report until 1929, at which point the findings were made public. These turned out to be to be another disappointment to the settler communities. While recommending a central authority of some sort for Kenya, Uganda and Tanganyika, the report in the end concluded that this group of territories did not have sufficient communication with the two Rhodesias or Nyasaland for all six to be included in a single union. It went on to give separate consideration to the possibility of closer union between the two Rhodesias and Nyasaland, but found against such a proposal, on the grounds that the centre of authority for an amalgamation of the three would naturally be Salisbury. The members felt that it would be unwise to recommend that any new areas containing a large black population be put under the government of Southern Rhodesia until that administration had demonstrated its ability to cope with the complex race problems that already confronted it.

Many Rhodesians were inclined to ask what solution there could possibly be to this ongoing dilemma. How could the aspirations of a large population of blacks groping hesitantly towards civilisation, and a smaller white population manifestly enjoying the rewards of civilisation, be reconciled? The Hilton-Young Commission attempted to provide the answer.

That one part of the community should govern the whole, or that one class should make laws for another, was deemed unacceptable. As articulated by African American writer and abolitionist Frederick Douglass with Ulster in mind: 'Protestants are excellent people, but it would not be wise for Catholics to depend entirely on them to look after their rights and interests'.[5] According to the Commission, the foundation and only sure defence of freedom lay in a proper balance of interests and powers in the State. In the future, settler capital and expertise was to be regarded solely in the context of its ability to develop native potential. White political domination would be tolerated only for so long as it served to bring the blacks forward sufficiently to assume their full share of government.

The popular argument against this — that without European oversight civilisation could not exist at all in Africa — was rejected. Ultimately minority government could only be tenable if it was built on the rule of justice that had the support and loyalty of the majority. So long as the systems of government in the settler colonies rested not on consent, but on privilege, they could not be indefinitely supported.

The Imperial solution was what came to be known as the Dual Mandate. Insofar as it was to be applied to south and south-central Africa, the Dual Mandate was to be an arrangement whereby both racial groups would be encouraged to develop their own self-governing institutions in their own separate areas — all under the guidance of the Imperial Government. Pivotal to the success of such a policy was the understanding that central authority would remain vested in the Crown until majority rule was deemed possible. Implicit was the fact that the white minority could never aspire to independence under the current form of administration. It seemed at the time that the Hilton Young Commission envisaged equal power sharing, but the obvious reality was that this also represented intrinsic and unequal privilege. However it went on to allude to the hope that if this dual policy could be followed to its natural conclusion, it would be:

> …only a question of time before the natives will have to be admitted to a share in the whole government which fairly balances that accorded to the immigrant communities ... if white and black can some day meet on equal terms, intellectually, socially and economically, the racial and economic antagonisms may be merged in a community of interests which will admit of some form of free representative government.[6]

This, then, was the blueprint for racial cohabitation, and the British Government expected its dependencies in Africa to adopt it if they hoped for any kind of future on the continent.

In June 1930, as this new vision of an egalitarian African society was sinking in, the white settlers of Africa were dealt a second blow. The new Secretary of State for the Colonies, Sydney Webb — the first Baron Passfield and a social reformer and prominent member of the Fabian Society — twisted the knife a little harder by publishing on behalf of the Colonial Office a paper he called Memorandum on Native Policy in East Africa.[7]

Passfield cut to the quick of the Southern Rhodesian race dilemma when he announced that certain experiments in land equality were to be tried in the Northern Rhodesia Protectorate whereby, in the disposal of Crown lands, there would be opportunity for acquisition without regard to race, colour or religion. The native in Northern Rhodesia was to be 'effectively and economically free to work, in accordance with his own wish, either in production in the reserves or as an individual producer upon his own plot of land, or in employment for wages.'[8] In layman's terms, this meant that black advancement was to be considered the first priority of any future race policy in the protectorate.

All this stung Southern Rhodesian whites deeply. Foremost they felt that the Hilton Young Commission had deliberately slighted a native policy that most in the country felt was making great strides, particularly in education, employment and the general encouragement of black development. And to such criticism they had a pre-prepared answer.

In Southern Rhodesia the framework of a dual race policy had actually been in place since the turn of the century. The 1894 and 1898 Orders in Council had both clearly stressed the right of blacks to fair and equitable land wherein 'native law' would apply. The appointment of a Secretary for Native Affairs, whose activities were subject to the Imperial veto, was also in keeping with the perceived need for a separate system of government for blacks. Furthermore, the Land Apportionment Act defined clearly the separate areas that both white and black would occupy. Why then was Southern Rhodesian race policy singled out for such obloquy?

Perhaps the views of N.H Wilson, Native Affairs official and leading race ideologue in both the Moffat and Huggins governments, might help to illustrate how far the official Rhodesian line strayed from the Imperial ideal.

We are in the country because we represent a higher civilisation, because we are better men. It is our only excuse for having taken the land. For us to turn round now and ask the natives to help us in directing the government of ourselves is ridiculous.[9]

The primary motivation for separate development, therefore, was not to nurture the capacity of the black man to govern, but to keep him at arms length — temporarily in principal but permanently if at all possible.

Beyond this, most whites in Southern Rhodesia were willing to be as pragmatic as necessary, so long as the final solution did not affect their generation. At all costs the standards of civilisation grafted onto the African landscape should be allowed to grow without hindrance. But in the absence of permanent white supervision, there were few whites that held out much hope. One had, after all, only to look at Liberia and Haiti among others to see precisely what black government would mean for the future of western, Christian, civilised standards.

23

Miscegenation

T he root of white race policy was fear — fear of economic competition, fear of political infiltration, fear of the barely understood fuzzy wuzzy, and of a voodoo society that existed entirely beyond their ken. Most of all, however, there existed a fear of social contamination. Nothing defined Rhodesian race consciousness quite as starkly as the dark and pervasive fear of miscegenation. In between the white and black populations of Rhodesia, occupying a shady hinterland of acrimony and denial, existed the coloureds and half-castes who were by-products of early frontier life. If one can picture the rigidity of race consciousness, prevalent in both white and black society at that time, it is not difficult then to understand the depth of emotion generated by this particular dilemma.

In the early years of the territory, coloureds and half-castes, although both of mixed blood, were distinct from one another. Coloureds were those of South African origin who had followed in the footsteps of the Pioneer Column, and in whose veins ran a mixture of all the races of the Cape. Half-castes, on the other hand, were the children of local women and pioneer men. In the order of things, Cape Coloureds presented no particular threat. They were found to be competent in the lower trades and provided a stopgap when local labour was unavailable. Half-castes usually existed as isolated individuals living with their black mothers in kraals, villages or labour compounds. They did not fit into the commonly understood doctrines of racial purity and, as such, they presented the administration with a unique conundrum.

The coloured population grew as a consequence of continued immigration and natural increase, which in itself did not unduly perturb local officialdom. If coloured people posed any problems, they tended to be in the matter of assigning them a social status. The difficulty in this lay in the fact that a class of poor whites existed in urban areas, who tended to live in close commerce with coloureds and openly mingled with them. The number of whites who, through misfortune, alcohol, low mental capacity or poor judgement, had come to be regarded as coloured, roughly equalled those coloureds who by dint of their industry, prosperity and light skin colour had come to be regarded as white. Coloureds were as anxious to be classified white as whites were anxious not to be classified as coloured. In this issue the stakes were high. The social advancement gained by a coloured individual or family, upon being classified as white, was as immeasurable as the devastation suffered by an ostensibly white family being classified as coloured. For a white child to be marked as coloured and assigned to a non-white school was a life-scarring catastrophe for both the child and its parents.

Not surprisingly then, instances of confusion and crossover were very common. This happened because of pale skinned coloureds, dark skinned whites and the notoriously haphazard methods employed to determined who was who. It could be the nap of the hair, the width and dimension of the nose or the fullness of the lips. As the newly- arrived Lord Baden-Powell observed of his first sight of a Rhodesian white: '…Boer hat, flannel shirt, and breeches — so sunburnt that it is hard at first to tell whether the man is English, half-caste, or light Kaffir.'

Classification was rigorously applied in schools, where the decision of whether a child was white or coloured was most frequently left to individual school committees. Evidence that a family mixed socially, or associated closely with coloureds, could be taken as proof that the children of the family were coloured. If one or other of the parents was deemed coloured it might not matter how Caucasian in appearance a child was. It often occurred that one child from a particular family would be accepted into a white school and another excluded. Neither was it uncommon for a child to be classified as white, then re-classified as coloured at adolescence, only to be white again as an adult. The exclusion of coloureds from white schools was reflected in the exclusion of blacks from coloured schools. There would be an outcry from parents in each case, apprehensive that their own contagion not be overstated, and anxious also that their children be placed as high up the race ladder as their complexion permitted.

An interesting case was that of Grace Maggio who lived in the Ardbennie industrial suburb of Salisbury where many coloured families lived. Grace attended Parktown white school, but was identified by her classmates as coloured and as such was ostracised. Her mother admitted to the school authorities that her grandparents were Cape Coloured, but was quick to point out that her husband was classified white and was serving in the armed forces as a European. It was decided after much heart searching that Grace was racially suspect. She was duly removed from Parktown and offered an alternative place in a coloured school. Mrs Maggio appealed to the Director of Education, but was told that in the interests of the child herself — whose life at a white school would clearly be unbearable — the decision could not be reversed. Mrs Maggio would not accept this and Grace was taken out of school altogether.[1]

An official census published in 1930 revealed that the coloured population in the country numbered upwards of 3 000 individuals. Much of this increase had latterly been due to the absorption of first generation half-castes. Coloureds were mainly urban dwellers so the problem of half-castes moved from the countryside into the towns. It was the Moffat government that found itself with the responsibility of dealing with it, and having for the first time to publicly address the thorny issue of miscegenation.

To get an idea just how thorny an issue it was, Moffat needed only to listen to the comments of his Chief Native Commissioner, Charles Bullock. Bullock observed that hybridisation, however gradual, could not be contemplated with equanimity. It was deemed appropriate that each race should develop (and be given full opportunities to develop) according to the potentialities that lie within its biological inheritance.[2]

Bullock was not alone in expressing concern for what was increasingly being seen as a social disease. The growing presence of coloured people in the cities, their ambiguous placement in the racial order, their grim squatter settlements and their tendency to draw in the less desirable half-caste element, brought the issue very much to the fore of government debate. The threat that a mixed blood community presented to white society was ill defined and naturally had greater moral overtones than political. The merging of half-castes into the coloured population made it difficult to deny that a moral disease was abroad. It was a disease that was deeply embedded and condemned almost as widely as it was practised.

When the Land Apportionment Act divided society into cultural zones, the coloureds were neither acknowledged nor offered any specific cantonments of their own. They found themselves equally segregated from both black and white with no quarter being offered by either. They were established in shanty settlements, in all of the main towns with the largest concentrations in Bulawayo. They were subject to the same petty racism as blacks and had their mobility and aspirations limited in the same way. When it came to facilities such as hospitals, prisons and schools, they were lumped in with blacks which offended them as much as it did the blacks. They were not black, and did not mix freely with blacks, but there was literally no place for them in contemporary Rhodesian society. Until a niche was found, the coloureds were likely to suffer even more than the blacks from the debilitating isolation of being stateless within society.

While the coloureds were maligned, it was not lost on those of clean conscience that they were the symptom and not the disease. As early as 1910 the police began collecting information on miscegenation. As data was compared it was noted with some relief that the main offenders tended to be Greek and Jewish shopkeepers, of whom three main types were identified. Firstly there was the minority who cohabited openly with black women; a larger number who regularly visited women in their huts; and finally a majority who made regular and covert use of local black prostitutes.

The first group was obviously regarded as the most dangerous because of the frankness of their behaviour and the number of children they produced. While casual fraternisation was not openly encouraged, it was accepted, especially in the countryside. But relationships of a settled nature were not to be so liberally tolerated. Since miscegenation between white men and black women was not illegal, there was nothing specific that could be done, although the police and Native Affairs officials were not above subjecting offenders to petty victimisation. Mixed race marriages required the consent of the Director of Native Affairs and this gave officials of his department ample opportunity to make their prejudices known. As part of an obligatory period of reflection on the gravity of their intentions, such men were often subjected to enormous pressure to reconsider — which in the end many of them did.

From 1914 onwards, the Native Affairs Department required that all headmen keep a list of white men known to be interfering with local women, and another of all mixed race births. Much thought was also given to the fate of half-caste children, still living as natives in the tribal areas. By 1930, these were thought to number about 700 individuals under the age of 15.

Local women's groups were the first to bring the situation to the attention of the government, and campaigned vigorously for laws that would force white fathers to acknowledge and accept responsibility for their half-caste children. It goes without saying that this met with strong resistance from a male dominated Cabinet and Assembly. Any legislation to limit or ban miscegenation — or indeed any type of pressure that would compel white men to recognise their half-caste offspring — would expose some highly placed in Rhodesian society to public ridicule, the threat of blackmail, or both.

While it was careful to point no fingers, the government was prepared to acknowledge the problem up to a point. Moffat in particular pressed for action to rescue half-caste children from, as he put it, being thrust back into the lower culture of their mother's people. He believed, as did many others, that white genetic material, no matter how degenerate, was still superior to any other, and as a matter of conscience its product had to be acknowledged.

After much hand wringing and nervous backward glances, the best the government could muster was a tepid series of responses. Where a half-caste child lived in a family with mixed race parents, the government did not interfere. Where the father was estranged, the child in almost every case lived with its black mother. A policy of removal was tried before it was in due course lost in a maze of official denial. Only a handful of children were ultimately institutionalised under Christian care, where they grew up with European values.

Moffat then proposed founding separate schools and orphanages specifically for half-caste children. However, the costs involved, and the denial factor prevalent in the male establishment, saw the issued fudged and in the end swept under the carpet. There was a strong feeling in government that creating institutions specifically for coloured people would necessitate the acknowledgement of a third racial group, that would further complicate an already tangled race dynamic. It is understandable that any public discussion on the question of miscegenation was apt to make legislators very uncomfortable, for many were rural men themselves, and it was possible that if the light became too bright, it would shine not only on Greeks and Jews.

So it was that children who were 'rescued' from black environments tended to be dealt with on an informal basis that dispensed with the need for any overt acknowledgement. The criterion was the attitude of the father and not necessarily the condition of the child. If a father wished to have the child removed from the mother's care, it was. Thereafter the mother would play no further part in nurturing the child and obviously would be encouraged never to see it again. Any legislation on the table tended to remain there while the office of the Attorney General pondered the problem of an acceptable definition for miscegenation. Years went by with no laws drafted. In the end, the simplest solution seemed to be not to awaken any differences in the minds of half-caste children and to allow them to be naturally absorbed into black society. The policy, therefore, was no policy at all. If a father chose to intervene, he did so at his own peril and as a consequence, few did.

In time, coloureds and half-castes established a separate identity, and found a niche in industry where they formed a socio-economic stratum of their own. They thrived on their status as social pariahs, creating both a vernacular unique to themselves and an outlook on life that was as colourful as it was irrepressible.

White concerns that coloured communities — both vice-ridden and violent — were often justified. However this merely added to a general atmosphere of mischief and humour that surrounded coloureds and that — paradoxically — endeared them to many whites. Politically, coloureds tended to veer to the right, but this was mainly as a consequence of contempt for blacks rather than any love of whites. In time the coloureds became an accepted part of the troubled racial dynamic of Rhodesia, although their acceptance has never been without a strain of poignant regret.

24

White man's burden

Much closer to home was the complex relationship that whites had with their domestic servants. An almost obsessive determination on the part of white immigrants to make use of this most colonial of facilities, was born out of two factors.

The first was that in the Victorian and post–Victorian period the goal of reaching the upper middle classes was best defined by the maintenance of domestic service. This ideal was imported to the colonies, where the facility became available to just about anyone with a white skin. In Rhodesia, this was profoundly felt due to the large number of British working class folk who brought with them their particularly well-developed class-consciousness. All of them were able on some level to look down on another social group, most for the first time in their lives. By 1904 the trend had taken such firm root that each European household employed on average more than two domestic servants. Some families would have more than this but there were very few that had none.

The second factor was that — in time — the prestige of keeping domestic servants became inverted to imply that, if a white family did not have servants, then they were living in a state of poverty. Therefore, even when the direst economic circumstances prevailed, at least one servant would be retained in a white household for no better reason than to keep up appearances.

By the 1930s, domestic service had come to define a large part of the celebrated Rhodesian way of life. White women were liberated from basic housework which made the isolation of their frontier lives a great deal more bearable. The colonial lifestyle also meant suburban living on a grand scale, characterised by large houses and extensive holdings. In time Rhodesian flower gardens were celebrated throughout the Empire. Expansive properties, spacious homes and extensive sporting facilities — these were but a few of the many luxuries that could never have been possible without cheap and willing domestic labour.

However, domestic service was governed by the strictest rules of propriety. In the 1950s a set of Federal guidelines for new immigrants was careful to include instructions to housewives without experience of employing male servants. They were cautioned never to allow their female children to exhibit any degree of nakedness, and for themselves to make their own beds, wash their own underwear and avoid appearing in a state of casual undress. This implied that women and female children were at some sort of risk at the hands of male servants. In theory this should have been so, for according to the census of 1911 there were over 6 000 African men living in Salisbury, but only 300 women. It was not inconceivable, then, that a lonely black man far from his home might be tempted by this most forbidden fruit. However statistics do not bear this out, and incidents of rape or indecent conduct, although they occurred, were very rare.

Nonetheless, under the Immorality Suppression Ordinance Acts of 1903 and 1916, an act of indecency — as applied to a black man — included raising or opening any window, blind, screen or the fly of a privy in order to observe any woman nude or semi-nude. This was later expanded to include voyeurism, flirtation and even friendships.

Whatever the mutual complicity, suspicion or risks that might have characterised the relationships between master and servant, it was in this quarter that the only real contact between the races took place. Social convention forbade any shared interaction and , even those men who married or cohabitated with black women, tended to do so with overtones of concubinage and chattel rather than in monogamy. The general view that each race held of the other was formed primarily at this point of contact.

Gertrude Page, who authored such Rhodesian classics as *The Rhodesian* and *Winding Paths*, wrote of a black house servant being beaten for wiping his nose on a tea towel. It is probable that incidents like this did occur, but they were certainly rare and never institutionalised. Doris Lessing in her novel *The Grass is Singing* went to some length to portray the unlikely tyranny of an unschooled white mistresses against her black servant. Hylda Richards in her portrayal of early farm life in Rhodesia draws more on the humour of mutual misunderstanding, than the usual attempts to depict the blacks as nose picking, belly rubbing incompetents, or the white housewife as a monster.

> In this way I came upon darkest Africa, Hylda Richards wrote. [1] She admitted that she did not like blacks, but having emigrated from lower middle class England, she apparently never contemplated living without them.
>
> My hope of being the beloved mistress of devoted slaves received a nasty shock. Like all newcomers I tried to spoil them so they would love me, but they just took advantage of my kindness and made incredible demands ...[2]

Far from ruling with an iron fist, Richards found it impossible to make any impact on her servants at all. A black male's disinclination to be bossed around by a woman of any colour found expression in many ways. Theft, indifference, lies, evasions and dumb insolence, were all weapons in a domestic servant's arsenal. To deliberately lay sauce and pickles for breakfast and marmalade for dinner, to sweep around things and spot no cobwebs, to give notice the moment he realises he cannot adequately train his mistress — all these drove the inexperienced Richards to distraction.[3]

Most labour — be it domestic, industrial or agricultural — was migrant. A kaleidoscope of different languages and cultures merged in the workplace. Sir Granville Orde-Brown, who was at the turn of the century the undisputed Empire expert on race and race relations, remarked on the subject:

> ... it is easy to hear a camp-fire conversation in the Congo during which conditions in the Union, Rhodesia, Tanganyika and Angola are all discussed and commented upon; brothers from Nyasaland may go one to the north and the other to the south, and may be trusted to compare their experiences on their return home.[4]

A language unique to migrant labour evolved which came to be known as Chilapalapa, or more commonly 'kitchen kaffir'. Chilapalapa was a pidgin language combining the common elements of a number of native dialects with occasional flourishes of English and Afrikaans. It developed initially on the Witwatersrand mines under the name Fanagalo, and it gave whites the sense that they could speak a native language and blacks the sense that they could speak English. In time it became the lingua franca of the workplace and was widely spoken throughout the Rhodesias and beyond.

Hylda Richards recorded an amusing conversation in Chilapalapa as she tried to explain to her boss boy the causes of World War-II. 'Manjie' [now] lo Germeni tells lo Austria, Mina bamba wena! [I catch you] and lo Austria say, Aikona! [No you won't] And lo English tells lo Germeni aikona enza so! [Don't do that!] Manjie lo Germeni bambele [grab] lo Austria.' ... and so the conversation continued until it ended with the boss boy gaining the gist of the story and concluding.

'Uh, uh! Lo Germeni meninge [very] cheeky!'[5]

Migrant labour was yet another of the strange anomalies of Southern Rhodesian race relations. While the Carter Commission and the subsequent Land Apportionment Act institutionalised a strictly separate system of development, all kinds of efforts were made to improve conditions in the reserves, to make it less attractive for young males to leave in search of work. However the counteractive imposition of hut taxes and the increasing demands for labour conspired to ensure that they did just that. Migrant labour had many different levels depending on its source, but since cities and towns were to remain white areas, all labour to some degree could be considered migratory.

There was internal labour migration from the reserves to the cities and a more regional movement that often saw labour originating in Northern Rhodesia and Nyasaland. These workers flooded into the Copperbelt, into Southern Rhodesia and in vast numbers further south to the gold mines of the Witwatersrand. The 1930s brought large-scale industrial development not only in Southern Rhodesia but in the north as well, creating a huge demand for labour. An entire industry developed around the movement of labour, involving private recruiting agents and modern transport networks, as well as comfortable rest stations along the most travelled routes.

The social cost to men and their families of long-distance migration was immense. In the early days tribesmen were torn away from their traditional life to work for enough money to pay their hut taxes, after which they would return to their lands and their families. By the 1930s, however, such attitudes had changed. The miniature industrial revolution, that was underway in both Rhodesias, rapidly undermined traditional structures of life by depopulating tribal areas of young and productive males. The wearisome journeys home and the material demands of kinfolk when they arrived, caused many to abandon their home areas for more modern lives in labour compounds and other fringe urban settlements. Many took wives or concubines from tribes different from their own and in due course discarded old tribal attachments for the new, integrated industrial generation of working blacks.

Rates of pay in Southern Rhodesia were higher than those in the north, and then, with a great deal more freedom of movement than now, many would travel huge distances to find suitable work. Large numbers of Nyasas moved south from the Shire Highlands and the 'dead north' of Nyasaland to find work in the cities and settlements of Southern Rhodesia. A labour caste system evolved with certain groups preferring — or being preferred for — certain types of work.

The removal of night soil from privies throughout Salisbury was the preserve of Tongas from the Zambezi Valley. Lawyer Hardwicke Holderness relates in his memoirs a story of an amateur Shakespearean practising her lines in the privy that backed up against a sanitary lane in Salisbury. 'Romeo, Romeo, wherefore art thou Romeo?' she keened, whereupon a crisp reply emerged from behind her. *'Mina aikona Romeo, Madam, mina Zambezi boy!'*[6]

Kingsley Fairbridge recorded the sight of gangs of Mozambican migrant workers working on the preparatory work for the new township of Umtali.

> Great gangs of boys from Nyungwe [ete] and Senna were working on the streets that were to be. Mabandawi and Magorongoza dug side by side, trenching the two streams that flanked the township; the deadly mud, packed with germs of malaria, was cast up beside the trenches.[7]

Before World War-I, Mozambican and Nyasa farm workers often followed white farmers down from Nyasaland to settle in Southern Rhodesia. This practice served to introduce local white farmers to the superior work ethic of the Nyasa, after which they tended to select Nyasas and northern Mozambicans for farm work in preference to whatever local labour was available.

The bewildering crosscurrents of labour movement and the rapid merging of communities were a feature of the postwar period. These activities, however, tended to diminish as the global depression of the 1930s made itself felt. The labour recruitment industry and its infrastructure fell away and was never quite revived. Migrant labour, of course, continued to flow, but it became victim to tighter political controls and covetous practices of governments jealous of their labour reserves.

Migrant labour also formed the bedrock of much black political opinion, in the period between the wars. The main detractors of political amalgamation tended to be black, with many of their concerns bound up in the fear of competition with labour from distant areas. As Nyasaland pioneered the migrant labour movement, so Nyasas brought back and disseminated the early breezes of revolution. Political consciousness travelled along a system of verbal arteries that ran from the Witwatersrand to Katanga and beyond.

Howard Moffat was the uncomfortable heir to a government charged with the task of regulating this disordered race-landscape. While this was not all that contributed to the aura of failure that tends to hang over his term, it represents much of what ultimately overwhelmed him. He was of missionary heritage and in his blood was the titanic social conscience of his forbears. It must then have been particularly difficult to be the hand that consigned the black man to a social and political wasteland. In many ways it was Godfrey Huggins who seemed born to the tasks of this time. From the backbenches, he contributed much of the weight that was used to push the country along the road that it must ultimately follow. Moffat went through the motions and completed his term, but was not dismayed when the day came for him to hand over power to Huggins.

25

Rhodesian hero and the golden years

Second man of destiny

By 1931 the effects of the global depression had reached southern Africa and although the worst impact had been delayed somewhat, by October of that year real hardship had begun to bite into the lives of the farming and working classes of Rhodesia. Moffat's political decline had begun, for apart from fumbling the race question, he was perceived as having acted indecisively when a second chance at amalgamation came around. Thanks to the burgeoning copper boom in Northern Rhodesia, a majority of southerners were then in favour of amalgamation. Without any help from the hapless Moffat, the Hilton-Young Commission had ruled out this solution and yet Moffat's government was still seen as being largely responsible.

The depression, meanwhile, brought about a rapid increase in white unemployment. The treasury pruned expenditure back as far as it could until Percy Fynn eventually scraped the bottom of the barrel by suggesting civil service wage cuts. This was thought at the time to be a reasonably safe proposal since the civil service was bound into government policy, and was the constituency least likely to fight back. Fynn, it seemed, had forgotten for a moment that the civil service constituency was not only his but also that of Godfrey Huggins. Huggins may have publicly eschewed any political ambition but this was beggared by the alacrity with which he seized the opportunity to fight. Fynn thoughtfully handed him a stick that he then used mercilessly to beat an already defeated Moffat.

Under a hail of invective, Fynn and Moffat duly submitted a bill to the House. Since civil service wages were protected by a reserve clause, a two-thirds majority was necessary for it to pass. After a handful of defections, the Rhodesia Party found that it had 20 members against the combined opposition of the Reform, Progressive and Labour parties holding nine. The speaker made up the total of 30 members. The governing party now needed the support of all its members if the bill was to pass — a fact that put Huggins in a very difficult position. If he supported the interests of his constituency, it would necessitate inflicting a defeat on his party. This would be nothing less that a vote of no confidence, that would require a general election to resolve. On the other hand, if he supported his constituency he would be failing his party.

Huggins made the best of it. He voted in favour of the bill but then immediately expressed his displeasure by crossing the floor. How his constituents reacted to this would decide whether he would take another step forward in politics or two steps back to his surgery. In the event, he held a constituents' meeting that turned out to be a vintage Huggins performance. After a half an hour or so of speaking, his audience was rolling in the aisles. A flawlessly timed offer to resign his seat was then overwhelmingly rejected. He returned to the backbenches as an independent for the time being, but mainly in order to keep an eye on things and see what happened next.

Rhodesian politics had proceeded until then as more or less a one party system that had been both necessary and commendable against the demands of transition, but now the time was ripe for the birth of a viable opposition. Bickering in the Assembly was usually put aside when the members stepped across the road to the Salisbury Club where lubricated interaction often resulted in more sensible policy. It was decided there that the current opposition — the Reform and Progressive parties — would bury their differences and unite with a smaller group called the Country Party, to form a united opposition under the banner of the Reform Party. At the first party conference, held in Gwelo in 1932, Huggins was elected leader. How Huggins' responded to this is open to speculation, but whether he liked it or not, he was from then on directly in line for the premiership.

A general election was scheduled for 1933. Huggins armed his campaign with two powerfully emotive issues and, with the moderation of a born gentleman, he lunged for Moffat's jugular. Firstly he enlivened the pot by adding to it the usual flavour of British South Africa Company wickedness, which both captured public attention and froze Moffat in his corner. This time the issue was mineral rights, which no less than the railway question, needled at the heart of national sovereignty. The fact of the matter was that mineral rights had been granted to the Company and recognised by the Constitution, and therefore the government of Southern Rhodesia had absolutely no legal say in the matter. This of course made it an issue that Moffat could neither avoid nor hope to win.

The second issue was race. As we have seen, race was a complicated hoodoo that continued to paralyse the country with irrational fear. With white Rhodesian men for the first time taking up picks and shovels, the question of the rights of white workers became explosive. Huggins proposed his twin pyramid scheme, so becoming the first politician to introduce race and segregation as a direct campaign issue. White workers blamed the government for unemployment and competition for the lower paid jobs and as a consequence, the working classes embraced Huggins' twin state theory with desperate hope.

Over the question of BSAC mineral rights, Huggins stirred up a storm. He conceded that the Company had paid for the construction of the railways, so there could be no doubt that the line belonged to the Company and if they wished to sell it when the day came, they were perfectly at liberty to do so. However, the mineral rights were an asset of the country and should belong to the people. It is interesting to note that once Huggins was retired and safely out of politics, he admitted that the natural conclusion of this would mean that the mineral rights belonged to the blacks. But during the 1933 campaign he made no mention of this and instead pounded the table at Moffat, daring him to act.

Moffat began rather hopelessly by asking the Company if it would submit the matter to the judicial committee of the Privy Council, which, after a collective shudder, the board of directors declined to do. The Company had no reason to humour Moffat since it stood on solid legal ground and everybody knew it. However, along with the rest of the world, it was short of liquid capital so it offered to sell out its rights for £2 million.

This was a reasonable deal and on 1 April 1933 it was struck. Moffat gained for the country a valuable financial asset that in future would realise a significant return, but for his efforts he was howled down for selling out and paying through the nose for what belonged to the country anyway. Huggins might have congratulated himself on a job well done — and he did.

The Ministerial Titles Act had been adopted at the previous session, causing the leadership title to be changed from Premier to Prime Minister. Since Moffat himself had become widely regarded as a liability to his party, he resigned in favour of his Minister of Mines George Mitchell, who then became the first and shortest serving Prime Minister in Rhodesian history.

The general election took place in September of 1933. Huggins lacked the support of the establishment but kept that of other strong sectors. Both the *Rhodesia Herald* and the *Bulawayo*

Chronicle kept public attention focused on the two main issues of economic recovery and sound, united and strong government. The Rhodesia Party had satisfied both these criteria in the past and, with predictable conservatism, the Argus maintained that only the Rhodesia Party could be relied upon to do the same in the future.

'It is abundantly clear', stated the *Rhodesia Herald*, 'that Mr Huggins has a large personal following, but the whole pith and marrow of the situation is that a team with one star player only is not a team upon which reliance can be placed.' There was a justifiable fear that no clear majority would be carried, and that either the Labour Party or the Independents would hold the balance of power. A resultant coalition could serve no useful purpose and would weaken recovery as world economic conditions improved.

In the event, Huggins' Reform Party won a narrow victory, giving it a slim but effective working majority. It captured 16 seats, the Rhodesia Party nine and Labour five. Huggins was sworn in as Prime Minister on 6 September, and began his term as the longest serving Prime Minister in British Commonwealth history.

Good times
Life in Southern Rhodesia was not entirely devoted to survival on a crippled economic landscape and machinations to grind the black man underfoot. As the roaring twenties plunged into depression, a golden age of verve and creativity grew out of adversity.

Salisbury, like most colonial capitals, managed to squeeze a third generation out of the Victorian experience — which for elite colonials had been among the most pleasant epochs in human history anyway. The combination of good medicine, an established white society, a sporting country and an excellent climate had made the Rhodesian experience particularly so. A wide-open country, with its natural beauty as yet unspoilt, lay before any white man who cared to enjoy it. White men administered the road from Cape Town to Nairobi and the territories in between were neither over-armed nor under-policed. Once again a certain moral blindness was required to enjoy it all, but many had it and many did.

The elite social network of Salisbury was still focussed on Government House. In the adjacent avenues, those with money and position built their signature brick and iron houses with their stern gables and expansive verandas. The most sought-after properties were those that could claim a glimpse of the Governor's residence, although Avondale, Newlands and Hillside were fast emerging as preferred suburbs. The crème de la crème — including civil servants, senior judges and wealthy industrial and professional men — for the most part resided on North Avenue. Their houses were gracious, spacious and practical. The rooms had high pressed ceilings, bay windows and ornamental fireplaces. Wide staircases with rich hardwood balustrades led from the arched hallways to the generous upstairs bedrooms. The acre-sized gardens were pleasantly lawned, each with an expansive fig tree or syringa, or a line of jacarandas to carpet jaded winter beds with a misting of mauve.

The elite wore evening dress to the cinema, and gloves were de rigueur for the ladies. Card dropping and other quaint Victorian or Edwardian traditions lingered on. Coat tails and couturier gowns were ubiquitous at the annual show ball. It was imperial England lingering under the gossamer sunshine of good times and plenty.

Among those determined to hang onto the last traces of gentility was the young and energetic wife of Sir Cecil Hunter Rodwell, who was Governor of Southern Rhodesia from 1928 to 1934. Rodwell had by then worked his way through a number of remote and charming postings that included the Pitcairn Islands, British Guiana and Fiji. Lady Rodwell, many years his junior, sat relatively lowly among the gubernatorial wives. The two had met in South Africa while she was touring in the cast of *Miss Hook of Holland*, and they were married after a courtship of noticeably short duration. As a consequence, and although reluctant to openly fete a chorus girl, the women of Salisbury north did all they could to compromise.

Lady Rodwell maintained her interest in the theatre and staged a handful of amateur productions, including Alice in Wonderland, that featured most of her family in the cast. She led the local bridge set and, in keeping with a questionable background, she fleeced the newcomers and raised many an eyebrow over points of sharp practice. The first genuine thespian in the small social community was a certain Christine Collings, who was the daughter of a wealthy mining engineer. Ms Collings had studied drama and dance in London and returned to Rhodesia keen to exhibit her achievements. Through Lady Rodwell she met a young doctor from Shanghai, Dr Paul Anning, who was also a keen amateur dramatist. The two soon tired of Lady Rodwell's rather gay view of drama and set about founding a serious stage movement, which later became the Salisbury Repertory Players, or Reps. On 17 February 1931, the Salisbury Repertory Players was consummated with the production in the Duthie Memorial Hall of two short plays, one by GK Chesterton and the other by Lord Dunsany. The small audience attending the premier was both curious and appreciative.

The undisputed doyens of the local arts movement, however, were Sir Stephen Courthauld and his wife Lady Virginia. Sir Stephen was a member of the wealthy British textile dynasty founded by his father George. Their time was divided between their London home of Eltham Palace and a country retreat called La Rochelle, in the hill country of Penalonga outside Umtali. The guest book at La Rochelle was a glass window etched by a diamond stylus with the names of many sundry imperial statesmen and royalty.

Sir Stephen did not join the family business but rather used its wealth to travel widely. He also committed much time and resource to local arts endowments. He and his wife built and founded the Courthauld theatre in Umtali, and were instrumental in the founding of the National Arts Gallery in Salisbury. The couple's perambulations between La Rochelle and their London home continued until Sir Stephen died in 1967, whereupon Lady Virginia moved to Jersey where she survived until 1972.

While the Governor of Southern Rhodesia netted a young and vivacious wife, his opposite number in Northern Rhodesia, Sir Hubert Young, was married to an entirely different kind of woman. Lady Young was an experienced pilot, and flew regularly between Livingstone and Lusaka in her own light aircraft. On 28 February 1935 she set off from Livingstone as usual on a routine flight, to join her husband in the capital. She had as her passenger the senior Government Medical Officer, Dr Kerby. In a moment of turbulence the aircraft compass locked and Lady Young became a little disorientated. She sighted a river that she assumed to be the Kafue but which turned out to be the Zambezi. With little fuel, no clear direction nor recognisable landmarks, she was forced after a period of anxious searching to bring the plane down in a maize field on the Southern Rhodesian side. Both pilot and passenger escaped with a few cuts and bruises but found themselves stranded in the middle of the bushveld with no idea of where they were.

As is customary, it was not long before a group of curious blacks appeared. They directed the pair back to their village where quite coincidently a white trader and locust officer by the name of G.W Cameron was visiting. He was carrying with him the essentials of tea, food and a mosquito net — which he lent to Lady Young.

The following morning Cameron sent a runner to alert the Native Commissioner, who resided at a station some 90 miles away in Gokwe. In the meantime the party set out and covered the short distance to Cameron's store on foot. A more comfortable night was passed before the three set out again the following day to march themselves to Gokwe.

Back in Lusaka, Sir Hubert was sick with worry, and mobilised detachments of the Northern Rhodesia Regiment, the local Native Affairs Department and thousands of villagers to scour the countryside. Aeroplanes from Southern Rhodesia as well as members of the Johannesburg Light

Aircraft Club joined in the search. Logically but unfortunately, efforts were concentrated along Lady Young's logged route on the wrong side of the Zambezi River.

While the hunt became more and more frantic, the lady herself, the doctor and the bush-wise local trader toiled south over the rugged terrain in the heat of late summer.

As news leaked out, the story captivated the public on both sides of the Zambezi, and indeed all over the world. The staff of the *Bulawayo Chronicle* were inundated with requests for news from overseas, while every report and every conjecture was devoured both at home and abroad.

The runner arrived in Gokwe not far ahead of the trio, who had by then been abroad in the bush for almost three days. The Native Commissioner passed the message to the outside world with the help of a ham radio operator in Bulawayo. A Westland Wessex of the Rhodesia and Nyasaland Airways was sent north from Salisbury with a package of supplies that it hoped to airdrop on the anguished party. The package included aspirin and champagne and certainly at least the latter would have been welcome had the Wessex been able to locate the group on the floor of the Zambezi Valley.

An Argus reporter by the name of R.F Windram, sniffing a scoop, was on his way to Gokwe from Bulawayo by car. He arrived at nine o'clock the following morning just in time to join the Commissioner on an improvised rescue mission. Naturally both men assumed that Lady Young was at Cameron's store, helplessly waiting to be collected and hurried back to the comforts of civilisation.

In his impatience to get his exclusive, Windram borrowed a bicycle from a local messenger and set off alone through almost trackless wilderness. His disappointment was acute when he arrived at Cameron's store almost dead from exhaustion to find it deserted. He had narrowly missed intercepting his quarry as the three dragged themselves in the opposite direction. When the Commissioner caught up, he made radio contact with Gokwe and discovered that Lady Young and Dr Kerby were en route and almost there. Feeling rather foolish, Windram and the Commissioner set off once again on the long slog back to Gokwe.

Lady Young and her companions arrived footsore and sunburned after six days of rough travel. They promptly boarded the waiting Westland Wessex and flew off to a hero's wecome in Lusaka. Windram turned his car around and made the long and painful journey back to Bulawayo to file his report. Doubtless Lady Rodwell read the story the following day, and would certainly have shuddered a little as she sipped her lemon tea on the sun-drenched lawns of Government House.

Hard times

By then the Great Depression had begun to bite deeply and the lot of the working man across the western world was the dole, hunger marches and soup kitchens. In Rhodesia too, the good life was by no means universal. Unemployment cut through the white population like the plague, and the best that could be said of it was that being out of work was perhaps less stigmatising in Africa than it might have been in Europe. It affected men of different social classes who shared the hard times as an equalising rite of passage. An unemployed train driver might easily find himself rubbing shoulders on the strip road construction programme with a penniless Cambridge Blue, while a travelling salesman with an uncle in the House of Lords might just as easily share a campfire with a down-at-heel veteran of the trenches.

These were temporary hardships and labour camp did not necessarily mean the end of the road for these men. A farmer did not automatically lose his farm if he stepped into the government's pay for a month or two. It was common enough for a destitute landholder to leave his boss boy on site while he worked on the roads or on a mine to tide the farm over. This happened even in the good times. Murray MacDougall, for instance, periodically worked as a transport rider as the heavy work of cutting his irrigation channel absorbed a never-ending amount of money.

In the tobacco industry the disaster of 1929 fed directly into the depression. That year alone 700 of the country's original growers were put out of business. By 1930, production had dropped to under 5.5 million lbs, as hundreds of speculators who had lost all their capital packed up and left the country. Others stayed but joined the work camps and waited for things to get better. Those who fled were usually the amateurs who should have known better, while those who stayed and survived certainly did know better by the end of it.

While Huggins might have appeared at times to be aloof to the struggle of many a broken pioneer, he did at least recognise the importance of the farming industry. Soon after he took office he confided to a study committee of the Empire Parliamentary Association:

> We, like other's countries, are having to subsidise the agricultural industry in every direction. I believe this to be right, because I think that any country which does not use the whole of its resources to maintain its rural population will probably find itself right out of the running as and when some sort of normality returns to the world.[1]

This was a wise philosophy. The colony had invested so much in agriculture already and by then, without it, there would probably have been nothing to underwrite a viable economic recovery.

As difficult as it was for specialist producers, they did not face the same hardships as traditional maize growers and cattlemen. When commodity prices collapsed, black maize farmers were able to produce more and sell for less using their extended families as unpaid labour. Nothing distressed a marginal white farmer more than unequal competition from a black man, and while some in the industry welcomed competition, those in maize clamoured for market controls — meaning white exclusivity.

Huggins was instinctively wary of government interference. His political philosophy had always tended towards limited government, but these were extraordinary times. During his first year in office he was confronted by powerful farming pressure groups that he could not effectively challenge so early on in his premiership. In 1931 the Maize Control Act controlled output by limiting the amount of land that could put down to maize — although production had already been regulated so that only white producers could profit. Huggins amended the Act in 1934, to further strengthen subsidies. He also responded to similar agitation from a vociferous body of white industrial workers by drafting the Industrial Conciliation Act of 1934.

Of course it is the squeaky wheel that gets the oil and although maize control benefited smaller white growers, it did so at the expense of large white producers and blacks in the purchase areas and reserves. Indigenous producers were cushioned to a degree by being able to produce cheaply and circumvent controls, tending to sell locally to white farmers and miners for labour and stock feed or to Indian traders for cash.

Tobacco growers, on the other hand, far from pleading for government intervention, dusted themselves down, realigned their leadership and contemplated the future with a combination of hope and determination. The government did help when it could, mainly through marketing control measures and by enforcing standards of quality, also providing funds for research and compelling growers to work as a united body. Growers who had established themselves and their markets and were making good money despite the reverses, did not universally welcome government involvement. It would be fair to say then that the 1930s in the tobacco industry was not only a period of measured recovery, but also one of internal review and restructuring. Partly as a result of this and partly due to the particularly perverse determination shown in the tobacco growing fraternity itself, recovery in the industry was rapid.

The imperial preference was set at 25 per cent for ten years, helping the tobacco harvest to climb to over 14 million lbs in 1932. Added to this, British advertisers agreed to phase out the claim that only 'authentic' American Virginia was used in the production of their cigarettes, which had the effect of re-igniting a surge of interest in Rhodesian tobacco. Growers gradually released their collective grip on one another's throats and started to smell a scent of recovery in the air. They quickly directed their attentions towards growing more of the capricious weed, that had so enriched and contaminated their lives. By 1934 a new record had been set with 26 millions pounds of tobacco being produced on Southern Rhodesian farms.

26

Same old idea and the usual problem

Huggins took up the office of Prime Minister feeling a sense of loss for the life that he had left behind — a fact which was not helped by his having also to accept a significant drop in income. In the interim, he continued to draw an allowance of £1 000 a year from his practice to augment an annual remuneration for the top political post of just £2 500.

In the beginning, Huggins tried not to abandon his medical practice entirely, and while in office operated on both the Governor of Nyasaland, Sir Harold Kittermaster, and the leader of his opposition — who complained of no ill effects as a consequence. However he was optimistic if he thought that the demands of office would allow him the time and latitude to continue practising medicine effectively. He had written and published for *The Lancet*, but that pleasure and privilege was also soon to be a thing of the past. History tends to portray Huggins as an excellent public servant, thanks to his old fashioned style of self sacrifice and perhaps this was so, but his biographers also hint that he approached his first official crisis hoping that his government would be defeated. In that case he would be able in good conscience to put politics behind him and return to his surgery with neither he nor the country any worse for the experiment.

The root of the crisis was twofold, and premised on a combination of a weak majority and an initial reluctance on Huggins' part to move too far or too fast. He was hindered not only by being a political amateur himself, but also by being surrounded by dabblers, at a time when politics in Rhodesia was beginning to emerge from its early roots as a cottage industry. Some of those standing to the right of his first cabinet expected more, and certainly there was much disappointment that Huggins did not immediately implement the explosive race policies that had helped win him office.

When he did make certain moves on the race issue, his amateurism was evident. He and his Chief Native Affairs Commissioner, Clive Carbutt, devised a plan to partition Northern Rhodesia into a grand native reserve, to which all of Southern Rhodesia's surplus blacks would be shipped. Northern Rhodesian whites would be invited to come south and be part of an exclusively white homeland. The Imperial Government was obviously taken aback when it was presented with such an enormous and quixotic scheme so early in Huggins' career — and quashed the idea immediately.

Despite such radical thinking, Huggins was still moving neither far nor fast enough for the fundamental wing of his party. At the Reform Party conference held in Gwelo in 1934, he found himself under attack from a belligerent clique of right-wing backbenchers. He had until then appeared hesitant and uncertain, but at this point he threw down the gauntlet and revealed to his party the terms under which he would be prepared to continue to lead it. 'As far as I am concerned', he said, 'I would rather return to the relatively peaceful life I have temporarily left. It is impossible to govern with the necessary strength in these difficult times unless I have adequate support.' That Huggins was prepared to resign his position as Prime Minister then and there, no one present at the conference doubted.

Thanks to this strong stand, divisions were temporarily patched up and a grumbling party marshalled into line. Although this would not be the end of his troubles, Huggins had for the moment successfully asserted himself, stating quite plainly that if the electorate wanted him to govern he would do so, but not at any cost. Knowing that a confrontation with the malcontents was inevitable at some point, he was inclined to grasp the nettle and provoke a breach sooner rather than later.

The moment came when Agriculture Minister C.S Jobling died unexpectedly, leaving a vacancy in the cabinet. Huggins clearly illustrated his lack of faith in his cabinet and caucus by replacing Jobling with a farmer, Captain Frank Harris, who was neither a party insider nor a parliamentarian. This prompted an immediate rebellion from established party members, who demanded to know why one of them had not been chosen to represent such an important portfolio. Huggins held his ground. He was Prime Minister, he told his party, and as such he reserved the right to choose whomsoever he deemed fit for the job. The difficulty was, of course, that the constitution required Harris to be a member of parliament. It therefore became incumbent on Huggins to ensure that he was elected. Help in this regard came from an unlikely quarter when, in a hint of political accommodations to come, the Rhodesia Party offered not to field a candidate against Harris in the by-election occasioned by Jobling's death.

The uproar was again quieted but tensions in the House remained high as Harris took his seat. Huggins then made rather thin use of the crisis by approaching the Governor for a dissolution of parliament. Chief Justice Sir Fraser Russell, who was acting Governor at the time, demurred stating that there was no precedence for dissolution purely on the grounds of an internal party squabble. It was editor of the *Rhodesia Herald*, George Ferguson, who offered a solution to the impasse when he wrote in a leader article:

> The best interests of the country would be served by party reconstruction … It is known that the Rhodesia Party is ready to work with Mr. Huggins. If he were to approach them to form an entirely new party by combining the Reform and Rhodesia Parties, there is good grounds for believing that his overtures would be more than sympathetically received.

Percy Fynn, leader of the Rhodesia Party, and a handful of his colleagues, were so impressed by the idea that they duly brokered a deal between Huggins and the Rhodesia Party. Three days later, following a meeting of the executive committee of the Reform Party, an amalgamation was announced. The Rhodesia and Reform Parties were to be combined into a new political alliance to be called the United Party, which would be led by Huggins. Sir Fraser Russell accepted this as grounds for dissolution and in November 1934 the country revisited the polls.

After the votes were counted it was shown that the United Party had been returned with 24 seats, giving Huggins an 18-seat majority. The old Reform Party won one seat while the Labour Party garnered five. With that, Huggins won a decisive hold over both the government of Rhodesia and its white hearts and minds, neither of which he would relinquish for another 20 years or more. The medical fraternity of Salisbury lost a surgeon, but the nation gained a credible Prime Minister and peered out of the first decade of responsible government with something of its old confidence returned.

* * *

Huggins was now suddenly much less of an amateur and to prove it he revived the old vision inherited from Rhodes. All the great colonial statesmen of southern Africa have dreamed at one time or another of a grand union of states stretching — if not as far as Cairo — then at least encompassing all of the British settled colonies of the south central region. Huggins was fortunate in that he approached the question with time to work at it, thereby improving the odds for success significantly. Unlike Rhodes, his version of the dream was secular, and unlike Smuts he was not pressed into a tight political corner. Although in some respects Huggins failed, it was he who over the following months and years came closest of the three to actually realising the dream.

From the point of view of many whites, the practical advantages of amalgamation with Northern Rhodesia were now much clearer, thanks in the main to copper, but also because of general progress in the north that made it less of a yawning black hole of no discernable value. To Huggins and his generation, the main problem facing Africa was its backwardness and the conservatism of its traditional institutions. Things had moved too far along for the Africans to ever contemplate recapturing their past, and yet quite evidently they could not be realistically expected to govern a modern society. Many colonials felt betrayed by the Imperial Government's conversion from an ostensible instrument of exploitation, to one concerned above all else with the wellbeing of the natives. They felt that for the defence of civilised standards, the Imperial Government should guard against any possibility that blacks might prematurely rush to power. If there was a vague sense in the colony, that government by blacks would one day be inevitable, few could imagine it happening within a century.

As the Hilton-Young Commission had confirmed, the problem that Southern Rhodesia faced whenever a proposal for closer union in central Africa was tabled, was her unbalanced race policy. His Majesty's Government had conceded all power to protect the natives of South Africa when the Union was formed in 1910, and the results of this were self-evident. Southern Rhodesia looked south more often than not in questions of race policy — which made the Colonial Office very careful to limit the spread of this sort of contamination further north. Both Northern Rhodesia and Nyasaland were British protectorates and so were governed directly from Whitehall under very different constitutions to the south. In both territories, blacks enjoyed somewhat greater freedom than in Southern Rhodesia, so both they and the Imperial Government were loath to see any compromise.

On the other hand, the rise of National Socialism in Germany and the possibility of war, had succeeded in focussing the mind of the British Government on Africa. Not only might calls from Hitler for the return of Germany's former colonies see the Huns once again pitching their tents in the middle of a British jamboree, but the natural sense of comradeship felt by the Boers for Germany, might see South African neutrality in the event of a war compromised. The idea of drawing the three naturally allied territories of the two Rhodesias and Nyasaland into a single state gained new appeal. Such an amalgamation would strengthen the British hand in central Africa at a time when global influence would be vital, while also acting as a political counterweight to a potentially aggressive South Africa.

South Africa's ideological withdrawal from British Africa was evident, not only in her empathy with fascism. It was also apparent in the introduction of trade tariffs in 1935, that put an end to much of the free trade that had been conducted between Southern Rhodesia and South Africa in the past. The effect of this in the event proved positive for Rhodesia, since domestic industrial capacity quickly increased, as goods once imported from South Africa started to be manufactured locally. As a consequence, Rhodesian industrialists also found new markets in Northern Rhodesia with its burgeoning mining interests and vibrant economy.

These were some of the important practical reasons for amalgamation. The visceral reasons were more obscure. Whites had begun to feel under pressure as the certainties of old seemed less relevant in a changing world. The sense that what they had built around them might not always be theirs planted a seed of fear in their hearts. This was particularly true of the working classes and the landowners, who found themselves searching for ways to restore their sense of security and stability. The isolationist and rather elitist Rhodesia of old now found herself vulnerable and craving the safety of size and influence.

Huggins opened the game in 1935, by introducing another of his quixotic solutions. He suggested a general amalgamation of the railway belt, that in principle, meant that the railway line and everything connected to it — including the Copperbelt — would come under Southern Rhodesian control. Since anything of consequence in Northern Rhodesia was located within 20 miles of the railway, and since the line more or less dissected the protectorate up its length, the country on either side could safely be deemed useless and tossed back to the blacks. This idea was not original, but it was cunning. It appealed to Southern Rhodesia, but not to her northern neighbour or, for that matter, to the British Government. The idea was politely filed away for future consideration, but attention had been captured and the ice broken.

A year later, Huggins put forward another, more sensible, proposal for a federation of territories, that would quarantine each from what it disliked about the others, but would unite them sufficiently for economic growth and political stability. The Colonial Office, probably relieved that this scheme was a little less harebrained, allowed the governors of the three territories concerned to meet informally over the question. Closer cooperation was discussed and broadly agreed to, although this would initially be limited to justice, customs, defence and other bureaucratic procedures. Although Huggins pressed for more and the governors themselves were supportive, this was as far as Britain was prepared to be pushed for the time being.

It is worth noting that, among the many factors of resistance to amalgamation, were the Southern Rhodesian blacks. They regarded the Northern Rhodesian natives as uncivilised and feared losing their labour market to a flood of these cheaper workers. Ironically, they also preferred the idea of uniting with South Africa for reasons of access to higher education and sharing in the social advancement that was taking place among blacks there.

A second and less formal governors' and inter-party conference was held at Victoria Falls in 1936, to which Huggins was also invited. A united Rhodesia was agreed upon and again pressure was exerted on Whitehall. The Secretaries of State for both the Colonial and Dominion Offices met and decided for the second time to appoint a commission to look into the question of closer political union, if not complete amalgamation.

This time the commission was chaired by Viscount Bledisloe, former Governor General of New Zealand, and he was assisted by the Kenyan writer and journalist Elspeth Huxley. The Commission recommended the acceptance of amalgamation in principle, but considered that for various reasons — principally differences in native policy — that the change should not be considered immediately. As an interim measure, increased cooperation between the two Rhodesias on an administrative, scientific and judicial level was encouraged. Federation as a lesser option was ruled out because of the basic constitutional incompatibility of the territories.

Although naturally disappointed, Huggins was not diverted. However he was forced to put the matter aside for the moment, to concentrate on other things. At that point, war interrupted the process and from 1939 until the end of hostilities nothing much of the scheme was heard. Instead, more practical home-based economic and political considerations took centre stage in preparation for the great and inevitable changes that would follow.

Global rearmament had created a demand for almost every primary product and raw material that the Empire could provide, and as base metal producers, the two Rhodesias were particularly well placed to respond. Copper was in high demand for use in tank, aircraft and battleship electronics. Between 1931 and 1939, increased copper production in Northern Rhodesia resulted in a consequent boom in Southern Rhodesian coal production and railway tariffs. While to a greater or lesser extent everybody benefited, these were golden times for the British South Africa Company. For the first time since it was floated in 1889, Rhodes' Chartered Company was making money hand over fist. Subsequently a deal was struck between the railways and the Northern Rhodesian copper mining companies to continue the transport of copper through the system for a further 20 years.

While all this might have been manna to an ailing economy, it was in agriculture that Huggins and his government still pinned their hopes. In the years leading up to the war, the agricultural industry had increasingly begun to benefit from thoughtful streamlining and creative legislation. As a primary producer, it was now in position to reap maximum benefit from the great changes affecting the world. In 1934, a second Maize Control Act bolstered existing legislation, while in the same year a Cattle Levy and the Beef Export Bounty Act were added to give supplementary assistance to ranchers. The Dairy Control Board regulated the dairy industry and in 1937, the government, in a departure from the Huggins doctrine of limited government, purchased the Bulawayo branch of the Imperial Cold Storage Supply Company. A further Act was passed, setting up a Cold Storage Commission with powers to control the industry for the export of frozen and chilled meats. In 1936 the Cotton Research and Industry Board was formed to control a crop that had otherwise flourished without the sort of state intervention that kept the rest of the agricultural industry afloat.

Like tobacco, the roots of cotton in Rhodesia lay in the ambivalent attitude that British manufacturers held towards their main suppliers in the United States. From 1910 until the outbreak of World War-I the American crop suffered a general failure that was only capped by the war. Britain again found herself looking to her colonies — principally Egypt and India — but a glance was spared for Southern Rhodesia too. The resulting boost to the crop helped it survive long enough to experience something of a mini boom from 1923 up to the end of the decade. By the 1930s, cotton was being reviewed as a cash crop since it seemed to have survived on its own merits and built markets on more realistic foundations than tobacco. Once again the advent of war and the inevitable economic restructuring that accompanied the mass mobilisation of armies, vindicated early optimism and poised Southern Rhodesia to reap the benefits.

Despite all this, however, tobacco remained the brilliant problem child of the Rhodesian agricultural family. Its fortunes had risen and fallen with bewildering regularity since Lord Grey politely coughed over the blue smoke of Hayward's cigar. By the 1930s it was apparent that the industry's main problem lay with its lack of internal cohesion and in a shortage of industry guidelines and conditions to tame the obstreperous few and curb chaotic fluctuations.

After the collapse of the cooperative system and the disastrous events of 1929, the tobacco industry resumed its preferred polarity. Individual growers worked in competition with one another, each establishing his own buying contacts and succeeding or failing on his own acumen. Some made a fortune while others — those Huggins called spineless, spoon-fed and inefficient — limped on in steady decline. An almost obsessive determination to remain free of buyer monopolies tended to nurture resistance to the development of any cooperative system of tobacco marketing. The effect of this was to maintain the industry in a half-formed state that crippled efforts towards general advancement. The auction system, which was universally accepted by the 1930s, had been so discredited by the Tobacco Warehouse debacle that producers remained unified only in resistance to it. As the decade progressed, a bitter dispute played out between growers who maintained their right to sell wherever and to whomever they wanted, and those who pressed for legislation to make it compulsory for all tobacco grown to be sold at public auction. Those successful growers who had thus far profited through individual contacts stressed that any merger would simply permit the weak to ride on the backs of the strong.

In the end it was the preference of the buyers and not the growers that swung the debate in the favour of the unionists. In 1933, a Tobacco Levy Act was passed that forced all growers to become part of the Rhodesia Tobacco Growers Association. Further industry regulation quickly followed with the Tobacco Pest Suppression Act and the Tobacco Research Act of 1935 that mandated both growers and government to contribute funds for further research into growing techniques and disease and pest control. Most importantly, the introduction of compulsory auction sales in 1936 brought the ever-divisive problem of marketing under control. The first auction floor opened for business on 11 April 1936. While dramatic success still continued to elude the industry, a sense of optimism was inescapable, as the tide of European politics began irreversibly to slide towards war. To the shrewd and the sanguine, it was clear that circumstances would gradually begin to shift the onus of commodity supply and demand from a buyers' to a sellers' market. By 1939 Southern Rhodesian tobacco, in keeping with primary industry throughout the empire, was ready to reap the bonanza of war.

* * *

The social and political picture of Rhodesia was somewhat less encouraging. By the end of the decade, Huggins had proved that he was an able administrator of a white colony, but he had still not made public a definitive native policy. Huggins is portrayed by his biographers as a great and gifted man with irrepressible humour and given to neither deep reflection, regret nor indecision. He tended to be less a man of his own ideas than a filter for the good ideas of others. The assurances of his hagiographers that he was fully abreast of black concerns and that he understood and appreciated their aspirations have an apologetic air about them that suggest this was no such thing. In reality the personal touch of his leadership existed only in relation to his peers. Despite holding the office of Minister for Native Affairs — as Coghlan and Moffat had done before him — he felt unsettled by the portfolio and preferred to deal with it through the Chief Native Commissioner.

If Huggins was never entirely reconciled to blacks, it can at least be said of him that he had a lot more to do with them than most. In the tradition of his profession, he regarded blacks as he might have looked upon the London poor: people who needed help, advice and sympathy, but who should never question or supplant their betters' opinions and prescriptions. This was Huggins' version of trusteeship. As the arch-paternalist he reserved the absolute right to guide with a firm hand the naughty children he was charged to protect. Whatever trusteeship might mean to any native or government official, the one thing that each held in common was that the black man was incapable of making intelligent choices on his own account.

As the decade matured, many questions were being asked about the effectiveness of segregation as a real and long term solution to the native problem. It had been noted that by then there were more blacks living outside the reserves than in 1931, when the Land Apportionment Act came into law, and no practical policy had so far evolved to stem, let alone reverse this trend. It was predicted that a build up of hostility in black society was inevitable, and that someday this might spill over into violence. Black urbanisation was, of course, unstoppable, and as long as whites were punctilious about immigration standards, there would never be enough of them willing to do menial work. That meant blacks would continue to flood into the towns and cities.

Thus, despite the removal of blacks from European areas continuing apace, Huggins was forced to push forward the deadline for the completion of the work by five years. The government acquired more land for native settlement and accelerated the construction of boreholes, schools and clinics.

Nevertheless, Huggins was forced to admit to the House that the final solution might not turn out to be so final after all. Complete separation had clearly been proved unworkable, and although Huggins refused to abandon the principal altogether, he was on occasions forced to concede that it required significant revision.

One of these revisions had been the Natives Registration Act that came into force in 1936 and introduced pass laws that limited black movement in white areas. Since in practical terms, blacks could not be stopped from working and therefore living in white areas, their movements were to be controlled and carefully monitored. In 1930 educated Christian blacks had lobbied missionaries to persuade the government to repeal the notice of 1906, that made it an offence for a black to use any sidewalk or pavement within any municipality. This pro-black-rights trend continued, until by 1938, acceptance of urban blacks had advanced to the point that Salisbury Municipality moved to provide housing for over 5 000 of the incumbent urban population. It did not, however, accommodate a further 6 000 (exclusive of domestic servants) who were living in various corners and commons, at the back of warehouses and factories and in 'private locations' adjacent to mines and industries.

While all this was a significant advance on the absolute denial of old, it had been difficult to achieve. The Land Apportionment Act declared that the cities were the white man's domain and only his interests were to be catered for there. It would require a much more open acknowledgement of black urbanisation before a formal native housing programme would be launched, and there was no evidence that this was about to happen. The problem of poor living conditions among urban blacks continued to be ignored until it was pushed into the forefront of the public debate by the urban unrest of 1945 and 1948. However, by the outbreak of war in 1939, Huggins and his government had at least concluded that physical separation as a theory was dead. The native problem had now become a build-up of black political energy that physical separation alone could not arrest. Around a framework of native policies, that were carefully crafted to avoid the slightest possibility of resistance, resistance was quietly forming.

Huggins and a handful of others at last began to notice the rise of a black intelligentsia. That most of the rank and file whites failed to take note of it had little to do with bare racism, and much to do with the frenetic pace of recovery in the run up to war. The war itself did not affect or limit the growth of the black intelligentsia, other than to allow it to proceed largely unnoticed. Blacks in fact found the war enlightening. The British were filled with the doctrine of freedom from oppression that they poured over the African as proof of British greatness. The blacks looked at the British themselves and thought very well of their philosophy.

For those blacks who observed the war from afar, the lessons tended to be political. For those who fought in it, the lessons were more direct. Black soldiers were astonished to discover that white men could fill the lower ranks of a vast institution and duly be slaughtered in large numbers. Furthermore, black Rhodesian soldiers — and indeed black soldiers from all over British Africa — fought German and Italian white men in many battles, and killed them. This naturally completely changed the black man's view of the white man's mortality. It was no less than the watershed for the surge of black political advancement that followed.

Ndabaningi Sithole, one of the first genuine political leaders to emerge from black society — and about whom much will be heard later — remembered in his autobiography a comment made to him after the war by a man he termed an 'Asiatic'. 'We owe our independence to Adolf Hitler...' was the comment, and a curiously intelligent one it was too. Sithole was inspired and wrote in response: 'The big lesson learned was [that] domination by any nation is wrong — and this is still echoing throughout the world, and it is being reinforced in many quarters in and outside Africa.'1

An event of significance occurred in March 1938 when the Rev Thomson Samkange received an invitation to attend the International Missionary Conference in Tambaram, Madras, as one of two delegates from Southern Rhodesia. In an India already sensing independence, Samkange would meet such celebrated revolutionaries as Pundit Nehru and the 'Mahatma', Mohandas Gandhi. He would also encounter others from Africa, like Albert Luthuli, and many more from diverse corners of the British Empire and the world.

Thomson Samkange was overawed by the apparent sophistication of the Asians he met at the conference. He realised as he interacted with delegates from China, Japan, India and Ceylon how backward the Africans must have appeared to them. From his long time friend Enoch Musa: '…it was an eye opener to him and to many other Africans. He saw that we were very low by comparison. The debates were very high. He didn't speak. He was learning. We still have not reached the edge of these things.'

Samkange was overawed but not discouraged. Indeed he was deeply impressed and stimulated by the open political dialogue of so many diverse peoples. Many of these groups were engaged in versions of the same struggle that the black people of Southern Rhodesia were only dreaming about. He sensed a daring theology in the unfettered exchange of ideas, and was challenged to express his views on nationalism, totalitarianism, Christ and communism, as well as such scarcely considered concepts as Christian Socialism. 'The European totalitarian state, and any extensions of it in Africa, must be met with the assertion that the demands of Christ are also totalitarian.'[2]

Before he left India, Samkange and other delegates travelled to Wardha where Gandhi's ashram was situated and he was introduced to the great man himself. He lunched at the Indian National Congress building and heard something of Ghandi's political philosophy of non-violent protest and non-cooperation.

When Rev Samkange returned home, those who knew him immediately detected a change in the tone of his language, for he had turned a vital corner. He had brought home with him the language of national freedom, and although at that point 'nationalist' may be too strong a word to describe him, the road to nationalism lay clear before him — and before a number of others too.

In the meanwhile, black Rhodesian aspirations and observations were clouded by white Rhodesian commitment to Britain, which was total. The heart and soul of a young nation went out to its kith and kin threatened by Nazi Germany. Huggins prepared to place the country on a war footing, and for this he felt it necessary to go to the electorate. Labour howled in protest claiming, not unjustly, that Huggins was trying to make capital out of a European war.

Huggins in fact could not take dissolution for granted and hoped that war might set a precedent. His reasoning was that a war might require the enactment of emergency powers, and should this be the case, a refreshed parliament would be required to carry it through. The Governor, Sir Hubert Stanley, was not obliged to agree with Huggins but he did so, and in April 1939 the country went to the polls. The new house was not unlike the old. The United Party won 23 seats with Labour emerging as the only opposition. The country was now virtually in Huggins' pocket to do with what he would. He built his cabinet with war in mind, and then dug in for the grim years to follow.

27

War, peace, hope and expectation

Rhodesians at war

When judged by the standards of even some of the minor combatants, Southern Rhodesia's manpower contribution to World War-II was small in absolute numbers but disproportionately high in percentage terms. Some 8 500 white men and 1 500 white women served in the allied forces, of whom 693 were killed. 14 000 blacks served in combat roles and suffered a loss of 126 lives. When the call to arms came, the response was so universal that the Minister of Justice and Defence was forced to introduce a system of selective conscription, aimed at limiting the depletion of essential services. This is probably the only time in history that conscription has been used as a means to keep as many men as possible out of uniform.

While her contribution in terms of men at arms may have been small, Southern Rhodesia's influence on the battlefront was once again significant. As in World War-I it had not gone unnoticed that Rhodesian youth were incubated with a command sensibility born largely of their practice in handling large local labour forces. As offensive as this fact might have been to certain liberals and Fabians in the United Kingdom, it was a commodity much sought after in wartime, and Rhodesian volunteers were put in command positions as both staff and field officers. In Rhodesia itself there were no requirements for officers to serve in the ranks as conditioning for command, since in Rhodesia the other ranks were black. A command capability was expected from white recruits from the onset. White Rhodesians, incidentally, were also widely used in the command of troops recruited in West, Central and East Africa. This was because, as Robert Tredgold put it: 'At least our men had seen a black man outside a Christy Minstrel performance…'[1]

Tredgold was also concerned that the white manpower of the colony should not be concentrated in a single regiment. It was important not to repeat the World War-I mistakes of East Africa, where the loss of manpower from the 2nd Rhodesia Regiment was so severe that the force was unable to continue as a cohesive fighting unit. The same fate had met the men of the Newfoundland Regiment at Beaumont Hamel during the Somme offensive when almost the entire regiment was wiped out in a single advance. There were also large Rhodesian losses in that offensive, particularly at Delville Wood together with savage South African casualties. The risk to Rhodesian manpower was spread by spacing volunteers widely in a variety of different reserves and regiments of the British Army.

The result of this is that it has become difficult, from the perspective of a general history, to point to any particular theatres or actions where Rhodesian servicemen contributed or excelled. Rhodesians served in one form or another in all the main theatres of the conflict and there is no doubt that they distinguished themselves and rendered a contribution disproportionate to the number of men who signed up.

British South Africa Policeman and future head of the intelligence community, Ken Flower, was one such example. He joined a small group of Rhodesians who sailed up to Berbera in the Gulf of Aden, to take part in the re-occupation of British Somaliland. Others served in Italy, Europe and the Far East. Yet others were engaged in the Western Desert, in the Long Range Desert Group and the exploits of the fabled Desert Rats of the Special Air Services. In fact David Stirling, founder of the SAS and architect of covert operations in North Africa, was a sometime Rhodesian who settled briefly in Salisbury after the end of the war. There he designed his own blueprint for a utopian and non-racial landscape in the form of the Capricorn Africa Society.

It was, however, in the RAF that perhaps the biggest Southern Rhodesian contribution was made. Hardwicke Holderness, of whom much more will be heard later, joined the Oxford University Air Squadron as a student in 1938, and served as a fighter pilot almost from the moment hostilities broke out. Holderness emerged as one of the most decorated Rhodesian servicemen and a hero of the Battle of Britain. Other Rhodesian aces included Wing Commander John Plagis and Flight Lieutenant Ernest Williams, each with 17 confirmed kills. William Maguire, Neville Bowker, Frank Holman, Perry St Quintin, Caesar Hull, George Buchanan, Eric Dicks-Sherwood, Johnny Deal and Percy 'Ping' Newton notched up 84 kills among them. Although never celebrated as an ace, future Prime Minister Ian Smith flew in North Africa and Italy before being shot down over the Po Valley, where he was briefly sheltered by Italian partisans. When it is considered that Australia fielded 83 RAF fighter aces, New Zealand over 100 and South Africa 58, the size of the Rhodesian contribution can be better appreciated.

Rhodesia has always claimed Sir Arthur 'Bomber' Harris, head of RAF Bomber Command, as one of its own. Born of Indian Civil Service parentage and schooled in England he went in search of his roots as soon as he was able to. At the age of 18 he went to explore the wide open spaces and the limitless possibilities of Southern Rhodesia. He farmed there in what was very much a pioneering period and would have had his own farm there if it had not been for the outbreak of World War 1. Instead he volunteered to join 1-Rhodesia Regiment as an infantryman and went to fight the Germans in South West Africa. He took part in some epic marches leaving him determined that he would never march into battle again. Inspired by the sight of both German and British aircraft dog-fighting overhead, he headed for England after the campaign ended and joined the fledgling Royal Flying Corps, later to become the Royal Air Force. By the end of the war he was a commanding 44 Bomber Squadron.

By the outbreak of World War-II Harris had risen to the rank of Air Vice Marshall. In 1941 he took over Bomber Command as an Air Chief Marshall. One of his first actions as commander was to change the nomenclature of his old 44 Squadron to 44 (Rhodesia) Squadron — the first squadron in the RAF to be equipped with the new Lancaster Bombers. Harris called himself a Rhodesian until the day he died and his loyalty to the country never wavered.

Thanks primarily to his adoption of the German practice of carpet bombing Harris was to emerge as one of the most controversial senior commanders of World War-II. His main object was to batter the German military and industrial machine into an early submission. To achieve this he deployed phalanxes of up to 1 000 bomber aircraft at a time on devastating night raids against German cities, with similar daylight raids being undertaken by the US 8th Army Air Force.

This tactic, although costly in civilian lives, manifestly succeeded. Under interrogation after the war *Feldmarschall* Albert Kesselring, commander-in-chief of the west, remarked that 'Allied air-power was the greatest single reason for the German's defeat'. This was a view echoed by many others, including, *Generalmajor* Kolb, formerly in charge of technical training at the Air Ministry, who commented no less equivocally: 'From the middle of 1940 onward, Germany was forced into major revision of its strategic plans of operation. The power of Allied day and night strategic bombing forced Germany on the defensive from that time on.'

For this achievement Harris received scant recognition and he was deliberately slighted by being the only senior British commander passed over for elevation to the peerage in the aftermath of the war. Many senior civil servants, some boasting only minor achievements except for time served, were and still are so honoured. The lesser figures being knighted, as was Harris himself, despite being one of the most influential figures of the war.

This snub was also extended to the men who had served under Harris during the dark days of the war. Bomber Command was engaged from 1939 through to 1945 with a staggering total loss of some 55 000 aircrew. On one terrible night a loss of 670 airmen was recorded — more than Fighter Command's total losses in the Battle of Britain. Harris' request for a special campaign medal for Bomber Command to recognise this sacrifice was refused which led to much bitterness among surviving bomber crews.

The controversy surrounding Arthur Harris and Bomber Command was triggered largely by socialist intellectual and MP for Coventry East, Richard Crossman. Crossman led a chorus of condemnation of the bombing campaign as a costly failure, even an atrocity — the fire bombing of Dresden being the most often quoted. The argument that strategic bombing was a tactic employed initially by the Germans over Warsaw, Rotterdam and London, and even Crossman's own constituency of Coventry, was largely ignored.

The United States 8th Air Force suffered no such scorn. With a comparable record of 26 000 men lost from their involvement in the campaign from December 1941— two years later than Bomber Command. They were quite rightly welcomed home as returning heroes. Strategic bombings remains to this day a cornerstone of American war strategy as can be seen by Vietnam and Iraq.

Harris, meanwhile, retired from the RAF in 1946 and moved to South Africa were he entered business.

In the mid 1950s he returned to England and from then until his death in 1984 he was received as an honoured guest at reunions. On such occasions he would remind the veterans of Bomber Command that they had been denied the recognition they deserved, to which he would invariably be rewarded with a standing ovation. At a dinner of the Air Gunners' Association, he responded to the emotion of the occasion by asking: 'Will you go back to Dresden, or Nuremberg or Berlin tonight?' According to one man present 'Every man there would have stepped forward and said: "Yes, sir, we will go.' And no one could have been in any doubt that they meant it.

The black Rhodesian contribution to the allied effort was made late in the war and began with the formation in 1940 of the 1st Battalion Rhodesia African Rifles. This battalion was the first Rhodesian regular unit, and recruits for it were drawn from both the Mashona and the Matabele, with black NCOs seconded from the British South Africa Police Askari Platoon. The officers were white and came mainly from the ranks of the BSAP and the Native Affairs Department. A training depot was built alongside Government House, and in 1942 large-scale training was undertaken both there and in the Eastern Highlands. At the end of 1943 the unit set off for Kenya for final training. Thereafter it became part of 22nd East Africa Independent Brigade, and after training with 82nd (West Africa) Division, the unit was shipped to Burma to be deployed against the Japanese.

The battalion first saw action in April 1945. Although the Japanese were by then already in retreat, they fought a determined rearguard action that blooded the Rhodesian soldiers with heavy casualties. Japanese commanders who had never before fought black men apparently complimented the battalion for its discipline and determination in battle. It was in Burma that the RAR regimental song of 'Sweet Banana' was born. When sung in sonorous chorus as only an assembly of black singers can, it tells of the delight to banana-loving palates of the local sweet variety of this fruit.

The signature and ongoing contribution that Southern Rhodesia made to the war, and vice versa, was her participation in the Empire Air Training Scheme along with South Africa and Canada. In the run up to the war pilot training had taken place on the British mainland but, once in the thick of the Battle of Britain, this became impractical. Pilots in training would interfere with air combat over Britain and add to the congestion of local airfields and facilities. The British climate was also not ideal for the large scale processing of trainee pilots. The clear skies of the dominions were an obvious alternative with the excellent climate of Southern Rhodesia particularly favoured.

The story of the Empire Air Training Scheme is also the story of the development of an independent air force in Rhodesia. Towards the end of 1935, flight training began at Belvedere Airport under the aegis of the 1st Battalion Rhodesia Regiment. By March 1936 Group Captain Arthur Harris was in Salisbury advising on the future course of flying training. It was Harris who suggested the establishment of a unit to train local territorial personnel who, in the event of war, it was agreed would be sent to Kenya for service with the RAF. On 17 July 1936, the Southern Rhodesia Government Gazette announced the formation of an air section to be attached to the Defence Force.

The unit could already boast four Hawker Audax and six Hawker Hart biplanes. Later another four Audax and two Hart aircraft were despatched from Britain, arriving just six days before the declaration of war. The unit was in due course renamed the Southern Rhodesia Air Unit. The first trainee pilots, a young Hardwicke Holderness among them, were awarded their wings in May 1938.

In August the following year, with the declaration of war imminent, the Air Unit was deployed to Kenya as planned. There it patrolled the Northern Frontier District, keeping an eye on the Italians in Somaliland. In April 1940, the unit was absorbed into the RAF as 237 (Rhodesia) Squadron. Two other Rhodesian-manned squadrons were formed as 44 (Rhodesia) Squadron and 266 (Rhodesia) Squadron.

In May 1940, agreement was reached between the British Air Ministry and the participating dominions, including Australia and Canada, and the Empire Air Training Scheme got under way. The Rhodesian Air Training Group eventually came to include four service flying training schools, an initial training wing, a combined air observers and air gunners school and a central flying school for instructors. By the end of the war over 7 600 pilots and 2 300 navigators had passed through the system in Rhodesia.

The infrastructure needed for the operation was massive, and Southern Rhodesia at that point had few such facilities. However, with a blank cheque from the British Air Ministry, the officer commanding, Lieutenant-Colonel Sir Charles Meredith, set about organising a huge building programme with an annual turnover of almost £350 000. This windfall provided quite a construction boom in an already steadily booming local economy. Then there were the 12 000 adult white males employed by the scheme — the majority from Britain — as well as 5 000 blacks and about 200 white women of the Woman's Auxiliary Air Service. Again, all these learners circulated a significant amount of revenue within the Rhodesian economy.

The boom in immigration that followed the war could be attributed directly to the exposure enjoyed by so many Britons and other allied nationals, to the pleasant climate and society of Rhodesia. All this contributed much to the rapid post war development of the country, but perhaps more than anything else, it produced an important symbolic understanding between Rhodesia and Britain. Since the Empire Air Training Scheme had been a combined project of the Imperial Government and her dominions specifically, this suggested that Southern Rhodesia had been upgraded from a mere self-governing colony to a de facto dominion. Why this was so important to the white sense of the future was that the other major dominions were sailing smoothly towards independence within the Commonwealth — and Rhodesia more than anything else wanted to follow this route. It was an extension of a hope that had been nurtured by the removal of the jurisdiction for Southern Rhodesia, from the Colonial office to the Dominions Office, in 1925. The country was then allowed certain limited freedoms, although without being officially recognised as a dominion. While much goodwill existed both in Southern Rhodesia and Whitehall regarding the concept of white self-determination, the Sacred Trust remained a barrier to the overt promise of independence. Neither the Southern Rhodesian nor the British governments had any idea quite what a barrier that would soon prove to be.

Fags before bullets

At home the war caused no less hardship and anxiety than it did all over the world. In spite of this, and in just a few key sectors, a profound economic revolution was triggered. With 1000 tons of copper required for the construction of a single battleship and two miles of wire needed for the electronics of one bomber aircraft, it is hardly surprising that the Copperbelt fuelled a boom, the effects of which were felt throughout the region. Britain's isolation, and the pressure on her war treasury, created an unprecedented demand for Empire products. Southern Rhodesian manufactured goods found a ready market north of the Zambezi, while prices for just about anything that could be produced shot skyward. Wankie Collieries worked at maximum capacity to fulfil orders for the blast furnaces of the Copperbelt and, as Rhodesian technical expertise and investment flooded north, dividends and remittances flooded south. Part of the economic revolution was the migration of black labour from the reserves to the cities and industrial areas, that again threw the formula of racial separation into disarray.

On the economic front the expected recovery took many forms, but it manifested most dramatically in the tobacco industry. Young tobacco baron and chairman of the Rhodesia Tobacco Association, Winston Field — of whom much will be heard later — flew to London in late 1938, to meet with representatives of the British tobacco industry. As a result of the prevailing political uncertainties, British manufacturers had lately begun to express a renewed interest in Rhodesian tobacco. In September of that year Neville Chamberlain met Adolph Hitler at his Bavarian lair of Berchtesgaden. So browbeaten was the British Prime Minister that he returned to London convinced there would be 'peace in our time'. Industrialists were less credulous and began cautiously anticipating a war and the severe restrictions that would follow. A dollar shortage would limit British access to American tobacco and this prompted executives to review the sterling area. Nestling in a bed of raw potential, the tobacco industry of Southern Rhodesia was waiting for just such a day.

Field was asked a simple question for which he had a simple reply. What would it take to effect a rapid increase in Southern Rhodesian production capacity? The answer was indeed simple: guarantee a minimum price of three shillings per pound at auction. Field was given a strong verbal assurance that this would be the case. Word quickly circulated and almost immediately the acreage under tobacco was increased by over 30 per cent.

It happened that heavy rains washed out the 1939 growing season, so yields proved to be poor anyway, and it was not until the record crop of 1940 that Southern Rhodesian growers were able to test the sincerity of the British commitment. In the event, few were surprised when the auction floors opened to find the British buyers reluctant to part with a penny more than absolutely necessary. Prices were depressed and there was no sign of meeting the promised three-shilling guarantee. Growers, of course, were quick to complain to the ministry. In response Frank Harris took one or two of the British buyers aside and reminded them of what had been agreed. He threatened that if the three-shilling minimum was not respected, he would close the sales floors and that would be it for the year. The threat worked and when the floors reopened the following morning, the price per pound had crept up to the magic figure of three shillings.

This marked one of the most significant moments in Southern Rhodesian history. For the first time in a long and tortured contest, British tobacco blinked, and the wilderness years were over. War rolled across Europe, and Britain was soon under siege. Nervous troops in every theatre demanded a steady supply of fags before bullets, and anxious urbanites chain-smoked as they peered out of the shelters at a rain of German bombs. As the tobacco manufacturers and buyers had anticipated, American tobacco became as scarce as her dollars, and every scrap of leaf that Rhodesian growers could produce was sold.

Tobacco farmers were already benefiting from the local war economy: price controls on inputs and heavy government subsidies for production, significantly cut overheads, but there was no concurrent control on selling prices. It was not long before the price of leaf on the auction floors more than doubled and continued to rise. It was the stuff of dreams. By late 1942 and early 1943 white tobacco farmers had leapt from an eccentric band of agricultural adventurers to the aristocracy of the Southern Rhodesian farming community.

Maize and beef producers, who had suffered price controls at both ends, were initially stung — and then increasingly envious. In an atmosphere of shortages and rationing, when sons and brothers were fighting over the skies of England, there was something odious about a class of cash-heavy back-country farmers garnishing their lands and homesteads with conspicuous wealth. The jealousy was short-lived however, for the tobacco boom lit a fire under the economic pot that was soon boiling furiously. By 1946, the value of tobacco exports for the first time exceeded gold. Two years later tobacco would be worth a staggering £11 million sterling, and had become the main prop of the Southern Rhodesian economy.

More than anything, tobacco money released a surge of creativity that revolutionised and modernised the general farming industry. It capitalised landholdings, funded experiments, bridged failures and financed research and the import of plant and livestock. It built homesteads, dams, weirs, roads and modern tobacco barns. It gave the country its signature richly textured and multi-layered agricultural landscape, and built an industry that, for the remainder of the colonial period, was the envy of farming communities everywhere.

The tobacco boom also had the effect of revolutionising Salisbury. The capital was situated in the heart of tobacco country and grew rapidly into the national centre of tobacco and agro business. In due course, the boom funded a surge of associated commercial, industrial and infrastructural development throughout the region. It would not be overstating the point to say that tobacco money built Southern Rhodesia.

Huggie's war

Despite being far from the front line, Huggins' own war was not without a good deal of turbulence. The boom proved to be something of an economic coming of age for him as well as for the country. As head of the administration he was forced, among other things, to grapple with fiscal problems that in the past he had always been able to delegate. With his best men away at war, he also tended to find himself keeping the company of old political dogs who, while preoccupied with stoking their spleen, were also bent on keeping their eyes alert for a sight of his jugular. As a result, Huggins fought a series of bruising political and economic skirmishes that not only consumed him with tedium, but also rubbed the last burrs of amateurism from the seams of his casting.

Huggins was by nature an imperialist and, insofar as he had any economic philosophy at all, it tended to follow the Victorian credo of hard work and free enterprise. He had never been given to sympathy for the weak, although during the difficult years of the depression, he had also come to realise that the weak are vocal and usually strong in numbers. Consequently, while he desired to see the pioneers of farming and industry prosper, he was also aware that he could not afford to alienate the unionists or the white working classes. While he tried to remain true to the free market and an open, uninhibited economy, he also found himself pressured, by the left wing of the House, to move away from the loose style of capitalism that had tended to thrive during the casual inter-war years.[2] State intervention was now part and parcel of modern economics, and if Southern Rhodesia wanted to be counted among progressive nations, Huggins would have to guide it through a period of painful and far-reaching reform. However, he decided to remain true to his natural pragmatism and took the view that success in the application of socialism lay in both stealth and moderation.

He started by putting price controls in place to protect consumers — particularly black consumers — against the inflationary tendencies of war. He did the same for the commercial sector, hoping to protect emerging industries from similar effects. As he did this he knew that he was provoking the conservative wing of the cabinet and risking a rebellion if he went too far or too fast.

His boldest move during the war years was the nationalisation of Rhodesia's only steel manufacturer, which at that time was owned primarily by South Africa's ISCOR (Iron and Steel Corporation). Again his objective was to protect the supply of raw and semi-raw materials to Rhodesia's own emerging industries, arguing that if ISCOR should temporarily withdraw production to concentrate on its own market — which under wartime expediencies it might easily do — it would strangle many local enterprises at the moment of their birth.

The government approached ISCOR but lengthy negotiations came to naught. Huggins then put before the House a bill providing for an ultimate appeal to the High Court if an accommodation could not be reached with the South Africans. Against significant opposition he argued that a country like Southern Rhodesia, with its formative manufacturing industry, should process its primary products under public control. Private capital could then use state manufactured semi-raw materials to benefit themselves and the country at large.

The bill empowered the government to acquire the Bulawayo works, and run them via a public board in a similar manner to the Electricity Supply and the Cold Storage Commissions. Huggins' decision was borne out some time later, when the industry expanded to include the Rhodesian Iron and Steel Corporation, or RISCO, which was founded in 1942.

The Cabinet then went on to review taxes. Applying the rather high-minded principal that no man should profit from a clash of arms, Huggins introduced an excess profits tax that enriched the Treasury, but served to wipe out much of the profit that businessmen and manufacturers had hoped to accrue from the war boom. The gold industry was targeted with a similar gold premiums tax, that was probably a little unfair, since the boom was largely in base minerals and not precious metals. Tobacco farmers also paid a special tax although they did not suffer price controls on the auction floor — besides which their gorging on profits was unstoppable anyway for the time being.

Under these stresses it was not surprising that Huggins' support base began to crumble. There were many men in powerful sectors who could not understand why the Prime Minister had gone to war against the breadwinners and architects of the nation's future prosperity. Finance Minister Jacob Smit, an Afrikaner shopkeeper and as uncompromising a right-winger as could be found anywhere, was dismayed by the government's gradual swing to the left. Through the grapevine he warned the Prime Minister of the possible consequences and made it plain that he felt Huggins had become a danger to both his country and his party.

Smit was a perfect example of a wartime appointment. It was not long after selecting him to join his Cabinet that Huggins realised he could not stand the sight of the man, and with his usual candour made no secret of the fact. Huggins, the airy intellectual, did concede on occasion that Smit was a credible treasurer, but he was also a dour, humourless and overtly religious individual — traits that could only frustrate and irritate a person of Huggins' temper. It was just this kind of bad feeling and infighting that caused the economic boat to slip its moorings.

Economically Huggins fought a good fight and ultimately held his own. Politically things were much the same. He came under attack from a variety of quarters, again mainly because the best of his men were away. He was surrounded in government by malcontents, as keen to obstruct one another as to thwart him. As a result, some of his Cabinet choices were made with a mind either to mollify one or other pressure group or simply out of desperation. This had the effect of further loosening his grip on the affairs of state.

It was in this tight corner that Huggins tried to affect some sort of an accommodation with the left wing of the House. He invited two prominent members of the Labour Party, Jack Keller and Harry Davis, to occupy the offices of Labour and Internal Affairs respectively. While hoping to nip a left-wing rebellion in the bud, what he actually achieved was to open an ideological split in the left wing that had not previously existed.

Labour happened to be divided between opposing versions of the same theme. The Anglo-Saxon working classes subscribed to socialism solely in relation to the rights of the white workers of Rhodesia. These men stood in bitter opposition to those left-wing intellectuals of a more Fabian orientation, who pondered race policy from an intellectual-liberal standpoint. The white workers, although labour in caste, were arguably the most entrenched racists in the country and it stood to reason that they and the Fabians would never meet in the same party on friendly terms. By inviting Labour into the Cabinet, Huggins widened the faultline, prompting a new squabble between those who supported participation in government and those who did not. This did not play entirely into his hands for in mid-term, and in the middle of a war, he needed strength to govern and not a divided opposition with one foot in and one foot out of government.

The situation would have been extremely perilous for the Prime Minister had it not been for a fortunately timed bout of labour unrest that erupted on the Copperbelt. While Huggins had been weakened, his degree of support was difficult to gauge, and in his response to a sudden call for help from the government of Northern Rhodesia, he was able to show that although he might have been down, he was by no means out.

The incident was interesting inasmuch as it presented another of those uniquely Rhodesian ideological conundrums. In 1942 the General Secretary of the Mine Workers Union (Northern Rhodesia), a certain Frank Maybank, formed an alliance with a group of Afrikaans speakers on the mines, who were supporters of the *Ossewabrandwag*, a South African fascist organisation bitterly opposed to the war. A strike was threatened by this clique, and in the nature of things, the forces available to the Administration to put them down were black. The Governor, Sir Eubule John Waddington, was obviously anxious not to interrupt copper production, but he was clearly wary of throwing black troops against white strikers. He had observed the trials and travails of Jan Smuts (currently serving his second term) at the hands of militant, nationalist white workers. If Waddington had used black troops to arrest these men, the result for Smuts could well have been a reversal of the very narrow majority that had brought South Africa into the war. This the Imperial Government could not afford.

It was at this point that Huggins received the cry for help from Waddington and saved the day by sending north a detachment of the white Southern Rhodesian Armoured Car Unit. The detachment effectively neutralised the rising and expedited the deportation of the ringleaders. The incident bolstered Huggins' personal image abroad, but added somewhat to lingering suspicions against him at home.

Despite this, there were few whites in Rhodesia who did not like Huggins, and even fewer he did not like in return. This handful of pariahs, of whom Jacob Smit was one, he tolerated with very poor grace. When the unity experiment with labour fell apart, Huggins found himself facing a sudden threat to his government from the right, rather than the left wing. In response to Huggins' determination to press on with his economic controls, an angry Jacob Smit broke away from the United Party to form a new ultra-right-wing political alliance that, in the pantomime of uniquely misnamed political parties in Rhodesia, was named the Liberal Party.

Smit thought he had read Huggins sufficiently well to gamble on dissolution. He judged the country ready for change, and with the two issues of Huggins' slide into socialism and the unregulated flood of blacks into the cities, he felt confident that he had a strong platform. Huggins, of course, would not be easily forced into a general election. As a son of England he knew a thing or two that an Anglophobe Afrikaner did not. He raised his voice above the hubris and disorder and appealed directly to the country for a show of patriotism. This strategy, although starting to wear a little thin, still worked surprisingly well.

Jacob Smit would not automatically have understood the power of British nationalism, but with the war moving towards its climax and most of the working men of the country abroad, an election would have been out of the question. Huggins outflanked Smit without difficulty, after which the latter was forced to resume his seat on the backbenches and reflect bitterly on a prime minister who was more than a little shrewder than he appeared to be.

While Huggins had slipped the noose for the moment, he was aware that the end of the war would demand political change. In the interim he was faced with the task of arresting the decline of his personal popularity, after which he could attend to the task of reuniting his crumbling party. He began this by reconsidering the now vacant office of the Treasury and decided to replace Smit with his old friend Max Danziger. Huggins had proved that he was a reasonable economic strategist, but the day-to-day business of fiscal management was beyond him. In trying to cooperate with Smit he had found him grasping, conservative and with a tendency to accrue rather than spend. Danziger was a man more on Huggins' intellectual level, and believing that one could do no better than having a Jew in charge of the fiscus, he put Danziger to work.

A brawny backcountry rancher by the name of Raymond Stockil quickly superseded Jacob Smit in the leadership of the Liberal Party. Stockil was a fairly typical product of Rhodesia, where he had gathered wide experience in mining and ranching — so much so that by the end of the war he was among a small clique of wealthy and influential farmer-capitalists who made up a key faction of the House. Huggins, on the other hand, with his dislike of cabinet reshuffles, was left surrounded by the tired old drudges of the United Party who were manifestly unequal to a bruising fight.

It was fortunate for Huggins that, at that particular moment, a certain Colonel Walker suggested to the Labour Party that black participation in the alliance was necessary. This promptly plunged labour into another round of bitter infighting and the party began to fall apart. By 1946 it had ceased to be an effective threat. Huggins was then able to concentrate his attention on the Liberal Party, and it didn't take him long to identify two contradictions in their manifesto.

Most importantly, the Liberals had picked as a battle cry, the demand for dominion status. As we have seen, this had been injected with significant momentum since the inauguration of the Empire Air Training Scheme, and throughout the war there had been strong hints emanating from Whitehall that dominion status would be granted to Rhodesia as a reward for her exemplary contribution. Now that the war was over, expectations were high, and there can be no doubt that a strong motivation existed in London to be true to the promise. However the question of native affairs as usual kept the brakes on.

The Liberals went further and demanded an end to the imperial veto, and the granting of rights to the minority assembly to legislate on behalf of the blacks. There was simply no possibility that Whitehall either would — or could — grant dominion status at that moment, and certainly not under a more restrictive native policy than already existed. Demanding both was amateurish and self-defeating and Huggins made a significant point of exposing this fact.

The second issue was the Liberal espousal of 'unbridled' capitalism while, at the same time, demanding state ownership of such industries as the Wankie coalfields and the railways. Likewise, this contradiction helped Huggins expose the Liberals as a dilettante alliance of loudmouthed amateurs.

All this notwithstanding, Huggins and the United Party barely survived the 1946 general election. The Prime Minister himself comfortably retained his seat, but his party suffered a series of defeats. The Liberals made an almost clean sweep of the rural constituencies, and cut deep inroads into the urban vote. Even Huggins' neighbouring constituency of Avondale fell. It had been a very close thing, but the United Party nonetheless held on to power with 13 seats against the Liberal Party's 12. Labour collected five but then promptly split, along familiar lines, into the right-wing Rhodesia Labour Party with three seats, and the liberal-intellectual Southern Rhodesia Labour Party with two. A recount helped Huggins a little with the removal of one seat from the Liberals — which increased the United Party majority to two seats. Despite this, Huggins found himself balanced on a knife-edge and he knew that hard times lay ahead.

28

The native comes of age

Largely unobserved by the white minority, the boom years of the war had set in motion a parallel revolution in black society. A young black student studying for an honours degree at Fort Hare University in South Africa — having defied the odds of poverty and discrimination to get there — defined the hope of the emerging black intelligentsia when, in a touchingly optimistic essay on the circumstances of the black race, he quoted from Booker T Washington's *Atlanta Compromise* address.

> No race that has learned to contribute to the markets of the world is in the long run ostracised.[1]

The student was Stanlake Samkange, the eldest son of Grace and the Rev Thomson Samkange, and when he returned to Rhodesia with one of the first university degrees to be won by a native of the country, the event marked the end of the beginning. Other gifted and accomplished young blacks would follow, and from among them the leadership of a future political struggle would be selected.

Stanlake Samkange's honours degree was a triumph that was brought about only through immense personal sacrifice. Nevertheless, he was to find, as he took up his first political office as secretary of the Southern Rhodesia Bantu Congress, that in the short term at least Booker T Washington had been mistaken. The work that blacks were doing, and the contribution they were making to the wealth of the minority, proved that it was indeed possible for a race to contribute to the markets of the world and still be ostracised. Ndabaningi Sithole, emerging from his own higher education and forming his own revolutionary ideas, saw the situation thus:

> On examination, the basic ingredients that go to make up the present African nationalism may be enumerated as the African's desire to participate fully in the central government of the country; his desire for economic justice that recognises fully the principle of 'equal pay for equal work' regardless of the colour of the skin; his desire to have full political rights in his own country; his dislike of being treated as a stranger in the land of his birth; his dislike of being treated as means for the white man's end; and his dislike of the laws of the country that prescribe for him a permanent position of inferiority as a human being.[2]

It is hard to believe that after just one generation of available tuition, a black man had been produced in Rhodesia who could articulate his condition so succinctly. Both Stanlake Samkange and Ndabaningi Sithole at that point bore favourable comparison to the great survivors and achievers of the black race such as Frederick Douglass and Booker T Washington himself. It is also interesting to note that the first black Rhodes scholar was not an African, but American Howard University philosopher Alain Locke.[3] Meanwhile, if any whites had cared to notice the rise of the black intelligentsia, there would have been as much amazement as concern.

In 1920 Ndabaningi Sithole was born into humble circumstances in the Matabeleland district of Nyamandhlovo. Largely self-educated, with some assistance from the Wesleyans and the Methodists, he attended the Newton Theological College near Boston Massachusetts where he studied theology for three years. Back in Rhodesia he was ordained at the Mount Selinda Congregationalist Church and began work as a school principal. At the same time he set to work on his sweeping political thesis, African Nationalism.

With Samkange, Sithole and many others to inspire them, young blacks were increasingly seeing education as the key to emancipation. While the gifted few were enjoying the sponsorship of the churches, many more were benefiting from improved native primary school education, and increasingly during the 1940s, secondary education too. By the mid 1940s, 100,000 black children in the country were estimated to be experiencing some level of tuition. Annually there were potentially more black job seekers flooding the labour market than there were whites living in the country, with many of these making their way into industry and commerce.

By the end of the war no fewer than 20 000 blacks were formally employed in urban industries with a further undisclosed number labouring on farms and in domestic service. In black urban settlements on the fringes of the cities, squatter communities and urban slums grew with frightening speed. The ambiguity of white attitudes to this was born out by the fact that no formal policy framework existed upon which to respond to it. The government was officially in denial and thus completely paralysed, allowing conditions for urban blacks to deteriorate steadily.

The evolution of an urban class of working blacks had been as rapid as the growth of industry itself. A generation of blacks had been plunged into the wage-earning economy and, for the first time, were influenced by such rapidly civilising factors as the cost of living. This alerted more of them than ever before to the reality that whites were rich and they were poor. The appalling conditions under which they were forced to live, and the pass laws that governed every moment of their waking lives stood in stark contrast to the liberties and lifestyles of their white Rhodesian colleagues.

Whites by and large maintained that, under the provisions of the Land Apportionment Act, the cities were their exclusive preserve. Blacks were to be tolerated only on a temporary basis and only if they could prove employment by whites. It became obvious, however, that a crisis was in the making and the native problem began to intrude directly on the lives of urban whites. Blacks were now impossible to ignore, and for the first time whites could see the native condition with their very own eyes — and the sheer numbers involved were frightening.

In 1941 Huggins published what he called his Statement on Native Policy in Southern Rhodesia. It is uncertain why he felt moved at that particular moment to define a policy that was in such rapid evolution, but in doing so he stressed certain key points. He stated that the blacks were not obliged to come to the cities if they did not want to, and that sufficient resources existed to sustain them in the native reserves.

The irony is that Huggins probably knew next to nothing about the native reserves. These designated areas, he observed, could support black clerks, nurses, interpreters, artisans and schoolteachers. However, the towns, like the European farms, were sacred, and the white communities they nourished were inviolate. He deviated from the hard line only once, to admit that the lines of parallel development separated by the Land Apportionment Act might not remain separate forever. What this ambiguous comment might have meant at the time was anybody's guess. While this was the Prime Minister's public position, he tended to take a more pragmatic line in private. A storm was gathering that demanded an immediate overhaul of defences. He articulated the fact, not very succinctly, that separate development had become impractical, yet neither he nor anybody else seemed able to offer a practical alternative.

Huggins' eventual response in 1944 was to appoint a commission under the chairmanship of retired Provincial Native Commissioner EG Howman. Howman was mandated to investigate economic, social, and health conditions of blacks in the urban areas. He duly took evidence from across the country and produced a report that stunned even those who felt they 'knew' blacks.

Howman approached white industrialists first and found that most agreed that some sort of change was inevitable, although they were divided on what form it should take. Productivity depended on labour stability and labour stability depended on the ability of the blacks to feel settled in the cities. The principal that blacks were to reside temporarily in white areas, while maintaining their permanent homes in the reserves, was proving too costly for both industry and the blacks themselves to sustain. Low wages paid in the past had been based on the belief that cash for blacks was 'pocket money'. The source of their sustenance was wives and children, who scratched at the soil of diminishing and impoverished plots on the reserves.

Things had changed from the old days though. Blacks were faced with many day-to-day expenses that more often than not made it uneconomical for them to work. Bearing in mind that their homes in the cities were not permanent, transport to and from the reserves was very costly. The material expectation of friends and relatives at home also impacted on the cost of working. Urban rentals for mean shacks and cabins were unregulated and therefore extortionate. It was difficult for a worker to maintain his loyalty to a particular employer under these circumstances, and difficult for employers to keep workers at work. All this came at a heavy cost in lost productivity to commerce, farming and industry and caused spiralling poverty among blacks.

On the social impact of slum dwelling, Howman reported that poverty was widespread, and the threat of disease and social disintegration imminent. 'Segregation', he observed, 'has not only tended to suppress family life, but to place the most strenuous obstacles in the way of those who have sought to set up homes in the urban areas and the consequences ramify into every field of the economic, industrial, moral and social order.'[4]

Huggins' reply was resigned. He told the House in November 1944: 'We have to realise that a permanent urban class is arising and is bound to grow in the future unless the people in the European towns are prepared to manage without any black assistance, and the time has passed when that might have been possible, so we must face the facts as they are.'[5]

Privately he responded with caution. Most importantly, he changed the Land Apportionment Act to make it mandatory for local councils to provide housing for black workers in the towns; previously they had been permitted, but not compelled to do this. This measure was counterbalanced by stricter pass regulations and tighter controls over the movements of blacks outside the reserves. There was no suggestion then of overhauling the Land Apportionment Act, and no evidence that any white man in the country was yet prepared to countenance it.

Before new legislation in the form of the Native (Urban Areas) Accommodation Act of 1946 could be published, an incident occurred which drew attention to the other pressing problem facing black workers. This was the question of low and unequal wages. It was the political aspirants like Ndabaningi Sithole who once again articulated the situation for the consumption of the masses.

> Men of different races may hold the same positions, possess the same qualifications, and be equally efficient, but their economic reward is not determined according to their merit, but according to the colour of their skins.

On Monday 22 October 1945, in virtually the first incident of its kind in Southern Rhodesia (1927 had seen a black miners strike in Shamva), the 2 400 African workers employed by Rhodesia Railways in Bulawayo came out on strike. The action was spontaneous, poorly organised and only lasted a few days, but Huggins took the warning very seriously. He appointed his friend and confidante — Minister of Justice and former Minister of Defence Robert Tredgold — as chairman of a house commission briefed to look into not only worker's demands, but also general conditions of living and employment.

Tredgold in due course produced a report that betrayed his amazement at the depth of a problem that hitherto he had no idea existed. An extract from his report illustrates this clearly:

> In its heyday, which was back in the early years of the century, the compound could not have been a particularly attractive residential provision. For the most part it consists of ill-lit and ill-ventilated barrack type rows of rooms. Now 2 173 African men and women are housed in accommodation which officially should house 1 450. Latrine and bathing provision is inadequate. Save in one section of the compound, there is no provision for cooking, which is done for the most part on homemade braziers in the open. Cooking in wet weather must be very difficult. Men and women are crowded in rooms without regard to hygiene or decency. For example, we found six males, three females and four children occupying one room 15 ft. x 17 ft. 9 in. x 11 ft. 6 in. high. This was by no means exceptional. In an attempt to gain a little privacy, partitions of old sacking or rags are erected which further reduce the light and ventilation. It is a miracle that no serious epidemic has originated here.[7]

Two years later, visiting South African government official JP McNamee, with plenty of his own examples to draw on, published this observation of black living conditions in Bulawayo:

> Some years ago, Sir Edgar Thornton, of the Union Department of Public Health, described a certain area situated immediately outside the boundaries of Port Elizabeth as 'the worst slum in the world.' He might well have qualified that statement had he seen the conditions of some of the shanty settlements in Bulawayo's industrial area.[8]

Tredgold recommended an immediate wage increase, and in a private letter to Huggins, further urged the government to deal aggressively with the reality of black urbanisation. A year later the government responded by drafting the Native Labour Board Act to create machinery to deal with labour disputes as they affected the blacks. Predictably, and justifiably, blacks and liberal whites interpreted this measure as yet another version of white superintendentship. It did not in any way compensate for collective bargaining as a tool to equalise wages.

In 1943 there had been a leadership change in the Southern Rhodesia Bantu Congress that would help set the tone for the radical years to come. The Congress was a native political organisation founded in 1934 by purchase area farmer Aaron Jacha, and like many other liberation movements founded in the British colonies, it was initially inspired by the Indian Congress Party. In recent years it had become moribund, due mainly to its preoccupation with the concerns of the current black elite. These members belonged to the first generation of partially educated black men who by the mid 1940s were beginning to age. Such men clung to the insistence that white domination could not be challenged. The leader of the movement, Solomon Chavunduka, was an excellent example of such a moribund theologist. The youth wing of Congress was deeply offended in April 1942 when Chavunduka commented thus in a speech:

> The European introduces the civilisation to the African and shows him the civilisational ladder, he asks him to come along behind him on the ladder, the African puts his foot on the

first step and probably on the second, but the power of his ancestral environment pulls him back so he discontinues his journey … the European looks behind and finds that his African brother is sitting, he gets disappointed and gives up hope.[9]

Chavunduka was ousted and the Rev Thomson Samkange was appointed in his place. Samkange's leadership was also doomed because he likewise tended to represent the respectable face of black nationalism. However in one vital area, his political philosophy differed from that of his predecessor. He believed that the future success of African nationalism lay in unification of the many separate voices that were then forming the character of African resistance. The focus of his efforts would be to unite that resistance under the single umbrella of Congress. Unity would thereafter be the catchword and the elusive grail of successful nationalism.

In his private communications with future Malawian leader Hastings Banda, Samkange was congratulated for being able to speak for all the blacks of Southern Rhodesia. How Banda formed this impression it is difficult to say, but in stressing it he did lay claim to the truism that a house divided cannot stand. Both men clearly recognised that African society — not only in Southern Rhodesia or Nyasaland, but continent wide — was apt to lend itself perfectly to the imperial policy of divide and rule.

Meanwhile, young men trickling out of regional and foreign universities, felt no awe for the white man. For them the 1940s was an exciting period of political mobilisation and awareness. Stanlake Samkange's triumphal return from Fort Hare University in 1947 was cause for national celebration. The black circulation *Bantu Mirror* reported the event enthusiastically. Young blacks were energised by their emerging political awareness and inspired by messages drifting down from the north. They heard the words of Booker T Washington and other black American intellectuals — some who had called for Pan African unity and freedom, and some who were still calling for it.

Fort Hare University, a South African all-black institute situated in the eastern Cape, turned out a steady stream of black nationalists. When he attended the university in 1949, Robert Mugabe found the campus awash with airs of freedom and nationalism. He was exposed for the first time to Marxism and the Ghandian philosophy of Satyagraha or the confrontation of tyranny with non-violence and non-cooperation. The political life of campus was dominated by the likes of Nelson Mandela, Oliver Tambo and Gatsha Buthelezi. Mugabe entered university as a humble schoolteacher, but left three years later as a powerfully motivated black nationalist.

The 1940s was also a period when black political expression slipped from the grasp of the intellectuals and became the property of the masses. The main issues of the time remained the franchise, and the amalgamation of Northern and Southern Rhodesia. Although these questions carried a strong moral appeal for men like Sithole, Mugabe and the younger Samkange, they were not the stuff of mass mobilisation. The common people brooded over more fundamental issues such as wages, living conditions, pass laws, forced removals and the land question. Thus in many ways the black elite were as estranged from the black working classes as the whites were. Calls for political unity, and other bookish pronouncements from clever sounding black youth, appealed to few at the grass roots. The months that were to follow would be a wake-up call for both the white and the black political leadership.

On a bright and pleasant spring morning in 1948 Bulawayo commuters were suddenly confronted by scenes such as had not been seen since the 1890s. From out of the locations an army of blacks waving knobkerries, metal pipes and bicycle chains moved through the early morning rush hour. Their objective initially was to beat up and harass any fellow blacks who appeared to be on their way to work. They mobbed cars with blacks in them and dragged them out. They moved through the residential precincts and entered houses to remove black servants who were given a rough reminder of whose side they ought to be on.

Some armed whites stood guard over their homes, but most stepped back and watched with awe as the usually passive natives commanded a moment of respect. Few whites were directly assaulted, although the *New Rhodesian* newspaper did report on an incident in downtown Bulawayo, where a white motorist trying to force his way through a mob blocking the road, was dragged from his car and assaulted. Author and historian Peter Gibbs described in his fictional account of the strike, *Stronger than Armies*, the moment when his hero confronts the truth:

> Phillip walked confidently up to the leaders and called, 'get outside the gate!' It was only necessary to command natives firmly and they obeyed. The little native held his ground. 'We will go very soon, *baas*,' he said, 'but first we must take the *baas's* cook who is working. We will not hurt the baas or his missus — not this time. That will come one day,' he added gratuitously. This was the first expression of hostility to his race that Philip had heard in his twenty years in the country. He was to look back at this moment as the split second in time when the world he knew entered a new era.[10]

Most whites, although conscious in general terms of growing discontent, were taken completely unaware by these events. The black political leadership had of course been in touch with developments, but efforts to form a coordinated response had not been successful.

Late in 1947, a number of white employers in Bulawayo had received a series of circulars from employees demanding a rise in wages, but few took any notice. Meanwhile, unknown to them or the city council, a large meeting of black municipal employees had taken place in October. Behind closed doors the assembly condemned the Labour Board, and resolved to call strike action if there was no satisfactory response to their demands.

Employers naturally refused to be badgered by their labour, although a round table meeting was held in Salisbury between various chambers of commerce, employers' organisations and municipalities which, as well as also criticising the Labour Board, undertook to settle wages. On 7 April, the *Bulawayo Chronicle* carried a loosely worded version of their terms that were vague enough to be misunderstood and ambiguous enough to be misapplied. The announcement was either ignored or rejected, and tension in the Bulawayo townships continued to rise.

Three days later, Congress held a meeting in Gwelo in an effort to limit growing factionalism. It was imperative that any action be credited to Congress as the authentic voice of the people. This failed for many reasons, the most important being that the organisation was staffed by intellectuals and run by blacks preoccupied by appearing accomplished and learned.

The Rev Samkange was forced to concede that neither he nor anyone else in Congress, nor for that matter in any other organisation, spoke for the majority of blacks. An increasingly desperate series of labour meetings in Bulawayo, and widespread calls for restraint, came to nothing. No single organisation was able to claim control of the strike, and when it erupted, the most than any of them could do was climb aboard and shout the loudest in the hope that theirs would be the voice accredited with responsibility.

The disturbances in Bulawayo quickly evaporated but a ripple spread to other urban centres. Forewarned, the authorities clamped down and the violent scenes of the previous weeks were not repeated. Huggins responded with a show of force, although he also quickly promised a review of wages. For the time being calm returned, but calls by nervous whites for 'a whiff of grapeshot' were loud and insistent. Many whites would reflect on those weeks as the turning point of a new era.

It was not only the whites who felt it. A contemplative Thomson Samkange made his resignation speech in July of the following year, saying:

We experienced in recent months a grave disaster in the widespread industrial disturbances. It is a warning that the new order of things has arisen in the colony of which [we] are warned by the Railway African strike ... Africans are awakening!

Indeed they were, and whites were suddenly acutely aware of the fact. Huggins tried to pacify his electorate. 'Our experience is not unique', he told them, 'we are witnessing the emergence of the proletariat and in this country it just happens to be black.'[11] To those demanding retribution, he recalled the days of showdowns with British labour. Any confrontation with Rhodesian labour would directly send the majority — who were migrant — back out of the country, and the rest back to their homes in the reserves, so he urged his fellow Europeans to face the facts and behave accordingly.

'Native problem' comes of age

Largely hidden from the majority, a small group of whites had for some time been trying to change perceptions on the race question. This was perhaps a local manifestation of a general leaning to the left that was reflected globally and had much to do with the World War. Many battle-scarred sons of Rhodesia had returned home after that experience, with a clear sense of the consequences of repression and a revived interest in addressing the race issue. Hardwicke Holderness and his childhood friend Pat Lewis were two such men.

It was clear that the native problem had evolved from a social into a political phenomenon. By the 1940s, the crisis had grown considerably in size and complexity, yet was no closer to being resolved. The only solution that the establishment seemed to have was ever more rigorous containment and repression. There had been a window of opportunity in the late 1920s and early 1930s, for blacks to be introduced into the administration on 'white' terms and without an obvious political agenda. By the mid 1940s this opportunity had been lost. There were educated blacks emerging into the political mainstream who owed nothing to whites and had no interest in collaborating with them. The country was booming, immigrants were flooding in and both blacks and whites were making money. Beneath the boom, however, a mood of pessimism continued to affect both races. By then, goodwill between them had become so deeply imperilled that to many there seemed no real chance that a community of interests could ever evolve.

In 1946 Holderness, Lewis and a number of others of like mind, began a programme they called the Rhodesia National Affairs Association. The Association began by holding informal lunch hour lectures in Salisbury designed to mould and inform public opinion. The initial sessions were well attended, and explored subjects pertaining loosely to race relations. One lecture was entitled The native as a human being and was delivered by Garfield Todd, of whom a great deal more will be heard. Another, by N.H Wilson, was entitled The various two-pyramid policies. Other subjects including education, agriculture, the franchise, conservation and health in the native reserves — were examined by a variety of local experts.

In the close personal atmosphere of politics in Salisbury, the Association was careful to keep the discussions reasonable and friendly. Holderness, however, tested the waters a little more deeply when, in 1948 he invited Gideon Mhlanga, schoolmaster at the new Goromonzi native secondary school, to deliver a lecture. Mhlanga was the first native of Southern Rhodesia to earn a university degree and, although he was perceived as a moderate, the organisers felt some justified apprehension. No one could say for sure how a white audience would react to being addressed by a black man and, more unpredictable still, was what that black man might be tempted to say. The organisers employed some discreet security in form of ex-heavyweight boxer Dave Linton who would be standing by in case of trouble. Thereafter they threw open the doors and hoped for the best.

Mhlanga chose as the subject of his lecture, the story of how he had acquired his degree — which he only completed when he was over 40 years old. To an audience brought up on accessible education, the tale was a sobering one. It was the usual chronicle of a black child struggling to sustain any level of instruction, and of his trials as an adult paying for or begging for higher education in South Africa. In relating his experiences he avoided militant language and maintained an attitude of humility and respect throughout. As Holderness closed a chapter on this subject in his memoirs he had this to say:

> How much we or the rest of the audience appreciated at the time the extent to which he was giving to white Rhodesians the benefit of the doubt is hard to say. The audience applauded enthusiastically, and that seemed fair enough.[12]

Emboldened by Mhlanga's reception, the National Affairs Association then took the experiment into the locations. The first lecture delivered to a full house of township blacks was on the subject of pre-colonial history. The second lecture followed the same topic into the post-colonial period, and was greeted by an altogether different response. As the speaker traced important themes of conquest and villainy, gasps of dismay escaped the lips of his audience. When the lecture was over the floor was opened. Questions were not questions at all, but lengthy polemics delivered by proud men who were heir to an entirely different view of history.

The white man's version of the recent past fell like hot lead on black ears. It was as hard for them to sit and listen to the white man's achievements being eulogised, as it was for whites to hear them derided. The gap was simply too wide and there was no common appreciation of events. The experiment was a failure and the township lectures were suspended, as the National Affairs Association retreated to safer themes and venues. Huggins might have chewed on his pipe stem, and chuckled as he sipped his Scotch at the deep end of the Salisbury Club. He had told them all along that it was a waste of time trying to stitch a suppurating wound and he had been right.

29

The Bengal Chancers

The gravity of the race crisis was widely perceived and from many quarters came many suggestions. One such quarter was Edgar Whitehead who was the member for Umtali and a gentleman farmer in the Honourable and Military tradition. He had been in the country since 1928 when he settled on a small farm a few miles outside Umtali. There he became a member of a small clique of upper middle class British immigrants, most trying to continue the imperial experience of the 19th century. They were whimsically known in the district as the Bengal Chancers, and they collected in their forested Avalon of the Eastern Highlands, nicknamed on occasions 'Poonafontein'.

Among this concentration of thoughtful and creative souls, eccentric solutions were commonplace. Whitehead had been in the Legislative Assembly since 1939 and was by then a thoroughly established character. He was a man of considerable intelligence and as a public servant it was not surprising that he applied much of this to the race problem. The solution that Whitehead eventually distilled from his lengthy contemplation was mass immigration.

Whitehead's suggestion was that the government and the white establishment discontinue the enforcement of the most stringent immigration criteria in the Empire. Certainly there was no crime in exclusivity, but in a contest of sheer numbers it was hardly the ideal weapon. Much of what made race a problem in Rhodesia, was the unease that the white man felt to be so outnumbered by his black compatriots. If white numbers could be massively increased then the entire premise of the native problem would evaporate. In addition, more whites would mean more skills and more capital — which in turn would mean more jobs and happier blacks. It was the perfect solution. It had to be borne in mind, though, that since Britain's human resources were finite, the net would need to cast more widely for likely immigrants.

Whitehead proposed that Rhodesia import a few of the hundreds of thousands of European war orphans who could be housed in the old Empire Air Training Scheme facilities, and introduced gradually into the economy of the territory. However, the conservatism of the white Rhodesian public proved stronger than their fear. Although the idea was cautiously accepted, it was whittled down to such a degree that it soon had no relevance at all. Whites in general either did not accept that blacks were an imminent threat, or felt that the risk of allowing in impoverished whites was greater. In truth the scheme was quixotic, and it would not be the last time that Whitehead would prove himself capable of tilting at windmills.

Nevertheless, post-war arrivals saw the white population surge from about 65 000, towards its peak in the late 1960s of nearly 300 000. Although this accelerated rate of immigration posed no threat to the blacks in terms of numbers, it did help the whites to put aside their woes and concentrate on a booming economy and a fantastic social revival. This wave of immigration, rather than reinforcing the old Bengal Chancers, tended to consist of urban, middle class artisans and professionals, escaping the sheer dross of a severely straitened Labour society in Britain.

In 1946 the government introduced the Aliens Act to further reinforce the exclusivity of immigrants. To many it was as good as trading the long-term future of the white man in Rhodesia for just a few more years of a lovely imperial dream. Thirty years hence the Rhodesian Government would welcome white immigrants from anywhere, but in the late 1940s the white political landscaped seemed to stretch forth into the future without a black blot anywhere on the horizon.

One person who met the correct immigration criteria was Clifford Dupont, who eventually became the first President of the Republic of Rhodesia. Dupont had been a practising solicitor in London, and as an engaging and amiable man, he felt the austerity of post-war England acutely. His gregarious manners, charm, sporting nature and political conservatism made Rhodesia a perfect choice for him, and he a perfect choice for Rhodesia.

Shortly after his demobilisation, Dupont happened to meet an old friend — a certain Dr John Hobday — who had emigrated to Southern Rhodesia a year or two earlier. In a dreary London underground station, Hobday engaged Dupont with a colourful portrait of the good life in the colonies. It was a tempting picture. Through Hobday, Dupont was introduced to an ophthalmic specialist who had also recently moved to Rhodesia, and again he heard much to recommend the country. Duly impressed, Dupont resolved to visit Africa soon to assess the potential for himself.

In 1947 an opportunity presented itself when the 2nd Lord Kitchener died, leaving his estate in some disorder. Acting on behalf of the family, Dupont travelled to Kenya, where the deceased had owned a number of properties. Before arriving in Nairobi, Dupont made a flying visit to Rhodesia, and after days of junketing, unexpected encounters with friends, distant relatives and old next-door neighbours, he was won over. He found the social engagements charming, the countryside beautiful and the frenzy of life and activity stimulating. Hundreds of others were arriving in the country daily and Dupont decided then and there to do the same.

In Salisbury he met up with a legal contact who interested him in the purchase of the Mayfair Hotel, situated on the corner of Fifth Street and Selous Avenue. The Mayfair was a substantial property selling for the reasonable price of £18 000. The city was awash with capital and Dupont was impressed at how easy it was for him to secure a loan. So before he had even settled in the country he found himself the owner of a large commercial property. Quite clearly Clifford Dupont was a man well suited to life in Southern Rhodesia.

Early in 1948, Dupont returned with his family and found to his surprise that conditions in Salisbury had changed considerably during his absence. The immigration boom had overtaken him and the country was overflowing with demobilised Britons trying to settle in. A chronic housing shortage meant that hotels accepted bookings for only four days at a time, which meant that new arrivals moved from hotel to hotel in four day-cycles, usually ending up at the Coronation Park camping grounds in a caravan or under canvas.

In that year alone, Dupont was one of 17 000 immigrants looking for a new life in the colony. The infrastructure groaned while massive profits were made, as old timers with farms adjacent to the capital reaped windfall profits by dividing and subdividing plots of land into stands and suburbs. Most of the newcomers concentrated themselves in the cities and, as a consequence, the growth of housing and industrial infrastructure simply could not keep pace with the demand.

This was the sort of problem that Huggins welcomed. To cope with it he formed a National Housing Board that came up with some creative accommodation solutions. One of these was to make use of the 'rammed earth' or pise de terre system whereby houses were built of clay stamped into moulds and finished with stucco. These were assembled rapidly and for a brief season became a common feature of the urban landscape. They were reasonably comfortable and gave the various municipalities time to survey and map out new suburbs. Huggins' response to complaints — and there were plenty of them — was as typical as it was indifferent. They were, after all, he remarked, better than the

Governor General's palace in Khartoum.

Clifford Dupont was probably luckier than most, for as a professional he was not pressed for funds. He found a half-built house in the neighbourhood of Lochinvar that he managed to buy reasonably cheaply. He then looked around — there was no further word in his memoir about the Mayfair Hotel, so possibly it could be described by a good man as a 'learning experience' — and saw that the social aristocracy and a good deal of the money was concentrated on the farms. He hired a farm manager and told him to go out and find a farm. In due course Dupont was shown a 2000-acre property near the Ngezi River, for which he fairly easily raised the money.

In later years he added to the property and, in time, became something of a local personality. He entered politics via the Liberal Party and followed the journey that saw the Liberals reinvent themselves as the Dominion Party and then the Rhodesian Front. Thereafter Dupont entered the cabinet and, like Huggins, became a much-loved character on the Rhodesian social and political landscape.

Huggie wins again

Huggins was still reeling from his near defeat at the hands of the Liberal Party. To recover his status, he seized on the last ace that could be wrung from the old game of settlers versus the Chartered Company. This final card was Rhodesia Railways, the outstanding grievance carried over by the white community against their unloved materfamilias of old. While it was a tempting trophy, Huggins did not forget that state ownership and other such diversions had been troublesome to him in the past, and so on this occasion he trod very carefully. He gauged that there was strong public sentiment in favour of state ownership and concluded that the odds were in his favour.

Happily also, the board of directors turned out to be willing to sell. Since the war the Company had lost interest in the railways, mainly because the whole system had begun to age and was in need of a comprehensive overhaul. The problems Huggins encountered on this occasion were not with the Company, but with an imperial Government anxious to protect the interests of the other two partners in the system. Bechuanaland and Northern Rhodesia relied no less than the south on the integrated railway system, and obviously the newly minted Labour Party regarded the trust as very sacred indeed.

The fact that British Labour, enamoured as it was with nationalisation, objected to nationalisation in the colonies was an irony not lost on either Huggins or the Tories. One can easily imagine the tone of the informal debates that would have taken place at the Salisbury Club during this time. A classic case of Britannia waives the rules. Such instances of British double standards were not rare and nor was this to be the last. Whitehall, however, overcame its objections in due course and Southern Rhodesia was given the go-ahead to buy out the other two partners.

The united railway system was purchased for a little over £3 million. A further £32 million was raised as a loan for covering debentures, the cost of overhauling the system and future development. Both Raymond Stockil and Jacob Smit howled in protest but their voices were smothered by a wave of national approval. For Huggins it was a triumph, and with it he was able to pack up and seal one of the most successful transactions of his premiership.

Huggins then briefly, and rather spuriously, turned his attention to another national controversy: the franchise. The Southern Rhodesian common roll — still in theory — allowed for the equal participation of blacks, and although they were limited by property and educational qualifications, the potential was there for greater numbers to qualify for the vote. It was not lost on the white electorate, that if this process continued, blacks would in due course swamp their vote with all the unthinkable consequences that would follow.

It was at this point that Huggins as a statesman and political leader reached a moral crossroads. He would by then have been aware that the moment to open government and the civil service safely to blacks had passed. There were, however, possible avenues of uninhibited black progress through the ranks of local leadership, the army, the private sector and in the professions. Freeing up the limitations of the franchise and letting blacks in slowly might also have reaped the reward of genuine racial unity. It would have taken a strong leader to do it, and, without doubt, Huggins had the wherewithal to be that leader. But whether it was because of his inability to confront the magnitude of such a change, or the fact that he never even contemplated it, the opportunity was never seized. Instead Huggins allowed himself to be influenced by the system currently employed in Northern Rhodesia.

In Northern Rhodesia British Protected Persons, as blacks in the main were classified as distinct from British Citizens, had no right of franchise and were governed entirely by the governor and the civil service. Huggins surmised that Southern Rhodesian blacks would be better served by a similar system adapted for local conditions. He therefore proposed that two white members with no functions other than to protect local black interests sit in an enlarged whites-only legislature. It had to be assumed, of course, that these two representatives would have the best interest of the blacks at heart.

It is surprising that Huggins chose to ignore the inbuilt contradictions in such an outdated political principal. Even more surprising was that he expected it would pass through the Imperial veto. The only possible explanation was that the whole thing was a ruse, for Huggins was certainly not above this kind of political gamesmanship. Knowing as he did that the critical point of the race issue had not yet been reached, it is possible that he felt it wiser to lay effective groundwork that would assist the next generation of white political leadership in what would undoubtedly be their primary preoccupation.

A pivotal part of this foundation would be the amalgamation of the region into a single, powerful and independent political bloc that would be better able to withstand the inevitable assault against white hegemony. To achieve this, Huggins needed to reassert his political dominance, for powerful leadership lies at the core of great history and with a minimal majority, great history would not be written by his hand. If the end justified the means, then so be it, and in this Huggins was setting no particular precedent.

A vintage political performance followed — one that yielded all the evidence necessary to prove that Huggins was indeed a great local and international statesman. In 1948 the government was defeated in the House over a trivial point of policy. The matter concerned allowing an inter-territorial currency board to build a vault and other buildings on Southern Rhodesian territory. Instrumental in its defeat was Jacob Smit, whose chief delight lay in fielding an effective majority in the House. Huggins, however, seized the opportunity. With the afterglow of the railway purchase still warm in the hearts of voters, he deemed the moment right to provoke a general election. To achieve this he created an enormous uproar in parliament over the defeat, by insisting that it represented a vote of no confidence. He furthermore demanded that the issue be run through the ballot a second time. On this occasion he had plenty of opportunity around the bar of the Salisbury Club to ensure that his friends contributed to yet another defeat. With this achieved, and Smit uncertain of what exactly had happened, Huggins successfully used the circumstance to petition for a dissolution, after which he took the country to the polls for the fifth time.

To the Prime Minister's immense satisfaction, the general election of 1948 swept Smit and the Liberal Party out of contention and returned the United Party with the most conclusive majority achieved so far. Huggins, the master political strategist — urbane, self-deprecating and pleasant to the last — triumphed once again. The United Party won 24 seats, the Rhodesia Labour Party one and the Liberal Party five. As the cherry on the cake as it were, Jacob Smit lost his seat, and Huggins never had to countenance his surly face again. The Prime Minister was now at last in a position to push forward with his dream of uniting the two Rhodesias.

The general election of 1948 was just one of three incidents that year that pushed the cause of amalgamation several steps closer. On 28 May a general election in the Union of South Africa ousted a complacent United Party under General Smuts and gave victory to the National Party by a slim majority. This was a triumph for the Afrikaners, but from the point of view of Imperial policy makers, it brought the whole question of a united central Africa to the fore and rekindled the idea of a British counterweight to Afrikaner nationalism.

The strike by black workers that took place in 1948, also reignited the question of political security in the mind of a white electorate daily drifting into a more conspicuous minority. It must be added, however, that neither factor was entirely conclusive, for there were as many whites in Southern Rhodesia who feared being overwhelmed by Northern Rhodesian blacks, as there were those who were keen to court a marriage to South Africa. Majority opinion, however, both in Salisbury and Whitehall, was now more or less in favour of amalgamation, and by the end of 1948 the question seemed to be not if, but when and how?

30

The last black moderate

As an aside to the efforts of the National Affairs Association, Hardwicke Holderness of the legal firm of Scanlen & Holderness, received an unexpected visit from black unionist and shopkeeper Charles Mzingeli. Mzingeli was seeking representation against the Subversive Activities Bill, due to be presented to the House at the end of 1950. The incident passed virtually unnoticed in Southern Rhodesia, but it played an important part in setting the tone of the race relations that would follow. This encounter between two largely unimportant players would perhaps be the last time that a black political leader attempted to work within the white system to bring about change. It was the point at which black leaders realised that cooperation was not only useless but counterproductive, and furthermore served only to undermine their own credibility in the eyes of their militant black constituencies.

The Subversive Activities Bill was essentially the white response to the strikes of 1948, and although in principal it was non-discriminatory, the bill was aimed squarely at countering a repeat of the native unrest of two years earlier. Mzingeli himself was leader of the Mashonaland chapter of the Reformed Industrial and Commercial Workers Union that, alongside Benjamin Burombo's Bulawayo-based African Voice Association, had formed the basis of black political resistance as it emerged in the late 1920s. Hardwicke Holderness described Mzingeli as a bespectacled, earnest, sensitive, touchy and probably quite lonely man. Holderness was prone to overcompensate for the overt insensitivity of his people in questions of racial entente, and tried to endear himself to blacks more sincerely than was often appropriate.

Mzingeli was of the old school. He was a trade unionist with a limited education, but a wide experience of life under different racist regimes. He worked as a 'house boy' in both South Africa and Northern Rhodesia. Whilst in South Africa he had come under the influence of the famous union leader, Clement Kadalie, a Nyasa who in 1920 founded the South African Industrial and Commercial Workers Union, or ICU. Mzingeli later brought this message home, and in Salisbury joined with others, such as Masotsha Ndlovu, in the formation and growth of a local chapter of the ICU.

In his memoirs Holderness records that when Mzingeli was due to call on him, he was careful to instruct his white secretary not to announce the black man as a 'boy' waiting to see him. He was also concerned about how his other clients would react to finding themselves seated alongside a black man in the waiting room.

The Subversive Activities Bill, meanwhile, was a carefully drafted document designed to read vaguely enough to pass the Imperial veto but to be sufficiently wide-ranging to cover any eventuality. Mzingeli handed to Holderness a memorandum on behalf of his union, listing its concerns and pointing out the discriminatory implications in a number of clauses. The memorandum then drifted into a more general overview of political conditions for blacks. It ended with a plea for parliamentarians to give serious consideration to the fundamental principals of democracy.

We desire to point out that the colour bar in industry as it exist now under the Industrial Conciliation Act, is one of the strong factor that the intention of the bill in question is intended to keep less privileged section of the community as perpetual drawers of water and hewers of wood. This is complete contrary to the principal of Human Rights and the rights which all those who participated in the battle against nazi and fascism to make the world safe for democracy. We desire to add that the native policy of this country which demand immediate overhauling if cooperation between African people and the government is to be maintained, has since 1941 deteriorated to a point far below reasonable measure, and the government is fully aware that African people are strongly opposed to such policy. Yet it now introduce a bill in order to make any protest illegal soon as such bill comes into power [sic].[1]

There was little Holderness could do but redraft the document, reflecting what he felt he knew about both blacks and parliamentarians. In later years he was to regret some of the phraseology he used — such as 'the African' and 'the more advanced African'. He did make a significant point, though, when he wrote of Mzingeli in the revised memorandum: 'It is not always easy for such an African to retain the confidence of his people when he advocates cooperation as the best method of achieving social justice.'[2] Holderness went on to muse on the folly of taking for granted the last generation of black moderates trying to reach out for common ground. 'If whites prove unable to take seriously and sympathetically someone like Mzingeli, they would be asking for leaders like him to be replaced by much more implacable ones who might really have something sinister about them.'[3]

In the end his representation made absolutely no difference, and for reasons that transcended the honest brokerage of two good men, the bill passed through the House. Holderness, of course, knew this in advance — or at least suspected it — as Mzingeli probably did too.

Mzingeli progressed only a short distance further in his career as a nationalist. Holderness' predictions proved to be valid, for very soon Mzingeli would be emasculated by the emergence of younger and more radical cadres. These newcomers founded the much more assertive City Youth League in 1953, and for the first time began issuing direct challenges against the basic laws of the country. In fact the very relevance of Southern Rhodesia's existence under minority rule was questioned.

31

Federation of the Rhodesias and Nyasaland

In 1953 Roy Welensky returned to the city of his youth from a long period in Northern Rhodesia, to serve in the Cabinet of the newly established Federation of Rhodesia and Nyasaland. Welensky had been born in Salisbury in 1907, and in those days his home had been on the south — or the wrong side — of the railway tracks that divided the middle and upper middle class neighbourhoods from the suburbs of the coloured, lower class and poor white artisans. Welensky had come a long way since then. As Booker T Washington observed, achievement can best be measured not in what is achieved but in what obstacles are overcome to achieve it. By that measure Roy Welensky achieved a great deal indeed.

In the years before World War-I, resources in Rhodesia were scarce and poverty among white immigrants widespread. Even by the modest standards of the times, Roy Welensky had a difficult childhood. He was born the youngest of 13 children to an itinerant Jewish hotelier and an Afrikaans mother. It was fortunate that he was vigorously constituted, for in the Rhodesia of those days — and particularly in the career that he chose — only the most robust were to survive.

When Welensky was just 11 years old his mother died after a lingering illness. It was during this melancholy period in his life that Roy met the man who would later become his political mentor, partner and friend. Godfrey Huggins attended the dying woman in her last days and in doing so he was particularly drawn to the rough, straight-talking but bright, agreeable and engaging Roy — a child whose days were otherwise spent swimming 'bare arsed in the Makabusi with the piccanins'.[1] Huggins must have sensed a higher strain of intelligence in the boy whom, during long conversations about this and that, had much to say about the British Empire and how fortunate a man might consider himself to be part of the great Anglo-Saxon union.

Welensky had hardly been born to such ideals — he didn't have a drop of British blood in him — but he adopted them completely as his life progressed. He would never forget those conversations with Huggins, and in later years was apt to describe himself as half Jewish, half Afrikaner and 100% British. In 1953 this fierce loyalty was rewarded with a knighthood in recognition of his contribution to the Empire. Like most Rhodesians, he was hostile to successive British governments, but never critical of the Pax Britannia or disloyal to the Crown.

Welensky left school at the age of 14 and drifted for a few years in a number of odd jobs. While still in his teens he entered the ring as a prizefighter. In 1926 at the age of 19 he won the heavyweight championship of the Rhodesias. He later joined the railways, first as a fireman, then as a mainline conductor, and in due course worked his way up to the position of engine driver. Soon afterwards, he left Southern Rhodesia and settled in the town of Broken Hill in Northern Rhodesia which was, and still is, a hub of the regional railway system. His political apprenticeship was served with the Broken Hill branch of the white Railway Workers Union, where he again worked his way up through the ranks, until in 1933 he was elected chairman.

Roy Welensky had a simple view of life. His intelligence, ponderous and untutored as it was, was nonetheless bountiful. His friend John Connell confirmed this in an introduction to Welensky's memoirs where he observed that the latter's brain had matured late but rapidly. Considering Welensky's grasp of imperial politics and a political career that earned him a knighthood, his brain was clearly a better instrument than his fist. As Connell put it, he was as morally courageous as he was physically stalwart.

While still on the footplate and only 31 years old, Welensky was elected to the Northern Rhodesia Legislative Council, where he became known as a 'thoughtful, constructive and vigorous, if often controversial, speaker'.[2] In 1941 he formed the Northern Rhodesia Labour Party and soon afterwards was appointed Director of Manpower for the colony. This appointment interfered with an undoubtedly genuine desire to fight in World War-II, but allowed the opportunity for an unlikely statesman to develop.

Throughout his life, Welensky remained a clear minded and forthright man. He and Huggins were the last of the principled men, whose candour and honesty lent them a community of purpose that endured as long as they both lived. Some say that the two were the last genuine colonial survivors who fought back to back to save the diminishing remnants of British Africa.

Their mutual personal battle began in London soon after Huggins' 1948 election victory. Towards the end of that year, he and Welensky happened to be visiting Britain as representatives of their respective territories, at a conference of African dependencies. By that time, Welensky was the recognised leader of the 'unofficials' of the Northern Rhodesia Legislative Council and, like Huggins, he was a champion of amalgamation. The conference was an all-Africa affair that also attracted members the emerging black elite, whom the British Government tended to regard as representative of the future of British Africa. Confronted by this fact, both Huggins and Welensky were eager to make their own representations for the future. Theirs was a version that neither Whitehall nor the nascent black politicians felt particularly comfortable discussing, for both men were advocates of amalgamation as a precursor to ultimate independence of their territories from the Crown under minority rule.

Welensky and Huggins represented the first genuine convergence of opinion between Northern and Southern Rhodesia on the question of amalgamation. Since 1915 many opportunities had come and gone, and to its advocates it seemed at times that the whole concept was ill fated. For example, on the very day that Huggins arrived in London to revive the question after his 1939 election victory, Hitler invaded Poland. Nine years would pass before the All Africa Conference of 1948 presented an opportunity for both men to fan a little heat into the dying embers of Rhodes' dream.

Welensky was the first to take up the bellows, visiting the new Secretary of State for the Colonies, Arthur Creech-Jones, for many years Labour's 'expert' on colonial questions. In his customary manner, Welensky put to him directly the question of amalgamation — with or without Nyasaland. In his response, Creech-Jones was equally forthright. No British government, he told Welensky, would allow Northern Rhodesia to fall under a constitution as imbalanced as that of Southern Rhodesia. Consigning several million blacks to the administration of a few hundred thousand whites was simply no longer an option. The new global forums and current realpolitik would not allow it.

Welensky then sought the advice of former Tory Colonial Secretary, Oliver Stanley, who confirmed the prognosis of his successor, but added for good measure that when he had been in office, he had given both Welensky and Huggins an instrument that could have been made to work. What Stanley was referring to was the Central African Council. The CAC was a kind of inter-territorial coordinating committee that had first been mooted by the Bledisloe Commission, as an alternative to amalgamation, and then adopted by Stanley soon after the war.

Oliver Stanley had always been clear in his opinion that amalgamation of the two Rhodesias —

under existing circumstances — was not practical. This was simply because Southern Rhodesia's race policy was consistently found to be incompatible with modern concepts of adult suffrage and democracy.[3] Recognising, however, that a degree of increased cooperation between the two territories was desirable, he announced the formation of the CAC to facilitate collaboration between the territories in fields that were non-controversial.

Huggins had accepted the CAC on the understanding that it was a preliminary arrangement to amalgamation. In the meantime he sat back to await the appointment of a new Colonial Secretary. When Creech-Jones occupied that chair he reviewed the situation, and in 1947 reported back to the House that conditions for blacks in Southern Rhodesia had not improved sufficiently for there to be any change of policy from that of his predecessor.

Welensky rejected the suggestion that the Central African Council compensated for actual amalgamation — to which Oliver Stanley shrugged and simply reiterated that full amalgamation of the two territories was impossible. After a moment's thought, however, he remarked that if the CAC was too soft an option, and full amalgamation too hard, then why not consider something in between? Why not, he suggested, consider a looser type of federal arrangement that might balance the advantages and disadvantages of full amalgamation?

After tramping the streets of London for an hour or two, in deep thought, Welensky dropped in on Huggins at his hotel and broke the news. Although depressed by this confirmation, Huggins was not particularly surprised. The issue of amalgamation was now plainly dead — a sad fact but true — so there was nothing to be gained by pressing it. The emphasis now would be on salvage and, if Stanley had thrown out a lifeline, then the obvious course of action was to swim for it.

Subsequently a meeting of interested parties was convened at Victoria Falls on 16 February 1949. Huggins was the only delegate who represented any government in office, for although delegates from Northern Rhodesia and Nyasaland were present, none had authority to speak on behalf of his government. The conference was chaired by Sir Miles Thomas, chairman of the Colonial Development Corporation, who was in the territory conducting an economic development survey, and was attending as no more than an interested party. Edgar Whitehead — by then Southern Rhodesian Minister of finance — and two other members of the Cabinet, accompanied Huggins. Welensky led a small delegation of Northern Rhodesian unofficials, while the Nyasaland delegation was led by wealthy plantation owner Malcolm (later Sir Malcolm) Barrow. No black delegates were invited because Huggins reasoned that the conference was a meeting of leaders of established political parties. Besides, the common voters roll in Southern Rhodesia still made no overt racial differentiation, so no special arrangements were necessary.

In the opening session, Welensky moved that the conference advocate a federation of Southern Rhodesia, Northern Rhodesia and Nyasaland. Barring a few points of discussion this is what happened. A constitutional framework around the Australian model was agreed, with the understanding that this would lead the proposed federation towards Australian-type independence. It was Malcolm Barrow who reminded the assembled delegates that it would be unthinkable to pursue the project without the support of the Africans. The closing communiqué went to some length to reflect this sentiment, and to stress that the rights of blacks under the proposed federation would be enshrined and protected. It was clear that criticism by blacks was expected to be universal — which indeed it turned out to be — although resistance from certain sectors of the white community was not insignificant either.

The inescapable fact, however, was that the United Kingdom Government had not yet been formally consulted, so rosy prognostications remained no more than that. Creech-Jones was a difficult customer and certainly not one to forget his sacred trust. He was a member of the Friends of Africa and the Anti-Slavery Society, and a past chairman of the Fabian Colonial Bureau. As a cabinet minister he tilted towards a liberal intellectual audience — confirmed later by an interview in which he alluded to the provisions of the Central African Council. He hinted strongly at his reluctance to abandon its work in favour of a closer union. He also said he had noticed considerable apprehension among the African population of Northern Rhodesia and Nyasaland.

Permanent white settlement needs to be controlled. Because Northern Rhodesia is a protectorate, the Africans have been guaranteed certain inherent rights and therefore in agricultural development there are certain definite restrictions so far as Europeans are concerned. Nevertheless, it is clear for the economic well-being and social development of the Territory the European must have a permanent place, and it has been British policy, while safeguarding the interests of the Africans, to encourage a degree of European development.[4]

Roy Welensky was never able thereafter to refer in his memoirs to Creech-Jones without a strong hint of venom. He even went so far as to make it known that if the Secretary of State ever tried to enforce such opinions in his territory he would need to do so at the head of an army.

Despite this, Huggins and Welensky both actively promulgated the doctrine of 'partnership', for certainly some visible effort was vital to prove goodwill in the building of positive race relations. Without it, federation would be a lost cause. Race had after all been the perennial bugbear, and was increasingly becoming the defining political conundrum of the age. The restrictions in this 'partnership' were clear, however, and rather despairingly Welensky tried to make them understood. In a speech to the Northern Rhodesia Legislature he had this to say:

> I am prepared to work in partnership with the African people, and for as long as I can see, in that partnership we will be the senior partner, but I will never accept that Northern Rhodesia will be an African state. Political rights, after all, mean very little to a man with an empty stomach … let us give them economic development and political rights can come later.[5]

His comments and vision were categorically rejected. Welensky was dismayed to look up midway through his speech and see the official members of the house stand up and walk out. It became startlingly clear to him at that moment that the gulf between Britain and her sons and daughters in Africa had become very wide indeed.

Welensky could not understand — probably until his dying day — why such clear and honest brokerage was construed as having evil intent. Surely in the interests of preserving the English-speaking civilisation that Rhodes had spliced onto the native landscape, the white man had to remain the senior partner? In the opinion of Roy Welensky and many men like him, whites could and must be trusted to foster the advancement of the voteless majority. The fact that the natives wanted total and immediate power was part of their immaturity, and it was incumbent on the Europeans to limit their zeal and dole out responsibility in modest measure.

Welensky and his ilk were not rich men, nor did they employ corruption and demagoguery as part of their political vocabulary — already a fact somewhat unusual in the African context. At the heart of the standoff on the federal question was fear and mistrust — fear that the black man simply could not balance and maintain a modern system of democratic government for the benefit of all. The failing of these men was that they simply could not construe, or ever be persuaded, that such a thing was possible.

Welensky's may have been a lonely voice but it was not without powerful echoes. Oliver Lyttelton, Colonial Secretary in the Churchill administration, was a firm proponent of amalgamation for the central African territories, and a believer in the principal of partnership. He repeated the orthodoxy that British skill and experience must for many years remain the foundation of a federal arrangement.

Ultimately Africans would be brought into the running, and into control of government, but the premature swamping of the white vote would only bring political and economic disaster in its wake.

Under a Labour government, British official opinion on the subject of federation and the broader question of governance, remained ambivalent and policy was left to drift for the remainder of 1949. Both Welensky and Huggins were at times tempted to abandon their efforts, since British indecision merely served to increase the tempo of black resistance. 'Since the war', Huggins lamented in a speech delivered later to the Southern Rhodesian Assembly, 'I have had several talks with ministers of the present British government and it became apparent to me that amalgamation was looked upon by them with even greater disfavour than by their predecessors in office. I say this with deep regret, but it is perfectly plain to me that we in this country are not considered fit and proper persons to whom the future destinies of the natives of Central Africa should be entrusted.'[6]

By then black resistance in the two protectorates had indeed attracted some very powerful advocates. A certain Nyasa doctor by the name of Hastings Banda, who was then practising medicine in North London, was increasingly being drawn into the power politics of resistance. The leader of the Northern Rhodesian Congress, Harry Nkumbula, was likewise articulating an increasingly powerful groundswell of black opinion. Another up and coming voice in the movement was a certain Kenneth Kaunda, who was supportive of Nkumbula, but also a forceful personality in his own right, and certainly a man to be watched in the arena of black nationalism.

Federation in itself gave definite focus and direction to black protest, which in each territory — notwithstanding varying freedoms of expression — was underpinned by the common principal that what the white man advocated must be bad for the black man. Many blacks were by then beginning to believe that a total handover of power was not only inevitable but imminent, and prevented only by local white obstinacy. Colonial rule in Africa appeared to be balancing on a knife-edge, and there was a strong sense that a little pressure applied in the right places could bring the whole aging edifice crashing down. This impression was not diminished by the almost senile benevolence with which the British Government smothered the restive nationalists. Kenneth Kaunda described the mood very well in a collection of his memoirs.

> ... the Mahatma Ghandi and I were equally fortunate in facing a colonial power which fell
> far short of being a ruthless tyranny. [Had] our struggle been in the Republic of South Africa
> or Salazar's Portuguese African colonies, it might have been a different story.[7]

Therefore throughout the region, the advance of Southern Rhodesian policy into the wider British Central African complex was feared. Beyond that fact, however, regional nationalists were not particularly concerned about Southern Rhodesia, for it was widely conceded that entrenched European interests in that colony would not be so easily dislodged. It was in the two northern protectorates, where the colonial weakness was most tangible, that efforts at destabilisation were to be focussed.

The question of federation was revived early in 1950, with a shift of party political fortunes in Whitehall. In February of that year Britain went to the polls, and although Labour survived, it did so narrowly. To Roy Welensky's immense satisfaction, Arthur Creech-Jones was one of a number of high profile casualties. His replacement was veteran miner's representative and union leader, James Griffiths. Griffiths was a socialist by temperament and positioned no nearer to the right of colonial affairs than Creech-Jones; but despite this and despite having no direct experience of Africa, Griffiths was a fresh face that promised new hope.

As a trade unionist Griffiths should have had more in common with Welensky than Creech-Jones. But Welensky found the new Colonial Secretary to be ego driven and determined to compensate for a lack of knowledge of Africa by pandering to every African he met. Helping to balance out this Mad

Hatterishness in the machinations of the Colonial Office, was intellectual moderate Patrick Gordon Walker, who was serving as Secretary of State for Commonwealth Relations. He was certainly welcome as far as Welensky was concerned.

Huggins, on the other hand, was quick to make contact with Griffiths. He proposed a second conference on the federal issue and the Secretary of State duly undertook to consider the matter. In November Griffiths announced that a conference of officials from the three territories was to be held in London early the following year. This was encouraging news, although Welensky and Huggins by then were conditioned to be cautious. With such a small parliamentary majority, it seemed inevitable that the Labour government would shortly have to return to the polls anyway. The announcement of another conference also prompted a renewed round of complaints by the black nationalists, that were all too clearly audible in Whitehall.

The promised conference was held in the Commonwealth Relations Office on 5 March 1951, and to the surprise of many, it roundly endorsed the principal of federation. This announcement might seem less surprising if one considers that it was mainly the radical black intelligentsia who opposed federation. This was in some ways balanced out by radical opinion among a minority of whites who favoured either going it alone or reconsidering union with South Africa. Griffiths could claim to be charting a course between the radical elements of both races, and in doing so maintaining a thoroughly British ambiguity of purpose.

Predictions of an early general election were proved correct, and the British Government chose as the moment to make the announcement the eve of the second Victoria Falls conference. Both James Griffiths and Patrick Walker had just flown to Victoria Falls, and were promptly thrown onto the back foot by the news. The conference immediately deflated, as its two principal delegates resorted to ponderous but empty and somewhat distracted pontifications. As soon as a seemly conclusion could be brought to the proceedings, they packed up their bags and hurried back to London.

The news was not all bad however. The general election brought in a narrow majority for the Conservatives and a Tory victory always tended to be good news for white Rhodesia. Winston Churchill was brought in to serve his final term at the age of 77and he could be relied on to be sympathetic to white Rhodesia. He appointed Oliver Lyttelton — the future 1st Viscount Chandos — as his Secretary of State for the Colonies. Lyttelton, we might remember, was something of a champion of white governance.

Lyttelton's Under Secretary was a young Jew by the name of Andrew Cohen (later Sir Andrew), who was perhaps best known as a leading light of the early anti-apartheid movement. Cohen was obviously not supportive of Southern Rhodesian race policy but was forced to concede that it was better than the South African version. In the years following World War-II, Afrikaner Nationalism had gathered tangible momentum, and what effect this would have on the territories to the north was of concern to the British Government. Cohen was one of few who recognised that if Southern Rhodesia was unable to find a suitable political accommodation in the north, she would be just as apt to look to the south — and he was right.

There were indeed many in Rhodesia who thought well of the South African apartheid solution. Economically, Southern Rhodesia's rapidly developing economy was better suited to union with South Africa than with the under-developed north. Moreover the two countries had been on the warmest terms since 1923. Huggins himself was friendly with South African Prime Minister Daniel Malan, and this alone suggested that Southern Rhodesia might throw in its lot with Pretoria if federation failed. Under no circumstances, though, could a career liberal like Andrew Cohen — with his personal sensibilities highly tuned to race persecution — allow this to happen.

Lyttelton, on the other hand, was a businessman and tended to view political issues in a pragmatic light. He looked at the economic circumstances of central Africa and saw three separate territories with complementary economies, but individually with all their eggs in one basket. Melded into a unitary bloc, their single economy would have sufficient diversity to attract investment and grow rapidly. He acknowledged African opposition but was not particularly moved by it.

Huggins again wasted no time in approaching the powers-that-be, and despite increasing black resistance, he was encouraged by the warmth of his reception in London. His visit resulted in the announcement that yet another conference was to be held in the capital that spring. This time the delegates would consider a final draft proposal that would then be submitted to the various governments for approval or rejection. It was further agreed that African representatives would be invited, and to this end Huggins summoned two prominent Southern Rhodesian nationalists — Jasper Savanhu, journalist, trade unionist and ex-secretary of Congress, and Joshua Nkomo. In his memoirs Welensky described Nkomo as a 'social worker', although Nkomo was then also the president of the Southern Rhodesian Congress.

Nkomo was indeed a rising star in the nationalist movement in Southern Rhodesia. Although a ponderous and self-opinionated man, he was emerging as the main spokesman for the black lobby. Born in 1917 in the Semokwe Native Reserve in Matabeleland, he was one of eight children of parents employed by the London Missionary Society. Nkomo completed his primary education in Tjolotjo Government Industrial School, before taking his first job as a delivery boy for the Osborne Bakery in Bulawayo. By 1941 he had saved up enough money to pay for one year of secondary education at Adams College in Natal where, as a 24-year-old, he had to endure considerable embarrassment attending lessons with children. He remained at Adams College thanks to a white clerk, who took him under her wing and paid for the remainder of his tuition. From Adams, Nkomo moved to Jan Hofmeyr School in Johannesburg where the same benefactor paid for a three-year course of study in social work.

In Johannesburg, Nkomo was exposed to nationalist politics and returned to Southern Rhodesia in 1947 as a nationalist himself. He was the first black man to be given the blue-collar post of social worker for Rhodesia Railways. Over the following two years he studied for an external degree with the University of South Africa, and his route to political prominence began — as Welensky's had — as a union organiser. Nkomo entered nationalist politics in 1952 when he succeeded Enoch Dumbutshena as President of the All Africa Convention.

In that capacity he continued the work of his predecessors in trying to unite all the diverse native organisations of Southern Rhodesia into one. As with Samkange and Dumbutshena, this effort was ultimately to fail.

Two black members of the Northern Rhodesia Legislature, P Sokota and DL Yambo, were also invited to the London Conference, but at the last minute they boycotted it and presented instead a prepared statement that outlined their opposition. Both Lord Salisbury, who had succeeded Lord Lionel Ismay as Commonwealth Secretary, and Oliver Lyttelton, who maintained the services of Arthur Creech-Jones as his advisor, chaired the conference.

The 1952 London conference was widely seen as the final furlong in the journey to federation — and submissions for and against grew shrill. In the run-up to the meeting, Lyttelton visited the region to assess for himself white and black opinion and, in a speech delivered to the National Affairs Association, he confirmed that the British Government remained solidly behind federation. Ex-Labour Prime Minister, Clement Attlee, also visited the region and in Northern Rhodesia met both Harry Nkumbula and Kenneth Kaunda. Attlee was forthright in telling both men that democracy as a principal was one only gradually absorbed, adding that the natives of central Africa had a long way to go before they could be considered competent to govern. Nkumbula protested that blacks had benefited from the good example of Britain but such flattery left Attlee unmoved.

The credibility of black nationalism had been damaged in the meantime by events further north. In

Kenya, after an extended period of oathing and arson, the Mau Mau terrorist movement had launched its campaign of mayhem and murder.[8] African methods of political enforcement gained — for the first time — global exposure, and the associated horror tended to confirm one or two of the choicer accusations made by whites against blacks. The fact that white excesses of violence and corruption were also exposed, did not necessarily sway settler communities further south to recognise any parallels or accept any responsibility.[9]

The Conference wound up at the end of January, and published its report as a white paper, defining the constitutional terms of Federation. Among the closing speeches, that of Joshua Nkomo was noticeable for its moderation. He warned, however, that his colleagues or his constituents, or both, might reject his own personal endorsement of the process. He obviously did not then expect the level of censure that he would receive. In some measure his career was undermined, and arguably never recovered. No sooner had he returned home than he changed his mind, and grew loud in condemnation of the Federation. It would not be the last time Nkomo would commit such a blunder.

The White Paper detailed a complicated division of legislative powers, that are too many and too tedious to list. Most importantly, though, the Imperial Government maintained the perennial veto on legislation, that differentiated between the races. Apart from that, each territory would maintain its own native affairs administration and apply its own separate race policy.

It was upon this last point that Southern Rhodesian Chief Justice Robert Tredgold quickly identified the signature weakness of the federal structure. He maintained that each member territory could not deal separately with an issue of such overriding importance to the Federation as a whole. He used the example of the American Civil War that had been fought — as much as anything — to equalise race policy across the breadth of the Union.

Furthermore each territory was to maintain its standing constitutional status. Southern Rhodesia was a self-governing colony while Northern Rhodesia and Nyasaland would remain British protectorates, ruled from Whitehall through a governor general. An African Affairs Board would be included within the framework of the Federal parliament to protect the rights and interests of blacks across the three territories. Raymond Stockil, as a Southern Rhodesian delegate, fought vigorously for a secession clause that would allow one or other territory to leave the Federation if they chose. This was roundly rejected because it would have undermined cohesion to the detriment of future loans and investment. It was argued that such a clause did not exist in any federal constitution active at that time — except for, ironically, the Soviet Union.

Defence became a Federal responsibility. Shortly before Federation came into being there was a hiccup when the Imperial Defence authorities said that without jet aircraft the Southern Rhodesia Air Force was useless and should be disbanded. There was a shortfall of money to buy the necessary jets but this was overcome by Northern Rhodesia contributing £200 000 which solved the problem.

As a compromise, a clause was included that allowed for re-examination of the constitution, at a time no less than seven and no more than nine years from the date it became law. The optimists took this to mean that the way was clear for dominion status — or even full independence in the Commonwealth — after a preliminary trial period. No one at that time was prepared to contemplate that it might equally be turned into a vehicle for the Federation's dissolution. Huggins won a symbolic victory when he secured the inclusion of a paragraph in the preamble, stating that, when the inhabitants of the territories so desired, the Federation could go forward with confidence towards the attainment of full membership of the Commonwealth. While this gave strong impetus to the push for independence, the provision made it clear that this could only happen if the inhabitants so desired it. To the British Government this implied all the inhabitants of the combined territories, while to the Federal Government it meant only those registered to vote. This became the blind spot that would bedevil any attempt in the coming years to solve the increasingly volatile race issue.

The conference's recommendations were debated in the House of Commons and passed with a narrow majority in March 1953. On 10 April, a referendum was held in Southern Rhodesia that saw almost 63% of the vote in favour. All three territorial legislatures were in agreement, and in the United Kingdom, the Rhodesia and Nyasaland Federation Act received royal assent on 14 July. The Order in Council was promulgated on 1 August. The Federation formally came into being on 4 September 1953 when Governor General Lord Llewellyn steamed into Salisbury railway station to a 19-gun salute.

The Federal motto was set on a coat of arms supported on either side by a sable antelope and a leopard, and read: *Magni esse Mereamur* — Let us deserve to be great.

Stanlake Samkange, then a chirpy correspondent with the South African black circulation *Drum* magazine, offered another interpretation: 'With partnership on our lips', he wrote, 'and apartheid in our hearts, may we appear to be great.'[10] Welensky's concluding comments were a little more reverent. 'We were, after all', he said, 'the successors and inheritors of Cecil John Rhodes.'

32

Huggie moves on

In the early years the Federation did indeed appear to be great. Huggins formed an interim government in which his loyal associate Roy Welensky served as Minister of Transport, Communications and Posts. In the meantime the two founded the United Federal Party (UFP) and fought the first Federal general election in December 1953. The UFP won 24 out of 26 seats — the kind of majority that Huggins was by then becoming accustomed to. Six specially elected black members — two from each territory — took their seats in the first Federal Parliament, as well as three European members — one from each territory — specially charged with responsibility for African interests. They had as their weapon the Whitehall veto that they were empowered to wield at will. Huggins formed his government with a clear mandate and set to work in earnest on this, the final phase of his long political career.

From the very outset a divided franchise revealed the anomalous structure of the Federation. Southern Rhodesia employed a common role that made no racial distinctions, meaning that the Federal vote in that territory was — in theory — open to blacks. In the two northern protectorates, only British citizens could vote — which disqualified almost all blacks, being as they were British-protected persons. While in practical terms this did not make much difference, it was nonetheless the point around which the early signs of stress in the Federation began to appear.

Huggins was given relatively fair weather to sail out his days. His personal prestige was sustained by an authentic majority, that allowed him to keep a firm grip on power in the manner of the aging autocrat that he was. The only opposition to his government came from the specially elected members of both races. Huggins saw the black members as political minors undergoing an apprenticeship, and was inclined to ignore them. They, on the other hand, saw themselves as a constituted opposition with an obligation to oppose and harass the government.

This they did, but Huggins' ballast was firm. His problems had more to do with finding good men to serve in his government than listening to those who had no chance of doing so. Four separate administrations were now in existence, and the pressure on local white skills was acute. The tendency was also for the best men to gravitate to the Federal Government — situated in the very pleasant capital of Salisbury — and this caused the territorial governments to languish somewhat. Huggins himself had settled into the sort of orthodoxy that rooted him in an earlier age. He scorned modern methods and kept the common touch that had served him so well in the past. Dealing with old soldiers like Winston Churchill and Clement Attlee tended to obscure him as to how out of step he had become. He couldn't see that the future was already upon him, and one or two of those around him began to feel that he was holding up progress.

If Huggins was an anachronism, there were aspects of his government that were no less misplaced, but which he could do nothing to change. Native Affairs, as one example, was still kept as a separate body of government that clung to the ample bosom of Britannia. At a time when racial partnership was not only a catchword but also a theme representing the very essence of the white man's survival, the government had no opportunity to make new and fresh contacts with blacks. Racial overlap occurred only in the home where the opinion of domestic servants, if ever sought, could not be relied on, and in the detention and processing of criminals and political troublemakers. The government had no access to the native reserves and the Native Affairs officials made a point of keeping it that way. Little empires formed with local white Native Affairs officials and their wives assuming the role of miniature monarchs. For blacks, looking at whites and forming opinions that would one day play out in their future politicisation, it was not a perfect example.

Another unsatisfactory situation was the exclusivity of the civil service. This again was something that the Federal Government itself could do nothing to change. In the first place the civil service was not centralised, necessitating four separate bureaucracies. With the exception of Southern Rhodesia, whose civil service was exclusive for different reasons, each was staffed by Colonial Service expatriates who were recruited directly from London. The civil service should have been centralised, as Huggins put it, so that Federal staff went home every night instead of every three years. The civil service might also have been the obvious place to begin the process of black advancement, for government service was seen as a virtual Holy Grail by blacks educated to blue-collar level. Later policies, aimed at fast-tracking a black middle class, would have been much more successful if a steadily advancing corps of black civil servants had existed to make up the vanguard.

Huggins suggested to Whitehall that the outside recruitment of civil servants cease, and that a combined bureaucracy be created to manage all Federal and territorial affairs. The idea was received by the British Government with very little enthusiasm and progressively whittled down to an inter-territorial Public Service Commission that had virtually no ameliorating effects on the problem. The exclusivity of the civil service remained one of a number of obvious partnership defects in the Federation that enraged blacks but could not be changed.

If anything blighted Huggins' federal days, it was the question of the positioning of a hydroelectric scheme on the Zambezi River. The economic successes of the Federation precipitated massive industrial growth that in turn put tremendous stress on the existing power grid. Until then all three territories had relied on thermal power generation, that itself depended on coal production at Wankie and the ability of the railway system to transport it. The Federation was fortunate in having the substantial Zambezi and Kafue river systems, both of which were potentially exploitable as sources of hydro-electricity.

Politics imposed itself on the issue when technical controversies spilled over into territorial partisanship. The dam controversy was in fact the only substantive political crisis since 1923 that had no race overtones. Refreshingly, it pitted one bloc of white interests against another. Discussions had been under way at different levels since 1941 over the question of which of the two options — the Zambezi or the Kafue — would be the most suitable. In 1953, while Huggins was still Prime Minister of Southern Rhodesia, he put his weight behind the Kafue scheme, although most of the benefits would accrue to Northern Rhodesia. The only question then was financing, the main weight of which would have fallen on the United Kingdom Government. However with the unification of the three territories, the financial burden shifted to the Federal Government itself.

Huggins maintained his support for the Kafue project and introduced a bill in the Federal Parliament to put the scheme in motion. Most members of the House were indifferent to the details — with the exception of Garfield Todd, who was by then Huggins' successor as Prime Minister of Southern Rhodesia. Todd challenged the proposal for the obvious benefits that the Zambezi option would bring to Southern Rhodesia. He initiated a geological survey that, at the last minute, located a viable site for a dam wall at the Kariba Gorge. Todd presented a sufficiently compelling case to cause Huggins to pause and reconsider.

Hoping to avoid controversy, Huggins appointed a group of neutral French consultants who produced a second report that presented the government with a dilemma. It was estimated that a dam on the Kafue would cost £55 million to construct, and although water volumes in that river had not been studied in any detail, it was estimated that 2 600 000 kilowatt-hours would be produced. Kariba, on the other hand, would cost an estimated £85 million but could be expected to produce 6 500 000 kilowatt-hours — more than double the Kafue output. The consultants advocated Kariba, with the Kafue project recommended only as a useful appendage.

By February 1955 Huggins had changed his mind. His apologists swear that his mind was swayed solely by technical arguments, while his detractors accuse him of predicting the breakup of the Federation, and arranging for Southern Rhodesia to end up with the choicest assets. Overnight, Northern Rhodesia was plunged into a state of virtual mutiny. Public meetings were held across the territory and threats to secede were as wildly made as they were greeted. The Northern Rhodesia legislature passed a motion that fell short of condemnation of the scheme, but expressed misgivings at what it regarded as partisanship in the Federal Government. The uproar was not eased by the revelation that the first power station was to be sited on the south bank. In the event of dissolution, control of the project would again revert to the south. The apologists insist that Huggins was swayed solely by the fact that the primary transport routes up from the south were the only practical ones for the movement of the massive plant and equipment required.

As things turned out, the enormous inland sea — at the time the largest man-made lake in the world — did indeed benefit Southern Rhodesia much more than her northern neighbour. Certainly, during the hot war that raged along the length of the Zambezi after the breakup, Southern Rhodesia would not have survived without control of the power utilities. Huggins held his ground, and for better or worse, the dam was built on the Zambezi with the turbines on the south bank.

In 1956 Huggins was raised to the peerage in recognition of his long political career and the undoubted contribution he made to the development of central Africa. Huggie became the 1st Viscount Malvern of Rhodesia, and of Bexley in the County of Kent. This unusual combination of geographic designations indicated his loyalty to his school — highly becoming of a statesman of his period — the home he had left long before, and his adopted country. Such an honour was appropriate for a man of 73 years old, enjoying the twilight of a distinguished career. In October of that year Lord Malvern resigned from the leadership of both the Federal Government and the United Federal Party, clearing the way for Roy Welensky to step up to the bar and begin, in many ways, the real work of the Federation. Godfrey Huggins maintained his place as a respected backbencher, and reigned on occasion as the much loved adopted son of the House of Lords. He retired to his farm in Arcturus and died in 1971 at the age of 88.

33

A liberal experiment

The rise and fall of Garfield Todd

Huggins' elevation to the higher podium of the Federal executive opened the way for a realignment of the political landscape in Southern Rhodesia. Within the sudden leadership vacuum, created by the formation of the Federal Government, the territory briefly took a new and unexpected ideological direction. The pivotal 1948 general election in Southern Rhodesia introduced a handful of new faces into the Legislature, all of whom were to influence the critical years ahead in one way or another.

One such newcomer, Humphrey Gibbs, tentatively entered the political arena as the United Party member for Wankie. Gibbs was a slight, wan, earnest, soft-spoken and civic-minded Englishman, who had been farming in the Matabeleland countryside since the 1920s. His election to the House served as his introduction to the general establishment, that he would in due course serve as valedictory governor. An equally earnest but somewhat less English farmer by the name of Ian Douglas Smith, also took his seat on the backbenches, but in his case as Liberal Party member for Selukwe. Smith, of Scottish descent, but very determinedly a Rhodesian, would emerge as one of the titans in the brief history of Rhodesia. He would also dominate its closing chapters as the only one of the eight Southern Rhodesian prime ministers to have been born in the territory. The careers of these two men will be discussed in much more detail in later chapters. Most important for the moment was the introduction, into the still relatively serene political establishment, of a 40-year-old New Zealand missionary by the name of Garfield Todd.

Todd was a most unlikely newcomer to a rather conservative political scene. That he became Prime Minister was almost unimaginable and can be largely attributed to happenstance and the lack of established political talent available for the territorial legislatures. Most important too was that for just a brief moment, there seemed to be an extraordinary willingness on the part of white Rhodesians to suspend their disbelief and give peace a chance.

It is worth noting that in the mid-1950s, white credibility and black indulgence had not yet reached the critical point that they would in later years. The black establishment was receptive to compromise, while the white seemed poised on the cusp of embracing genuine race partnership. All that was needed, it seemed, was for the right brand of courageous leadership to drive both races across the Rubicon. To achieve this would take a prime minister, not only capable of tearing through the perception of white supremacy, but one who could force his brethren to accept once and for all the peril of their situation. Many liberals on both sides of the race divide hoped that Garfield Todd was this man.

It was during his hunt for such good men during the lean years of the war, that Huggins first persuaded Todd to run for the Shabani seat. Todd had then been settled in Southern Rhodesia for just

14 years, serving as head of the New Zealand sponsored Dadaya Mission in the southeast of the country. As a missionary, Todd inhabited a world separate from his fellow legislators and far removed from the world of most whites. He lived and worked with blacks on a simple, interactive and human level. He knew many of the emerging nationalists personally and as an educator, he was often the first white man many of his students had ever met. Ndabaningi Sithole recalled his first encounter with Todd in his book, *African Nationalism* — the foreword to which was written in 1959 by Todd himself. Sithole found the missionary gruff, doctrinaire and partial to corporal punishment, but above all infinitely kind and fair.

As a New Zealander, Todd's colonial credentials were impeccable, and the inevitable stigma that hung over his vocation was diluted somewhat when he bought a 90 000 acre cattle ranch in the vicinity of his mission. This purchase won him membership to a significantly more muscular club than the church, but how much this aided the momentum of his political career it is hard to say — although in a party still largely dominated by farming interests, it could not have hurt. The fact that Huggins was always very personable towards Todd — which was wholly in keeping with his nature — was also significant. It was said that Huggins was scandalously candid when discussing affairs of Cabinet with the young MP. To most observers this was a sure sign that he had no intention of including Todd in it.

Garfield Todd might have been content to remain on the backbenches, and Huggins might have been content to keep him there, had not the exodus of white political talent to the Federal Government opened many opportunities at the territorial level. This was true for all three territories, but most notably for Southern Rhodesia. Huggins, of course, vacated his seat as Southern Rhodesian Prime Minister, opening the way for many members of his cabinet and loyal parliamentarians to follow him. This left the territorial cabinet and legislature scraping the barrel for viable candidates — which is not to imply that Todd was a scraping, but there can be no doubt that were it not for the manpower shortage, his political career is unlikely to have begun, let alone carried him to the highest office in the territory.

In the event, a ballot was held at the United Party Congress in Bulawayo in August 1953, where Todd's name was among only a handful of candidates. Standing against him was ex-cabinet minister Julian Greenfield who made no secret of his preference for a place in the Federal cabinet alongside Huggins. Greenfield stood only to test Todd's popularity and by no means did he want to win. The first round of voting hung on a split decision with the deciding vote being cast by the party chairman. Greenfield's desire to lose precipitated a second ballot and while the two candidates enjoyed a friendly lunch at the Bulawayo Club, Todd won the majority. To his great surprise and the consternation of many, he found himself leader of the party and de facto prime minister.

Todd was not exactly swept into office on a tide of popular support. Whites on the whole regarded his victory with circumspection, although, at a point of national indecision, there were obviously enough people who were willing to give him the opportunity to try. The black response to Todd's rise seemed somewhat out of proportion to its significance. In fact, for a group desperate for some real evidence of race partnership, he seemed to be the answer to a prayer. He was not widely known in either the black or white community, but his missionary origins and the uncertain temper of the times, caused him to be heralded in certain quarters with the joy of desperation. This in turn probably imbued Garfield Todd with an exaggerated sense of his own destiny. However, it would not be long before the reality of race politics silenced the celestial trumpets and brought him down to a temporal level with a painful bump.

The vehicle of Todd's political journey was, of course, white Rhodesian public opinion, although after 1956 and Roy Welensky's ascension to the office of Federal Prime Minister, the driver was less often Todd than Welensky. Todd and Welensky had humble origins in common, and the latter was only a year older, but that was as far as their commonality extended. Todd had experienced a gentler youth in the family brick-pottery works in New Zealand, and was an attractive and charismatic man. Welensky enjoyed no such advantages. Todd represented the left wing of the centre movement and Welensky the right.

By the time Sir Roy — he received the KCMG in 1953 — assumed the leadership of the Federal Party and became Federal Prime Minister in 1956, Todd had been Prime Minister of Southern Rhodesia for two years. The two men then took up opposing ends of a tug-o-war — as Todd himself put it — to grab the African people by the scruff of the neck and drag them into the 20th century.1 By this, Todd presumably meant both black and white Africans. His view of the 20th century was probably more accurate than Welensky's whose opinions tended to be rooted in the views of men like Huggins. Both believed in partnership but Todd did not necessarily see this as a master–servant style of partnership. He defined the white man's mission as one of leading the black man over the difficult road to social maturity towards eventual and full inclusion in the political process.

Sir Roy — obese, not in the least attractive and without the nimble intellect of Todd — was nonetheless a forceful man and an altogether more ambitious and authoritative politician. From the moment that Todd was elected head of what was in effect a sister party to the United Federal Party, he became a threat to Welensky's ambitions. These were not only selfish ambitions, but also the expression of Sir Roy's view of the ultimate place of the white man, in the future of British central Africa. Initially Welensky had seen Todd as a potential rival to succeed Huggins as Federal Prime Minister but later, when that did not happen, he saw Todd possibly mounting some sort of ideological challenge, to upset the applecart of white regional dominance. This could only undermine Welensky's plan to guide the Federation to independence under the aegis of long-term, if not permanent white rule.

An undeclared war was therefore implicit from the moment that Sir Roy assumed office as Federal Prime Minister. He and Todd grappled like scorpions in a bushfire. Whichever of them won they were both palpably doomed. This more than anything else lends an air of tragedy to the political careers of both men, but more poignantly perhaps to that of Todd because he was the one who might have led Rhodesia to a future that brought social justice without bloodshed.

The land and the fallen Dutch woman
An examination of Southern Rhodesian political activity during the period of the Federation not surprisingly reveals a continuum of the evergreen preoccupation with race. The 1930s and 1940s had seen a smoothing of many of the most jagged edges of race policy, but as often happens, artificial solutions tend to lead to artificial problems.

When the Land Apportionment Act was adopted as the bible of race development, signs of stress quickly began to appear in the holding capacity of the native reserves. One fairly obvious solution was to make available some of the vast and unused tracts of white land. This had been proposed more than once, but was never taken seriously,on the basis that it would simply delay the problem and not solve it.

The problem of overcrowding in the reserves had both a complex and a simple history. The simple history was that the white man had invaded the black man's country and taken the choicest land. The more complex version was bound up in traditions of land and land usage among the blacks themselves. Black farmers had a notorious reputation for wasteful and destructive agricultural practice, that made the whites loath to cast pearls before swine. To the blacks, however, the land represented far more than a practical means of livelihood and its misuse or otherwise was irrelevant. The land was a nation's foundation of social identity. It was the burial place of the ancestors and the currency of power. If it was misused — and without question it was — this happened because it simply reflected past agricultural tradition that had evolved at a time when land was unlimited.

In 1902, the black population of Southern Rhodesia was no more 500 000 souls, who cultivated an area of perhaps 500 000 acres and grazed an estimated herd of about 55 000 head of cattle.[2] Obviously at that time there was no particular pressure on land. By 1941, not only had the black population tripled, but an estimated two million head of native cattle now grazed land delineated by law, to less than 38 million acres. Without laws to force proper land management in the reserves, native commissioners could merely urge the destocking of cattle. This obviously struck a hollow note with many a black man who could point to rich and empty lands in the European areas. However, be that as it may, as things stood the signs were all beginning to point towards a crisis.3

Concerns for the wellbeing of the native reserves, and the landscape in general, were not new. As early as 1913 the Chief Native Commissioner had felt obliged to comment on the question of land tenure in his annual report.

> The conversion of native land tenure from the communal to the individual system is the true basis on which the progress of the natives is to be evolved …[4]

As chairman of the newly formed Natural Resources Board, Humphrey Gibbs, made it his particular vocation to create a wider awareness of conservation matters. Until the 1950s his efforts had been aimed mainly at his fellow commercial farmers. During the consolidation years, most of these had put matters of survival before the intelligent use of the land. By the late 1940s, those days were largely behind them. In his first and perhaps only substantive speech to Parliament, Humphrey Gibbs tried to turn the attention of his fellow legislators to conditions in the reserves.

> I have been to most of the [native] reserves when associated with the Natural Resources Board. I do not suppose the house realises their deplorable state and the enormous amount of work to be done.[5]

Work had in fact been under way for some time, thanks mainly to the efforts of the missionary schools. The most progressive of these was the American Missionary Board training centre in Mount Selinda. One of the most colourful individuals at work here during the 1950s was E.D Alvord, a native of Salt Lake City in Utah, USA, and one time Pacific Coast wrestling champion. Since 1919 he had been in the employ of the American Missionary Board, trying to introduce progressive farming methods to the local blacks.[6]

Alvord's methods were simple, and on his own experimental plots dramatically successful. On the occasions that he demonstrated his high yields on marginal land to black farmers, they were invariably impressed — despite a depressing majority who dismissed any scientific explanation in favour of witchcraft. Alvord instructed the pupils who had carried out the work of digging manure into the soil, to describe the process to his audience, but the youngsters explained in translation that the manure was a ruse and that Alvord crept out in the night to sprinkle medicine on the soil.

Alvord pioneered the principal that rural blacks could not be forced to transcend these superstitions surrounding their agricultural practices and that a black farmer needed to 'see things demonstrated on his own level, within his reach, by demonstrators of his own black skin and kinky wool'.[7] He put in place a system of training black agricultural demonstrators, by taking a piece of land strained by overuse and applying natural fertilisers available to the humblest farmer. He demonstrated how, within three years, the land could be completely reclaimed.

By 1921, Alvord had established at the Mount Selinda School a five-year course in agriculture — the first of its kind in Rhodesia — and a four-year rotation of crops on a school demonstration site.

By 1924 he had compiled his experience into a booklet entitled *Helping the Heathen to Help Himself*. Included was a blueprint for promoting agricultural development, better housing, improved water supplies and better home sanitation for the native areas. The Southern Rhodesia Government later officially adopted this groundbreaking publication as standard.

The message of conservation, however, had no meaning when nothing could be done in practical terms to force the blacks to cooperate, and this could only be achieved by limiting their rights over their land in some way. However, sacred to the Orders in Council defining Southern Rhodesian self-government, was the understanding that this would never happen. Thus it was that the Native Land Husbandry Bill was cautiously introduced into the house in April of 1951.

This proposed statute represented an amalgamation of all the intelligence so far gathered on the subject of land management. Contained within it was a wide reaching law intended to achieve nothing less than an agricultural revolution. It summed up the teaching of 30 years and made it possible for the first time to enforce what hitherto had been mainly a matter of persuasion.

The bill proposed granting the government powers to divide up the land in the native reserves, and to allocate it in equal lots to every individual who had rights in the reserves. In some areas this would amount to as much as 60 acres per head, while in more congested reserves, allocations could be as little as one and a half acres. Grazing rights for as many cattle as it was calculated the land could support, would supplement rights to the land. These rights would be held by an individual and would be negotiable but not divisible. They were to be transferable and heritable, although the holder could be forced to sell, if he had three times been convicted of failure to protect his land or use it properly. It was envisaged that eventually the stage would be reached when cultivation would be prohibited, except by the registered holders of farming rights on specified plots.

The bill was intended to come into effect in stages. In a typical area, a survey would first collect information regarding the number of residents, the number of families entitled to cultivate, the amount of land available and how much was fit for cultivation. This would make possible decisions as to the size of an arable holding, and the number of cattle that might go with each. There would be a great deal of preparatory work in the form of demarcating holdings, contouring and terracing and the provision of boreholes and dip tanks. If successful, a whole new class of professional black farmers would be created. In time the system would leave no place in the reserves for those who presently alternated between the countryside and the city, achieving very little in either.

The dark side of the plan was that there would be very many people dispossessed, and whole generations would grow up with no access to land at all. This was fine insofar as it presupposed the emergence of a permanently urbanised class of working blacks, but it was self-defeating ultimately because the Land Apportionment Act forbade this.

Blacks wholeheartedly, and almost without exception, rejected the Native Land Husbandry Bill. The reasons for this were as many as they were obvious. Apart from destocking and dispossession, the devolution of the powers of land allocation from the traditional chiefs to the Native Affairs Department was very unpopular. The Commissioner and the members of his department, would gain wide discretionary powers on top of what many blacks felt was already excessive power. Along with this, there was a sort of subconscious feeling that no matter what the white man did or said, it should be rejected on principle.

Hardwicke Holderness was again approached through Scanlen & Holderness, this time by the Southern Rhodesia African Association, to prepare a memorandum listing black concerns about the bill for the consideration of a Select Committee. The Southern Rhodesia African Association was one of the early raft of indigenous alliances, in this case purporting to be the voice of traditional native authority.

While the chiefs had suffered much erosion of their influence since the advent of European administration, they still retained some residual authority. One or two chiefs — Chief Mangwende in this case — still spoke with a powerful moral voice. Chief Mangwende was a relatively modern and progressive man with an equally progressive and educated wife. He was among a handful who bridged the divide between the disaffected urban class of mainly young blacks, and the more conservative element still desiring dialogue with the government. For those few with the gumption to try, it was a thankless task, attempting to reconcile obligations that the traditional leadership had towards the administration and their loyalty to their people. Like Charles Mzingeli before him, Chief Mangwende's voice would soon be stilled by the young, educated and militant nationalists. Although it was perilously close, the moment of the complete usurpation of traditional authority by the nationalists had not yet arrived.

Mangwende's decision to engage a professional lawyer to compile a memorandum, came about thanks to some novel advice given to him during a meeting of the National Affairs Association. United Party Member of Parliament, Dendy Young QC, a mercurial personality, pondered Mangwende's thoughts on the bill and delivered his opinion. While the bill was necessary, he said, and the likelihood of changes being brought about as a result of black concern was low, he suggested the chief nevertheless make a representation to his member of parliament.

The first meetings between Holderness and various chiefs were salutary, and in the mood of times something of a forlorn re-enactment of Rhodes' earlier triumphs. Holderness eventually met with over 100 chiefs, who were largely illiterate and uncertain of what exactly they wanted to say, but were very eager to say it. The general unease about the Native Affairs Department increasing its powers over them gradually opened a dam burst of grief, to the point that the interpreters and legal drafters were quickly overwhelmed, causing the process of compiling a coherent memorandum to take weeks.

The memorandum began with a lengthy recapitulation of the concerns of the government over the land issue. This was to ensure that the blacks completely understood the problems and realised that there were no easy solutions. Although it was accepted that not every native had an inalienable right to land, it was also true that most were unable to provide secure conditions for their families in the cities. It was pointed out that this insecurity would cause black workers in the towns to rush to claim land in the reserves, believing this would be their last chance to do so. This in itself would create unreasonable pressure on the land. Certainly there were few blacks who would give up their right to land in the reserves, if their existence in town was dependent on their jobs. What if they were dismissed? What if they grew old and could no longer work? It had become absolutely vital that some satisfactory tenure for blacks be made available in the cities.

Besides this, the memorandum urged that blacks be allowed an official voice in the deliberations. They could be given places on the various boards of assessors, while the native councils could be the chief vehicles for administering the law. Acknowledging their own inadequacy in terms of effective local government, the chiefs urged also that a college be set up to educate them in the effective administration of their own affairs at a local level.

A clearer and more open invitation to co-operation could not have been made but — as was inevitable — the members of the select committee would not read into the memorandum the voices of the rural blacks themselves. Most members thought they were listening to the opinions of the 'clever boys' from the towns, and as an outspoken liberal, Hardwicke Holderness would probably have been regarded as a clever boy himself and his input examined with suspicion.

The select committee did take up a few of the recommendations — and amendments were made accordingly, so it could not be said that the entire effort was wasted. But it was not an unqualified success either and probably — and perhaps predictably — the Southern Rhodesia African Association members were disappointed. The experience confirmed the underlying reality that one could not expect to get far without voting power and representation.

In the meanwhile, Holderness and other liberals involved in the National Affairs Association, added another arm to their outreach. It would be interesting to examine this briefly since many names of future radical nationalists were first heard in the context of the Interracial Association of Southern Rhodesia.

The Interracial Association was founded in 1953 by — as Holderness remembered it — a multi-racial collection of people from a variety of backgrounds.[8] Such a gathering would have been both unnecessary in the past and impossible in the future and was feasible only in that brief decade when the concept of partnership was untested. A British missionary and fellow of Magdalene College Oxford, Guy Clutton Brock — who had been for some time involved in a multi-racial community at St Faiths Mission in Rusape — was a founder member, as was Charles Mzingeli. V.S Naidoo, a schoolmaster and adherent of Rabindranath Tagore (the first non-European to win the Nobel Prize for Literature) and Ramakrishna (one of the three great leaders of the Hindu revival in the 19th century), was a rare representative of the Asian community that — briefly — by habit was dissociated and secretive in Rhodesian society. Coloureds were an obstreperous section of the membership and were often at odds with others over such deeply embroiling themes as whether they preferred to be known as coloured or Eurafrican.

The black members gave the impression that they were willing to be partners in this effort only for so long as it was convenient. In the meantime they groomed themselves and one another for a more radical political approach. George Nyandoro, Nathan Shamuyarira, James Chikerema, Leopold Takawira, Jasper Savanhu, Chad Chipunza, James Z Moyo and others, were then virtually unknown to the white Southern Rhodesian public. However, within 20 years they would no longer be moderates, and to whites their names would resonate as the bastard children of the revolution and the whores of both Moscow and Peking. This ominous position was presupposed even in the Interracial Association's founding statement of principals, wherein a clear warning was struck:

> The Africans who are in the majority, may expend their energy in opposition to the Europeans instead of working constructively to acquire the gifts of their civilisation. The Europeans may become the 'Herrenvolk' and the Africans 'Black Nationalists'.[9]

The truth of this would be made clear by, among others, Leopold Takawira, who would remark, on the eve of Southern Rhodesia adopting a new constitution in 1961, that:

> The African, with the aid and sympathy of the Asians and a few Europeans, is seeking ways and means of saving himself from the Sandys-Whitehead conspiracy. Some of the means chosen will, to the onlooker, seem crude and queer. But who really should morally criticise the clumsy strokes of a drowning man? The hunted African has now reached a point where he cannot advance any farther. He is faced with the problem of either sitting down to meet his death or facing the enemy in trying to escape.[10]

Another tentative observer of this interracial entente — the Moses who had yet to take up his staff — was Robert Mugabe. Mugabe impressed Guy Clutton Brock with his articulation and chilly appraisal of the Association's efforts. 'An extraordinary young man', as Clutton Brock put it, 'an ascetic, reluctant to come out from his shell, and with it something of a cold fish'.[11]

Mugabe also attended the meetings of another fringe organisation dedicated to racial coexistence: the enigmatic Capricorn Africa Society that was founded by the legendary British Special Air Services commander, Colonel David Stirling. Stirling settled in Southern Rhodesia after the war and was dismayed to unearth what he considered to be a false paradise. He was an egotistical and wilful man whose vision, more elaborate than that of the Interracial Association, defined the usual tableau of a union of states under some vague formula for racial and political coexistence. As whimsical as Stirling's version of reality might have been, it still presupposed the acceptance — by at least a majority of whites — of the truth of their situation and this, at that time, was asking too much.

The impact of even this cautious effort was conspicuously shattered when in 1957 a Rhodesian-born black by the name of Patrick Matimba, a printer by trade, returned from study overseas with a Dutch-born wife, Adriana van Hoorn. It was the first time such a thing had ever happened and initially Matimba and his wife faced something of a dilemma. Wherever they tried to settle, they would be in contravention of the Land Apportionment Act, and in the first instance the couple had no choice but to seek the hospitality of Guy Clutton Brock and his wife Molly in their multi-racial community of St Faiths Mission near Rusape.

The presence of the two in Rusape did not take long to reach the attention of local MP Norman Straw. Straw took exception to Matimba, a standpoint shared by many whites in his constituency. As far as they were concerned, the Brocks were already a brace of race traitors who were living cheek to jowl with the blacks and even going so far as to eat their food. The marriage of a black man to a white woman was simply a step too far. The law did not prevent it, but as many had suspected, it would be precisely over this type of hurdle that the notion of racial partnership would stumble.

Norman Straw was a United Party member and the difficulty for him — apart from his visceral outrage for which there was no legislative cure — was the Dominion Party that had emerged from the ashes of the old Liberal Party. The Dominion Party was poised as a contender for power in Southern Rhodesia and Straw's seat would be the first to go if he was seen to be sanctioning something as subversive as this. He brought the matter to the attention of the caucus, and some anxious deliberations followed on what exactly ought to be done.

As things stood, the Immorality and Indecency Suppression Act contained a slight imbalance insofar as it banned extramarital sex between a black man and a white woman, but offered no such censure for white men doing the same thing. It was decided for lack of any alternative action to make the grandiose but politically impotent point of equalising the law to make extramarital sex between the races illegal for both men and women. The object was probably to provide a vehicle for the condemnation of miscegenation in general, since nothing cut quite so cleanly to the quick of white racial consciousness than the image of a black man copulating with a white woman.

The debate drew in few advocates of reason except, strangely, Winston Field, who was then a Dominion Party MP in the Federal legislature. Field's reaction was to dismiss all the fuss and urge his fellow honourable members to keep things in perspective. Dominion was the name of his party and dominion its objective. The distasteful peccadilloes of an errant Dutch woman were entirely irrelevant and he said as much.

Garfield Todd, however, was forced by the fury of the right to give the matter more recognition than was due. With the help of the CID, the Prime Minister ordered an informal inquiry into the extent of miscegenation and prostitution in the country. He was told when the report was complete that the traffic in commercial sex was confined mainly to coloured women and a growing number of blacks. Those few white women who were operating were doing so on a higher level and at the better hotels. The CID therefore recommended no change in the law since it was hardly justified by the few respectable white males who transgressed it. Furthermore, Todd was reminded as others had been before him, legislating against miscegenation would merely expose the offenders to ridicule and the threat of blackmail.

An amendment to the law was nonetheless discussed in the House in May 1957. The flurry of anxious debate that followed, revealed the depth at which this type of issue was felt among whites. A few, such as a certain Dr Alexander, were more reserved, observing that in his 30 years of practice in the countryside, he had only dealt with four cases of white women falling pregnant to black men. What's more, on each occasion these were women of low mental development, who were isolated on marginal farms with no meaningful social outlet available other than within the labour compound. A psychiatrist, the doctor said, would have dealt better with these cases than a high court judge.

Todd, of course, was a missionary, a multi-racialist and a liberal advocate of black advancement. To him such a retrogressive debate must have been very difficult to take seriously. He plunged directly to the point in his own speech when he told the House that at first glance the issue was one of morality, and was being presented as such to him, but in truth it was not an issue of morality but of racism. His suggestion to equalise the law over the question of miscegenation was to repeal it altogether, and acknowledge the rights of human beings to interact as they chose. The simplicity of this, and its undoubted truth, did not sit well with the House. Analysts of Rhodesian politics have often pointed to this moment as the beginning of the end — not only of racial partnership, but also of Todd himself. The House voted in favour of the amendment, although in the event no change was made to the law. Notable, however, was the fact that Garfield Todd voted with the minority, and that a majority of both his cabinet and backbenchers voted against him.

34

The franchise

In March 1957 a report was published that would pit the territorial government against the Federal, and Garfield Todd against Sir Roy Welensky. The issue was the franchise, and the long festering question of black representation. Huggins had in 1951 temporarily resolved the issue by increasing the monetary qualification from an annual income of £100 or property worth £150 — as it had been set in 1914 — to £240 and £500 respectively. This had been intended only as a temporary measure to protect the franchise until a more permanent solution could be found. Despite this, the number of Africans who could meet the voter qualifications was steadily rising.

In 1953 there were only 441 registered black voters on the common roll, against a total white electorate of 48 870. In June 1957 there were 764, and by mid-August of the same year the number had risen to 1060. Asian and coloured voters combined, exceeded the black total with 1164 individuals registered to vote. While still minimal, the increases were steady enough to register concern among white legislators.

The fundamental need at that moment was to convince the growing band of black nationalists that whites were genuine in their desire for partnership. To achieve this, blacks needed to be convinced that real change could be fought for, and realised from within the political establishment. And the only way that this could happen was for the franchise to be opened up a lot more than it already was.

Sir Robert Tredgold, by then Federal Chief Justice, was a man of widely respected integrity and endowed with sufficient breadth of character to appeal to the trust of both whites and blacks. For this reason, on 28 December 1956, Todd appointed him as chairman of a commission to consider and report on a system of representation whereby power could be kept in the hands of 'civilised and responsible persons'.[1] The wording of this mandate was vague enough to obscure to nervous whites the fact that Todd was in fact seeking a more liberal franchise.

'Civilised and responsible persons', of course, could mean different things to different people. Todd was anxious to pull the wool over white eyes and give the impression that his primary concern was to protect the franchise against black encroachment. He was reported in the Rhodesia Herald as declaring that the majority of black voters were barely literate and that it was:

... the responsibility of the Government to safeguard the position without further delay and it is working towards that end.[2]

This was in striking contrast to the actions and words of Roy Welensky who was at last attending to the issue of the broader Federal franchise. It will be remembered that a dichotomy existed within the Federation between the voting laws of Southern Rhodesia and her two sister territories to the north. The Southern Rhodesian common roll was in theory open to all, while under the gubernatorial systems in the north, voting was restricted to British citizens and not British Protected Persons. This created a theoretical imbalance across the Federation for which an equally theoretical solution needed to be devised. This was Welensky's responsibility.

In direct contrast to Todd, Welensky's objective was to establish a more restricted access to the vote, however he tended to couch the verbiage around the issue in politically liberal terms for the ears of Her Majesty's government. This type of posturing was one of the more bizarre features of the times, for in order not to upset the white voters, discreet liberals like Todd were forced to appear reactionary, while genuine reactionaries like Welensky were forced to appear liberal. While it was not possible under these circumstances for the two men to draw their ideological differences out into the open, it was this differing view of the franchise that set the stage for the struggle between them.

When his report was finally released, Tredgold appeared to have adroitly struck the necessary balance. Obviously a system of universal suffrage was impossible, and in his analysis Tredgold confirmed this, adding that limiting the franchise to those who could exercise it with reason, judgement and public spirit was justified. He went on to observe that recent events in Africa had proved that appeals to nationalism were highly effective in channelling the black vote in a detrimental direction, and if simple natives were prepared to so easily squander their own political wellbeing, how could they be expected to understand and protect the interests of the white man? Tredgold was also quick to admit that the application of a race-orientated franchise was inherently wrong, and could only be tolerated in a civilised society on the understanding that it was a strictly temporary expedient.

'An uneducated peasant', he wrote, 'from a remote area, might possibly be able to form some sort of judgment upon the personal qualities of a candidate. But under our system of parliamentary government, that is not enough. A voter must be able to form an opinion as to the true merits of the policy for which the candidate stands. This he certainly could not do.'[3] As for its recommendations, the Tredgold Commission proposed that the country neither divert from the common roll nor be drawn into any system of separate race representation.

Under Welensky's proposals for the Federation, two voter categories would be established: ordinary and special. Two voters rolls — the general roll, predominantly European, and the special roll, predominantly black — would serve the electorate. The general roll would vote for 44 members out of a 59-member legislature, while voters on the special roll would elect eight special black members and one European member from Southern Rhodesia who would be specifically concerned with black interests.

Tredgold's recommendations were more complex and successfully maintained the concept of the common roll, but only just. He recommended a sliding scale starting with an income qualification of £60 a month with sufficient literacy to fill out a form; this progressed to an income of £40 a month with a primary education, and finally £25 a month with four years of post-primary education. He then proposed a 'special' qualification of £15 a month with literacy. The special vote would be subject to devaluation in order that its influence could not count for more than half of the total votes cast by the other three classifications.

Todd was pleased with the recommendations of the Tredgold Commission and, although it remained to be seen how the matter would be treated in the House, it at least set the tone for positive change.

In truth, however, the hope that this change would be sufficient to convince the blacks of their future in the current system, and tear them away from the piper's call of black nationalism, was at best a slender one.

As expected, the report was greeted in the House with caution. While it was widely understood that change was inevitable, the desire to complain about it was often too strong to resist. The special qualification received equally special attention, with many different variations on the same theme being suggested. All of these were contorted to appear as fair as possible while taking care to ensure that no possibility of a political threat to white hegemony emerged. The enfranchisement of wives on their husband's qualifications attracted an amendment put forward by Norman Straw to exclude those in polygamous marriages — which would bar a majority of black females, no matter what their general ability to qualify might be.

Meanwhile, these digestive difficulties were being anxiously monitored from abroad. Naturally Welensky was openly hostile to the entire concept, but the British Government cautiously took the view that Todd and Tredgold were well meaning if a little misguided. The Commonwealth Relations Office tended to support Welensky and even the United States Consul General in Salisbury made it known that he thought Todd was rushing things. This may have been so, but Todd seemed to be the only one to realise that time was perilously short. In fact, it was not inconceivable that time had already run out. What Todd had accomplished was in truth no more than a cosmetic advance, and certainly not enough to wholly — or even in part — satisfy blacks desires. For this small victory he had had put his head on the block.

On 21 August 1957 the bill was passed with modest amendment to the special qualification, and the ban on polygamous marriages was thrown out altogether. The special qualification became an income of £240 per annum with literacy. A fifth qualification of a standard eight education was also added. Instead of operating on a sliding scale, the influence of the special vote would be moderated by 'closing the door' when votes registered on these qualifications exceeded 20% of the number of ordinary voters.

The bill did not pass without some brinkmanship from Todd, and not without political cost to him either. While the issue was still under debate, he delivered a speech to the Interracial Association where, with dangerous candour, he made his personal feelings abundantly clear. He assured his audience that it was not his intention to let European standards decline, but rather to invite an increasing number of blacks to rise to them. He remarked that each man, after all — as Tredgold had been bold to point out — has a right to find his place in the sun.

> We are in danger of becoming a race of fear-ridden neurotics. Rhodes felt that when a man had so far accepted civilisation as to be a working, wage earning citizen, sufficiently educated to read and write, he was entitled to a voice in the government of the country. The Federal Government, to our great disappointment, announced the continuation of the racial pattern. Southern Rhodesia must uphold Rhodes' liberal dictum of equal rights for all civilised men, regardless of colour.

Todd then went on to threaten that he would no longer be prepared to lead his party if anything less than this was achieved.

The Act was promulgated on 18 October 1957. Five members of Todd's caucus turned their backs on him and voted with the opposition. If nothing else this sent the Prime Minister a clear message.

Todd had crossed the Rubicon but he was standing on the far bank alone. He had moreover exposed his political naiveté by revealing himself beyond a shadow of doubt to be a liberal. Furthermore, by choosing the Interracial Society as his platform, he identified himself with the most liberal bloc of the white electorate. This not only antagonised his cabinet and party colleagues but also rendered his leadership a political liability in the eyes of the nation.

This moment can be regarded as another critical turning point in the history of Rhodesia. It was the moment at which white Rhodesian society, having accepted partnership in principal, began to reject partnership in practise. It was also the moment that blacks began to realise that the small flame of hope nurtured under Todd was guttering on the verge extinction.

It is no coincidence that on 12 September 1957 two Rhodesian African nationalist organisations, the Youth League and the All African Convention we4re combined to form a new polit6ical organisation called the African National Congress of Southern Rhodesia (ANC). Its inaugural congress was held a month after the franchise reform was published. This occurred on Pioneer Day, the most revered date on the Southern Rhodesian calendar.

Joshua Nkomo was elected president, James Chikerema vice president and George Nyandoro secretary general. Nkomo said afterwards '... we decided to do what was being done all over the world to free the masses from domination by the [white] minority.

The ANC preached non violence as an open policy, while beneath the surface embarking on plans to cause riots and civil disobedience. They covertly joined with the African National Congresses of Nyasaland (Malawi) and Northern Rhodesia (Zambia) to plan a policy of violence to erupt simultaneously in all three territories in a joint effort to break up the Central African Federation.

* * *

Welensky had by then just completed a series of meetings with the United Kingdom Government, and, three days before the publication of the Tredgold report, he returned from Britain having secured a number of valuable constitutional concessions. Interesting among them was the enlargement of the Federal Assembly from 36 to 60 members, which had the immediate effect of diminishing the value of the eight seats held by blacks. Further to this, the British Government agreed the following: it would not legislate on behalf of the Federation except upon its request; it would allow the Federation greater control over its external affairs; it delivered a categorical statement against any territory seceding from the Federation; agreed that the civil service would be locally based; and finally that the Federal Constitutional Review Conference, permitted by the Orders in Council, would be held sometime in 1960. Welensky was explicitly assured that, during the conference, a programme to enable the Federation to achieve full independence within the Commonwealth would be discussed.

All these were important political achievements that, in contrast to Todd's apparent fumbling, presented Welensky as a forceful Prime Minister able to stand up to, and indeed dictate terms to Her Majesty's Government. The white population of the Federation was also emboldened into believing that they no longer needed to delve too deeply into partnership, and that the handful of cosmetic changes already under way, along with a chorus of cooing assurances, were all that was needed to calm the British and guide them in the direction of granting independence. After this the blacks could like it or leave it. Of Welensky's minor concessions to the UK Government the most important was his assurance that in due course a 'reasonable number' of Protected Persons would become eligible for the franchise.

The Federal Electoral Bill was duly put before the Federal Assembly, and was carried on 31 July 1957 with no second reading. It became law the following year. The new law amounted to 'differentiating' legislation, so it was immediately referred to the British Government by the African Affairs Board. Almost as if by prearrangement, the Tory government brushed aside Labour objections and the bill was approved. Blacks were once again outraged, and this time their outrage spread across the entire breadth of the Federation.

Welensky had no reason then to suspect that the British Government would be anything less than true to its word, and as a consequence he felt that he had little to lose by alienating the blacks a little more. In due course his own political naiveté would be his Waterloo, but for the time being he felt quite secure in office and optimistic about the future.

This was in stark contrast to Todd, who at that moment was in crisis. Since the Patrick Matimba affair and Todd's unwillingness to countenance any change to the law, his intentions in the light of the liberalised franchise were suspect. He had earlier amended the Land Apportionment Act to accommodate the changed circumstances of the Federation. These amendments were: provision for the multiracial university that was one of the signature achievements of the Federation; the loosening of restrictions in city centre hotels to allow for black visitors and delegates to the Federation; and the granting of leave for Advocate Herbert Chitepo — the first black man to qualify as a advocate in Rhodesia — to occupy chambers in the city centre.

These were small victories but again they came with a heavy political price tag. To balance things out, Todd issued stern warnings to the ANC to keep within the law, and he responded vigorously to black labour unrest. This was reminiscent of action he had taken a few years earlier in what Huggins described as a 'trigger-happy' response to black labour unrest. Indeed, on 1 February 1954, when 9 000 black workers at the huge Wankie collieries went on strike for a cash payout instead of the food rations given to them, Todd tried to make the point that he was not too soft on blacks, by sending in the police and the army.

The white minimum wage at that time was some 30 times the black minimum so in large part the workers' grievances were fair.[5] The police were given powers to search all premises and make preventative arrests, to expel from the district for 30 days any persons suspected of agitation, and to imprison for one year any person 'committing an act or making a declaration calculated to provoke the stoppage or hindrance of essential services'.[6] In a softer tone Todd added an assurance to blacks who might have been shocked to receive such a hard smack from the Sunday School teacher. 'The gap between black and white standards of living', he told them, 'must be narrowed as quickly as possible.'[7] Despite this performance he failed to assuage the unease felt by his colleagues, who perceived that his concern rested primarily with the wellbeing of the blacks.

This view of Todd was crystallised by his complete and utter lack of personal racism, and the obvious esteem in which he was held by various native organisations and influential blacks. He had led the white population of Southern Rhodesia in a certain direction, but found that they would not follow him all the way. Todd was drifting down the same road as his Matabele predecessor Lotje. When the ramifications of the truth he had recently spoken became too much for the nation to bear, he would be taken out and morally executed.

Todd and Welensky now occupied such diametrically opposing positions, that one or other of them had to go. How great a role Sir Roy played in the rebellion against Todd that followed, is difficult to pinpoint and has remained a matter of speculation. Since Welensky was able to achieve the worst for Todd by doing nothing at all, it is possible that he did a great deal. The tide of fortune was running so strongly in his favour that all he needed to do was ride the swell on his considerable bulk while ignoring the cries of a drowning Todd.

It might be remembered that the United Party — which Godfrey Huggins had helped to form out of the ashes of the Rhodesia Party almost 30 years earlier — had given birth to the Federal Party, when Huggins moved on to fight the first Federal election. Because they shared both an ideological root and many common branches, the United Party — lately known as the United Rhodesia Party — and the Federal Party were sister organisations. A suggestion had been on the table for some time that the two parties should merge. It was noted also that the only opposition in the territory, the Dominion Party, was set up to fight both the territorial and Federal elections from a single platform.

Todd was ambivalent about the proposed changes but allowed himself to be swept along by the mood of his party. He did this in spite of knowing that a merger would dilute what limited support he still enjoyed in his own chapter. The matter was discussed at the annual conference of the United Rhodesia Party on 20 September 1957, where Todd was not alone in realising that a merger would weaken his position. Welensky had considered it too. Although Welensky still regarded Todd as a political threat, he saw him at this stage less as a rival than as a liability in the upcoming Federal and territorial elections. It was obvious that Todd had succeeded in antagonising all but a narrow minority of left-leaning liberals, but even as a mere territorial prime minister, he still had the capacity to bring the current Federal Government to its knees.

Two dissidents in Todd's caucus orchestrated a challenge to his leadership in the House. Consensus could not be reached, however, and the motion did not carry. The decision to merge with the Federal party was agreed to and then referred to the Federal Party Congress, that was to be held in Ndola in November of that year. There was broad support in the Federal Party for a merger, so there seemed no doubt that it would proceed. At that point Todd travelled to the Eastern Highlands for a short break, leaving behind a brooding cabinet. His timing was clearly a blunder since it left the field temporarily open to Welensky and his allies.

Welensky returned to Salisbury from Ndola in buoyant mood, having achieved his plans for a merger. It was broadly agreed within the territorial cabinet, that the chances of Todd leading the new party — now called the United Federal Party — to victory at the next election were negligible. Passions ran high and Todd was shocked on returning from Inyanga to hear reports of an open revolt. Passions soon cooled though, and when Todd confronted the rebels the following day, language was restrained and the mood muted. He agreed to a number of concessions including some tough action against the ANC — by then aggressively mobilising in the countryside — and an agreement to accept an amendment to the Immorality Act. As part of his closing speech to the caucus he declared:

> I speak with humility, but with conviction and some knowledge, when I say that my removal from office at this moment would be widely interpreted to indicate a rejection of Southern Rhodesia's moderately liberal stand, or at least a step back from it. I know also that to the great African section of our population this is how the position would appear... The position today is disturbing and serious. On the race relations side it cannot be denied that my leadership of this party represents to the African almost his sole hope that Partnership is not an empty word but a genuine and honest policy held by a majority of Europeans in this country...
>
> I know that enormous pressures are being built up to have me removed from office and if they are successful I believe that my going will remove a deterrent which at present exists against extremism of a kind we abhor. This is a simple and sincere statement of fact and responsible men will wish to consider it.

Todd then went on to commit exactly the same blunder, and then added two more to it. In mid-December he left with his wife for a month's holiday in the Cape, departing on the very day that regulations were published, setting out a 30% raise in the native minimum wage that Todd had more-or-less decreed. Why he chose this particular moment to tamper with native wages it is hard to imagine, but in doing so he immediately lost what limited big business support he had hitherto enjoyed. Perhaps more damaging still, he handed his cabinet colleagues the perfect pretext to support claims of dictatorial behaviour. Moreover, on the eve of his departure, he informally met with Joshua Nkomo, Ndabaningi Sithole and Guy Clutton Brock, the only white member of the ANC. This unauthorised and unrecognised meeting did Todd enormous damage in the eyes of his party. Ian

Smith, whose derisive language towards Todd in his memoirs, *The Great Betrayal*, hints strongly at the general antipathy felt towards him, commented on the meeting thus:

> The question came to a head when his cabinet colleagues discovered that behind their backs, he was involved in talks with Joshua Nkomo and the Reverend Ndabaningi Sithole, the leaders of the newly revived Southern Rhodesia African National Congress, which was engaged in a massive intimidation campaign in the battle for support among their own people. Clearly this placed them in the category of terrorist leaders.[8]

The United Federal Party was now entirely controlled by Welensky supporters. It was therefore not difficult over the Christmas period, and with all these issues in mind, to generate broad condemnation for the Southern Rhodesian Prime Minister while he was away. As the general election loomed, calls for Todd's purge grew shrill.

Todd returned to the colony on 9 January 1958 to be met at the airport by one of his MPs, Patrick Fletcher, who bore the news that the resignation of the Cabinet was imminent. At first Todd did not take the matter too seriously, but as the day progressed he realised that he was dealing with a genuine crisis. The following morning a Cabinet meeting was held and Todd found himself under sustained attack. This time the main avenue of complaint was irregular procedure in the granting of a minimum wage rise to the blacks. In the event, it was shown that Todd had, albeit somewhat vaguely, followed the necessary procedure. Thereupon the attack became more general, but aimed more-or-less at his pandering to the rights and wellbeing of the blacks. Individual complaints were wide-ranging, but the entire Cabinet did agree on at least one thing: Todd had become an electoral liability and could not be relied upon to lead the party to victory at the upcoming general election.

Todd calmly asked each member if they intended to withdraw their support — to which every one replied in the affirmative. It seemed that the Prime Minister was faced with a fait accompli and the rebel cabinet supposed that he had no choice but to resign. As a matter of form he was given 24 hours to think it over. To the consternation of the members, he commenced proceedings the following day by turning the tables and accepting the resignations of the entire Cabinet. On 14 January he announced a new cabinet, but with the writing on the wall for him, there was no air of permanence about the haphazard assembly of men named.

Meanwhile, battle lines had been drawn. Todd's unexpected display of tenacity simply polarised the party and precipitated the crisis. The last act was played out at a specially convened party conference held on 8 February 1958, attended by several hundred delegates. The original structures of the United Rhodesia Party had been superseded by the creation of the United Federal Party and Todd found himself facing a largely hostile convention packed with Welensky supporters. Most of the original members of the United Rhodesia party stood by their chief and, had the vote rested with them, there is every chance that Todd would have survived. More than 200 black members of the United Federal Party also pledged their support to him.

On the first ballot, after a combative speech lasting two hours, Todd was gratified to see his main rival, Patrick Fletcher, bringing up the rear in a field of three. On the second ballot Todd retained his 129 votes, but all Fletcher's support switched to the 'dark horse' candidate, Sir Edgar Whitehead. Whitehead received 193 ballots, and to his immense surprise became the party leader and de facto prime minister. Throughout the entire meeting Welensky maintained a determined silence — a performance very different from his usual style. Bearing in mind that a single word from him could have changed Todd's fate, his silence was considered significant.

The closing comments of the episode, however, go to Garfield Todd himself: 'In Africa, there is never enough time', he said. 'The hands have come off the clock, and it is later than we think.'

My luck has always been on the thin side

T he political fortunes of Sir Roy Welensky were so bound up in the fortunes of the Federation that, to conveniently wrap up his contribution to the region's public affairs, also serves to wrap up the story of the Federation itself.

The golden years of the Federation were its first years of strong economic growth and apparent political progress. These early successes tended to confirm in the minds of its architects that the experiment was working, and that the Central African Federation could look forward to a long and prosperous life. To whites in general there seemed every reason to suppose that a trial period of continued supervision by Whitehall would lead seamlessly to full independence in the Commonwealth. For the duration of Huggins' leadership, there was the air of a respected old man completing his valedictory term. It seemed that the substantive political issues, expected in the run up to the Constitutional Review Conference, could be attended to after he had gone. Not surprisingly, then, things began to go conspicuously sour almost from the moment that Huggins hung up his briefcase and Welensky took over. Sir Roy could therefore hardly be blamed towards the end of his term when he was heard to lament that his 'luck had always been on the thin side'.[1]

Welensky may have been a victim of bad luck — some men are — or he may have been simply too wedded to inappropriate policy — as some men also are. What is certain is that, in common with most whites aspiring to take the helm of government during these transitional days, Welensky was a man out of step with his times. The likelihood is that his fate combined all these elements, but most importantly it was just a matter of unfortunate timing. On 26 July 1956, just four months before Welensky was due to take over from Huggins, General Gamal Abdel Nasser upset the British applecart by seizing the Suez Canal Zone. After a year of gathering tensions in the Middle East, Britain was plunged into her first serious foreign policy crisis since World War-II, and the first in recent history that she did not eventually suppress.

One of Welensky's first tasks in office was to offer Prime Minister Anthony Eden the full support of the Federation in his dealing with the Suez Crisis. Federal support was cf little consequence however, and in due course Britain was humiliated. The event shattered British faith in her ability to rule, and illustrated in the harshest light the fact that she was no longer a global power. Nasser's comments at the end of the crisis were instructive.

> We cannot under any circumstances remain aloof from the terrible and sanguinary struggle going on in Africa today between five million whites and 200 million Africans. We shall not stand idly by in the belief that it will not concern us.[2]

The first of the 200 million Africans achieved their liberty when the Gold Coast was granted independence on 6 March 1957 as Ghana. The first black statesman to emerge from under British

(Above) The BSAP fort at Mafiking commanded by Colonel Hore was captured by Boer General Eloff. Eloff afterwards surrendered it to Colonel Hore. The fort was the low building on the right.

(Above) The Relief of Mafiking. E Squadron Rhodesia Horse parades after the relief. Major General R.S.S Baden-Powell takes the salute.

(Left)Rhodes died in South Africa on 26 March 1902. Picture shows his funeral procession passing through Bulawayo en route to his grave in the Matopos. The ruts made by the gun carriage's steel clad wheels in the soft rocks of the Matopos can still be traced.

(Right) 1899. Volunteers of E Squadron Rhodesia Horse off to fight in the Anglo-Boer War

(Above) The Rhodesia Horse was formed during the Matabele War. This contingent under Lt Maurice Gifford was readying to proceed to assist with the Relief of Mafiking.

(Right) Rhodes while cut off in Kimberly during the siege, ordered the building of a heavy gun in the De Beers' workshops to counter the Boer artillery. It was named Long Cecil and could fire a 30lb shell.

(Right) Rhodes' grave in the Matopos as seen many years later.

(Left) View from Jameson Avenue, Salisbury. 1902.

(Right) Constable in the Southern Rhodesia Constabulary parading in front of the Baker Avenue Police station, Salisbury. 1902.

(Left) Opening of the Queen Victoria Memorial Museum and Library, Salisbury.1902.

(Right) E.H Smith, a pioneer tobacco grower standing at the entrance to his flue-curing tobacco barn. 1903.

(Left) Victoria Falls bridge under construction. It was completed in 1905 and strengthened in1930 to take a roadway.

(Right) Manica Road East, Salisbury. 1910.

FIRST STREET - SALISBURY.

(Left) First Street, Salisbury. 1910.

GOVERNMENT HOUSE, SALISBURY.

(Right) Government House, Salisbury. 1910.

(Left) The Duke and Duchess of Connaught arriving at the Drill Hall, Moffat Street, Salisbury. 1910.

(Right) The Salisbury Gardens. 1910

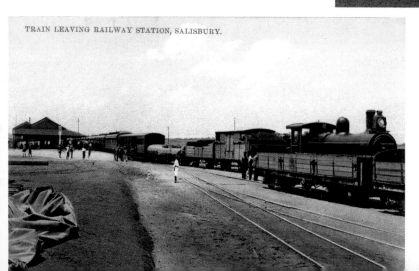

TRAIN LEAVING RAILWAY STATION, SALISBURY.

(Left) A train leaving the Railway Station, Salisbury 1910

(Right) The Mazoe Mail coach outside the Salisbury Post Office. 1912.

(Left) Fighting for King and Empire. South African and Rhodesian troops crowd the rigging of a troopship as it prepares to set sail from Cape Town to Windhoek in German South West Africa.

(Right) Infantry, probably the 1st Rhodesia Regiment, being inspected after landing Walvis Bay.

(Left) South African and Rhodesian troops digging entrenchments at Walvis Bay. They were rarely used in defence against German attacks.

(Below) The sturdy all-steel British-supplied Henri Farmans were unaffected by South West Africa's harsh climate. Private Arthur Harris (later Sir Arthur 'Bomber' Harris) was so envious of the pilots because of the exhausting route marches the Rhodesians had undertaken, that he vowed never to march in war again. After the campaign he went to England and joined the Royal Flying Corps. He ended the war as the squadron leader of 44 Bomber Squadron RAF. We will hear more of him later.

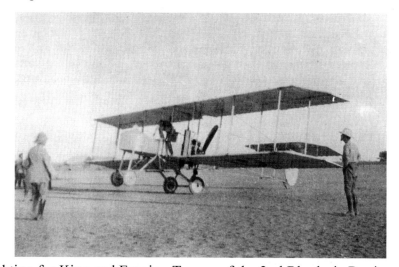

(Below) Fighting for King and Empire. Troops of the 2nd Rhodesia Regiment parading in Salisbury in preparation to leaving for German East Africa to fight the foe. A British South Africa Police column under Colonel Murray, was similarly preparing to move north. 1915.

(Right) 2nd Rhodesia Regiment entrains at Salisbury for the north.

(Left) Rhodesian troops wading through a swamp.

(Right) Rhodesians who had already fought at Salaita and Latema, preparing to march on Tanga.

(Left) Capt F.C Selous with his company of the 25th Royal Fusiliers shortly before he was killed in action on 6 January 1917.

(Right) Members of the 2nd Rhodesia Regiment after their withdrawal from East Africa, departing Salisbury to fight on the Western Front. 9 September 1917

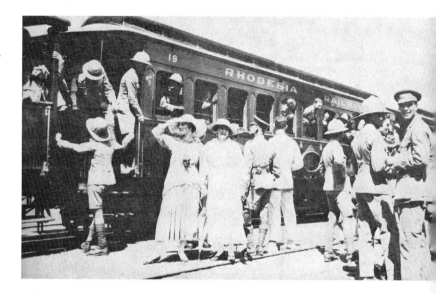

(Left) Fighting for King and Empire. For six days and five nights of absolut hell the South African Brigade (which included Rhodesian troops) fought to hold Delville Wood. 121 officers and 3 032 men went in. Two officers and 140 men either walked or were stretchere out. Picture shows troops digging a communication trench through what remained of Delville Wood The Rhodesians were decimated.

(Right) Battle of
Menin Road. German
POWs passing through
a dressing station
while British, Aus-
tralian, South African
and Rhodesian troops
look on. 20 September
1917.

(Left) A raiding party
with an officer lead-
ing the way amidst the
bursting of German
shells.

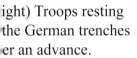

(Right) Troops resting
in the German trenches
after an advance.

(Left) Fighting for King and Empire. Rhodesian troops serving with the King Royal Rifle Corps fought in Salonica. Picture shows Bulga shells bursting on an English position.

(Right) Salonica. A means of transporting the slightly wounded.

(Left) Salonica. A despatch rider is held up in the dang zone while gas shells burst in front of him. Note the ga masks.

(Right) Rhodesian and Union delegates, April 1922. Back row: J.H.Eakin, W.M. Leggate, D. Hawksley, Hon P. Duncan, Rt Hon F.S. Malan, G. Johnson, F Moore, J.W. Weller. Middle: E.C Baxter, P.D.L Fynn, Raleigh Grey, Rt Hon, Sir Thomas Smartt, R.G. Garvie, Sir Randolf Baker, J Stewart, Capt E. Lane. Seated: J.G. McDonald; R.D. Gilchrist, H.T. Longden, Sir Drummond Chaplin, Rt Hon General Smuts, Sir Charles Coghlan, Mrs T.Jollie, Sir Bourchier Wrey.

(Left) Responsible government delegates to London in 1921. Back: W.M Leggate, P. Rewton. Front: R.A Fletcher, E.P Goghlan and J. McChlery.

(Right) Mrs Tawse Jollie. She was the organiser of the Responsible Government Party in 1920 and the first woman elected to a legislative assembly in the British dominions.

(Left) Sir Charles Coghl. taking the oath as Rhodesia's first prime min ter after Rhode sia was grante responsible government by Britain in 192.

(Right) The staff at British South Africa Police, Goromonzi. 1933.

(Left) Southern Rhodesia's tobacc auctions in progre

(Right) Sir Godfrey Huggins (later Viscount Malvern) held the Southern Rhodesian premiership from 1933 to 1953 when he became the Federal Prime Minister, handing over to Garfield Todd. He remained in this office until 1956 when he retired and handed over to Sir Roy Welensky. His continuous service as a prime minister was a British Commonwealth record.

(Left) In World War II, because of the savage casualties suffered by Rhodesians in World War I, it was decided that servicemen would be sent in small numbers to serve in a spread of South African and British units to avoid history repeating itself. Rhodesians served with South African forces during the Abyssinian campaign.

(Right) Rhodesians were an important element of the Long Range Desert Group during the Western Desert campaigns.

(Left) Rhodesians served with the British 8th Army (Desert Rats) during the Western Desert campaigns fought against the Italians and Germans. Picture shows the bombardment of Bir Hakeim. 1942.

(Right) 237 (Rhodesia) Squadron, RAF, flying into a desert sunset during an operational strike. A future Rhodesian prime minister, Ian Douglas Smith, served with distinction in this squadron.

(Left) Air Chief Marshall Sir Arthur 'Bomber' Harris became AOC-in-C Bomber Command on 22 February 1942 and he fought the bomber war decisively until the collapse of Germany, playing one of the most important roles in the defeat of the enemy. He re-titled his old squadron command from World War-I as 44 (Rhodesia) Squadron RAF, He described himself as a Rhodesian until the day he died.

protection was the visionary academic, Dr Kwame Nkrumah, and his coming out was celebrated in grand style.

One particular guest at the independence celebrations in the Ghanaian capital of Accra, was the diminutive Nyasa medical doctor, Hastings Banda. Banda had risen from relative obscurity in the run up to the Federation thanks to his organisation and leadership of the general protest. He was a medical doctor twice qualified, first at the Meharry College in Tennessee, and again at the University of Edinburgh. In recent years he had established a busy general practice in Harlesden, north London. He was a physically unprepossessing man, habitually dressed in a dark, three-piece suit, a homburg hat and a pair of dark sunglasses. What he lacked in physical stature, however, he made up for in conceit and gumption. If Kwame Nkrumah had been a dream to the Colonial Office, then Banda was about to become its nightmare.

As much as Hastings Banda was awed by the deep symbolism of Ghanaian independence, he was charmed even more by the cries of 'Saviour' and 'Messiah' that followed Kwame Nkrumah wherever he went. This adulation ignited a notion in the little doctor's mind, that one day he could also be a black nationalist Messiah. Consequently it took little persuasion for him to abandon his medical career and return home, when the call came for him to lead the Nyasaland African National Congress.

It is noteworthy that Banda had been out of Nyasaland for so long that he was no longer fluent in his native language His birth was never recorded, so his age was always a matter for speculation. It is probable, however, that he was about 56 at this time.

It is unlikely that Banda would have entered the trenches of the national struggle if he had not been fairly confident of victory. All that was lacking was a likely pretext upon which to stage as dramatic a return as possible, and fortunately for him and his backers, Sir Roy was about to provide just that.

Welensky realised that events in Ghana — and similar plans for many African colonial territories — all served to fire the blood of local nationalists. The ease with which countries to the north appeared to be slipping through the fingers of their colonial masters, was spreading hope throughout central and southern Africa. Welensky was anxious to douse any similar hopes that might be gathering momentum in British central Africa.

For the time being the Crown seemed eager to confirm its ongoing support for the Federation. However, Britain was increasingly adrift in unpredictable seas and her course was progressively less reliable. It will be remembered that in April 1957 Welensky visited London for the purpose of pressing for his five major constitutional concessions, the most important of which was that Whitehall would not countenance a motion for any territory to secede from the Federation. Welensky had been anxious that the Colonial Office be quite categorical on this point — and he had won the point. He also succeeded in obtaining a firm date for the convening of the Federal Constitutional Review Conference. It had originally been scheduled for 1962 but he persuaded Whitehall to move it forward to 1960. Most importantly he secured a clear understanding that the principal objective of the Conference would be to examine the conditions under which the Federation would move towards complete independence, and once again this was categorically confirmed.

With all this in the bag, Welensky returned home in victorious mood. He had good reason to believe that he had pinned the British Government down on the question of the Federation's future, and that the territory could now survive the daunting possibility of a Labour government with some degree of confidence.

Welensky was not immediately aware, though, of the negative effect that all his apparent political success was having on the blacks. The concessions were widely viewed in that quarter as a betrayal by Her Majesty of her sacred trust. The Crown was seen to have capitulated in the face of white pressure, which indicated that when it came down to it, the British would always see things in favour of their kith and kin. This was not altogether untrue, but there were other factors in the mix too. What the blacks of the three territories did not take into account was that the Central African Federation was the only British overseas possession with an army under local command.

More than once Welensky had been heard to utter darkly that some of the more outrageous British suggestions would need to be backed up by an army. At the very least he had the power to declare unilateral independence. So as long as the blacks in the territory were passive, London had much to gain by keeping Welensky quiet. However the blacks were aware of this fact too, and consequently began to formulate a strategy significantly less passive than hitherto. They had also recognised the significance of the impending Federal Constitutional Review Conference and concluded that they had but a narrow window of opportunity to make their voices heard in Whitehall.

More fuel was thrown on a gathering rebellion by the passage of the Federal Election Act. This appeared superficially to be an advance but was in reality much less than that. By then most blacks had lost faith in the franchise, to such an extent that it scarcely mattered how the Act was framed. The new franchise represented the kind of differentiating legislation that was a cue for the African Affairs Board to refer it to the UK Government for review. In due course the Board was heard but overruled after a lively debate in the House of Commons. The Federal Election Act, as well as the Constitutional Amendment Act of a year earlier that had facilitated it, were approved. Church of Scotland Missionary the Rev Andrew Doig — a member of the African Affairs Board — resigned in disgust, declaring the Board a farce.

In the meantime, Dr Hastings Banda returned to England from Ghana and there waited for the appropriate moment to, as Welensky put it, 'make his messianic descent on the land of his birth'.[3] Sir Roy had obviously heard the talk swirling around on the subject of Banda. It is unlikely that the doctor was born with delusions of grandeur but his consequent behaviour indicated that they sat very well with him. To the whites of Nyasaland, the signs of demagoguery were there for all to see, and indeed whites throughout the Federation could not help but see shades of their own future in the strutting arrogance of a black popinjay, who had a mission-funded education and an overpowering desire to rule.

In London, Banda was apprised of the concessions granted to the Federal Government in April and the apparent impotence of the African Affairs Board to uphold its mandate. In September 1957, a memorandum demanding major reforms to the Nyasaland territorial constitution was prepared by the ANC and presented to the Governor, Sir Robert Armitage, a man not well disposed to unpleasant surprises like this. Armitage emerges from biographical accounts, as a timorous gentleman who had recently had his fingers burned in Cyprus. He apparently hoped that a term in a colonial backwater such as Nyasaland would be a tonic for his nerves. He therefore very gingerly put it to the Congress that its proposals were too advanced, the aim of an all-African government by 1960 impractical and the expectation of universal adult suffrage highly unrealistic.

Congress then invited Armitage to put forward proposals of his own, which he promised to do, but not before consultation with the other Federal partners and the Colonial Secretary. He then sat on the issue until November when he received a second deputation from the ANC. The Governor assured his visitors that he was due home on leave the following spring, whereupon he would take the matter up with the Colonial Secretary.

This time Sir Robert was as good as his word, but was perhaps guilty less of consulting than passing the buck to the Colonial Secretary, Alan Lennox-Boyd (later Lord Boyd). Lennox-Boyd in turn sat on the matter for a further month or two, perhaps pondering the usual expedient of a Royal Commission. Before he could act, Banda arrived at his desk with an ANC delegation from Nyasaland, who made it clear that delays in the matter were no longer acceptable. The pace of change was gathering its own momentum and the British ought either to swim with the tide or get out of the water. A decision on the matter still rested ultimately with Sir Robert Armitage, so Lennox-Boyd assured

Banda and his associates that he hoped to receive the Governor's recommendations by August.

Welensky, in the meanwhile, was powerless to intervene. The focus of tension was Nyasaland and the issue therefore resided with the territorial government. He may have publicly expressed satisfaction at Armitage's progress, while privately he was riddled with misgivings. Although he still hung his faith on the British Government's undertakings of the previous year, he was painfully aware that on the fate of Nyasaland — the territory that no one, not even itself, had wanted in the Federation in the first place — hung the fate of the entire union.

Banda decided that the moment was ripe and prepared for his long anticipated return. The date of his expected arrival was 29 June, and lavish preparations were made to greet him. Placards proclaiming him President General Designate of Congress were circulated while a crowd of 3000 gathered on the tarmac in keen anticipation. When the aircraft finally touched down Banda did not appear. A rumour quickly began to circulate that communications had been tampered with and that a plot existed to kill the Messiah. The aircraft was searched from top to bottom and dark threats to burn it were uttered when no sign of the doctor was unearthed.

Banda was in fact at that moment addressing a meeting in London and arrived only a week later, stepping out onto the apron in Blantyre to the thrilling sight of 5 000 rapturous blacks greeting him as their saviour. He was immediately absorbed in a flurry of speeches and press conferences, before making his way to Government House to meet Sir Robert Armitage.

So Anglicised did Hastings Banda appear that Armitage was at first relieved to assess him not as a hot-blood rabble-rouser, but a man of moderate temperament and high intellectual gifts. For Banda, by then probably already in or near his 60s, this was initially no disadvantage and he affected the public position that self-government was to be achieved only with the consent of the Crown, and by means of negotiation and non-violence. These typically moderate sentiments were heard time and again, but translated as they had to be into the local language, they usually assumed a much darker and more revolutionary tone. In the meantime a full meeting of the ANC was held in Blantyre where Banda was unanimously elected President General of the Party.

A few weeks later Armitage announced that he had no immediate announcement to make. It was no less than Banda had expected and events thereafter began to move quickly. The doctor began a series of public meetings, and although maintaining at all times a moderate tone, the security situation in the territory began to deteriorate perceptibly. Public meetings were tense, and a new mood of insolence towards the white settlers took root as violent incidents flared throughout the territory.

Faced with an upcoming general election, Welensky did all that he could to calm the situation. He also made it clear to the British that, while he was at all times willing to discuss constitutional changes, they would be strictly moderated and not driven by any violent reaction in the countryside. A government White Paper was published on September 17 1958 on the question of Northern Rhodesian constitutional reform. Welensky appealed to the British Government through informal contacts, to either modify or delay the release of the new proposals in the light of the fact that he would soon have to face the polls. The two northern territories already sat on a knife's edge and he did not need either a white or a black backlash. Despite his misgivings, however, the United Federal Party made a clean sweep, winning 46 out of 59 seats, after which Welensky settled in on his unsteady throne so see the crisis through.

Tensions in Nyasaland eased somewhat when Banda left the country in early December, to attend the All Africa Peoples Conference in Accra. He was jubilant when it was announced, largely for his benefit, that 'The Conference declares its full support of all fighters for freedom in Africa.' He was feted, honoured and occasionally humoured before returning to Nyasaland in a mood of much increased belligerence. In his speeches and press interviews, he repeatedly forswore violence, but to this he now commonly added that violence could not be ruled out if it proved to be unavoidable.

In his memoirs of the fight for the Federation, Sir Roy Welensky's slide into despair becomes evident as he begins to dwell on the events of 1959. He was still hearing various earnest voices in the British Government talking of their commitment to the Federation and their determination to see it work, but at the same time he could not fail to notice signs of backsliding. He had the power at his disposal to deal with the unrest and would have done so had he not been bound by a plethora of frustrating limitations imposed on him by the Crown. As the man of Africa, he had so often tried to make the British see that whites on the ground were better able to deal with African affairs than out-of-touch bureaucrats in Whitehall. He could see exactly what was happening but was powerless to intercede. He gnawed his fingernails over Soviet and Chinese power plays in Africa that in some ways succeeded in magnifying the simple moral issue at hand into something much more terrifying.

Banda, meanwhile, was touring the Nyasaland countryside and setting the hearts and passions of his people aflame. He had shaken himself free of all restraints and was soaring in a revolutionary ferment. Violence in the countryside was escalating, although it was still isolated and spontaneous and more-or-less within the capacity of the local constabulary to suppress. During a particular meeting, however, 50 female activists were arrested, in response to which Banda and his aide, one H Chipembere, incited the crowd to descend on the police station in Zomba and violently effect their release. The incident was the worst of its kind so far, and prompted a revision by the Federal authorities of security measures in the territory.

Regular Federal troops, territorials and the Air Force were put on standby in expectation of a rapid escalation of unrest in the months to follow. It was an anxious time. At a Congress conference, held at the end of January 1959, menacing threats were made against internal dissidents and 'quislings' while at the same time a call went out for 'brave men' to undertake a renewed campaign of violence. Clearly Banda was goading Armitage as the Governor himself slipped deeper into paralysis.

Welensky arrived in Blantyre, took Armitage by the ear and tried to shake some sense into him. Banda was clearly courting arrest and detention, but since Britannia was no tyranny bristling with malice, the doctor had little to fear from it. On the other hand, the thought of having to resort to such action produced symptoms of apoplexy in Armitage. A joke born in Ghana was then in circulation among the Nyasa nationalists: 'When the British start arresting, full independence is around the corner.'[4]

It was agreed in Congress that when that day came, a committee of four would take control of the Party and signal a pre-planned campaign of sabotage and violence. Prior to that, a low-level state of unrest would be maintained in preparation for a major push. Prisoners from Zomba jail would be released on a signal to their prison guards and would augment nationalist manpower. There was an expectation that help would come from neighbouring countries, but what form this would take was obscure. On 21 February Federal troops were airlifted to Blantyre as a precautionary measure. The British press was in ferment as comparisons to the gore and horror of the Kenya Emergency and the excesses of the Mau-Mau were liberally made.

On 23 February pamphlets condemning the use of Federal troops were circulated throughout Limbe and Blantyre. On 26 February Edgar Whitehead declared a State of Emergency in Southern Rhodesia under the provisions of which the police rounded up and placed in preventative detention more than 500 officials and members of the Southern Rhodesia ANC which was declared an unlawful organisation and banned. This was simultaneous to the banning and rounding up the leaders of the African National Congress of Northern Rhodesia and the ANC Nyasaland.

Joshua Nkomo, commencing a pattern that would become noticeable in the future, happened to be out of the country at the time and avoided arrest. On this particular occasion Nkomo was out of the country attending the All-African Peoples Conference in Accra, where both he and Banda made their international debuts. Nkomo lingered in Accra longer than was necessary before travelling on to

Egypt. There he was persuaded — as he himself explains it — by Egyptian friends to resist his natural impulse to return to detention in Southern Rhodesia, but instead to travel on to London in order to open an external office of the ANC. Without doubt friends at home would have counselled him differently, but he found Britain a great deal more pleasing than a detention camp. It was inevitable that one day he would be forced to face the whirlwind — as every revolutionary must — but to the maximum of his ability he put off that disagreeable day.

Nkomo's first visit overseas also answered a question that had fascinated him since he was a boy. Based on his experience in Rhodesia and South Africa, he had often wondered who did the work in England. The answer was revealed when a white maid who called him 'Sir' attended to him in his hotel. This was as gratifying to Nkomo as discovering that he could apply for the dole as a Commonwealth migrant. This he did, although he claimed in his autobiography that he found living off the British taxpayer demeaning. The Egyptian Government had already given him a substantial donation for his personal expenses.[1] In fact he continued to live for some time on donations and gifts from various sources, that in combination allowed him, among other luxuries, to educate his children abroad.

None of this withstanding, Nkomo made active progress in London. His list of foreign supporters and benefactors was impressive for a novice, and included Labour MP and chairman of the National Executive Committee, Ian Mikardo, and future Labour member for Eton and Slough, Baroness Lestor of Eccles. He was also well received by the Anti-Slavery Society, the Fabian movement and in many other homes and forums linked to the Socialists and the Labour Party. Detention in Southern Rhodesia — and even just the grubby day-to-day struggle of activism in the townships and reserves — held very little appeal for Nkomo.

In the north of Nyasaland, a mob had taken over a customs post at Fort Hill on the Tanganyika border and occupied airfield runways to frustrate the landing of Federal Troops. On 27 February the first shootings occurred.

The incident happened during the sitting of a tribal court. A local chief was repeatedly interrupted by a mob as he tried to deliver judgement on three men who had broken local agricultural rules. A detachment of the Kings African Rifles was brought up and in a confusion of tear gas and controlled gunfire, one protester was wounded and another killed. Later, the British South Africa Police killed two more people, breaking the proud record of the BSAP of not having fired a shot in anger since the turn of the century.[5] All in all there were 11 casualties during the 12 days of the revolt of which six were fatal.

On March 3, Armitage finally declared a State of Emergency. White women and children were airlifted out of the territory and troops deployed to strategic locations. The ANC and its women and youth leagues were proscribed, and in a stealthy dawn raid the principal Congress leaders and coordinators, including Banda, were arrested and flown to detention in Southern Rhodesia. The planned uprising was stillborn, and what conflagrations escaped the pre-emptive clampdown were efficiently doused. It was a shrewd piece of work and Welensky, with some justification, was proud of himself.

If that had been the end of the affair, Welensky would have had excellent grounds for self-congratulation, but unfortunately it was just the beginning. Naturally the Crown despatched a Commission of Inquiry to look into the episode, and the Devlin Report drew not altogether unpredictable conclusions. It was Harold Macmillan, successor to Sir Anthony Eden as British Prime Minister, who most vitally concluded that the Nyasaland emergency was a turning point for the British view of central Africa. It had become clear to Macmillan that humouring Welensky and the whites was not going to be the easy panacea that had been hoped. Black voices had become altogether too loud, angry and insistent. The Nyasaland Emergency had taught the British Government exactly the lesson that Banda hoped it would. They would from then on have to listen much more carefully to him than to Welensky.

This was also exactly the kind of thing that Welensky had tried to guard against with his insistence on a clear undertaking from the British regarding their view of secession. It remained now for him to discover precisely how unreliable Her Majesty ministers could be. With just a subtle shift of emphasis, the stride of the UK Government did not alter discernibly, although a change of direction was unmistakable. Once again all eyes were directed at the Constitutional Review Conference, now no more than a year away. In the Meanwhile, circumstances on the ground had changed profoundly.

Secession had now become the clarion call of all nationalist protest and now that it had been silenced, Banda's voice was louder than ever. The matter had been drawn into the sphere of British party politics, and with Labour gathering confidence and casting around for a casus belli, it would be unbecoming of Macmillan to hand the means of his own defeat to the opposition. What was to be done? The Prime Minister did not have to ponder this question for long. A Royal Commission of Inquiry was of course the answer.

36

Monckton Commission

T he proposed commission was vaguely defined at first as being a tool to prepare the ground for the Review Conference. This immediately alarmed Welensky who felt, quite rightly, that the ground had already been prepared. His impression had been that terms of independence were to be discussed and that secession by any territory was not to be countenanced. So what had changed? The answer, of course, was everything!

Welensky resolved to fight any suggestion of a new commission tooth and nail, and so he did. When it became apparent that the commission — due to be chaired by Walter Monckton, a lawyer, close friend and university colleague of the British Prime Minister — would go ahead anyway, Welensky applied himself to trying to steer the Commission's terms of reference into the narrow space previously agreed.

Labour Leader Hugh Gaitskell became the most ardent advocate of terms of reference that were as wide as possible — which shielded Macmillan somewhat from the tempest of Welensky's rage. The Monckton Commission, Macmillan said, would set about finding ways to make the Federation work. If, however, it was unable to do so within its terms of reference, it would no doubt say so.1

It is perhaps incidental that at the British polls on 8 October 1959, the Conservatives increased their parliamentary majority to 100 seats, for it was too late by then to alter the course of events in central Africa. The Monckton Commission arrived in Salisbury in February 1960 and spent three months gathering evidence throughout the Federation. In early April it returned to London and six months later its report was published.

In the meanwhile, a hint of some behind the scenes shenanigans came to light as a result of two import incidents. In the first, Banda was visited in prison by his legal advisor, a British QC by the name of Dingle Foot. During the course of a wide ranging interview, Foot let it be known to Banda that the Monckton Commission, although tethered by certain limitations, would not be squeamish about giving serious consideration to the advantages of Nyasaland seceding from the Federation. Unknown to Foot or Banda, the room had been bugged and in due course Welensky felt the earth shift a little more beneath his feet.

The second incident was less covert. Welensky's by then highly developed mistrust of the British was tuned to an even finer pitch when Macmillan twisted the peg and insisted that Banda be released to give evidence to the Monckton Commission. Welensky gnashed his teeth and resisted but had limited grounds to refuse. Macmillan then set off on his now celebrated Winds of Change tour of Africa, and nothing that he said during his addresses quenched the ardour of black nationalists.

Before dawn on 1 April 1960, Banda was released unconditionally and flown to Blantyre where he met with Armitage and the new Colonial Secretary, Iain Macleod. The two found Banda mildly chastened but unmoved over the question of constitutional reforms. Macleod was able to inform Welensky, after two days in close conference with Banda that he believed the ANC President would endeavour to keep the peace. Even if Banda was unwilling to concede on any of his demands, he was at least prepared to move forward at a measured pace.

Upon that, Banda set off on a publicity tour of Britain where on arrival he promptly announced to the press that the Federal Constitutional Review Conference was to be held in the summer of 1960 and that he intended to press for both immediate self-government for Nyasaland and secession from the Federation. Macleod was unimpressed and assured Welensky that despite this grandstanding, Banda would do what he was told. It is hard to imagine that Welensky drew much comfort from this.

At the end of June 1960 a shocking series of events seized the attention of the region and the wider world. It was the first open and uncensored display of African independence at work. If the Nyasaland Emergency gave the whites of the Federation an unsettling glimpse into the future, it was the Congo crisis that wrote the facts in large letters. Surely the most supremely misguided words ever uttered on a political stage were those spoken by Patrice Lumumba on the day of Congolese Independence.

> We are going to show the world what the black man can do when he works in freedom, and we are going to make the Congo the centre of radiance for the whole of Africa.[2]

If these lofty words were supposed to impress gathered dignitaries — including King Baudouin of Belgian — with promises of progress, peace and liberty, then all were soon to be sorely disappointed. Those apologists, who over the years have cried out that the handover was bungled, ought first to remember that it was bungled mainly because it was driven by too much haste. This was the determining lesson learned by the Federation whites who anxiously watched the ensuing tragedy unfold.

The sequence of events that had led up to the crisis had a cautionary ring. The Belgian authorities appeared to take fright at increasing black agitation, and jettisoned the Congo territory without making any meaningful efforts to prepare the ground. Neither the military nor the civil service were adequately conditioned for self-government and within four days of the handover, the country began its descent into anarchy. The military ran amok and by February 1961 Lumumba was dead and the country fractured along regional and tribal lines. European refugees streamed south into the Federation, bringing with them ever more lurid tales of rape and slaughter.

In the Congo, the United Nations was drawn into the only real hot war of its existence to date. The conflict claimed the life of UN Secretary General Dag Hammarskjold, whose aircraft was lost while flying from the Congo to the Federation to meet with Moise Tshombe. Tshombe was the leader of the breakaway Katanga province and Welensky's protégé in the affair, and while Welensky was widely suspected of having been behind the incident, no evidence to support any hypothesis of foul play has ever been found.

More than anything, the tragedy confirmed the worst fears of whites in the remaining occupied territories. Rampant excesses among liberated blacks and the complete breakdown of law, order and any civilised standards shocked whites to the core. It utterly confirmed their determination to make no political concessions to the blacks. If the natives could reduce the relatively orderly Belgian Congo to a smouldering heap in a few months, what could they do to any one of the territories of the Federation?

In July 1960 a new party was born out of the ashes of the reformed African National Congress in Southern Rhodesia, and with it came a touch of the Congo. The National Democratic Party was the ANC under a different name, and no sooner did the news of its birth circulate than the townships of Salisbury and Bulawayo erupted into an orgiastic celebration of violence. It was an inauspicious backdrop to the publication of the Monckton Report, which was released in mid-October.

It would be wrong to say that Welensky was entirely surprised by what he read when he sat down to ponder the findings. Monckton gave much unsolicited praise for some of the obvious achievements of the Federation, devoting endless verbiage to that which was commendable. However, all that was swept away by the few concluding paragraphs. The text returned to the stale, intractable and inescapable reality of black resistance. *Drum* magazine summed up the Monckton Report thus:

> ... their 175 pages of history-making reading can be summed up in three terse words: 'It won't work.'[3]

The architects of the Federation, including Lord Chandos, Andrew Cohen and not least, of course, Huggins and Welensky — with the added help of such observers and well-wishers as Clement Attlee and Sir Miles Thomas — had still not succeeded in satisfying the blacks that their best interests were being served. Improvements brought about by the Federation had either not been sufficient or the disadvantages were too great. 'I know my Africans', remarked Sir Edgar Whitehead from within his perennial fog, 'and they are not interested in politics.'[4] Such illusions are deadly, and Kenneth Kaunda said as much. 'Call an elephant a rabbit', he warned, 'only if it gives you comfort to feel that you are about to be trampled to death by a rabbit.'

By the time he finished reading through the report, Sir Roy would certainly have felt severely trampled. The rabbit was not in this instance an obstreperous black man but the British themselves, who were — or who at least ought to have been — the staunchest allies of white Britons. The inference of the Monckton Report was clear. If a majority of citizens of a territory decide that remaining in the Federation has become untenable, then that territory ought to have the right to leave. The nature of this majority would not, as Welensky and so many others had sought to insist, be the narrowly representative electorate, but all who had a voice and could raise it.

Welensky's voice in the midst of it all pealed betrayal, and of course he was right. The Monckton Commission had totally exceeded its terms of reference, and underlining this was a more bitter betrayal still. Time and time again Welensky had been assured that Her Majesty stood squarely behind the survival of the Federation. She would under no circumstances do anything to in any way undermine the future of her subjects. *Drum* cruelly lampooned Welensky's predicament in the pages of the November 1960 edition:

> Roy Welensky, heavyweight champion of the rough-neck Rhodesia of the 1920s, has just been knocked groggy by a blow harder and more painful than any punishment he ever took in the ring. And Welensky, who swapped his fighter's gown for the striped pants of the Prime Minister's office — and held onto the title of central Africa's "White Hope" — is making the same cry as every fighter who ever got licked and didn't like it: 'Throw out the ref.'[6]

One wonders whether the poison chalice handed to Welensky tasted any worse than it did to the handful of British politicians whose job it was to bring the curtain down on the British Empire. Never again would Britain stand proud in the region. Never again would the sun-scarred men in khaki ever feel their Britishness without some revulsion. The men of Rhodes' stature seemed to have given way to a bevy of vacillating yes-men and this was indeed the end.

37

Another one bites the dust

The Federal band, of course, marched on for a few more choruses. In his memoirs Welensky tried with good grace to plough through the galling details of his own disengagement. Nyasaland had always been something of a liability, he wrote, and the union was in many ways better off without her. But this was not to be. Symbolism had overtaken practicality, and with Nyasaland now feverishly negotiating its secession and independence, there seemed no reason to suppose that Northern Rhodesia would not to do the same.

The next step in the political process was the long awaited Federal Constitutional Review Conference. It was held at Lancaster House in London, the funeral parlour of the British Empire, on 5 December 1960. By then, of course, the dye was cast. A new constitution for Nyasaland had already been agreed and Banda had succeeded in securing a black majority on the Legislative Council. His objective at the conference was to smash the Federation, and rarely did he miss an opportunity to say so. An air of hopelessness settled on the countenances of all the white delegates as they glumly waded through the performance.

As was his wont, Banda enlivened matters by carefully choreographing a headline catcher. The idea was that he would walk out of the conference hall with his entire delegation at the optimum moment. However, the chairman frustrated the plan by steering the proceedings away from any potentially provocative areas. With a press conference already arranged, Banda was forced in the end to throw his papers arbitrarily in the air and shout 'To hell with the Federation!' Then he gathered his entourage and hurried off to meet the press.

The incident was more comic than dramatic and thoroughly in keeping with Banda's aptitude for histrionics, but no one was laughing. Banda was not supposed to be a comedian but a national leader of undeniable influence who had to be taken seriously. Clifford Dupont, who observed the incident, related the story in his memoirs, but was careful to add that he had always regarded Banda as the wisest and bravest leader of any African state. At that time these were few and the competition was unimpressive. Banda would in due course evolve into the closest thing the whites had to a friend in the region and his sensibilities needed to be protected. Dupont perhaps revealed more than he intended when he added the comment: 'I will not embarrass him with any details beyond stating that I value his friendship.'[2]

By then events had utterly emasculated the Conference, and it broke up after 12 days, having achieved almost nothing. The statutory imbalance created by Nyasaland's new status demanded constitutional reviews on the part of the two remaining territories, and it was with some relief that the assorted delegates parted company and set off in their various directions to undertake this.

After Banda's successes, blacks in Northern Rhodesia were rapidly energised. They could sense devolution and so could Roy Welensky. However, by then the Federal Prime Minister could barely muster the energy to protest. He was forced to drink from the poisoned chalice again when Duncan

Sandys, Secretary of State for the Commonwealth, obliged him to release the remaining Nyasaland detainees still held in Southern Rhodesia. As Sir Roy wearily warned, it would, this simply precipitated an immediate deterioration of the security situation in Nyasaland.

During these dark days Welensky more than once pondered a unilateral declaration of independence. Anticipating something along these lines, Macmillan placed a British air and ground force on standby at Nairobi Airport. Welensky was alerted to this, and although hoarse from weeks and months of shouting, he raised his voice again. Macmillan promptly faced a right-wing backlash in his party and was forced into some infantile back peddling — the entire episode doing him little credit.

After interminable wrangling, a formula for a new Northern Rhodesian constitution was presented in July 1961. It conceded more to the whites than seemed justified by recent events and incidents of sabotage, arson and violence soon engulfed the protectorate. The uprising, in the unique style of Kenneth Kaunda, now leading the pack, was named the Cha-cha-cha Campaign.

Kenneth Kaunda had by then risen to the leadership of the Zambia African National Congress, which was banned in March 1959 after serious civil unrest in the countryside. In June Kaunda was arrested and imprisoned for nine months, first in Lusaka, and then in Salisbury. On his release in 1960 he formed and was elected President of the United Independence Party (UNIP). By February 1962 another constitutional formula had been devised that succeeded in giving the nationalists an almost guaranteed majority in the house, and a black majority was indeed the net result of the general election that took place in October 1962. Kenneth Kaunda and Harry Nkumbula, leader of the ANC, formed an uneasy coalition government with the aim of breaking away from the Federation and formulating a one-man-one-vote constitution.

Banda's story, meanwhile, was from that point on somewhat predictable. As much that Welensky and many others had predicted would happen did happen, all had ample occasion to say 'I told you so'. 'One man one vote once' was the Rhodesian version of the nationalist joke and Banda did nothing to disown it. He became prime minister of an independent Malawi on 1 February 1963, president in 1966 when Malawi was declared a one party state, and president for life in 1971. In his 31 years of autocratic rule over one of the world's poorest countries, he was reputed to have amassed over US$320 million worth of personal assets. After the breakup of the Soviet Union he was forced to allow multi-party elections and in 1994 was resoundingly beaten at the polls. At the age of possibly 94 — nobody could be sure — he finally released his grip on power and seven years later died in a South African hospital.

Welensky, meanwhile, had swum heavily against the tide by supporting Moise Tshombe during the Congo crisis. Tshombe was the leader of the breakaway Katanga Province which housed the richest mining areas, including the sister industry to the Northern Rhodesian Copperbelt. Tshombe was the enemy not only of many local factions in the Congo, but of the international community too. His efforts, and no doubt those of Welensky in supporting him, were seen abroad as trying to draw the valuable real estate of Katanga into the Federal sphere of influence.

In this matter the international community could say what they liked; but as far as Welensky was concerned, it had been he who had confronted the crisis on his northern border and he who had tried to deal with it. The high profile association between he and Tshombe, however, did little for either man's long-term credibility. After having his aircraft hijacked to Algeria by unknown persons, Tshombe died there under house arrest in 1969 at the age of only 50.

Sir Roy was forced in 1962 to acquiesce to the secession of Nyasaland from the Federation and a year later the process was repeated in respect of Northern Rhodesia. The Central Africa Federation writhed in its death throes for a few more months and was formally dissolved on 31 December 1963. After just over ten years, the great experiment in amalgamation was at an end.

The front line was now the mighty Zambezi River, and over the next two years much political reorganisation would take place ahead of the great race war that was to follow.

38

An illiberal experiment

The Whitehead era

It is probable that Edgar Whitehead thought more of himself in his appointment to the highest office in Southern Rhodesia than was warranted. It would have been in his nature to suppose that he had been chosen not as 'anybody other than Todd' but because of his intrinsic abilities and his natural leadership qualities. Neither of these attributes was present in noticeable quantities — which did not stop him plunging into his new role without a moment of self-examination.

While he may have assumed command, Whitehead was a captain without a compass. It might be said that the ship of state was entering the roaring forties and there were better men on board than he to steer it around the Horn. The times no longer belonged to the liberal and intellectual classes of middle England, but to the white political brawlers and the black nationalists. These were the right and left wing men of steel. To them Whitehead was a morsel of cannon fodder about to have the stuffing completely blown out of him.

Edgar Whitehead's background was superior to Huggins' in the subtle weights and measures of British society, and in theory he ought to have stepped in at a higher level. He was born in Berlin in 1905 to a father in the diplomatic service and educated at Shrewsbury and Oxford. Like Huggins, it was poor health that brought him to the colony, and like Huggins he suffered from hearing difficulties. His deafness, though, was worse than Huggins' and he had the added disadvantage of extremely poor eyesight.

Whitehead had a kind of bumbling, gnomish quality about him that was not helped at all by thick spectacles that magnified his pale eyes. He was a confirmed bachelor, possibly because of his awkward looks and somewhat gruff manner, but also perhaps because he could rarely abide being corrected and was seldom inclined to concede a point. References to alcohol also tended to feature large in most recollections of him.

In his uniquely unforgiving way, Ian Smith remembered that when Whitehead had had a few drinks he tended to 'fumble and stumble'.[1] Smith's favourite beverage was tea, so no doubt Whitehead found him equally gauche. Alec Douglas Home, then Leader of the House of Lords, likewise recalled that once when Whitehead visited him for a chat, he consumed 13 bottles of beer between the hours of eight o'clock and midnight.[2] Robert Blake, in *A History Of Rhodesia*, noted that Whitehead was in the habit of proving his self-discipline by giving up alcohol for one month of the year, and the month he usually chose was February because it was the shortest.[3] Less charitable was Rhodesian intelligence chief Ken Flower who observed that Whitehead used to upset government officials who were summoned for consultations in the small hours of the morning, only to find the Prime Minister drunk.

In matters of human, and in particular race relations, Whitehead was equally enigmatic. Hardwicke

Holderness made the point that Whitehead's previous job in the ministry of finance had been perfect for him. 'It enabled him to make full use of his talent for statistical and economic analysis without having to worry about the more illogical aspects of politics concerned with people and their susceptibilities.'[4] Holderness went on to surmise correctly that Whitehead's relationship with blacks stretched no further than his house and garden help and the men who worked for him on his farm. He was out of step with the times and innocent of the trauma to blacks that his ouster of Todd had caused. He blundered into the role of race arbitrator with great confidence in himself — based however on nothing but the most superficial understanding of the task. He was the enemy of Todd, so he was the enemy of the black people. He had nothing with which to counter this view because he had no idea that it existed. With his anchor sunk deep in the British establishment, he shared no common ground whatsoever with the blacks of Rhodesia — and little with the majority of down-to-earth white.

Whitehead was otherwise isolated and at the very least somewhat eccentric. He was an intellectual, confident of his gifts, and as Huggins once observed, quiet but basically quite conceited.[5] From 1930 onwards he had farmed on a reasonably large scale in the Vumba area outside Umtali, and lived alone in a large farmhouse remembered for its haphazard arrangements and generally poor state of organisation. He was a prominent member of the Umtali District Farmers Association and the Eastern Farmers Federation.

His political career began when he won the Umtali North seat for the United Party in the 1939 election. Shortly thereafter he left the territory to serve abroad for the duration of the war. In 1945 he returned with the rank of lieutenant-colonel and was appointed High Commissioner for Southern Rhodesia in London. Recalled to Rhodesia to serve as Minister of Finance, he was instrumental in the railway purchase, and was one of the principal architects of the Federation. The truth of his arrival in the office of Prime Minister of Southern Rhodesia was voiced by Bennie Goldberg — a Jewish lawyer of the wealthy Goldberg farming family of Odzi, and Federal Minister of Education — who remarked on the sidelines of the UFP Party Congress:

In the final analysis if we have to choose between Todd and a donkey, then it's the donkey![6]

If the new Prime Minister hoped to use his term of office to dispel the idea that he was an ass, then his first manoeuvres did not succeed. Whitehead was not holding a parliamentary seat when he was voted in as leader of the UFP and it became incumbent on him to win one as soon as possible.

First he formed a government in which he offered Todd a cabinet position — an offer that Todd duly accepted. And then, in a rather rash display of self-confidence, he forswore a safe seat in his own constituency of Umtali and arranged instead to challenge a vacancy in the Bulawayo constituency of Hillside. Compounding this error, he called to his support the predictably loyal voice of Todd. Todd was a Matabeleland man and Whitehead imagined he would appeal to the Bulawayo voters. The effect, however, was quite the opposite. A by-election was held in April and on the polling day Whitehead lost by 87 votes to a Dominion Party candidate. He now found himself in the embarrassing position of having to call a general election, the date for which was duly fixed for 5 June.

The Hillside by-election convinced Whitehead — as probably the last man in the country to realise it — that Todd was a political liability and had to go. Todd was not aggrieved at this and moved into a secondary career as the multiracial champion in an area of local politics that offered him neither voice nor public forum. He existed from then on as a celebration of the possibility of multiracialism, if never the tangible fact. However, his allies gathered around him. Principal among these were Hardwicke Holderness and his legal partner Pat Lewis who together proposed reinvigorating the old United Rhodesia Party to fight the upcoming election on the uncensored race philosophy of all three men. Holderness had come in on the seventh session as the UFP member for Salisbury North —

which had been Huggins' old seat. This was also the seat that Whitehead, now exercising extreme caution, selected for himself, but being obviously unable to afford the possibility of another defeat, he was running with Lord Malvern's public endorsement.

Other high profile liberals in the new Todd stable included John Moffat, the son of the ex-Prime Minister; Alan Henderson, son of the Matabele Rebellion hero; and most importantly from a financial point of view, Sir Stephen Courthauld. Such an august gathering of (actual) liberals had not been seen before in a single club, and as figurehead, Todd was no less than the martyr tossing the last of his reputation to the judgement of the synod. Large in the new party's manifesto were these clear words of truth:

> Africans are becoming part of the machinery of the modern state which Europeans have established here, and from time to time the old legislation has to be changed to give them some voice and responsibility in its affairs. If the change is made in time, their desire for cooperation and partnership will be retained. If not, they will be forced to become racialist and hostile, and eventually a seed bed for communism.[7]

As campaigning progressed, Holderness appeared initially to be advancing steadily in a constituency that he both knew well and had served conscientiously while with the UFP. He could only be criticised for being a little too determined to ram his message of multiracialism down the throats of his constituents. Whitehead, alarmed by reports that he was trailing in the safest seat he could have chosen, thought it prudent to publish a photograph not of himself on the UFP pamphlets, but one of Huggins. What's more, this was not the venerable Lord Malvern of the day but a younger Huggie who had fallen so like oil on troubled water in years gone by. Whitehead had nailed his colours to the mast — and it worked.

In the election, Holderness lost Salisbury North to Whitehead and the new United Rhodesia Party proved itself stillborn by winning not a single parliamentary seat. With it was buried the active political careers of most of its principal architects. The result was 17 seats to Whitehead and the UFP and 13 to the Dominion Party. It was less than Whitehead hoped for but it was enough.

Although hardly embittered, Holderness' memoirs betrayed a weary resignation. 'Whatever hope there might have been of white Rhodesians finding common political ground with Rhodesian blacks ceased to exist on 5 June 1958.' History would prove him right. Rapprochement was dead, and no one who was above desperate jingoism believed that bloodshed could now be avoided.

Rising voice of the African nationalists

W hitehead approached his term of office determined to succeed where Todd had failed. In a sense he believed that Todd had forgotten that liberalism in Africa meant not advancing the interests of blacks as much as pacifying their fears. He nonetheless found himself heir to the same old conundrum, although now with conditions on the ground significantly worse than they had been under Todd. He adopted Theodore Roosevelt's maxim of 'talk softly but carry a big stick', although unfortunately, circumstances were such that he was forced to wield the big stick long before he was given a chance to talk softly, and by then it was likely that no one was listening.

1960 would turn out to be an eventful year for everybody, largely thanks to the formation of a new political party to supersede the banned Southern Rhodesia ANC. Since Joshua Nkomo was still abroad, and the other main leadership figures were languishing in detention, control of the National Democratic Party (NDP) fell to a modest trade unionist turned nationalist by the name of Michael Mawema. The event was celebrated in the July issue of *Drum* in characteristic style. 'Congress is dead — long live the National Democratic Party!' Thus shouted the opening sentence of an article entitled 'New Party Rises Up Out Of The Ashes'. The article went on:

> That is the cry ringing around the locations, townships and reserves of Southern Rhodesia. The Party's rallying call? The same one that is sweeping Africa from Cairo to the Cape, the catch-phrase that is turning Africa upside down and inside out: 'One man, one vote!'[2]

Meanwhile, the blood of black Rhodesian nationalists was continuing to be stirred and heated by events occurring elsewhere in southern Africa. Towards the end of 1959 the South African Pan Africanist Congress staged a national protest against local pass laws. PAC leaders and their followers defied these laws and predictably a large number of arrests were made. The process was mainly peaceful except in the Transvaal township of Sharpeville where police opened fire on a group of demonstrators who were surrounding a police station and attempting to tear down the fence. When the dust settled, 69 people were dead and 180 wounded. Later that same day a large crowd of PAC supporters in the township of Langa in the Cape reacted on hearing the news by rampaging through the district and attacking police. Police again opened fire and a further three people were killed and 40 injured.[3]

This chapter in the South African revolution sent an unexpected message north. On the one hand, political agitation seemed to be achieving spectacular results in seeing off a British government that was in any case anxious to leave Africa. On the other hand it appeared to simply entrench the resistance of a white minority determined to stay. Southern Rhodesian blacks were buoyed by optimism and preferred to believe — contrary to the facts — that their future would follow the pattern of their Federal partners. In Southern Rhodesia, revolution was in the air and energised blacks were anxious to test the waters. However, there were many among them who were moderates and intellectuals, and these, supported by *Drum* magazine, sounded a more cautionary note.

> The NDP is not so starry-eyed as to believe that it can deliver independence to the Blacks of the colony in five minutes, or even in five years. Unlike the two territories in the north, and unlike the Federal Parliament itself, no black man has ever stood for — let alone won — a seat in the Southern Rhodesian Assembly. It may take ten years, maybe 15, to get into power. We're ready to sweat out our period in the wilderness.[4]

The leadership of the party and the black media may have been pragmatic, but their grass roots supporters and the wider urban population were less inclined to be patient. On 19 July 1960 the so-called 'March of the 7 000' took place in Salisbury. A demonstration, ostensibly to protest against the earlier arrests of the nationalist leaders, began in the Highfield Township, from where marchers made their way in growing numbers towards the city. There it was intended that they would demand a meeting with Whitehead himself. However progress was halted at 2:30 a.m. by a heavy police cordon at Stoddart Hall in Harare Township, where those assembled were informed that Whitehead would address them at that location the following day.

Upon receiving this news some dispersed while others settled down to wait. As word of Whitehead's agreement to meet a black delegation spread, a crowd formed, until by mid-morning upwards of 40 000 people had gathered in the vicinity of Stoddart Hall. Among them was Robert Mugabe who had recently returned on leave to Southern Rhodesia from Ghana, were he had been teaching, as part of Ghanaian President Kwame Nkrumah's programme of Pan-African outreach. Mugabe at that point was not politically active and was attending the demonstration not as an NDP member or activist but as a 'distinguished guest'. With him were members of the leadership including Leopold Takawira — a close friend of Mugabe and chairman of the Salisbury branch of the NDP — who was standing in for Nkomo who was still abroad.

As a member of the small but growing clique of educated blacks in Southern Rhodesia, there was naturally a place for Robert Mugabe at the table of nationalist leadership should he have wanted it, but at that stage the 36-year-old schoolteacher was yet to overcome a distaste for politics. He had come home to present his 29-year-old Ghanaian fiancé and fellow teacher Sally Heyfron to his mother, after which he fully intended to return to his teaching post in the Ghanaian port town of Takoradi.

Whitehead, meanwhile, had no intention of facing either a mob or a delegation. His response was to call up a territorial battalion to protect key points of the city and otherwise to deploy the BSA Police in a show of force. This fact was broadcast on the radio along with a sweeping ban on public meetings in any of the Salisbury townships. The crowds already gathered in Harare Township received this news with disquiet, while at the same time they noticed a build up in the numbers of security personnel at the scene. This continued until by early afternoon Stoddart Hall was completely surrounded by police riot detachments supported by dogs. The crowd then fragmented into a series of political meetings with a variety of young men jostling to be heard on a number of makeshift podiums.

Mugabe was urged to speak, and he did. At first his voice was weak and uncertain as he discoursed vaguely about his experiences in Ghana, painting a picture of the free African society that he had witnessed, and drawing strength from the crowd thickening around his podium. In due course his oratory gathered strength and began to crystallise as he mesmerised his listeners with his vision for a future Rhodesia. At that exact moment a seed was planted, for as Mugabe urged all men to become part of the struggle, he recognised that this call could not reasonably exclude himself.

Mugabe was held to the podium where a militant crowd determined he would remain until some positive response was received from the government. Whitehead, however, was not in a particularly positive mood. He was unnerved by a situation that was turning out to be much more than a petty labour dispute or the usual localised demonstration. The event had become a city-wide economic boycott that he was urged to rapidly contain. But he had neither the nerve nor the articulation to appear before a mob of baying blacks, particularly after they had spent the day stewing in the heat and were in no mood to compromise.

By late afternoon a Royal Rhodesian Air Force spotter plane was seen circling overhead and soon afterwards police and dogs moved in. The crowds were pressed back and dispersed towards their townships, but in places barricades had been erected, and running battles were fought. By evening the initial disturbances had been quelled with the arrest of 130 blacks and dozens more injured. However, the instability in and around the black townships of Salisbury continued for almost a week.

By the weekend, unrest had spread to other centres, the worst being Bulawayo. NDP meetings were cancelled at short notice by the courts but too late to arrest a momentum that had been building for some days. Frustrated demonstrators mingled with the Sunday morning crowds and before long feelings began to run high. Beer halls were drunk dry and European bottle stores besieged by thirsty and unruly demonstrators. The city centre and white areas were protected by a six kilometre long cordon of police and territorials, so the demonstrators laid waste to the townships in an orgy of black on black violence. White territorials were called up and deployed on protection duties.

Historian Peter Stiff, who was a serving BSAP Inspector during this period, remembers that police attempted to handle the situation in Salisbury under strict instructions not to shoot — which otherwise would have broken the BSAP record of never having fired a shot in anger in the territory since 1896. Instead baton charges were employed which pitched riot policemen against fleet-footed black rioters who easily melted away. In 24 hours a year's supply of tear smoke canisters (the description 'tear gas' was still discredited by memories of World War-I) was used, and extra supplies had to be hastily flown in from Britain. A white policeman, Sergeant Ron Dowling, who found himself isolated within the mob, shot and wounded a rioter in self defence when his life was threatened. Commissioner of police, Colonel Basil Spurling, ordered the policeman's suspension from duty and instructed that the shooting be put down as an accidental discharge.

Later riots that broke out in Bulawayo saw the record of the police not opening fire was finally broken with the deaths of 12 blacks. Riots followed in Gatooma and thereafter in Gwelo. Dowling was quietly reinstated and not another word was said about the matter.

Law and order

The big stick was formalised in law by the promulgation on 2 December 1960 of the Law and Order (Maintenance) Act. This new instrument replaced the Public Order Act which had proved ineffective in dealing with the escalating unrest. It equipped the British South Africa Police with a formidable legal arsenal and gave it enhanced power to deal with the deteriorating political situation. The taking unlawful oaths to commit capital offences (shades of Kenya's Mau Mau), making statements threatening or encouraging violence, inciting a strike in essential services, carrying offensive weapons or materiel without lawful authority, the importation of dangerous weapons, undermining police authority, making subversive statements, throwing articles at motor vehicles, intimidation and many other actions became criminal offences. It also allowed for the detention of individuals and the proscription of organisations deemed a threat to public order and national security. In particular, Sections 50 and 51 conferred the power to restrict persons on the orders of the Minister of Law and Order. This cleanly bypassed the judicial process and gave the ministry and the police freedom to detain agitators, troublemakers and intimidators.[5]

It can be said with reasonable accuracy that the Act was promulgated not to clamp down on political dissent but to deal with the shocking violence inflicted by blacks against blacks at that time.

Sir Robert Tredgold, as just one who regretted the new Act, and who as Federal Chief Justice would have been obliged to arbitrate in appeals against it, resigned in protest. 'This bill outraged every basic human right', he wrote in his memoirs, '… it will remove the last vestige of doubt about whether Rhodesia is a police state.'[6]

Whitehead and his government defended the action by reminding the likes of Tredgold that before the promised liberalisation could take place, law and order had to be assured. In fact Edgar Whitehead was caught in a balancing act that at times was much more complicated than simply trying to beat the blacks into silence. He also had to prove to Whitehall that he had a scheme for a universally acceptable system of government that would keep that silence once pressure was lifted.

As with most other whites, Whitehead's mind was focussed almost entirely on the holy grail of independence under minority rule. Nyasaland was beginning to negotiate independence as part of her withdrawal from the Federation; Northern Rhodesia would do likewise, and white Rhodesia saw no reason why it should not be granted the same privilege. With the increasing irrelevance of the Federation, a series of territorial constitutional reviews would take place, and it would be during the Southern Rhodesian Constitutional Conference, to be held in Salisbury on 31 January 1961, that Whitehead hoped to strike the necessary balance. His aim was to negotiate a constitution acceptable to both the governed majority and the ruling minority. His main constituency was white, and for a majority of whites indigenous rule remained acceptable in principal, inevitable in fact, but nonetheless in reality a very a difficult pill to swallow. For blacks the question had not become not if but when, and few among them had much use at that stage for compromise.

In fact at that point the opportunity to find a formula for a peaceful resolution to the crisis had passed. This fact was observed and commented upon frequently by the likes of Todd, Holderness and others of the liberal clique, who were no doubt agreed with by others such as Sir Robert Tredgold and Godfrey Huggins who, from the safety of retirement could afford to be frank. Whitehead was still in active service, however, and was less perspicacious. He was Prime Minister and thus heir to the great illusion, and he approached the constitutional conference with optimism.   Rhodesia's most recent plea for independence could be traced back to the birth of the Federation. Huggins had believed then, with some justification, that Federation was the better alternative to immediate independence that was on the table for Southern Rhodesia. This followed almost categorical assurances from Britain that in exchange for services rendered to the war effort, Southern Rhodesia could expect independence. However, for Whitehead to try and remind Britain of this promise after the breakup of the Federation would clearly have been a waste of time. In his day Huggins had been aware of the risk of this, but had made the calculation that Federation would be a better solution for the time being. He hoped that it would lead to the independence, not just of Southern Rhodesia, but also of the entire Federation as one unitary nation. Choosing federation, therefore, proved in the end to be a missed opportunity, for had Huggins seized the moment when it was ripe and ignored the temptation of a greater central African union, the history of Rhodesia may well have had a very different conclusion.

A majority of whites held firm to the understanding that implicit in their decision to take part in the Federation was the condition that, in the event of its failure, Southern Rhodesia would be granted automatic independence. Independence was also widely seen as the only way for the territory to find the peace and quiet it needed to pursue incremental political reform. It is also fair to say that the reluctance of the British Government to grant independence was not seen then as a particularly serious obstacle. Whites perceived that some easing of the more obvious constitutional restrictions against blacks would be sufficient to surmount it. Before the Constitutional Conference could take place, however, two events — both somewhat off the political radar — occurred that would increase the pressures on Edgar Whitehead and drive Southern Rhodesia further to the right.

At the end of October 1960 the National Democratic Party held its inaugural congress after nine months of already very active existence. It took place at the Goodwill Centre in Salisbury's Harare Township, where 200 delegates packed this Asian and Coloured community hall. It was a hot Sunday and in the dusty street outside, crowds milled around awaiting the outcome.

Four key resolutions were passed. Firstly, the Party committed itself to a general election boycott until such time as a system of universal suffrage was in place. Secondly, the congress called for a constitutional review conference to be attended by all political parties. Thirdly, it was decided to call on the British Government to suspend the current constitution and intervene in ongoing tensions until such time as a new constitution could be drafted. And lastly, the congress demanded the repeal of all restrictive and discriminatory legislation.

More importantly, Robert Mugabe made his political debut. He had arrived at the Goodwill Centre as a distinguished visitor, but left as the new publicity secretary of the National Democratic Party. A less emphatic ballot took place to elect the president, and after much jostling and a degree of uncertainty and dissatisfaction, Joshua Nkomo was returned to the top position in absentia.

Thus Robert Mugabe was welcomed into the nationalist fold, but by no means was this welcome universal. Mugabe was then, as he consistently remained, an introverted intellectual with a chilly, Machiavellian detachment. This alerted those more astute amongst the delegates to a potential for autocracy that would indeed later mature to the benefit of the revolution, but to the detriment of many revolutionaries. He was the utter antithesis of the European political norm. Whites had been searching for a moderate to bridge the gap, while all along, the blacks themselves had been waiting for Mugabe.

Mugabe was not a physically impressive man. He appears from old photographs to have been an awkward and angular-featured individual with a pronounced weakness of the jaw. In group shots he appears detached and slightly improbable — almost as if his image had been pasted in a later and entirely different context. Early pictures of him on a makeshift podium — alone but in complete command and fixed in a posture of fevered oratory — are the only ones that betray a hint of his true nature. Competition for the power positions in early black political organisations was naturally intense and at times even deadly, so during this formative period Mugabe deliberately kept himself aloof. As he had done since his university days, he watched — either cautious of getting involved or instinctively waiting for the optimum moment.

Among the few who had access to Mugabe was Leopold Takawira. The two met after Mugabe graduated from Fort Hare in 1951 when Mugabe worked as a teacher in a variety of local mission schools. Takawira had at one time been a novice pries,t but by the 1950s he applied himself almost entirely to politics. He was a bold man of a deeply traditional nature — older than Mugabe and as a consequence tending to be more of a moderate. This was evidenced by his early involvement in the Interracial Association, and his willingness to join David Stirling in the Capricorn Africa Society as an executive officer. Along with many other young blacks, he would soon respond to the increasing polarisation of the races by becoming one of the founding members of the National Democratic Party.[7]

Apart from providing friendship, Takawira was also Mugabe's first political mentor. It was he who took the raw materials of the younger man's bookish political philosophy and moulded them into tools for work in the field. By this route Mugabe found himself drawn to Marxist theory, and in due course was writing to England for copies of Marx's *Das Kapital* and Friedrich Engels' *Conditions of the Working Class in England* and *The Communist Manifesto*.[8] He also began to attend meetings of the Interracial Association and the Capricorn Africa Society, but as usual kept to the fringes with no more than his curiosity aroused.

To whites Robert Mugabe gave no access. Although always polite, he was cold, detached and even a little unfriendly. With his origins deeply steeped in the mythology of revolution, it is interesting to note that his past reveals a child deserted by his father, and with an overt and emotional dependence on his mother. At that time he was often slighted for being a small and overly serious youth, evidently weighed down by manly concerns far too early in life. It was during this period of early struggle and hardship that the slow incubation of his hatred for whites appears to have begun. He was disinclined as an adult to give even those well meaning among the enemy the benefit of the doubt. Entente was entirely irrelevant to a man who by then recognised that only confrontation would succeed. To him the black man could look to none but himself for his future salvation.

Mugabe's early reluctance to plunge into activism had as much to do with an ideological dichotomy than fear or uncertainty. He was then — and claimed to be in later years — a committed Catholic. As such, and despite his reading, he found the teachings of communism incompatible with his faith. He subscribed to the principal of reversing the imbalances of history, but the ideological vehicle in common use at the time was not to his taste.

In 1955 Mugabe, in part to disassociate himself from demands that he join the struggle and in part to earn more money, left Southern Rhodesia and for three years taught at the Chalimbana Training College outside Lusaka. There he studied in his spare time for a third degree. In 1958 he was offered a teaching post at St Mary's Training College in the Ghanaian port town of Takoradi. He was stunned by what he saw happening in Ghana. To a man brought up under an invisible ceiling, it was a wonder to see blacks in controlling positions in government, the civil service, the military and the private sector. It was the moment when it truly came home to him that such a thing was possible in Rhodesia.

In May 1960 he took advantage of the generous expatriate leave conditions offered by the Ghanaian Government, and returned to Salisbury with his future bride. By then the lessons of Ghana had been learned to varying degrees by all the natives of the continent. Interracial experiments had been filed away as failures and a new mood of confrontation on both sides had taken root. The NDP was four months old at that time and still under temporary leadership. Nkomo would not return to the territory until November of that year and the party was vigorously aggressive and spoiling for a fight.

Joshua Nkomo's return — only, it must be said, after stern entreaties from other members of the leadership — was the second event during 1960 that would influence the immediate events of the struggle. It escaped widespread publicity although it was nonetheless acutely observed. Nkomo reappeared 22 kilograms heavier and somewhat more educated. He accepted a very delicate mandate when he agreed to represent the NDP at the forthcoming review conference. This would be the first major diplomatic tournament of his career and it would put all of his newfound sophistication to the test.

New constitution: 1961

The new Commonwealth Relations Secretary, Duncan Sandys, was chosen to chair the much-anticipated constitutional conference. Sandys was both a charming and guileful politician with a reputation for achieving the apparently impossible. This was fortunate since from the outset he had his hands full with Edgar Whitehead. The Rhodesian Prime Minister opened proceedings by insisting that the chairman bar the participation of the NDP — which was obviously impossible since Whitehead himself had not yet banned the party. In any case, what then would be the point of having a conference? The entire proceeding was premised on a broad-based acceptance of any draft constitution, so limiting or excluding black participation would clearly have rendered the whole enterprise moot. Space was duly made for the NDP around the negotiating table where Joshua Nkomo, Herbert Chitepo — now an executive member of the NDP — and its financial secretary

Ndabaningi Sithole, — each took their places.

Whitehead was mollified at first, and then pleasantly surprised. His first substantive encounter with a civilised black man turned out to be less a tossing of the bones than a refined and instructive interlude. Herbert Chitepo in particular was a highly impressive individual, an advocate and a quiet, pleasant and easy-going man. Sithole tended to be suspicious and doctrinaire, which a charitable assessment would reveal to have had more to do with nerves than aggression. Nkomo was tall, overweight and avuncular. Despite his reputation he remained pleasantly approachable and entirely at ease in his surroundings.

Sandys chaired this mixed assembly with extraordinary skill and in due course did indeed succeed in achieving the impossible. Nkomo and his colleagues accepted the draft constitution, although in fairness to Nkomo his acceptance was not absolute. His words were that he was prepared to 'give the new constitution a chance', and after a rather ineffective walkout and a muted return, the NDP closing statement on the negotiations stated:

> We could not be party to the franchise as it stands. This leaves us with the issue of franchise still as the greatest field of political operation. It is a subject for political pressure. But although we did not approve of the franchise, the attitude we adopted was not to impede or encourage the introduction of these proposals. The onus is on the UFP to prove the truth of its intentions in the implementation of these proposals.

This was a victory for Sandys but it came at a price. In exchange for relinquishing almost all of her reserve powers in terms of legislation and African affairs in Southern Rhodesia, Her Majesty's government accepted certain verbal undertakings to make discriminatory practices illegal and to enshrine a Declaration of Rights in the Constitution. In terms of the franchise — which was of course the definitive issue — the common roll was finally split in two with a complicated set of procedures designed to increase black representation without permitting an overall majority. This was achieved by enlarging the House from 30 to 65 seats and introducing A and B voters' rolls. Qualifications for the B roll would be similar to those in the existing special vote. The two rolls would exist in a relationship of reciprocal devaluation ensuring that B roll votes never exceeded 25 per cent of A roll returns.

However, no sooner had the ink dried on his signature than Joshua Nkomo was badly scalded by recriminations from within the NDP. He was bitterly chastised for putting his name to what was seen by others as a latter day Rudd Concession. A now famous telegram arrived for him from Leopold Takawira who had succeeded him as the NDP representative in London.

> We totally reject Southern Rhodesian constitutional agreement as treacherous to future three million blacks. Agreement diabolical and disastrous. Outside world shocked by NDP docile agreement. We have lost sympathy of friends and supporters. We have undermined Northern Rhodesia constitutional conference. Unless you take firm stand in Sunday council meeting, future means untold suffering and toil. Pray you denounce uncompromisingly and reject unreservedly conference agreement. Demand immediate reversal of present position. Future of three million Africans depends on immediate action.[10]

Nkomo reeled under such an attack on his first executive action as President of the NDP. His initial instinct was to try and defend his position but in due course he realised that it was indefensible, and in the end opposition to it was so widespread that he had no choice but to climb down. Within a week of the conference the NDP executive met and overturned his decision. Takawira in London took the lead in the attack, while at home it was Mugabe who had most to say. He chose a moment in the middle of an acrimonious meeting of the party executive to deliver a bitter harangue against the leader. Nkomo, the great grandson of Lobengula's chief rainmaker, husband to the granddaughter of his chief councillor, was forced to sit and listen to his publicity secretary openly denigrate him. When he could take no more of it he stood up and left the conference muttering dark threats about unspecified action. It is doubtful that Nkomo ever forgave Mugabe, Takawira or himself for what had transpired.

Nkomo then flew to London to confront Takawira, and although what was said is unrecorded, on his return he was contrite. He remarked to the press regarding his volte-face: ' … a leader is he who expresses the wishes of his followers; no sane leader can disregard the voice of his people and his supporters.' He might have added to this his political backers, for it was no doubt as much due to threats from Kaunda, Banda and Tanzania's Julius Nyerere that Nkomo was forced to utter those flavourless words.

As far as the outside world was concerned, the party held ranks and maintained a united front. As *Drum* reported in April 1961:

> It has been suggested by some Europeans, and also by some Africans, that "Nkomo is on the way out". It appears to be wishful thinking. The boat may have rocked slightly, but no one was thrown out.[11]

With these early upsets the dynamics of the liberation struggle could already be seen at work. After their first encounter, Mugabe and Nkomo would never be entirely reconciled. It was astonishing that Nkomo's political career did not end at that moment, but against all the odds it survived. Chitepo would achieve some prominence but would be allowed to rise only so far while Ndabaningi Sithole would in due course wilt under the radiance of Mugabe's ambition and personality.

Despite his change of heart, however, Nkomo could not alter the fact that his signature was on the agreement and the draft constitution stood as it had been agreed. All that remained was for it to be submitted to a referendum. The NDP initially agreed to participate in this but only under certain conditions. These were the release of all ANC detainees still being held after the February 1959 arrests and the lifting of a ban on rural meetings. Whitehead refused both conditions and the NDP duly voted to boycott the referendum altogether. This was of no particular importance to Whitehead since the agreement had been signed and the British had fallen into line. Now he could simply shrug his shoulders and say of black resistance that he and his government had at least tried.

Whitehead was now able to concentrate on a unity strategy that had been gestating in his mind since he took office. So far he had had neither the time nor sufficient sympathy from the public to reveal it, but with the independence constitution under his belt, he felt better placed to test the water. The campaign would be aimed mainly at the black vote in the upcoming election and was to be called 'Build a Nation and Claim a Vote', or simply 'Build A Nation'. This was effectively a clarion call to the black middle classes to join with Whitehead to crush radical nationalism. In return they could expect a process of gradual indigenisation.

It is a perennial political truism that stable democracy is built on the middle classes, but Whitehead seemed unaware that almost nothing resembling a black middle class existed in Rhodesia.

40

The first and last Rhodesian

Ian Douglas Smith was 41-years-old and serving as Chief Whip for the United Federal Party in the Federal Parliament. Of 400 delegates attending a special preparatory party congress gathered to discuss the proposed draft constitution, he was the only to stand up and raise his voice in objecting to it. This was probably because he was the only member of the party who had actually read the draft constitution from beginning to end. What he discovered — or at least failed to discover — was any mention of Rhodesia's automatic right to independence in the event of the failure of the Federation. Bearing in mind that the Federation was already collapsing, this was a very important omission.

In politics Smith was an enigma. He was a bloodhound and an unrelenting and detail-conscious prophet of the black and white. It was in his nature to sniff a strain of loose rhetoric in some political statement or other, seize upon it and then wring from it the last drop of its hidden perfidy. Such was the case with his understanding that Rhodesia was to be granted independence on the failure of the Federation. Smith decided that he would be the one who reminded the Crown of its obligation. Indeed he had apprehended more acutely than any other, the real reason for Britain's apparently spineless and mendacious behaviour. He could see that slapping his forehead — as Welensky had lately been prone to do — and uttering ever more shrill entreaties, would not ultimately achieve much. His instincts told him that the only viable policy from then on would be to pick a fight with the British and see who came out on top.

From the position of Federal Chief Whip, Smith began to stir the pot and give voice to changes that were taking place in white Rhodesia. It did not concern him particularly that Nyasaland was slipping out of the Federal family, nor was he particularly aggrieved at the loss of Northern Rhodesia. However to lose Southern Rhodesia in a moment of complacency would have been a dreadful catastrophe. In this belief Smith was not alone. As he made it his business to protest, he was gratified to find himself with an audience of like-minded men. The common motivation amongst them was a deep disquiet at Edgar Whitehead's apparently reckless experimentation with their future.

Smith, like Mugabe, was neither qualified nor politically mature enough at that juncture to seize the crown. He was a son of the soil, a sportsman, a veteran World War-II fighter pilot and a Christian parent, but politically he was a novice. For the time being he needed a more established figurehead to lead the charge. In the first instance he sounded out Roy Welensky who, not surprisingly, demurred. Sir Roy was in fact still technically engaged in Federal matters, and to interfere with territorial issues would have been inappropriate. Smith prodded an already bruised Welensky a little too painfully by suggesting that the moment had come for men of principal to have the courage of their convictions. Welensky responded sharply, reminding Smith that he more than most had shown the courage of his convictions, and could be accused by no-one of lacking a fair sense of the direction things were headed. Besides, the Northern Rhodesian Constitution was under debate and that was of more immediate concern for the future of the Federation than the status of Southern Rhodesia.

Smith clearly needed to look further. Although Clifford Dupont was a farmer, he could hardly claim to have roots in the soil. Unlike Smith, his farming tended to be more of a social vehicle than an authentic agricultural venture. His political views were distinctly right of centre, and although he and Smith were on friendly terms, Dupont was also a little too blithe and unpredictable for a determined straight shooter like Smith. It must be remembered that Smith was not looking for a leader — merely someone who resembled a leader — and in this regard Dupont could not entirely be trusted.

Winston Field was another possibility. Although Field had led the Dominion Party in the Federal Parliament, his credentials seemed at times to be obscured by a certain personal introspection. Furthermore, the Dominion Party in Southern Rhodesia under William Harper, tended to be amorphous and no more than a holding pen for the colony's current crop of non-aligned voters. The only common theme within it was that dominion was still a popular prescription for the political problems of both Southern Rhodesia and the Federation. Beyond that, and despite undeniable charisma, Field seemed to have very little to offer in the way of genuine, dynamic and aggressive leadership. Therefore he was perfect for the job.

Such was the action playing out behind the scenes of the white conservative lobby. On centre stage, as the missiles rained down, Edgar Whitehead was still playing the lead. His performance was as dire as most had predicted, but in the classic style of the British middle classes, he was determined to carry on regardless. As Smith quietly sat in the wings and drew the new map of Rhodesia, Whitehead prepared to deliver his finale.

Last of the British liberals

The referendum on the new Southern Rhodesian draft constitution was held on 26 July 1961. Opposition to it was not limited to the nationalist factions and significant disquiet was also felt among whites. Bill Harper's Dominion Party led the white opposition, based mainly on the claim that the voting clauses in the constitution would for the first time introduce an official race aspect to the franchise. This was indeed true since no legal race restriction had existed prior to this, although it would arguably now be easier for a viable body of black representatives to achieve a voice than at any previous time. The Southern Rhodesian Dominion Party 'Vote No' campaign was countered surreptitiously by the United Federal Party (although this fact was furiously denied by the UFP at the time) with a flurry of last minute campaign posters that were liberally pasted around the towns and cities. They read: 'Vote No for Nkomo'.

Whitehead nonetheless succeeded in winning a resounding victory with 41 000 for and 21 000 against — a result which left the Prime Minister with exactly the kind of victory that Huggins would have pulled out of the hat. Unfortunately Whitehead did not pause to consider the underlying causes of such a swing in his favour — as Huggins would certainly have done.

While Whitehead had sold the new constitution to the electorate as a march down the road to independence, in his own mind he saw it as part of the process of black advancement. Whites, however, had voted for independence and not black advancement. Whitehead received advice from various quarters but was in no mood to take it. Meanwhile, far away and over the rainbow, a chain of events was under way in the nationalist camp that would have dismayed Whitehead had he only been aware it.

The night before referendum police riot squads were deployed into the township. Whitehead visited and addressed one of them commanded by Inspector Peter Stiff. He stressed that they should not use their firearms because heavy-handed police action would likely reinforce the 'No' vote. Stiff told the Prime Minister that he could rely on the police using minimum force, but if the necessity to use firearms arose, he would not hesitate to give the order. In the event he did.

Joshua Nkomo had earlier held a well-attended rally in Highfield Township to announce the boycott, after which he met privately with *Drum* correspondent Noel Mukono at Empandeni Mission where his family were staying. During a wide-ranging interview, Nkomo made a specific point of introducing and holding up a toothbrush. As he explained to Mukono:

> I shudder whenever I see a toothbrush. Not one African among our entire three million can make a toothbrush, or even a pin. What sort of education system is that? We must scrap this system of government for a better, democratic one approved by the majority of citizens. The NDP can provide such a government. We have our plans set. We are ready.[1]

In a clear sign of things to come, the NDP mounted a boycott of the constitutional referendum and conducted a rigged poll of its own. The way this 'black referendum' was conducted gave a clear illustration of the political methods likely to be employed by the black nationalists in the future. Two booths were set up and marked respectively 'Yes Vote' and 'No Vote'. The party youth wing were extremely active in rounding up location residents and herding them towards the 'No Vote' queue where they were circulated from the booth to the back of the queue several times during the course of the day.

All day the 'Yes' booth was surrounded by an ominous force of thugs ready and willing to mete out party justice to anyone foolish enough to vote 'yes' for Whitehead.

An hour after the close of their polling the result of 471 in favour and 370 000 against, was announced. This indicated that there had been some impossibly quick count! Later than evening Special Branch under the protection of a riot squad raided the NDP offices at Machipisa Shopping in Highfield Township. Not unexpectedly, they found the so-called ballot boxes unopened, proving the whole NDP exercise had been a complete sham.

Had Whitehead read Nkomo's toothbrush interview, his comments would have sent a ripple of amusement through the Salisbury Club. But he had not. As he had frequently stated, he did not read the native press. Instead he stumped from one end of the country to the other in a state of blissful ignorance in order to sell his policy of rapprochement to as many moderate blacks as he could find — which was not many.

Nkomo, in the meanwhile, was not without certain fragile delusions of his own. He was about to discover that others besides himself suspected the skill, sophistication and modernity of Rhodesia's blacks. In the same month as the referendum he visited London where he called on an under-secretary in the Commonwealth office — Andrew Buxton Cavendish, the 11th Duke of Devonshire, a nephew of Harold Macmillan and the son of Edward Cavendish, who had been the author of the infamous Sacred Trust speech delivered to the House in 1923. Andrew Cavendish urged the NDP leader to try and make the 1961 Constitution work, explaining that notwithstanding the vexed race question, Rhodesia was a well ordered, functioning and viable country with an economy second in strength in the region only to South Africa. Its industrial base was growing apace under the momentum of British capital, and he, Cavendish, found it hard to imagine a situation whereby the Britain would sacrifice all this to the uncertain temper of a black majority. Nkomo's party, he warned, ought not to expect power in the immediate future.

This unexpected dousing came as a shock to Nkomo who had fully expected a friendly encounter with the under-secretary, during which his own future premiership would be discussed. In fact he had said as much to Noel Mukono when the two met over the toothbrush interview. His exact words on the matter were: 'The first thing to do when we take over, which is not far away of course, is to embark on an extensive educational programme.'

His initial disappointment was quickly followed by a nervous tremor, for if he agreed to work within the constitution, what sort of reaction could he expect from his Party? At that moment his nemesis was extremely active in Salisbury. Nkomo had an airiness akin to Whitehead's in matters of party politics — in sharp contrast to Mugabe who was a natural and had in fact been hard at work organising the NDP along bona fide party lines. This time, more than any before, Nkomo's heart rebelled against going home. This time, more than any other, though, he absolutely had to.

As might be expected, Robert Mugabe's response to the news was cold but determined. He revealed plans for an immediate campaign of violence in the townships and the countryside. The British, he told his colleagues, needed to be made aware of the fact that their economic interests would be better served by a freely elected black government than a nation of unfranchised blacks in open revolt. To emphasise this point, the new Land-Rovers that party organisers were given to traverse the country, wore slogans pasted onto their doors that read: 'One Man One Vote; Freedom Now, Now, Now'.[2] Nkomo, meanwhile, brought up the rear in the rhetorical contest of anger, with the muse that if economic development in Southern Rhodesia was an obstacle to black rule, then blacks should destroy that development.[3]

The customary vehicle for havoc and destruction in the townships was the so-called Youth Wing — many of its members being in their 30s or 40s.

Out of this motley corps of youth, young unemployed delinquents and sundry political enforcers — some of whom would never see 40 again — Mugabe formed the NDP Youth Wing. These were to be both the storm troopers of the party and its informal political commissars. They were carefully instructed by both Mugabe and his aide-de-camp Simon Muzenda in the aims and ideology of the Party. They were then sent out into the field to stage a demonstration of force followed by a programme of intense politicisation.

The Party line was Marxist but not exclusively. It also sought to rejuvenate black ethnicity through vaguely remembered traditions of old, and by drawing to itself young intellectuals who worked to write black history in their own language, promoting a strongly ethnocentric vision. A study of Shona orthography was undertaken and among many others, Herbert Chitepo made use of the revised written language to record an epic poem entitled *Soko risina musoro*, or The tale without a Head. Ndabaningi Sithole, besides his thesis on African nationalism, wrote a strongly nationalist novel entitled *maNdebele KaMzilikazi*, or The Ndebele of Mzilikazi. Influential Shona writer Solomon Muswairo produced a fictional portrayal of the Nehanda legend in his novel *Feso*. The book was deemed subversive by the government and taken out of circulation for the remaining period of white rule, but nonetheless they found favour among nationalist ideologues and others keen to institute a revival of indigenous oral tradition. The Oxford University Press published all of these titles on behalf of the revolution.[4]

There was, of course, a dark and more persuasive side to the Youth Wing. An early youth leader, Rugare Gumbo, in his report of a particular night's work, adequately illustrated this. The mission was the 're-education' of black small business owners in Fort Victoria who had decided to join the 'Build a Nation' campaign launched by Whitehead in the aftermath of the Constitutional Referendum. Most advertised their involvement by displaying government posters in their cars, busses, shops and workshops.

> We started working at six o'clock pm. We attacked Gondo's butchery, we attacked the beer hall, we attacked everything we thought would advance our cause. For the first time we ignited a riot in the little town of Masvingo [Fort Victoria]. Thus the first ever political violence in Masvingo was our work. A number of people were injured in the incident.[5]

When the violence began, followed by a public announcement of the new NDP policy of 'positive action', Robert Mugabe became a household name overnight. He had been under police observation for some time and an earlier scuffle at Salisbury Airport involving the police and members of Mugabe's entourage resulted in a rare display of intemperance. It was reported that Mugabe waved his finger at a policeman and uttered the heresy: 'We are taking over this country and we will not put up with this nonsense.'[6]

Meanwhile, the NDP Youth League were unleashed on the black population in an orgy of murders, beatings, arson, intimidation and assaults. The white population, although aware of the lawlessness through the media, were shielded from the worst of its effects by the police. Mugabe's orders that white-owned stores and business were to be boycotted were heard but largely ignored. Fearsome examples were made of black collaborators and quislings. These were identified as United Federal Party black members, black members of the police or armed services and even chiefs. One such example was Chief Mtoko who in November 1961 was burned to death in his hut for being perceived to support the Build a Nation Campaign.

Elspeth Huxley, author of a trilogy of memoirs of life in colonial Kenya and member of the Bledisloe Commission, wrote a letter to the British *Sunday Times* in which she lamented: 'Intimidation by Congress members has been widespread and ugly and it has not yet been eliminated. "Join us or we will come tonight and burn your house" is the usual form.' The *Sunday Mail*, sister newspaper to the *Rhodesia Herald*, added its voice to the chorus of concern: 'National Democratic Party terrorism has spread to a fantastic limit in Southern Rhodesia.' The *Rhodesia Herald* itself called for action: 'When will Sir Edgar Whitehead move against the thugs and hooligans who are making life unbearable for everybody who does not believe as they do?'[7]

Whitehead was in despair. He was driven around Highfield on a tour of inspection during which he kept a waste paper basket beside him to put on his head in case he was stoned.[8] In the meantime he tried hard to salvage his campaign by portraying the violence as undirected criminal thuggery. This was a hard theory to sell since the NDP clearly enjoyed widespread support, the proof of which lay in the fact that its protests, rallies and demonstrations were all well-planned, effective and well-attended. The violence was also by no means misdirected — in fact, quite the opposite. It was a well-applied and efficient tool of political enforcement. To the dismayed whites who watched, it was a terrifying glimpse into the future. It would by no means be the last time that black on black violence in the midst of the struggle would bewilder whites. They would never truly grasp the meaning of the aggressive factionalism that attended all black political activity, especially as its proponents were ostensibly united in a war against whites.

Drum chose to observe the non violent methods of protest that were from time to time evident in the midst of the general fratricide:

> Extra-parliamentary protests began in earnest. A general strike failed but only after troops were called out. In July 1961, the NDP submitted themselves to a one day fast and crowds at mass meetings in the major towns were urged to remove their socks and shoes. "Today you have removed your shoes," Robert Mugabe told them, "tomorrow you may be called upon to destroy them altogether, or to perform other acts of self denial. If European-owned industries are used to buy guns which are aimed against us, we must withdraw our labour and our custom, and destroy those industries."[9]

The following month a number of churches practising segregation, were subject to multiracial 'kneel-ins', while in November a general boycott of municipal beer halls was observed. Rural unrest was blamed on protests against the Native Land Husbandry Act, and indeed many of the most hated icons of suppression such as dip tanks were destroyed. *Drum* magazine again reported:

... the adroit use of symbolism ... to create the unity and identity, fervent in its appeal, that a nationalist movement needs to grow.'[10]

As all this was going on, some aspects of the white response did nothing to help. On Pioneer Day 1961, a nationalist demonstration interrupted the official ceremony traditionally held in Cecil Square. A sit-in was staged by a group of unsmiling but otherwise well-behaved blacks. In the confusion that followed, a pioneer widow paraded herself alongside the group with a young white man in attendance holding aloft a placard reading: 'Join the Zimbaboon Club'.

A little later a well-dressed white man wearing the tie of the Police Regimental Association appeared on the fringes of the sit-in and began to disdainfully toss handfuls of peanuts into the knot of sitting blacks. As he did so he observed bitterly to the few whites who were standing within earshot: 'Look at the monkeys. They're not really hungry. You can see they're well fed. They don't want the peanuts.'

A moment later a young white constable made his way towards the lonely figure and after whispering a few words into his ear, quietly led him away.

Lovemore Chimonyo and the Freedom Sitters, a group co-founded by Federal University academic Dr Terence Ranger, led the Pioneer Day sit-in. This was just one of many provocative actions Dr Ranger was responsible for in his personal crusade against racism. The 33-year-old professor was hurled fully clothed into Salisbury's municipal swimming pool after invading the whites-only facility in the company of a handful of blacks.

Terence Ranger was an Oxford educated Londoner who had at one time taught at the Royal Naval College. In 1957 he took up a position at the new University College in Southern Rhodesia and three years later applied for Federal citizenship. In the interim he wrote a pamphlet entitled *Crisis in Southern Rhodesia* in which he was heavily critical of the government. His view was that only immediate political action could avert a tragedy. Sluggishness on the part of the Passport Office in processing his citizenship application, immediately became apparent. For a white man to be a prohibited immigrant in Rhodesia was a rare distinction in those days, but as Ranger's polemics were becoming public property, Minister Malcolm Barrow let slip that citizenship was a privilege and not a right. A few days later Ranger's application was denied.

Ranger then threw down the gauntlet and joined the NDP. As a final act of separation he issued a defiant public statement: '... it has been an arrogant assumption on the part of the European that the ideal society in Southern Rhodesia is a European one ... I am showing that I am prepared to live under African leadership.'[11] Whitehead's government soon indicated that it was not prepared to countenance his rabble rousing and in December of that year his house was raided by the police before being deported.

Ranger's partner in the Freedom Sitters, Lovemore Chimonyo, was a spry character who brought some much needed humour to the dry business of race protest. He was a short and slightly built man with an extravagant beard who affected a Stan Laurel style of loose-limbed buffoonery. Chimonyo had in the past sat on a whites-only public toilet and declared: 'Here I sit until the law is changed.'

On a different occasion, Chimonyo and his group invaded the lesser sanctum of whites-only bars. Over the course of a three-day pub crawl, he and a handful of followers entered every bar in the white neighbourhoods of Salisbury. With the exception of one pint of beer flung in his face and a messy brawl in the southern suburbs, he and his friends were surprised at the generally cordial welcome they received. In one or two bars they were actually served a drink, and once or twice even stood a round.

In the interests of freedom of worship, Chimonyo one day exchanged the seat of his pants for his knees when he attended a service at the Dutch Reformed Church. The incident might well have been the first of its kind in 300 years of Dutch Reform history in southern Africa. Despite worshippers being scandalised, violence was forsworn — although Chimonyo was persuaded to leave the church in a hurry. This series of incidents prompted a bout of frolicking journalism in the black press. *Drum* celebrated Chimonyo's crusade thus:

> Grieve not for Lovemore, friends, he can take it. A few months ago this man with a drooping beard and the bellowing voice, was the talk of the nation, celebrated as the freest of the freedom sitters. He wore his way through trouser seats as he sat his way around town.[12]

However the antics of Lovemore Chimonyo and the Freedom Sitters accounted for virtually nothing towards the eventual banning of the NDP when it came, it was more the raised fist and inflamed oratory of Robert Mugabe and his fellow party leaders. As party leader, Nkomo was frequently upstaged and often forced to trim his sails and ride hard ahead of a reactionary wind. On 9 December 1961 the NDP was proscribed under the Unlawful Organisations Act and its assets and funds were seized. Mugabe's dirty work in the trenches now proved itself valid. A little over a week later the activation of a new party was achieved with barely a break in the stride of positive action.

The Zimbabwe African Peoples Union was the first organisation to make explicit use of the revolutionary name 'Zimbabwe'. It was also the first to use a languorous Z in its acronym — ZAPU. The NDP was laid to rest at a political rally held at the Cyril Jennings hall in Highfield, but before the meeting was broken up by the police, a black Mark Anthony whose name did not survive the incident, spoke somewhat above the heads of police observers.

> Sons and daughters of the soil, lend me your ears. I come to bury the NDP and not to praise it. The evil that parties do lives after them; the good is often interned with their bones. So let it be with the NDP. The noble Sir Edgar has told you the NDP was seditious: if it were so it was a grievous fault, and grievously has the NDP answered for it. Here, under lives of the NDP and the rest [sic] — for Sir Edgar is an honourable man. Come, I speak in the NDP's ashes. It was my party, faithful and just to me: But Sir Edgar says it was seditious; and Sir Edgar is an honourable man.[13]

Joshua Nkomo was re-elected to the leadership. He reappointed his executive with the addition of two new honorary members — George Nyandoro and James Chikerema, who were both still in detention following their arrests under the February 1959 State of Emergency.

Meanwhile there was no check on the level of violence and unrest, which in fairness to the Whitehead government, was the motivating factor for the introduction of the much-maligned Law and Order (Maintenance) Act. Attacks against blacks, the burning down of schools and churches and the destruction of rural infrastructure continued unabated. Whitehead deployed more police and stiffened the law, which at that time held over 4 000 people in detention — a record that would never be equalled.[14]

Strangely, Sir Edgar did not immediately ban the new party. He seemed willing — perhaps because he had staked his political future on the new black vote — to give it the benefit of the doubt. For a further nine months the wreckage of inter-black violence obscured the delivery of his political vision, until in September 1962 he finally issued the anticipated banning order.

1962 was a bad year for the Prime Minister. Among other things, a rumour in circulation had it that, during one of the security and intelligence briefings that he was subjected to each week, he was so distraught that he wet his pants. The Special Branch later learned that Whitehead suffered from a nervous bladder condition that was aggravated by tension.[15] White voters were uncertain exactly what to make of it all, but the feeling was strong that Sir Edgar had lost his way.

For a second time, nationalist assets and funds were seized and most of the leadership placed under restriction. Special Branch found it very curious that ZAPU appeared unscathed by this second round of asset seizures, and questions were asked about exactly where Nkomo was sourcing his funds. While his travel expenses alone amounted to a considerable sum, he was also found to have imported a brand new Rambler sedan, and later a new Vauxhall, both of which were shipped from England and paid for with cheques drawn on a London bank.[15]

These facts kept a stew of rumours boiling and things got even hotter when Nkomo once again just happened to be outside the country when his colleagues were rounded up and placed under restriction. On this particular occasion he was in Lusaka on the final leg of an international trip. According to his own explanation, he was revisiting friends in Egypt with the intention of sourcing arms and cash for the struggle. This explanation was at least partially true for he was indeed given a rather motley collection of firearms that included Lanchester machine, ammunition and grenades. Amazingly the ZAPU leader carried all this hardware with him on a scheduled Air France flight without being intercepted.

While Nkomo was in Lusaka, Kenneth Kaunda put it to him that he was under a moral obligation to return home immediately. After all, detention and persecution were part of the usual burden of leadership and he was no exception. Nkomo agreed, but then flinched and instead drove north to Dar es Salaam hoping that Tanganyikan leader Julius Nyerere would be more sympathetic. By way of explanation Nkomo pleaded that he had travelled back to Dar es Salaam to collect more weapons. Whatever the reason, Nyerere was unimpressed and gave Nkomo the bad news that a revolutionary's place was behind bars.

There was no fire of passion for this sort of thing in Nkomo's heart, and it took a third diplomatic visit to force him to pick up his cross and trudge back up the hill. Ndabaningi Sithole was a rising star in the Party, a godly man and a true zealot. To then have Sithole detouring on his return journey from a conference in Athens to urge his leader to fight was more than the big man could bear. The ZAPU president tried one more time to rescue the situation by pleading the cause of a government in exile, but he was shouted down and in due course forced to return to Rhodesia.

Back home, and restricted to the Sobukwe Reserve near Kezi, Nkomo continued to ruminate on the theme of a government in exile. The more he thought about it the more it appealed to him. He summoned the ZAPU executive to a meeting — which incidentally caused some inconvenience and danger to those breaking their own restriction orders to attend — and urged his colleagues to leave the country and join him in Tanganyika. There the executive would have the freedom to effectively coordinate the struggle.

Mugabe was dismayed and led an immediate rejection of the proposals. Others followed with varying degrees of commitment. Shaking their heads in wonder, the nationalist elite turned and made their way back to their restricted areas. Much anxious discussion followed concerning the apparently wavering Nkomo. There were no doubt a few who favoured the idea of life in an exiled shadow cabinet, but no public admissions along those lines were made. The triumvirate of Mugabe, Sithole and Takawira were committed to pursuing the struggle at home and no potential unpleasantness in the immediate future would be enough to divert them from their course.

With nothing much to do for the moment but observe events in the opposing camp, the nationalists sat back and watched a similar leadership struggle playing out in the Southern Rhodesian Parliament.

End of the road

The all-important constitution brokered by Duncan Sandys in January 1961 turned out to be significantly less than it seemed. It took some time for this fact to be discovered, and when it was, it came as more of a shock than a surprise.

Edgar Whitehead had campaigned for a 'yes' vote in the referendum after the British had given the most earnest assurances that the new constitution contained the terms of independence. The Governor, Sir Humphrey Gibbs, and Sir Roy Welensky — who was busy overseeing the collapse of the Federation — had both endorsed this. In fact, Welensky's exact words on the subject have since been immortalised.

> The provision of the new proposals are that future amendments to the Constitution will rest with us here in Southern Rhodesia. I wasn't going to leave that power in London for all the tea in China, because you might have a Labour government one day which would be quite agreeable to making changes we could never accept.[17]

According to Welensky, the new constitution ought to have seen the removal of all Whitehall's substantive reserve clauses, and prevented it from legislating for Southern Rhodesia without the latter's consent. In other words, the territory would have as much independence as it needed and could have hoped for. But would Sir Roy never learn? Had he forgotten perfidious Albion?

If the British had duped Welensky once, they had fooled him a dozen times. Duncan Sandys had indeed made it clear that the draft constitution was a major step in the direction of full independence. However, in the light of recent violent events and some still happening, what possible value could a statement like that have?

Somewhere between agreement and drafting, the British had slipped into the draft text an amendment so canny and so apparently minor that it would evade even the studious attentions of Ian Smith and others and in fact would take months to be discovered. Section 111 retained for Her Majesty the right to intervene by Order in Council notwithstanding anything to the contrary drafted elsewhere in the Constitution.

By the time this little amendment had been discovered, the agreement could not be reversed, and by then the usual suspects had become such a familiar and tedious chorus that even they quickly gave up the cry. The Constitution was then presented as just a little less than full independence. Whitehall had successfully reserved enough power to ensure that it would have to put up with the Zimbabwe nationalists and the white Rhodesians at odds for a long time to come. It was a catastrophe that for the umpteenth time brought home to white Rhodesia that Britain could simply not be trusted.

While on the surface it might have appeared that Britain was simply incurably duplicitous, in fact the situation was much more complicated than this. While Lord Devonshire had admitted to Nkomo that Her Majesty was not prepared to countenance an entirely black government, it had also been made clear that she was equally unwilling to hand over absolute power to the whites. It was difficult then for either side to accurately determine whose interests the Crown was serving. The answer lay with the fifth column involved in the Rhodesia crisis. This was a combination of diverse interests represented mainly by the newly liberated nations of the world. These, by dint of numbers rather than wealth, had begun to dominate the moral high ground of the two main international forums, namely the United Nations and the Commonwealth. In combination this group was known as the Afro-Asian bloc and it was from this source that intense pressure was being applied against the British Government.

The story began early in 1961 when Joshua Nkomo delivered a petition to a United Nations committee, calling for the body to implement its Charter on the granting of independence to all colonial territories. Specifically the petition protested Britain's handling of the 1961 Southern Rhodesian Constitutional Conference — to which Britain in turn protested that because Southern Rhodesia had been self-governing since 1923, she alone was responsible for her internal affairs. With this in mind, the right of the United Nations to discuss any issues relating to the internal affairs of such a self-governing territory was questioned. The UN committee, however, came out in favour of Nkomo, maintaining that Southern Rhodesia was not a self-governing territory within the terms of the Charter and was therefore a valid subject for discussion.

Not surprisingly, the loudest voices within the Afro-Asian bloc tended to be the recently liberated African nations, particularly Tanganyika, Ivory Coast, Sierra Leone, Guinea, Nigeria and Liberia. A sub-bloc within the Afro-Asian grouping comprising countries bordering Rhodesia declared their nations to be the 'Frontline States'. As the Winds of Change gathered pace, so the volume and insistence of these voices increased, although predictably unity among them was not absolute.

Hastings Banda was too old and too comfortable to be a revolutionary gunslinger. He slipped out of the club soon after its formation and declared himself to be a pragmatist. Seretse Khama of Botswana also tended to keep a healthy distance between himself and the two main firebrands, Kenneth Kaunda of Zambia and Julius Nyerere of Tanganyika. Of the pair, Kaunda was probably the coolest burning while Julius Nyerere — a strong willed, ascetic and powerfully authentic revolutionary — held the torch firmly. He would maintain this grip throughout his own political education and remain an implacable enemy of white Rhodesia.

Theoretically the voices of these nations — small, weak and sometimes disreputable — carried as much weight on the international stage as did Britain's. The days of the Pax Britannia when Whitehall could slap down or ignore the protests of its minions were over. During the course of the following year the United Nations General Assembly would hear again from Nkomo; from Paul Mushonga, the leader of a splinter group known as Zimbabwe National Party; and Garfield Todd. As a result, a sub-committee on Southern Rhodesia was formed. It was chaired by India and included members from India itself, Mali, Tanganyika, Tunisia and Venezuela. Its role was to liase with the British Government and monitor progress towards acceptable independence for the territory as well as to 'discuss future action'.

The committee sat until April 1962 and in its report observed that the 1961 Constitution needed revision since it did not provide adequately for African representation. It also forcefully urged Britain to convene another conference to draw up a new and universally acceptable constitution.[18] Togo, meanwhile, submitted a draft resolution to the General Assembly calling for the release of all political prisoners in Southern Rhodesia and the lifting of the ban on ZAPU. A formal resolution to this effect was passed and adopted on 12 October 1962.

From this it can be seen that Britain was under increasing pressure from countries and groups with an interest in decolonisation. This was incomprehensible to most whites in Central Africa because of the obvious fact that most, if not all black African countries had deeply questionable standards of their own for the protection of human rights. Nonetheless this was how things stood, and Britain was anxious not to rock the international boat — and even more anxious not to oversee a collapse of the Commonwealth. Churchill's signature on the Atlantic Charter and the pressures of the Cold War and Moral Rearmament all served to place Britain between a rock and hard place. Her Majesty was by no means disinterested in the well-being of her subjects overseas, but her government was manifestly shackled by the realities of the post-war political landscape.

Eventually a handful of those subjects began to see the writing on the wall. Among other rumours, word was abroad that Roy Welensky was planning to declare unilateral independence for the two remaining territories of the Federation. Ian Smith was privy to the plan but did not support it since in his view the Federation was a spent force, and it was high time that Southern Rhodesians began preparations for a new future. This, of course, could mean many things, but one thing it meant for certain was that Edgar Whitehead had to go.

The smell of insurrection spread like blood in the water and as Smith began slowly to circle the beleaguered Prime Minister he was soon joined by a school of like-minded and influential men. Swimming with his head barely above the waterline, Whitehead had scant idea of what was underway beneath.

41

A new chapter

Having suffered Welensky's rejection, Ian Smith approached Winston Field to carry the standard of the breakaway group into the future and was gratified to find Field ready to do so. Both men in due course resigned their Federal commitments, to begin the business of building the political defences of Southern Rhodesia. If Welensky managed to hold the Federation together, he could count on the support of each, but if he failed then an alternative refuge would be in place for him, and any other central African white man who wished to take it.

Smith then made a point of visiting the aging but extremely wealthy farmer D.C 'Boss' Lilford, who had both the political leverage and the financial means to underwrite the creation of a new party. With little persuasion Lilford came on board and shortly thereafter the ship was launched. With this first lurch of the gunwales a steady stream of Federalists began to jump their sinking ship and swim over to the new alliance.

A meeting of prominent citizens was called and widely heeded. From it a committee was selected to organise the congress of a new party. Smith proposed Winston Field as chairman, ostensibly for reasons of his respectability, wealth and establishment appeal. Rumours had already begun to circulate that Smith had ambitions beyond being Field's deputy. Clearly, Smith heard the rumours and was at least a little embarrassed by them, for years later in his memoirs he stringently maintained that his support for Field was both genuine and absolute.

The Rhodesian Front Party was formed in March 1962 under Field's leadership and quickly built a strong following among a younger and clearer-thinking body of whites, not unlike Smith himself. Welensky, whose party had been bled white by the consequent defections, held a rather meaningless general election for the Federal Parliament in April of that year. In sharp contrast, the Rhodesia Front confidently prepared itself to fight its first general election in Southern Rhodesia in just a few months hence.

As all this was under way, Edgar Whitehead had begun to prune away dead legislation in an effort to expedite a political breakthrough. All the while he refused to acknowledge the collapse of law and order, and a complete disintegration of communication between the races. The NDP had stated — and clearly illustrated by then — that it intended to boycott every future election held under the 1961 Constitution. With his fingers in his ears and his eyes clamped shut, Whitehead pursued the black vote in as determined a manner as he ignored evidence of a gathering white backlash. As his platform groaned under increasing disaffection, he assured a United Nations Trusteeship Committee that there would be a majority of black voters within 15 years. On the eve of the election he went so far as to inform the electorate, the relevant members of whom were far out of earshot, that he would include a black member in his next cabinet.[1]

Were it was not for the fact that Sir Edgar was fiddling while the capital burned, a lot of what he had achieved was what Garfield Todd would like to have achieved, but failed. And while the fate of

Todd was a lesson not to be ignored, the Immorality Act was abandoned and the Industrial Conciliation Act modified, to allow for black trade unions. In addition, racial distinction in future wage negotiations was disallowed, public swimming facilities became multiracial and the middle levels of the civil service were opened up to blacks.

The Land Apportionment Act was the most important and most emotional piece of legislation on the statute book and to tamper with it would stir up old and deeply entrenched fears. Even here, Whitehead plunged in unperturbed and, after some preparatory work by a Commission of Inquiry, initiated a repeal of the Act as a pillar of his re-election campaign.

The Prime Minister also pressed ahead with his 'Build a Nation Campaign', despite the obvious fact that the NDP had largely succeeded in mobilising a boycott of black voter registration. It was evident to anyone, with a mind to observe, that few if any blacks would vote — a verity even Whitehead was finding it difficult to ignore. He was genuinely astonished to discover that quite a large proportion of blacks seemed to prefer the idea of rule by a bunch of radical nationalists than by well-meaning whites. He also began to realise that he might just have alienated a good number of white voters, for the sake of pandering to blacks who were now not going to vote anyway.

On the other side of the fence, the Rhodesian Front based its campaign on the preservation of the Land Apportionment Act. Forced integration was rejected, as was unwarranted haste in preparing the black man for political responsibility. The grandstanding of Nkomo, Mugabe and others added significant weight to this position, in the eyes of a nervous and overwhelmingly white electorate. Another weapon in the RF arsenal was the fact that Winston Field, with his good looks and quiet self-confidence, stood in stark contrast to the dry, bumbling and myopic Edgar Whitehead. Field did not directly reject black political advancement but counselled against what he saw as dangerous zeal on the part of the Prime Minister. Ironically Sir Edgar was also accused of being too soft on law and order.

Despite overwhelming evidence to the contrary, Whitehead remained confident of victory. He attacked the RF with the bizarre accusation that it intended to break up a Federation already crumbling to dust. The British Government had by then agreed to the secession of Nyasaland, so Whitehead was among a diminishing handful who could not read the writing on that particular wall.

The results of the ballot of December 1962 therefore, came as a profound shock to Whitehead but to few others. The Rhodesian Front won 35 seats to the United Federal Party's 29, while 14 were won by a brave handful of black UFP candidates, who stood in the electoral districts. The registered black voters made up a tiny proportion of those who would have been qualified to vote and, even among those, the majority abstained on the day. It was estimated that if a mere 5 000 blacks had cast a vote, the UFP would have been victorious.

Thus the final irony was awarded to Nkomo and Mugabe, for between them they ushered in a victory that, in years to come, would cost the blood of tens of thousands of innocents.

42

A family divided

Feuding nationalists

The collapse of the Federation, the rejection of partnership and the rise to power of the white right, set the stage for race conflict. In the order of things, however, war against the whites would have to wait until a civil war had been fought between the black political factions themselves.

In an ideal world, an ordered progression of nationalist politics — such as the British tried to promote under the rules of trusteeship — would have advanced through political partnership to eventual benevolent black majority rule, after which everybody would have lived happily ever after. In Southern Rhodesia this process had been rendered impossible by a white minority unwilling to relinquish control, creating by a rigorous process of natural selection a species of violent black extremists.

The few survivors of black internecine political strife were now the predators who were grimly determined to brawl their way to the top of the pile. From the moment that Rev Thomson Samkange assumed the leadership of the Southern Rhodesian ANC, the efforts of men like him — to try and achieve a united voice — had been confounded. Tribal orientated blacks lived under a formula of division and whites were always more than willing to help them along this path.

When the Rhodesian Front was voted into power, Joshua Nkomo remained leader of the only substantive black opposition. Nkomo was no fool, and allusions to his sensuality and corruptibility, should not serve to imply that he was either weak or stupid. Although he was among the least impressively educated of the black leadership, he was unquestionably a natural leader. His failing was that he yearned for power without the desire to bloody his knuckles in an open fight to get it. His seconds often had to do quite a lot of shoving to get him into the ring; but once he was there, he never failed to give a good account of himself.

The story of Nkomo's fall from grace began at the 1961 Constitutional Conference and, as we have seen, continued in August of 1962 when he angered his executive by summoning them to his place of restriction, in order to press for a government in exile. The plan was heard by his colleagues and rejected. To them that was the end of the matter, but with Nkomo the thought persisted. His current term of restriction was tedious but hardly catastrophic, and if it turned out to be the last, all would be well. However under a Rhodesian Front government, the odds were excellent that he would visit the inside of a detention camp regularly, until inevitably he finished up in prison — which was a dreary prospect for him indeed.

Nkomo therefore never forgot his government-in-exile scheme, and at the first opportunity renewed the appeal to his executive, careful this time to couch the scheme in suitably revolutionary language. He argued that the permanent restriction of the nationalist leadership would stifle the movement and render useless the sacrifice of liberty and life. On the other hand, if the executive established itself abroad, it could do what it wanted in furtherance of a direct liberation struggle, with the aid and support of friendly governments.

Nkomo's motive may have been self-serving but his logic was sound. It would be difficult to disagree unless one fundamentally believed that a liberation struggle was unnecessary. In truth most of those allied against Nkomo felt that way. With the collapse of the Federation, all evidence suggested that the white man was on the run. Thereafter elaborate political structures, beyond those necessary to sustain a campaign of civil unrest would be superfluous. A bit of noise, fist waving and gratuitous destruction ought to be enough to bring the whole edifice crashing down.

Soon after their release from restriction, Mugabe, his wife Sally and Nkomo were rearrested on various charges under the Law and Order (Maintenance) Act. Each was arraigned and released on bail pending trial. Detention for all moved several steps closer and, with this prospect in mind, Nkomo began to appeal more urgently to his comrades. Indeed he had begun to feel so strongly about the matter that he was willing to risk the consequences of a blatant deception.

Nkomo convinced the executive that Julius Nyerere had invited him to form a government in exile, for which Tanganyika would provide all the necessary support. He clearly did this in the belief that if he arrived in Dar-es-Salaam with the entire leadership of ZAPU, Nyerere would be forced to accept it as a fait accompli, News of the move spread among the party executive and had the desired effect. The newly independent African states exerted a powerful moral influence over the nationalist movement, and if the future brought war, the patronage and support of the Frontline states would be essential. As a consequence, direct orders from the likes of Julius Nyerere tended to override internal policy, and thus the ploy was reluctantly endorsed.

It is unlikely that many regretted leaving the trenches once the decision had been made. Exile meant pan-African exposure, financial support from sympathetic governments and the prospect of uninhibited political activity. This was a temptation that was hard to resist. Mugabe had mixed feelings about the decision. He would have gone to prison as willingly as Christ to the cross, but at that time Sally was pregnant and if he could shield her from exposure to an increasingly aggressive political environment, he would.

In the event, Sally Mugabe was spared nothing. Her right of passage was to be as bitter as could be predicted and no better or worse than her husband's. When the proposed cabinet-in-exile began trickling into Dar es Salaam during April of 1963 they found Julius Nyerere shocked and angered. He protested that at no time had he given encouragement to an idea that, in his opinion, was neither desirable nor welcome. When news of the arrivals reached Kenneth Kaunda, he also made it known to Nkomo in Dar-es-Salaam that the move was unacceptable. Both he and Nyerere stringently maintained that the abandonment of the country by almost the entire nationalist leadership would be devastating to the struggle, and the executive was urged to return to Rhodesia as soon as possible.

Sithole, Mugabe and Takawira were understandably enraged. Despite one or two members of the leadership rallying to his defence, Nkomo was left isolated and mortified by the turn of events. He might have escaped overt criticism if the gambit had succeeded, but clearly it had not, and since he could offer no credible explanation, he chose to offer none at all. Sides were drawn, communication collapsed and the matter was left to fester.

In his autobiography, published in 1984, Nkomo blamed Nyerere for having lied, for being a pacifist and for regarding the author as a rival in pan-African affairs. He accused him of being an egomaniac, determined to highjack the struggle for Zimbabwe as part of his own liberation crusade. Throughout the remainder of his memoirs, Nkomo is charitable and philosophical, and he describes no one else in such mean terms. But he was never able to find it in himself to forgive Nyerere — and perhaps vice versa.

In the meantime, Nkomo's party colleagues tried to establish themselves in Dar-es-Salaam, with neither money nor support. They could hardly believe that their president had manufactured such an elaborate ruse, but for all intents and purposes it appeared that he had. The view of the executive was not made known to him immediately, but when a written response was finally circulated some three months later, the language it contained was revealing. The document was authored by Ndabaningi Sithole, and in part read:

> Mr Nkomo is very much afraid of going to jail, and this fear of jail causes him to evade taking the necessary decisions which any leader in his position is expected to take. The white settlers have exploited this fact to full advantage. Because of this fear, Mr Nkomo has deserted the people at the time when they most needed bold leadership and does not count the cost.[1]

An even more bitter denunciation was reserved for the visit of a six-man ZAPU delegation to Addis Ababa to attend the inauguration of the Organisation of African Unity. It was an inauspicious debut for Nkomo. Against a backdrop of criticism, he was cautioned by the organisation against disunity, and urged to return to Rhodesia forthwith and reclaim the struggle.

Nkomo thereupon made a virtue out of necessity and left Dar-es-Salaam immediately prior to an executive meeting of the exiled leadership, where he could expect his own conduct to dominate the agenda. He was fortunate in that he did not happen to be facing charges in Rhodesia at the time, so he was not arrested on his arrival at Salisbury airport. He then wasted not a moment in attempting to reclaim the initiative.

A probable reason why Nkomo was not immediately detained on his return to Rhodesia, charges or not, was Winston Field himself. Field sat somewhat to the left of his cabinet and caucus, and was initially reluctant to make use of the security powers he had inherited from Edgar Whitehead. Cabinet had in fact passed stiff new amendments to the Law and Order (Maintenance) Act that further limited black political activity, and added a mandatory death sentence for acts of sabotage. It would only be a matter of time before Nkomo would be arrested but at this juncture, time was of the essence.

Nkomo took full advantage of his liberty to discredit the rebels and promote his own version of events. The existence of a plot against his leadership was confirmed when he intercepted a series of telegrams from Dar-es-Salaam, decrying his actions and urging the party to prepare for a change of leadership. To this his response was swift and decisive. He had succeeded in jumping into the ring some weeks ahead of his opponents, and his fists were flying. On 6 July 1963 he addressed a rally in Salisbury where he publicly named 11 officials — some of whom were present — as enemies of the organisation. Three of these — Enos Nkala, Henry Hamadziripiri and Maurice Nyagumbo — had already served terms ranging from two and four years, and were justifiably astonished to be so named. It was a risky and divisive tactic. In a later press conference, Nkomo also announced the suspension from the party of Takawira, Sithole and Mugabe. A telegram was sent to the rebels in Tanganyika that read simply:

> Messers. Sithole, Takawira, Malianga and Mugabe, you are hereby suspended until the decision of the Conference of Peoples Representatives. You will be informed of the date and place of the Conference.[2]

In Dar-es-Salaam the response was equally rapid. Messages of solidarity were sent to the 11 banned members pledging support. The executive committee voted to replace Nkomo with the Rev Ndabaningi Sithole. Among three dissenters was Jason Moyo who, like James Chikerema, would remain steadfastly loyal to Nkomo for the time being. Chikerema was directly in line for the deputy presidency of the party, and although somewhat pedestrian in his ways, he had also recently been appointed ZAPU's head of Special Affairs. This was the organ of the party charged with recruiting and training a military wing for the purpose of waging an armed struggle.[3]

It is noteworthy that around this time a certain Tobias Bobylock Manyonga was intercepted in a police roadblock near Shabani Mine. Police had received a tip off that he was carrying arms and so his car was searched. It had been to Manyonga that Joshua Nkomo had entrusted the gift of arms from the Egyptians. The search revealed a small consignment of two Lanchester sub-machine guns that were later linked by serial numbers to those taken over by the Egyptians during the seizure of the Suez Canal Zone from the British. There was also a quantity of grenades and ammunition.

Nkomo issued a challenge to the seven rebels to return to Rhodesia and face the struggle as he himself had done. He knew that Sithole, Takawira and Mugabe were facing charges and would in all likelihood be arrested immediately. Despite this, Ndabaningi Sithole was not long in making his appearance in Salisbury and as expected, he was arrested the moment he touched down. However, a few days later he was released on bail, and was then at liberty to turn his attention to the rebel agenda. Nkomo, of course, had by then hijacked the main stage, leaving Sithole to ponder his next move with neither money nor support.

To be fair, the Rev Sithole was hampered less by resources than by deeply felt principles. He had risen steadily on the tide of nationalism and thanks in some measure to his groundbreaking book, *African Nationalism*, he was regarded as something of a founding father. But could he really be counted among the predators? Was he willing to lie, manipulate and sacrifice — the kind of Machiavellian tactics that Nkomo was employing as the struggle for leadership reached its furious climax? The passage of the next few years would prove that Sithole was not of the right cut for this fight — a fight that would ultimately prove immensely difficult and damaging for him.

History has tended, justifiably, to portray Ndabaningi Sithole as a foil. He was gullible, nervous, fumbling at times, and a regular target for lampooning. His name was twisted with glee by a generation of white schoolboys into such effronteries as 'rubber-dingy-shit-hole' while their fathers referred to him as *indaba maningi*, which translated from Chilapalapa meant 'big trouble'. However, for the moment at least, Sithole was the anointed leader and like it or not his job was to face down a buoyant and trumpeting Nkomo.

Nkomo applied enormous energy to the consolidation of his position, before the rebels could gather strength, and to a large extent he succeeded in out-manoeuvring them. On 10 August 1963 he called a substantive party conference at the Cold Comfort Farm, a widely sponsored multiracial experiment, situated just outside Salisbury. Although Sithole was invited he did not attend. A snake symbolically representing him was killed by a mob drawn from a huge crowd of party faithful.

To replace the now banned ZAPU executive, Nkomo formed what he called a People's Caretaker Council (PCC). Although not strictly a political party, it would serve as a standard under which the surviving elements of ZAPU could reform and go forward. Within the new PCC was a caretaker cabinet to which Nkomo was elected life president with absolute power.

On the same day, a handful of press and nervous supporters met outside the modest Highfield home of Enos Nkala, to hear Ndabaningi Sithole announce the formation of a breakaway party. The new organisation was to be called the Zimbabwe African National Union, or ZANU, and would be led by Sithole himself, with Robert Mugabe as general secretary. The national response to this news was at first subdued.

Nkomo held mass rallies throughout the country outlining a new policy of isolating the government. Sithole remarked of him:

Mr. Nkomo has fallen into the unfortunate habit of concealing the truth from the members of his Central Executive so that in many cases these members have found themselves deceived and hence have become embittered against him.[4]

As the news was digested, the townships and countryside of Rhodesia erupted into another vicious bout of fratricidal violence. ZANU, meanwhile, wasted no time in committing itself directly to the armed struggle. Masipula Sithole, younger brother of Ndabaningi, described the aftermath of the split as a horrible and murderous affair.[5] His view was reflected in a report issued by the Commissioner of Police later in the year that read in part:

In 1963 there was almost a state of civil war between supporters of rival nationalist parties in the African townships.[6]

The dynamics of the civil war were complex and in no small way influenced by gang warfare and youth delinquency. There was no ideological difference between the two parties that mattered a whit to the masses. The common enemy wore a different skin colour and could be easily identified. But because of an inability to come to grips with him effectively, it became all too easy for the masses to channel their anger and frustration inwards. The pages of *Drum* make it clear that the mood of the nation was depressed.

This is a civil war of sticks and stones and sneers. Old friends and neighbours are divided — and sometimes even families. Salisbury, with its big and tribally cosmopolitan population is worst hit — this is a city divided ... the sticks crack down and the bricks arch lazily through the air ... The police move in and cart away the injured ... No one wins and the government is left with rare (sic) excuse to clamp down on nationalism.[7]

So it was. The war was driven by militant youth who are always to be found at the vanguard of political division. The PCC youth called themselves the *Zhanda*, a corruption of the word gendarmes, while the ZANU youth styled themselves the Zimbabwe 1st Battalion. *Drum*, reflecting the dismay of a large section of the black establishment, was apt to call both the 'highly irregulars'.[8]

In December 1963 Robert Mugabe, with his new son now three months old and his wife on her way back to Ghana, set off on the return journey from Dar-es-Salaam to Salisbury. He travelled in the company of Herbert Chitepo, who was to be retained as his legal counsel. Mugabe knew that he would be facing severe consequences on arrival and in this he was not to be disappointed. He was arrested immediately and remanded in custody pending a trial that would last from January to March of 1964.

In keeping with his investiture into the hard core of African nationalists, Mugabe turned his court appearances into a political platform. He refused to retract his subversive statements and instead added more of the same, including a richly worded denouncement of the 'hanging' clauses, now incorporated in the Law and Order Maintenance Act. He was sentenced to 21 months in prison, and as he began his term, it would probably not have surprised him to know that he was not to see the proverbial light of day again for nigh on a decade.

Within three months, over 150 ZANU and ZAPU leaders — including Joshua Nkomo — joined Mugabe. The comfort-loving Nkomo was sent to serve his time at the Gonakudzingwa Detention Centre, in the hot and dreary southeast of the country; Ndabaningi Sithole joined Mugabe in Sikombela Detention Centre. In August 1964 ZANU joined ZAPU on the list of banned organisations.

On the evening of 4 July 1964, Petrus Oberholtzer was driving with his family along a lonely Melsetter road when he came upon a makeshift roadblock. While his wife and three year old daughter remained in the Volkswagen Kombi, Oberholtzer stepped out and walked forward to investigate. On reaching the obstruction he bent down, picked up a boulder and hurled it into the bush. He was astonished when the boulder, or one like it, was promptly thrown back, followed by a fusillade of rocks and stones. Realising he was under attack he rushed back to his vehicle and was reaching for a rifle when a petrol bomb exploded over the car.

The embattled Oberholtzer then turned to confront a shrill group of black men who had emerged from the undergrowth and were bearing down on him. Before he could bring his rifle to bear, a knife was plunged into his chest. As the group fled with his firearm, Oberholtzer was able to enter his vehicle, mount the roadblock and drive for a short distance before he lost control and died. When help arrived a note was found inserted in a cleft stick close to the scene. 'Confrontation Smith' it read, 'Crocodile Gang will soon kill all whites. Beware!'[9]

All but one of the culprits was rapidly brought to book. A second escaped from police holding cells. Two were later hanged despite universal pleas for clemency and a Queen's Pardon. The event counted as the first politically motivated attack on a white since the rebellion of 1896. Rightly or wrongly, it has been cited as the moment that the war proper began. Whatever the real or symbolic importance of the Oberholtzer killing, it succeeded in galvanising the police into nipping in the bud this kind of black militancy. This they did very successfully and the first round of the struggle without doubt went to them.

The Oberholtzer killing blew the lid off what had previously simply been civil unrest. This and the earlier discovery of arms in the boot of Tobias Manyonga's car, led to an immediate tightening of border security along the Zambezi boundary, leading to further arms shipments being unearthed in both private vehicles and long distance haulage trucks. A rash of grenade attacks in Bulawayo followed, as activists tried to dispose of their accumulated ordinance. In September 1964 a ZAPU group staged an abortive attack on the Kezi farmstead of former chief magistrate Farewell Roberts. The attackers fled but were tracked for some 30 kilometres and arrested by a diligent and unarmed black police sergeant.

Around this time, semi-organised groups, also known as Zhanda, started to be infiltrated into Rhodesia from Zambia with the ill-defined objective of attacking white farms and strategic government installations. In the main they were armed with nothing better than petrol bombs, and these were more often than not used against soft black targets rather than white. It was clear at this stage that the nationalists still entertained the forlorn hope that a few aggressive acts would cause all whites to pack up and leave the country. Perhaps also they hoped that, at the first signs of widespread black violence, a general revolt would occur. The British South Africa Police acted with both speed and precision against this rather amorphous and ineffectual organisation.

Effective intelligence, combined with good police work, ensured that this phase of the struggle was speedily brought to an end. As surviving Zhanda fled north across the Zambezi to regroup and reconsider their strategy, the Rhodesian security services could congratulate themselves on a job very well done. The Central Intelligence Organisation (CIO) founded by Winston Field and headed by Ken Flower found itself adept at penetrating the external nationalist networks. Special Branch did the same within the country. These groups were riddled with informants, the most senior reputed to be Jason Moyo, whose code-name was Number One. No less important was the disunity and amateurism of the nationalist leadership, and the poor quality of men initially called to arms.[10]

With scant resources and few established networks, the early recruiters tended to focus on the large black Rhodesian expatriate community in Zambia. There was no evidence in the beginning of a popular movement, since the majority of early recruits were either press-ganged or duped with promises of educational scholarships. They were dismayed to be delivered instead to training camps in Tanzania. There they were given guns, run around the paddock for a day or two and then told they were going back to Rhodesia to fight.

It took very little for these men to betray their comrades once it occurred to them that their life expectancy was likely to be severely curtailed. It was no particular secret that the probable consequence of poor strategy and overtly political priorities was the death of the foot soldier. With nothing to lose, this cannon fodder was itself responsible for many of the catastrophic security leaks, that led directly to failed operations.

Both guerrilla factions were unwelcome in Zambia, so their newly minted fighters were shunted south as soon as possible. Their first obstacle was the challenging geography of the Zambezi Valley — along with the Security Forces and National Parks personnel who diligently patrolled it. If insurgents did manage to escape detection and penetrate populated areas, their newly acquired foreign manners and unfamiliar dress immediately gave them away. The temptation to use their weapons for hunting or local banditry was also very strong, which again made them vulnerable to detection. Locals were also rewarded for information and therefore frequently sold out insurgents whom they did not know or necessarily care for.

In due course a measure of peace returned to the countryside and the city streets of Rhodesia. Obviously this did not mean that the spirit of resistance had been broken — far from it — but simply that the optimistic and disorganised phase of the struggle had passed. The nationalist leaders now accepted that the revolution would be won only after a long and tough fight. They needed to retire to some quiet place to work out their differences and plan a better strategy.

Smith picks a fight

On 29 March 1963 it was finally announced in London that Northern Rhodesia had been granted the right to secede from the Central African Federation. The 40-year process of self-government in Southern Rhodesia had reached a crossroads. This was probably the bitterest day in the life of Sir Roy Welensky, who had endured so many bitter moments. The news was given him by the First Secretary of State for Central African Affairs, Richard Austin 'Rab' Butler as the two met at 10 Downing Street for a luncheon with the Prime Minister. Welensky promptly spun on his heel and stormed out. He explained later: 'I cannot accept the hospitality of a man who has betrayed me and my country.'[1]

Welensky put behind him his long battle to keep Northern Rhodesia in the Federation and shifted the focus of his attention to the south. He spoke powerfully for Southern Rhodesia's right to independence, recognising in common with almost every other white man in the region that his own future was bound up with the survival of the territory.

'If Labour come into power in Britain', he said with burning memories still vivid in his mind, 'at least they might stab us in the breast and not in the back.'[2]

It was his determination and also that of the new territorial government in Salisbury that if the Federation collapsed, then Southern Rhodesia must at any price be saved from the wreckage.

The two northern partners were by then moving seamlessly towards independence, but the future of Southern Rhodesia still lay mired in doubt. Many whites maintained that if independence was to be the condition of federal dissolution, then that principal must apply to all. They also took it for granted that it was their responsibility to control the pace of majority rule according to Rhodes' maxim of 'equal rights for all civilised men'. They expected too — not unreasonably since it had been the general understanding — that the terms of the 1961 Constitution would be the basis for independence. This was simple, unequivocal and in the mind of white Rhodesia, perfectly reasonable. That the blacks had turned around and repudiated the agreement the moment it was signed was simply more evidence of their political immaturity.

Winston Field was sworn into office on the understanding that he would hold the British to their promise. It was probably not widely known at the time that he did not in fact share the majority opinion of his Cabinet and caucus. Privately he felt that if achieving independence from Britain was likely to create a conflict with the colonial power, then it would be a retrogressive step.

It was obvious in the current global climate, that Britain could not grant independence to Southern Rhodesia on the same terms as the north. Besides, there was no real need at that time to buck the status quo. The country was governed under very lenient terms and the white minority enjoyed many liberties. The country would be able to move towards majority rule at its leisure, and should a war erupt as a consequence of black zealotry, it would be a British war with British troops fighting it. Independent status would relieve the Crown of that responsibility and Rhodesia would then face renewed terrorist activity from a position of isolation and relative weakness.

Under a groundswell of white nationalism, Field did not feel that he had much choice in the matter, and he duly responded to pressure to take the fight to the British.[3] The next event in the Federal calendar was the dissolution conference to be held at Victoria Falls some time in June. There the breakup of the Federation would be formalised and its assets divided up. The Rhodesians decided to use this event as a lever and at the end of March, Field despatched a letter to Rab Butler defining the position.

> I have now carefully considered the Southern Rhodesian attitude towards the Conference and I wish to state that the Southern Rhodesian Government will not attend the Conference unless we receive in writing from you an acceptable undertaking that Southern Rhodesia will receive its independence concurrently with the date on which either Northern Rhodesia or Nyasaland is allowed to secede, whichever is first.[4]

Sir Roy Welensky backed this up by stating that if Field chose to boycott the conference, he would withdraw the attendance of the Federal Government delegation too. This would, of course, make it very difficult for the British Government to proceed. Rab Butler fudged and suggested more talks — to which Ian Smith responded by throwing his hands in the air and asking what more there was to talk about.

Field calmed his deputy and made his way to London alone to meet with Butler. His resolve was stiffened by repeated exhortations from Smith and Clifford Dupont, then Minister of Justice, to accept no compromise. The only ground he had leave to give was that independence outside the Commonwealth was acceptable if Britain feared the reaction of the Afro-Asian members of that Club.[5]

When the two men met, Butler admitted that granting carte blanche independence to Southern Rhodesia might well precipitate the breakup of the Commonwealth. Field was quick to remind him that most Commonwealth countries were now either one-party states or dictatorships that, under the principals of the Commonwealth, ought to disqualify them from presenting any opinions at all. Butler declined to be drawn and instead pleaded with Field to attend the dissolution conference. If he agreed to do this, Butler undertook to visit Salisbury en route to Victoria Falls to finalise proposals on independence.

Field was naive enough to accept this and returned to Salisbury to the angry disappointment of his Cabinet. He preached caution — and reminded his colleagues that he could play the dissolution conference card only so far. If Butler broke up the Federation without a delegation from Field's government attending, Southern Rhodesia would be frozen out of the distribution of Federal assets. At stake was the bulk of the armed forces, including the Air Force, as well as the railways, Air Rhodesia and the Central African Power Corporation. In the event, Welensky made a favourable award to Southern Rhodesia, his minimum condition for attending the conference, which was agreed to by the British as a necessary price for Zambian independence.

No matter how he might protest to the contrary, Field had swallowed Butler's bait and it was not long before he felt the first pull on the line. A week before the conference was due to be convened, Field received a message from the British High Commissioner reporting that Butler's health was poor, and he wondered whether Field and his delegation would spare him the effort of travelling to Salisbury and meet him in Victoria Falls instead.

Field was sympathetic and saw refusal as churlish. He persuaded the Cabinet to his point of view, although Clifford Dupont was heard to remark that Butler had probably never felt better in his life. However the Southern Rhodesian Government was clearly made up of amateurs, not one of whom had ever held any kind of public office. None could hope to match in guile and cunning a career politician like Butler.

What follows is Ian Smith's account of the meeting and it concurs with the recollections of those on his side. It was subsequently repudiated so violently by Butler and the British Government that there has ever since been some doubt over the facts. According to Smith, Butler began with a lengthy eulogy that he quotes as follows:

> In view of your country's wonderful record of 'responsible government' over the past forty years, during which time you have conducted yourself without blemish, managed your financial affairs in an exemplary fashion, and above all the great loyalty you have always given to Britain.[6]

The colonials were assured that Her Majesty's Government was carefully considering Southern Rhodesia's request that independence be granted no later than Northern Rhodesia's and Nyasaland's. Gratitude was also expressed to Field and his colleagues for attending the conference, despite the fact that no direct promise of independence had been given.

All eyes then turned to Smith who thought for a moment before asking if an agreement was about to be signed. Butler retreated a little and pleaded that in familial affairs that there must be trust. Smith could see this for what it was, but by then he probably didn't care. A unilateral declaration of independence had already begun to visibly permeate the national debate and Smith gives no hint in his memoirs that he was in any way opposed to this course of action.

Field then rose and, speaking largely for himself, accepted Butler's trust and shook his hand on it. Smith's parting comments to the First Secretary were sterner. 'Let's remember the trust you emphasised', he said, 'if you break that you will live to regret it.' — rough language indeed to use on a British Secretary of State.[7]

As the year progressed, Smith and several of his fellow ministers began to sense that Field was drifting. The Prime Minister did not dispute this but argued that his drift reflected a similar mood in Whitehall. It was widely expected that Macmillan would retire and Field argued that it would make sense to wait until this happened, and deal more aggressively with his successor. As it turned out, he was right. In October 1963 Macmillan retired on grounds of ill health and Alec Douglas Home moved into 10 Downing Street.

Ian Smith was immediately despatched to London to test the waters. He met Duncan Sandys — who had taken over responsibility for Southern Rhodesia from Rab Butler — and the two immediately established a mutual antipathy. Three days later Smith met Home and received a more cordial welcome from a man with whom he had much more in common. Home, however, was not particularly empowered as an unelected prime minister to act, besides which the familiar bogey of resistance from the OAU and the Commonwealth reared its head — and again no firm conclusions were reached.

Home, showing great sensitivity, tried to explain to Smith that Afro-Asian resistance was not the only factor at play. A less easily definable mood that could best be interpreted as a desire to atone for past wrongs, had taken hold in Britain and Europe. It manifested principally in a strong determination to see justice done in relation to subject populations overseas. Smith could air to his heart's content how Rhodesia had managed a superior style of democracy to any other in Africa, but this, he was assured, would make no difference whatsoever. Smith then pressed for what he saw as the simple honouring of past commitments, pointing out that the consequences of appeasement would mean the destruction of Rhodesia. Again Home could not be moved but promised that he would offer, via Duncan Sandys, something for Smith 'to take home with him'.

However when he and Sandys met later, Sandys simply reiterated — with much less sensitivity —

the difficulties that her Majesty's Government was facing. He urged flexibility on the part of the Rhodesian Government, suggesting greater inclusion of blacks in government. To this Smith replied that under the 1961 Constitution — which Sandys himself had negotiated — the legislature, and by extension the government, was accessible to all Rhodesians. Had the nationalists not boycotted the process, more of them would be in government already. Sandys agreed, but like his superior he was not impressed.

Smith then flew back to Salisbury as confused by British sleight of hand as his Prime Minister had been. He was struck by the gloomy realisation that the current Conservative government was no less a slave to the party political machine than any before it. It was obvious that the administration was bent on preserving the dignity of Britain in the face of her rapidly diminishing powers, and the only substantive power remaining to her in world affairs, was the authority she exercised over the fate of Southern Rhodesia.

Efforts to expedite financial concessions, promised as part of the dissolution of the Federation, became deadlocked for no good reason until in the end Smith was forced to return to Salisbury with neither money nor independence. Shortly after his return a letter from the Commonwealth Relations Office reached Winston Field. In it Sandys proposed a meeting to include the prime ministers of Canada, Australia and Tanzania. Field's government protested that the Rhodesian question was a matter entirely between Her Majesty and itself and certainly they could see no place for Julius Nyerere on any panel of arbitration. Sandys' suggestion was rejected.

Frustrations within the Southern Rhodesian Government were in due course directed internally, and the victim was Field, who found himself in an impossible position. Thanks to his disinterest in a bloody tussle with the British he was out of the step with the majority hawks, and also more than a little touched by the recent fate of Garfield Todd. Increasingly he was seen to be abdicating his authority and decisions to Ian Smith.

Smith was, of course, the natural leader and the one who best reflected the national mood. He was by then already receiving petitions from the caucus to consider the Prime Minister's ouster in favour of himself, but for the time being he demurred. For reasons perhaps more cosmetic than practical, he groomed a weary Field for one more encounter with the British. The latter was despatched to London with instructions to threaten Whitehall with 'unspecified action' if immediate independence was not granted. 'Unspecified action' in this context was obviously intended to imply a unilateral declaration of independence.

Field's final trip to London as Prime Minister marked the melancholy end of a disenchanted journey. His mission was doomed by the fact that a general election in the United Kingdom was imminent, and general paralysis in Whitehall inevitable. Certainly there would be no point in Field pressing Sandys or Douglas Home for a decision, when both men were likely to be on the backbenches in a fortnight. Field returned to Salisbury with nothing achieved, and although Smith could have done no better, Field's reputation suffered irreparably.

Relations between Southern Rhodesia and Britain grew strained, and the mutual rhetoric became increasingly shrill. In due course a message from Whitehall was received in Salisbury, warning of the consequences of any unilateral declaration of independence. It was this direct allusion to that scenario that triggered open discussion of it for the first time, and — almost overnight — UDI became the talk of the nation.

Growing frustration at Winston Field's inaction prompted questions about his competence, that in turn prompted questions about his loyalty. The parliamentary caucus broke up into conspiring cliques that reformed around the leadership of Ian Smith. Field pleaded for patience and restraint in precisely the same forum that Smith was calling for action. In an apparently unemotional decision, the caucus voted out Field, and although long standing friendships ostensibly survived, he and his colleagues parted company. Governor Humphrey Gibbs, himself feeling matters slipping under a rising tide of white nationalism, urged Field to seek a new mandate. Field, however, had by then completely lost heart, and had no intention of hanging on for political crumbs like another Garfield Todd.[8]

In London, Field's ejection was seen for what it was and the effect of it was to bring the spectre of UDI a step closer. There was anguish in Whitehall just as there was throughout the free world. Clearly this was more than a simple change of leadership — it was a shift to a virtual war footing.

44

Third man of destiny

Smith's first visit to Britain as Prime Minister was the tour de force of a man with little legitimate political leverage but an enormous amount of personal appeal. He was determined that he would tolerate no political chicanery, but acting with some cunning of his own he sent ahead of him a group of local chiefs on a goodwill visit, first to India and Pakistan before Britain. Sensing the ruse, Douglas Home declined to meet with the chiefs and instead handed them over to Duncan Sandys.

Within the British establishment itself the gesture was well received. Smith was an easy man for the British to identify with as they mourned the passing of the great days. He was a warrior with proven loyalty to the Queen and a scion of the establishment who had grown strong in the tropics. He still spoke the almost forgotten language of men like Rhodes and Jameson, of Kitchener, Lawrence, Churchill and Montgomery. With his ponderous speech but nimble intelligence and with eyes that gazed through the scars of imperial battle, the hero-starved British public took him easily to their hearts. That the British Government did not do likewise was related more to politics than sentiment, for with all his charisma and his compelling combination of courage and tragedy, Ian Smith spoke on behalf of a dying institution.

To introduce Smith to one or two current realities, the British Government sent him a message telling him that the Commonwealth would not be inviting him to attend its annual Prime Ministers' Conference, to be held in London. It had been a convention throughout the life of the Commonwealth that the Southern Rhodesian Prime Minister attended as a de facto dominion prime minister. This had been the case with both Huggins and Welensky as Federal Prime Ministers and Smith's exclusion was a clear warning of an imminent sea change.

On a personal level Smith was cut to the quick. It was a heavy blow for a man whose entire life's philosophy had revolved around his faith and belief in the British Empire. The snub was felt no less acutely by the nation. In fact it was from that moment that the settler community of Southern Rhodesia started to become 'Rhodesian' as distinct from 'British'. Their loyalty to the Crown remained unshaken but thereafter this deliberately excluded the government of the day.

On a practical level Smith shifted his diplomatic focus and stopped over in Lisbon on his way to London. With the possibility of UDI, he needed to gauge carefully the mood of his two immediate neighbours, for as a landlocked country, Rhodesia could not survive without the help of Mozambique and South Africa.

There are many historical reasons why Portugal might have rejoiced to see a comeuppance served on Cecil Rhodes' legacy. However, in the years that followed the early unpleasantness, the governments of Mozambique and Rhodesia had developed a tradition of friendship and cooperation. Rhodesians flooded into Mozambique for their annual holidays, while Rhodesian transport and communications depended as much on Mozambique as on South Africa. Mozambique in turn had come to depend on the revenue from both this and the rail link through Rhodesia to the Copperbelt.

Portugal knew which side its bread was buttered and quickly declared itself in favour of any government in Rhodesia, whether it had declared unilateral independence or not.

This endorsement notwithstanding, the future of Mozambique was bound to the future of Portugal — and Portugal was under no less pressure than Britain to jettison her overseas provinces. Portugal did not tolerate self-governing colonies so all her overseas territories were governed directly from Lisbon. If push came to shove, Smith wanted to be sure of support from metropolitan Portugal as well as Mozambique.

Then there was South Africa: intelligence assessments of UDI that had been lately landing on the Prime Minister's desk offered no hope of the action succeeding. The reasons for this were many and included uncertainty regarding the Governor as commander-in-chief of the Security Forces — and indeed the loyalty of senior service commanders themselves. But mainly the Central Intelligence Organisation believed that Smith and his confederates had misjudged the mood of South Africa.

It might reasonably be supposed that, for purely ideological reasons, South Africa would support any efforts by Rhodesian whites to prolong their rule; and on the surface at least this appeared to be the case. While South Africa was not blind to the strategic importance of a buffer between herself and the black tide, she had other considerations to take into account. At no time did any official of the South African Government encourage UDI, and indeed it was made known that any assistance Rhodesia might expect from South Africa would be given reluctantly and only because of an accident of history and geography.[1]

Talks in London took place between Home and Smith on 7 September 1964. Smith could immediately see that Home's government was in an even tighter spot then than it had been during Field's visits, and it may have been small comfort for him to learn that the Commonwealth standing invitation episode had not been an entirely British initiative. The British Prime Minister was under immense pressure and Smith could sense that he was speaking largely with the voice of the Afro-Asian Bloc.

The issue now centred on the ability of the Rhodesian Government to satisfy the British that any change of status had the full support of the majority. Smith pointed to the ostensibly multiracial franchise and proposed a referendum of the electorate — which brought both men more or less back to square one. It seemed unnecessary for Home to explain to Smith that the majority meant the real majority, and certainly there was no point in Smith reminding Duncan Sandys that in 1961 he had negotiated a constitution on behalf of all the people of the country. A British general election was due in a matter of weeks and Home was disinclined to add his body to a battlefield already littered with Conservative corpses. In a somewhat defeatist frame of mind, both he and Sandys were content to let the issue drift. Smith was not prepared to do anything of the sort and devised a strategy to elicit black opinion, even though the Conservatives were not particularly interested in hearing it. He moved forward carefully but with no deliberate chicanery, since in those days Smith fully trusted the merits of his case. He genuinely believed that the nationalists were extremists, their followers thugs and the rest of the blacks reasonably moderate. The problem as he saw it was that a straightforward referendum held solely for blacks would fall prey to nationalist intimidation.

What Smith thought he knew about black opinion was anyone's guess — but he did know a thing or two about black politics. As Tredgold had observed of an earlier political generation, it would — and usually did — take very little to sway black opinion with the use of terror. It could be taken absolutely for granted that, following the announcement of such a referendum, levels of violence in the black areas would spiral. Therefore Smith instead looked to the chiefs to speak on behalf of the people.

The problem in this lay in the fact that, over the years since the occupation, the nation's traditional leadership had undergone a gradual induction into government service. Of late they had been chosen, appointed and removed when necessary by the government. They were given ceremonial uniforms and paid a regular stipend as virtual civil servants. There were a handful who could claim independence, but the majority had by and large been compromised. Smith heard numerous warnings, not least from Duncan Sandys, that a Council of Chiefs would not be considered an acceptable test of black opinion. Despite this though, he went ahead and ordered the convening of a Great Indaba to which over 600 chiefs were summoned.

The event took place on 22 October 1964 in Domboshawa, just outside Salisbury, where for five days the assembled chiefs debated the desirability of independence under the terms of the 1961 Constitution. Representatives from Australia, Austria, France, Norway, Portugal, Sweden, Greece and South Africa observed the event, but not a single official delegate represented the government of the United Kingdom. From the days of Cecil Rhodes and the much-loved Godfrey Huggins, how had it come to this?

A week before the Indaba, Britain had gone to the polls and, from the ashes of the Profumo Affair emerged a reinvigorated Labour phoenix. Prime Minister-elect Harold Wilson's victory was less than a landslide but it gave him the keys to Number Ten. This meant that Rhodesian whites could now expect to be stabbed in the chest as well as in the back. Naturally Wilson dismissed the Great Indaba as a publicity stunt, as he settled into office and began to weigh up Ian Smith.

Smith was given his black endorsement when the chiefs returned a solid verdict in his favour. Without doubt this result did reflect the limited scope of moderate black Rhodesia. Soon after the Indaba, a referendum of the white electorate was held over the same question and this returned a practically unanimous vote in favour. No mention of UDI was made at any time during the campaign, except to make clear that the referendum was not to be considered a vote for UDI ... as if anyone needed to be reminded that the blacks boycotted the ballot almost entirely.

Harold Wilson

At last there seemed to be two protagonists in office in Salisbury and Whitehall who were sufficiently secure to deal with one another. In the beginning, however, both governments were slow to break the ice — for the ice was particularly thick in that season, and the political waters dividing the two, colder than they had ever been.

The reason for this was largely the campaign platform upon which Wilson had chosen to fight the British general election. Perhaps not anticipating the difficulties ahead, he had revealed his hand very early on by committing to paper a radical position on Rhodesian independence. In a more or less open letter to a largely unknown nationalist by the name of Dr Elisha Mutasa, he laid bare the facts in a handful of ill-chosen words:

> The Labour Party is totally opposed to granting independence to Southern Rhodesia so long as the government of that country remains under the control of the white minority. We have repeatedly urged the British Government to negotiate a new Constitution with all the African and European parties represented in order to achieve a peaceful transition to African majority rule.[2]

These were indeed the facts laid bare — the same facts that had hampered the goodwill of men like Macmillan and Home, and would no doubt hamper Wilson now. Neither of Wilson's most recent predecessors would have been so frank about their positions, nor would Wilson be in the future, but the damage was done and the damage was severe.

The letter was unearthed and made public in the midst of the Great Indaba and immediately British credibility in respect of Rhodesia plummeted. Whites saw Harold Wilson as displaying a cavalier attitude to a problem that he evidently did not understand. It was, of course, probably asking too much of him — as an intellectual liberal — to have any real feeling for the crisis at that early stage. He could have offered no particular support for the continuance of white domination in the region, but it would not have been too much for him to keep his mouth shut at such a vital juncture. Smith, for his part, could have shrugged the matter off but he was in a fighting mood and made no particular effort to deny it. Traditionally Labour had been no friend of white Rhodesia and early communications between the two prime ministers tended to confirm this status.

Smith received an apparently cordial message from incoming Secretary of State for Commonwealth Affairs, Arthur Bottomley, who was shortly due to travel to Zambia for talks with Kaunda. Bottomley suggested that prior to his Kaunda meeting, he and Smith should meet in Salisbury for a round of familiarisation talks. He added the proviso that he would only consider doing so if the meeting included Ndabaningi Sithole and Joshua Nkomo.

This was a bad start and the offer was immediately rejected. The two nationalists, Smith reminded Bottomley, were imprisoned not for political reasons but for their criminal malfeasance. The chiefs, who at that moment were winding up their indaba, represented black opinion in Rhodesia. Bottomley could meet as many of these men as he wished with the blessing of the Rhodesian Government. Bottomley was effectively silenced by this but a letter followed from Wilson expressing regret that Smith had chosen to snub his Secretary of State. Wilson then invited Smith to visit London for talks, which Smith declined claiming pressures of work.

Wilson must have been stung by something in the tone of Smith's reply, for his own response was immediate and angry. In effect it was a demand that Smith at once stated in writing, that there would be no unilateral declaration of independence, failing which the British Government would issue a public statement warning of the serious consequences of such a step.

Smith would have been quite within his rights to ignore this outburst, but he went one better and demanded from Wilson — in light of his letter to Dr Mutasa — that the British Prime Minister state in writing the exact position of his government on the question of Rhodesian independence. Neither statement was issued and after Wilson had taken a moment taken to regain his composure, he lowered the pitch and tried again. He assured the Rhodesian Prime Minister that if the two governments were to meet, Smith would not find the British unwilling to compromise.

As far as Smith was concerned, the question had been settled previously, most recently at the 1961 Constitutional Conference. Furthermore, the wishes of the black majority had been expressed through the Great Indaba, and whites had spoken in a referendum held shortly afterwards. All were in favour. What precisely, Smith demanded to know, was there to talk about? After a fortnight of reflection, he wrote Wilson a scathing letter demanding that his British counterpart — once and for all — submit a definitive reply on the question of independence.

'Once and for all', of course, is a concept alien to politics and Smith should have realised it. Wilson's reply when it came was laconic and stated simply that various items of financial aid promised to Rhodesia as part of the dissolution were premised on the understanding that relations between the two governments remained stable. Under current circumstances, however, irresponsible talk of UDI had undoubtedly thrown a shadow over future financial relations.3

Smith was enraged but before he could build up an honest head of steam, the squabble was interrupted by the death of Winston Churchill in January 1965. For the duration of the mourning period no member of the British family tree could in good conscience concern itself with any other official business. The break in personal hostilities came as a relief to both Smith and Wilson, while the funeral would force the two to at least shake hands. This, it was hoped, would draw some of the sting out of all the early unpleasantness.

In his prime ministerial clothes, Harold Wilson was undoubtedly a devious character. As an Oxford don he was well respected and as a liberal ideologue even more so, but as a political strategist he relied to an unhealthy extent on half truths, misrepresentation and deceit. Smith, on the other hand, was unusually straightforward for a politician and, if forced on occasion to manipulate the facts, he was rarely guilty of ignoring them. Moreover Smith had no intellectual pretensions, while Wilson at times seemed to have nothing else. Even before they met, the two men developed a deep mutual loathing. Smith despised Wilson because he felt that the British Prime Minister was allowing himself to be pushed around by the Afro-Asian bloc, and Wilson hated Smith because he was right.

There was nothing that Wilson could do to prevent Smith coming to London to attend the funeral, which he did. It was noted, however, that the Rhodesian leader received no invitation to a luncheon hosted by the Queen at Buckingham Palace the following day. To his credit, Smith took this apparent snub in his stride and lunched with friends instead. He was pleasantly surprised when the Queen's equerry found him in the restaurant and handed him a note expressing Her Majesty's regret at the misunderstanding and her hope that he would honour her by attending the luncheon immediately. Of course he did and the moment he arrived the Queen came over and could hardly have been more gracious. Shortly afterwards the two were joined by Prince Philip, and both showed great interest in Rhodesia, about which they were well informed.

If Smith's version of events is correct then Harold Wilson's hand was likely to have been behind the oversight, although Wilson naturally claimed that Smith had the invitation in his pocket all along. No one will ever know for sure, but on the surface Smith's seems the more plausible account. Rightly or wrongly, Harold Wilson was cast as the petty villain — a role he would play often and well from then on.

Once the embarrassment was put aside, Wilson made a virtue out of necessity and suggested to Smith that since they were both in town they surely ought to meet. As an afterthought he suggested that Smith and his party use the side entrance to 10 Downing Street so as not to alert the press. Smith agreed and recalled in his memoirs that a cordial and restrained meeting between the two concluded in an agreement that Bottomley and the Lord Chancellor Lord Gardiner would visit Rhodesia. There they would meet a cross section of the public, but Smith warned that their contacts should not include any nationalists detained on criminal charges.

For his part Wilson remembered that he found Smith 'extremely difficult, extremely sour and not a little bit offensive'.[4] He further records sitting through a virtual sermon as Smith gave vent to considerable spleen against his 'obsessional aversions'. These included the present and past British Governments, the United Nations and both the Commonwealth and its independent community of states.[5] Wilson also maintained that immediately after the meeting, Smith ran into the Australian and Canadian Prime Ministers and to them denied having met Wilson at all. When Wilson heard this he was forced to ponder the 'character of the man with whom I am dealing'.[6]

The following month Arthur Bottomley and Lord Gardiner duly arrived in Salisbury, and did indeed make a concerted effort to meet as wide a spectrum of the population as they could. As well as gathering opinion, it seemed the two were preoccupied with helping the decision makers understand the British terms for independence. These terms included the principal of unimpeded progress to majority rule; guarantees against retrogressive amendment of the Constitution; immediate improvement in the political status of blacks; progress towards the ending of racial discrimination; and the most vital point — that the British Government was completely satisfied that proposals for independence had the support of a majority of the population. This would all become known as NIBMAR, or No Independence Before Majority Rule.

From what Bottomley and Gardiner were able to gather, there seemed to be no clear consensus in the country. Those chiefs they met struck a note of caution by reminding the pair of the deep political decay that had struck wherever nationalist governments had prematurely been given control. They warned that the same fate almost certainly awaited Rhodesia. This was the most conservative opinion available from blacks but it nevertheless represented a very valid point. The nationalists demanded that power be handed to them immediately while a majority of whites insisted that it remain exclusively with them. One group had the power and the other had the numbers. It was a very tricky situation indeed.

Back in Britain Bottomley chose to gloss over much of what he had heard and presented a conciliatory report to the House of Commons. This in turn prompted Wilson to send a placatory message to Smith, but it still did not avoid expressing doubts about the validity of the Great Indaba.

Smith knew he now had a fight on his hands and decided that the moment was right to seek a fresh mandate. The ensuing campaign revealed a far deeper politicisation of the white population than had hitherto been seen, or indeed suspected. It also revealed how conclusive the swing of opinion to the right had been. After a ballot held on 7 May 1965, Smith was amazed at both the voter turnout and the subsequent result. If he had hoped for a substantial endorsement, he must have been very pleased indeed when the Rhodesian Front swept all 50 A-roll seats. The combined opposition was no opposition at all. Of the 15 B-roll seats, 13 went to black candidates, one to an Asian and one to a white independent.

In one fell swoop the Rhodesian Front had become omnipotent. The British were forced to sit up and take notice while the Afro-Asian bloc in both the United Nations and the Commonwealth was dismayed. The Indian charge d'affaires to Rhodesia told the Governor, Sir Humphrey Gibbs, that his government saw the election as a prelude to UDI and the Indian mission in Salisbury closed its doors forthwith.[7]

In July 1965 Minister of State Cledwyn Hughes arrived in Salisbury with the rather vague objective of finding grounds to reopen dialogue. To Smith and his Cabinet colleagues, dialogue was now little more than an irritating diversion. It was incumbent on them to give a hearing to any new British initiatives, but this was done with a patent lack of enthusiasm. Smith conceded only that he would accept the formation of a senate to house some black members who would wield a constitutional blocking mechanism. With a possible bicameral solution in mind, Bottomley replied that the proposals were under consideration. He suggested that a meeting between himself and the Rhodesian Prime Minister would be desirable, and amid dire warnings of growing Rhodesian impatience, Smith agreed.

Delegations from the two governments met in London in early October, but from the onset the Rhodesians were regaled by demands for constitutional amendments that would have left the 1961 Constitution virtually unrecognisable. Smith repeated his willingness to allow black opinion to be expressed through a senate but would be pushed no further than this. Wilson then suggested the repeal of the Land Apportionment Act which was clearly impossible. It was again obvious to the Rhodesians that Wilson had no intention of conceding a settlement that either de facto or de jure would leave power in the hands of whites.

At this point it is not inconceivable that Wilson also saw UDI as the cleanest solution to a growing problem. He believed — and said so — that a rebel Rhodesian government would be brought to its knees by economic action in a matter of weeks. He prevaricated, pondered and smoked copious quantities of Rhodesian pipe tobacco but he could not be drawn to make a definite commitment. The series of meetings ended with a blunt communiqué.

Despite intensive discussion, no means has been found of reconciling opposing views. No further meeting is planned.[8]

An interview with Smith had been scheduled by the BBC to appear on the popular weekly current affairs feature *Twenty-Four Hours*, and in an obvious effort to avoid a damaging buildup of sympathy, Wilson at the last minute caused the interview to be cancelled. True to form, he denied this but was drawn to admit it later — not that there was ever any real doubt.

Before leaving London Smith made contact with old friends in the Conservative Party and through leaders Edward Heath and Selwyn Lloyd he proposed a treaty that would guarantee no regression of black political rights. Wilson accepted the suggestion — although it is unlikely that he took it very seriously — and proposed a final meeting to hammer out the details. The two men duly met in an atmosphere somewhat more cordial than hitherto. However, except for a vague commitment by the British Prime Minister that he would consider the new proposal, no serious movement was recorded.

Wilson then immediately poured cold water over the suggestion in a television appearance where he reiterated the dangers of UDI and the likely consequences to Rhodesia should it be declared. He concluded with a heartfelt but no doubt strategic plea:

> I know I speak for everyone in these islands, all parties, all people, when I say to Mister Smith: Prime Minister, think again.[9]

Smith's response was just as emotional. In what he termed an eleventh hour petition to the British Government, he repeated his Cabinet's terms of settlement and appealed to the Queen to act with goodwill and decency in the treatment of her kith and kin abroad.

These submissions had an air of finality about them, yet there was more to come. Wilson contacted Smith and showing some signs of alarm, suggested that he and Bottomley fly out and try one more time to find common ground. This appeared to be little more that a propaganda ploy designed to portray Wilson as the reasonable party. He could not have been under any illusion that this was indeed the eleventh hour, but it has never been demonstrated that he was seriously interested in averting a rebellion.

Wilson arrived in Rhodesia on 25 October at the head of a large and impressive entourage and wasted no time in trying to stretch and manipulate Smith's offer of a treaty. This merely succeeded in infuriating Smith who was highly sensitive to any hint of political manipulation. Wilson then embarked on an extravagant tour of inspection of the country. Before leaving, he handed Smith a letter from Her Majesty the Queen. The letter was handwritten and read:

> Dear Mr Smith,
>
> I have followed the recent discussions between the British Government and your government with the closest concern and am glad to know that Mr Wilson will be paying you a visit.
>
> I earnestly hope that your discussion in finding a solution to the current difficulties succeeds.
>
> I would be glad if you would accept my best wishes and convey them to all my people in your country, whose welfare and happiness I have very closely at heart.
>
> Yours sincerely,
> Elisabeth R.

It is unfortunate that Smith took this to imply that Wilson had somehow subverted the traditional impartiality of the Queen. To believe this, Smith's faith in the British must have been damaged beyond repair. Yet this was the impression he gave and it added yet more grist to the anti-British mill.

Some satisfaction was felt when Smith learned that Wilson's discussions with Sithole and Nkomo had been both difficult and acrimonious. He hoped this would help the British Prime Minister to realise that the Rhodesian Government was dealing with a mob of unprincipled fanatics. Wilson was told by the imprisoned nationalists that they would entertain nothing less than the immediate use of British force to effect majority rule. In reply Wilson made it plain that the use of force was out of the question. Lord Devonshire had earlier stressed to Nkomo that an overnight handover to majority rule was not in Britain's immediate plans, and nothing had changed. A military strike would necessitate an immediate handover and that was much further than Wilson was prepared to go. In the absence of a phased and constitutional exchange of power, the blacks would simply have to wait.[10]

On the back of this hard message, Wilson was guilty perhaps of improvising a smokescreen. He discovered that neither Sithole nor Nkomo had been fed by the prison service on the day that they had been brought to Salisbury to meet with him. They had been kept in a holding cell for most of the day with no refreshments at all. Wilson made a huge fuss over this incident — no doubt because it diverted attention from matters for which he might be held accountable. The nationalists faced open-ended prison terms that were likely to end only when they toppled the government and, of this, he could offer no immediate prospect. By making it known that military force would not be contemplated in the event of UDI, Wilson provided impetus to Smith and his colleagues to press ahead with it.

In the end Wilson could come up with nothing better then than to propose a royal commission of inquiry with ample terms of reference, and to this Smith warily agreed. Wilson conceded that if the commission produced a report favourable to the Rhodesians, then there would be little he could do but accept it. If this was to be believed, it was music to Rhodesian ears. The principal was agreed upon and Wilson departed, leaving Smith with the feeling that it all seemed a little too good to be true.

Soon the terms of reference arrived in Salisbury for Cabinet approval. A codicil had been attached stating that Whitehall would not commit itself in advance to accepting the report. In other words, if the British did not like what they heard they would not accept it. This, of course, simply put the situation right back to square one.

Smith and his cabinet, meanwhile, continued laying the groundwork for UDI. Wilson greased the wheels by confirming in an address to the British nation on 30 October 1965 that force would not be used against Rhodesia.

> If there are those in this country who are thinking in terms of a thunderbolt, hurtling through the sky and destroying their enemy, a thunderbolt in the shape of the Royal Air Force, let me say this thunderbolt will not be coming.[11]

45

Kith and kin

Calls for a violent solution were not confined to the humble chamber of a police holding cell in Salisbury. As demoralised and depressed as the two nationalist leaders might have been, they were well informed and knew that they had powerful support elsewhere. Seen in this context, it is possible to feel some sympathy for the way in which Harold Wilson handled his difficult relationship with Ian Smith. He not only had the partisanship of his own legislature to consider, but also persistent pressure from within the United Nations and the Commonwealth. Canada and Australia, with their own skewed history in such matters, were to be found aggressively campaigning against white Rhodesia in both forums. By 1965, the issue was so dominating proceedings in the Commonwealth, that there were fears that the organisation was evolving into an African pressure group. If accusations of treachery and disloyalty made against Britain by white Rhodesia were true, then it seems odd that Wilson should have fought so hard on behalf of the British Government for the sole right to handle the Rhodesian crisis.

The pressure against the British Government remained unrelenting. On 5 May 1965 the UN Security Council adopted a unanimous resolution calling on Britain — and indeed warning her — not to accept a unilateral declaration of independence by Rhodesia. During the London Commonwealth Prime Ministers Conference of that same year, Dr Kwame Nkrumah weighed in by proposing a six point plan, recommending that if a constitutional conference embracing all parties was not convened, then Britain should suspend the current constitution, put in place an interim and representative government and prepare the country for a general election based on universal suffrage. The doyen of the African revolution, Julius Nyerere, gave powerful vocal support to this plan, adding his reproach to Britain for failing to use force in Rhodesia as she had done in Cyprus, Kenya, Aden and British Guiana. He was dismissive of Wilson's claims that the logistics and risks of mounting a military invasion were prohibitive.

Time and again the kith and kin argument was used against Wilson, and in truth it was not an entirely false argument. Wilson knew that Her Majesty's Armed Forces would fight where they were ordered to, but he also knew that no command on earth would make them happy about it. Rhodesian whites were seen in many influential quarters as being vilified for nothing more than keeping aloft the shredded banner of Anglo-Saxon dignity. If Smith was gambling on this perception he was doing so with very fair odds. The mood of the British public was well illustrated by a cover of *Private Eye* magazine featuring a cartoon by Gerald Scarfe; Smith was depicted with his unbelted trousers down, forcing a black man's face to his backside; the caption read: 'Kith my arse!'[1]

Black leaders were inclined to feel that they had kissed too many white arses already and through the young Organisation of African Unity, their voices were growing increasingly strident. At its Assembly of Heads of State and Government meeting held in Accra on 25 October 1965, the assembled leaders, including such notorious demagogues as Mobuto Sese Seko, declared that they were deeply concerned with Britain's apparent support of a minority and racist government. Rhodesia, the organisation declared, was a threat to world peace. A resolution was adopted, deploring the refusal of the United Kingdom Government to meet with firmness the threat of a unilateral declaration of independence. It further called on Britain to suspend the 1961 Constitution and take the necessary steps — including armed force — to resume the administration of the territory. Failure to do this would result in members reconsidering all political, economic, diplomatic and financial relations with Britain.[2]

* * *

The OAU resolution was under debate as Harold Wilson was winding up his eleventh hour visit to Rhodesia. As he left Salisbury, he had a strong feeling that Smith was about to do the unthinkable. He must have hoped most fervently that a rebel government would collapse — as he had widely predicted it would. If it did not he was in for a very rocky ride indeed.

Advance preparations for a unilateral declaration of independence were now openly under way. Foreign reserves were moved out of England and placed in South Africa. Those service chiefs and senior civil servants whose loyalties were suspect were urged to resign, and indeed after the declaration a handful did. Governor Sir Humphrey Gibbs found himself in a most uncomfortable position, for his loyalties were divided between the Crown that he served and the country he had adopted in the 1920s.

Gibbs was a farmer by vocation and was a reluctant participant in politics. This was evidenced by the fact that he underwent only one parliamentary session as an MP before returning to the land. He had accepted the office of Governor on the understanding that the appointment would be brief. He could not in 1959 have known that he would soon be drawn into one of the most entangled affairs of empire since the American War of Independence.

Gibbs made no secret of the fact that he was cold on the issue of UDI, and so did Welensky — even though both fully supported the concept of independence under the 1961 Constitution. Sir Humphrey's first instinct on the matter was to resign. Obviously, however, Whitehall needed a dependable presence in Salisbury and Gibbs was repeatedly advised by both government and opposition politicians to sit tight. Alec Douglas Home gave him the rather forlorn advice that he would be justified in taking any measures that were open to him to secure respect for the Constitution, but what these might be was never said.

Gibbs sounded out Ken Flower — the phlegmatic head of the Central Intelligence Organisation and another who consistently opposed UDI — on the likely reaction of the armed forces, if he tried to oppose unilateral independence. Flower confirmed that the options were few. Technically Gibbs was empowered to declare a UDI government illegal and call on the chiefs of staff to enforce the restoration of legality. Although Flower had no doubt that the service chiefs would follow the Governor's lead, he expressed some doubt as to the willingness of the average Rhodesian trooper to exchange his tangible loyalty to Smith, for some theoretical allegiance to the Crown.

The judiciary too was placed in a difficult position. Some on the bench advocated the issuing of a common statement that they would regard UDI as illegal while others maintained that this would represent unwarranted interference in the political process. The conundrum was solved by a message from the Lord Chancellor, saying that it could not be considered treasonable for judges to remain in office in the event of UDI.[3]

The government, meanwhile, tried to gain complete control over the media and in the case of the electronic services, it succeeded. By the end of 1964 the Parliamentary Secretary for Information had purged the television and radio stations to the extent that they had both become virtual propaganda arms of the government. The Argus press maintained its long history of independence, although a certain necessary caution began to characterise its criticism of the government.

After securing an undated proclamation of a State of Emergency from the Governor, Smith put the police and armed forces on standby, as preparations continued for a declaration early in November.

On 10 November as the full Cabinet was discussing the impending break, the British High Commissioner appeared with an oral message from Wilson to Smith. However, it shed no new light on the situation and offered no new hope. After the meeting, all ministers were sent home, with instructions from the Prime Minister to give the matter a last night of reflection. The following morning, as the Cabinet assembled to give final consideration to the matter, a telephone call from Harold Wilson came through. Smith had a protracted conversation with him, but again nothing new was put on the table and it was painfully clear that stalemate had been reached.

Smith joined his colleagues in the Cabinet Room and put the leading question to them. Was it to be Yes or No? Each minister around the table nodded his head. The decision was unanimous. Rhodesia would make a Unilateral Declaration of Independence forthwith. It was 11 November 1965, the eleventh hour of the eleventh day of the eleventh month — the deeply symbolic moment when Armistice in World War-I had been declared 47 years before. Rhodesia was on its own.

46

UDI — the beginning of the end

Arguably the man most unfairly burdened by UDI was the Governor. On the morning that UDI was declared Smith and his closest political ally Clifford Dupont visited Gibbs where Dupont was saddened to see the Governor so visibly distressed. He was moved by what he described as the situation in which 'this loyal Englishman, who had spent so much of his life in Rhodesia, found himself'.[2] In this, Dupont might easily have been describing himself, and indeed a majority of other Rhodesian whites, including most who had signed the declaration. What made Dupont a Rhodesian and Gibbs, who had arrived in the country nearly twenty years earlier than Dupont, a loyal Englishman who had spent so much of his life in Rhodesia, was Gibbs' subsequent reaction to and refusal to accept the illegal declaration.

When the matter came out into the open, Gibbs' wish was to dispense immediately with his responsibility as Governor and resign. 'Gentlemen,' he told his visitors, 'you realise that I cannot condone your decision. I presume you want me to retire to my farm and see if I can get any more milk out of my cows?'[3] Smith and Dupont, relieved no doubt, both smiled and agreed that this would be for the best. Gibbs was relieved too, since he had no desire to engage in a battle of wills with Smith and his new government. He asked for a few days grace while he went up to Inyanga for some rest and contemplation before making any announcements.

He arrived home from Inyanga to find that Chief Justice Sir Hugh Beadle had hurriedly returned from a visit to London, with a plea for him from Whitehall. Sir Humphrey held the governorship of Southern Rhodesia in a caretaker capacity, having accepted the appointment in the belief that legal independence was around the corner. Suddenly, however, his position had become much more than ceremonial and clearly could not be relinquished while the country was in such legal hiatus. It was imperative to the British Government that their representative should remain in office.

The decision was confirmed on 15 November when Gibbs informed the Rhodesian Government that he was to stay on as the legal governor, in order to support the current constitution. By this announcement, Gibbs effectively dismissed Smith and his Cabinet, leaving Rhodesia with no legitimate government. Gibbs paradoxically advised officials of the judiciary, the armed forces and the police that it was their primary obligation to maintain law and order in the country. Otherwise, his comfortless instructions were to just sit tight and hold the fort as best he could. Sir Hugh Beadle joined him at Government House in a gesture of official solidarity.

The local Cabinet's response was to supplant the post of governor with a functionary who was somewhat less than a president, and had the awkward title of Officer Administering the Government. The officer so named was Clifford Dupont who took the oath of office two days later. He remained in his ministerial home in Salisbury while Gibbs continued his occupation of Government House in what was termed 'his private capacity'.

Immediately after Dupont's appointment, the Government set about establishing the terms of its own existence. It promptly abolished any right of appeal to the Privy Council and vested the right to alter the entrenched clauses of the Constitution in a two-thirds majority, and not by a referendum of each of the racial groups as before. The existing franchise for the moment remained unchanged, as did the Constitutional Council, the Declaration of Rights and the inviolability of the Tribal Trust Lands. Gibbs was informed that the Rhodesian Government was in effective control of the country and that any instructions that he received from Whitehall no longer had any validity.

Sir Humphrey's occupation of Government House began what became known as the Battle of the Books. The Government provided books in all the main centres so that citizens could sign an expression of loyalty to the person of the Queen — but in effect the new Rhodesian Government. Gibbs, on the other hand, opened a book at Government House and invited loyal citizens to express their allegiance to him as the Queen's representative. The Government books received a great many more signatures, but qualitatively Gibbs triumphed. Lord Malvern, erstwhile Godfrey Huggins, made a significant point of putting his signature in the Governor's book and, with his encouragement, many others of the old establishment followed suit.

For three and a half years Gibbs lived in a state of virtual house arrest in the large and empty Government House. He seldom left the property, worrying that if he did some government official would creep in and lock him out. This was not an idle fear, for although no such attempt was made, the government did have his telephone lines disconnected and his official car and salary discontinued. He was connected by telephone only to London and the British mission in Salisbury. Any efforts he made to publicise his situation were frustrated by a heavy-handed censorship of the media.

The Argus press was not accustomed to this type of treatment, and responded by producing editions of the *Rhodesia Herald* and other newspapers with more blank spaces on the pages than print. Even Huggins was censored from airing his views, and when finally his opinions were published, it was in the *Times* of London and he had some sobering advice for his successors.

'Surely they have the wit to learn', Huggins wrote, 'if they can learn anything, that what a revolting minority can do, a revolting majority can do so much better.'[4]

It was Lord Malvern and others of the old school, like Sir Roy Welensky, who maintained a fund to support Sir Humphrey throughout his vigil. Smith's administration could easily have removed him from Government House if it had felt the need, and perhaps for Gibbs' own sake that would have been for the best. His protest cried out for some sort of solution, but the Government did nothing. It was an awkward situation: Gibbs could not publicly back down and for many reasons, some sentimental and some political, no one in government really wanted to force him out.

Gibbs received visits from several high ranking military officers. All reaffirmed their loyalty to the Crown and urged Gibbs to issue a warrant of arrest for Smith and Dupont. However, even if he had wanted to, Sir Humphrey clearly had no power to attempt this. As Ken Flower among many others had warned him, the brass did not necessarily speak for the rank and file. It is notable that Brigadier Rodney Putterill had found it necessary to reprimand Rhodesia Light Infantry commanding officer Peter Walls, for allowing his men to wear paper hats reading: 'RLI for UDI' at a 1964 Christmas party.[5] Any attempt to arrest the military conspirators would obviously be an open invitation for a coup d'etat. Therefore the Governor had no option but to dig in and sit it out, which in the end was precisely what he did.

Sanctions

On the political and diplomatic front, UDI triggered a bitter struggle between Britain and her wayward colony. These were some of the words that Ian Smith chose in a radio broadcast to announce UDI:

We Rhodesians have rejected the doctrinaire philosophy of appeasement and surrender. The decision which we have taken today is a refusal by Rhodesians to sell their birthright. And, even if we were to surrender, does anyone believe that Rhodesia would be the last target of the Communists in the Afro-Asian bloc? We have struck a blow for the preservation of justice, civilisation and Christianity; and in the spirit of this belief we have this day assumed our sovereign independence. God bless you all.

Thus Ian Smith staked out the twin terms of his revolution. The first was an appeal to a sense of patriotism that could only exist among a handful of the Rhodesian whites. To the few like himself, who had been born in Rhodesia and had acquired some sense of genuine belonging, his words rang true. To the majority who were immigrants, it would seem to stretch a point mightily to assume that they were committed patriots. This was not the land of their ancestors, nor even of their parents. Of the 16 ministers who were party to the decision to declare UDI, only six, including Smith, had actually been born in Rhodesia.[6]

Smith also attempted to obscure the fundamental issue — the failure of the black and white races of Rhodesia to coexist — with a crusade against communism and the threat it posed to the entire Christian world. If communists had infiltrated the Afro-Asian bloc, as Smith and others implied, then it was only in keeping with the mood of the times. If nothing else, the natural cupidity of Africa offered very stony ground for Marxism, and if moral and material support were not forthcoming from elsewhere, then Africans were as communist as it was necessary to be.

Smith might have fooled a handful of Rhodesians with this sort of propaganda but he certainly fooled nobody else. What he wanted to say — and what a majority of whites probably heard him say — was that the utter and proven catastrophe of black rule must be avoided in Rhodesia at all costs. He took pleasure in noting that as the news became general, the Commonwealth and the United Nations both exploded with the wrath of a smoked beehive.

Harold Wilson was quick to try and douse the fury by assuring his international partners that it was the intention of the British Government to restore legality promptly and freedom to Rhodesia. To this, Smith later added in own peculiar style of commentary — spiced, as it so often was, with an awkward seam of truth: 'Had he [Wilson] been truthful he would have admitted that there was more freedom in Rhodesia than in any other country in Africa.'[7]

Although this was undoubtedly so, Smith refused point blank to accept the contemporary political realties that went with it. As Lord Devonshire had said in 1923, and Conservative Colonial Secretary Ian Macleod repeated during the Nyasaland crisis:

> No amount of colonial development and welfare, and no rate of economic improvement, could be an adequate substitute for a government with which the majority of the nation felt identified.

This became the adopted policy of both the Conservative and Labour parties with regard to any grant of independence to Rhodesia. Rhodesia's record of good governance over the previous 40 years was commendable and certainly unique, but not in the slightest bit relevant.

An unforeseen consequence of UDI was to make it politically and morally acceptable for the guerrilla factions to wage their freedom struggle by any means against the illegal and indeed pariah government of Rhodesia. No less of a blunder was to make it impossible in the long term for friendly countries, namely Portugal and South Africa, to give the kind of support they were able to render to a legal government. Moreover, no country would risk recognising an illegal declaration until Britain did, and Britain could now never do so. Every discussion henceforth hinged on a return to legality.

This would mean Smith handing power back to the Governor — something that was out of the question. Under the proclamation of UDI, constitutional links between Britain and Rhodesia had been severed completely for the duration of the struggle.

The qualitative value of Smith's actions can best be judged by a simple question. Since it had proved impossible to persuade successive British administrations that good government was more important than self government — this when Rhodesia was negotiating as a lawful government under the 1961 Constitution — how could it hope to do better as an illegal government under an illegal constitution?

A debate to formulate a rapid response to UDI was held in the House of Commons on the very day that independence was declared. Wilson made the point that although Rhodesia had seized her independence, she might have improved her chances of a soft landing by sticking with the Crown. Wilson, of course, realised that despite this a severe mauling at the hands of the Afro-Asian bloc was inevitable:

> The problem will be to avert excessive action by the United Nations. As for the economic sanctions, I think that it will be right for us to concentrate on trying to get other nations to follow our lead rather than seeing them get too far ahead of us.[8]

With almost unprecedented haste the British Parliament endorsed the Southern Rhodesia Act of 1965 which stated that the territory continued to be a part of Her Majesty's dominions and by Order in Council gave power to the Government to impose economic and other sanctions.

An assortment of sanctions was quickly rolled out and implemented. The British High Commissioner was withdrawn from Salisbury and his opposite number was expelled from London. Economic measures included a moratorium on the export of arms and spare parts and on British aid to Rhodesia. Rhodesia was removed from the sterling area and its access to the London capital market was halted, as was the export of British capital to Rhodesia. Export credit guarantees were withdrawn and Rhodesia was suspended from the Commonwealth Preference Area, along with an import ban on such products as Rhodesian sugar and tobacco.

However, crucial omissions from the list of banned products were various strategic minerals and Rhodesian beef. There was no mention of a fuel embargo either — a measure that would have been pivotal to the rapid success of any economic measures.

Whitehall now felt that it had done what was required, by applying a prescription tempered with traditional British moderation. But the free African nations, empowered by liberation, and happy to see their former master squirm, had no intention of allowing matters to be handled solely by British diplomacy. As the economic sanctions were being rolled out they were immediately condemned as inadequate. Wilson had threatened to deal firmly with a rebel Rhodesian government, but in the event his bark was rather louder than his bite; in the words of a wit of the time, he threw the book at the Rhodesians one page at a time.

Black diplomats beseeched the Security Council to take action, and the UN body was happy to comply. Within a week two new UN resolutions had been passed. The first called on all member states to neither recognise nor assist the rebel government. The second declared Rhodesia a threat to international peace and security. Both stopped short of any direct criticism of the British response, and no mandatory sanctions were imposed. The only abstention was France, which maintained the position that Rhodesia was a purely British problem.

The Rhodesia question also dominated the agenda of an emotional OAU Council of Ministers meeting, held in Addis Ababa a month later. The Council imposed a deadline on the United Kingdom to crush the rebellion, failing which all the member states of the OAU threatened, to sever diplomatic relations. It was also mooted that consideration be given by all member states to the possibility of using African force to assist the people of Zimbabwe.

Hastings Banda, who was about as non-aligned as an African president dared to be, had a good chuckle at the suggestion of military involvement. Ten Rhodesian mercenaries, he told his colleagues, could whip 5 000 so-called African soldiers. If Smith commanded it, the Rhodesian Army would conquer the whole of east and central Africa in a week.[9] This was probably not a total exaggeration, for even the British were less than sanguine about their chances against a belligerent Rhodesian Army. Gingerly, however, a squadron of RAF Javelins nosed south to Zambia to ease the mind of Kaunda who was convinced that the Rhodesians were about to invade his country.

The restructuring of relations between Britain and Rhodesia once again exposed the ludicrous and the ironic. Because Zambia still relied on Federal air traffic control, it was Salisbury that greeted the British pilots and guided them safely into Lusaka airport. Regular visits were then made by both RAF and British Army personnel to Victoria Falls and Kariba, culminating in several Christmas and New Year's Eve parties where Smith and Rhodesia were warmly toasted. Moreover, the RAF pilots and commanders made it amply clear that any order given to attack Rhodesia would be ignored.

As the weeks slipped by, Harold Wilson felt no easing of the pressure. Having taken with a pinch of salt African threats to sever diplomatic relations, he was astonished when 13 of their number did. Somalia, it was reported, borrowed a guide to British diplomatic procedure from the British Embassy in Mogadishu to familiarise itself with the process.[10] This was not the end of it either. As Wilson addressed the General Assembly the following morning, 20 African delegates stood up and walked out. The Prime Minister paused and watched the silent exodus before he gathered his composure and continued.

> Today we see some of our friends, passionate to intervene and unable to do so, directing their understandable anger not against Rhodesia but against Britain. All right, I understand that. But the British Government is not going to be deflected from the course that we are convinced is right, in which I believe the whole British people are behind us …

On this, a further 100 delegates from various OAU states stood up, and left the Assembly. Oh how the mighty had fallen!

In response to it all, Wilson — to his credit — did not give away much. He agreed to expand the scope of British sanctions, to include a ban on the import of most minerals including copper, chrome and asbestos — and the all-important oil embargo was put in place. This was still not enough to stop a two day emergency Commonwealth conference held in Lagos in January 1966 — the first in the history of the organisation not held in London — where these new measures solicited a surly but largely acquiescent response. The Rhodesia crisis was exhaustively discussed and once again calls were made for Britain to use force to end the rebellion. Wilson clung to his assurances that the rebellion would be over in weeks rather than months, but as weeks passed, and then months, his hopes of a Rhodesian collapse began to fade.

Arguably, Harold Wilson saved white Rhodesia. His piecemeal imposition of economic sanctions gave the country time to catch its breath before the full weight of the embargo was felt. Whether this was due to regard for British kith and kin or simply a failed policy, it is hard to say. Certainly Wilson received no gratitude. He was the man white Rhodesians most loved to hate, and forever more they would jeer and gloat at the now pathos Albion.

The British Government went on to freeze Rhodesian assets held in the United Kingdom, although the Treasury had already transferred the country's foreign reserves to South Africa. In reply, monies that were due to be paid to Britain as loan repayments, interest and dividends were diverted into a fund until it became appropriate to release them. Rhodesia was left flush with liquidity and supremely self-confident. Edgar Whitehead, who by then had left Rhodesia, and was enjoying his retirement in Britain, wrote an article in the *Spectator* that ridiculed British sanctions and was harshly critical of the British people.

> They have forgotten what they would have done to anybody in 1940 who suggested that they should give in to Hitler, because if not they would be subjected to sanctions and a shortage of petrol.[11]

The British Treasury raised the bar further, by stopping payment to their pensioners living in Rhodesia. The Rhodesian Government responded by making a point of ensuring that all Rhodesian pensioners living in Britain received their full benefits. Britain cut off fuel supplies to Rhodesia so Rhodesia cut off fuel supplies to Zambia. The British Government was then compelled to deliver emergency fuel shipments from Tanzania and Mozambique, to Lusaka by RAF transport aircraft. It cost the British taxpayer 4 000 gallons of aviation fuel to airlift 2 500 gallons of petrol.[12] For Zambia the effect was catastrophic and there was much more to come. This was just the first blow in a 15-year beating that Zambia was to suffer at the hands of Rhodesia. Her crime was to be a member of the Afro-Asian bloc, that also happened to be a black neighbour of Rhodesia.

For its part, Rhodesia had more to worry about than sanctions in the first year of UDI. Of far greater concern was a severe drought that came at an unfortunate time. It affected most gravely those areas of Matabeleland and the dry southeast where cattle ranching was the traditional industry. Despite a huge effort to relocate cattle to wetter areas, to load beef into the cold storage system, and to transport vast quantities of fodder, catastrophic losses of cattle were recorded.

To keep fuel flowing, many of Rhodesia's old friends, including not a few in Britain, were willing to buck the system and supply what they could. The British Government was subject to repeated accusations that it was conniving with oil companies to circumvent its own sanctions. According to Liberal politician David Steel:

> Those who shipped in oil were not hostile powers. They were British companies, backed by the British Foreign Office, with the connivance of British Cabinet Ministers and the knowledge of the Prime Minister.[13]

Sources inside Mozambique and Portugal were quite candid about British and American involvement in the supply of fuel to Rhodesia. British businessmen Tiny Rowland, chairman of the ubiquitous Lonrho (London/Rhodesia) Corporation, revealed that about 60% of total supplies reaching Rhodesia, originated from Royal Dutch Shell and British Petroleum.[14]

The first few months of the oil embargo were obviously the most critical. Fuel rationing was quickly introduced, while companies and individuals from all over southern Africa came to Rhodesia's aid. Random shipments drawn from a variety of sources helped the country to surmount the initial shock of the embargo. Naturally the effort was not entirely benevolent and significant amounts of money changed hands. Enterprising Portuguese entrepreneur, Jorge Jardim, built a duty-free filling station a few miles east of the border town of Umtali, and estimated that 300 tons of product a month was moved across the border. Jardim and other Portuguese expatriates also controlled the main Sonarep oil refinery outside Lourenço Marques, through which most of Rhodesia's fuel would be routed for the next few years.

By the end of 1966 Rhodesia was listed as an official threat to world peace. The Royal Navy was tasked to mount a blockade off the coast of Mozambique to prevent fuel destined for Rhodesia landing at the port of Beira. Without a guarantee that he would receive full cooperation from both Portugal and South Africa, it is hard to imagine what Wilson hoped to achieve by this. The first two tankers carrying fuel for Rhodesia, the *Joanna V* and the *Manuela*, appeared on the horizon and docked in Beira without interference from the Royal Navy ships.

Purpose-built receiving facilities for Rhodesian petrol were speedily built at the port to avoid contaminating the Portuguese with any obvious evidence of their assisting Rhodesia. However, the expense of constructing this tank farm was wasted, when Jardim and his confederates pressured the Rhodesians not to take delivery of the *Joanna V* and *Manuela* cargoes. Ostensibly the reason was to again avoid compromising the Portuguese, but actually it was to divert the business back to the Sonarep refinery. Jardim owned a controlling interest in this plant and stood to make a fortune — which he did. In fairness it was also true that the same fuel could easily be consigned to South Africa from this depot before being redirected to Rhodesia. This was ultimately what happened and after some months of streamlining, this particular organ of the sanctions-busting machine worked without a hitch. In due course fuel rationing in Rhodesia was relaxed and eventually it disappeared altogether.

Despite sanctions, Rhodesia remained open for business on just about every front. Such vital strategic exports as chrome and tobacco, adjusted to the changing climate of business better than anybody could have hoped. To the average white man in the street, the disappearance of imported whisky and chocolate from the shelves, and a scarcity of certain spare parts, seemed to be the only noticeable effects of economic sanctions. It became a matter of pride to refuse Scotch whisky and anything else from the United Kingdom even when it was available.

In some respects, sanctions were proving to be positive for the people they were aimed at. A rapid diversification of industrial production provided substitutes for goods that had been embargoed. A natural aptitude for tricky business was discovered in the commercial sector and many entrepreneurs made fortunes for themselves. Generally, the economy continued to be buoyant and morale remained high.

White Rhodesians loved audacity with a stiff splash of deeds of derring-do, and sanctions-busting offered plenty of opportunity for this. Circumventing sanctions consisted mainly of the kind of back door dealing that saw Swazi veterinary documents attached to Rhodesian beef bound for black African markets. Chrome destined for the United States was routed through South Africa where, through relatively simple sleight of hand, it acquired a South African identity. Rhodesia was a reliable trading partner and her terms of trade were favourable. Old friends and business links were camouflaged and kept mobile. For all intents and purposes Rhodesia was limited in her international trade only by what she could absorb and produce. For a few it was a thrilling subterfuge, but for the majority it was business as usual, and plenty of it.

Apart from numerous companies and individuals in the UK, there were many others still willing to trade with Rhodesia. The French ignored sanctions thanks to an evergreen willingness to thumb their noses at the British. Italians joined the party because of the significant number of Italians in Rhodesia, and likewise the Greeks who were virtually all involved in one way or another with trade. The Portuguese held the line thanks to the interdependence of the Mozambican and Rhodesian economies, and the fact that President Salazar was determined to see anti-colonialism fail in southern Africa.

Jack Malloch, the legendary fighter ace and comrade-in-arms of Ian Smith, was the *Boys' Own* hero who regarded sanctions-busting as a game he could excel at. Apart from the mundane distribution of Rhodesian beef and produce around Africa, he worked covertly on behalf of the government — and indeed on behalf of quite a few governments. He was the genuine article and his exploits are the stuff of a dedicated biography, though for the purposes of this narrative, one or two are worth mentioning.

After World War-II, Malloch scraped together enough money to buy a handful of surplus military aircraft and, in 1964 he formed the semi-commercial, semi-official airfreight company Air Trans Africa, later with undisclosed financial help from the CIO. The main object of the company was, of course, to bust sanctions, but thanks to Malloch's extraordinary network of connections all over Africa — and indeed all over the world — he was also an intelligence handler's dream.

Air Trans Africa operated Lockheed Super Constellations, Douglas DC-4s and DC-7s. Historian Peter Stiff, who knew Malloch personally and conducted security work for him, remembers: 'He went where the money was and where nobody was competing for cargoes ... he flew for the Belgians in the Congo, gladly assisted the French in central and west Africa, the Portuguese in Angola, the CIA wherever and the British MI-6 in the Sudan and other Arab countries.'[15] Most notably Malloch became a lifeline for the besieged government of independent Biafra, a state in the Nigerian Federation that fought a bitter secessionist war from May 1967 to January 1970. Soon after the outbreak of this conflict, the Rhodesian CIO opened an air bridge between Libreville in Gabon and Uli in Biafra. South Africa provided logistical help and military training to the government of Biafra and also used Jack Malloch's aircraft for transport in and out.

A curiosity of the Biafran crisis was that both the breakaway republic and Nigeria itself were financing the war with identical currency. The Nigerian Central Bank was forced to withdraw and replace the existing banknotes, which would render Biafran reserves worthless. Every available aircraft was stuffed full with banknotes that were shipped to Switzerland to be exchanged at a discount on the international market. A new Biafran currency was minted and, on behalf of the CIO, Malloch was contracted to fly it in. However during a routine fuel stop in Lome, the Togolese capital, Malloch's aircraft was inexplicably impounded, the banknotes confiscated and the crew arrested. For the next five months Malloch was held in a fetid Togolese prison while the CIO, with the help of the French, negotiated his release. Having lost his aircraft, Malloch did what was by then expected of him or any other true-blue Rhodesian maverick. He flew into an unidentified black country and stole a DC-7 that he knew was parked regularly at the far end of an airstrip.

In this way Malloch acquired fresh aircraft to replace the many that disappeared, burned on the tarmac, rendered politically or mechanically inoperable. The acquisition of replacement aircraft was in itself a triumph over sanctions. He freely spent CIO funds, that were given equally freely to keep the intelligence and sanctions-busting operations moving at full capacity.

Jack Malloch's love of aviation brought him back to his roots, when he recovered a Spitfire that had been mounted on a plinth outside New Sarum airbase and completely restored the aircraft. One day in March 1982 Malloch disappeared in his Spitfire and some time later was discovered dead in the wreckage. If his service in 237 (Rhodesia) Squadron RAF, during World War-II can be said to be the beginning, then surely dying behind the controls of a classic World War-II fighter aircraft was as apt an end as any man of action could hope for.

Bush War

The ZANU leadership detained at Sikombela Detention Centre at last recognised that they had a fight on their hands, and met to formulate a military strategy that would coincide with the momentum of UDI. A number of directives were issued to the leadership abroad concerning the future conduct of the armed struggle. The most important of these was the Sikombela Declaration, that authorised Herbert Chitepo to establish a dedicated war council to be known by its Shona equivalent of *Dare re Chimurenga*. The Dare was to be appointed for the purpose of coordinating a rational approach to the armed struggle, and Chitepo was to add to it both a revolutionary council and a guerrilla army. It will be remembered that two years earlier James Chikerema had been similarly appointed by

ZAPU as head of 'Special Affairs', which echoed the proposed functions of the ZANU Dare by creating a structure within the party specifically for the purpose of recruiting and arranging for guerrilla training.

By 1965, ZANU was still labouring under the general mistrust of the main Frontline leaders who saw it as an upstart splinter group guilty of splitting an otherwise united movement. It was therefore only with considerable difficulty that Chitepo was able to raise the funds necessary to source weapons and establish training facilities. Utilising his Tanzanian connections, he was eventually able to secure facilities at Intumbi Reefs, a disused goldmine of the German colonial era, not far from Mbeya. There William Ndangana and Felix Santana — the two survivors of the Crocodile Gang, and both relatively salted veterans by then — commenced training an initial intake of 24 men.

Unfortunately for them, some devils of old had followed the intake to Intumbi, for within the group were Rhodesian agents which effectively meant that before the recruits even laid their hands on a weapon or stepped back into Rhodesia, they were as good as dead. They crossed the Zambezi into Rhodesia in April 1966 with orders to make their way inland to Sinoia. There they were to split up into separate attack groups and proceed in-country on a variety of missions. The first group was briefed to destroy the Feruka Oil Refinery on the outskirts of Umtali, but was tracked and arrested before it could get anywhere near its target.[16] The second set off towards Fort Victoria but was likewise accounted for almost immediately. The third remained at large for longer by integrating with the local tribesmen in the Zvimba area. The fourth, calling itself the Armageddon Group, made camp on a large commercial farm in the Sinoia area owned by Noel Edwards.

According to intelligence chief Ken Flower, this fourth group was under Special Branch observation. Despite a half-hearted attack on a police station and an even weaker attempt to disrupt the national power supply by destroying an electricity pylon, it did not represent a significant threat. Therefore, Flower argued, little was to be gained by making martyrs of the men, particularly since the war was at a stage where intelligence accumulation counted for more than operational kills.[17] However, information reached Special Branch that, after a meeting with ZANU contact men who were due to drive up from Salisbury on 27 April, the group would mount its first planned attack against a white farmstead. This of course escalated the urgency of the matter.

Apparently some disagreement existed within the Operations Coordinating Committee. Flower implied that the Commissioner of Police, 'Slash' Barfoot, made the case that the BSAP — acting alone — was the agency best able to handle any aspect of subversion. Barfoot was anxious to be seen as actively complying with the Government's demand for 'the toughest possible action against terrorists'. Suggesting a passing breeze of inter-service rivalry, it seems that the BSAP wished to remind both itself and the country at large, that it was the senior regiment in the country and still the most effective line of defence. All this, though, remains a matter for speculation because many sometimes conflicting accounts of the same incident are available.

It is unequivocal that, as the matter was debated, Chief Superintendent John Cannon, then Officer Commanding BSAP Lomagundi District — the immediate area under which the incident fell — urged Commissioner Barfoot to invite the army to conduct the operation. The police, it was argued, were at that time poorly armed relative to the insurgents. The latter could deploy modern Soviet-supplied automatic weapons against the police armoury of Sterling sub-machine guns, World War-I vintage Lee Enfield .303s and Greener single shot shotguns. Cannon's suggestion was vetoed, on the grounds that the group were law-breakers and it was the duty of police and police reservists to arrest or kill them.

In the event, helicopters were deployed by the Air Force and an air-supported ground operation — conducted primarily by police regulars and reservists — accounted relatively easily for all seven gang members. There were no Security Force casualties or damage to the helicopters. More difficult to handle were the ramifications that followed. The Operations Coordinating Committee meeting, held immediately after the operation, was tense and combative with accusations and counter-accusations of bad faith. It was later agreed that any incidents that drifted beyond the control of a single service would be dealt with by the combined operations of all arms of the Security Forces. Some portrayed this as the BSAP — thereafter deciding to seek the assistance of the army as and when necessary. However, it was suggested by others, Flower among them, that it was a trimming of the powers previously enjoyed by the BSAP as the nation's first line of defence. Whatever the case, the incident catalysed the birth of the Joint Operational Command (JOC), the structure under which the war would be fought from then on.[18]

From the nationalist perspective, the incident was both a tragedy and a godsend. The group of seven died with undoubted courage, and as Flower had predicted, they earned the tributes of their comrades, leaders and the general black public. Even Flower conceded that the nationalists had learnt the necessary lessons with great courage and commitment, noting that guerrillas continued to penetrate the country knowing full well that most of those who had preceded them had been killed or captured.

The 'battle' was awarded a depth of significance by the nationalists that far exceeded its merits as a military operation, and was fully exploited for its obvious propaganda value. The Battle of Sinoia (Chinoyi) provided the first necessary crop of martyrs to found a war mythology. Most importantly though, it allowed ZANU to claim first blood vis-à-vis ZAPU in the shooting war. The day, 28 April, is now celebrated annually as Chimurenga Day, and in ZANU history remains the official start of the Liberation Struggle, or Second Chimurenga.

The single group of guerrillas still at large made their way to Johannes Viljoen's Nevada Farm situated between Sinoia and Hartley. On 18 May 1966 Viljoen responded to a loud knock on his front door, where he was confronted by a group of armed men. His wife joined him on the verandah and after a brief and incoherent harangue, the two were abruptly gunned down. The couple's young son crawled into a cupboard and survived. The extensive counter-insurgency operation that followed lasted through most of 1966 and eventually all members of the gang were either killed or detained.

Around the same time as the Nevada Farm incident, another ZANU incursion was recorded that once again highlighted not only the astonishing intelligence successes that the Rhodesians continued to enjoy, but also the reckless courage of the early insurgents. Four guerrillas secreted themselves in the back of a removal van travelling from Lusaka to Salisbury, but were intercepted by Special Branch. A combined force of Rhodesian SAS and Special Branch operatives stood ready as the vehicle was waved down. Once the exits were surrounded, the attackers hidden inside were given the chance to surrender. They initially gave the impression that they would, but suddenly weapons appeared and they opened fire. Moments later they were cut to pieces in a brief hail of return gunfire.

ZAPU was also probing the nation's defences at this time. During July and August 1966 a total of five separate ZAPU groups crossed the Zambezi River from Zambia at various points. They carried with them orders to make for specific Tribal Trust Lands, where they were to set up bases in order to recruit and train locals. Again their activities were monitored from the outset by local intelligence, and with the exception of one group of eight who were arrested some months later, all were accounted for relatively quickly.

Terrorist activity was not confined exclusively to blacks. There were incidents recorded of white assistance or participation in a number of attacks. Perhaps the most interesting was that involving the mixed race couple of Patrick Matimba and his Dutch-born wife Adriana. In August 1966, the couple rented a suburban house in Salisbury with Adriana Matimba posing as a middle class woman, and Patrick as her chauffeur. In due course Adriana checked into five separate city centre hotels, in each of which she planted a crude incendiary device. There was some damage to the rooms but nothing that threatened the structure of the buildings. After this the two slipped across the border into Zambia where Patrick went on to make a more productive contribution to the struggle and Adriana settled into motherhood.

The closing months of the 1960s saw the morale of the early guerrilla units shattered. With their leadership imprisoned and their forces in tatters, the two political parties withdrew to consider their situation. In due course this resulted in a radical reappraisal of their military tactics. For the time being, however, the apparent lull in terrorist activity lured the Rhodesians into believing that the war was as good as won. But much was going on behind the scenes. This was the moment when the nationalists finally came to terms with the fact that they had a real fight on their hands, and many hearts must have weakened at the prospect. Herbert Chitepo was quoted in an interview published in a Danish newspaper, as observing: 'It is useless to engage in conventional warfare with well equipped Rhodesian and South African troops along the Zambezi River.'

Truer words were never spoken.

47

British ship of State

Harold Wilson fought a second general election at the end of May 1966, and was returned to power with an improved majority. Thereafter much of his early uncertainty was eased. It was now time to wash the spit off his jacket and take more direct control over the Rhodesian crisis. Kenneth Kaunda predicted this surge of confidence when he assured his colleges in the OAU: 'Now you will see. Harold Wilson will do the right thing.'[1] Harold Wilson certainly did intend to try and do the right thing. It just happened that it was not quite the right thing that Kenneth Kaunda had in mind.

The first peace envoys to wend their way to Salisbury, in the aftermath of UDI, were sent by the Conservative Party. Ex-Chancellor of the Exchequer Reginald Maudling had already made the Tory position on Rhodesia clear: economic sanctions could not work without the active commitment of South Africa. In the unlikely event of South Africa pulling the plug on Rhodesia, it was predicted that hard line support for Smith would simply solidify, and stifle the emergence of any alternative and potentially moderate parties.

Former Lord Privy Seal Selwyn Lloyd arrived in Salisbury on a fact-finding mission in February 1966. He reached the conclusion that the crisis was solvable, and that grounds existed for the British Government to consider opening negotiations with the rebels. Hesitant contacts were established through the civil services of both countries, as behind the scenes 'talks about talks' took shape. These contacts continued through 1966 as a way was sought — as Smith put it — to find a peg upon which Wilson could hang his climb-down. Not least of these was Wilson's oft-repeated pledge that he would never negotiate with an illegal regime. This begged the question of who he was then to talk to. Mercifully Humphrey Gibbs was still holding his appointment, so it was through him that the first high-level contacts were made.

The talks about talks were suspended briefly to accommodate the Commonwealth Prime Ministers Conference in Lusaka. The opportunity was nonetheless taken for an under secretary in the Commonwealth Office, Sir Morris James, to call on Gibbs and make it known that the Labour Government was now determined to resolve the crisis through negotiation. The Governor passed this cautiously welcomed news on to the rebel administration.

On 19 September Commonwealth Secretary Herbert Bowen arrived in Salisbury, in the company of Attorney General Elwyn Jones, to set the stage for formal negotiations. Talks were held but an acceptable compromise remained elusive. Broad agreement was reached over a timescale and the general terms of majority rule, but the question of a return to legality remained the principal bugbear. The British insisted that the current Rhodesian parliament be dissolved, and that a governor be appointed by the British to assume control. This step was to be followed by the stationing of British troops in the country for the purpose of maintaining law and order. Since the Rhodesian Government could discern no failing with either their maintenance of law and order or their execution of government, both conditions were rejected.

It was the perception of Smith, his cabinet and a majority of the white citizens of Rhodesia that UDI had so far been a success and, despite sanctions, the country was gaining economic muscle. It was generally agreed that Britain, and Wilson in particular, needed a negotiated settlement more than Rhodesia did. But obviously, not being too keen to help Wilson out of his dilemma, Smith simply sat on his hands. Parallel to this, an incident occurred that was so absolutely unnecessary and so ill conceived, that it is surprising any kind of contact between the two governments survived.

Armistice Day 1966 coincided with the first anniversary of Rhodesia's independence. The day was as usual commemorated in London, but a ban had been placed on any official Rhodesian participation in the royal ceremony, traditionally held at the Cenotaph in Whitehall. Whatever animosity there might be between the two governments, there was simply no call for a mean spirited and petty action like this. It was vintage Harold Wilson that by no stretch of the imagination could it have been an expression of popular British will. Rhodesians black and white had participated in both world wars and had militarily supported Britain in many other conflicts and disturbances. Rhodesia's right to both attend the ceremony and participate was inviolable.

The Anglo-Rhodesian Society organised its own wreath-laying ceremony later that afternoon with a Salvation Army band providing the martial music. This continued until 1979. It didn't take long for a feeling of dislike and deep distrust of Wilson and his government to set in, not only among the Rhodesian rank and file, but also for the first time with the Crown loyalists and the old guard.

Oblivious to the significance of the incident, Wilson busied himself planning his next encounter with Smith. The British PM believed that the unresolved questions could be bridged by his not inconsiderable powers of diplomacy. He made the curious decision of choosing as a venue, a warship anchored at the British enclave of Gibraltar. Winston Churchill might have used the tactic to impress a victim in the days of Empire, but Smith was hardly that type of victim and the days of Churchill had long passed. The invitation was issued through Sir Humphrey Gibbs and Sir Hugh Beadle, in order to give the appearance of regularity.

Despite his apparent self-confidence, Wilson was under no illusion as to who he was dealing with. As the Rhodesian delegation was piped on board *HMS Tiger*, he gave Beadle and Gibbs the nod, but gravitated immediately towards Smith. He took his counterpart aside and urged him to be conscious of the seriousness of the current situation, adding that clarity of mind and maturity at this moment was vital for the future of Rhodesia. This immediately put Smith on the defensive. Prickly at best, he tartly reminded Wilson that, unlike his strictly theoretical stake in the affair, he himself was a Rhodesian, a patriot and a landowner. As such he had more reason than anyone on board to be aware of the seriousness of the current situation.

Smith was not in the slightest overawed by his surroundings. He was certainly more comfortable in the company of naval officers than the bookish British Prime Minister. Wilson had served as a civilian in the supply department throughout the war, and had absolutely nothing in common with men of the uniformed services. Smith, on the other hand, was warmly received by the ship's officers and invited that evening to the wardroom for drinks. There he was toasted with assurances that — with the possible exception of one man who could be tossed overboard with no particular loss to the kingdom — support for Rhodesia on board ship was absolute.

Thus the tone of the next few days was set. *HMS Tiger* slipped anchor and steamed out of harbour, while the two parties searched for the wit to cut through the Gordian knot. The stumbling block remained the question of a return to legality. Wilson insisted that power be handed over to the Governor who would then form a new government that, it was hoped, would be more broad-based than the current one. This idea was obviously repellent to the Rhodesians since a 'broad-based' government could mean anything at all, even that the next Prime Minister might be either Joshua

Nkomo or Ndabaningi Sithole. It also meant, perhaps more importantly, that should the process break down — which it almost certainly would — the white Rhodesian electorate would have relinquished the sceptre and would be powerless to reclaim it.

The Rhodesians suggested instead that a test of acceptability on a revised constitution should be carried out. Assuming that a general endorsement was achieved, the two parliaments could then legislate simultaneously. Wilson held firm that he was unable to deal overtly with an illegitimate government, and that a return to legality was imperative before further progress could be made. Smith's reminder that he was dealing with the Rhodesian Government at that moment was taken for the supercilious observation that it was. Wilson pleaded the difficulties that he was facing at the UN and the Commonwealth, to which Smith replied that these were problems of his own making. In due course the discussions broke up in some acrimony with no advances being made.

48

Detained nationalists

Black reaction to the 1966 *Tiger* negotiations was predictably hostile. Between October and November of that year a series of OAU meetings in Addis Ababa resulted in yet more fulminating condemnation of Britain. The announcement was made that the member states 'bitterly and unreservedly' deplored the Anglo-Rhodesian talks in Gibraltar. They were condemned as 'a conspiracy aimed at recognising the independence seized illegally by the rebel settlers.'[1]

While Smith and Wilson butted heads in the Mediterranean, and in Ethiopia black nations gathered to demonstrate their unremitting rage, a personal tragedy was unfolding in Salisbury Remand Prison.

Toward the end of the year Robert Mugabe was visited in prison by his sister Sabina who brought the news that Mugabe's young son, Nhamodzenyika, had died of a severe bout of cerebral malaria at the home of his father-in-law in Ghana. Mugabe was devastated and immediately drafted a request for temporary release in order to travel to Ghana and bury his son.

His appeal found unexpected support from Detective Inspector Tony Bradshaw of the Special Branch — unexpected since Mugabe and Bradshaw had had a number of bruising confrontations in the past. Bradshaw was confident that Mugabe would honour any undertaking he made to return to detention. He also sensed that an act of human charity such as this might soften the position of the intractable and unbending jailed nationalists. He was probably right. Mugabe might indeed have returned from Ghana in a more responsive frame of mind, and from then things on could have been very different. But in the atmosphere of the time, it was a long shot that predictably missed.

In later years much was made of this inhuman denial of a man's paternal rights, but the truth is probably more prosaic. It would have been bending the rules too much to allow a prisoner compassionate leave, with no more surety than his own word that he would return to prison from a friendly foreign country. If the child had happened to die in Rhodesia there is little doubt he would have been granted the leave he sought.

Understandably the episode did nothing to diminish Mugabe's hatred of whites and, in fact, probably influenced his outlook from then on more than many at that time were prepared to admit. His early biographers tend to claim that anger did not contaminate the sorrow in his heart, but time was to prove that he was less of a saint than a Machiavellian power broker. The myth of his Ghandi-like purity of spirit was never any more than that.

In the meantime, Sally Mugabe, now with no particular reason to confine herself to home, made her way from Ghana to Britain and sought the solace of activism and study. A bleak picture is often painted of this colourful West African woman, as iron-spirited as her husband, cast up lonely and isolated on cold foreign shores. She won a scholarship to study secretarial science in London, and did so initially with special permission from the Foreign and Commonwealth Office. However, in due course, Home Secretary Mervin Reese divined that her marriage to Mugabe gave her no claim to Rhodesian citizenship and therefore no claim to British protection, and she was ordered to leave the country.[2] In her remaining time she spent long, Dickensian hours bent over volumes in the British Library reproducing in her own handwriting texts, quotes and references that Mugabe needed in his prison cell some 5 000 miles away.

Education was also the solace and cornerstone of Mugabe's prison regimen. In total he accumulated seven university degrees while in various prisons and detention centres, and he also insisted on education programmes for all the ZANU nationalists incarcerated with him. Few achieved what he did but some, like Maurice Nyagumbo, advanced their education quite significantly — certainly more than they ever would have on the outside. More significantly, they were given a rigid political education by Mugabe himself, who administered the lessons as he learned them. If prison is a university of crime, then political detention is the most intense college of political indoctrination available.

It was by these methods that Mugabe succeeded in maintaining his own equilibrium, and to a great extent the mental stability of his comrades. It is worth remembering that Mugabe was not in any actual position of leadership at this time. Ndabaningi Sithole remained the President of ZANU and Mugabe was his General Secretary. Despite this, an examination of the testimonials of many nationalists who were in prison with Mugabe, reveal that it was to him they turned for guidance. The growth of a powerful and charismatic revolutionary leader had begun.

Of his education, Mugabe himself remarked with double edged self-effacement: 'I do it for myself and Zimbabwe because I know one day we both will need these degrees.'[3] That Mugabe's self-effacement was but skin deep is illustrated in the biography of Mugabe's future deputy, Simon Muzenda. The episode describes a fight that broke out between emotionally burdened men.

> Tekere stood up and kicked Nkala, who was sitting down, in the ribs. Some of us tried to stop the fight from breaking out. But Mugabe thought the two had been at each other verbally for too long. He therefore persuaded us to leave them alone so they could fight it out. They boxed each other to exhaustion. The guards who might have stopped the fight were nowhere to be seen. By the time the guards appeared they had really messed up each other and Tekere's face was swollen completely. In fact, Tekere had been knocked to the ground about two or three times. Nkala was the far better boxer of the two. The last time he rose from being floored Tekere retired from the fight and went to sit quietly by himself. When Nkala challenged him to continue the fight he refused. Mugabe said, 'If you leave people to fight it out, they release their anger completely.'[4]

Another story, this time lifted from *Drum* magazine, revealed the no-less dreary fate of ZAPU President Joshua Nkomo. Nkomo was also interned with the core of his executive, but sojourned relatively quietly and led no selfless charges towards the accumulation of knowledge.

> At a recent chiefs' indaba on the future of Rhodesia one man spoke of a place where the body of a poisonous snake was buried. It was dangerous to go near that place, he said. The 'snake' he referred to was nationalism and the place was Gonakudzingwa in the Sengwe area. Here waits banned leader Joshua Nkomo now facing four years restriction.[5]

Conditions in restriction camps such as Gonakudzingwa and Sikombela were primitive and uncomfortable, but not overly confining. Restrictees were usually dumped in very isolated locations, given basic rations and left with the materials to construct their own crude shelters. The compounds were unguarded most of the time, with police visiting only once a week to conduct a roll call and bring fresh rations. Otherwise the internees were technically limited to a certain perimeter, although in practice they were free to move around the district at will.

The lack of close surveillance of nationalist restrictees was a major error made by the Government, as was confining the leadership of different parties together. The forced fraternity gave each executive the opportunity to meet daily and continue the process of planning and executing the struggle. Separation of the leadership only happened when certain of them were convicted of offences under the Law and Order (Maintenance) Act, upon which the offenders were usually required to serve prison terms in either Salisbury or Gwelo. Besides this, the leadership remained in a position where they could make reasonably easy contact with one another, and with others on the outside.

Gonakudzingwa was remote and the ZAPU leadership was more effectively isolated than ZANU at Sikombela. At the end of 1964, *Drum* magazine spent a weekend at Gonakudzingwa and found Nkomo inactive and morbidly depressed in the heat. A handful of women were attached to the camp, and it was these that undertook most of the labour, so for the men there was very little to do. Accommodation consisted mostly of tin huts that were either too hot or too cold, while the landscape of drab lowveld woodland and scrub stretched unbroken into the blue distance. Nkomo spent his days seated in the shade of a tree with his transistor radio and a pair of binoculars beside him. He listened to the news, watched elephants browse in the distance or an occasional lion also seeking shade. Nkomo had turned a few shades darker by then but appeared not to have lost any weight. Historian Peter Stiff recalls rumours regarding the tendency on the part of the authorities to ensure Nkomo had more than ample food in the hope that he would suffer a heart attack, while Nkomo himself remembers tablets given to him by his doctor to help him lose weight that kept him awake at night with a surplus of agitated energy. He spent much of his time alone, fingering a volume of *Samuelson's Economics* and drinking from a bottomless bucket of brewing tea.

'So we sing.' Joseph Msika, fellow restrictee and PCC Secretary for External Affairs, revealed. 'Don't be baffled that we are singing when we should be sobbing. We sing our sorrows out. Go anywhere in Africa where people are in sadness, and see them sing their sorrows out.'[6]

There certainly was much to be sorry about. *Drum* was soon to be banned, along with all other avenues of nationalist expression. The leaders were in detention, police informers were everywhere and freedom fighters were falling like dominoes. *Drum* had this to say before it temporarily closed the book on Rhodesia.

The Government had gone about its business well. The nationalist movement that could once raise a 20 000 crowd with a whisper, was long since split within itself and since its leaders had been carried away to distant restriction, informers seemed to abound. Fervent revolutionaries who took trips to foreign guerrilla warfare training centres — in Ghana, East Africa, even China — got back only to walk into the arms of waiting security police.[7]

49

HMS Fearless

Regardless of who would administer a transitional government, Ian Smith was at first tempted to accept the *HMS Tiger* proposals. Back in Salisbury he put the matter to his Cabinet colleagues and insisted that they return a unanimous vote before a final decision was made. To give them all an extra hour or two to think things over, he scheduled the vote for the afternoon session, upon which everyone went home for lunch.

Initially the pundits could have called a clear majority in favour, but by afternoon the mood had changed. A vote was held and a negative result was returned, although not by any means unanimously. With that the *Tiger* proposals simply slipped off the radar. Analysts in the meantime — which at that time included just about everyone — gathered around bars and watering holes all across the country and were intrigued by rumours that Janet Smith had led a lunchtime revolt. Friends of the Smiths usually found Janet to be more of a political hardliner than her husband, and myth has it that over lunch she contacted all the Cabinet wives and orchestrated a parlour rebellion. This is the popular version of why progress stalled in 1966. The more prosaic version is probably the more factual.

Wilson could not be held completely over a barrel, and a negotiation without any compromise is hardly a negotiation. The Tiger proposals were not unreasonable and Ken Flower had an excellent theory on why Smith ultimately slammed the door. Flower believed that Smith appeared strongest when he was saying 'no'. He would say 'no' not so much because it was the correct answer, but because he was afraid of being proved wrong after saying 'yes'. According to Flower, Smith's method of negotiation was not to negotiate at all. If any accommodation was possible it was left entirely to the other side.[1] While this was not invariably the case, the tendency did seem to exist. Smith appears to have squandered many opportunities by a combination of uncertainty, tenacity and an inability to horse trade in the universally accepted political tradition.

Smith would soon be forced to make concessions — and many of them — but for the time being he was under no particular pressure to do so. No doubt this also contributed to the hiatus. By the end of 1966 any white resistance there had been to UDI had largely fallen away and Rhodesians, in the time honoured British tradition, were knuckling down and getting on with it. Smith could instinctively sense that with the dust well settled, his grip on the hearts and minds of white Rhodesia was firm.

The killing of Oberholtzer and the Viljoens had brought it home to whites that they were facing a direct physical threat. As bungling as the guerrilla war had been so far, it was war nonetheless. A common enemy, clannishness and high morale, created a strong bonding. To not support Smith implied support for Wilson and no one cared to be guilty of that. For a long time Smith was able to use this solidarity to paper over a general political stagnation, while whites were only too happy to rally behind a strong and determined leader.

However well things seemed to be going internally, the fact was that Rhodesia remained in political isolation. After two and then three years of independence, no country in the world had yet made any serious move towards recognising the rebel colony. On the right of the caucus, some discussion took place regarding the correct moment for Rhodesia to declare herself a republic. Smith did not discourage this talk and in fact gave it considerable momentum when, in February 1967, he appointed a commission under Salisbury lawyer Sam Whaley to consider a new constitutional framework. At the same time he made the observation that the door to negotiations with Britain was now fully slammed and locked.[2]

Be that as it may, Rhodesia could not exist forever as a political outcast. While he publicly aired his Churchillian determination to never surrender, Smith was not immune to the jitters, and the *Tiger* proposals were never entirely discarded. Perhaps the wives were never told, but quietly the outlines of Wilson's proposals were returned to the table, where they remained as a basis for future negotiations.

The first signs of renewed contact between the British and Rhodesian Governments came with a visit to Rhodesia in mid-1967 by Lord Alport. Alport, former British High Commissioner to the Federation, held meetings at different times with both Ian Smith and Humphrey Gibbs, and after three weeks returned to Britain to report mixed results. His broad conclusion was that perhaps some progress was possible. On this thin margin, Wilson authorised Gibbs to begin preparatory talks with Smith. Smith remained tight lipped and publicly rather indifferent, but he peered through a door ajar and was relieved to see that the British were still there.

Smith had recently returned from a holiday in South Africa, where he had for the first time met South African Prime Minister John Vorster. Smith generally had a very narrow field of vision when it came to people whom he did or did not like. Most of his diplomacy over the UDI crisis tended to fall into the latter category — besides which UDI was such an emotive issue for Smith that he simply did not have the capacity to absorb anything other than praise for it. Vorster unfortunately had little praise to offer so he did not qualify as a friend.

However, events were under way that would force an increase in security cooperation between the two whether Smith cared to ask for it or not — or for that matter, whether Vorster cared to offer it or not. In 1967 ZAPU entered into a temporary military alliance with the South African ANC. This was mainly to allow ZAPU to assist a large number of trained *Umkonto we Sizwe* (Spear of the Nation — the revolutionary armed wing of the ANC) cadres to move through Rhodesia on their way to South Africa. The benefits of such an alliance were not easily understood by the rival organisations of both groups. A statement issued jointly by the Pan Africanist Congress (PAC) of South Africa and ZANU stated:

> You cannot hope to gobble up a regular army all at once in a conventional style war, as our brothers tried to do, and still claim to be waging guerrilla warfare.

SAANC was counselled to wage its own war at home and give no excuse to South Africa to deploy force into Rhodesia. Time and again ZAPU functionaries and historians have tried to drive home the point that South African force was already deployed in Rhodesia prior to this, and that the strategic alliance between the two revolutionary movements did not bring the fact about. There is no evidence whatsoever of this having been the case, and there can be no doubt that the actions of ZAPU and *Umkonto we Sizwe* (MK) in this regard were instrumental in the deployment of South African armed police units to Rhodesia.

Meanwhile, during July of 1967, a combined force of 200 combatants of ZAPU's military wing and the SAANC's MK crossed the Zambezi River at the third gorge below the Victoria Falls and from there sought to establish a route south through the Wankie National Park. Once again, it was not long before their presence was detected by vigilant game control staff, and throughout August the first of the dramatic combined operations involving all the regular units of the Rhodesian security forces, including the BSAP,b played out.

Operation Nichol was a ruthless and bloody affair that pitted the seasoned Rhodesian Security Forces against a newly inspired, well-trained and determined enemy. Despite having the advantage of air power the security forces were sobered to tally seven of their men dead and 13 wounded. For this they could claim a mere 30 ZAPU men dead but many more were captured. In spite of the unacceptably high Rhodesian casualties, *Operation Nichol* had stopped the incursion firmly in its tracks and was marked down as a successful operation.

Soon afterwards the offer of South African security assistance was made via the CIO. Smith quickly accepted it in the face of surprising resistance from the hierarchy of the Rhodesian military who were convinced that they should go it alone. The offer was made as a result of pressure from South African military sources and ran somewhat contrary to Vorster's better judgement. But it was an opportunity and Smith was not immune to the political value of a security relationship with South Africa. Soon thereafter a detachment of 2 000 SAP members under the guise of ' riot police' arrived in Rhodesia. They were supported by SAAF helicopters (disguised as police helicopters) to help reinforce the Zambezi River line.

The obliteration of their first major incursion did not immediately put paid to ZAPU's alliance with the SAANC. As an eventful year drew to a close, the two combined their forces once again. A more conventional approach was taken this time, with the initial priority being to lay supply lines into Rhodesia. It was hoped that this would allow an attack force in the Zambezi Valley to remain undetected long enough for them to find a way up the escarpment and into suitable cover on the Highveld.

Their strategy was no more successful than previous efforts. A patrolling game ranger, David Scammel, detected signs of human movement in the valley almost immediately. Scammel had noticed an unusual pattern of game movement in his patrol area, which was caused by a handful of insurgents shooting for the pot. Their movement through the valley was also confirmed by spoor, showing the unique figure-of-eight tread of their Cuban-manufactured boots.

The army was alerted and the general location of the group quickly established. Once again a rapid mobilisation of army and police units was coordinated before an extensive operation codenamed *Cauldron* swung into action. *Operation Cauldron* saw a series of running battles during March and April 1968 which culminated in the death of 69 guerrillas and the capture of 50 for the loss of just six members of the Security Forces.

The next major action occurred in September 1968, and although accounts differ as to the strength of the attacking force, upwards of 90 cadres crossed the Zambezi River at widely separated points. This formation was presumably to test Security Force ground coverage, but within hours of a successful crossing, at least one member hived off and made his way to Chirundu Police post where he reported to the local police inspector that he was an undercover Special Branch agent. Trackers then promptly located the insurgents and an operation codenamed *Griffin* accounted for the entire group.

Notable in this operation was the death of South African police constable Daniel du Toit who, according to one account at least, stood up in the middle of a fire fight and called out to the enemy: 'Come and get me, kaffirs.'[3] This they did and Constable du Toit died of a gunshot wound to the head. Of the guerrillas, 39 were killed and 41 captured.

Rhodesia was entirely dependent on her neighbours — South Africa significantly more than Mozambique — for outside access and material support. However the possibility of South Africa weighing in with armed force could never be taken for granted. Although help was offered and frequently supplied, it still hovered uncertainly on the fates, as Vorster loosened or tightened his grip on Smith. Under the necessary veneer of cordiality, the two were destined to remain consistently at odds over the question of UDI for the duration of Vorster's term. The minutes of their first meeting were never made public but on his return Smith was noticeably depressed. For years afterwards he grumbled about the unwillingness of South Africa to fully throw her weight behind Rhodesia. One of his favourite lamentations was how much easier it was to deal with his enemies on the battlefield than his friends in the conference room.

Smith clung to the position that, whilst he was willing to pursue a settlement on the basis of the *Tiger* proposals, sanctions would not persuade him to resume discussions. In fact, far from bringing Rhodesia to its knees, the blockade was probably hurting the weakened British economy more than the Rhodesian. The major stumbling block was the question of the Government returning to 'legality', and the basic unacceptability of the principal of 'No Independence before Majority Rule' or NIBMAR. If a compromise on this score could be arrived at, then a settlement would be possible.

For the remainder of 1967 Wilson continued to hedge, because dropping NIBMAR would have invited all the usual histrionics from the Commonwealth, and not inconceivably a left-wing revolt from within his own government. Visits were made and contacts maintained, but by year-end no substantive movement had been recorded.

Smith's jitters were revealed in his New Year message of 1967/8 when he admitted to the nation that Rhodesia could not indefinitely sustain the current state of uncertainty, and that a solution urgently needed to be found. In response to this the question of a Rhodesian republic was once again raised and debated.

Alec Douglas Home slipped in and out of the country during February, visiting a variety of people including the Governor, Lord Malvern, Winston Field, Robert Tredgold, and of course Ian Smith. Neither did Home spare Smith the usual unwanted advice. Although genuine and bipartisan concern for white Rhodesia did exist at the highest level of the British establishment, the Rhodesian Prime Minister was warned that time was running out.

In the meanwhile, national attention was briefly diverted by the release of a High Court judgement — supported by a majority of the appellate division — confirming the local de jure status of the UDI government. This strengthened the country's claim to independence and edged it closer to the status of a republic. Thanks to the fact that now in its own eyes Rhodesian independence was legal, Chief Justice Sir Hugh Beadle separated himself from the British constitutional resistance and withdrew as Gibbs' constitutional advisor, thereby further isolating the beleaguered Governor.

In June, Wilson prevailed on an old friend and RAF associate of Ian Smith, Max Aitken — son of Lord Beaverbrook and heir to the newspaper dynasty — to make a secret visit to Salisbury to try and nudge the process forward. With him came Lord Goodman who was legal advisor to both Aitken and Wilson. Although warned that he was in danger of painting himself into a corner, Smith was once again in no mood to compromise. After consultations with Smith and others, Aitken and Goodman were prepared to concede that no settlement with Rhodesia would be possible until the terms of NIBMAR were dropped. Smith also stood his ground on the matter of a return to legality until such time as he heard what new proposals Harold Wilson had to offer.

Wilson's next discernable move was to send a senior Labour official, James Bottomley (no relation to Arthur), who came to gauge the Governor's opinion and test the temperature of the water surrounding the Rhodesian Cabinet. Bottomley found Smith still receptive and willing to work around the Tiger proposals, but the vexed question of a return to legality and NIBMAR remained the principal stumbling block.

In September 1968 a message was received by Gibbs stating that Wilson, bravely taking the initiative in the face of powerful opposition from the left wing of his own party, wanted to meet with Smith in the near future. Ignoring some obvious lessons of déjà vu, the British PM again proposed that the venue be a Royal Naval warship moored in Gibraltar harbour. The meeting was duly set for 9 to 13 October aboard *HMS Fearless*. On this occasion the Rhodesians were given their own accommodation on *HMS Kent* moored alongside.

On this occasion Wilson was courteous and considerate and took care not to ruffle Smith's feathers, but in other respects the meeting was more or less a repeat of the previous one. Apart from Sir Humphrey Gibbs and a handful of cabinet ministers, the Rhodesian delegation included arguably the most hard-line official in the Government. Secretary for Internal Affairs Hostes Nichol made no secret of his admiration for the South African system of race management and advocated the creation of Bantustans for the future accommodation of Rhodesian blacks. In the opinion of MI6, he had been included in the delegation purely to minimise any chance of the conference succeeding. This was a confusing accusation considering other indications that Smith very much desired a settlement. Nevertheless, Nichol's contribution was extremely negative and led to questions over Smith's sincerity. Perhaps he was again reluctant to be the one making concessions.

It is also interesting to note that the previous problem of the return to legality barely featured on the agenda of this conference. The British were prepared to drop the six principals of NIBMAR, requiring instead only a commitment to majority rule, a fact which should have seen the Rhodesians rubbing their hands in glee. The only point they could find to take issue with was a matter previously agreed during the *Tiger* talks, namely that any individual who cared to do so could make an appeal to the Privy Council on matters of legislation. It was upon this apparently innocent clause that the conference stalled. Smith could not concede that a British court should be permitted to usurp legislative decisions that were the province of the Rhodesian Parliament.

The *Fearless* talks were as good as it would ever get, and Smith under the circumstances could not reasonably have hoped for more. Nonetheless the meeting broke up with a communiqué announcing that a gulf remained between the two parties, but that efforts to bridge it would continue.

For Wilson, the issue was filed away in preparation for another bruising Commonwealth Conference followed by another general election. Smith made this parting comment on the last substantive Wilsonian contribution to the Rhodesia saga:

> It was clear to us throughout the talks that the British were obsessed with the question of black majority rule and that this dominated all their thinking. They are prepared to accept that the white man in Rhodesia is expendable.

There was indeed little question that the white man in Rhodesia was expendable — if not entirely, then at least in a governing role. Smith's closing remark in an address to the nation on 19 November 1968 revealed either an astonishing level of naivete or an attempt to keep his audience as far removed from reality as possible.

> We Rhodesians believe that there is a place and a future for all Rhodesians, black and white.

Perhaps Joseph Msika, just then in the company of Joshua Nkomo and other restrictees at Gonakudzingwa restriction camp, expressed in this regard a rather clearer personal view of the facts on the ground.

... unless there are drastic changes, my white fellow Rhodesians will have to leave the country in their pyjamas — through the kitchen window.

Warfare by other means

On 7 November 1968 the three leaders of ZANU — Ndabaningi Sithole, Leopold Takawira and Robert Mugabe — were briefed on the details of the *HMS Fearless* talks by two British Cabinet ministers. George Thomson and Maurice Foley had flown in for the specific purpose of gauging nationalist opinion on progress. The meeting was held at the New Sarum Airbase, largely to avoid official eavesdropping. In the interests of further privacy the five men walked the length of the tarmac where they held their meeting under a tree at the furthest end of the runway. It was an animated encounter and for the British, a largely unsatisfactory one.

The two British ministers were informed promptly and without equivocation that the black political representation of Rhodesia rejected British efforts to reach an accommodation with Smith. The fact that Harold Wilson had been willing to grant independence to Rhodesia on the basis of the 1961 Constitution so dismayed the three locals that Takawira had to be restrained from assaulting one or both ministers. Thomson's assertion that half a loaf was better than none almost brought foam to Takawira's lips.

Mugabe then brought up the issue of force. Why, he asked, was Britain loath to suppress the rebellion in Rhodesia when she had been so willing to use her armed forces in Aden, Cyprus, Kenya and the Suez? To be reminded of Suez was painful, while the mention of Aden brought back memories of white Rhodesian military assistance there. Thomson resorted to the plea that logistically Britain was simply not capable of launching a military assault against a regime that was both armed to the teeth and well entrenched. Mugabe scoffed at this rationalisation and spat the heresy that the real reason was kith and kin. Although shocked denials followed, everybody knew that Mugabe was essentially correct.

It is interesting to note here that political historian Paul Moorcroft, who lampooned Smith's immortal comment, 'Never in a Thousand years', in his book, *A Short Thousand Years*, served as a political instructor at the Royal Military Academy at Sandhurst. He had occasion to ask hundreds of junior officers whether they would be prepared to use force against Rhodesian troops, and an astonishing 90% said they would not.

Mugabe was wrong only inasmuch as he assumed that the underlying reason was racism — or at least white on black racism. The same body of junior officers were no less adamant that they would not hesitate to use force against any 'white' member of the Irish Republican Army. It was a question of kith and kin and it was a question of 'Britishness'. It would be naive to suppose that a British soldier would not find it easier to draw a bead on a black man of unknown origin than a Briton like himself. White had killed white in monstrous quantities in two world wars, when no fraternalism had frozen the trigger fingers of either side. Irishman and Englishman would grapple unto death over issues of Irish sovereignty, but over Rhodesia — a land embracing the European gamut from Volgograd to Galway — the question was more complicated, and then, as now, defied any attempt at explanation.[5]

Mugabe inadvertently let Maurice Foley off the hook when the former was probing the extent to which the British feared that South Africa would attack any British occupying force. Foley responded that he had no doubt they would. In reality though, he could not possibly have imagined that South Africa would commit herself militarily to Rhodesia's defence against Britain when she was barely able to muster enough common cause to keep Rhodesia supplied with fuel. But it was the best he could come up with at that moment, and it at least brought the ugly matter to a close.

Thus an unsatisfactory encounter ended with sullen farewells. The three depressed and dissatisfied nationalists were walked across the tarmac and driven back to Salisbury Remand Prison, while the two British Ministers boarded a waiting aircraft and flew home to London.

The united front that the three ZANU leaders presented that day was not indicative of the general state of the revolution. In fact, the nationalist leadership in detention was in crisis, with the main point of stress being the personal temptations of Ndabaningi Sithole.

Sithole was by 1970 entering his fifth year of incarceration with no end in sight, and for all the loss of life and liberty, there was no apparent weakening of the regime. The imprisoned men living life one day at a time had very little reason for optimism. So far the armed struggled had been crushed with depressing ease, which meant that the detained nationalists had to accept that the duration of their detention would very likely parallel the duration of the Smith regime.

It was apparent that the common man had turned his back on the struggle. For the most part blacks were relieved that the infighting of the late fifties and early sixties was over. A consequence of this, however, was that the country was now swarming with sell-outs and informers. Almost every day captured guerrillas were sentenced to death and executed for a struggle that no longer seemed to have any hope of success. To these stresses were added the more mundane concerns of families struggling on the outside to cope, wives seeking comfort and financial support elsewhere and children running wild.

So it was that rumours of a curious nature began to reach the ears of Ndabaningi Sithole. As Alexander Solzhenitsyn once remarked: 'The thoughts of a prisoner — they are not free either. They keep returning to the same things. A single idea keeps stirring'.[6] Word had begun to circulate that Sithole's wife was fraternising with Portuguese soldiers encamped on his farm south of Chipinga. As unlikely as this was, the news tormented Sithole. It compounded the normal pressures of maintaining his mental balance in prison, coupled with unavoidable evidence that his grip on the leadership of the Party was slipping. For this there were many reasons, but principally it was because he was tribally isolated. He could not have failed to notice that meetings and discussions paused or ceased as he passed or walked into a room. Such discussions often focussed on the fact that a leader originating from a small tribe confined to the extreme east of the country — the Ndau — would limit the Party's national appeal. Both Mugabe and Takawira were from larger and more representative tribal groupings, and many members felt that one of them would be a better leader.

Less tangible was the hint of weakness in Sithole's character that could no longer be obscured by his intellectual achievements. Once the struggle had degenerated into a brawl, it would be inevitable that the brawlers would rise to the surface — and manifestly Sithole was not one of them. Perhaps more telling was the schism that had opened between Mugabe and Sithole after the inaugural congress of ZANU held in 1964. A vote for the presidency had pitted a minority of Mugabe supporters against Sithole. Mugabe, then relatively unknown, had not gathered sufficient support to stand and had to accept the lower position of General Secretary. Since then there had been no love lost between the two men and now, of the two, Mugabe was beginning to emerge the stronger.

One day Sithole was admitted to a local hospital for routine treatment. His ailment was minor, and as he was being attended to, he fell into conversation with his white doctor. The doctor enquired about the health of Sithole's wife, and Sithole replied that she was well. The doctor said he was glad, and remarked in an offhand way that he was sorry nothing could have been done to prevent her miscarriage.[7]

Sithole was returned to prison in a state of shock. If the way to a man's heart is through his stomach, then the way to his stomach is through his wife. The gambit worked perfectly and an already emotionally weakened Sithole quickly lapsed into depression. In the quiet of his confinement he began threshing his mind to find a way to shorten the revolution. As he did so, the forces of law and order were at work in ways even more devious.

Sithole used a certain Mrs Cele as a courier for his communications with the outside world. Unbeknown to him, Mrs Cele was a salaried police informer who routinely passed his correspondence on to Special Branch. Therefore, when Sithole came up with a desperate scheme to assassinate Ian Smith and his Law and Order Minister Desmond Lardner-Burke, Special Branch was immediately on to him.

Initially Sithole kept the idea to himself but, in about June 1968, he identified Maurice Nyagumbo as a possible confederate. Nyagumbo was a recklessly bold nationalist of poor education and limited intelligence, but known for being a solid soldier and a fanatical revolutionary. Nyagumbo thought the scheme was marvellous and immediately agreed to help. Sithole would pursue outside contacts while Nyagumbo was left to organise what funds he could through a certain Dr Mundawarara. Sithole's instructions to his contacts — and to Special Branch — were ridiculously explicit, besides which Nyagumbo bungled his way through a series of intelligence leaks and mishaps. Special Branch agents collating all this must have wondered whether the whole plot was not some kind of a joke.

Nyagumbo secured the princely sum of £300 while Sithole wrote to a Mr X in Salisbury, instructing him to employ 'some of our hard core criminals' to carry out the assassination.[8] Up to 30 letters were ultimately smuggled out of prison by friendly warders and passed on to Special Branch. There they were accumulated until the inevitable day when, in front of their astonished associates, Sithole and Nyagumbo were arrested and moved quickly into isolation.

Both men were taken into separate interrogation rooms and told that they were to be charged with treason. Sithole realised that he was now in terrible straits. Instead of open-ended jail time, he now faced a mandatory death sentence. It was accepted that Nyagumbo was of little political value and in due course charges against him were dropped. Sithole, on the other hand, was presented with a deal that he could hardly refuse. In exchange for leniency he agreed to try and persuade his colleagues to abandon the armed struggle, and commit themselves to working for change within the Constitution.

Sithole's trial took place from 3 to 12 February 1969, during which time he was permitted to visit his colleagues in prison in order to present his proposals. His argument was simply that it would be more effective for the Central Committee to orchestrate the struggle with limited freedoms on the outside than with no freedoms at all. Early faith in a quick collapse of the regime had been proved wrong, and there was nothing to be gained by them all rotting for years in prison as they waited for change.

His colleagues greeted Sithole's volte-face with dismay. It was said that Takawira was reduced to tears. When Mugabe recovered his speech, he brutally denounced the Party leader, pointing the way for others to condemn him as corrupt, weak, cowardly mad or all of the above. Sithole listened but remained unrepentant. 'That's all right', he said, 'you have turned down my constructive suggestion. But I want to assure you that I am not going to spend all the six years in prison. I am going to work hard to extricate myself.'[9]

To the white prison chaplain a deeply depressed Sithole later confessed, 'I'll hang for this, unless I can do something to form the basis of my defence.'[10] As his trial progressed, he held his line and agreed to renounce violence in word, thought and deed. For that he escaped with his life. He did not, however, escape his six-year prison sentence.

While public lamentations were staged for the benefit of the rank and file, it is unlikely that Mugabe or any of the leadership felt particularly distressed to see Sithole go. He was a moderate and as such had outrun his usefulness. Conversely, Mugabe was increasingly seen to be forswearing any veneer of moderation.

A few days after their encounter with Sithole, the Central Committee held a meeting where they unanimously rejected Sithole's leadership. In a further closed session Mugabe was elected Party leader. Fearing any appearance of disunity, Mugabe insisted that the matter be kept under wraps. For the time being Sithole would simply be frozen out of committee business — not difficult since he would be locked up in a prison cell for the foreseeable future.

A little later Mugabe's personal ambitions were given another boost when Leopold Takawira suddenly died. It had been apparent for some time that his health was deteriorating, and in the last year of his life he suffered chronic weight loss for reasons never diagnosed, but that were indicative of diabetes. One morning he collapsed and it was some four hours before he was examined by a doctor who then transferred him to Salisbury Hospital. In a sad aside to this tale, it happened that Takawira's wife worked at this hospital, but was neither informed of her husband's condition nor of the fact that he had been admitted. The first she knew of the incident was when she was told the following morning that he had died during the night.

With the disgrace and fall of Ndabaningi Sithole, the virtual collapse of the armed struggle and now the death of one of the principal founders, a sense of hopelessness descended on many in the prisons and detention camps. Indeed, at the close of the decade the struggle for Zimbabwe entered its darkest days.

50

Lords Home and Pearce

For white Rhodesia the new decade opened on a much more optimistic note. On 2 March 1970 the country declared itself a republic, and Humphrey Gibbs and his wife Molly were at last able to close the visitors' book, put the whole ugly business behind them and retire to their farm.

It had not been an easy decision for the Rhodesian electorate, nor was it a unanimous one. Smith had all along been ambivalent as the heads of services asked him, and each other, what this new order could possibly achieve. Most, though, allowed themselves to be carried along on a tide of patriotism that obscured many more practical and important issues. On the whole, the country consummated its independence with this declaration of a republic with little or no regret. The economy was registering growth, the armed insurgency had been crushed and immigration remained steady. No one was under any illusion that a republic would prompt recognition, but it was generally felt that neither Britain nor Rhodesia had much to offer one another any more. The Rhodesian green and white flew over Government House, Clifford Dupont was appointed first President and a bicameral constitution that recognised — but did not promise — that racial parity would come into effect.

The United States was the first to distance itself from the new Republic. Britain quickly followed, as Wilson wearily fed himself to the lions once again in an effort to limit the ferocity of the international response. Both countries vetoed a Security Council resolution demanding tougher action against Rhodesia. In the meantime Smith took the country to another general election. The Rhodesia Front again won all 50 A Roll seats, which was a thumb against the nose to the international community that again gave Smith an open mandate.

Things looked up even more when Harold Wilson was swept out of power in June 1970 by a Conservative election victory that occurred just three months after Smith's. This development immediately excited the pundits and breathed new life into the search for a settlement. Incoming Prime Minister Edward Heath had no particular interest in Rhodesia and handed the whole problem over to an old hand in the matter: Sir Alec Douglas Home.

Sir Alec had spent a year in office as Harold Macmillan's replacement, but under Heath he joined the Cabinet as Foreign Secretary. He was a sportsman and an ex-county cricketer so it could be expected that Smith's rapport with him would be better than it had been with a port and tobacco-drenched intellectual like Wilson. When given the authorisation to treat with Salisbury, Home moved fast and within six months was able to report to the House that preliminary contacts with the Rhodesian Government were on course to establish whether detailed negotiations were possible.

Talks that continued through 1971, often between Smith, Max Aitken and Lord Goodman, were informal and very friendly. A sense of common destiny between the Rhodesians and the Tories seemed to have been revived to the satisfaction of both, and a cosy little process saw the British trim their negotiating position down to a virtual handover. Not a single black opinion was given or sought, so an accommodation was easily reached. On 15 November Sir Alec himself flew into Salisbury and after lengthy behind the scenes discussions, a final agreement was reached, and then signed, in less than a week.

It was stipulated that there would be no interim administration and no appeal to the Privy Council. NIBMAR was whittled down to the principal of parity, with black advancement protected only by Rhodesian guarantees. It was a giveaway. The problem that nobody really thought was a problem was the broad-based test of acceptability. Smith had already conducted a survey of black opinion that he maintained was valid, so he felt reasonably sure of his ground. Home suggested a Commission of Inquiry and Smith was happy to agree.

The information that Smith had available to him regarding black opinion was mainly filtered through the Internal Affairs Department. CIO reports of a black backlash were also delivered, but Smith preferred not to acknowledge these. The more soothing observations of Internal Affairs persuaded him that the black man in the street, if pressed, would choose his government in preference to a radical black nationalist takeover. So confident was he, in fact, that he authorised the release of a large number of detained nationalists who were then allowed to interact and organise without restriction. In his autobiography Smith claims that the people in Highfield — that traditional hotbed of highbrow black politics — were openly celebrating (the Home/Smith Agreement).[1] The only concern that he had was to get the Commission operating as soon as possible, before the nationalists could regroup and mobilise.

The Commission of Inquiry was to be chaired by former Lord of Appeal, Lord Edward Holroyd Pearce. Sir Alec Douglas Home agreed that it had to commence its work as soon as possible. Smith acted swiftly and placed on standby the entire state structure of Rhodesia. By year end, however, there was still no sign of the Commission. Repeated inquiries from the Rhodesian Government were met by oddly vague assurances that the Commission had been constituted and would be despatched to Rhodesia in due course. The arrival was further delayed by the festive season and it was not until early in the new year of 1972 that the commissioners finally made their way to Salisbury. By this time, of course, Smith's fears had been realised — the released nationalists had had those vital weeks to organise a vigorous campaign of violence and intimidation, and they did.

Because of the opportunities presented by both the Smith/Home agreement and the Pearce Commission, black party politics took an interesting turn at this juncture. There appeared to be a difference of attitude between ZANU and ZAPU in terms of their exiled chapters and those that undertook party work internally. The radical voices tended to be heard on the outside while the more moderate seemed to be restricted to within. Outside there was a tendency to consider no option other than war, while inside the lines of communication remained open in a number of ways. Also, there was a practical political vacuum in Rhodesia. No forum of organised political resistance was at liberty to meet what was seen as another British attempt to legalise an illegal regime. The recently released nationalists reacted quickly and formed a bipartisan platform they called the African National Council. This new ANC was conceived to represent both ZANU and ZAPU in exile. It would be staffed reasonably equally between the two parties and be chaired by someone unblooded by any past confrontations. Such a man was required to be sufficiently unthreatening to forestall a ban for long enough for the group to mount an effective campaign.

The person selected for this job was 46-year-old Abel Muzorewa, a Methodist Bishop and the first black man to have ascended to the bishopric of any denomination in the country. If the intention was to name as leader a dilettante with neither political aptitude nor any pleasing physical attributes, then Muzorewa was certainly well chosen. He was a short, bespectacled man of the type of which political cartoonists are fond. He emphasised these characteristics with a fondness for outlandish dress and a prevaricating and indecisive state of mind — all of which burdened him with a discernable aura of failure. The ANC, however, was not conceived with permanence, and if the opposing political establishment did not take Bishop Muzorewa particularly seriously, then that was so much the better. Despite his unpromising credentials, Muzorewa did succeed in leading a spirited campaign against the Smith/Home proposals, that surprised everybody with its unity and focus. Almost everywhere that the Pearce Commission ventured it was met by ANC-organised demonstrations that, although largely peaceful, were unequivocal in their rejection of the settlement terms. The ANC catch phrase was: 'Reject this settlement. We will get better terms later on.'[2] Thus to the dismay of both white Rhodesia and the British Foreign Office, the Pearce Commission was forced on 12 March 1972 to conclude that the settlement was not acceptable to the Rhodesian population as a whole. The Commission's final report observed:

> We are satisfied on our evidence that the proposals are acceptable to the great majority of Europeans. We are equally satisfied, after considering all our evidence including that on intimidation, that the majority of Africans reject the proposals. In our opinion, the people of Rhodesia as a whole do not regard the proposals as acceptable as a basis for independence.[3]

Black rejection of the Smith/Home proposals was primarily based on the fact that consultations had excluded them. Didymus Mutasa, a middle ranking nationalist, put it simply: 'We rejected these proposals simply because they are not honourable...' He then went on to add. 'We want equal rights in our country. It is not something that we should ask for cap in hand, but what every human being is entitled to.'[4] Across the board, blacks rejected lukewarm commitment to majority rule as some ill-defined principal relevant to future generations. They demanded majority rule — without conditions — immediately. Smith simply could not accept that a black rejection of the settlement proposals was genuine — an opinion that a majority of whites were quick to endorse. Not only had the ANC and other nationalist bodies applied their usual alchemy of violence and threat, but also they felt that the vast majority of blacks simply did not understand the question. The concept of a ballot and the idea of individual thought and opinion, Smith explained, simply did not exist in native culture. He swore then, and swore until his death, that the blacks of Rhodesia supported him. In herding the masses towards rejection of the proposals, a small group of radicalised nationalists had robbed the white tribe of a rare opportunity for legitimacy...he maintained.

Maybe Smith and his white constituency were right. They were certainly right when they rammed home the fact that the vast majority of workers and peasants, then — and possibly even now — did not really understand the notion of individual suffrage in all its varied ramifications. It is open to question whether this implies that — with knowledge — the opinion of the black masses would have been any different. On certain levels the nationalists did indeed beat, burn, rape and murder their way through the campaign. What is certain is that despite this, the whites were completely quarantined from the nuances of black thought and opinion.

As is common in situations such as this, the material result ranked second in significance to the symbolism. To the blacks this was the first time that their opinion had been directly consulted en masse, and the first time they had uttered a unified and clearly audible reply. To the whites it naturally came as a tremendous shock. For the first time many of them were forced to swallow the fact that blacks were not content to be their meek acolytes. Nor would they willingly fall in behind white leadership with a compliant acceptance of their own social and political inferiority. It was the moment, many whites would agree, when they sensed that a high water mark had been reached. From that moment on, imperceptibly at first, whites found themselves swimming against the tide.

51

The losing war

Portuguese decline

By the 1970s the mutual dependence of Mozambique and Rhodesia had grown to include matters of internal and joint security. The Portuguese laissez faire, that had for so long made social relationships across the border so pleasant, also made the business of forcing the Portuguese to attend to their own security situation frustrating. Portugal remained committed to her 'overseas provinces' to a far greater extent than any other European power still holding them, but that determination did not always seem to filter down to the men-at-arms holding the line. Both of the Portuguese African possessions south of the equator were under threat from nationalist activity, and in the case of Mozambique, this was spearheaded by the Front for the Liberation of Mozambique, or FRELIMO, founded on 25 June 1962.

FRELIMO was a unity movement of three regionally based nationalist organisations: the Mozambique African National Union, the National Democratic Union of Mozambique and the National Union of Independent Mozambique. The merger formed a broad-based guerrilla movement under the leadership of Eduardo Mondlane. Mondlane was killed by a book-bomb in 1969 and was succeeded by the ruthless but charismatic Samora Machel, under whom FRELIMO achieved its greatest successes.

The organisation's administration and rear bases were situated in Tanzania from where, with the help of the Soviet Union, it began in October 1964 to infiltrate insurgents south into Mozambique. Thanks to a long and wild border region, these incursions were relatively easy to execute. The insurgency, however, ran into trouble in the Tete Province, when fighters were forced to cross the Zambezi River and thus over-extend their supply lines.

For four years the war in northern Mozambique fizzled along in a hinterland way beyond the pale for most urbanised whites in the country. Construction of the huge Cahora Bassa hydroelectric project was under way on the Zambezi River, and the Portuguese were always quick to dismiss suggestions that the war in any way inhibited progress. Of course this was not so. FRELIMO's strategy necessitated crossing the Zambezi River and this depended in the long term on it controlling Cabo Delgado and Niassa Provinces, and there seemed to be no reason to suppose that it would not succeed.

Much of the Portuguese apathy that was evident on the ground came about as a consequence of a somewhat feudal attitude to war. Increased prophylaxis against malaria had, by the turn of the century, changed Mozambique from the suicidal military posting it had once been to a very pleasant sojourn for Portuguese officers posted abroad. The moment that the killing started, however, fewer of these men tended to report for duty on the front line. The two main port cities of Mozambique, as well as a handful of smaller coastal towns, were sublimely pleasant. There, more often than not, were to be found the billets of officers who had no interest in sweating it out with the *povo* who were facing the dangers of an armed insurgency.

Therefore they were young, conscripted peasants who knew little and cared less about Mozambique who fortified the front line. These men, poorly led, sparsely provisioned and unmotivated, were consistently pushed forward to take on the brunt of the guerrilla insurgence. It was not surprising then that FRELIMO made steady advances. By the end of the 1960s FRELIMO had effectively occupied all the territory from the line of the Zambezi River north to the Tanzanian border. Then, in 1968, after four years of war, FRELIMO opened up a new front in the Tete Province below the vital Zambezi line. This was a severe blow to the Portuguese, but far more so to the Rhodesians. The Zambezi was the Rubicon and FRELIMO had crossed it. Thereafter any friend of Samora Machel, who had an interest in piercing the soft flanks of Rhodesia, could rely on FRELIMO protection and support.

It was at that moment that Rhodesian security concerns ceased to be containable. The Zambezi ran the length of Rhodesia's border with Zambia, and was a perfect defensive line so long as the war remained confined between the 25° and 30° parallels. Further east was a land border with Mozambique and if guerrillas could simply step over it without having to cross the Zambezi, then Rhodesia would have a whole new problem on its hands. Of vital importance as the 1970s dawned, was to keep FRELIMO north of the line, with or without Portuguese co-operation.

As it happened the Portuguese accepted Rhodesian help but with the proviso that no suggestion be made that Portugal could not cope with its own security demands. While it was not officially acknowledged, Rhodesian military activity in Tete Province began in earnest in 1970. Ostensibly this was in the form of combined operations with Portuguese units, but in practice the Rhodesians were generally on their own.

Rhodesia used its regular units — primarily the SAS and RLI — supported by the Air Force and units of the Rhodesian African Rifles (RAR). In January 1972 a Tactical HQ was set up in the Makonde Protected Village (*Aldeamento*) south of the Zambezi River, from where the RAR patrolled the south bank and the SAS the mountain areas to the north.

While the Portuguese fought the war with great flourish, they did very little to actually engage the enemy. Despite this almost total unwillingness to fight, they obviously still found it difficult to acknowledge that they were losing the war. Ken Flower recalled overhearing General Costa Gomes, the man in charge, ask his military attaché if the Rhodesians really expected the Portuguese to live like animals in the bush. 'No, Senhor.' The attaché replied. 'It is the example that is quite magnificent, and it suits the Rhodesians who are Anglo-Saxons, but they don't really expect that sort of behaviour from us Latins.'

To explain the apparent Portuguese incompetence and lack of engagement in the field of military campaigning, it helps to briefly examine the background to the Mozambique war. Between 1961 and 1974 Portugal was confronted by the almost impossible task of supporting three simultaneous and determined counterinsurgency campaigns in Africa. These were in Guinea Bissau, the smallest campaign of the three; Angola, the largest; and Mozambique. Portugal was neither a wealthy nor a highly developed country, and although the maintenance of her 'overseas provinces' was key to her national prestige, the financial and human cost of suppressing national resistance in all three was crippling. Key also was the limited experience, and indeed inclination towards war that Portugal had shown in the modern context. Since World War-I, when the East African Campaign had briefly spilled over into her territory, the Portuguese had not fired a single shot in anger.[1]

While the SAS and RLI were treating FRELIMO to the only real fighting of the Mozambique War, Rhodesian Special Branch and the CIO were scanning mountains of recovered intelligence to establish whether any sort of strategic alliance existed between FRELIMO and ZANLA.

The answer came in March 1972 as Special Branch began receiving reports of the arrival of a small

ZANLA reconnaissance group investigating a possible route south through Mozambique. The Portuguese were steadfast in denying that there was any ZANLA traffic through Tete, but they were probably the least likely to know. They did agree, however, to mount a combined operation with the SAS to investigate the reports.

The Portuguese were then sent on a fallacious patrol some distance away while an SAS team, commanded by Lieutenant Bert Sachse, mounted an unhindered attack on the Matimbe Base. There they found the evidence that they had been both hoping for and dreading. While it was difficult to discern from the bodies of the dead exactly who were FRELIMO and who were not, a search revealed a passage in a notebook that read: 'Go tell Evensi that the Zimbabwe boys have arrived.'[2] Evensi Mashonganidze, founder of one of many local apocalyptic churches, was a guerrilla contact already known to Special Branch. However, even if he had been apprehended and questioned on the matter, it is unlikely that he would have been able to add much to the simple gravity of the intelligence.

A situation report was radioed through to Salisbury but the CIO remained sceptical. Nevertheless, Special Branch was immediately deployed in force to the northeast to investigate, and CIO scepticism soon evaporated as the truth gradually came to light. No one could quite believe just how far the nationalists had progressed in laying the groundwork for a new phase of the armed struggle. An arms cache was discovered, then another, followed by local testimony revealing the steady portage of large quantities of war material over the preceding months. Arms were even unearthed in a Salisbury industrial site, thereby exposing unacceptable intelligence failings on the part of the Rhodesians.

A parallel mobilisation and politicisation of the masses had also been under way. It had now proceeded to the point where manpower and ordinance for a respectable war could be transported into Rhodesia, and hidden in the countryside without a whiff of it reaching the noses of either Special Branch or the CIO. The security establishment was stunned. So was Ian Smith. On 4 December 1972, in a mood of rare solemnity, he made a broadcast to the nation in which he said:

> The security situation is far more serious than it appears on the surface, and if the man in the street could have access to the security information which I and my colleagues in government have, then I think he would be a lot more worried than he is today.[3]

Operation Hurricane

Almost at the moment that Ian Smith uttered these words, the first group of 21 armed men slipped into the country and immediately moved into pre-prepared hiding places in the Chiweshe Tribal Trust Land northeast of Centenary. A tough and motivated young field commander by the name of Rex Nhongo led the group. Nhongo's initial objective was to fire a few shots at soft targets in order to see what kind of a hornet's nest could be stirred up. After a brief reconnaissance he selected as his first target Centenary farmer Marc de Borchgrave's Altena Farm. Altena was subjected to a few minutes of machine-gun and rifle fire before Nhongo and his team slipped back into hiding.

De Borchgrave and his family took temporary refuge on a neighbouring farm, Whistlefield, which was also attacked a few days later. The hapless de Borchgrave and his hosts survived this second attack, although a young Rhodesian soldier, Corporal Norman Moore, was killed by a landmine blast during a follow-up operation. Soon afterwards three more white soldiers fell victim to a second landmine. In the meantime, Nhongo and his men moved back into the anonymity of the Chiweshe Tribal Trust Land to wait on events.

The immediate Security Force response was the setting up of a Joint Operational Command (JOC) codenamed *Operation Hurricane*. Troops and equipment were moved into the area in the expectation of another quick sortie. This time, however, the army found no trace of the enemy. Local villagers had nothing to say, protecting their *vafana* (boys) with a stubborn wall of silence.

It was at this point that the blacks of the countryside were confronted by some of the blunter realities of the struggle for their hearts and minds. They faced the guerrillas at night and the Security Forces during the day. Revealing intelligence about terrorist movements invited brutal retribution, flavoured with some of the darker creativity of black Africa. Failing to do so could bring about a beating or the confiscation or destruction of property by the Security Forces.

There were two schools of thought in the armed services regarding the correct response to dead intelligence sources. The first was the more forceful approach: 'keep the blacks in their place', while the second was the more pragmatic: 'keep the blacks on-side'. For the rural population it was a very sharp dilemma. Although the balance of terror unequivocally lay on the side of the insurgents — very few among the Security Forces could or were willing to compete with the guerrillas in the use of extreme terror and cruelty which was routinely applied by both ZAPU and ZANU throughout the war — an encounter with either side was never likely to be pleasant.

The people's war

The theories of Mao on the subject of people's wars are filled with simple rules of human engagement. The mantra is simple: an armed insurrection cannot succeed without the active support of the masses. In Rhodesia's war too there was to be no elitism. Borrowing from Mao, it became clear to the nationalists that revolution must remain of and for the people and could only be fought with the full integration of the people and their militias. One of the first to hear and ponder this message was Josiah Tongogara, who was undergoing a period of training in China. Like Rex Nhongo, he was a tough and charismatic guerrilla leader who would in due course take over full military command of ZANLA (Zimbabwe African National Liberation Army). Having listened and learned, Tongogara returned to southern Africa in the glow of an epiphany.

Simply sending guerrillas to confront Rhodesian troops — without first educating the local people on the nature and aims of the struggle — could only invite suspicion and confusion. Significant preparatory work would need to be done. The vital first step was to begin a programme of instructing political commissars, and then infiltrate them into the tribal areas in order to politicise the masses. Not before the common man fully understood and identified with the aims of armed struggle could fighters be safely deployed into the countryside.

This simple but profound lesson came on the heels of a long period of introspection within both major political parties. Herbert Chitepo revealed in 1972 that his party intended to reverse the errors of the past by politicising and mobilising the people before mounting any attacks against the regime. He went on to state that the object of any direct military action from then on would not be an attempt to defeat the Security Forces in battle, but to harass and attack vulnerable targets — the effect of which would be to force the Rhodesian Army to over-extend itself. In this way white manpower needs for defence would serve to override the demands of commerce and industry with the result that the country would eventually collapse. It was a simple strategy that had every chance of succeeding — particularly since the opening of the Tete front in Mozambique.

The Tete region was now under FRELIMO control. The difficulty was that the movement was led by the Castroesque revolutionary Samora Machel. Machel remained hostile to ZANU, which he regarded as a splinter movement of ZAPU and a dangerously divisive influence. The offer to capitalise on Tete was initially extended exclusively to ZAPU, as the first and only legitimate liberation movement. However ZAPU was inert at that time. This is partly explained by its Soviet alignment, but it had also been plunged into a leadership crisis, of which we will hear more later. ZANLA, on the other hand, was equipped and ready; it waited only for permission from FRELIMO to mobilise south of the Zambezi. For some time Machel maintained pressure on James Chikerema, the ZAPU leader in exile, but in the end he began to sense that a vital opportunity was being lost.

At that point he began to entertain ZANU contacts until in due course he permitted a limited number of ZANLA fighters to occupy rear bases and commence operations in Rhodesia. These were the 'ZANU boys' unearthed by Special Branch in Tete in the aftermath of SAS operations.

Prior to this, ZANU had been covertly deploying reconnaissance groups into the tribal trust lands of the Rhodesian northeast, in order to begin the process of preparing and politicising the people for war. Of this period Ken Flower wrote, with the benefit of white observations of the time, that this process led inevitably to 'intimidation in its very worst forms'.[4] Chinese war philosopher Sun Tzu put it more succinctly: 'Kill one, frighten a thousand'.

ZANLA methods of political enforcement were as sinister and brutal as any in Kenya or the Congo — or China for that matter. Cadres who returned to Rhodesia on these political missions were often deployed outside their home areas lest sentimentality intrude on what needed to be done. Perpetrators of this type of violence morally transitioned from guerrillas to terrorists with the use of killings and torture that were at times aberrational, and the Rhodesians were quick to label them thus. These units usually announced their arrival in a district with a harsh application of this sort of violence, followed by a period of intense political education. The combined message was inescapable and few members of the audience failed to hear it.

ZANU doctrine itself was also highly persuasive. It played on a cocktail of common grievances — losing the land to the whites was a powerful example — seductive promises of restitution, a subtle allusion to Marxism alongside much stronger references to the historical significance of the struggle. The latter concept was supported by an ideological revisitation to the shrines and mediums of the spirit world.

The most important point of religio-historical significance was the fact that the new phase of the war was opening in the seat of the old Mwane Mutapa Empire, that had also been the home of Mbuya Nehanda, executed along with Kagubi during the Mashona Rebellion. Mbuya Nehanda was by then a powerful historical figure whose significance had been magnified by her execution, and was now absorbed into the iconography of the liberation struggle. In early 1972, ZANLA guerrillas made contact with an elderly woman who had been reputed for the last 60 years to be the reincarnated spirit of Mbuya Nehanda. They introduced themselves to her as the vanguard of the second Chimurenga, and were told by the spirit of Nehanda that her medium was to be transported across the border into Mozambique from where both would assist in the planning of the struggle.

By the 1970s, respect for traditional authority had been severely compromised by the Chiefs Councils where traditional chiefs received government pay. People therefore looked to the spirit mediums more than ever. Mediums were more than just a link to the spirit world — they were the archivists of the nation's traditional institutions and a vital force in the preservation of a common identity. They were also the last surviving indigenous authority that the guerrillas could cite to validate both themselves and the struggle. The degree to which this succeeded was best reflected in the numbers of young people beginning to present themselves for guerrilla training. Political Commissar Josiah Tungamirai later remarked on the effect of this spiritual endorsement of the struggle.

> Once the children, the boys and girls in the area, knew that Nehanda had joined the war, they came in large numbers.[5]

In a radio broadcast aired in January 1973 Ian Smith explained the phenomenon to the nation to the best of his ability, and probably to the satisfaction of most whites.

> ...they found a few witchdoctors of doubtful character and of little substance, and succeeded in bribing them to their side.[6]

Of doubtful character or not, the Security Forces were suddenly chasing invisible terrorists. No one was changing sides and no one was talking. Farms were being attacked, roads mined and vehicles ambushed, but no one knew anything. To the tribesmen the awful consequences of treason at the hands of their liberators had already been demonstrated. Besides, there were few by then who did not at least partly identify with the aims and objectives of the struggle. The inevitable frustration that began to build in the ranks of the Security Forces found expression in collective punishment, as troops lashed out at innocent people who were rarely innocent. Blacks became practical liars thanks to the nature of their circumstances and their blank faces and stubborn denials tended to prove beyond doubt to sceptical interrogators that they knew something.

On 19 January 1973 emergency regulations came into effect. These gave power to the government and government agents to impose collective fines, confiscate cattle or burn villages where members were suspected of aiding and abetting terrorists.[7] Two weeks later the police closed down all the beer halls, clinics, schools, butcheries and stores in the Chiweshe Tribal Trust Lands. A month later the maximum penalty for supporting terrorism was raised from five to 20 years' imprisonment. In May these regulations were incorporated as amendments to the Law and Order (Maintenance) Act, and in September the Act was amended again to impose a mandatory death sentence, or life imprisonment, for terrorist activities. The sentence for recruiting terrorists was increased to 20 years and provided for the forfeiture of property as an additional punishment.[7] All this could be taken as an admission by the government that it had lost the battle for the hearts and minds of the people. It was a rare man or woman indeed who chose to risk fearful retribution at the hands of the *vafana* by leaking information to Special Branch.

To deal with this problem, Salisbury borrowed a strategy from earlier British conflicts. The use of containment camps was the crude manifestation of a simple principal: isolate the fighting men from the support base of their homes and women-folk and the struggle would soon collapse. This strategy was originally applied during the Anglo-Boer War and it worked very well. Later it was tried — with more questionable results — in Malaya, and later still in Kenya. The model most closely followed by the Rhodesian Government was the *Aldeamentos* system used in Mozambique up until the end of colonialism. In simple terms, people were herded together — ostensibly for the sake of their own protection — in fortified camps that were termed Protected Villages rather than containment camps.

By mid-1973 four Protected Villages had been established in the northeast that compacted thousands of villagers into tightly cramped spaces. The overcrowded conditions arose because of inaccurate population estimates, and the ad hoc nature of construction. In essence the method was to create an area demarcated by security fencing into which, with government help, people were able to build their own dwellings that more or less conformed to the basic mud and thatch model. The final result resembled a huge village compound surrounded by a fortified military perimeter. A separate branch of the Security Forces was formed to administer the system, which came to be regarded as something of a poor relation of the Army. In due course this Guard Force tended to become a receptacle for conscripted whites who were of limited capacity either physically or intellectually. These would often be school leavers who were then given command of poorly trained and apathetic black 'troops'.

The South Africans serving in the northeast were also not immune to the frustrations of these new rules of bush warfare. On 14 December 1973 a lamentable incident occurred that briefly threw north-south cooperation into jeopardy. A patrol of South African Police in the Chiweshe Tribal Trust Land came upon an African woman gathering wood while carrying a baby on her back. They questioned her but did not receive satisfactory answers. Thereupon a white constable seized the child and cut its throat with a Swiss Army Knife. The traumatised woman walked to Bindura Police Station to report the incident and a docket for murder was opened.

The subsequent interrogation of black BSAP details attached to the South African patrol confirmed the incident. Initially, South African commanders were bemused that such a fuss was being made over the death of a black infant. They certainly could see no justification for the subsequent arrest of the guilty man. On arraignment of the defendant in the High Court, the commanding officer of the South African CID, accompanied by legal advisors, arrived in the country to examine the evidence and interview their men. Within a few days the Rhodesians were informed at the highest level that the matter, if pursued, would not be beneficial to Rhodesian relations with South Africa. A few days later the constable was released and repatriated.[8]

* * *

Closer to home the government was also showing itself willing to lash out at the ghosts of an invisible war. Ian Smith closed the border between Zambia and Rhodesia on 9 January 1973, warning that it would remain closed until the Zambian Government acted to stop the movement of guerrillas across the Zambezi. This action was seen as a sign of uncertainty rather than strength and, if nothing else, it forced Kenneth Kaunda to accept, willingly or otherwise, that he had finally been sucked into the struggle for Zimbabwe. Before long, however, Smith was forced to reconsider. Closing the border immediately affected regional transport networks and clearly should not have been done without consultation. With his only two friends grumbling in his ear, Smith had no choice but to announce the reopening of the border. Kaunda made the most of a bad business and announced that the border would remain closed, and it did.

The foreign press was another target of unwarranted official attacks. In March 1973 journalist Peter Niesewand was jailed and later deported, convicted of divulging official secrets. He had filed a routine report for the UK *Guardian* that highlighted Rhodesian military cooperation with the Portuguese, a fact that the Rhodesian Government had been consistently denying. Niesewand, a Gwelo native, continued to report on Rhodesia from outside the country.

In another indication of internal stresses, a minor rebellion took place in 1973, when Alan Savory, a young Member of Parliament, ecologist, territorial officer and pioneer of the Tracker combat unit, conspicuously broke ranks. Savory made the point that although the guerrilla movements were politically aligned with the Eastern Bloc, the war was primarily a civil conflict between Rhodesians. He warned that there was nothing to be gained by avoiding this reality by insisting that the war was a fight against communism. He further cautioned that brute force and tough talk would ultimately lose the war. For the first time in Parliament, it was Savory who referred to nationalist insurgents not as 'terrorists' but as 'guerrillas'. To win the war, he told the House, the guerrillas only required that the masses remain passive. For Rhodesia to win, it would be necessary for the bulk of the population to actively support the Government, and there were few in the country who believed that at that stage this was even a remote possibility.

Savory went on to echo the CIO mantra that a political solution was imperative, and proposed the idea of inviting the guerrilla leaders to a constitutional conference. This stirred up the bile of the right wing RF majority, who were irrevocably committed to the hard-line. It was unfortunate that Savory chose to press this message right after three Security Force members were killed in action.

The Prime Minister was equally unlikely to endorse Savory's suggestions, and with typical hyperbole he described them as 'the most irresponsible and evil I have ever heard.'[9] Ken Flower put it another way, aiming the blame more directly at the government: 'RF policies, moving towards apartheid, have embittered Africans, or at best, turned them into neutrals waiting to see whether the terrorists are 'Freedom Fighters' or whether the Security Forces emerge victorious.'[10] Increasingly it began to appear that the odds against a Security Force victory, even if it was a simple matter of long-term containment, were growing very long indeed.

The Rhodesian war machine and pseudo operations

So far responsibility for the hard fighting had been concentrated in the hands of the regular units — the BSAP, SAS, RLI and RAR. While killing terrorists had been a productive sideline of counter-terrorism, the main effort had always been focussed on prevention and intelligence gathering. Now killing terrorists was becoming at least as important — if not more important — than the accumulation of intelligence. In the early 1970s the main problem had been to find isolated groups in remote tribal areas so that they could be pinned down and engaged. For this the CIO formed small experimental pseudo groups to penetrate the guerrilla networks operating within the country. The idea was to conduct close surveillance with a view to compromising and ultimately destroying the enemy. In due course the Army took control of the programme and, in 1973, the Selous Scouts Regiment was formed as a mixed race special force unit intended for internal covert operations and for the infiltration of enemy formations. To achieve this a small Special Branch unit was attached to it. There job was to interrogate captured guerrillas or sympathisers and otherwise to gain information which was used to direct their military partners onto enemy targets.

The Selous Scouts operated within the general Rhodesian military structure which at the time represented a formidable arsenal of force — second on the continent only to the South African Defence Force. By the end of 1972 the Rhodesian Security Forces numbered almost 5 000 regular Army and Air Force personnel supported by 10 000 white Territorials and some 8 000 BSAP members of both races. The BSAP itself was supported by 35 000 mostly white police reservists. The regular Army consisted of two battalions, one of which was the all-white Rhodesian Light Infantry (RLI) and the other the white-officered Rhodesian African Rifles (RAR).[11]

It was with ample justification then that white Rhodesia felt confident in the ability of its Security Forces to contain and limit the current security threat. In this they succeeded, but containment increasingly appeared to be the key word, and unlike previous operations, *Operation Hurricane* proved to be ongoing. Guerrilla units were living among tribesmen who sheltered and fed them, and through whom the re-supply of war materiel was easily managed. Targets were selectively chosen, and direct confrontation avoided wherever possible. The interrogation of captures revealed the location of large caches, while ongoing intelligence work made for increased successes. Nevertheless, the threat was not eliminated, and while many insurgents were being killed, many Rhodesian soldiers and civilians were also dying.

While for most white Rhodesians these were disturbing developments, the threat remained confined almost entirely to the northeast, and the majority continued to enjoy the Rhodesian way of life. Fuel rationing was gone, immigration was exceeding emigration and the economy was for all intents and purposes beating sanctions. White Rhodesians were reasonably confident that the security threat would soon be crushed as it had been in the 1960s. The nationalists were still at each other's throats and indeed seemed to spend more time posturing and grandstanding than trying to win a war.

Kenneth Kaunda had recently and quite unexpectedly handed 129 guerrillas over to the Rhodesians. He was responding to ongoing inter-camp warfare in Zambia that was beginning to interfere with civic life and annoy the President a great deal. The intelligence services also seemed to be more or less back on track and usually had a good idea of what was going to happen before it happened. All this fed a false sense of confidence that had much to do with economic well-being, and tended to deflect attention from the unchanged political circumstances of UDI.

Most whites probably decided that they would wait for the war to be won, then see how it affected the general state of UDI. Exports were topping pre-UDI levels as inflation hovered at around 3%. A high profile and extremely satisfying coup had been the recent acquisition — for the national carrier — of three Boeing airliners that were flown in covertly by Air Trans Africa. White immigration figures for 1972 indicated an 8 500 person net gain. Defence expenditure amounted to just 12% of the budget, which certainly did not seem excessive for financing a war.

For those with a mind to read between the lines, however, indicators of stress were becoming increasingly visible. September 1973 saw an abrupt and unexpected immigration turnaround with the first net loss of whites recorded since the Great Depression. Army Commander Lieutenant General Peter Walls was heard to comment that shortages of European manpower were beginning to affect important expansion plans for the Security Forces. These were the first echoes of Chitepo's threat to force the Rhodesian armed forces to over-extend themselves. But expansion plans went ahead anyway. Early the following year the National Service intake was doubled and white men over 25 who had been living in the country for more than five years became eligible for call-up periods of up to a month. Even this did not entirely cover the bases, and it was later decided to raise a second battalion of the RAR.

These measures were both seen and explained as healthy contingencies, for after all the country was at war. Nothing so far had seriously threatened the white establishment and nothing obvious was on the horizon. However, many who should have been looking were not, and in an atmosphere of tight security many others were simply ill informed. About 8000 whites had come in and 8000 could just as easily leave. Two friendly neighbours protected Rhodesia's rump and her eastern flank, but the security situation in Mozambique was perilous. Surprisingly few put two and two together and a year or two of pleasant complacency seemed to colour the whole future with roses.

Struggles within the struggle

Privately Sir Alec Douglas Home had been as dismayed as Smith to hear the report of the Pearce Commission. Publicly he took the attitude that henceforth it was incumbent on Rhodesians of both colours to settle their differences internally. The British should only be approached to endorse what had been found to be mutually acceptable. Desperate to shed the Rhodesian albatross, Home nominally kept the 1971 proposals on the table but otherwise took a step back, and hoped against all precedent that the Rhodesians could find a solution to their own problems.

In taking this attitude, Home either forgot or ignored the fact that most of the main nationalist leaders were in prison, and whether he knew it or not, the external situation was no more positive. The liberation movements were in utter crisis. With a tried and tested determination to undermine any gain, ZAPU was busy leading both itself and ZANU down the road to virtual ruin. The main culprit in this particular chapter of nationalist disunity was James Chikerema.

Chikerema was an authentic nationalist with an impressive record of service. He had been the founder and first president of the African National Youth League before he slipped down a rung, to become vice-president of the newly formed ANC, and later a mere executive member of ZAPU. These eclipses were due primarily to his lack of education but were not helped at all by the fact that he tended to be a snappish, difficult and rather paranoid individual. In an effort to arrest his own decline, he insinuated himself close to Nkomo. But since Nkomo had just narrowly survived a leadership crisis himself, he was no less paranoid. Most of his best men had either been sacrificed or had crossed the floor, and because Chikerema was both loyal and not particularly gifted, he was a perfect choice for deputy president. The mass detention of the top leadership was a further godsend for Chikerema, and as the parties shifted their focus to Lusaka, he naturally moved to occupy the leadership of ZAPU in exile. If ever there was a moment for him to make a name for himself, this was it.

Circumstances, however, appeared always to conspire against Chikerema. He had been a founding father of the party and once back at the helm, he felt that he was owed more respect than he was being given. He had neither the charisma nor the intelligence to earn respect, and nor could he compete anymore with the handful of new and genuine rising stars in the party. Chikerema was outclassed and it irritated him enormously. But Nkomo had given him power of attorney, so when in a corner he simply ruled by decree. Others who had also been loyal to Nkomo were not overawed. Two of these — Jason Moyo and George Silundika — formed a front in opposition to Chikerema and a power struggle was born.

Chikerema's most celebrated blunder occurred in 1970, when he accompanied a British film crew into a guerrilla camp in Zambia. As he toured the camp, cameramen were allowed to film men in training who would soon be infiltrated back into Rhodesia. When Moyo was briefed on this he was appalled. Exposing to the media the men who were about to fight a vigilant enemy was incomprehensible. Doing so without first consulting with the executive, and then with Kaunda — who had always fervently denied that any guerrilla bases existed on his territory — was in both cases a major breach of faith.

This blunder demonstrated Chikerema's basic lack of sophistication. Had he given the matter any thought, he would immediately have recognised his folly. But having failed to do so, the only response in his arsenal was to maintain vigorously that his actions had been correct. The incident provoked an open rift in the party. A document was released by the executive entitled 'Observations on our Struggle'. Jason Moyo was the author and his comments were not so much observations as a series of bitter denunciations of Chikerema. The latter was personally cited as being guilty of leadership failings, of showing a disregard for security and for allowing a damaging complacency to take root in the heart of the party.

Chikerema's response was too immediate for it to have been properly considered. A document of his own entitled *Reply to Observations on our Struggle* was circulated. In it he offered a handful of tart rejoinders in validation of his actions, adding fulsome accusations of tribalism, corruption and immoral conduct. He ended with an announcement that he had dissolved the entire leadership structure of ZAPU, and henceforth would be assuming absolute control. Moyo replied, noting the extraordinary number of times that Chikerema had used the words 'I' and 'me' in his exhortations, and expressing regret that the tone of the exchange had been allowed to sink to the level of personal insults.

Chikerema's coup was declared 'null and void' by a majority of the executive and as might have been expected, the factions split and shots were fired. Several dozen fighters were killed as militancy swept rapidly through the camps. The violence came to a head in March 1971 with an assassination attempt on George Nyandoro in the centre of Lusaka. Nyandoro was a fellow pioneer member of ZAPU and an important Chikerema faction supporter.

Chikerema was again put on the defensive and soon found himself forced out of the party offices. With a rapidly dwindling support base, he became desperate for some shred of a viable strategy. Then he remembered old calls to unity from the Frontline States and the OAU. As he thought about it he forgot all about previous claims he had made that ZANU was a splinter party and of no political importance. He led the tatters of his faction in an approach to ZANU, pleading the necessity for some sort of a unity agreement.

ZANU itself was at that stage reasonably united, but most importantly it was actually focussed on fighting the war. While a coup in ZAPU was obviously to ZANU's ultimate benefit, Chitepo and the ZANU leadership could not at the same time appear to be ignoring any genuine overtures of unity. It was also unfortunate for ZANU that Chikerema succeeded in attracting a few its members to his side, principal among whom were Nathan Shamuyarira and Godfrey Savanhu. This dilution precipitated a split in ZANU that in turn gave birth to a third political party — FROLIZI, or the Front for the Liberation of Zimbabwe. FROLIZI was formally launched on 1 October 1971, at more or less the same time as the centrists of both parties were uniting within Rhodesia to form the African National Council.

In theory, FROLIZI ought to have superseded both ZAPU and ZANU. To support this position Chikerema claimed the existence of a 'letter' from Nkomo stating that he had been in contact with Sithole, and that both men had agreed to step down in favour of Robert Mugabe. Chikerema also maintained that Chitepo had received a similar letter but he was denying its existence to preserve his power ambitions.

FROLIZI was immediately denounced by both ZANU and a reconstituted ZAPU. However its formation was well received in the OAU where it was accepted as an authentic 'unity' party. Thanks to this, ZANU was forced to come around and in a press statement issued on 7 October it grudgingly accepted the new party, but rejected any suggestion that ZANU had been superseded by FROLIZI.

This so-called front is not a united front at all; it is a nepotistic grouping of cousins and relatives who are determined to sabotage the liberation struggle and so help the Smith regime in its futile attempts to divide the people of Zimbabwe further.[1]

ZANU warned against hasty recognition of FROLIZI by the OAU, but the organisation was not listening. The OAU had been pressing for a bipartisan front for some time and generally welcomed developments. In light of this ZANU issued a second press release.

The OAU and all states sympathetic to the liberation of Zimbabwe must resist the temptation to recognise one movement as the sole vehicle for liberation, and therefore, the only one to be considered for aid.[2]

This was at the root of the issue for both sides. Recognition by the OAU had long been denied to ZANU — which was ironic because it was ZANU — virtually alone — that was attempting to engage in the armed struggle. While it actually fought, FROLIZI pondered strategy from a distance. Chikerema acknowledged that OAU recognition would come only on the heels of action in the field but he was slow to act. He claimed that his fighters were being 'systematically' deployed after extensive 'scientific' analysis.[3] Ultimately, the only recorded FROLIZI action of the war was the murder of a Wedza farmer. After some nine months of its existence, the *Times of Zambia* asked what had actually become of FROLIZI.

In March 1973, a Joint Military Command was formed in terms of an OAU agreement that obliged the three liberation movements to declare their loyalty to a single command structure. All three swore to this, but their fingers were crossed behind their backs and the organ never functioned. To all three parties, the OAU was what the Imperial Government had once been to Cecil John Rhodes: carping, complaining, suspicious, reluctant, but also ever present and ever abiding. In the end things returned more-or-less to normal with FROLIZI and ZAPU doing very little, and ZANU continuing to fight the war essentially alone.

By late 1972 the more considered predictions of the liberation leaders were proved to be correct. FROLIZI became a victim of its own irrelevance and so did Chikerema. In due course the ZANU deserters rejoined the party on the understanding that none could hold an elected office for two years. By 1974 FROLIZI was effectively dead.

* * *

Whatever the external contradictions might have been, the centrists of both parties inside Rhodesia voted to preserve the composition of the African National Council, arguing that it had served a useful purpose so far and ought to be allowed to continue. The party had not been banned, and Bishop Abel Muzorewa appeared — if not exactly as a rival to the established nationalist leadership — then at least as a credible voice in a political vacuum. For Smith this was in some ways fortunate, for he would have found it very difficult to follow Home's advice if there had been no internal leader or organisation with which to engage.

As Smith relates the story, Muzorewa emerged from the startling success of the 1972 'No' campaign with improved confidence — and a great deal more ambition. It was agreed by the ANC leadership that the mandate of the party would be extended, but there was much internal disagreement as to what direction it should take. A section of the growing black middle class was willing to accept the 1971 proposals, on the grounds that the 'no' vote had been emotionally inspired and was unfortunate. After a reasonable cooling off period, it was argued that most blacks would probably see the sense in accepting the terms. There were others who felt that the 'no' vote had been provisional and was intended only as a negotiating position. Yet others held that the situation was far too fresh for there to be any proposals at all. How, it was asked, could there ever be a formula acceptable to the Rhodesian people as a whole when at that stage a whole did not exist in Rhodesian society? The people of the country were either black or white, and what pleased one could be relied upon to displease the other. It was felt that far more pressure was needed before Rhodesian whites would even begin to ponder genuine parity, let alone majority rule.

By early 1973, however, a degree of consensus appeared to be emerging. Among the rank and file a majority felt that the ANC leadership ought to be doing more to engage the government. Smith himself was also heard to ponder why the ANC had made no direct approaches since the departure of the Pearce Commission. Muzorewa indicated that he would like to do so but was hampered by internal opposition. Smith helped clear the way by arresting and locking up the principal hardliners. Muzorewa protested weakly at this but quickly resolved to move on regardless. 'The need of our country to return to normality and to reach an honourable settlement', he explained, 'is greater than the temporary suffering of our brothers…'[4]

So it was. On 17 June 1973 the first official meeting between Muzorewa and Smith took place in an atmosphere of frank exchange. Muzorewa officially pressed a list of eight demands and a fortnight later Smith officially rejected them. Neither man was particularly startled since, high on the list, was a demand for the repeal of the Land Tenure Act. Other demands included immediate parity in Parliament, the urgent release of all political detainees and an amnesty for all members of ZANU and ZAPU based abroad. These, Smith carped — with the weariness of a schoolmaster who had spoken for the thousandth time — added up to nothing less than the old parrot cry of 'one man, one vote'.[5]

Smith's position was that the 1971 proposals, as they currently stood, were non-negotiable. On 1 August, a further 20 senior officials of the ANC were arrested, and a political meeting that the Bishop had been due to address was banned. Despite all this, Muzorewa declared himself still in favour of talks, and a fortnight later he and Smith released a combined press statement that read as follows:

> The Prime Minister and Bishop Muzorewa met on 17 August 1973 to discuss the question of the constitutional settlement. The Prime Minister gave Bishop Muzorewa a solemn undertaking on behalf of the Government of Rhodesia that if the 1971 proposals for a settlement are ratified, they will be fully honoured by the Government. Bishop Muzorewa accepted the undertaking and stated that he had complete trust in the Prime Minister. In these circumstances Bishop Muzorewa in his capacity as President of the African National Council gave an undertaking that he accepted the 1971 proposals for a settlement, and that he would urge the British Government, on behalf of the African people, to implement the proposals.[6]

A few days later the arrest of nine more ANC officials was announced. At the same time Muzorewa and Smith appeared together to announce that they had agreed on a set of principles that would lead to an equitable solution to Rhodesia's problems. The principles again fell some way short of majority rule and again it was evident that compromise was not in Smith's scheme of things. Muzorewa was prepared to accept parity as a working alternative to majority rule, but the meaning of parity in the context was not defined. He did manage to wrest a further six parliamentary seats from Smith, in addition to the 16 black members already sitting, plus the possibility of a further six after a period of review. All of this was put to the ANC executive at a meeting held in Highfield. It was swiftly rejected. The result was announced by firebrand Publicity Secretary Edson Sithole, who — predictably — was arrested soon afterwards.

Word of the negotiations was not particularly well received by the exiled leadership. The three parties were by then in the thick of their own internal trauma, so their response was muted and did not materially alter the direction of the ANC's policy. It was only in March, when the opinion of the ZANU executive in Salisbury Prison was heard, that the rug was brutally pulled from under Muzorewa's feet.

> We have been receiving persistent reports that the ANC's stand in negotiations falls far short of majority-rule-now, and all the other traditional nationalist demands. Working on the assumption that such reports are correct, we ourselves here are inclined to look upon the ANC and its involvement in negotiations as disastrous and posing the greatest threat to African political interests in a situation currently being militarily improved in the African's favour and which ought to be left to mature for our maximum exploitation when the regime and its supporters are sufficiently ground down to yield meaningfully.[7]

All the ZANU leaders in Salisbury prison including Ndabaningi Sithole signed the message. In respect to the moral authority of ZANU, no more contacts were reported between Smith and Muzorewa until 1975 when circumstances had altered considerably.

53

Spiral of terror
A bloodless coup

Until late in 1973, Rhodesian intelligence had been assessing the security situation in Mozambique from the point of view of containment. Now the situation had changed drastically, and they had to look at it in terms of what they believed was an imminent collapse. The implications for Rhodesia of a Portuguese defeat in Mozambique did not bear thinking about. Much of the confidence felt by Rhodesian whites was based on the fact that a limited front in the northeast was relatively easily controlled. With the addition of 1 000 kilometres or more of hostile border, the situation would leap from a comfortable status quo to a full-blown war that Rhodesia would be unlikely to win.

Ken Flower was amazed — as he constantly seemed to be — at how determined the Rhodesian Government was in resisting the truth. First there had been a rejection of ZANU cooperation with FRELIMO in Tete, then the belief in the loyalty of the blacks of the northeast, and now it seemed that the government was determined to ignore an imminent collapse in Mozambique.

It was not as if there was any shortage of concrete evidence. By the end of 1973 the initial deployment of a single company of troops in the *Operation Hurricane* area had grown to 20 — and this did not include additional air and BSAP support as well as the SAP units. Addressing a meeting of intelligence officers and the Joint Chiefs of Staff of both Rhodesia and South Africa, Flower sounded an ominous warning.

> With every year that has passed our enemies have become more united and in some respects more efficient, whilst the component parts of southern Africa have become more vulnerable and in some respects more disunited.[1]

By adopting this approach, Flower had hoped to draw the South Africans into the Rhodesian dilemma. It was not only the fate of Rhodesia that hung in the balance, but the future of white domination in southern Africa as a whole. He rejected out of hand the illusion that the war pitted communism against the western, Christian, capitalist order.

> Communism as such does not constitute as great a threat to our respective governments, to the white man in southern Africa, as say, African nationalism.[2]

The South Africans, however, proved as difficult to impress as the Rhodesians. They seemed already to have written off Mozambique, and perhaps by extension Rhodesia too. Pretoria was now leaning towards the use of charm and dialogue, and even the Portuguese military command itself did not seem to have wholly comprehended the crisis. On a visit to Mozambique, Flower described a quixotic scene in a Portuguese Army ops room with a high-ranking general present.

…he stood beneath flashing lights as he surveyed the wall maps liberally decorated with coloured pins. Carried away with his own enthusiasm, obsessed with pretentious plans, the deployment of troops and the portrayal of tactics, he then faced me, reluctantly turning his back on his playthings, and exclaimed:

"Is it not magnificent!"

And I thought: "What has his 'magnificent' battlefield got to do with the men who are dying out there in the African bush."[3]

In the northeast the killing was indeed well under way. Besides black civilian deaths which tended to slip into a less visible category, Rhodesian Security Force casualties were mounting. By April 1974, 45 deaths had been recorded in the armed services Roll of Honour A handful were road or air accidents and a number caused by land mines, but most were deaths in action. Of these 28 were white and the remainder black. White civilians were also contributing to their own column of statistics. With the widespread use of landmines, commercial and security traffic in the northeast had so diminished that it had begun to affect the economy adversely. Random farm attacks were also increasing in frequency, making the northeast a very dangerous place to live and work.

White security concerns generated a boom in the fencing industry countrywide. It also prompted a surge of creative engineering that produced some of the most memorable icons of the Rhodesian War. Initially, ordinary farm vehicles were simply packed with sand bags to limit the effect of a landmine blast. However, powerful Russian and Chinese anti-tank mines continued to claim lives. To combat this, the police, and later engineering concerns scattered around the country, started producing such classics as the Rhino ambush and mine-protected vehicle.

The Rhino, designed by Chief Inspector Don Hollingsworth, was a Land-Rover chassis upon which the standard cab and flatbed had been replaced with a heavily armoured pod and roll bars. This concept proved to be very effective against both landmines and the increasing incidence of roadside ambushes. Soon Rhodesian roads were filled with a variety of similar vehicles, some homemade, with the various designs, called Hyenas, Leopards, Crocodiles and Hippos.

Ambushes were no less of a deadly hazard on lonely country roads than landmines. As the war progressed, barely a day went by without news of this one or that one surviving or succumbing to an ambush. Ordinary civilian vehicles, of course, were highly vulnerable to both ambushes and landmine blasts, and again it was farm workshops that came to the rescue. A number of eccentric solutions were devised that were eventually narrowed down to the use of multiple firing barrels arranged in a variety of configurations that were then mounted onto cars, trucks and pickups. Each barrel was primed with a 12-gauge buckshot cartridge, and in case of an ambush, could lay down a brief but devastating curtain of fire.

Such was the day-to-day life of whites struggling to survive in the hostile northeast. Home security equally taxed the creativity of backcountry farmers. Screens were fitted across windows to inhibit the casual tossing in of hand grenades. The perimeter of the homestead was typically tightly corralled with barbed wire and diamond mesh security fence. A kill zone carved out of the bush beyond could be illuminated by powerful security lights at the flick of a switch. The price of menacing dogs was high, and Rottweiller, Doberman or Rhodesian Ridgeback puppies were usually booked several litters in advance.

A coordinated community defence system very quickly supplemented early individual arrangements. Police Reserve patrols mounted by local men, linked together all homesteads into a central control system based at a local police camp. Agric Alert was a primitive but very effective radio link that allowed for some communication, a regular morning and evening roll call, a panic button and a sense that the isolation around each distant homestead was relieved a little.

Periodically, a creative or paranoid individual went overboard with home security arrangements.

An occasional addition to the standard precautions was a series of 200 litre fuel drums packed with a mixture of explosives, concrete and odds and ends of scrap metal and deployed along the perimeter. An electronic trigger could completely or selectively detonate these homemade bombs that were capable of killing everything — including dogs, horses and cattle — within 100 meters. In most cases an outside bunker, fortified with sandbags, was also available for a last stand against intruders.

With all this going on, white farmers, soldiers and the Government were not impressed when the Catholic Church raised its voice to comment on the rising incidence of Security Force violence against black civilians. Bishop of Umtali Donal Lamont aggravated an already chary white parish by describing the racism in Rhodesia as a 'pernicious heresy'. The Catholic Commission for Justice and Peace alleged torture, assaults and destruction of property — charges that were forcefully rejected by the Government, as were calls for an independent inquiry, on the grounds that those injured by such action had full recourse to the law.

The Government also claimed with some justification that Catholic exposure of violence in the northeast was one-sided, and neglected to mention the regular and horrendous acts of political torture and terrorism, that were daily perpetrated by the guerrilla factions against their own people. In 1974, the Ministry of Information released a propaganda leaflet entitled *Anatomy of Terror*, that illustrated in the most graphic terms the reality of terrorist activity in the countryside. The text began with the admission that 'this is not a pretty book', and indeed it was not. A gallery of ghoulish imagery depicting some of the worst incidents of torture and savagery committed on the frontline, succeeded in awakening the darkest fears of suburban white expatriates. This was black on black violence, and it was wanton, depraved and deeply disturbing.

Unfortunately the Rhodesian Government's plea of being a civilised minority confronting a pagan invasion, was sometimes smudged by legal but nonetheless questionable acts. In May 1973, three guerrillas who had been involved in the Altena and Whistlefield farm attacks, were sentenced to death for those attacks, and for the murder of Corporal Norman Moore. Appeals and protests were loud, with ZANU arguing that Moore had died as a consequence of an act of war and that the three guerrillas should be deemed prisoners of war. This argument was dismissed, although ultimately the men were reprieved .

Donal Lamont himself almost fell victim to the same device that had killed Corporal Moore. He had become such a thorn in the flesh of the Rhodesian Government that at some level of the security services the decision was made to kill him. Acting on intelligence that he was about to embark on a programme of visits to Catholic missions in the southeast, Special Branch arranged for a landmine to be placed in the road he would travel. God was with his servant that day, however, and Lamont stopped his VW Beetle a few hundred metres shy of the mine to chat to some children. A mine-protected troop carrier passed him, continued up the road and was destroyed in the explosion that followed. Thanks to 3cm of armour plate, no Rhodesian soldiers lost their lives. Donal Lamont was soon thereafter prosecuted under the Terrorism Act and deported.[4]

* * *

In the meantime, Rhodesians were slowly beginning to take seriously warnings that the flame of a 500-year Portuguese occupation of Mozambique was guttering. It seemed that just at the moment when Rhodesia needed her neighbour most, metropolitan Portugal was about to falter.

As the first quarter of 1974 drew to a close, Ken Flower found himself flagging too. His spirit had been tested by months of futile diplomacy trying to form a tripartite response to the security threat that he knew was coming. He found the Portuguese stalwart in their refusal to yield, but at the same time swamped by the military threat and growing disaffection within the armed forces. South Africa remained inert and fatalistic, being mainly concerned with looking into the future to find some platform for peaceful cooperation with black Africa.

On 24 April 1974, Flower's aircraft was the last to leave Lisbon airport on the eve of a bloodless military coup. This event of major international significance became known as the Carnation Revolution. This serene name was born of the fact that soldiers of the *Estado Novo* were greeted on the streets by crowds carrying red carnations indicating overwhelming popular support for the revolution.

The *Estado Novo* had chosen to occupy Portugal's colonies beyond the 1960s essentially because the maintenance of a colonial empire was part of the historical vision of the regime's ideologues. Maintaining these colonies had involved Portugal in costly wars, not only in Mozambique but also in Angola, Guinea-Bissau, São Tomé, Príncipe and Cape Verde. These conflicts served no real purpose in a changing world but they did spark the coup that left a huge question mark hanging over the future of military campaigning in Africa.

It was now past the time when Rhodesia could effectively influence either the military or the political situation in Mozambique, and all that she could do now was wait, hope and wonder.

54

Men of steel

Detente

In the aftermath of the Portuguese coup, the fate of Rhodesia began to fall into the hands of two men. Each had an army and a vision of righteousness, dangerously intertwined with a personal determination to prevail. Robert Mugabe, the flint hard and ascetic revolutionary, listened from his jail cell to the tales of collapse in Portugal with quiet satisfaction. Ian Smith, his absolute antithesis, received the same news with deep a sense of foreboding.

White Rhodesia initially took comfort in the hope that the loss of Mozambique would be regrettable, but not necessarily fatal. South Africa was the economic colossus, and despite Pretoria being a little slow on the uptake in matters of mutual security, Rhodesia was confident that the fall of Mozambique would change this. So far, South African military assistance had been offered to Rhodesia without strings attached. The operational brilliance of the Rhodesian Army and the superb little war it was fighting, was the cause of much envy among sister units in South Africa. For the chance to participate and gain operational experience, South African commanders were quite often willing to deploy their elite Special Forces to Rhodesia without the authority — and at times even without the knowledge — of their Government. This helped considerably and was never unappreciated, but the Rhodesians needed massive military assistance from South Africa to really clean up the region. Curiously though, this had never been forthcoming.

Manifestly this now had to change, and there was virtually no other subject of conversation across the length and breadth of Rhodesia. South Africans would at last weigh in to support their brethren holding the white line at the Zambezi River. John Vorster was due in Salisbury for talks with Ian Smith, around the middle of 1974, and it was widely anticipated that the South African Prime Minister would take the opportunity to roll out some sort of revised security policy for the region. In the Rhodesian nationalist camp, expectations were not dissimilar, and Muzorewa was advised to take a step back from his negotiations with the Smith regime, to see how the new political map of the region would be drawn.

Abruptly the calm of expectation on the Rhodesian political landscape was ruffled, when the extreme right of Smith's parliamentary caucus hatched an unexpected rebellion. A noisy faction led by RF party chairman, Des Frost, echoed intelligence advice to the office of the Prime Minister take the war directly to the terrorists. It was necessary to give the insurgents, then visibly massing in the Tete Province, a sound thrashing, so that any talk of a negotiated settlement in the future would be backed by a few hard facts. While a political rebellion was not viewed kindly in the country, most whites could indeed appreciate the need for some sort of vigorous and salutary action against the the guerrilla forces at that point. Smith was among these, but as he prepared to lead the country into uncharted territory, he was not about to let his House majority slip away. On 31 July he took the country to the polls once again. The results proved that when push came to shove, the electorate was still behind him and the Rhodesian Front was rewarded with yet another clean sweep of every white parliamentary seat.

When John Vorster arrived just a few days after this rousing display of public support, Smith was girded and confident. With military and security matters foremost in his mind he was ready to tell his South African counterpart that the time had come for South Africa to put her muscle behind the iron fist. Despite the obvious lack of mutual affection, Smith was confident that good sense would prevail and for the sake of the common good he was prepared to put aside his personal feelings and place his leadership at the disposal of the South Africans. But if he expected security matters to dominate the meeting, he was about to be sorely disappointed.

As the two settled in, Smith was quickly alerted to an air of apprehension surrounding the topic of military and economic support. Vorster seemed not to be listening to the tough talk, and consequently that part of the meeting was brief. Smith soon found himself doing much more of the listening than the talking, and as Vorster warmed to his theme, Smith began to find himself almost at a loss for words.

Vorster was enlarging on a theme of cooperation and common markets in Africa, explaining that current realpolitik did not countenance war ... and that if the white man was to remain viable on the continent it would be through capital, political integration and trade. As he spoke, Vorster was gazing into the middle distance where he seemed to see the ghosts of Rhodes, Smuts and Huggins. His vision of a grand political union was different only in that he saw it as a commonwealth, held firm by the weighty economic ballast of Pretoria, and sailing north into the dark infinity of Black Africa under the flag of detente.

At the core of detente lay John Vorster's hope that if he were perceived to be an honest broker over the Rhodesia question, South Africa's own racial policy of apartheid would be overlooked. For this not to appear juvenile in its naivety, it ought to be remembered that the South African economic machine was vastly superior to anything else in Africa. By necessity most countries to the north had lifelines plugged into it — even though it was in everybody's interest to keep this fact a secret. Although Vorster was probably not blind to the fact that glaring political misalignment could at times override common sense and self-interest, he thought the odds were good enough to give it a go.

Smith had been told nothing of this beforehand, probably because he would not have appreciated hearing that Pretoria was gambling with the future of white Rhodesia, even though this fact was not yet acknowledged. For Smith to have the news broken to him thus — when he had all but guaranteed to his constituency that South Africa would now come onside — was brutal almost beyond endurance.

Ken Flower stated in his memoirs that his South African opposite number had for some time been urging him to make it known to Smith, that Vorster was working towards achieving a 'solution' in Rhodesia. He needed one before South Africa itself was pushed towards a similar process over the future of South West Africa. It is unlikely that Flower failed to pass the message on to Smith, and therefore strange that Smith in his own memoirs claimed no prior knowledge. Stranger still was the fact that behind the scenes, work towards achieving detente had been going on hush-hush for some time.

Vorster had sensed that of all the local black leaders, it was Kenneth Kaunda who was most likely to respond positively to his scheme, and through 1967-68 he worked hard behind the scenes to try and improve relations with Lusaka. In reply, Kaunda had laced a hostile response with pointed criticism of South Africa's apartheid policy. But despite this, he was indeed a good choice of starting point. Although typical of his kind in trying to consolidate power and crush democratic opposition, Kaunda was not overtly corrupt, and his desire to see Zambia prosper was genuine. Bridge building and peacemaking were also components of his personal philosophy — gleaned no doubt from his devotion to Satyagraha. By the middle of 1968, his hostility had cooled, and he was prepared to concede that solutions proposed for Rhodesia were not necessarily applicable to South Africa.[1] He added enigmatically that although a white victory in Rhodesia was now impossible, a black victory was not necessarily desirable.

Detente was born alongside the first whispers of the revolution in Mozambique, and to these Kenneth Kaunda was among the first to be alerted. In September or October of 1973 he was contacted by the British peer Lord Colyton, who in turn introduced him to a group of dissident officers of the Portuguese Army. A probable collapse of the Portuguese Government was predicted which, if it happened, would result in the inevitable collapse of colonial rule in Mozambique. Kaunda's help was requested in negotiating a truce with the nationalists, of whom FRELIMO was identified as being just one. Sensing correctly that Samora Machel would accept no solution short of complete military victory, Kaunda demurred and kept this information to himself.

He did, however, have an inkling that the information might stir up some useful panic in South Africa, and leaked it to Lonrho chairman Tiny Rowland with whom he was on good terms. Rowland, a major player on the continent, was uncommonly well connected among all of its leading African plutocracies. He duly passed the information on to fellow Lonrho director Marquard de Villiers, who happened to be a personal friend of John Vorster. Over a game of golf De Villiers casually briefed Vorster on the word regarding Mozambique. He however exaggerated the situation to the extent of assuring the Prime Minister that a new constitutional blueprint was already on the table. Vorster had less than a month to digest this news before the predicted political collapse in Lisbon took place.

The event added urgency to Vorster's quest for a solution in Rhodesia, and at the same time further softened Kaunda's view of detente. The fact that a white victory in Rhodesia was now impossible, and a black victory undesirable, suggested to Vorster that Kaunda was thinking about the middle ground. This was precisely the language of detente, and Vorster was happy to hear it. The fact that Samora Machel had led FRELIMO to an almost complete military victory in Mozambique, suggested certain things about his nature that did not bode well. The name 'Machel' had spread through a hero-hungry black population of South Africa like wildfire, and the rise of another charismatic autocrat in Rhodesia was to be avoided at all costs.

These developments affected John Vorster deeply. Obviously Kaunda was now presenting himself as the voice of black moderation, and this made Lusaka the perfect bridgehead between South Africa and the glowering black masses north of the Zambezi. This was the good news. The bad news was that Smith was a white Samora Machel, with a name that resonated with equal cachet. Call a toast to Ian Smith in any bar from Table Mountain to the Orkney Islands and glasses would be raised in salutation. Before Smith could upset the whole balance from within, Vorster had to find some way to ease him out.

As far as future policy towards Mozambique was concerned, South Africa had two important factors to consider. The first was that migrant labour from Mozambique made up about 25% of the work force on the mines of the Witwatersrand. The second was an uninterrupted flow of power from the Cahorra Bassa hydroelectric plant situated on the Zambezi. Another consideration was that the port facilities of Lourenço Marques provided an important overflow for South Africa's own busy ports. There was little to be gained by upsetting any of these traditional areas of cooperation.

Vorster concluded that any hostile response towards a Marxist takeover in Mozambique would be counterproductive, so he had no choice but to consider constructive engagement. There were so many paradoxes in this situation, that at times it was hard to keep up. In a quid pro quo with Mozambique, it did not take a genius to predict that South Africa would put Rhodesia on the table. Mozambique had as much to lose as South Africa by drawing an ideological frontline, so again things looked grim for Rhodesia. That Kaunda would be delighted to see an end to Rhodesian attacks on his country also went without saying.

As he listened to all this, some facts prima facie and others implied, Smith felt the ground lurch beneath his feet. He could hardly believe what he was hearing. As Vorster sketched out his vision, Smith heard an echo of the old parrot-cry, and it was coming from where he least expected it. Conciliation and compromise — two words that Smith had no use for — underlined Vorster vision. He assured his incredulous host that it was these two concepts that would usher in a new era of peace and cooperation in southern Africa.

What did all this mean? To Smith it mostly meant the end of any immediate plans to escalate the war. With Mozambique on the brink, South Africa was Rhodesia's only ally and as bleak as the garden path might have looked to him, Smith had no choice but to follow the South African leader down it. Before he took the first step, however, he tried his luck with a different plan.

While in Lisbon, Ken Flower had unearthed a scheme under discussion by senior members of the military intelligence establishment. These were among a minority who believed that the new military government had conceded too much too quickly. They were proposing a plan to divide Mozambique into two separate cantons. FRELIMO could have all of the country north of the Zambezi. South of the river the Portuguese would form a federation with both Rhodesia and South Africa — or better still an enlarged southern African super state. Smith had grasped this straw despite Flower advising him that he personally judged the moment to have passed. The Portuguese Government was already in negotiation with FRELIMO and an obvious momentum towards disintegration was being formalised by two willing partners. FRELIMO wanted power and the Portuguese wanted to give it to them. How could a federation — or any sort of complicated redrawing of the map of Africa — ever be taken seriously?

Vorster certainly did not take it seriously. As Smith assured him that the Portuguese were 'onsides' he listened uncomfortably, promising Smith that he would take the idea back to Pretoria and air it to his Cabinet. However, despite Smith tugging on his coat tails from time to time over the next few months, he offered no further encouragement.

* * *

On the battlefield, meanwhile, the intensity of reprisal and counter-reprisal grew, and as manpower shortages in the armed services became critical, any and every type of force multiplier was considered. The Selous Scouts and Special Branch were behind most of these ideas and were highly creative and successful in employing them. One such scheme turned the tables on the terrorist's tendency to rob rural stores. Operatives fitted transistor radios, much coveted by guerrillas in the field, with secret homing transmitters effective within a radius of 50 kilometres. The transmitters were usually only active when the radios were turned off which meant that any follow up by Fireforce could be conducted in the fairly certain knowledge that the guerrillas were asleep. This theme was developed a little further, when a charge of plastic explosive was fitted into each radio so that when the on/off switch was activated a prescribed number of times, the charge would detonate. These were called 'road runners' after the propensity of Wily Coyote to explode several times during the course of a cartoon episode.

Exploding bicycles was a tactic the Selous Scout used during a number of cross-border raids. Bicycles packed with explosives were left lying around in Gaza to be picked up by FRELIMO patrols. Usually the devices were detonated by weight on the saddle or ringing the bell, and before FRELIMO and ZANLA fighters got wise to it, a good number were despatched. The fact that quite a number of civilians fell victim to these ruses spoiled only slightly the pleasure of hearing that many important guerrillas had been killed. As a first entry into chemical warfare, the Rhodesians poisoned natural waterholes in the dry southeast of the country. The water stank once poisoned and even animals wouldn't drink it. The purpose was to deprive infiltrating terrorists access to drinkable water during their long, dry march from Mozambique's Gaza Province. The rains broke not long afterwards scouring out the poisoned pans so the scheme was abandoned.

To spread the use of chemical warfare into the wider conflict, the security services had their own local expert on poisons, the late Bob Symington, professor of surgery at the University of Rhodesia. He was amateur toxicologist with a small but well-appointed laboratory in his Borrowdale home. He was also a high-ranking territorial officer and as such had a direct connection to the Ministry of Defence. As early as the last quarter of 1974, Symington was working with the Ministry to devise a system of exterminating guerrillas, using various poisons. At the same time authorisation was handed down to the CIO, to commence a top-secret programme to deploy chemical weapons. Ken Flower was Director General of the CIO and answerable only to the Prime Minister, so if Flower was au fait with the operation, so must Smith have been. The chemical warfare programme was placed under the aegis of the Selous Scouts and was installed at their Bindura Fort to keep it from prying eyes.

The first major application was to impregnate clothing with parathion, an organophosphate absorbed into the bloodstream through hair follicles. A person wearing a treated article of clothing such as jeans, a t-shirt or underpants could be expected to die within four or five days.[2] Poisoned clothing, tinned meats and soft drinks were supplied to ZANLA contact men via pseudo groups. Consumables were laced with the thallium, a poison that attacks the peripheral nervous system. Thallium was also a favourite of chemist-turned-crime-writer Agatha Christie. Cigarettes were poisoned by treating the filters with anthrax spores.

By the middle of 1977, it had become apparent that Rhodesia was losing the war, and as a consequence the chemical programme was expanded. Special Branch distributed poisoned food and clothing in a highly secret programme that utilised rural stores that were commonly raided by insurgents. Storekeepers were usually ignorant of the deployment and as a consequence quite a few accidental deaths were recorded in the general population. In June 1977, the Operations Coordinating Committee requested the officer commanding the Special Branch unit attached to Selous Scouts, to provide detailed figures for deaths of guerrillas that could be attributed to poisoning. The figures supplied indicated that 809 individuals had succumbed to this method in a period of six months.[3] Many members of Special Branch believed that more terrorists were being accounted for by chemical means than by conventional Fireforce attacks.

Biological attacks were also part of the strategy, and claimed an unknown but significant number of lives. The Selous Scouts introduced cholera bacteria into the water supply for the FRELIMO and ZANLA camps at Madulo Pan not far from Malvernia. By sabotaging pumps and pipelines, the Scouts forced the guerrillas to use tainted ground water. Unaccountable cholera outbreaks were reported in various parts of Rhodesia as a consequence of ongoing deployments of spore and the natural spread of the disease.

Anthrax was also used by the Selous Scouts to infect cattle in the Malvernia area. The spore would then be passed on to humans consuming the meat. The distribution of anthrax was carefully controlled in Gaza lest infections move to the Kruger National Park to the detriment of wildlife and South African goodwill. Selous Scouts Special Branch officer Jim Parker, in his book *Assignment Selous Scouts*, confirmed that anthrax was deployed in Matabeleland north to infect or kill cattle, in order to deprive infiltrating ZIPRA forces of food. Veterinary Department personnel, unaware that the Scouts were responsible, had a very difficult time containing outbreaks in the Tribal Trust Lands. The disease was more easily controlled on white ranches where there was better access and security.[4]

By October 1979 the isolation unit at Gwelo Hospital was overflowing with cases of anthrax poisoning. Patients from Lower Gwelo, Que Que, Zhombe, Gokwe, Selukwe, Shangani — even some from as far away as Fort Victoria — were treated. There were 10, 753 recorded cases of anthrax poisoning in 1979 and 1980, and 182 confirmed deaths. These figures were compiled from

treated cases and in reality must have been much higher.[5] Whichever way, they far exceeded cases
recorded in the rest of the world combined.[6]

55

Arbitrary executions of their own men

For Ken Flower the dark atmosphere of the moment was brightened a little by a trip to Portugal in the company of the Rhodesian Minister of Defence. In September, invitations had been sent from Lisbon to both Salisbury and Pretoria asking each country to send a senior official and a minister to Portugal to be briefed on Portugal's future overseas policy. The South African delegation included Foreign Minister Brand Fourie and the head of the South African Bureau of State Security, General Hendrik van den Bergh. Ken Flower travelled in the company of the elegant and entertaining P.K van der Byl who had just assumed the dual portfolios of defence and foreign affairs.

PK, as he was familiarly known, was an interesting character and something of a remnant of the old Honourable and Military. He was a flamboyant and colourful hardliner, whose public antics and social credentials placed him at the very centre of the local elite, although as a politician his accomplishments were mixed. While born and bred in South Africa, he affected the airs and graces of an English gentlemen which caused frequent offence to the South Africans he was in contact with in the course of official business. His first Cabinet position had been as Smith's Deputy Minister for Information, where he proved his commitment to the concept of UDI by zealously applying press censorship and streamlining the public media in the direction of Rhodesian independence.

His relationship with Smith was a close but curious one. Since Smith himself was known for a conspicuous lack of personal charisma, PK was often presented at the fore as the official and unofficial spokesman for the Government. This did nothing to dispel the general impression that the Rhodesian Government was being run by the lunatic fringe. British journalist Max Hastings, then reporting on Rhodesia for the *Evening Standard*, described Van der Byl as an 'appalling' individual, and ventured to add that he and Smith would both have been comical were it not for the fact that they held the power of life or death over so many people. Within a fortnight of this, Hastings was on an aircraft back to London.[1]

With his flamboyance and artificial imperium, PK was frequently lampooned and derided both within the country and without, but he never seemed to care, and remained a much-loved Rhodesian character throughout the UDI period. This applied particularly on the frontline, among the rough and ready contingents of Rhodesian fighting men. In his capacity as Minister of Defence, he made a regular point of mixing and identifying with the troops, and on such occasions would be choppered into forward bases, dressed in immaculately pressed battle fatigues. He would occasionally sport a rifle, but more frequently a swagger stick and a bottle or two of imported whisky. As he addressed the assembled troops with a tumbler of Scotch in one hand and a Dunhill cigarette in the other, he would effuse with such Churchillian flourish as: 'If the battle should wax fiercer, there can be no question of surrender. We shall contest every river, every crossroads, every village, every town and every kopje.'[2] With that he would rock back on his heels and grin from ear to ear. The officers would discreetly hide their smiles while the men of the ranks would roar with laughter — and that, it seemed, was what really mattered.

In many ways, PK spoke for precisely what the whole business of white Rhodesia was all about. He offered a lesson to his compatriots that, no matter what was done, or what was said, or who was killed or maimed along the way, none of it was to be taken too seriously. [3]

* * *

Sadly, however, undeniable evidence that the whole edifice was beginning to crumble was all that Van der Byl and Flower were able to bring back with them from Portugal. A series of meetings held in Lisbon were humourless, sober and depressing. The Rhodesian and South African delegations were told by Overseas Minister Dr Costa Almeida that Portugal now regarded her position in Africa as untenable, and the current policy regarding Mozambique was to negotiate the best possible deal and get out. He added, rather naively that, in his view, nothing of consequence would change. Predicting that most Portuguese nationals would remain in Mozambique, he assured the Rhodesians that current relationships in the region could be preserved without difficulty.

This was obviously not going to happen. The Rhodesian property market was booming with the sudden influx of Portuguese refugees flooding into the country, and the same was true for South Africa. Flower, who was a Portuguese speaker and familiar with the rat holes of Lisbon, sought out a prostitute and asked her what the common man thought of the overseas empire. During the course of the evening she introduced him to many ordinary people, who supported the view that the nation would be better off without it. Later, seeming somehow to have missed the gravity of the moment, Van der Byl urged Flower to slip a pornographic magazine into General van den Bergh's luggage, hoping that it might be confiscated by customs at Jan Smuts Airport to Van den Bergh's consternation. Flower demurred, although the story circulated to the amusement of Parliament and members of Salisbury Club for a long time. It proved to be the only cheerful part of the whole business.

The agreement negotiated between the Portuguese Government and FRELIMO in Tanzania, was signed into existence in Lusaka on 7 September 1974, just five months after the coup. The accord made provision for a transitional government that, with desperate haste, was sworn in a fortnight later. Mozambique was to be administered under the caretaker leadership of FRELIMO's Paris representative, Joaquim Chissano, in preparation for a formal handover.

A few months later an attempted right wing coup by disillusioned whites in Lourenço Marques, upset an uneasy peace. It precipitated a brief slaughter of Portuguese nationals before those who survived fled the territory. They left behind economic and infrastructural ruin, from which Mozambique never really recovered. FRELIMO inherited six Alouette helicopters that were handed over to the new air force by the Portuguese, but these did not remain in Mozambique for long. Disgruntled Portuguese pilots flew them across the border into Rhodesia and handed them over for an undisclosed sum in hard currency.[4]

As indigenisation took root, Rhodesians found themselves peering over the ramparts of the Eastern Highlands, to the sight of blacks making their own decisions and running affairs all over Mozambique. For the whites, impromptu visits to the superb beaches, the best game fishing in the world, the fattest prawns and the *vinho verde* — the pleasures that had accounted for quite a large part of the good life — were abruptly halted. Not for the first time in recent months, white Rhodesians began to wonder if there really was a future for them in Africa.

In the wake of this another sombre chapter was soon opened. Smith hosted South African Foreign Minister Dr Hilgard Muller, on a visit ostensibly to report on the progress of detente. Muller's visit followed the same pattern as Vorster's had before him, and he and Smith sat in the congenial surroundings of Government House and exchanged the usual pleasantries. Muller was conspicuously lavish in his praise of Rhodesian political maturity, and went on in this sotto voce way to tell Smith how well Vorster was progressing with his detente efforts among the frontline presidents, and how pleased he was with Rhodesian cooperation. All of this circumlocution alerted Smith immediately to the fact that something extremely unpleasant was afoot.

The success of detente had been premised on Kaunda's desperation for an end to the Rhodesian war of attrition. Although Smith had gone out of his way to be accommodating in this respect, it was now required of him to move a little further to give Kaunda what he needed to force Nkomo and Sithole to the negotiating table. If Kaunda was to deal with these two men, he needed them to be in Lusaka. This meant that Smith would have to release all the leading nationalists from detention and allow them to leave the country.

Smith's heart sank, but this was the stark reality of the situation, and Hilgard Muller sat back to give his host a moment to digest the tasteless fact. Unpalatable as it was, Muller nevertheless had every reason to suppose that Smith would fall into line. To drive home the point that Rhodesia's dependence on South Africa was now absolute, Muller threw in a couple of further points for Smith to chew over. South African Railways carried the bulk of vital Rhodesian imports and exports and the system could be rendered unworkable by congestion without difficulty. Even more distressing, a tangible hostility towards Rhodesia had started to appear in the mood of the Afrikaans language press, a fact which strongly suggested that Pretoria was priming her northern neighbour for bad news. Complaints in South Africa were now frequently being heard, about the increasingly heavy political and economic burden of supporting Rhodesia's hopeless bid for survival. Rhodesia was still unrecognised and still boycotted, almost a decade after the declaration of UDI and was still the focus of unrelenting African and Asian pressure. South Africa's own social imbalances were also now increasingly being taken into account in a liberal-leaning world. She needed to concentrate on her own survival and many in the Republic felt that the moment of separation was near.

For the little that it was worth, Smith's flagging spirits might have been buoyed by a display that proved he was still held in very high esteem south of the Limpopo. He was in the habit of timing his visits to South Africa to coincide with the best of South Africa's international rugby fixtures, and on a visit to Ellis Park Stadium, he received a standing ovation from over 70 000 fans — a much greater welcome than that accorded to their own prime minister.

Another fact that might have lent Smith some comfort in these dark days, was that his principal enemy was also squirming under the unwanted interference of his sponsors. As Smith regarded Vorster, so Mugabe had come to regard Kaunda. The two had never met but Mugabe was deeply distrustful of a man so given to compromise. He would soon meet his nemesis in person, and nothing about the meeting would change his mind.

Mugabe makes his move

After almost five years of hiatus, the question of Ndabaningi Sithole's leadership of ZANU resurfaced when, having served his term, he was released from confinement and returned to the general prison population. In the yard he found the entire prison establishment in a ferment of both hope and fear over detente, and rumours that all-party talks were imminent. While most of the rank and file thought excitedly about possible release, the executive was concerned mainly by the fact that the party could not approach talks, with the leadership question unresolved. Therefore, soon after his release in March 1974, Sithole was summoned before the Central Committee to present his version of the events of 1969. There was nothing he could do to resist other than not attending a meeting of the council on which he would not be invited to serve as chairman. In his absence a resolution condemning him was drafted and a copy smuggled out of prison.

Sithole was now in a tremendously difficult position. His years in confinement had given him much time to ruminate, and although he could have thrown in the towel — and perhaps should have — he instead opted to tough it out and maintain the constitutionality of his leadership. Refusing to attend meetings might have proved his determination not to be pushed around, but it left him isolated. A few days later a second meeting was called and — this time — Sithole did make an appearance. He came across as haughty and contemptuous but, as he read a rather fumbling vindication of his earlier actions, his hands shook and his voice was querulous. It was an unconvincing performance and when the floor was opened he was denounced to his face. A second resolution was passed that came within a hair of ousting him. It was agreed instead that he would no longer be permitted to discuss party or national business with any outsider, except in the company of another member of the executive.

This unsatisfactory state of affairs continued for a month or two, with Sithole keeping largely to himself and the main clique of his antagonists doing what they could to isolate him. In due course he held a routine and private discussion with a Special Branch officer, after which Sithole was immediately questioned by his colleagues. He retorted again that his censure was unconstitutional and he was under no obligation to explain his actions to anyone. On 1 July, most of the Central Committee was transferred to Que Que prison where agitation for Sithole's dismissal began in earnest.

The pretext for another round of attacks came again with Sithole's determination to pursue a pragmatic line, in the face of what he believed was an unnecessarily uncompromising stance by Mugabe; and certainly Mugabe was not the man to interpret the spirit of detente for the people. Sithole made it known that he thought one-man-one-vote ought not to be an immediate goal, but rather a slogan to be used in mobilisation and negotiation. The chance of a settlement on the basis of one-man-one-vote was so remote that Sithole felt the concept ought not to be the guiding ideology of the party. A power struggle continued until early November, when a full meeting of the executive was held, and there Sithole was formally suspended from office. Having orchestrated the dismissal, Mugabe cleverly abstained from the actual vote, claiming that the action was unconstitutional. His concerns were noted but the action went ahead regardless.

In the meantime, events on the outside were moving rapidly. Later in July, Sithole was visited in Que Que prison by a member of the Special Branch, Detective Inspector Peter Moores, who informed him that a temporary release had been authorised, allowing him to travel to Lusaka for secret talks with Kaunda. Mugabe happened to be in the same room writing an examination, and immediately intruded on the meeting. He refused the invitation on Sithole's behalf on the basis that negotiations were only possible between free men. Whether Sithole liked Mugabe's intervention or not, he had to agree. The following day Nkomo, Muzorewa and others boarded a South African executive aircraft and flew to Lusaka, leaving the ZANU leader alone and isolated in his prison cell.

The nationalists travelled in the company of Mark Chona, Kaunda's urbane right hand man who was the younger brother of Mainza Chona, one time Zambian Prime Minister and promoter of the one-party state. Mark Chona, who was something of a rising star in the Zambian establishment, was still smarting over an unfortunate and rather crude encounter with Ian Smith. He had been charged with the difficult task of liaison between the Frontline leaders and Smith, in negotiations to secure the release of the nationalists. Smith was understandably irritated at this latest turn of events and dismayed at being forced to authorise the temporary releases. He received Chona with a minimum of courtesy and after a moment or two of terse conversation he thrust a forefinger into the Zambian's face and promised that if any kind of unity ever came about within the liberation movement, his guest could return to Salisbury and cut the finger off.

Kaunda and Nyerere were equally irritated when the combined contingent of Zimbabwe nationalists arrived in Lusaka without Sithole. There was certainly no point in trying to negotiate unity without the most important half of the whole. As politically valid as Mugabe's point about the negotiations of free men might have been, it was also a major inconvenience. More telephone calls were made and Peter Moores once again found himself driving out to Que Que prison.

Mugabe did not receive the renewed summons well, but the authority of the Frontline leaders remained absolute and could not be ignored. It was agreed that he himself would attend the meetings in the company of fellow Central Committee member and Secretary for Youth, Moton Paul Malianga. The two were flown to Salisbury in a Rhodesian Air Force Dakota, before being put on a waiting South African aircraft bound for Lusaka.

The following day the two briefly met Nyerere, who demanded to know where Ndabaningi Sithole was. The circumstances of the leadership crisis were explained, and as Mugabe had expected, he faced a gale of criticism for staging an unconstitutional coup. Nyerere took the view that if the ZANU executive wished to suspend its leadership it was its own business, but the move had to be sanctioned by a party congress and endorsed by a democratic vote. On this Machel and Kaunda agreed. Mugabe tried to hold his ground but as a virtual unknown he was easily overruled. The meeting was fraught with animosity and from it a future of cold relations was born. Mugabe and Malianga were promptly sent back to Rhodesia without even the courtesy of being told the reason for the summons, or being allowed to meet Chitepo or any other members of the exiled leadership.

On his return to Que Que, Mugabe called a Central Committee meeting to lay out the terms for Sithole's visit to Lusaka. Sithole's attendance was authorised but on the strict proviso that he was to travel as the party spokesman and not as its leader. To reinforce this point, the hapless Maurice Nyagumbo was detailed to be his chaperone. Nyagumbo's job was to ensure than nothing out of order was said, and that it was clearly understood that Sithole was travelling strictly in his private capacity. The two were then flown to Lusaka where they met a waiting Kenneth Kaunda. Kaunda tried to reveal no hint of the purpose of the summons but let enough slip for Nyagumbo to surmise that the object was the establishment of unity between ZANU and ZAPU.

Nyagumbo was not a gifted man, and his fame in the movement came not from his intelligence but his commitment, courage and tenacity. He was also testy and combative at times, and as a result many of the years he spent in prison resulted from verbal or physical assaults against white officials. Kaunda was known to broadly support Nkomo and ZAPU in the battle of the parties. Nyagumbo therefore took 'unity' to mean 'ZAPU' and accused Kaunda to his face of favouritism and of promoting his 'useless friend' Joshua Nkomo. A noisy and acrimonious exchange followed, which ended with Sithole pulling the two apart and later severely reprimanding Nyagumbo for lowering even further, Kaunda's opinion of ZANU.[5] Kaunda was infuriated and insulted by the episode and would have sent Nyagumbo home via a lengthy spell in a Zambian prison had Sithole and Chitepo not intervened on his behalf. Against his better judgement the Zambian President allowed Nyagumbo to accompany Sithole and Chitepo on to Dar es Salaam.

Chitepo spoke for all of the exiled leadership when he lamented the leadership crisis and Mugabe's coup. Here the seeds of yet more unpleasantness were sown and although, in fairness to Mugabe he had not been alone in fermenting the coup, he had led it and had benefited from it more than anybody else. Needless to say, from that moment on, Herbert Chitepo joined the growing list of men Mugabe did not like. After a long and emotional appeal from the exiles Nyagumbo agreed to return to Rhodesia to repeal Sithole's suspension until such time as a formal congress could be held.

Nyerere and Kaunda were finally able to address a complete gathering of the Zimbabwe nationalists on the subject of unity between the various factions. It was time, Nyerere told his audience, for the liberation forces of Zimbabwe to present a common face. An immense amount had been achieved on behalf of the revolution of late, and the Frontline leaders were disinclined to countenance failure simply because of divisions within the various liberation councils. Nyerere's plea was sincere and heartfelt. Samora Machel added the sombre warning that if ZANU did anything to frustrate unity — or indeed persisted in trying to marginalise Sithole — he would personally see to it that ZANLA's forward bases in Mozambique were closed down and the several thousand ZANLA men already deployed in his country arrested and detained.

From the ZANU perspective, unity was again not a particularly welcome development. The party was actively engaged in the war and, in the hands of Chitepo and Tongogara, it was being prosecuted with increasing confidence. Exhaustive preparatory work had been undertaken in terms of mobilisation, training and politicising the masses. With the long Mozambican front now opening up it was to be expected that ZANU would resist peace talks with other movements, that had collectively done little or nothing to further the liberation struggle.

This feeling did not seem to impact Sithole who was elated by this renewed exposure. He had been liberated to speak his mind, and this was precisely what he intended to do, whether what he said made sense or not. He enthusiastically endorsed the concept of unity between the liberation movements and toured the forum shaking everybody's hand. The ZANU delegation watched their leader's happy handclapping with utter dismay and no doubt with a much clearer understanding of recent events.

Back in prison, Sithole continued to make the most of his last summer of sunshine. He thoroughly enjoyed chairing a Central Committee meeting that suspended the terms of his suspension and reinstated him as party leader. Then, at the beginning of December, the moment arrived for which he and so many others had been waiting. Under intense pressure from South Africa — and under the terms of détente — most of the jailed nationalists were released.

Smith moreover declared himself willing to discuss the question of majority rule, if the nationalists would in turn agree to honour a cease-fire. This was precisely what Chitepo feared; he and Tongogara could sense a movement towards compromise, that could only result in a dilution of absolute liberation. While Chitepo was committed to détente because of pressure applied by Nyerere, Kaunda and Machel, this did not stop him grumbling fitfully in the company of James McManus of the UK Guardian who scribbled notes. To his dismay, he was later quoted in that newspaper discussing the question of majority rule.

…that is not majority rule tomorrow, next week, next year or whenever. It is now.[6]

Smith drew little comfort from the fact that Chitepo was severely rebuked for his outburst, and reminded by Sithole that majority rule was simply a negotiating position. The leaders could chasten Chitepo but the words could never be unspoken.

After four days of closed-door horse-trading, the four nationalist parties emerged with an apparently credible unity accord. All four agreed to combine under the umbrella of the now United African National Council (UANC) to be led ostensibly by Bishop Muzorewa. A Unity Agreement was signed on 8 December by Sithole for ZANU, Nkomo for ZAPU, James Chikerema for FROLIZI and Muzorewa for the ANC.

Smith probably hoped that Mark Chona would fly into Salisbury to cut off his finger. Who, Smith might have asked, could possibly take Bishop Abel Muzorewa seriously, as the overall leader of the Zimbabwe nationalists? This circumstance alone was a clear indication that the whole agreement was a sham. If it was on Muzorewa's say-so that a ceasefire was to come into effect, then Smith would not be ordering his swords to be beaten into plough shears any time soon.

As if to prove this point, an incident took place that was at once tragic and politically disastrous for Rhodesia. The occupants of a police Land Rover moving cautiously up the Rushinga road were astonished to see a ZANLA detachment walking openly towards them. A very wary white patrol officer responded to being flagged down, after which a curious exchange followed between him and the guerrilla leader.[7] The detachment commander introduced himself as Herbert Shungu, and added that he was interested in learning more about the ceasefire. Shungu was duly loaded into the Land

Rover and driven to an interview with the local Officer commanding Special Branch. A wide-ranging and cordial discussion was recorded which ended with Shungu agreeing to return to the bush in order to bring in his detachment.

Shungu did not return, and nothing more was heard of him until late December, when he waved down a South African Police patrol on the Mazoe low level bridge. Aware of his earlier approaches, the SAP men were reasonably friendly and responded in due course to his assurances that they could safely lower their weapons. The moment that they did so, the ZANLA detachment opened fire, killing five members in cold blood. The only survivor was a black BSAP constable who saved his own life by leaping into the swollen waters of the Mazoe River. Shungu then spent an entertaining few days taunting Security Forces in the Rushinga District over a captured radio, until the batteries ran out.

Despite the loss of life, the incident came as something of a well-timed relief to Pretoria. Central to detente was the withdrawal of South African manpower from Rhodesia, which had until then been a difficult operation for Pretoria to order. Force levels had been reduced considerably over the preceding months, but a complete withdrawal would have offended the fraternal article of faith that continued to exist between South African and Rhodesian whites. The Herbert Shungu affair brought the matter to a head and, in the wake of it, Smith was summoned to Cape Town to be briefed on 'new developments'.

In an atmosphere of foreboding, a Rhodesian delegation flew out of Salisbury on the morning of 16 February 1975 and headed for the Cape. Prime Minister John Vorster received them at Groote Schuur and ushered them into a side room where they were confronted by a coterie of cabinet ministers. There was of course the usual preamble, tea and trivialities. Eventually the tension was broken by the news that everyone was expecting. South Africa intended to pull all of her armed units out of Rhodesia with more or less immediate effect. Smith was told that South African personnel were increasingly feeling that they were fighting for a cause they did not support. It was generally felt that Rhodesia had fallen 'out of step with South African policy!'

This comment probably had much to do with the fact that Vorster had been receiving petitions from his supporters questioning why young South Africans were dying for a system that was already allowing black participation. This, taken to its logical conclusion, meant that Rhodesia had already defined its future under the principal of majority rule, so why waste South African lives?

Smith smiled bitterly, for these people after all were supposed to be his friends. What if Bantustans were immediately created in Rhodesia, he asked. What if institutionalised apartheid was forced on Rhodesian blacks? Would the South African forces then feel more comfortable? Vorster was not amused. It was precisely this sort of thing that he hated about Smith. As Winston Churchill had once quipped of Labour Chancellor Sir Stafford Cripps: '…he has all the virtues I dislike and none of the vices I admire'. After the meetings Smith and his delegation were invited to a luncheon at Groote Schuur — but all found they had lost their appetites.

Nhari Rebellion

The political detainees had been released more or less as a result of South African pressure and, as a consequence, they walked the streets without the blessing of the Rhodesian Government. Watching over their every movement was Special Branch looking for any excuse to lock them up again. Some of the nationalists left the country and others dropped out of the struggle, but a few remained in the public eye to achieve what they could before the next axe fell.

Joshua Nkomo launched himself into an energetic reorganisation of ZAPU. Sithole remained leader of ZANU, but was powerless to direct or contain Mugabe — who also threw himself into a general reorganisation. Mugabe knew that more than anyone, he risked jail by political organising. His main objective was to recruit as many young people as possible, to build up ZANLA's fighting forces in Mozambique. This was extremely risky work, for if he put one foot wrong he might well disappear permanently. He knew that he had to move fast and then time the moment perfectly to get safely out of the country.

After a decade of neglect, the internal structures of ZANU were moribund. But in Lusaka the party was well led and well organised by Chitepo and Tongogara. These two appeared to at least have the existing military structure well in hand, and while they were around, there was little that Mugabe could achieve in Lusaka. Mozambique, however, was fast gaining significance as an extensive new front against Rhodesia. It remained to be exploited in its entirety and, with this in mind, Mugabe set to work.

At that time Mugabe benefited from the fact that he was held in relatively low esteem by the Frontline leaders. It gave him the opportunity to work toward his own ends without interference. Chitepo, Sithole and all the others were, by then, the acolytes of one or other of the Frontline leaders, and had little scope in that position for independent action. They were also powerless to explain the enormous confusion that détente was creating throughout the party, and in particular among the fighting men now in hiatus on the front line.

Most ZANLA operational groups were not equipped with any means of radio or telephone communication, so information from Lusaka reached them by carrier, word of mouth or rumour. Détente was a subject of regular campfire discussion, and with the cease-fire on or off or on again, no one really knew for sure what was going on. The high level negotiations between the fat cats in plush capitals seemed very far away. When the supply of war materiel ebbed to a trickle, speculation on the frontline became negative and then angry. Arms supplies had in fact dwindled largely because of an expectation in Lusaka and Dar-es-Salaam that peace negotiations were imminent, but the fighters were never directly informed of this and, consequently, disaffection spread rapidly through the ranks.

The best information reaching the fighters in the northeast and in Tete Province, tended to be that originating from Special Branch. To the Rhodesian Security forces — who were suffering none of the disadvantages of poor resupply, poor leadership and poor communications — detente and the cease-fire meant simply boredom and inactivity. To Special Branch personnel, with time to spare in their forward positions, the situation offered a unique opportunity to try and advance matters with a little judicious trickery and disinformation.

As the Portuguese abandoned their garrisons throughout Tete Province, Special Branch began establishing friendly contacts with incoming FRELIMO units. Initially the Rhodesians found FRELIMO receptive, and in due course a reciprocating cross-border accord came into effect. FRELIMO soldiers took to crossing regularly into Rhodesia to buy food and liquor, while Special Branch were allowed to move fairly freely in Mozambique, learning what they could about ZANLA movements.

In September and again in November 1974, Special Branch made contact with various ZANLA sectorial commanders operating out of Tete, and from someone called Raphael Chinyanganya — nom de guerre Thomas Nhari — they learned a great deal. Nhari was a competent commander and a committed ideologue, and as such his rise through the ranks of the armed forces had been rapid. He had been active on the front line since the Altena attacks, and he and a certain Dakari Badza, were the current commanders respectively of the Nehanda and Chaminuka Sectors of the northeast. It was from these two that Special Branch received its first confirmation of the ZANU leadership crisis in Sikombela, Salisbury and Que Que prisons. After several conversations, Special Branch urged the two men to align themselves to the Sithole faction.

It also came to light that a power struggle had broken out in Lusaka between Chitepo and Tongogara. This was separate, but parallel to the usual friction between the nationalist parties that the CIO with its Lusaka-based operatives took great pleasure in aggravating. The intelligence on internecine strife within ZANU presented an opportunity for Special Branch to infect the wound with a picture of a leadership that had sold out, of fat cats who junketed from one end of the world to the other while the fighting men of the revolution died, neglected, in the bush. The fact that Herbert Chitepo's official vehicle was a VW Beetle of uncertain vintage, and that Mugabe was applying the full force of his character to the job of rebuilding the structure of the struggle, hardly alludes to champagne lifestyles. But it didn't matter. The propaganda assault was very effective — more effective in fact than the Special Branch men operating on the fringes of Mozambique could have dared imagine.

Thomas Nhari was an ex-schoolteacher who at one time aspired to study law, but was educated only briefly before the money ran out. He was then unable to secure sponsorship, so he drifted into teaching. In 1967, he was smuggled out of the country by ZAPU, narrowly forestalling his arrest for crimes against law and order. He sojourned briefly in Lusaka before joining ZANU and shipping out for training in Moscow.[1] After returning to the struggle in southern Africa, he felt that his natural place was not on the front line but in the high command. His frustrated ambition and resentment played him easily into the hands of Special Branch, and he became prime material for manipulation. His simmering anger was harnessed to generate an effective alchemy of insurrection and, before too long, he was observed to be contemplating a coup.

Nhari's bitterness and personal frustration was also widely reflected in the rank and file, and it was not entirely unjustified. The political leadership of ZANU had always exhibited a shocking indifference to the welfare of the fighting men. It was therefore not difficult for Nhari to raise a small force, willing to march on Lusaka and mete out a little salutary justice. Events gathered momentum very quickly, and Special Branch was able to retreat back across the border and watch as a bloody rebellion unfolded.

Nhari's initial objective was to take over the main rear base of Chifombo, situated in northern Tete Province not far from the Zambian border. Initially it seems that Nhari, along with his protege Badza, set off alone because the angry men were not yet angry enough to risk a confrontation. The two were caught, and after receiving 15 lashes each and Badza losing his command, they were returned to the frontline.

By November 1974, when the 'unity' talks were due to begin in Lusaka, the two were ready to try again. This time they marched north at the head of a body of 30 armed men. There was a great deal of confusion and acrimony during the seven-day march, and a number of shootings and other abuses that were directed at waning supporters. Nevertheless they managed to take over Chifombo base by force of arms. Two commanders, Lovemore Chikadaya and Peter Nywenya, who attempted to oppose the rebellion, were buried alive by their comrades just outside the perimeter of the base.

Nhari appointed a nine-man military high command, that would also be headed by him, ostensibly as Josiah Tongogara's replacement. Nhari's first decision was that all members of the High Command in Lusaka, including Tongogara himself, were to be apprehended and brought to the front line to serve as ordinary cadres.[3]

Tongogara happened to be visiting Romania in the company of Herbert Chitepo at the time, and news of the coup only reached him on his return in early December. Once back in Lusaka he took the news directly to Ndabaningi Sithole, who he found depressed and rather indifferent. Sithole urged Tongogara to keep the news to himself in case the story broke and interfered with the unity talks then under way. When asked what should be done, Sithole shrugged and remarked that 'if there had been a coup then there had been a coup'. If Tongogara had been ousted, then the party would sponsor his education abroad. Sithole had probably lost interest in military matters by then, due no doubt to his belief that a settlement was imminent.

Suspecting that Chitepo was one of the 'big fish' behind the rebellion, Tongogara avoided seeking any advice or leadership from him, and instead set about coping with the crisis himself. From a personal point of view it was the first direct challenge to the High Command, and in particular to his own command of the military. Mugabe was in Salisbury, and not at that point considered to be in contention, while Chitepo had been wrong-footed by Sithole's release and was searching for a plot under every bush. Sithole was the anointed one, but he was largely powerless to influence events, so for the moment the mantle had fallen on Tongogara to rescue the party and the struggle from descent into total anarchy.

In the meantime, the rebels arrived in Lusaka in two trucks, heavily armed, drunk, belligerent and broke. They demanded money from Tongogara who refused, but he agreed to meet the group at a bar just outside Lusaka, where a large number of armed men were drinking heavily on 'Kalashnikov' credit. The meeting then moved on to a house in the suburb of New Kabwata, where Tongogara was read a document listing the grievances of the rebels. He was menaced to accept a change of leadership and promised that if he did not do so, he would receive a 'surprise' within 12 hours.

Kenneth Kaunda was probably more surprised than anyone when news of all this reached him. He was also furious, as he often seemed to be in those days. Both guerrilla armies were tolerated in Zambia only on the strict proviso that they did not carry arms — the logic of this being simply that the Zimbabwe nationalists were wielding more firepower than his army, and he could not afford a civil war.

Back in New Kabwata, Tongogara was holding his ground. He reminded the rebels that he was their commander, and ordered them to put down their weapons. Nhari then attempted a compromise and offered Tongogara the position of coordinating secretary in a new command. This was refused, and Tongogara sent the rebels off with orders for them to sober up and return to the ZANU offices the following morning, when he might be willing to listen to them.

Tongogara's 'surprise' was delivered the following evening. When he arrived home from a reception in the company of Rex Nhongo, the pair were ambushed by Nhari, Badza and an attack group of about eight rebels. Tongogara and Nhongo escaped under a hail of gunfire by taking to their heels in different directions. When a police detail arrived to investigate, the rebels fled. Tongogara entered his gutted home to find his wife and child missing. Later the rebels returned to the scene in one of their trucks, but immediately ran into a reinforced police detail. After a brief firefight Nhari and his companions were disarmed and arrested. The following day Nhari led Tongogara and the Zambian police to where the former's family were being held. Two of his older boys had been tied to a tree while his wife had been stripped to her underwear and tortured.

It was notable that Nhari and his followers had made no hostile advances against Herbert Chitepo. Whilst on a visit to Malawi, Chitepo had been arrested by the head of ZANLA's internal security, apparently on the orders of Tongogara, but was released a short while later as no fault could be found. However the incident betrayed more than a little of the growing tension within the party.

Tongogara's response to the attack was rapid and decisive. The rebels at Chifombo were disarmed by FRELIMO, and Tongogara entered the camp on Christmas day at the head of a force of newly trained cadres. Badza, Nhari and another rebel named Mathew Nyanga were executed on the spot. By this time most of Nhari's force had deserted or returned to the party, pleading that they had been coerced by threats. Many were dealt with in brutal purges that claimed the lives of upwards of 150 guerrillas and party officials. Tongogara took no personal responsibility for the deaths, remarking casually that these were men who had 'died at the hands of the party'.[4]

The violence that erupted in the aftermath of all this seemed out of all proportion to the size of the rebellion. No one, least of all Nhari, Tongogara or Chitepo, had realised the extent to which tensions had been building within the party. Increased Rhodesian military successes, the short-term success of the protected village programme, and an unregulated flood of poorly trained recruits from Zambia all added to this. The politics of revolution was only part of the reason for the slaughter. Factionalism, tribalism, suspicion and violence seemed always to flower, when two or more nationalists gathered for a political purpose.

No two accounts of the Nhari Rebellion have drawn the same conclusion and, since most of the actors were either killed or silenced, much of what actually happened and why remains speculative. What is clear, however, is that the rebellion triggered a catastrophic bout of violence and murder in Lusaka, that dismayed the Zambians and the Frontline leaders who were all initially powerless to intervene.

With the ink barely dry on the definitive unity agreement, it was a manifestly ridiculous situation. In Lusaka the factions of ZANU were literally tearing out each other's throats. Special Branch and the Rhodesian Government were naturally delighted, and Smith remained attached to his finger, although he doubtless would willingly have sacrificed a digit or two just to see the look on Mark Chona's face. On 13 March, Kaunda summoned Herbert Chitepo and demanded that he end the derangement. Chitepo had just returned from his brief imprisonment, and admitted to Kaunda that there was nothing he could do. He was stained with complicity in the Nhari Rebellion and, against this, his minority tribal background offered no protection at all. By then he even had reasonable grounds to fear for his life.

Just five days later this fear proved justified when, a few minutes after 08:00, the morning calm of the Chilenje South suburb of Lusaka was shattered by a massive car bomb explosion. The blast destroyed Chitepo's VW Beetle, killing him and a bodyguard outright. A flying wheel also killed the child of a next-door neighbour. For Kenneth Kaunda, usually a tolerant and mild-natured man, this was the last straw. The Zambian police launched a programme of arrests and detention, and one or two extra judicial killings of their own, to which the Rhodesian CIO added what disinformation it could.

The day after Chitepo's burial, the mass arrest of ZANU members began. Seventy high-ranking ZANU and ZANLA officials were taken into custody and ZANU's Lusaka offices were closed down. All ZANLA military bases in the country were ordered evacuated. Just in time, Josiah Tongogara and several of his high-ranking commanders slipped quietly across the border into

Mozambique. Kaunda then announced that an international committee of enquiry was to be appointed to get to the bottom of the matter. Closest to his heart were whispers that somehow he himself had been behind Chitepo's murder. He was known to dislike the man, and certainly he vocally championed ZAPU in favour of ZANU. Whatever the commission turned up, one thing was for certain — it would not blame Kaunda.

Samora Machel, on the other hand, was fond of Chitepo and was irritated by the accepted wisdom that Tongogara was behind his murder. When he heard that the OAU had endorsed the proposed commission, he ordered that Tongogara and three other members of his high command return to Lusaka to assist it. On their arrival all four were promptly arrested.

African interrogation methods can usually be relied on to be simple and to the point, and Tongogara was reported to have been tortured to the extent that his back was broken. Sadat Kufamazuba, one of Chitepo's two bodyguards and the only survivor of the explosion, was taken into custody and severely beaten despite grievous injuries sustained in the blast. Others were beaten routinely, starved and sleep-deprived. Kaunda was a peaceful man by his own reckoning, but the whole thing had gone just too far. A little bit of rough stuff was a small price to pay to restore order in his capital, and to provide sufficient grounds to kick ZANU finally out of the country.

The Commission began its work in July 1975. On 8 March 1976, ten days before the first anniversary of Chitepo's murder, the report of the Commission was signed and presented to Kenneth Kaunda. The findings pointed the finger squarely at members of the ZANU Dare Chimurenga and the ZANLA High Command. Josiah Tongogara was explicitly named, along with four other people. The underlying logic was presumably that Tongogara ordered the hit to better align himself for the ultimate leadership of a free Zimbabwe.

Now the entire command and control structure of ZANU was in disarray, as well as being homeless. Ultimately more than 1300 ZANLA guerrillas were detained in Zambian prisons, as ZANU's war against Rhodesia virtually ground to a halt.[5] Robert Mugabe responded by issuing a statement blaming the Zambian Government for complicity in Chitepo's murder, and announced an end to the participation of his faction of ZANU in de
tente, or any future negotiation with Smith.

Mugabe blamed the Zambians and the Zambians blamed ZANU, but in private there were strong suspicions that the Rhodesians had somehow been responsible. It is in the nature of covert operations that the truth is always obscure, but Ken Flower, who in 1985 published his memoirs of his time in Rhodesian intelligence, claimed that the CIO had set up the assassination — although of course he could have been lying. Liberation historians David Martin and Phyllis Johnson produced a book in the same year that purported to finally put the matter to rest, but it did no such thing.

Martin and Johnson's book was closely followed by another, written by respected Rhodesian War historian Peter Stiff — See You In November — that records the operations of an alumnus of the British SAS with the nom de guerre of 'Taffy'. Following Ken Flower's admission that he knew the circumstances of Chitepo's death, Taffy revealed that he indeed was the CIO-sponsored assassin of the ZANU leader. Taffy was in fact Alan 'Taffy' Brice whose identity was held secret by all until his death in 2006. Brice had been leading a CIO in Zambia for years and using homemade and often unstable devices, he had been regularly vandalising targets in the capital to make it appear that ZANU and ZAPU were engaged in ongoing tit-for-tat attacks. He was never exposed by the Zambians, and in a short but fruitful career, was responsible for considerable mayhem.

Herbert Chitepo was an enigmatic character who appears very differently to his various biographers. Clearly, he was a soft-spoken, educated and erudite man. He was a nationalist, angered at the sight of injustice, but never scarred or driven to extreme behaviour. Conversely, and perhaps in the interest of demonising his victim, Stiff quotes Brice as having a very different view of Chitepo.

Thousands of tribespeople were tortured, mutilated or murdered on his orders. He had no qualms about personally engaging in such things...the victim, who had been discovered in chains and close to death, had named Chitepo as his torturer. Chitepo, he testified, had personally wielded a red-hot poker and unspeakably mutilated him. Chitepo was reported to have enjoyed the interlude.[5]

Chitepo may well have had a sadistic streak, and it was certainly true that on his watch many innocent people on his own side were tortured and killed; but this was part of the revised guerrilla strategy. Moreover it was in keeping with the accepted philosophy of terror. As observed by Colonel Walter Kurtz of the Viet Cong, in Francis Ford Coppola's epic *Apocalypse Now*: 'You have to have men who are moral ... and at the same time who are able to utilise their primordial instincts to kill without feeling ... without passion. If I had ten divisions of those men', Kurtz went on, 'our troubles here would be over very quickly.'[7]

This of course is distinct from the sociopathic violence that was not absent on either side of the struggle. But if Chitepo was Public Enemy Number One, it was only because the Rhodesians were not yet familiar with Robert Mugabe. If they believed that Chitepo was the most likely candidate for a future Zimbabwean presidency — which would certainly have justified his murder — it would not be long before they began to regret his absence.

Brice later expressed remorse at the unintended death of a child, as a consequence of the blast that killed Chitepo. 'Such is war, the innocents suffer along with the antagonists'.[8] The same could no doubt be said of a handful of dissidents, who may or may not have had their chestnuts roasted by Chitepo.

The ZANU leader

One man who was certainly not grieving Chitepo's death was Robert Mugabe. Because Kaunda was washing his hands of ZANU, Mugabe found the way open to pursue his own objectives more fruitfully. With Chitepo dead, Sithole discredited and Tongogara in a Zambian prison, Mugabe was at last beginning to sense that his star was rising.

Mugabe was still very active in Rhodesia, but also aware that it was only a matter of time before he was rearrested. With the suddenly altered dynamics of the struggle, he had now to think very carefully about his future. Zambia was out of bounds, not only because of Kaunda's banning of ZANU but also because Mugabe wanted no part of detente. It was a policy designed to appeal to the moderates and in his estimation it would not and could not succeed for that very reason. Of all the Frontline leaders, Mugabe identified Machel as his only kindred spirit — although this admiration was yet to be reciprocated.

Machel was a militant, a Marxist and an advocate of the total solution. Mozambique had not been handed over to majority rule — it had been handed over to FRELIMO. The new military was not known as the Revolutionary Armed Forces of Mozambique, or any other such nomenclature, but simply as FRELIMO. FRELIMO was as ubiquitous and all-powerful as the Russian Communist Party, and Machel was its Vladimir Lenin. It was this more than anything else that excited Robert Mugabe's 'most 'umble' ambitions. With the battlefront now extending from Mukumbura to Vila Salazar, he could clearly picture the next phase of the war. Virtually uninhibited access to Rhodesia would give the force incumbent in Mozambique the edge to win the war. Mugabe therefore made up his mind that when things became too warm for him in Rhodesia, it would be to Mozambique that he would flee.

When Ndabaningi Sithole and Maurice Nyagumbo were rearrested in March for their own recruitment drives — and also on the improbable charge of plotting to kill their comrades — Mugabe judged that the moment had arrived for him to make his escape. As Special Branch trawled the townships looking for him, he put the finishing touches to his plan. Early in April he and a loyal associate, Edgar Tekere, slipped out of Salisbury and travelled to Inyanga in the company of a Catholic Sister called Mary Aquina. In Inyanga they were sheltered by an elderly but thoroughly revolutionary Manyika Chief by the name of Rekayi Tangwena. After a week or so, Tangwena guided the little party on foot past Security Force patrols and ambushes into Mozambique.

There news reached Mugabe that, after a terse bout of shuttle diplomacy, the South Africans had secured Sithole's unconditional release. Mugabe had not anticipated this, and the news put an immediate brake on his plans. Sithole was evidently still recognised as party leader and was expected to attend the 1975 OAU Foreign Ministers Conference to be held in Dar-es-Salaam later that month. With him he took the main focus of ZANU, and since he still enjoyed the recognition of Machel and other key members of the OAU, a wrong-footed Mugabe was aggrieved to find himself alone in hostile territory, with absolutely no claim to diplomatic protection.

When Machel heard that Mugabe was an uninvited guest in his country he was less than delighted, and immediately ordered that the fugitive be placed under 'protective custody' until some sort of assessment of the situation could be made. The most pedigreed revolutionary in southern Africa still suspected Mugabe, and still more or less supported Sithole, but was shrewd enough to realise that there was rarely smoke without fire. Before any permanent decisions were made about Mugabe's future, Machel intended to wait and see who emerged out of the hiatus as the stronger man. In the meantime Mugabe was interned in the pleasant but isolated surroundings of a villa in the small port settlement of Quelimane.

Mugabe made diligent use of his time by familiarising himself with the various ZANLA placements scattered around the country. Moving around as covertly as he was able to, he presented his credentials to the local commanders and fighters, while at the same time he assessed for himself how the army worked and its general state of battle readiness.

Although Mugabe had never been a particular friend of the proletariat, he made a point of taking an interest in the mechanics of war in exchange for the chance to dispense a little political re-education. Netting droves of new recruits and refugees who were flooding east, he turned many impromptu meetings into political rallies, and in due course more and more people began to look to him for guns, training and leadership. Within six months of leaving Rhodesia, he had successfully organised upwards of 10 000 Zimbabweans residing for one reason or another in Mozambique. With his genius for organisation he created the bedrock of a movement that would endure for the duration of the war and beyond.[9]

57

Farce at the Victoria Falls

As Mugabe was preparing for total war, others in the movement were treading obediently towards the detente goal. Preparations were under way for the much-anticipated constitutional conference, that was supposed to be the crowning achievement of Vorster's policy of rapprochement. By then unity was acknowledged as a farce, and Abel Muzorewa a farcical unity leader. The presidency of a free Zimbabwe was now an open race and at that point each man had as much chance as the next of winning it.

The choice of venue for the conference was quaint. It was a railway coach parked precisely on the border between Zambia and Rhodesia on the picturesque railway bridge that spans the Zambezi Gorge just below the Victoria Falls. The choice symbolised the fact that neither side was prepared to give an inch. Bishop Muzorewa was to lead a large delegation of nationalists under the guidance of Kaunda, while Smith — with everything to lose and nothing to gain — wearily mustered his forces and agreed to the arrangement on the say-so of John Vorster.

For Smith the moment was a bitter one. Both his own instincts and his military commanders were warning him that compromise was incompatible with the facts on the ground. It was the optimum moment to flood Mozambique with fire, and crush the armed struggle finally and conclusively. When that had been done, dialogue could then be pursued from a position of strength. However, Smith could not give that order, for had he done so, his Security Forces would have had to win the war with just the bullets in their guns. Supplies from the south would have cease immediately and Rhodesia would effectively be sealed up as tight as a drum. Smith had no choice but to tether his dogs and trudge north to indulge in yet more wasteful and irrelevant dialogue.

The conference was held on 25 August 1975 and was as much a pretext for Vorster to meet Kaunda face-to-face for the first time, as it was an opportunity for Rhodesia to align itself with prevailing world opinion. When the Rhodesians arrived it was clear from the number of international journalists filling local hotels, that the event was to be a South African media circus. The parties were to meet in a luxurious South African Railways salon with an equally plush dining car coupled to either end. One was for the Rhodesians and the other for the nationalists, and each was stocked to the roof with the best delicacies, wines and liquor that South Africa could provide.

On the morning of the conference, Vorster flew up from Pretoria in the company of Foreign Minister Hilgard Muller. It had been planned that he and Kenneth Kaunda would open the conference with their mutual blessings, and after preliminary speeches they would retire and not interfere in any way. Smith was briefed by Vorster that the object of the conference was merely for each side to appoint representatives who would meet in Salisbury at a later date, and actually get down to negotiating a new constitution. In this way appearances would be maintained and everyone would walk away happy.

When the Rhodesian delegation of six ministers arrived they were confronted by an assortment of

40 or more nationalists. Everyone except Mugabe was there, and everyone was trying to get the best seat. Vorster, who was not a small man, also squeezed himself in, followed by Kaunda who grinned, sweated and nodded as the South African Prime Minister wished them all God speed. The two then retreated to another carriage in order to assess one another and await results from the salon.

Bishop Abel Muzorewa opened the conference and, at complete variance with his usually timid nature, he began to thump the table. He stated clearly and forcefully that one-man-one-vote was to be the basic prerequisite for any agreement — which had most definitely not been part of the brief. It is easy to picture Smith raising his eyebrows and exchanging a glance or two with his colleagues. He might have peeked at his watch, drummed his fingers or gazed through a window at the magnificent falls. All the other demands — a general amnesty, freedom of campaigning etcetera — hardly seemed worth listening to. For the Rhodesians, the conference was as good as over. All this was a contest of relevance among the competing nationalists themselves and had nothing to do with him.

While Smith was being buffeted by the turgid dialogue, the meeting between Vorster and Kaunda went well. They soon moved out of the overcrowded and overheated carriage and made their way to the Mosi-o-Tunya Hotel in Livingstone, where a crowd of cheering locals lined the route waving placards applauding Vorster and his revolutionary leadership. After tea with various Zambian worthies, Vorster thumbed his nose at the Rhodesians by driving Kaunda across the bridge into Rhodesia, where less formal talks were held. Later Vorster was guest of honour at a luncheon in Livingstone.

Smith also proposed an adjournment for lunch, which prompted a dash for the dining salon on the Zambian side. The Rhodesians then wandered off to complain to Vorster, but by that time the South African could hardly have cared. The press had left the scene, he had thoroughly broken the ice with Kaunda and, in fact, was already on a flight back to Pretoria. The nationalists settled in to make merry in their dining salon, while on the opposite bank, the Rhodesians contented themselves with a reflective beer or two on the veranda of the Victoria Falls Hotel.

Later that afternoon Smith revisited the conference venue to see what chances there were of resumption. There were none. He found the nationalist salon in a shambles with no sign of the delegation. Smith had little time for alcohol and even less for its effects, so he noted with resigned distaste that the free South African liquor had been obliterated. Objecting to this behaviour was a waste of time though, for those on his side had already come to expect such foibles of the black man, and besides them no one else was interested. They were African, it was their country, and they were going to have it back. Those were the simple facts.

(Right) The Rhodesian African Rifles, grenade throwing training in Burma.

(Left) An RAF Lancaster bomber, taking part in a 1 000 bomber raid on an oil refinery near Bremen in 1944. Rhodesians served in squadrons throughout Bomber and Fighter Commands, not all of them in the Rhodesian designated squadrons because of the danger of large numbers being wiped out during particular operations which would have adversely affected morale at home.

(Right) Rhodesia supplied many officers and NCOs for the West African Brigade fighting in Burma. Picture shows Allied troops crossing the upper Chindwin in the Sittaung area.

(Left) Rhodesians fought with both South African and British Armies in the fight for Italy.

(Right) Rhodesians also took part in the D-day landings and the long haul across Europe which led to the German defeat.

(Left) The Federal Assembly being opened by the Governor-General of the Federation of Rhodesia and Nyasaland, Lord Dalhousie on 3 September 1953.

(Right) The Kariba Dam project began in tandem with bush clearing and the removal of wildlife from the areas being flooded. Here an unappreciative snake is captured.

(Left) The Kariba Dam. June 1959.

(Right) The new Canberra bombers of 5-Squadron Royal Rhodesian Air Force playing its part in Commonwealth Defence in Cyprus. 1959.

(Left) The Southern Rhodesian cabinet pose for a photograph in 1957. (L to r): G Elman-Brown, P.B Fletcher, Prime Minister R.S.G Garfield Todd, C.J. Hatty and A.R.W. Stumbles. In January 1958 the four ministers would revolt against Todd prompting his eventual replacement by Sir Edgar Whitehead.

(Right) Lord Malvern welcomes British Prime Minister Harold Macmillan to Salisbury. January 1960

(Left) Joshua Nkomo (right) and Ndabaningi Sithole walk out of the Southern Rhodesian constitutional talks on 15 May 1961. History might have taken a different course if Nkomo had stayed.

(Right) Disaffection in Southern Rhodesia in July 1960. The BSA Police face up to rioting mobs in Salisbury, Bulawayo, Gatooma and Gwelo. The police had not opened fire in the course of their duties since the rebellions of 1896, but in 1960 there was no other way to restore law and order.

(Below) Constitutional accord. On 1 June 1961 Prime Minister Whitehead and the British Commonwealth Secretary Duncan Sandys, announce that they had reached complete agreement on a new constitution for Southern Rhodesia. This was endorsed with enthusiasm by the largely white electorate but the blacks were not satisfied.

(Left) Joshua Nkomo flying home after talks in Britain.

(Right) Speaker's procession, Southern Rhodesian House of Assembly.

(Left) Lord Home gave Sir Roy Welensky and the Federal Government 'unstinting help and understanding' with regard to the serious problems they faced.

(Right) Sir Edgar Whitehead and Sir Roy Welensky discuss common problems.

(Left) Sir Arthur Benson, Governor of Northern Rhodesia,, wrote a secret indictment of the Federal Government and sent it to the Colonial Secretary, Lennox Boyd.

(Below) The crisis years for the Federation. The verdict of the Monckton Commission was that territories should be granted a qualified option to secede. Weelensky rejected this but it was a mortal blow to the Federation.

(Left) Kenneth Kaunda of Northern Rhodesia forced the pace of constitutional change. When Britain granted D Hastings Banda and Kenneth Kaunda the right for their territories to secede, spelt the end of the Federation.

(Right) The Federal break-up. Sir Roy Welensky and Sir Athol Evans drink a toast to the Federation at the final banquet held in Salisbury on 12 December 1963.

(Left) Dr Hastings Banda, President o Malawi and Winston Field, the new Rhodesian Front Prime Minister of Southern Rhodesia discuss common ground after the break-up of the Federation. 1964.

(Right) Southern Rhodesian Prime Minister Ian Smith, Commonwealth Secretary Arthur Bottomley and British Prime Minister Harold Wilson meet in Salisbury to make a last ditch attempt to avoid a Rhodesian Unilateral Declaration of Independence. 25 October 1965.

(Left) Harold Wilson and Arthur Bottomley meet African leaders at New Sarum Airport. Joshua Nkomo has his arm in a sling. 17 October 1965.

(Right) The signing of the Unilateral Declaration of Independence (UDI), 11 November 1965. Seated (l to r): Gardner Burke, Du Pont, Ian Smith, Harper, Lord Graham. (Second row): Howman, Van Heerden, Musset, Rathall, Rudland. (Back row): Phillip Smith, Dillon, Lance Smith, Van der Bijl, Dunlop.

(Above) Sir Humphrey Gibbs, last governor of Southern Rhodesia.

(Right) Clifford du Pont became the Officer Administering the Government replacing Governor Sir Humphrey Gibbs when UDI was declared. He became President when Rhodesian was declared a Republic on 2 March 1970.

(Below) Black urban disturbances after UDI. Bulawayo 25 November 1965.

(Right) Fruitless talks with Harold Wilson on HMS Tiger in 1966.

(Left) Fruitless talks with Harold Wilson aboard HMS Fearless in 1968.

(Right) President Clifford du Pont takes the salute at the foot of Rhodes' statue in Jameson Avenue, Salisbury, 11 November 1970.

(Left) In late 1971 Lord Home agreed to a Commission of Enquiry headed by Lord Pearce to test Rhodesian opinion regarding a settlement. It was agreed that it would begin and end its work in December 1971. The British Government, however, dilly-dallied for weeks on end which gave the black nationalists time to orchestrate an intimidation campaign to force the black population to say 'No'. When the Commission finally completed its work in mid-March 1973, not surprisingly, it reported that the majority of whites were in favour, but the majority of blacks were not.

(Right) Advocate Herbert Chitepo was orchestrating ZANU's war effort in Zambia. In March 1975 he was assassinated by a team of Rhodesian Central Intelligence Organisation operators headed by ex-British 22-SAS operator, Alan 'Taffy' Brice. It was conducted in such a way that Zambian security thought it had been carried out by ZANU. This resulted in the organisation being kicked out of the country and their war effort being disrupted for a year.

(Left) South Africa's Prime Minister John Vorster was relied on by Britain, America and Zambia to pressurise Prime Minister Smith into submission.

(Right) One of Vorster's
ideas was the abortive
conference held in a
South African Railways'
coach parked in the cen-
tre of the Fall's bridge.
It was a disaster.

(Left) The 500th meeting of
the Rhodesian Operations
Co-ordinating Committee
in June 1976. Seated (l to r)
Walls (Army), Sherren (Police), Mussell and McLaren
(Air Force) and Flower
(CIO). 13 month later the
committee, re-born as Combined Operations, appealed
to Smith to seek a political
settlement before the situation reached 'a point of
no return'. Smith didn't
listen and the situation soon
reached the predicted stage.

(Right) The 3 March Agree-
ment (1978). Seated (l to r)
Muzorewa, Smith, Chirau,
Sithole. Behind Muzorewa
and on his left Mundawarara.
Behind Smith: David Smith.
Behind Chirau: Ndweni,
Gaylard the cabinet secretary
leafs through papers.

(Left) The gang of three intent on selling Rhodesia down the river. David Owen (left), Don Jamieson — Canada's Minister for External Affairs and Pik Botha (right front).

(Right) The Lancaster House conference, Autumn 1979. Bishop Muzorewa's on left, Lord Carrington and the British delegation in the centre and the Patriotic Front on the right.

(Left) Lord Carrington gives an excited smile at the signing of the Lancaster House Agreement on 21 December 1979. He is flanked by Bishop Muzorewa and Sir Ian Gilmour, with Joshua Nkomo and Robert Mugabe on the far right.

(Right) Josiah Tongogara, ZANLA army commander. At Lancaster House he displayed a willingness to work with whites much to Mugabe's disapproval. He arranged for his assassination in Mozambique shortly afterwards.

(Left) Lord Soames became the British Governor charged with implementing the Lancaster House Agreement.

(Right) British police and British and Commonwealth military personnel were sent to supervise the majority rule elections.

(Left) The winner of the elections, Robert Gabriel Mugabe. A brutal an[d] murderous campaign was mounted by Mugabe's political commissars who spread out into the country are[a] during the election run-up. They we[re] supposed to report to assembly poin[ts] in terms of the Lancaster House Agreement, but they didn't. This was frequently reported to Governo[r] Soames but he took little or no notice. The British Government wante[d] Rhodesia out of its hair. This left th[e] commissars free to ruthlessly murde[r] dissenters and threaten death to thos[e] likely to vote against Mugabe and h[is] ZANU-PF. No wonder Mugabe wo[n] the election hands down. And look what has happened to Zimbabwe since!

(Below) The Rhodesian Security Forces, both black and white, comprising policemen, soldiers, and airmen doggedly fought black nationalist guerrillas for seven years from 1973 to 1979. The enemy were well supplied with weapons by the Soviet Bloc and China. The guerrillas of both Mugabe's ZANLA and Joshua Nkomo's ZIPRA adopted [a] strategy of using terror against black and white civilians. During the war there were 21 782 terrorist attacks, mostly against blacks, recorded. The Rhodesian Security Forces never lost a battle, but world sympathy for the black Nationalist's cause resulted in the[m] losing the war.

Disappearance of a nationalist
The Mgagao Declaration

The collapse of the Victoria Falls conference had the dual effect of freeing up the Rhodesian Security Forces to get back to the business of war, while at the same time softening Ian Smith's attitude to Joshua Nkomo whom he had begun to view as a possible ally. If he was going to be in negotiation with somebody, then Nkomo was probably the best of a bad lot. Muzorewa would obviously have been better, but for the time being he seemed to be mesmerised by his ambitions. To get through to Nkomo and set the stage for some sort of contact, Smith, used the reliable and ever resourceful Ken Flower, to act as his front man in Lusaka.

Among the first to notice this new ploy was the ANC's publicity secretary, Edson Sithole. His earlier criticism of Muzorewa's willingness to reach an agreement with Smith had seen him arbitrarily detained. Sithole was also not silent on his conviction that the Smith regime had ordered the murder of Herbert Chitepo. Sithole went to the length of announcing, at the burial of the murdered nationalist, that the killing had ruined any possibility of a negotiated settlement. He now loudly decried contacts between Nkomo and Smith which inevitably marked himself in both camps as a problem.

Edson Sithole was another of those humble men who by grit and determination had educated himself, and then risen through the ranks of the liberation movement. He was a short but spry and energetic character who bore more than a passing resemblance to the old terrier himself, Dr Leander Starr Jameson. As a consequence of being detained in Whitehead's roundups in February 1959, Sithole missed the opportunity to study abroad. While in detention he studied for an LLB through the University of London and in 1963 sat and passed the Rhodesian Bar examination. Politically he was a radical, holding early office in the Youth League, the ANC and ZANU before joining Muzorewa's centrist African National Council. He was deeply distrustful of Joshua Nkomo, and vigilant against any effort by ZAPU to use the ANC for its own ends.

Of course his suspicions where not without foundation. Nkomo was being actively encouraged by the Rhodesians to — more fruitfully in some way — provoke a breach that would give him the opportunity to demand a congress, after which it was assumed that he could fairly easily manoeuvre himself into the leadership. Muzorewa, who had left Rhodesia soon after Victoria Falls to tour the United States, soon received word of this. On his return in September he called for a meeting at which Nkomo was expelled, along with one or two other members who were loyal to him. This turned out to be a coup for Nkomo, who immediately called his own congress, where he was nominated as leader. His version of the ANC was then renamed the ANC-Z in order to distinguish it from Muzorewa's — all of which made the Rhodesians very happy.

The ANC-Z represented ZAPU and, for the time being, the Rhodesians were content to let it exist. This was not only because of their renewed contacts with Nkomo, but also because the entire party structure was riddled with police informers. Nothing Nkomo did, thought or planned remained a secret to Special Branch for long. On 1 December 1975, he and Smith went so far as to sign a 'Declaration of Intent to Negotiate a Settlement', an accord that lived on in precarious health for a year or so until it was superseded by events. In the meantime one of the least creditable episodes of the war took place.

Edson Sithole was a regular visitor to the Quill Club in the Ambassador Hotel in Salisbury — a popular bar and watering hole for journalists, fringe nationalists and other interested parties. At about seven o'clock on the evening of 15 October 1975, Sithole arrived outside the Ambassador in his BMW, with his secretary and girlfriend Miriam Mhlanga. As the two stepped out of the car they were approached by a pair of white individuals who identified themselves as members of the Special Branch. Such approaches were commonplace for a high profile nationalist like Sithole, so at first he was not unduly concerned. He and Miss Mhlanga followed the men to a VW Kombi parked against the curb. They were then seized and bundled inside before the vehicle was quickly driven away.

It happened that the Secretary General of the Catholic Commission for Justice and Peace (CCJP), Father Arthur, witnessed the incident. He also saw a black man climb into Sithole's BMW and drive it away. The vehicle was later found abandoned outside Umtali, perhaps to give the impression that Sithole had fled into Mozambique. Neither he nor Mhlanga were ever seen again.

The CCJP promptly hired a private investigator to look into the disappearance and, before long, a black army corporal was identified who signed a sworn statement to the effect that he saw Sithole at the main Selous Scouts Inkomo Barracks a short time after the abduction. Henrik Ellert, author of the authoritative *Rhodesian Front War*, presents the theory — substantiated no doubt by inside knowledge gained as a member of the BSAP throughout the war — that the Selous Scouts conspired to abduct and 'turn' Sithole in the same way they turned captured guerrillas. It was unfortunate that Father Arthur witnessed the incident, because this may have prompted the decision to eliminate Sithole. The witness who saw Sithole at Inkomo Barracks was sent to Malawi for his own safety, but was returned as favour to the Scouts by Malawi Special Branch. He was also never seen again.

* * *

Both Smith and Mugabe felt an urgent need to restart the war as soon as possible. For the Rhodesians this was simply a matter of reissuing orders, but for the nationalists it was still a question of resolving crippling internal contradictions. On the surface, things had simplified inasmuch as they had temporarily returned to the basic formula of two parties, ZANU and ZAPU. ZAPU's military wing, ZIPRA, was still the weaker of the two, but ZANLA was also in conspicuous disarray. Most top ZANLA commanders had either died in the purges, or were imprisoned in Zambia, and the political leadership was technically in the hands of Ndabaningi Sithole. To try and claim the loyalty of the surviving armed forces, Chikerema, Muzorewa and Sithole formed a brief alliance that they called the Zimbabwe Liberation Council (ZLC). The Council attempted to visit camps in Tanzania but found access denied. Instead, during October 1975, 43 commanders at the Mgagao Camp, held a series of closed meetings to consider the catastrophic leadership crisis that had overwhelmed the party, and to determine a policy to break the deadlock. Out of these meetings, emerged arguably the most important document of the entire liberation struggle.

The Mgagao Declaration effectively ended Ndabaningi Sithole's leadership of ZANU by explicitly condemning him, Muzorewa and Chikerema on behalf of the military, which collectively accused them of bungling, vacillation and indecision. The ZLC was dismissed for what it was, Zambia was condemned for her lack of support in the war, and an appeal was made to the OAU Liberation Committee — as well as Tanzania and Mozambique — to allow ZANLA to restart the war. In the event that the request for supplies, safe haven and transit facilities was rejected, then the cadres wished to be deported back to Rhodesia to fight with sticks and stones.

We cannot afford to just stand and stare at the Smith regime and allied forces of reaction whittling away every ounce of rights of the people of Zimbabwe. If we cannot live as free men, we rather choose to die as free men.[1]

The most important feature of the Mgagao Declaration, however, was its response to the leadership crisis, about which it had this to say:

An executive member who has been outstanding is Robert Mugabe. He has demonstrated this by defying the rigors of guerrilla life in the jungles of Mozambique. Since we respect him most, in all our dealings with the ANC leadership, he is the only person who can act as a middleman. We will not accept any direct discussion with any of the three leading members of the ANC we have described above. We can only talk through Robert Mugabe to them.[2]

While less than an actual anointing, this statement nonetheless opened the door to the leadership of the Party for Robert Mugabe. It was the moment he had been waiting for, and as far as Samora Machel was concerned, the decision had been made.

The Mgagao Declaration left one or two loose ends. Most importantly, the fact still remained that the OAU had authorised the supply of weapons and materiel only through the ANC, which made it necessary to form another of those empty corporations to facilitate the movement of assets. A brief military alliance came into being that purported to reflect the broader unity accord. ZANU and ZAPU were the principal partners — since the UANC had no army of its own — and a new, integrated command system to be called the Zimbabwe Peoples' Army, or ZIPA, came into being. came under the command of Rex Nhongo who, although only 27-years-old, had proven himself to be a commander of exceptional courage and ability. The undisputed strong man of the region wanted final and personal confirmation of the new direction, and for this Samora Machel sought the counsel of the imprisoned Josiah Tongogara. He put to Tongogara the simple and direct question: To whom did the fighting men of ZANLA owe their primary loyalty? To this Tongogara replied without hesitation: Robert Mugabe. Thus the last strands of the Gordian knot were severed and Mugabe leadership became de facto if not yet entirely constitutional.

Mugabe was of course elated when he heard. In his first memorandum to the party — to his party — he could not contain a desire to gloat. As he did so, his signature language permitted a ray of dark light to escape.

Indeed we have seen no less a person than the Commander-in-Chief of our ZANLA forces [Ndabaningi Sithole] perform an unprecedented dramatic and counter-revolutionary feat as he somersaulted to a disgraceful surrender, deserting, thereby, the very Forces he had helped to build. In the process, he joined forces with the enemy…and thus became an unmitigated traitor to the whole revolution.[3]

As usual the merger of the two guerrilla armies was a mirage and a split was not long in coming. Fighting between ZIPRA and ZANLA soon erupted in Mozambique, and in due course elements of ZIPRA defected and made their way back to Zambia. ZANLA complained that ZIPRA was determined to commit as few men at arms as possible to the new offensive, in order to retain the bulk of its force to support Nkomo in a conventional war if his negotiations with Smith failed.[4]

With that, it was understood that each army would fight its own war, and ZANLA again found itself at the bottom of the list for the distribution of Soviet military support. Mugabe was forced to re-examine ZANU's external network which took him in new directions in search of arms and financial backing. He forged relations with Red China, Romania and Yugoslavia, sourcing arms, money and training. In due course four of the Frontline leaders paid him a visit in Quelimane and formally conceded that détente had failed. All agreed that there was now no alternative to total war.

* * *

Guerrilla incursions rapidly began to spread throughout Manicaland Province, which ZANLA had divided into several of its own operational zones. From north to south these were: Takawira Sector, Chitepo Sector, Tangwena Sector, Monomatapa Sector and Musikavanhu Sector. Below these, adjacent to the Gonarezou National Park, were three further sectors that were numbered and not named. This was because they were situated in tribally divergent areas where ZANLA commanders were reluctant to use Shona names for fear of giving offence to local people. The Government covered the same area with two Joint Operational Commands codenamed *Thrasher* and *Repulse*. Tanzanian-trained guerrillas earmarked for deployment in Manicaland were shipped south from Dar-es-Salaam to Beira, and from there driven to a large rear base on the Nyadzonia River not far from Chimoio. Those intended for the Tangwena and Monomatapa Sectors were trucked north, while those heading east into Musikavanhu Sector infiltrated on foot.

Their activities were not long in being felt in Rhodesia. On 2 February 1976, an 11-ton truck belonging to Chipinga Tea Estates was destroyed by a mine, killing the driver and his assistant. Had the truck encountered the mine on its return journey, it would have been packed to the gunwales with contract tea pickers — most of whom would probably have been killed.[5] A police follow-up section was ambushed the following morning, and later that month a group of guerrillas attacked Hogwe Farm near Chipinga. On the evening of 29 February, guerrillas entered the Pungwe Hotel in the Honde Valley and opened fire randomly, injuring seven people. A passing Special Branch vehicle was spotted by a guard detachment positioned outside the hotel, and raked with fire, killing three black personnel.[6]

On 3 March, Samora Machel closed the border, announcing that Mozambique was now in a state of war with Rhodesia. Surprisingly, the Rhodesians did not anticipate this and lost 2 300 pieces of railway rolling stock — one sixth of the company's entire complement. As sanctions bit deeper into the national economy, such losses were not to be taken lightly.[7]

In the early evening of 18 April, four South African tourists riding two motorcycles came upon the scene of a robbery on the Fort Victoria-Beit Bridge road. A group of 12 guerrillas had set up a makeshift roadblock and were in the process of robbing the occupants of two cars that had been travelling towards Salisbury. The South Africans did not immediately grasp the seriousness of the situation. One of them became belligerent with the group leader and was shot dead. Two of his companions were gunned down a moment later, while the fourth, a woman, was seriously injured but survived. The two motorcars — that were the original focus of the robbery — seized the opportunity and sped off to raise the alarm.[8]

The entire eastern front peeled open, exposing the soft underbelly of Rhodesia. The magnitude of this can scarcely be imagined without looking at a map, and seeing the crisis of vulnerability that this presented to the agricultural and economic heartland of Rhodesia. The war suddenly reached into the lives of a great many more people, who had hitherto been unaffected. The renewed public anxiety soon resulted in calls for the war to be extended across that border. In a series of statements during the course of the next few weeks, Smith allowed something of the gravity of the situation to seep out. In a televised broadcast on 6 February he announced that, following the most serious incursions so far seen in the hot war, it had become evident that the eastern front had been activated. This development added fuel to rumours already circulating, that the Cubans were disembarking en masse in Beira and bringing with them tanks and Sam-7 missiles.

Meanwhile, as an indication that international sanctions were at last beginning to bite, long-established international cigarette brands abruptly disappeared from the market in favour of new local brands that had no licensing requirements in terms of quality and packaging. Dispensing with silver foil and cellophane would, it was hoped, save the government US$1 million in foreign currency. The disquiet generated by this most visible effect of sanctions, was overlaid by some British humour — the cigarettes were a fine blend of camel dung and khaki weed. Nonetheless the event was one of many that hinted strongly at tough times to come. The cost of living had risen by 2% in January, the petrol allocations were cut by 20 per cent following the closure of the Mozambique border, holiday allowances had been slashed, and the Rhodesian cricket team was pushed down to third place on the Currie Cup table.[9]

Smith warned that hit-and-run attacks against white farms would escalate, mine incidents would increase and a barrage of psychological warfare could be expected, in an attempt to convince Rhodesians of the hopelessness of their cause. Furthermore, South Africa now manifestly could not be relied upon in the event of all-out terrorist war.

'Unfortunately', Smith lamented, 'there is no Churchill alive today to bring home to them [Western Powers] the folly of such appeasement.'

The Prime Minister then revealed the degree of his own nervous anxiety, by letting it be known that he would actually consider abandoning UDI if it could be was proven to him that it was essential to do so. A little later he obviously thought better of this, for on 20 March 1976 he made what was perhaps the most iconic utterance of his career: 'I don't believe in majority rule ever in Rhodesia,' he said ' ... not in a thousand years.'[10]

The iron fist

D uring 1975 the Selous Scouts, born a pseudo terrorist unit, began to slip deeper into the role
that would later build much of its legend. Responsibility for external operations had tended
in the past to fall on collaboration between the SAS and the CIO, but as the war progressed,
the all white SAS steadily lost ground to the racially mixed Selous Scouts. Clearly SAS patrols could
not easily merge into populated landscapes when attacks or reconnaissance were necessary, and this
put them at a severe disadvantage.

A second factor that often allowed the Selous Scouts to exceed their original mandate, was the fact
that Commanding Officer Lieutenant-Colonel Reid Daly, enjoyed something of a personal rapport
with Army Commander General Peter Walls. At times Walls was influenced by Reid Daly beyond
his better judgement, and that of other top military commanders. Reid Daly was among many who
argued that the war could only be won through aggressive action carried directly to the enemy. While
this was not a particularly original theme, Reid Daly was convinced that the Selous Scouts was the
natural unit to carry out this kind of work — and indeed to a large degree this had already been
proved.

In September 1974, the Scouts were successfully deployed on an ad hoc operation to kidnap a
high-ranking ZIPRA official from Francistown. In March 1975, a small force of 20 Scouts crossed
the northeast border into Mozambique where intelligence indicated the existence of an important
staging post for guerrillas moving to Rhodesia. The mission was experimental, and the group set off
on the understanding that air support would be countenanced only if severe casualty evacuation was
required. It was also understood that the Government would disclaim responsibility for any failures
or personnel captured by the enemy. In the event, after a hard march, the Scouts arrived at the base
to discover that cholera had done their work for them. Those guerrillas who had not died of the
disease had fled. This operation was followed a few months later by another small patrol that entered
Mozambique through the cordon sanitaire, and successfully kidnapped a low-ranking FRELIMO
official and a ZANLA contact man.

Although these incursions were satisfying, they achieved relatively little due to severe limitations
imposed by the Defence Ministry, which itself was limited by the Cabinet. PK van der Byl had
meantime taken over the Defence Ministry and, as one of the principal hawks in Government, he was
among those who advocated taking the war directly to the terrorists. Reid Daly was also pressing for
permission to penetrate deeper into Mozambique with greater force, and his petitions were heard
with a great deal of sympathy by, among others, Van der Byl. Thanks then to determined lobbying
by the Minister, and with a rapidly increasing volume of terrorist attacks being felt all along the
eastern border, the Government began to appreciate the inevitability of giving the Selous Scouts and
other units the green light to cross the border.

The South Africans, however, were still determined to tread as lightly as possible in the region, so caution remained the key word during any Rhodesian cross-border strikes. Restrictions included the previously imposed moratorium on air support, as well as a limit on attacks beyond five kilometres of the border. No attacks whatsoever were to be undertaken against FRELIMO. On this understanding, Reid Daly retreated to his command bunker and deployed the first serious attack group.

On 17 January 1976, a small group of Scouts inconclusively attacked a staging camp and, a month later they raided another transit camp close to the three-cornered frontier of Rhodesia, Mozambique and South Africa. Again, with only three kills confirmed, these attacks hardly justified the input. The Scouts were nonetheless gathering important experience and intelligence and, at the same time stirring up a healthy ferment along ZANLA and FRELIMO supply lines.

The probing attacks tended to confirm to Samora Machel that the open relationship he had tried to entertain with Rhodesia was paying no dividends. It was at that point that he closed the border and committed Mozambique to upholding international economic sanctions. The CIO quickly responded to this by establishing a Mozambican pseudo resistance group that was christened *Movimento Nacional da Resistência de Moçambique* (MNR) and later as the *.Resistênicia Nacional Moçambicana*, or Renamo. [1]

The MNR was devised as a tool to destabilise the FRELIMO Government, and to punish it for hosting ZANLA guerrilla activity. But it also had the beneficial by-product of creating a widely dispersed intelligence network within Mozambique itself. The first MNR training camp was located outside Rusape, in Rhodesia, and fell under the command of CIO liaison officer Peter Burt who was formally based in Lisbon. The camp was later moved to a farm at Odzi close to Umtali. The first batch of operational men was drawn from the ranks of former Portuguese pseudos, known as *Flechas* (arrows). A former FRELIMO detachment commander, Andre Matangaidze, known as Commandant Andre, was placed in overall command. The group's first operation was planned as a solution to a manpower shortage, and was mounted by a combined force of MNR and SAS on the sinister-sounding Sacudzo Re-education Centre. Approximately 500 anti-FRELIMO dissidents were freed and invited to join the MNR — and about 300 did.[2]

The MNR then went on to do what African guerrilla movements tend to be good at — pillaging, raping, torturing and slaughtering. The wholesale banditry so offended Machel that he complained bitterly and frequently on the international stage. As a reward for his resolve in upholding international sanctions, Mozambique was offered UN financial compensation for her fiscal losses. It has been suggested that this was also to persuade Machel to assist Mugabe, in his struggle for dominance over ZIPRA,[3] but it is unlikely he needed any persuasion. London gave an initial sum of £15 million to this cause, which prompted PK van der Byl to comment on the absurdity of a Marxist regime being paid by Britain to destroy what had once been the pride of the British Empire.[4]

The MNR would never have been as effective as it was without the support of the Rhodesian SAS, that provided operational credibility to a guerrilla organisation lacking genuine popular support. Historians of the Rhodesian war have tended to press the case, that the creation of the MNR was a successful strategy simply because it did tap into a deep pool of latent discontent; but the author finds this unlikely. FRELIMO was ubiquitous and dominated government, the military and the police. It started out as a unity movement, but evolved into a Cuban-style communist party based on a personality cult centred around Samora Machel. Opposition to it was cruelly discouraged and where it did exist, it usually operated on tribal or ideological lines. Organisations expressing opposition, tended to have an intellectual flavour with neither broad cohesion nor any real military potential. There was a vague hope in Rhodesia that popular resistance would crystallise around the MNR, but without Rhodesian material support — and later South African — the military activities of the MNR would and did evaporate.

Ken Flower was the person most directly responsible for the birth of the MNR and, as with the

Selous Scouts, he was dismayed by the monster that grew out of his original idea. As time passed, Mozambique stumbled from a colonial war, to war with Rhodesia, and to a bitter civil war that was aided and funded almost exclusively by South Africa. FRELIMO survived, but the cost in human suffering was immeasurable. Flower felt a certain responsibility for the many thousands of lives destroyed in these conflicts, and he carried the guilt with him to his grave.

ZANU, in the meanwhile, set up a propaganda broadcasting service called the Voice of Zimbabwe. VOZ utilised the services of a homegrown Lord Haw Haw, in the form of Scotsman Ian Christie, who from his studio in Maputo relentlessly vilified the minority government in Salisbury. In competition, and in support of the MNR, the CIO set up a Portuguese language alternative called The A Voz da Africa Livre (Voice of Free Africa), that broadcast over a massive transmitter based outside Gwelo, nicknamed Big Bertha. This station gathered such a following in Mozambique that, in due course, a distressed Samora Machel commissioned East German engineers to block it. Such was the zest of Big Bertha, however, that even with the most sophisticated equipment this effort failed.

The Selous Scouts flying column raids into Mozambique continued. A second attack on Caponda Base was followed by the first flying column attack. In May 1976 Scouts assaulted targets in Gaza Province using Mercedes Unimogs, disguised as FRELIMO vehicles. This was followed in June by raids aimed at Mapai and Chicualacuala. The latter operation involved sending a unit into South Africa posing as tourists, so that they could enter Gaza through the Eastern Transvaal. This particular operation degenerated into a brawling firefight, that resulted in the death of a Scout and serious wounds to two more. Helicopters were authorised to pick up casualties, while an air strike was guided in to neutralise resistance. This alone allowed the remainder of the attack force to make good their escape. The enemy body count helped to compensate for these reverses: ZANLA guerrillas lay dead with 18 wounded. This had been the most spectacular operation so far, although the first that had claimed a Rhodesian life.

It had been noted that the main conduit of insurgent traffic into the Thrasher operational area, was through the Honde Valley, a picturesque catchment in the lee of Inyangani Mountain that — on the Rhodesian side at least — was thickly populated with native villages interspersed with a handful of commercial tea estates. The question of how to plug this human flow taxed the minds of military command, until the routine interrogation of a captured guerrilla revealed the existence of a sizable ZANLA base vaguely indicated to be on the Pungwe River. More detailed questioning of captures revealed that this installation was the main logistics base for ZANLA guerrillas being channelled into the Thrasher operational area.

The Rhodesian Air Force was then requested to conduct an aerial survey of the Pungwe catchment area, to pinpoint the base. Since the days that Frank Johnson and Dr Jim had paddled down that same river in their underwear, things had changed significantly. The landscape was now densely inhabited, which made locating the position of a base in the midst of it all very difficult. The operation consumed a great deal of Air Force reconnaissance time with very little to show for it.

The base was in fact sited a few degrees wide of where intelligence reports had originally indicated, and in the end it was accidentally located during a flight diversion around bad weather. Images were produced of 800 or more people mustering in a substantial emplacement, sited by a tributary of the Pungwe called the Nyadzonia River. The discovery generated tremendous excitement in security circles, as the practicalities of dealing with such a large concentration of manpower were pondered.

Eventually another flying column attack was prescribed, and in the early hours of 9 August 1986, the Nyadzonia Base was assaulted by a motorised force of 84 Selous Scouts in a small complement of Ferret armoured cars, and ten heavily armed Unimogs disguised as FRELIMO vehicles. The raid has since become iconic, and was arguably the definitive Selous Scouts operation of the war. It was a clinically conducted attack that inflicted catastrophic casualties on the occupants of the base, with no loss of life by the Selous Scouts.

Exactly how many people died in the attack on Nyadzonia Base has never been accurately established. According to the United Nations High Commission for Refugees, 675 died and 675 were wounded. The equal number listed as dead and injured implied, as Reid Daly suggested, a case of over-simplified mathematics on the part of ZANLA and FRELIMO. Ex-ZANLA guerrilla Alexander Kanengoni witnessed the aftermath and gave his haunting impressions in an article written some years later for the Zimbabwean *Sunday Times*.

At Nyadzonia, it took us over a week to bury the nearly 2 000 people who had perished in the horrendous incident. And as we walked away from the horrible place, I was afraid to turn back and see the thousand or more sobbing shadows with their heads bowed, following us, refusing to be left behind and got [sic] forgotten.[5]

Kanengoni was one of many who claimed repeatedly and insistently that the dead of Nyadzonia were refugee women and children. The Rhodesians were adamant that those killed were either trained terrorists or recruits in training. In fact Nyadzonia was without doubt a military installation, and Edgar Tekere later confirmed this fact in an interview conducted for Granada Television as part of the *End of Empire* series. Further corroboration was provided the following year when a combined SAS/RLI raid on Chimoio in Mozambique, unearthed the official ZANLA report on the incident which listed 1 028 killed, 309 wounded and 1 000 missing. The report strongly suggested that the Nyadzonia Base had been a full ZANLA military facility.[6]

In the face of the evidence, Ken Flower still maintained that the base had been nothing more than a staging camp where some low level training took place. As he later put it when the matter was revealed to the Rhodesian public:

OCC's communiqué was 'terse', because we were not prepared to take responsibility for lying about the nature of the raid, and we could not devise a formula which would account for the death of such a large number of unarmed, untrained people.

In the aftermath of the raid Flower virtually disowned the Selous Scouts. As Director General of the CIO he was sternly professional in his duties, but his personal bias did not tilt in favour of the Government. He later expressed regret at what he considered to be the blunders and excesses of the Rhodesian War. What perhaps upset him most was that, having been instrumental in designing the Selous Scouts blueprint, he had no control over the unit evolving into a formidable strike force. The Nyadzonia incident caused a rift between he and Selous Scouts commander Reid Daly that spilled over into acrimony and distrust between the Selous Scouts and the CIO, and was a rift that would never heal.

Flower maintained in his memoirs that there was no evidence to suggest that the Nyadzonia camp had been anything more than a staging camp, where some low level training took place but this does not accord with the facts that have subsequently come to light

Year of the people's storm

Unwanted interference

Three days after the Nyadzonia raid, the border town of Umtali suffered a bombardment launched from Mozambique. A few rockets and mortars fell about the city in an action lasting about 40 minutes or so, hardly matching the firestorm that had provoked it. The gung-ho humour of white Rhodesians under siege, was illustrated on a T-shirt that featured a beer bottle fitted with mortar fins above a caption reading: 'Come to Umtali and get bombed!' These T-shirts became collector's items, and were shipped internationally in large quantities as souvenirs of the Rhodesian War.

The political fallout of the Nyadzonia raid was much more severe. Condemnation was universal, and not surprisingly so, for the astonishing success of the raid that had translated into such grotesquely lopsided casualty figures, made it impossible for the operation to be seen internationally as anything other than a genocidal attack. Be it refugees, women, children, guerrillas — trained or untrained, armed or otherwise — it hardly mattered. It was a propaganda coup for ZANU, and sympathy was ruthlessly milked worldwide. Almost incidental was the massive cost in human life, as both sides bickered over who between them was the worst, the most inhuman and degraded, in a war increasingly without rules, and probably no different from any other war.

Rhodesians at that point could scarcely have given a damn what the wider world thought about the revised tactics. It was clearly evident that international support for the liberation agenda of the black nations of Africa reeked of hypocrisy. While the OAU vilified Rhodesia, chairman and commissioner of the UN Commission on Human Rights — one Idi Amin, dictator of Uganda — feasted on the blood of his countrymen in fits of killing, that had overtones of psychosis rather than race or politics. The Congo, renamed Zaire, was mired in catastrophic corruption, the Central African Republic had become the canvas upon which one man, Jean Bédel Bokassa, writ large his insane ambitions and Francisco Marcías Nguema of Equatorial Guinea set a yet unbeaten record of violence, demagoguery and corruption. It was only when South Africa began to raise her voice in irritated protest that the Rhodesians were forced to listen and comply.

The Rhodesian ambassador was summoned to an audience with Vorster, who expressed his strong disapproval and disappointment that the Nyadzonia raid had gone ahead without his prior clearance. If it was Ian Smith's inclination to ignore the rebuke, he could hardly ignore the subsequent removal of South African helicopters and aircrews on loan to Rhodesia, nor the chronic backlog of rail traffic south of the Limpopo that continued to hold up vital Rhodesian imports.[2]

In political terms, the Nyadzonia raid signalled the start of a second period of direct and unwanted South African interference in the Rhodesian crisis. This time the issue was related to a belated acceptance on the part of South Africa to establish a common defence against communism. To his credit, Vorster was now prepared to accept that mistakes had been made, but in rectifying them he was again willing to use Rhodesia as collateral.

The Marxist takeover in Mozambique had proved to be very tricky to handle and so detente was for the time being quietly buried. With this lesson learned, Pretoria viewed the imminent communist takeover of Angola in a much less benevolent light. The transfer of power in Mozambique had been relatively simple, mainly because FRELIMO had suffered no competition. In Angola, however, the situation was very different. Three powerful liberation groups contested the immediate political fate of this large country — in itself a recipe for bloody and almost perpetual civil war. In turn, this dynamic offered huge potential for the Soviet bloc to become involved in the region.

It was at this moment that United States interest in Africa accelerated to the point of engagement. Prior to this, the main theatre of the Cold War had been Southeast Asia. Whatever manoeuvring the Soviets and Chinese had been contemplating in Africa, tended to be forestalled by white minority regimes that could be relied on to defend their ideology to the last man. However by the mid-1970s those men were falling at an alarming rate. Mozambique had been the first, Rhodesia was on her knees and South West Africa could expect the fight to arrive on her borders at any moment. The time had abruptly arrived for the US to act.

It was onto the stage, therefore, that American super-statesman Henry Kissinger stepped. With little appetite for direct military intervention after the Vietnam experience, he chose to rely on cordial relations between the US and South Africa to influence events. The political risks of backing South Africa, in a war against the MPLA in Angola, were significant, but substantially less than the risk of another Vietnam. Secrecy would be vital since Kissinger could hardly try to win friends and influence people in the region, while he was in bed with South Africa.

A pretext for South African military involvement came with the arrival by the shipload in Angola of Cuban 'military advisors'. In August 1975, South Africa — with covert CIA assistance — launched an invasion codenamed *Operation Savannah*, that rolled up 3 000 kilometres of Angolan territory in 33 days. It stopped short of Luanda because the river bridges had been blown ansd no bridging equipment was available. This effectively handed Angola to the MPLA and its communist backers.

Washington's worst fears were realised, as details of American involvement began to surface. In the face of almost universal black condemnation, Kissinger was forced to look around for a foil, and it was on Rhodesia that his eyes fell. He proposed a deal to Pretoria that John Vorster could hardly refuse. American support for anti-Marxist forces in Angola would continue. No political pressure would be applied in the short term over the future of South West Africa. In addition, the United States would strive to overcome international resistance to the granting of $460 million in IMF credits to South Africa. (The significance of this can be seen by the fact that this one grant exceeded the total IMF allocation to all of Black Africa for that year, and was less only than record loans granted to Mexico and the United Kingdom[4]). In exchange for all this largesse, South Africa had to ratchet up the pressure on Rhodesia.

In the first week of September, Smith was summoned to Pretoria to be briefed on the results of Kissinger's recent tour of the region. Kissinger had determined that any approaches he might make to Smith would be done strictly in accordance with current British policy. He therefore made a point of meeting British Prime Minister James Callaghan before flying to Pretoria to meet Smith.

Between 1976 and 1979, James Callaghan remained a rather anonymous presence at Number 10 as far as Rhodesia was concerned. His apparent indifference to the Rhodesian problem was predicated on a belief that, as long as Smith was in power no meaningful settlement was possible. While serving as Harold Wilson's Foreign Secretary, Callaghan had sent an exploratory mission to Salisbury, to assess Smith's attitude and had been convinced by the report that Smith himself was the main brake on progress. His policy then was largely to disengage his government from any involvement, until such time as Smith was either voted out or toppled. His attitude to Kissinger's overtures was somewhat rueful. He was willing to share what insights his government had on the subject of Rhodesia and outline the minimum British conditions for independence. After that he wished the American Secretary of State the best of British luck.

Vorster put to Smith the new minimum conditions when the two met in preparation for later discussions with Kissinger. Smith now had no choice but to accept the principal of majority rule within two years. It was made clear that independence would only be granted after majority rule, and elections held under the principal of universal adult suffrage. Vorster added for the record, that negotiations towards that end should be authentic, not protracted, and not used as a means either to buy time or thwart genuine progress. Implicit was the fact that Vorster concurred with James Callaghan that toppling Smith would be the first step towards a Rhodesian settlement and Vorster would no doubt have taken pleasure in personally arranging for Smith's replacement. However Kissinger had dismissed any suggestion of the Rhodesian Prime Minister's early removal — which in Vorster's view required Smith to be grateful.

What Smith was offered, in simple terms, was a return to legality under the constitutional authority of the Crown. The country would be governed by decree of a Council of State, comprising three blacks and two whites, or vice versa, while a white Chairman could or could not hold a casting vote. This Council of State would function as a transitional government, until a majority rule election could be held within a maximum of two years.[5]

Smith had been prepared for the worst, and in a way he was relieved. The war was moving towards its decisive phase, and two years was a long time. He warned Vorster for the record that Rhodesia was prepared — if pushed too far — to fight on to the bitter end. Vorster nodded and accepted this threat for what it was. South Africa held all the cards and could bring Rhodesia to her knees in a fortnight. Vorster also knew that the ringing cries of patriotism and fighting to the death, sounded good, but the people doing the fighting would quit long before the last man was put in the line. Smith confirmed this view when he reflected later in his memoirs on that particular meeting with Vorster: 'If Rhodesians believed it was a sell out', he wrote 'there would be a mass exodus of skills, expertise, professionalism and investment, with resultant disaster.'[6]

This was indeed the root of Smith's dilemma. Such a comment hardly describes a nation of patriots willing to fight to the death, but instead reveals a rather discerning population of expatriates who, if circumstances became too difficult or hazardous, could leave the country and make their homes elsewhere. Certainly African whites did exist, and Smith was as much one of these as any; but even he could relocate to Britain, Australia or South Africa if conditions became impossible. It is instructive to note that only 50 000 or so of the 250 000 plus whites resident in Rhodesia were holders of a Rhodesian passport.[7]

Kissinger, meantime, followed up his talks with Callaghan, with a whirlwind tour of Black Africa. In April he visited Kenya, Tanzania, Zaire, Liberia, Senegal and Zambia, where he delivered his keynote policy speech. In it he announced a new era in United States policy towards Africa, while at the same time issuing a stern warning to Salisbury that it could expect no support from the United States. To those countries experiencing hardship as a consequence of their support for the armed struggle, he promised that financial assistance would be forthcoming. The Frontline States could also look forward to generous compensation, for their help in bringing the Zimbabwean nationalists to the negotiating table. On 16 September, he began a second high profile visit to the region before making his way to South Africa, for his much-anticipated meeting with Ian Smith.

Smith officially flew down to watch an All Blacks/Springboks international rugby match at Ellis Park, that John Vorster also attended. The current state of relations between Salisbury and Pretoria was clearly illustrated when Smith was pointedly not invited to watch the match from the comfort of the VIP box.

The President of the Rugby Union apologised, saying that he had been asked to put me aside from the main party. Fortunately, that kind of thing has no effect on me, but those who were accompanying me were taken aback at the pettiness and discourtesy.[8]

Later, in a far more courteous atmosphere, Kissinger and Smith met at the American ambassador's residence, in the upmarket Pretoria neighbourhood of Waterkloof. Kissinger was, of course, widely distrusted in Rhodesia, but on this occasion Smith made the rare concession of taking the American Secretary of State at face value.

Dispensing with formalities, Kissinger quickly assumed a confidential air, and guided an apprehensive Smith into a side room. There the two held a brief private discussion, during which the American unburdened his mind. In the view of the United States, he told Smith, an unresolved conflict in Rhodesia would ultimately lead the entire region into a much wider racial and ideological war, and the US had no particular interest in being dragged into another of these. 'We are fighting world communism' he said, as if Smith did not already know this. 'The day will come when communism will rule the world: all we are doing is holding out for time.'[9] Smith was given no opportunity to plead his case, for the essence of what was said to him was simple and direct and did not invite discussion. The monologue was concluded, with an apology for the fact that what was on offer was patently not attractive. 'Mr Prime Minister', Kissinger said with his lugubrious accent: 'This is the first time in my career that I have asked anyone to commit political suicide.'

Kissinger went on to explain that what he offered, was the best that could be achieved under the circumstances. He also made the point that this was probably the last chance for white Rhodesia to find an acceptable settlement. If it failed, Smith and his people would be cut adrift to face the consequences of a bleeding war alone. Furthermore, if the offer was rejected, Smith could look forward next to dealing with Jimmy Carter, who was poised to topple the precarious administration of Gerald Ford. Kissinger was later criticised for referring to Smith as 'Prime Minister' when technically he was not recognised as such. The Secretary of State commented: 'I called him Mr Prime Minister … I did not think it would do any damage to say that because the whole purpose of the exercise was to deprive him of the position as Prime Minister of Rhodesia.'[11]

If Kissinger delivered the uppercut that turned Smith's knees to water, then it was Vorster who laid him on the canvas. When the South African Prime Minister put in an appearance at the meeting, he made it clear to Smith that Pretoria could not continue to support Rhodesia either financially or militarily. Not only was this becoming a strain on South Africa's own economy but it was also adding to the weight of diplomatic pressure, that the country was feeling in the aftermath of the Soweto riots.

Vorster then went on to demand an immediate decision on the matter. Unpleasant scenes followed when Rhodesian Cabinet Ministers Jack Musset and Des Lardner-Burke momentarily lost their composure and verbally attacked Vorster, who had to leave the room briefly. He returned with his dignity ruffled, but his position unchanged. Kissinger, in his more polished style, added the same note of urgency. Smith reluctantly agreed, but he was quick to add that he anticipated either constipation or backsliding from the blacks. Vorster assured him this would not happen, since Zambia and Mozambique were desperate to bring an end to the war. Smith had little say about this, for to do so would have antagonised Vorster ,and would anyway have been a waste of time.

The unbearable tension was broken for a moment, by a contrived and somewhat theatrical leap onto the stage by Kissinger's wife Nancy, who embraced Smith and engaged him in a moment of intimate conversation. Whether this was stage-managed to disarm Smith or was, as Nancy professed, simply that she was an admirer and sympathiser of Smith and Rhodesia, is probably irrelevant. Kissinger's work was done and his closing comments revealed what could only have been a genuinely felt sadness. As a Jew, Kissinger could not but feel empathy for a game fight, on the part of a plucky minority. 'For what must have been the most painful day of their lives', he wrote later, 'the Rhodesians behaved with great dignity.'[12]

Back home, Smith was apt to echo Churchill in his search for hope. Since there was no choice in the matter, his Cabinet and parliamentary caucus accepted the plan, and on 24 September, he sat down in front of a camera and delivered a sombre address to the nation. 'This is not the end' he assured his people. 'It is not even the beginning of the end. But it is, perhaps, the end of the beginning.'

* * *

The critical weakness in the Smith-Kissinger agreement, was that it had been agreed to by Smith and Kissinger alone. No local black opinion had been sought or given, which to the Frontline leaders was a forgivable oversight. So anxious were they by then for a general agreement, that they were willing to ignore many of the obvious inconsistencies. Nyerere, however, could not resist querying a few difficult points, one of which was an agreement that the ministries of Defence and of Law and Order remain in white hands. Another was a two-tier system of government, with a white chairman of the proposed Council of State. It was noted that on both these points Kissinger had exceeded a previously agreed mandate.

Nevertheless, the plan was generally accepted on the Frontline, but only on the basis of it being a minimum negotiating position. Mugabe, of course, laughed when he heard the news. To a jeering audience of guerrillas he had this to say: 'What is required is the total destruction of Smith's army and immediate replacement by ZANU forces ...we shouldn't worry about the Kissinger-British proposals. They can put in any puppet government they want, but a puppet government cannot contain us.'[13]

Although this was tough talk, the truth was that Samora Machel and Kenneth Kaunda were indeed nearing a point of critical load. They were anxious that the guerrilla leaders were made aware of the fact that Frontline sponsorship and support was not to be viewed as open-ended. In the aftermath of the Nyadzonia Raid, Machel went further and summoned all the nationalist leaders to Maputo to hear their views and to rub their noses in the soil of war.

Machel was a warrior and unafraid of the face of conflict, but if the nationalists were to expect solidarity from Mozambique in the face of such attacks as these, what were they going to give in exchange? After taking a moment to express his sorrow at the loss of life, Machel went on to reprimand his audience for their unseemly bickering in the face of such a determined enemy. He then arranged a trip to Nyadzonia to display the mass graves, the broken, the wounded and the dying. It was educational for some to see such sights, most for the very first time. Robert Mugabe was among these. It was equally salutary for him and others to note that of the conscious injured, none were willing to talk to or even greet anybody but Mugabe.[14]

Following this lesson, the nationalists were transported to a meeting with all the active Frontline leaders in Dar-es-Salaam. After the sobering lessons of Nyadzonia, it was hoped that once and for all the feuding parties could be driven towards a formula for peace. Negotiations that might follow the Kissinger agreement would have at least a passing chance of success, if everyone could work together. After a stern briefing, Nyerere and his colleagues left the Zimbabweans alone, with instructions not to emerge from the meeting unless an agreement had been reached.

A long and bruising closed-door session produced yet another antipathetic union, that was ratified in early October, and became known as the Patriotic Front. This arrangement represented the militant nationalists with Mugabe unhappily wed to Nkomo. The others were left to find a home somewhere in the shadow of these two. The race for the presidency of a free Zimbabwe had officially become a two-horse affair.

The Geneva Conference

O n 29 September, British Foreign Secretary Anthony Crosland announced the convening of a British sponsored conference, to be held anywhere in southern Africa that suited all parties. Since no such venue could be agreed on, it was ultimately held in Geneva. The British Government, by now utterly disillusioned by the whole Rhodesian affair — and perhaps feeling the first pains of another Northern Ireland — noticeably dragged its feet. As James Callaghan had indicated, there was virtually no prospect of success as long as Smith and his hardliners remained in power, and this was even more valid now that the militant nationalist factions were united under the ostensible leadership of Mugabe. A fair indication of British indifference was the choice of chairman for the conference: Ivor Richard was a corpulent, well meaning and pleasant man, but as an MP and relatively lowly ambassador to the United Nations, he was not of the upper strata. He had neither the political qualifications nor the moral authority to arbitrate between two such seasoned political brawlers as Robert Mugabe and Ian Smith.

Geneva was to be Mugabe's international debut, and while he held out no particular hope for a settlement, he was anxious to fly his colours well. He was also no doubt anxious that the air of determination he exhibited in Switzerland would reflect the new drive and militancy that he brought to the struggle. Nkomo arrived very much in his shadow, but alert to any opportunity to prove that he was an equal partner. The two were prepared to agree on one thing only — and that was complete opposition to the Kissinger proposals. Bishop Muzorewa represented the African National Council, and although he had no substantive support, he kept beside him two symbolically empty seats: one for Edison Sithole who had by then been missing for a year, and another for Enos Nkala who was still in detention.

Mugabe's opening move was fairly illustrative of his underlying aggression. He insisted that Ndabaningi Sithole under no circumstances, be permitted to attend the conference, and certainly not under the aegis of ZANU. Sithole, whom Mugabe had taken to calling the Reverend Herring, still enjoyed some residual sympathy and support from, among others, Nyerere — and Nyerere insisted that he attend.[1] Mugabe then made his own attendance conditional on Josiah Tongogara, and others still detained at Mpima Prison being released to join his delegation. This was agreed and Tongogara was released. It was, incidentally, the first time that he and Mugabe had met in person.

Alongside these principals, a rather forlorn delegation of influential Rhodesian whites known as the 'Five White Presidents' attended, with a mandate to represent Rhodesian agriculture, commerce and industry. One of them was Hardwicke Holderness whose mission it was to reconcile the Rhodesian Front delegation with any of the nationalists interested in reconciliation.[2] There were few of these and Robert Mugabe was manifestly not among them. From the outset, Mugabe's objective was to make any settlement or agreement impossible and to this end he tested the range of his guns on Ivor Richard.

Mugabe searched for and found immediate fault with the chairman. He claimed that Richard was too junior to chair such an important conference, and demanded his replacement. Richard was dismayed but held his ground. Upon failing to have him replaced, Mugabe began to heap pressure on him. He insisted that the Rhodesian delegation be recognised only as members of the British delegation, putting Richard in an extremely awkward position. Smith was predictably outraged when Richard, rather hopefully handed him his official nametag as a member of the 'Smith Delegation'. Smith immediately had a new set of cards printed correctly naming his party as the 'Official Rhodesian Government Delegation'.

Thus the ill-fated Geneva Conference began. Smith early demonstrated his ability to match Mugabe by making it clear that the sole item on the agenda was the interim government as agreed in Pretoria according to the Kissinger plan. John Vorster released a supporting statement, declaring that a viable settlement could only be achieved within Kissinger's five principles.

It gave Smith some satisfaction to note that, as the conference opened, the Rhodesian Army struck at camps in Tete and Gaza; not a murmur of protest was heard from Pretoria. In fact there seemed to be a general change of attitude on the part of the South Africans, who now appeared far more willing to co-operate. On the strength of this, Smith made it his business to brook no negotiation. He stuck rigidly to the period of two years for the implementation of majority rule, while Mugabe tried to press for a handover within one. Smith also made the provocative point that Kissinger had made mention only of majority rule, without specifying that this should mean black majority rule.[3] Not to be outdone Mugabe countered by outlining to the press his vision of a future Zimbabwe.

'…we are socialist', he said, 'and we shall draw on the socialist systems of Mozambique and Tanzania … In Zimbabwe, none of the white exploiters will be allowed to keep an acre of their land.'[4]

Smith fired back with a stab at Mugabe's slight frame and rather shambling, effeminate gait. Mugabe, Smith said, was '…riding on cloud nine with a camouflage terrorist uniform. I don't think he has heard a shot fired in anger in his life.'[5]

Smith, of course, was quite right. Mugabe was not by any means a man's man, but he could order others to nonetheless, and proof of this came right in the midst of the conference itself.

At 20:30 on the evening of 20 December, a ZANLA platoon entered the labour compound of the Aberfoyle Tea Estate in the Honde Valley, and gathered together all the men, women and children they could find. These innocents were then marched to the gates of the Eastern Highlands Tea Factory where 27 men were gunned down in front of their horrified families. Nine of them were migrant workers from Mozambique and eight from Malawi, with only ten of the murdered men being Rhodesian.[6] The incident sent a clear message to the black workers of the district and another to the assembled press and delegates in Geneva.

It would not be entirely fair to say that Smith and his party were jubilant at this turn of events, but the killings could not have been better timed to illustrate in the sophistication of Geneva, what kind of murderous thugs they were dealing with. A satisfying uproar was accompanied by tight-lipped silence from the nationalist camp, as journalists were quickly flown out to Rhodesia. Retribution meted out by the Rhodesian Security Forces was as usual swift and effective. In internal counter-insurgency operations, 321 terrorists were killed, compared to 304 for the whole of 1975. Externally, the SAS, the Selous Scouts and the RLI, launched *Operation Mardon*, a series of attacks against targets in the Tete and Gaza provinces of Mozambique. A number of separate camps were attacked and large numbers of ZANLA personnel killed for the loss of two Rhodesian soldiers. Huge quantities of weaponry were recovered.

In the aftermath, not a whisper of complaint was heard in Geneva, London or Pretoria. South Africa had pushed Rhodesia to Geneva and now it was incumbent on the Republic to make sure Rhodesia survived long enough to effect an all-party settlement. Within a few days, another combined SAS and RLI force neutralised Mavue Base in Mozambique, killing 31 terrorists. In early December the two units attacked a camp at Rambanayi in Mozambique, severely mauling a platoon of Tanzanian troops stationed there. In direct response to the Honde Valley killings, the SAS mounted a raid on the adjacent town of Mavonde in Mozambique, killing 44 members of ZANLA.

In spite of all this, the foot-dragging in Geneva soon returned and the general deadlock persisted. Smith temporarily gave up and in early November left for home. He informed Ivor Richard that he would return as soon as there appeared to be some commitment to progress. A few weeks later he did return, but only to find Richard just as bogged down and irritated as before. His failure to pin the Zimbabwean delegations down to a firm agenda was abject, and in early December he too flew home to London to consult with the Foreign Office. This left the conference in limbo for a few days until Anthony Crosland announced a brief adjournment for the Christmas season. With palpable relief the various delegations packed up and went their separate ways. The conference never reconvened.

Ivor Richard attempted to stimulate renewed dialogue by following the Rhodesians back to Salisbury. However, what had died in Switzerland could not be revived in Rhodesia. Having gone out of his way to honour the Kissinger plan, Smith could see no point in trying again. As far as he was concerned, the British were 'now conniving with communist terrorists in their unscrupulous plan to achieve their evil objective'.[7] Richard left Rhodesia with something of a flea in his ear, and was apt to wonder if the British role in the Rhodesian crisis was finally over.

On his way back from Geneva, Joshua Nkomo slipped into Rhodesia without being immediately arrested. In Geneva, Mugabe had as manifestly eclipsed Nkomo quite as he had unnerved Smith. Smith and Nkomo therefore saw much wisdom in reaching an accommodation between themselves, that would block any possible avenue of progress for Mugabe, a man who, each for his own reasons, both men had adequate grounds to fear.

As 1976 drew to a close, the atmosphere of general failure did not appear to depress the Rhodesians quite as much as it did the British. Vorster seemed to have lost interest in Rhodesia temporarily, but there were no complaints about that fact north of the border. The Security Forces were raiding ever deeper into Mozambique and enjoying increasing success. If there was a window of opportunity to fight the war without limitation or restraint, the white Rhodesian public were prepared to climb through it. Most still believed that a political solution was possible, but only after the nationalists had been sufficiently chastened to trim their negotiating sails. So, as Smith and Nkomo resumed dialogue, the war went on.

62

Mugabe stamps his mark

Mugabe's insistence on the release of Tongogara had not entirely been an act of altruism. His main objective was to use Tongogara to gain full control of the military. Under the aegis of ZIPA — the Zimbabwe Peoples' Army — military affairs in ZANU had fallen under the influence of a group of young commanders, who neither trusted Mugabe nor saw him as a viable military leader. Smith had not been the first to notice that Mugabe was something of a military poseur.

Under no circumstances could Mugabe be described as being a man of action. He did once or twice try to wear camouflage and carry an assault rifle, but the effect was more comical than dramatic, and lacking a noticeable sense of humour, he could never hope to pull it off in the manner of PK van de Byl. To those who knew him well, Mugabe was judged more by his muscular intellect than his limp handshake. As far as he was concerned, it was better to be feared than loved, and increasingly he was — although not yet by the young commanders of ZIPA. It was to counter such overt disrespect that Mugabe needed a genuine man of action such as Tongogara to stand by his side.

In the run-up, and in the immediate aftermath of Geneva, Mugabe's leadership remained unconsummated. Machel had indicated his approval but had yet to lift his protective custody or invite Mugabe to Maputo. It was also true that Mugabe had inherited a military establishment that was uncertain of its direction, tending to factionalism and dissatisfied with ineffective civilian leadership. The Mgagao Declaration had identified Mugabe as a strong leader, but the first two executive decisions he had been forced to make –the formation of the Patriotic Front and attending the Geneva Conference — did not appear to confirm this. For the sake of all the observers of Mugabe's coming out, he needed to reveal his capacity to wield an iron fist, and to show that his style of leadership owed less to Ghandi than to Machiavelli.

Mugabe's main antagonist in the armed wing was a certain commander by the name of Dzinashe Muchingura. Muchingura was a Marxist ideologue who had devised a blueprint for a people's revolution that was to remain the property of the masses. He did not espouse a movement led from the rear by an effete intellectual such as Mugabe, nor for that matter by any of his political lieutenants who were branded in the camps as the *zviGananda*, or bourgeois — as opposed to the fighters themselves who were the *vaShandi*, or workers.

Mugabe was quick to claim his due from Tongogara and, in exchange for his reappointment as supreme military commander, the latter pledged his full support to Mugabe as commander-in-chief. This released Mugabe to concentrate on party organisation, confident that Tongogara would assert his authority over the army. Tongogara duly achieved through the medium of violence, a strategy that impressed Machel, Mugabe himself and of course as those in the ranks of the military.

In January, a meeting of the ZANU Central Committee was held in Beira with internal contradictions high on the agenda. Dzinashe Muchingura and several others were arrested and held in Maputo with neither trial nor representation. A further 90 were arrested in various camps throughout Mozambique, and yet more in Tanzania.[1] As expected, this provoked a badly organised coup attempt that was promptly and extremely harshly put down by Mugabe loyalists commanded by Rex Nhongo. A number of abducted party officials were released, as a further 133 coup plotters joined their comrades in detention.[2] Tongogara was now in control of the army and Mugabe was in control of Tongogara, and all was as it should be.

* * *

Mugabe moved to Maputo and established his offices on the Avenida Lenin, in a building gifted to him by Samora Machel. He applied himself as a matter of urgency to prying loose blockages in the supply pipeline of ammunition and equipment to the military. By May 1977 he was feeling confident enough to openly chastise the OAU for dragging its heels over the question of material support. July saw him in Peking (Beijing), cementing a military alliance with the Chinese, and later establishing additional accords with Yugoslavia, East Germany and Romania. Sally Mugabe became active and applied herself to the care and rehabilitation of black Rhodesian refugees who by then were arriving in Mozambique in large numbers. She sourced humanitarian assistance, mainly from Western European countries that provided medical, hospital and other non-military facilities to guerrilla and refugee camps springing up all over Mozambique.

Despite heavy attacks from the Rhodesians, political uncertainties and leadership struggles, a planned offensive for the 1976/77 wet season successfully spread the line of conflict down the eastern flanks of Rhodesia. Mass disaffection of blacks inside Rhodesia combined with a growing sense of empowerment to ferment an almost unstoppable flood of recruits. By then both Tanzania and Mozambique were providing ZANU with significant transport and logistical support to enable it to absorb most of this number into basic training. Over and above the provision of forward bases and transit facilities, Mozambique also laid on air transport for recruits moving between Tete and Tanzania, while the Tanzanian Government shipped trained guerrillas south by sea on board the locally owned SS Mpanduzi.[3] Massive holding camps for the arming and deployment of trained men grew up in such locations as Chimoio and Tembue.

While all this was happening around ZANU, Nkomo was also hard at work building up a more conventional strike capacity as an insurance policy against white duplicity, ZANU treachery or any other obstacle to power. As ZANU's central military philosophy echoed the Chinese principal of the human wave, Nkomo worked along more conventional Soviet lines. He and a handful of Russian advisors implemented a military policy that became known as the 'Turning Point Strategy'.

While ZANLA commanders focussed on mass recruitment, ZIPRA set about selectively enlisting personnel, who had the capacity to be trained in conventional and semi-conventional tactics. ZIPRA's arsenal contained sophisticated armaments, including recoilless artillery, tanks and aircraft, as well as Strela shoulder-fired heat-seeking missiles, that were being supplied by the Soviets. Units were upgraded into brigade and detachment formations, with a view to preparing them for conventional military assaults. Commanders were coached to lead from the front and ZIPRA units were to be despatched into the field with the advantage of mobile communications equipment. This was a luxury almost completely unknown to the more basic ground fighter units of ZANLA. It was because ZANLA fought deaf and blind that few groups courted open contact with the Rhodesian Security Forces, and why casualty statistics were often so hopelessly lopsided.

By late 1977 and early 1978, ZIPRA forces were operational throughout Matabeleland. Reconnaissance patrols penetrated into the Midlands and Victoria Province, and soon as far inland as the Urungwe and Karoi districts. By crossing the Zambezi at Kanyemba. and moving into the Sipolilo and Makonde districts of Mashonaland, ZIPRA began edging into traditional ZANLA turf and in effect opening up a new front. The forward base for operations in these areas was Kavalamanja, situated a short distance outside the Zambian town of Luangwa.[4] Therefore, from Kazangula around three quarters of the border areas to Vila Salazar, the war was being fought in absolute earnest.

63

The murder season

In Rhodesia, the effects of the new commitment to the war by the nationalists were not long in being felt. The Bristow family of the B-J-B Ranch situated in the southeastern Lowveld were woken in the early hours of the morning by a rattle of automatic gunfire. Norman Bristow had been expecting something like it for some time, and in disciplined order he herded his family into a sandbagged bunker situated outside the homestead from where a police reservist — known as a 'brightlight' — was already returning fire. Bristow and his wife joined in the firefight while their 14-year-old son calmly worked to reload their weapons. At the end of a 90-minute engagement a shot from Lena Bristow's rifle claimed at least one victim in the darkness. Abruptly the firing stopped as a dozen or so unidentified gunmen melted back into the African night.

This sort of attack was repeated almost nightly somewhere or other in the contested border regions, and just as often a farm worker or two would be shot or worse, as a 'sellout' to enforce the rule of terror. Most were relatively benign compared to events that occurred at St Pauls Mission in Musami on Sunday 6 February 1977. That night armed men arrived at the mission compound, marched nine members of the white clerical staff — three of whom were women — out into the open and shot them. Only Father Dunstan Myerscough survived.[1] The guerrilla faction most likely responsible, Robert Mugabe's ZANLA force, pointed the finger at the Selous Scouts, as the perpetrators of the murders. The accusation had excellent propaganda value and gained wide currency, but was later disproved by the discovery of a notebook on the body of a guerrilla that contained accurate details of the incident. One might be forgiven for thinking that this was a very convenient discovery, but it is important to remember that without radio communications, ZANLA operational units received orders and communicated with their forward bases in Mozambique by writing notes.

A month after the St. Paul's incident, another two white Roman Catholic missionaries, both women, were shot dead by terrorists.[2] Also that month, several white civilian deaths were reported as a result of homestead attacks and vehicle ambushes. At the end of September a white population, growing increasingly desensitised to reports of violent death, were shocked anew to open their newspapers and read a report on the senseless murder in Chipinga of six-month old Natasha Glenny. The baby had been bayoneted to death while tethered to the back of her black nanny, who at first tried to hide her and then said that she was her own albino child.

1977 limped to its end but the killing continued. The death toll since 1972 stood at 115 white and 2 000 black civilians. Security Force deaths for the same period were 574, along with 3 596 confirmed guerrilla kills. There was no doubt in anybody's mind that the good times were well and truly over. White Rhodesia, after 87 years of existence, was in the throes of a last and bitter bid for survival

Despite the spiralling slaughter, there was still some residual optimism that the future could be decided on the battlefield. In fact, 1977 opened with a series of high profile Security Force successes that buoyed the spirits and gave Rhodesia the impression that she had again seized the upper hand. The 1976/77 guerrilla offensive had been ordered on the assumption that the Rhodesian Government would be too preoccupied with political distractions to attend to its military preparedness, but nothing could have been further from the truth. The Rhodesian Army, at that point streamlined, motivated and at the peak of its battle fitness, was enjoying an international reputation as the deadliest little army in the world. Cries from abroad, that it was stocked with mercenaries, was in fact evidence of the willingness of adventurers from all over the world to serve in and identify with this elite force, on financial terms no different to any other serving Rhodesian trooper. Pundits compared it to the Israeli Army, but Rhodesians were confident that it was far superior. It was in fact ZANLA that in particular was suffering political interference, as a trickle of ill trained, poorly equipped and indifferently commanded cadres crossed the border into the waiting arms of Rhodesian Security Forces. If they survived border patrols and ambushes to penetrate the country these men were usually quickly run to ground and killed in the kinds of numbers that satisfied even the hardest-line prophets of a total military solution.

However the truth behind the statistics was less triumphant. The level of recruitment and the sheer numbers of enemy combatants now entering Rhodesia, made any celebrations of victory premature. The war was being lost and no amount of desperate jingoism could change that fact. Those who did not support Smith seemed to be those even further to the right than he, while the more moderate voices were either shouted down or ignored. The truth — so carefully hidden — was best unearthed in the national immigration/emigration statistics.

In 1976 Rhodesia suffered a net loss of over 7 000 whites. This total would increase through 1977 to almost 11 000.[3] Notwithstanding the effect that this was having on commerce and industry, its more vital impact was felt in the military. 'Regrettably', Ian Smith wrote in his 1997 autobiography, 'there were signs that our white community, for the first time, was beginning to have doubts about our future.'[4]

Doubts indeed. By mid-1978, enough white families were opting for the 'chicken run', or the 'wise owl route' as some called it, meant that the country was losing the equivalent of one company of territorial troops a month.[5] 'Gapping it' was becoming a more frequently chosen option for white, suburban, middle-class Rhodesians, who had never traded in their British, Italian, Greek or South African passports. Apart from the handful of whites who could call themselves fully indigenised, those who were not leaving were those who could not. Some were finally trapped by a dire shortage of foreign exchange, that did not afford them the resources to begin again elsewhere. The gathering tide of exodus even included plans by the military for a possible evacuation. In mid-1978, Lieutenant-Colonel Garth Barrett took over as SAS commander, and was told that in the event of a catastrophe — for example an unconditional handover to Robert Mugabe — plans were in place to airlift to South Africa the personnel and families of both the SAS and the Selous Scouts.[6]

Minister of Defence Reginald Cowper, who in 1976 had raised the age limit for military service from 30 to 34, set the tone for the new year by raising the age limit again. It was now legislated that all fit men, Asian, white and coloured, up to the age of 50 were liable for call-up. In September, Phase One National Service that affected mainly school leavers, was extended from one year to 18 months. As a gesture of compensation, the territorial reserve commitment was reduced from 190 to 120 days a year.[7]

Those whites — with a mind to stick it out — applied themselves to saving the country as they had done since 1972. However, blind faith in Smith was wearing thin and instead of trusting their futures to him, whites increasingly began to look at the facts for themselves. National solidarity was strong and morale high, but the political dispensation was largely unchanged since the days of Huggie and the Howman Commission. It was clear that a solution to the race dilemma was no closer than it had ever been and the establishment had clearly run out of ideas.

Ian Smith sought the comfort of his worst and only friend. At a meeting with John Vorster in Cape Town, he revealed his intention to work with the moderate black leaders in the hope of reaching an internal settlement. Vorster was sympathetic — or at least appeared to be — but restated his preference for an Anglo-American solution. When he told Smith that he had been working behind the scenes with the British and Americans to try and get the Pretoria agreement back on track, Smith's heart sank. Vorster's main hope now lay in the new British Foreign Secretary David Owen, who had taken over the office on the death of Anthony Crosland. Vorster spoke warmly of the new man as an improvement on his predecessor, but to Smith that probably was not saying a great deal. A reliable and trustworthy officer of the British Government, was a rare creature that Smith and his Cabinet would need to see to believe.

Thus, with another unsatisfying encounter under his belt, Smith returned to Salisbury. No sooner had he arrived than he began to look around for likely partners to include in an internal settlement. Bishop Muzorewa and Ndabaningi Sithole both loomed large as non-aligned freelancers looking for a new home, and to flesh out their possible contribution, Smith identified a handful of chiefs with both moral ballast and influence. Before he had gone too far with this process, the new and improved British Foreign Secretary flew into Cape Town to familiarise himself with the neighbourhood. Smith was duly invited to Groote Schuur in order to assess David Owen's merits for himself.

At 38, Owen was the youngest Foreign Secretary to be appointed to the British Cabinet since Anthony Eden. Young, dynamic and pedigreed, he was an alumnus of Sidney Sussex College, a medical doctor, a Fabian and a scion of the upper-middle class establishment. He had not achieved his ministerial position through any particular track record and so had much to prove. He was therefore anxious to stamp his particular mark onto the Rhodesian crisis.

Naturally Smith arrived in Cape Town predisposed to disliking him, and he was not disappointed. In his own words Smith found Owen 'one of these petty little men trying to fill a job which is too big for him'.[8] 'Petty little man' was probably unfair, but certainly Owen was trying to fill a job too big for him. It was not just at that preliminary meeting, but throughout his involvement in the Rhodesian drama that Owen revealed a very patchy understanding of the history of the affair and no real grasp of the racial and interracial nuances at play. It did not take Smith very long to establish this, and moreover he found Owen evasive, vague and somewhat less than his own man. In fact, by his own admission, Owen was simply the vanguard of another Anglo-American initiative and could do nothing without American approval.

Once again Smith flew home with a lot to think about. A few days later Owen caught up with him in Salisbury. He brought with him his own jerry cans of petrol in order to avoid breaking British sanctions. His meeting with Smith achieved nothing other than to enrage white Rhodesians with such verities as publicly describing terrorists as '…essentially men of good will driven to take up arms'. Although he rejected the Patriotic Front's claim to being the only legitimate voice of the revolution, he was equally adamant that neither Nkomo nor Mugabe could realistically be excluded from any internal settlement.[9]

Owen was not the only player in the Anglo-American team apparently running in the wrong direction. US Vice President Walter Mondale held a meeting with John Vorster in Vienna in May 1977, the object of which was to confirm American interest in Africa in the wake of Henry Kissinger's diplomatic journey across the continent. Mondale immediately broadsided Vorster with the contention that South African race policy was no less repellent to the world than Rhodesia's. He then tried to browbeat the Prime Minister into dictating to Smith some vague settlement that the American seemed to be inventing on the spot.

Vorster was both offended and unnerved. Mondale's arrogance — and his flagrant ignorance —

were fairly reflective of the Carter administration's overall African policy. While Kissinger had been pursuing a global political strategy, Carter's policy was simplistic, and aimed above all at the African-American vote. As Carter's black ambassador to the United Nations, Andrew Young, observed: the hand that picked the cotton picked the president. With all this wisdom ringing in his ears, Vorster flew home from Vienna a little less certain of himself, and far more favourably disposed towards Smith than at any time hitherto.

 Meantime Andrew Young was nominated to be David Owen's partner in the Anglo-American initiative. Young represented an odd but potentially very good choice of envoy to serve as African peacemaker. Although hampered by poor timing and circumstances, he was noticeably less inclined than many of his black countrymen, to view the African situation as simply 'black man good, white man bad'. He was a pedigreed civil rights activist and one-time ally and friend of Martin Luther King. He had been educated in a segregated school system and understood racism. He later became a student of both King and Ghandi, and adopted non-violence as his political mantra.

It was sad that Young was deliberately paired with the British Foreign Secretary for reasons no better than the obvious race symbolism. In due course, like Owen, he was seduced into viewing his mandate — for want of anything else — as primarily a vehicle for personal advancement. The terrible twins, as they became known in local diplomatic circles, would suffer throughout their mission the consequences of Walter Mondale's intemperate comments to John Vorster. Vorster, on both his own and Smith's behalf, was now inclined to lie low and let the nasty liberal rash in Washington cure itself in the usual way. At that time he was beginning to suffer ill health, and it was becoming apparent that his hard-line Defence Minister, PW Botha, was influencing many of his major decisions. Indeed, on 20 September 1978, Vorster resigned in favour of Botha, which tended to leaven the body politic of South Africa even more in favour of general white supremacy.

More or less free of South African pressure for the moment, Smith equally had no interest in discussing an external settlement with anyone. He had at last seen an opportunity to sprint for the touchline, with the over-inflated bladder that he was calling 'Internal Settlement'. Sceptics and observers predicted that the ball would rupture long before it fell to earth, but Smith lunged for the gap notwithstanding and proceeded to run for his very life.

It is important to note that most, if not all, leading members of the Rhodesian security structure were sceptical about the outcome of the war. The inaugural meeting of Combined Operations (ComOps) was held on 20 July 1977, to discuss the Intelligence Coordinating Committee's assessment of the threat to Rhodesia for the quarter 1 July to 30 September 1977. All branches of the Security Forces were represented: Lieutenant-General Peter Walls, appointed Commander of ComOps and chairman of the meeting; Ken Flower, Director General of the CIO; Commissioner of Police, Peter Sherren; Lieutenan-.General John Hickman, Commander of the Army, and Air Marshal Frank Mussell, Commander of the Air Force.

The fact sheets handed out to each man made depressing reading. Rhodesia's actual physical survival was hanging by a thread. Security Force successes were astonishing but were not keeping up with guerrilla deployments, and certainly not making an appreciable impact on the outside threat. ZANLA was accelerating attacks in key operational areas, while, under Cuban and Russian tutelage, ZIPRA was fast building a conventional capacity. It was predicted that by the end of the quarter the number of guerrillas operating in Rhodesia would outnumber the Security Forces.

Whites were fleeing the country, the internal security system was buckling, and it was becoming increasingly difficult for ComOps to conduct the war, protect civilian life and property, as well as monitor vital rail and road communications. Large areas of the country — particularly along the border with Mozambique — were then under effective guerrilla control. As Herbert Chitepo had predicted, Security Forces simply did not have the manpower to garrison the entire country.

This was all made known to Smith and the Cabinet, in a top-secret memorandum dated 20 July

1977. The document, signed by all the heads of services who attended the meeting, was entitled Military and Police Implications of the Quarterly Threat, 1 July 1977 to 30 September 1977.10 In it the service chiefs stressed the need to expand the Protected Village programme to limit local support to the guerrillas. They warned that if the current levels of guerrilla deployments continued — along with the ongoing haemorrhage of white manpower — the war would in due course become conventional. It concluded that a purely military solution no longer existed.

> Of over-riding concern is the present inadequate and diminishing force level with resultant urgent need for additional manpower to even contain the situation, let alone prevent its inevitable deterioration.
> No successful result can be attained by purely military means. It is now more vital than ever to arrive at an early political settlement before the point of no return beyond which it will be impossible to achieve any viable political or military/political solution.[11]

Although not stated explicitly, the document underscored the ComOps view that an internal settlement that excluded the main warring parties, would be a waste of time, and at that point time was of the essence.

Smith seemingly glanced at the memorandum — effectively put it to one side and continued on precisely the course that he had already set for himself. The government information services supported him, with ongoing propaganda that Rhodesia was winning the war without difficulty — which was a vital reassurance if white Rhodesians were going to continue giving total commitment to it. In later years, many would question the ethics of service chiefs who filed the memorandum away, said and did nothing, and went on pretending that it was a jolly good war. Had the general public been made aware of the fact that their security commanders were wont to give up the fight at that point, another two years of bloodshed might have been avoided. These were the most ferocious years of the war during which thousands lost their lives. A military coup was certainly out of the question, but a staged leak, or even a clear statement, might have saved the reputations of otherwise loyal men.

64

Internal settlement

Smith's new squad was a C-team of political desperadoes who had nothing to lose and everything to gain by signing up. Ndabaningi Sithole was visited in Malawi by a senior CIO representative who invited him to take part in internal negotiations, on the condition that he restate his denunciation of violence. Without wasting a moment, Sithole put a telephone call through to the *Rhodesia Herald* and stated for the record that he was opposed to terrorism — this just hours after his latest plea to the OAU for money and arms had been rejected.[1]

After a decade in the political wilderness Sithole was inclined to grasp at any straw that came to hand. Smith offered him perhaps his last opportunity to lift the premiership of an independent Zimbabwe right out from under the noses of his opponents. He arrived at Salisbury Airport on 10 July 1977 to a disappointing reception and, with no point in making a speech on the tarmac, he was hurried on to an equally bleak rally staged in Highfield where less than 2 000 souls put in an appearance to greet him.

In truth it hardly mattered. Smith's choreography did not include Sithole taking anything from anyone. He had written Bishop Abel Muzorewa into the part of first black prime minister, with Sithole and a handful of chiefs tossed in to flesh out the chorus.

Muzorewa was the next to be invited to join the ensemble, and, of him, Smith's opinion is written clearly in his memoirs. To paraphrase: a black leader is incapable of acting without constant reference to the opinions of his followers. In the case of a strong leader, this complies with accepted democratic principals but, where a weak leader is concerned, it smacks of appeasement. This sort of behaviour would in very short order turn a leader into a follower, which was precisely what Smith wanted in a puppet black prime minister.[2]

This then was the blueprint for an internal settlement. The dynamics were easy to interpret while the absence of the Patriotic Front made the general motivation fairly obvious. Such baby steps were, however, hard to make, and caused a terrible pain in the caucus. Before Smith could get to work, another rebellion broke out on the backbenches that threatened to derail the process even before it had begun.

An evergreen voice of discontent in the RF was its past chairman, Des Frost. On this occasion, Frost teamed up with two prominent local farmers to form a new party called the Rhodesian Action Party. Nine RF members defected to the RAP, earning the rebels the rather unoriginal appellation of the Dirty Dozen. This was the long expected white backlash against the Kissinger proposals. The engine of the protest was a large body of Afrikaner dissenters who were absolutely irreconciled to any talk of black majority rule. It was the most serious challenge to Smith so far and, in response, he called a general election. On 31 August, Smith once again fought the good fight and won. The RF swept all 55 white seats, giving Smith the fresh mandate he needed and effectively a free hand to reinvent the future.

Shortly afterwards, Smith received a brief and unexpected visit from the new South African Foreign Affairs Minister, Pik Botha. Botha was on his way to London to meet David Owen and Jimmy Carter's Secretary of State, Cyrus Vance. Botha was a straight talking man and approached Smith with none of the forbearance of his predecessors. He fixed the Rhodesian Prime minister with his steel blue eyes and warned him in clear terms that time to find a peaceful solution to the Rhodesian crisis had run out. Whatever else Smith thought or hoped would come from the South African, Botha made it clear that in his opinion there would now have to be losers, and Smith correctly took this to mean that one of those losers would be himself.[3]

Just as Pik Botha was flying out of Salisbury, the Anglo-American team of Owen and Young was flying in. This was their first substantive visit to the country and, to an already irritated Ian Smith, they presented a dossier of suggestions for a solution to his problem. As might have been expected, Smith found the new proposal the work of enthusiastic amateurs and had difficulty taking any of it seriously. Despite lengthy diplomatic procedures between Washington, London and various African capitals, all that Owen and Young had achieved in their desire to please everybody was to please no-one. Smith, with so much else on his plate, once again had to sit and listen to the old parrot cry of one-man-one-vote.

Freshly packaged and stamped with a new label, the latest Anglo/American proposal read like a cheaper version of the old. It was a variation of the usual constitutional manipulations to get blacks in and whites out, without appearing to take away or give anything to anybody. Ultimately it made absolutely no difference whether a prime minister or a president led the country, how a bill of rights might or might not protect minority interests, or whether the outlawing of racial discrimination would compromise the civil service and the judiciary, it was in proposals for the transition — the return to legality — that both Owen and Young revealed the extent to which they had not been paying attention.

A pivotal difference between Kissinger's superior diplomacy of a year earlier and these amateurish efforts, was a failure to recognise that without South Africa the Rhodesians could not be forced to do anything. Walter Mondale had temporarily closed this avenue, so hell could freeze over before Ian Smith would hand over the policing of a transitional government and a cease-fire to the 'liberation forces'. This was the basic theme upon which the Owen/Young proposals had been premised, and the simple point upon which Smith could not be pinned.

The Anglo-American overture also, of course, represented Robert Mugabe's minimum negotiating position, and he knew perfectly well that Smith would laugh any such bid off the table. As Smith was trying to forge an internal alliance, Mugabe's strategy was total war, and neither man had any time for the work of a pair of amateurs. Smith handed the proposals over to his legal experts for formal consideration, and largely forgot about them while the co-leaders of the Patriotic Front released a document asking: 'By what faith can an election booth be regarded as democratic, free and impartial if it is surrounded at its four corners by Smith's policemen, his soldiers, his district commissioner and his judges?'[4] For all intents and purposes that seemed to be the end of it.

Still wanting nothing more than to get on with the job of building his internal alliance, Smith was once again distracted, this time by an intriguing invitation discreetly delivered through the offices of Tiny Rowland, to meet Kenneth Kaunda for talks in Lusaka. Clad in caution and with great haste and secrecy, Smith and PK van der Byl left Salisbury and flew to the Zambian capital, where an avuncular Kaunda met them at the airport.

Kaunda's objective in arranging the meeting was to present himself as an honest broker between the Rhodesians and the nationalists, and in particular the faction loyal to Joshua Nkomo. Kaunda believed that Nkomo had emerged from the trials of the past few years a renewed and sanitised revolutionary, with a desire to negotiate and to reach a pragmatic solution. Closer to the truth perhaps was that he, like Muzorewa and Sithole, sensed the danger of being eclipsed by Mugabe — and if

460

a shortcut to power could be found, Nkomo would be happy to take it.

From the Rhodesian point of view this was welcome news. What had so far beggared the internal settlement was the fact that broad-based authenticity would not be achieved if substantial leadership for the transition could not be found. If everything that was being said was true, Nkomo would certainly bring an element of authenticity to the negotiations that neither Sithole nor Muzorewa was really capable of. On the chances of such an alliance succeeding, Smith was given contradictory intelligence. The CIO opined, contrary to Smith's better judgement, that no settlement of any sort would work without Mugabe. Furthermore, throwing a dominant Nkomo into a race with Sithole and Muzorewa was likely to precipitate an implosion. Also, the fact that Mugabe controlled more than half the liberation forces, guaranteed at the very least that such an arrangement, although it might alter the balance, would not stop the war.

Nonetheless, Smith was very keen to explore the matter further, and then perhaps meet with Nkomo. However, news soon leaked and the first to hear it was Nyerere, who duly passed the intelligence on to Mugabe. Both men were furious — Mugabe, both because Kaunda had presumed to speak on behalf of the Patriotic Front and because Nkomo was manoeuvring behind his back. And Nyerere, because Kaunda had approached Smith outside the aegis of the Frontline alliance. It was not long before Muzorewa and Sithole were also alerted, which immediately ignited the predicted histrionics. The first thought to strike each man was that if Nkomo came on board, neither would have any real chance of leading the alliance to the presidency.

Like everybody else, Nkomo lived with a healthy terror of Mugabe. The moment he was directly confronted by the ZANU leader, he retreated and denied any suggestion of infidelity. The only lesson that Smith and P.K van der Byl found worth taking home, was that Kaunda was by then so desperate to bring an end to the war that he would do almost anything.

On 24 of November 1977, Smith made a formal announcement that that he had invited three 'internal' black leaders — Muzorewa, Sithole and Chief Jeremiah Chirau — to the conference table. The moment was deeply significant, even if a strong taint of compromise hung about it.

Operation Dingo

On the morning of 23 November, a day before Smith's announcement, SAS paratroopers and a modest strike force of heliborne RLI commandos attacked the main ZANLA headquarters positioned outside the town of Chimoio, some 60 kilometres over the Rhodesian border. Chimoio was by far the biggest ZANLA facility in Mozambique, and according to Rhodesian intelligence estimates, it accommodated between 9 000 and 11 000 enemy troops. A second and smaller base at Tembue, situated further north some 225 kilometres into Mozambique, was also attacked, in a logistically difficult operation that went ahead immediately after Chimoio. An accurate body count of casualties proved impossible, although the figure was generally agreed to be very high. By the time the Tembue Raid was pressed home, the guerrillas stationed there had heard about the Chimoio raid and had largely fled the scene. A figure of 1 200 kills — announced in a Security Force communiqué — was an estimate but was probably far from accurate.

For ZANU, the propaganda value of the attack was again colossal. The publicity was zealously disseminated worldwide, and arguably outweighed the human cost in terms of its long-term significance. The *Zimbabwe News*, ZANU's in-house newspaper with a love of rich invective, had this to say about the raid:

> The racist enemy forces of Ian Smith supported by those of Johannes Vorster, the Racist Prime Minister of South Africa, attacked two of our transit camps... where our people have been engaged in serious self reliance projects like agriculture, poultry, piggery, health and

crafts...the enemy also destroyed farming equipment such as harrows, planters and tractors...[5]

The report went on to fancifully implicate French, South African, Israeli, British and West German forces in the attack. The British, for their part, found it difficult to disguise their respect for the attackers. With traditional Anglo-Saxon support for the underdog, David Owen could not help remarking: '...it might show the Patriotic Front that the Rhodesian Defence Force is not on its back.'[6] Mugabe was affronted by the comment but not unduly concerned. He knew that Owen was wrong. The Security Force, like the rest of the white establishment in Rhodesia, was indeed on its back, but he was shrewd enough to acknowledge in the wake of the most recent attacks, that the dying Rhodesian donkey still had a few savage kicks left in it.

* * *

In his New Year message to the nation on 31 December 1977, Ian Smith outlined the criterion that he had laid down for his talks with the internal nationalists.

We are seeking safeguards which will ensure that a future Government will not be able to abuse its power by resorting to actions which are dishonest or immoral.[7]

On this note, talks to find an internal settlement commenced in earnest. Those participating were Bishop Muzorewa, Dr Elliot Gabellah, James Chikerema, Ndabaningi Sithole and two local chiefs: Jeremiah Chirau and Kayisa Ndweni. Sithole and Muzorewa were the principal players and, in them, Smith had the raw materials he needed to play one weak personality off against another. Both coveted the premiership, each was consumed with suspicion for the other and each was prepared to out-compromise everybody else to achieve power.

Elliot Gabellah was a local businessman and black MP, who could not be expected to achieve much, other than to pack a top-heavy ship with ballast. The same was true of the two chiefs, of whom Jeremiah Chirau represented traditional Shona opinion and Kayisa Ndweni the Ndebele position. Chirau was a venerable and grandfatherly soul who lacked any real passion for victory, and Ndweni lacked any broad-based appeal. James Chikerema tagged along, but played no meaningful role in the process, except possibly as a spoiler when it was all wrapped up.

Between Muzorewa and Sithole, Smith stood a good chance of negotiating a fair constitution. Of course 'Fair' in this context meant giving the moderates the trappings of power, while keeping the instruments of state under white control. Nothing could be fairer than that. Whether he hoped this would silence the extremists or satisfy the world community is hard to say, but at the very least it would alter the complexion of the war from appearing to be a race struggle to being a black-on-black civil war.

Sithole retained the name ZANU, and unexpectedly attracted to his side many of the disaffected elements of the UANC — in particular those among the Ndebele. This gave him a rather brief and dangerous boost in confidence, that prompted him to contact Kaunda and probe the possibility of engineering Mugabe's eviction from the Patriotic Front. If this happened, Sithole would presumably be able to jump into the ZANU seat and lead the party and the alliance to victory. Kaunda would have been very happy to comply, but his fingers had already been burned. Besides this, as Samora Machel's man, Robert Mugabe was effectively beyond his reach.

Thereafter, both Sithole and Muzorewa slipped compliantly into character. They took to the stage, making tough statements over irrelevant issues, while the important questions were slipped past the public with a minimum of debate. Rhodesian Front demands laid bare the essentials of a new constitution. Whites would elect one third of the existing parliamentary seats with power to block any changes in the constitution. They would remain in control of the police and the army, civil servants would enjoy career and pension guarantees, and a bill of rights would protect white interests. They would maintain the right to hold dual citizenship while the existing — and almost exclusively white members of the bench — would dominate the judiciary.

While all this positive work was under way, Smith received another unwanted communication from the British Foreign Office. This time it was an invitation to attend an all-party conference, to be held in Malta in late January. Owen and Young had been watching from the sidelines, and felt it necessary to try and find a way to include Nkomo and Mugabe in the deal. Smith felt under no pressure to attend and so he did not. The invitation was also extended to Mugabe and Nkomo as joint leaders of the Patriotic Front. Although Nkomo was as happy as ever to be seen on the world stage, the invitation was as inconvenient for Mugabe as it had been for Smith.

Despite losing every battle, Mugabe was still winning the war. He could sense with perfect clarity the moment that Smith would be brought to his knees. The weakness in his position was the Frontline States and, if South Africa had temporarily climbed off Smith's back, Nyerere and Kaunda were still riding heavily on Mugabe's. If they deemed it was appropriate for him to explore every avenue for a peaceful settlement, then he had no choice but to appear to be in compliance. Mugabe had other worries too. In the event of an internal settlement, Britain might lead the way in recognising a puppet government — which in turn would inevitably lead to the lifting of sanctions, and probably the end of the war. There was also the fact that that he had again only narrowly survived a military coup.

Rebellion in the guerrilla camps was never far from the surface. Although Mugabe was without doubt committed to the war, there was often a feeling that he was less than committed to the warriors. Investigations following the attacks on Chimoio and Tembue, revealed indifferent defences and very poor, if any, emergency procedures in camp. This prompted not only considerable private criticism of Mugabe, but also fermented an explosive discontent in the ranks. Ever the political tactician, however, Mugabe took the opportunity to conduct a general purge of his party structures. He was in the midst of this when he was summoned to Malta to meet the Anglo-American team.

The quality of Mugabe's political apprenticeship would be tested in the months to follow, for Malta was just part of a complex dependency on international goodwill that he simply could not afford to neglect. If he had to humour the professional egos of a couple of political novices, it would seem a small price to pay to keep the Americans and the British on his side. As he had expected, though, the affair was a charade. Without Smith, Muzorewa or Sithole on board, no real progress was possible. But to sustain the Owen-Young effort, Mugabe agreed that a United Nations peacekeeping force might have a role to play. He balanced this concession by insisting that his army would play the dominant role in any transitional arrangement. 'The trouble with Mugabe', Andrew Young later admitted, 'is that when you've got a Jesuit education mixed with a Marxist ideology, you've got a hell of a guy to deal with.'[8]

Back in Salisbury, Smith was not without challenges of his own. His claim to intimately understanding the mind of a black man, was being severely challenged. Most of his time lately seemed to be spent putting out fires, mollifying egos and promising everybody everything. He was also not insensitive to the fact that his partners were playing to a large audience of blacks, who were looking to them for signs of genuine progress. Obviously Muzorewa and Sithole were the main players, but pandering to them tended to create pressures elsewhere in the alliance, that also needed to be smoothed over. It was only with considerable skill that Smith managed to keep the whole bipolar coalition together.

Bishop Muzorewa had a tendency to fudge, sulk and obfuscate, but he was perhaps the easiest of the four to deal with. What little genuine resistance Smith did encounter came from Ndabaningi

Sithole, who was at least not an absolute novice. He was the author of the benchmark work African Nationalism and shared his genuine political pedigree only with James Chikerema. Nevertheless, Sithole was worn out physically and emotionally, and in the end he conceded far more than he should have. In fact both he and Muzorewa — in the end — let almost everything of value slip through their fingers.

A few days before the internal accord was brought into being, the OAU Council of Ministers spoke on behalf of the Afro-Asian bloc, and elucidated the general view of the internal settlement talks. The Council passed a resolution, rejecting and condemning the process as aimed at perpetuating white minority domination in Rhodesia.[9]

On the morning of Friday 3 March 1978, the parties to the internal settlement gathered at the Governor's Lodge in Salisbury and prepared to sign the accord into being. Amid a flurry of excitement and press cameras, Muzorewa mingled in the sunshine, clearly happier to be in the glare of political celebrity than buried in the trenches of bare-knuckle diplomacy. He went around singing enthusiastically: 'I am in the mood for signing!'[10]

He then rummaged in a carrier bag and produced what Ian Smith described as 'one of those colourful embroidered fancy dress costumes which he had gathered in one of those countries to our north'. In this dramatic but hardly authentic outfit, Muzorewa approached the business at hand. After five copies had been signed, Smith was rather taken aback when the Bishop, coutured in his fancy dress, publicly praised the Rhodesian Prime Minister for his forbearance during a difficult period. Smith admitted later that a tart rejoinder had hovered perilously close to his lips. However, as in a rugby game, he conceded that one tackles one's best friend with the same zest as any, and he let the moment pass with a smile.

65

The killing goes on:
Elim Mission massacre

T hus an unwieldy transitional government came into being. Each ministry thereafter fielded a black and white co-minister — which had both a symbolic and a practical purpose. Obviously it struck the right racial balance, but it also served to ensure that black politicians worked under white guidance, before they could assume full office. It was hoped that a general election, under the rules of universal adult suffrage, would take place at the end of the year. Meanwhile, the primary short-term objective of the Transitional Government was to gain international recognition. While Smith stayed behind in Rhodesia to manage affairs, all the other signatories departed in various directions to sell the merits of the internal settlement abroad. Smith's job was too delicate to abandon, for proof of success would come only if the settlement succeeded in ending the war.

To this end an intense propaganda campaign was rolled out and, under the terms of a tentative cease-fire and a general amnesty, guerrillas were encouraged to come out of the bush, disarm and pledge their allegiance to an internal party. A parallel effort was made to encourage whites to at last reconcile with their black neighbours. A three and a half minute advertisement appeared on the nation's television screens, depicting many areas of existing racial co-operation such as in the military, in hospitals, in the Internal Affairs Department and with children at play. Scenes of interracial openness were filmed in soft focus and played to the words and music of South African recording artist Neville Nash's composition *Harmony*.

Apart from being a boon to Neville Nash and certain local advertising agencies, the campaign achieved very little. Neither did the Beverly Building Society's morning radio language clinic that tried — after nearly 90 years of colonisation — to teach the white Rhodesian public a new Shona or Sindebele word each day. Both efforts wilted against a flame of ongoing violence, as the relentless killing went on.[1] The nightly news broadcasts on radio and television passed this information on to a Rhodesian public growing daily more distraught. The anonymous reportage also counted out the deaths of blacks 'caught in the cross fire' or 'running with terrorists'. These became inconsequential when every night the Security Forces would regret to announce the death of Lance Corporal so-and-so of 4-Company Rhodesia Regiment, Corporal this of 1-RLI or Flight Lieutenant that of the Rhodesian Air Force. The list of white youths falling in ones and twos, sometimes threes and fours — and occasionally more — began after a while to tear at the hearts of a wondering nation. Whites were alternately mollified and threatened by the likes of P.K van der Byl, who expressed his bitter contempt for the Yellow Routers with utterances such as:

> ...if the cause our soldiers died for should be lost, then an intolerable and shameful burden of responsibility will rest on the shoulders of those who fled and [will] haunt them for all of their days.[2]

If many whites were groping for a justification to say honourably to themselves and to their friends 'so far and no further', then that moment came on 23 June 1978, when terrorists of disputed origin arrived at the Elim Pentecostal Mission in upper Vumba, some 20 kilometres outside the border town of Umtali. Their savage work that night would both scar and disgust the nation, even as it brought home to many sceptics on the outside some of the raw facts of this dirty little war.

At about 20:30 that evening, the uninvited visitors instructed the black students in the school to pack up and go to their quarters. The British staff, consisting of three male and four female missionaries plus four children, were escorted onto the playing fields where they were summarily beaten and bayonetted to death. One woman, 28-year-old Mary Fisher, survived her beating and a variety of stab wounds, before crawling into the bush where she was found the following morning by Security Force details. She died later at the Andrew Fleming Hospital in Salisbury.

The bodies were left by the authorities, more or less as they had been found, in order that the full impact of the night's horror would confront the international press, as it arrived. P.K van der Byl personally accompanied a batch of journalists, hurriedly mustered by the Ministry of Information, and the gruesome scenes shortly decorated the front pages of newspapers around the world.

The epilogue was nothing if not predictable. A war of words erupted as fingers were pointed and blame apportioned. The Conservatives in the House of Commons blamed the Patriotic Front and castigated David Owen for supporting terrorism, while Labour led the way in blaming the Selous Scouts. Mugabe, the Marxist Jesuit revolutionary, pleaded the utter impossibility of him or his followers being responsible for such gratuitous brutality. He plucked from the slough of conflicting opinion, a claimed eyewitness who attested to the fact that the killers had not been bona fide ZANLA.

The guerrilla tendency to keep minute notes on operations, either cleared the air or thickened the plot, depending on who was reading the evidence. However, Luke Madjuimbo, a ZANLA guerrilla killed in a later operation, was carrying a notebook with a passage that read: 'We killed 12 whites including four babies, as a remembrance of Nyadzonia, Chimoio, Tembwe and in Zimbabwe massacres.'[3]

66

A new and improved Foreign Secretary

If this was the state of play by the middle of 1978, then it was evident that the war was not about to end. Clearly Britain and the world community could offer no recognition of the internal settlement, and there matters rested. An OAU Council of Ministers meeting was held in July, at which every encouragement was given to the Patriotic Front. Just in case there was any doubt, the United Nations passed a resolution, declaring the internal settlement 'illegal and unacceptable' and calling on all member states to withhold recognition.[1] ZANLA was also quick to deal with any of its members who might be responsive to calls to surrender. Any units deemed suspect were either eliminated or withdrawn.

While recognition was unlikely, the internal accord did cause some disagreement in the House of Commons. The opposition Conservative Party displayed considerable sympathy towards the efforts of Smith and Muzorewa, and considerable animosity towards the Patriotic Front. The same was true in the House of Lords. Although falling short of a call for actual recognition, Lord Peter Carrington, then leader of the opposition in the House of Lords, told the House:

> It must be said that there has been inadequate recognition of the remarkable achievement
> of the internal settlement and too much support for its opponents.[2]

Carrington went on to suggest that if the Patriot Front was excluded from the process, it was because it had excluded itself. There should be no support for those promoting the use of arms over dialogue. Labour had the final say, and David Owen reiterated that an acceptable solution could not realistically exclude the Patriotic Front.

That month a high-powered team of Field Marshal Lord Carver — the proposed British resident commissioner — David Owen, Andrew Young and American Secretary of State Cyrus Vance, visited Salisbury. They arrived after briefly meeting the two principal leaders of the Patriotic Front in Dar-es-Salaam. Nyerere had previously assured Young that Nkomo and Mugabe were willing to accept the broad terms of the Anglo-American proposals. However, on meeting Mugabe, the four found him as insistent as ever that the dominant role in any transitional arrangement would be played by his forces. By then in full dress rehearsal, Mugabe opened proceedings by demanding a complete renegotiation of the entire agreement.

As a consequence, the meetings that followed had a somewhat theatrical flavour. Smith might have been tempted to say 'I told you so' but he held his counsel. His personal account of the meeting nonetheless oozed hatred towards Owen, who swept into the venue with an air of grand self-importance, and pushed past several important white members of the Transitional Government in order to lavishly greet every black member present. This included an office messenger, who took the unexpected courtesy for what it was. Cyrus Vance did much better. He sincerely complimented

Smith on how clean, well planned and well run Salisbury appeared to be — in stark contrast, he added, to all the other African capitals that he had visited.

Smith found Andrew Young to be the only other genuine and committed member of the delegation, and forgave him such naiveties as confusing Mugabe's very British over-refinement with a gentleness of nature. Young could be relied upon to be utterly honest, a trait Smith found singularly lacking in the politicians he had lately been forced to deal with. When Bishop Muzorewa and others in the Executive Council asked Young and Cyrus Vance how they assessed Mugabe's position, Young was candid in replying: 'He is fighting for personal power.'[3] Such frankness had no place in the politics of the moment and, at Owen's request, Vance tactfully excluded Young from the press conference held after the meeting.

The first major internal challenge to Muzorewa as head of the Executive Council, arose when a sharp young lawyer by the name of Byron Hove began to make his voice heard. Hove had been summoned by Muzorewa from his practice in London, to fill the position of co-minister of Justice, Law and Order. He soon began to challenge the establishment with a series of provocative statements.

> We must bring in a situation where the laws reflect the broad interests of all the people in this country. I am aware that in this country the Police Force has been used as an instrument to enforce the Rhodesian Front laws which it has done enthusiastically. This has to stop…the white community and all law enforcement agencies need to adjust to a new situation. Blacks do not need to because they have always wanted fairness and justice.[4]

While whites waited to see how Muzorewa would deal with this, Hove overnight became the one member of the Transitional Government with any credibility. Even if some question marks hung over the integrity of his comments, Muzorewa had a rare opportunity to publicly support a black dissenter. Instead he paced the floor under a terrible weight of indecision and, under pressure from Hove's co-minister Hillary Squires — a man of acknowledged anti-British feeling and something of a right winger — he eventually issued Hove with an ultimatum. It was demanded that he either retract his statements or face dismissal. Hove opted for dismissal and returned to London. Realising his error, Muzorewa hinted loudly that he might demand Hove's reinstatement, but he lacked the courage to do so — and by then it was too late anyway.

As the year progressed and the war raged on, Smith was forced to conclude that the internal settlement had failed. The effect on Muzorewa and Sithole was a widening of the rift between them, as both came to realise that if they were to compete effectively, they would need armies of their own. As for Smith, he again found himself thinking about Joshua Nkomo. He increasingly saw Nkomo's participation as the only possible catalyst to a general acceptance of the settlement. Although he kept this thought from his Cabinet, he gave Ken Flower and his deputy Derek Robinson, the job of fixing a new round of contacts with the ZAPU leader. On Saturday 5 August, Robinson managed to engineer a meeting between himself and Nkomo in London, at which he proposed discussions between Nkomo, Kaunda and Smith. Nkomo was in agreement, and a meeting was duly scheduled to convene in Zambia the following weekend. Smith boarded a top-secret flight from Salisbury to the Zambian capital, where a lengthy closed-door session took place at Government House.

Kaunda, and a Nigerian Foreign Ministry official by the name of Brigadier Garba, co-arbitrated the talks. Nigeria stepped out of costume a little in agreeing to be part of this conference, but not a murmur was heard from the rest of the continent — not even from Mugabe. The outcome was what Smith termed a 'workable plan' to bring both Nkomo and Mugabe into the existing arrangement. For Smith, the move was enormously risky. Nkomo was in agreement but Mugabe's opinion was untested. Even if the ZANLA leader came onside, a power struggle between the two would be inevitable. It certainly appeared unlikely that either would countenance co-operation with the other as a legitimate means of progress. All this taxed Smith's mind heavily. Should he or shouldn't he? What was he to do?

It did not help much, when a few hours delay in his departure, gave Smith a brief glimpse into the future. He took the opportunity to wander through the corridors of Government House, that he had known so well in his Federal days. He found the rooms unkempt, the paint peeling, dust on the pelmets and the pictures askew. How different it all was from the days when the white man had kept the lawns trimmed, the linen starched and the curtains clean. From a bathroom window, he looked out over shantytowns that had grown up in all directions. There, but for the tenacity of a handful of brave white men, would go Rhodesia.

A day or two later, harsh reality returned to the proceedings. Plans for a follow-up meeting were cancelled, as Nyerere blustered at his exclusion, and Mugabe expressed concerns that Nkomo was getting ahead of himself. Smith might easily have shaken his head at the tedium of it all but he had other problems mounting. The Transitional Government almost collapsed, at the news that Nkomo might soon arrive to lead it. Smith himself was also beginning to quail a little bit at the thought of what he might have done. By giving Nkomo encouragement, he had cracked open the lid of Pandora's box, and he could now think of a hundred reasons why he should promptly slam it shut again.

A little later, Mugabe and Nkomo met face to face for the first time in a long while. Mugabe had already been briefed by the Nigerians, which spared Nkomo the discomfort of having to do so himself. He nonetheless had to offer some sort of explanation. If Smith was on the verge of surrender, he pleaded, then why not engage him? Why not indeed? Nkomo suffered that fearful finger being thrust in his face, and was warned that if he became one of Smith's puppets he would be treated accordingly.

Those who could be termed puppets in the Transitional Government, incidentally, had never been left in any doubt what Mugabe thought of them. 'Those African Stooges, Smith's four Yes Men…are nothing less than traitors, who stand condemned by the suffering revolutionary masses of Zimbabwe. Their own children will spit on their graves.'[5] And these were Mugabe's public utterances; what might he have had to say in private.

On 3 September 1978, a Russian Strela SAM 7 missile brought down an Air Rhodesia Vickers Viscount. Shortly after an 18:00 take off from Kariba, the Hunyani took a direct hit on the heat exchanger/jet pipe assembly that knocked out both starboard engines. As the passengers for the most part maintained their composure, the pilot struggled to control the stricken aircraft long enough to bring it down in an open field in the Urungwe Tribal Trust Land. The Viscount plunged into the bush killing 35 of the 53 passengers aboard. Ten survivors were later murdered on the ground by a ZIPRA unit deployed in the vicinity to mop up survivors. Because this aircraft was over booked, a second Viscount was lined up for take off with General Peter Walls on board. It has often been asserted that Nkomo had a highly efficient intelligence network to be in possession of this flight information, but in fact it had been reported in the general press.

Ken Flower detected in Ian Smith a mixed response to this tragedy. First he sensed a great release of tension, for Smith had truly not wanted to grasp the nettle of engaging Joshua Nkomo in government. This outrageous incident now put it beyond consideration no matter what might have been the potential political advantage. Other sources contradict this, and state that although the atrocity compromised the process for a while, it did not ultimately destroy it. Secondly, of course, Smith, in common with the outside world, reeled at the horror of the incident.

Smith prepared himself to receive the condolences, and to hear condemnation of the savagery from international governments and NGOs. But curiously nothing of the sort happened. The silence that followed astonished white Rhodesia, and as its meaning became clear, a feeling of tremendous isolation and abandonment overcame the nation. More incomprehensibly still, Nkomo freely admitted during an interview with the BBC that his party had been responsible, although he denied any suggestion that his forces had perpetrated the subsequent murders. He laughed nervously when answering the question. The Viscount, he claimed, was a valid military target, since the aircrew and most of the male passengers on board were territorial reservists, who were themselves guilty of murder. The British Government said nothing at all and Nkomo walked away from that infamous interview without a breath of censure.

In the white Commonwealth and in Britain itself, there was much sympathy expressed for Rhodesia by the common people. However this did not change the fact that governments, global Christian organisations and charitable bodies, were noticeably reserved in their criticism of ZAPU. The ZAPU representative to the UN, Dr Callistus Ndhlovu, contradicted his leader by admitting that ZIPRA had in fact killed the ten survivors, but he did not accept that this was murder.[6] The UN meekly accepted this account of the affair without condemning the organisation. It was the Anglican Church in Rhodesia — which was by no means as militant as the Catholic, and certainly not as clearly aligned — that took the lead in exposing the shameful silence.

* * *

For some time there had been growing concern in ComOps at the evident build up of ZIPRA conventional forces at various camps in Zambia. In response, CIO's Alan Brice and Chris Gough of the Selous Scouts, separately conducted detailed reconnaissance of a large ZIPRA training camp situated on a farm on the outskirts of Lusaka, known as Westlands Farm, or Freedom Camp. The base had been sited close to the Zambian capital and local Air Force and Army bases, in the hope that the Rhodesians would be wary of attacking it in such a position. Prior to the Hunyani tragedy this might have so, but things had changed. On 19 October, four Rhodesian Canberra bombers, eight Hawker Hunter strike jets and four helicopter gunships launched a surprise attack on Westlands Farm.

While the attack was under way, a Canberra bomber circled menacingly above Lusaka International Airport and suggested to ground control that both civil and Air Force aircraft should remain grounded for the duration of the raid. At the same time, a more conventional series of airborne attacks neutralised two additional camps: Mkushi, some 125 kilometres north east of Lusaka, and one known as CGT-2 — about 100 kilometres east of Lusaka. The combined kills for all three operations were estimated to be over 1 600 ZIPRA guerrillas.

Once again the Rhodesian armed services had proved that they were a force to be reckoned with. Hats were lifted to their effectiveness and precision in some strange quarters. The Zambian *Daily Mail* commented:

> One striking aspect of the attack was that though the bombing was quite heavy, vehicles passing by were not affected, except that many motorists abandoned their cars and trucks along the main road.[7]

The *Times of Zambia* quoted a railway official, who was also impressed that rail traffic using the line adjacent to the attacks was not disrupted. As satisfying as the whole episode might have been, however, it ultimately made no difference to the general direction of the war. Mugabe did not share the sense of quiet admiration expressed by the local press. 'Confronted by the reality of an imminent downfall', he raged in an address to the Tanzanian Association of Journalists, 'Smith has turned into a sadistic killer who tortures, kills and massacres not to survive but because he can no longer survive.'[8]

While the pot loudly condemned the kettle, the question of an approaching deadline for majority rule elections could not be ignored. To Smith and his partners in the Transitional Government, this put the issue of ending the war at the top of the agenda. Their biggest obstacle was Mugabe's opposing agenda, that was defined by an ongoing determination to fight.

To Muzorewa and Sithole, ending the war meant more than simply the achievement of peace. It was the test that would define the degree of support that each enjoyed within the guerrilla factions, for if either could gain credit for ending the war, then he would be as good as anointed. For white Rhodesia, the question was one of recognition. The ending of both international isolation and the economic sanctions, had become the Holy Grail. For those determined to stick it out, a dramatic improvement on current circumstances was vital, to arrest the daily haemorrhage of white manpower.

When Rhodesian Minister of Information, Immigration and Tourism, Wickus de Kock, joined the 'dismal jimmies', and took his 'precarious loyalty' to South Africa, he did so staunchly defending his right to make a personal decision to reject majority rule.[9] Although widely condemned and given a very rough crossing by customs officials at Beit Bridge, his was a decision that many others of principal were also beginning to contemplate. By June 1978 the emigration figures indicated that in the first half of that year 6 493 Rhodesians had packed up and left the country.

The list of white civilians killed was growing too. Farmers, technicians, foresters, hoteliers, traders, miners and ordinary citizens travelling between towns and cities, were picked off with depressing frequency. By the beginning of 1978, armed convoys had begun escorting residents of outlying areas backwards and forwards. Regular convoys were run between Bulawayo and Victoria Falls, Fort Victoria and Beitbridge and Kariba and Salisbury. Even journeys between Salisbury, Bulawayo and Umtali were carried out strictly in daylight hours, and usually with a small group of heavily armed friends.

The internal militarily situation was deteriorating at a critical rate. Each week virtually every Joint Operational Command meeting reviewed gains by the guerrillas, and intelligence reports of incursions, running into hundreds of men. Of late, guerrilla groups that were able to negotiate the frontier, had a good chance of proceeding to their destination unmolested. Large areas of the countryside had become no-go areas, where heavily armed military convoys found themselves doing precisely what the Portuguese had done a decade earlier. Men were content to fire randomly into the bush and move out of kill zones as quickly as possible. In a progressively defeatist mood, *Operations Thrasher* and Repulse became known as Thrashed and Repulsed.

By 1978 guerrilla incursions were effectively penetrating every sector of the country. With 'gooks' now causing havoc in the towns and cities, an unprecedented security regime was implemented, including the mandatory searching of anyone entering public buildings. Urban blacks were subjected to some rough treatment, just in case their loyalty lay in the wrong quarter.

Despite these precautions, a bomb blast in a Woolworths supermarket in Salisbury killed 11 people and injured 70 — all black. On the evening of 7 September, Umtali experienced another mortar and rocket attack. This time four people were injured. A few weeks later another 40-minute bombardment saw one hundred and fifty projectiles of various sorts landing in scattered locations throughout the municipal area. It was the loudest and most sustained attack against the city so far. Nevertheless, the majority merely turned over and went back to sleep, so inured had they become to the nocturnal fireworks.

On 11 December 1978, a unit of six ZANLA combatants successfully penetrated the Salisbury industrial quarter and fired several RPG-7 rockets into the bulk fuel storage containers. This caused a gargantuan explosion, and an ensuing blaze that, over the course of a week, consumed several months' supply of precious fuel. police officers attached to the Special Branch close security section — who were assigned to protect Ian Smith — were heard to remark that they had never seen the Prime Minister looking so haggard.[10]

Because Manicaland lay along the Mozambique border, it was arguably the hottest area of the country. By early 1979, the tea estates of the Honde Valley had ceased production, and white personnel concerned themselves with nothing more than socialising and discussing security at the club, getting the kids to and from boarding school and keeping themselves alive. The untended tea bushes grew unruly and the factories shut down. Briefly a system of forced labour came into being, as the Rhodesian African Rifles (RAR) unit that ostensibly controlled the valley, forced locals to work so that the guerrillas could see they were not doing so willingly. The killings went on, however, and protected villages provided no protection at all. Whites were attacked in their homes, on the roads, and periodically projected skyward by a landmine blast. Comrades Kid Bazooka, Roy Rogers and Coconut Jongwe were guerrilla leaders who enjoyed almost total hegemony. A large dog baboon, that nightly surveyed his empire from atop a phallic volcanic plug in the valley, was the only worthwhile target the army could find. Every evening a barrage of rifle fire would meet the old gentleman as he took his seat across the valley from Operations HQ. Maybe the marksmen were not trying particularly hard since intelligence later suggested that he had survived the war.

It was perhaps the forestry industry in Manicaland that suffered the most. Forestry also most acutely defined the gradual crippling of the Rhodesian economy, and the gallant but utterly hopeless efforts of many to keep it alive. Estates that cloaked thousands of hectares of hill and mountainside along the frontier provided an unassailable sanctuary for insurgents. Isolated industrial sawmills and factories were heavily fortified, as were the even more isolated homesteads. Ambushes on lonely estate roads, and homestead attacks, claimed the lives of a disproportionate number of whites in forestry communities. The ease with which a box of matches could destroy vast plantations of trees, also rendered the Eastern Highlands the most lucrative quadrant for guerrilla activity.

Social occasions at the various country clubs were characterised by a variety of heavily armoured private vehicles in the car parks, outdoor playgrounds that were off limits to children, and custom-built gun racks in the bar that were stacked high each evening with personal weapons. Bizarrely, the most frequent gatherings of friends and neighbours took place at the wakes and funerals of others who had been murdered.

The Melsetter district was probably the hardest hit of all. Eight employees died violently on the Charter Estates alone while 26 white civilians in the area were killed in one way or another. Whites, of course, suffered and died more visibly than the blacks but many blacks were also menaced and killed. Their deaths would usually be more brutal, in order to serve as a salutary warning to those working for white managers and white owned estates. The public decapitation of a black husband and wife took place on one particular estate, because the couple's daughter had married a policeman. Throughout the region, beerhalls were attacked and robbed, labour compounds terrorised, people abducted, terrorised and killed and rural buses regularly ambushed or blown to pieces by landmines. Blacks living this nightmare had a singular disadvantage — under no circumstances would the authorities allow them to bear arms. Their isolated dwellings of mud and thatch construction, or geometric rows of tin Nissan huts in fenced-off labour compounds, offered absolutely no protection at all.

The predicament that the residents of the border areas of Manicaland found themselves in, was reflected in many variations throughout the country. For example, in the southeast, where individual blocks of ranch land could run to hundreds of thousands of acres, the picturesquely sited homesteads rendered isolated pockets of white life desperately vulnerable. It was here that a now elderly Garfield Todd was still hanging in and still fighting the good fight.

In December 1978 Todd wrote a letter to the *Rhodesia Herald* that the newspaper declined to carry, but it was published elsewhere and reflected the gut feelings of many others. The old man wrote: 'This is the saddest and most frightening Christmas Rhodesia has ever known.'[11] The courage of the many who held out in these communities was matched by the many more who did not. No less courageously, many succumbed to pragmatism and abandoned their landholdings either for the cities or the yellow route.

67

Operation Favour

T he warnings Smith had been given that his Internal Settlement partners carried no weight against the leaders of the armed factions, began to prove correct. So far only a handful of guerrilla fighters had surrendered, and if not remedied, this situation would soon undermine the nationalist bona fides of both Muzorewa and Sithole. It was perceived that many combatants wanted to come in, but were waiting for some sign that a significant number of their comrades were doing the same. Both Muzorewa and Sithole approached General Walls for assistance. Walls issued a directive to Lieutenant Colonel Reid Daly and Chief Superintendent Mac McGuinness of Special Branch Selous Scouts, to concoct a scheme that would give the impression that large numbers of guerrillas were indeed surrendering. The plan was dubbed *Operation Favour*.

In essence the scheme required Selous Scout pseudo operatives posing as fighters to come in from the bush, and receive training at specific receiving and holding centres. A gale of publicity would reach the ears of genuine guerrillas in the countryside who, it was hoped, would respond by flocking to hand in their weapons and themselves. The Selous Scouts SB initially acquired two farms for use as holding centres. The first was in the Plumtree area and the second in the Mudziwa area near Bindura. Later, another two farms near Beit Bridge and Enkeldoorn, were acquired specifically to house and retrain Sithole faction supporters. The areas around the farms were 'frozen' or insulated from orthodox military activity. They were termed 'free zones' to give the impression that those housed there were 'liberated' ZANLA or ZIPRA forces who had been retrained and redeployed.

In due course, pseudo call-signs began to arrive and take up residence. They were then trained by Selous Scouts instructors to be 'guerrillas'. Muzorewa and Sithole were charged with gathering their armed supporters, and channelling them to the various holding centres. Since neither had any particular core of armed support, both sought to flesh out the numbers with urban rowdies, who were promised food and pay and the seductive drawcard of weapons and training. In April 1978, 100 political detainees were released from Wha Wha and Chikurubi maximum-security prisons, and added to the swelling rabble of bogus returnees. Upon the completion of their training this third force of unaligned gunmen became Security Force Auxiliaries (SFAs) and were deployed into the countryside to represent the armed wings of Sithole's ZANU and Muzorewa's UANC.

The real ZANLA did what it could to expose the ruse. A group of ZANLA guerrillas waylaid two auxiliaries in the Wedza TTL, when they strayed from their group in search of alcohol and women. The two were 'turned' and sent back to call the rest of the unit on the pretext that the ZANLA detachment wanted to surrender. A little later a large group of auxiliaries walked into a well-laid trap. They were disarmed and their hands wired behind their backs. Since it was quite clear what was planned, a good many were able to run and lose themselves in the bush. However, 41 of their number were executed on the spot and their bodies left on the side of the road. The ZANLA group then moved off taking the SFAs arms and equipment with them.

On 2 May the Executive Council repealed all bans on ZANU and ZAPU. This was followed by another wide appeal for guerrillas to lay down their arms and surrender. The *Rhodesia Herald* was in the forefront of the propaganda offensive.

> The time has come to bring an end to the fighting. We guarantee their [the guerrillas] safety if they come in peace.[1]

Nothing happened except for a perceptible rise in guerrilla attacks. Special Branch then turned to the *mujibas* — a force that might be described as the pilot fish of large guerrilla deployments. Mujibas acted as a kind of informal youth brigade made up of young rural toughs, not quite combatants, but loyal to the cause and useful as contact men, runners and fags. Trying to indoctrinate them against the revolution, however, was like shouting against the tempest. Youngsters with their eyes on proper weapons did what needed to be done, chanted what was told them to chant and swore loyalty to whomsoever asked. They were duly trained, deployed as SFAs — and thereafter left to their own devices.

By virtue of the sheer numbers of volunteers that the programme was attracting, plus those press-ganged or coerced in some way to sign up, the operation was deemed a success. In due course it was decided that the SFAs should be reoriented, stripped of their Warsaw Pact identity, given Nato weapons and integrated into the Security Forces proper.

Sithole then revealed that he had men training in Uganda under the army of Idi Amin. This shady group, known as the Zimbabwe Strike Force, were ZANU men who had refused to fight alongside ZIPRA, and had been sent from Zambia to Uganda for 'training'. In *Operation Favour*, however, numbers were numbers and it was not particularly important who they were. The CIO chartered Jack Malloch's Air Trans-Africa to fly to Entebbe, collect the contingent and bring them home. These men were billeted in the Gokwe area, but became a problem when they began to terrorise the local area and resisted efforts at integration.

A simple no-nonsense strategy was devised to deal with them. Word was circulated that a high-ranking ZANU official would be arriving to address the group, and the commander was instructed to muster his men at the airfield, where the official was due to land. The group was told that they would receive their pay at the same time. A large force of 10-Battalion Rhodesia Regiment troops quietly took up positions around the airstrip, while stop groups were deployed in the bush beyond. Two 11-ton army trucks with their canvas canopies down, moved into position. When the entire rogue group was assembled, a spokesman with a loud hailer ordered the men to lay down their weapons. The group hesitated and in the confusion did not immediately comply. Flaps were thrown aside to reveal a heavy machine gun mounted on each truck that commenced to spit fire. Most of the guerrillas were cut down in the opening salvos but a few managed to escape. These were picked off in ones and twos as they ran into the waiting stop groups. Within a few minutes 180 men were dead.

Under new orders, the Shona auxiliaries were given the name *Pfumo re Vhanu*, or Spear of the People, while Ndebele factions carried the same name in their language — *Umkonto wa Bantu*. A spear and shield emblem was assigned that was worn on brown fatigues. By the end of the transition, the Spear of the People had become an orthodox military formation comprising 10 500 men.

Operationally the SFA programme was a disaster. Although garnished with military apparel and armed with Portuguese manufactured G3 rifles, the new operatives had not been effectively re-educated and — almost to a man — retained their original loyalties. Because the unit was essentially made up of urban riff-raff, these loyalties were mainly to themselves. However, those who were originally aligned to ZANLA or ZIPRA, maintained that alliance and desertions were commonplace. Security Force details were increasingly reporting fleeting contacts with guerrilla groups, among which were men using G3 and FN rifles.

So far *Operation Favour* had been conducted behind closed doors. A handful of rather optimistic supernumeraries to the SB Selous Scouts, who were part of the Psyops (Psychological Operations) programme, thought that the moment was ripe to break the story to the Rhodesian public. ComOps was doubtful but gave the go-ahead for a Rhodesia Broadcasting Corporation camera team to be present at a rally, to be addressed by Bishop Muzorewa. It was intended that they would selectively film and interview Security Force Auxiliaries loyal to the UANC.

Rhodesian whites, waking up to read the Sunday papers, were shocked to be confronted by a large photograph of Bishop Muzorewa holding a communist AK47 assault rifle and addressing a rally in the Msana 'free zone'. Clearly visible in the background were the surly faces of his SFAs.

After a day of ruminating over this, the public was dealt another blow when Rhodesia TV personality Johan Meiring interviewed on camera a highly disreputable-looking guerrilla, who claimed to be the new District Commissioner of Msana Tribal Trust Land. 'Comrade Max' was in fact a decommissioned pseudo operator who was being occupied with odd jobs around the Selous Scout Fort at Mount Darwin, and had lately been dusted down for this role. Warming to his theme, Comrade Max waved his arm around and declared that no white man was to be found within his 1000 square kilometre zone. He claimed to run '…the educational system and deal [sic] with civil problems as well as maintain order.' Meiring closed the interview in deference to his subject by claiming that, in the Msana free zone, Comrade Max was the boss. The next day the *Rhodesia Herald* posted a huge banner headline reading 'DC Max is the boss!'

After a moment of stunned silence Parliament erupted in disbelief. The secret had been very closely guarded and apparently not a single parliamentarian had been briefed. Minister of Defence and ComOps Roger Hawkins was quick to put the record straight, and in a speech to the House on 16 August assured the members that Comrade Max was not a District Commissioner, and all civil offices concerned with Msana TTL, and indeed throughout the country, were intact and functioning.

As concern died down, white Rhodesians came to acknowledge the existence of the SFAs, and to accept that it was just a sign of the times. In September 1979 the SFAs were deployed to Protected Villages and keeps around the country. This helped to free up the Internal Affairs Guard Force to patrol and protect the nation's vital communications links. The auxiliaries were used and touted as an extension of the Security Forces, but everyone took them for what they were. The Rhodesians had created private armies in order that Sithole and Muzorewa might blend into the militant culture of black nationalism. This at the very least was a tacit acknowledgement on the part of the authorities that the standards of 'Western civilisation' no longer applied. Future elections, it was assumed, would be run by African rules.

* * *

Perhaps the last ballot to be held in Rhodesia under these coveted Western standards, was the rather perfunctory referendum on 30 January 1979. The ballot was organised to test the response of the white population to an ultimatum they really had little choice but to accept. What Smith offered was a choice between black majority rule, heavily tilted in favour of the white minority, or oblivion.

The majority rule constitution was unveiled on 30 November, for the perusal of the last white dominated Rhodesian electorate, and in presenting it to his constituency, Smith endured a significant amount of abuse and censure. As he spoke at various venues throughout the country, he was accused of selling the whites down the river — although he and everybody else correctly took this as bark and not bite. It was too late by then to change the course of events, and there was no alternative route to choose anyway. Black majority rule was the future and it would come sooner rather than later. As late as it was though, white Rhodesia still felt that to some degree it had the right to define the rules of black government to suit itself. Smith's solution was the best that anyone could have hoped for. After all, old Smithy could always be relied upon to get the best deal. Had he not stated quite plainly in Geneva that majority rule did not preclude responsible government?

The new constitution required that the new black Prime Minister select a percentage of his Cabinet from political parties other than his own, which ought to have guaranteed the Rhodesian Front a strong showing on the front benches. Also, any effort on the part of a black government to indigenise the civil service, would be halted by a Public Service Commission whose chairman and members would be white. The principal agencies of government — Law and Order and Defence — were categorically to remain in white hands. Further, the Prime Minister would be obliged to select his military commanders on the advice of a board appointed for the purpose, the members of which would be made up of the retiring commander, one other commander, and a third, appointed by the Prime Minister. Property rights were to be protected, which meant there would be no change in the current land tenure system. Any change in the constitution would require an 80 per cent majority — which in effect would mean the support of every black member of the House as well as six whites. All in all, the entrenched rights of whites to live as they had and to govern by proxy were protected. If an incoming black Prime Minister sought to tear up the terms of the new constitution, he could be immediately arrested and removed from office. Despite a rough referendum campaign, 57 000 out of 67 000 whites voted in favour of the proposals.[2]

68

The toilet window

1979 was launched by Robert Mugabe as *Gukurahundi* — the year of the people's storm. He wrote in an emotional epistle to his cadres in the field:

The enemy is battered and dazed. Let us now move towards him with all our mustered reserves, remembering always that ours is a people's war, fought by the people and for the people.[1]

So it was. The finally tally of dismal Jimmies for 1978 was 13 500, an increase of 3 000 over the previous year.[2] What once had been the 'chicken run' now became the 'owl run' — the route taken by the wise at night. An old observation used by German Jews was heard again in Rhodesia: 'The pessimists left the country and the optimists went to the gas chamber.' And another: 'When the Jews start leaving it's time to go; when the Indians start leaving it's too late.' All the usual gags were in circulation, and all illustrated in one way or another that things were rapidly going downhill.

On 2 January, 27–year old James Jolliffe opened the annual score card when he was shot dead during a guerrilla attack on his trading store in the Gatooma district. The following day, 39–year old District Commissioner David Mirams was killed in a landmine blast. Five days later another landmine blast in the Odzi area claimed the life of Rosemary Hacking. The day after that, 54-year-old year old Petrus Blignaut and his 47-year-old wife June were killed in a vehicle ambush in the Selukwe area. Their 17-year-old son engaged the guerrilla group, and beat them off in a fierce firefight. On 30 January, Beatrice Farmer Japie Smit and his wife Connie were killed when their vehicle was ambushed near the couple's farm. On 1 February animal health inspector Lukas Koen was ambushed and killed while visiting a farm in the Umvuma area.

To even the score somewhat, a daring raid on the Munhava oil storage depot in Beira was staged by a team of Rhodesian SAS assisted by South African Special Forces. Such acts of daring never failed to uplift flagging Rhodesian spirits. The attack was a seaborne assault, with the naval component provided by South Africa. Operators using RPG rockets and heavy machine guns with tracer rounds, started eight major oil fires that ironically were later extinguished by South African contractors.[3]

The highlight of the 1979 killing season was the action of 15-year-old Churchill School pupil Jamie Scott. Scott and a friend were ambushed while riding tandem on a motorcycle. Scott was hit five times. He survived the first shock, then using only an unreliable Heckler & Koch G3 rifle, he drove his attackers off with a full frontal charge. Apart from achieving the status of a living legend at every white school in the country, Jamie was honoured by the nation with the Conspicuous Gallantry Award — the highest given to a civilian during the war. Sadly, the medal was later sold to defray medical expenses incurred as a consequence of Scott's severe injuries.[4]

The low point of the year was the downing of a second Air Rhodesia Viscount — the Umniati, shot down on 12 February by a ground-to-air missile. The circumstances were virtually identical to the downing of the Hunyani some five months earlier, except that this time none of the 59 passengers and crew survived the crash. Less mirthful on this occasion, Nkomo claimed that his men again believed General Walls to be on the flight, which he maintained made it a legitimate military target. This appeared to be a curious confusion of facts since the same rationale had been used in the case of the Hunyani. Following this second tragedy, aircraft leaving Kariba Airport spiralled to high altitude over the lake before proceeding south. Heat dispersal devices were also fitted to the engines of civil aircraft to confuse the controls of heat-seeking missiles.

Perhaps the most brazen and dramatic cross-border raid of the entire war was mounted with the object of killing Nkomo. *Operation Bastille* of April 1979 involved an SAS flying column that was transported across Kariba and driven through Zambia to the capital, Lusaka. A well co-ordinated lightning raid virtually destroyed Nkomo's suburban house, yet the intended target managed to slip through the net, claiming that he had escaped through the toilet window. Speculation persisted that he had been tipped off, for it challenged the imagination to suppose that a man of Nkomo's bulk had been able to squeeze through the narrow aperture of a toilet window unobserved while bullets and bombs were flying around him.

A few months after the Umniati incident, a senior ZIPRA intelligence commander by the name of Elliot Sibanda, codenamed Black Swine, was abducted by the Selous Scouts in Botswana and returned to Rhodesia. After recovering from a gunshot wound to the abdomen, he became an important — in fact probably the most important — intelligence source of the entire war.

What Black Swine had to offer came as a complete surprise to ComOps. A specially convened meeting of the inter-services committee was briefed by a member of Special Branch, on a new and potentially deadly development. The apparent lethargy with which Joshua Nkomo and ZIPRA had so far conducted the war — a frame of mind that had earned ZIPRA the nickname matshowshowe, or shuffling walker — was in fact part of a deliberate strategy. The deployment of guerrillas into the field was limited so that large numbers could be held back in order to build up a powerful conventional capacity.[5]

With the support and guidance of Nkomo's Soviet backers, ZIPRA mechanised infantry would then invade Rhodesia via the two bridgeheads of Victoria Falls and Chirundu. Initially, the airports at Kariba, Victoria Falls and Wankie would be seized, after which conventional troops would be flown in using Libyan transport aircraft. Once territorial control had been achieved, the right to form a government would be announced from a position of strength. Nkomo let it be known fairly widely that he anticipated being in full control of Salisbury by May 1979.[6]

Security forces were promptly deployed along the northern border to bolster security and pre-empt any such possible deployment.meantime ComOps went to work planning some suitable response to nip Nkomo's elaborate scheme in the bud. The plan that swiftly came to the fore was to hit Nkomo personally, and if possible kill him. This was the umpteenth time a hit of this nature had been mooted since Nkomo's release from prison, but except for the Lusaka raid, it was always called off for one reason or the other. The CIO's main assassin, Alan Brice, who had had many opportunities to kill Nkomo, was one of many who were angered and frustrated by the constant indecision. Typically the final go-ahead was given for a mission only when achieving it had reached its maxim degree of impossibility.

In fact it is not difficult to imagine that the situation regarding Joshua Nkomo presented Smith with a conundrum. Public anger demanded that something be done to revenge the downing of the two Viscounts, but as long as Smith was trying to negotiate a settlement with Nkomo, he was loath to swop the kid gloves for the mailed fist. This is merely conjecture, of course, but if true it would explain how Nkomo continued to survive.

An old parrot cry

The first election to be held under the rules of universal suffrage, passed off with a minimum of fuss. The Patriotic Front deployed a combined total of 10 000 armed men into the field but failed to disrupt the process.[7] Nkomo's instructions to his commanders were to ensure that every man with a gun equalled one thousand with a vote.[8] Between 17 and 21 April 1 869,000 votes out of a possible 2 862 000 were cast in an atmosphere more relaxed than anyone had a right to expect. There was a 63% turnout and in the event, only 19 out of 932 polling stations suffered attacks, none of which was put out of action.

Smith and his Information Department were at pains to make it known how unique an achievement this was. That the conduct of the ballot had been universally endorsed as free and fair, was in itself a fact unprecedented in Africa. Internationally the charade was dismissed for its irrelevance, although white Rhodesia nevertheless clung to the hope that they might just have pulled off the impossible.

The results were as expected, and Bishop Abel Muzorewa emerged as the Prime Minster elect, with his UANC winning 51 out of the 72 black seats.[9] Ndabaningi Sithole's ZANU won 12, the Rhodesian Front 28 and Chief Kayisa Ndweni's United Federal Party took nine. Ahead of Ndweni in the popular vote but winning no seats was Chief Chirau's Zimbabwe United Peoples Organisation.

There were many international parties publicly feigning indifference, despite which the result was met with intense interest when it reached the foreign press. No sensible claims of misconduct were made, although it was observed that due to the general state of war there had been a lack of genuine campaigning. British observer Lord Boyd returned a verdict that the election had been as fairly conducted as possible, and as Britain thoughtfully rubbed her chin, and the UN waited on her lead, the awkwardly named Republic of Zimbabwe-Rhodesia was born.

On 31 May, Ian Douglas Smith celebrated his last day in office, and a day later Bishop Abel Muzorewa took occupation of the Prime Minister's residence. In keeping with his occasional flirtations with the absurd, Muzorewa arrived in a replica pioneer-era ox wagon with a spear in his hand, and his signature West African robes over his suit.

If the robes had originally been more theatrical than appropriate, then the ox wagon was even more bizarre, and it is hard to imagine why Muzorewa should have chosen this particular symbol with its emblematic overtones of colonialism. The *Rhodesia Herald* gaily documented the event in the following day's edition. A photograph spread across the front page featured the Bishop on his journey through town, dressed up as a bantam cock — as Ian Smith put it — who cringed at the ghastly spectacle and wondered not for the first time whether he hadn't made a disastrous mistake.[10]

Not everyone was convinced of British fair play and, as might have been expected, Ndabaningi Sithole cried foul. At a press conference held in his ZANU offices, the defeated chairman read out an angry statement in which he alleged grave irregularities and demanded a commission of inquiry. In the meantime he refused to take up his 12 seats, and was delighted when eight of Muzorewa's MPs led by James Chikerema rebelled. The Prime Minister's parliamentary majority had instantly evaporated. Sithole, meanwhile, petitioned the high court to declare the election null and void. In rapid retaliation he was subjected to surveillance, searches and random arrests. This, plus the Security Force massacre of his auxiliaries, ensured that in due course he meekly took up his seats in the House.[11]

* * *

A month later, white Rhodesia's ray of hope began to shine a little brighter. In the British general election, the Conservatives seized a narrow 44-seat majority in the Commons that swept out James Callaghan and brought in Margaret Thatcher. Thatcher wasted no time in attending to the Rhodesia question and announced that her government would take immediate steps to ascertain whether the country was now in compliance with the six principals of NIBMAR. She hinted very strongly that recognition and the lifting of sanctions were probable.

Both the British and Rhodesian Governments knew that Nkomo and Mugabe had been warned by Nyerere and Kaunda that, if the elections achieved a significantly positive result, support for the armed struggle might have to be withdrawn. The moment therefore seemed propitious for Britain to act in Rhodesia's favour, and if she was indeed tempted to recognise the internal settlement, she was in good company.[12] Intelligence sources suggested that the governments of France, Germany and other less influential European states were willing to support Zimbabwe-Rhodesia against the Patriotic Front. However, they would only recognise the Muzorewa government if Britain took the lead.

These developments caught Jimmy Carter on the wrong foot. His had not been a spectacular term of office and the odds were fair that he would not serve a second. Eventually, of course, one of the happiest marriages in political history would be consummated between Ronald Reagan and Margaret Thatcher. If Reagan had already been in office at that time, he would almost certainly have followed Senators Jessie Helms of North Carolina and S.I Hayakawa of California in supporting Muzorewa's position. In any case, a US Senate resolution that supported recognition of Zimbabwe-Rhodesia was passed on 15 May. But Carter himself was guided by the hand that picked the cotton, and he cautiously announced that he would make a decision on the matter the following week. That brief lapse of time made all the difference.

The final furlong

T
here was a moment when the Rhodesian public, some in hope and some in fear, held their breaths. The best possible news for white Rhodesia was the return to power in Britain of the Conservative Party. These were desperate times, and the distant voice of Roy Welensky had by then become very faint indeed. Even those old timers — Smith not least among them — who remembered the Federal days, greeted the news of a Tory victory with a deep sigh of relief. The *Rhodesia Herald* made much of the event:

> …the Iron Lady will be able to put some steel in the souls of Western politicians in general and President Carter in particular.[1]

Jimmy Carter, with his eye fixed firmly on the US black electorate, simply waited and watched. Margaret Thatcher was undergoing a metamorphosis under the heat and pressure of real politik and was emerging tougher for it. Before she could think much about white Rhodesia she was forced to consider the value of British economic investment in black Africa. She had early on set the tone of her Government's view of Rhodesia when discussing the question with Commonwealth Secretary General Sonny Ramphal. She described both Nkomo and Mugabe as terrorists, and when Ramphal tried to correct her she replied: 'Well of course they are terrorists. They are just like the IRA.'

Ramphal communicated this view to the leaders of the Afro-Asian block and two days after the Conservative victory virtually every Commonwealth ambassador signed a letter to the British Government warning against recognition of Muzorewa's administration.[2] Thus it was that while Ian Smith was receiving comforting prognostications from other members of the British establishment, both Thatcher and Carrington were being pulled in the opposite direction. If Nkomo had once been told that Britain could not afford to hand Rhodesia over to blacks, Thatcher was now hearing that she could ill afford not to.

The economic gravity of black Africa was centred on the oil fields of the Niger Delta and Abuja, where Nigerian kingpins controlled most of the region's cash flow. Black Africa had earlier frowned on Nigerian General Garba's effort to assist in a possible compromise between Nkomo and Smith, and that criticism had been raised an octave when the effort failed. In the aftermath Garba was chastened, the breach quickly healed and Nigeria ushered neatly back into line.

In May 1979 it was announced by Nigerian Military Leader Olusegun Obasanjo, that Nigerian public contracts would henceforth be denied to British firms. This moratorium would remain in effect until such time as majority rule was established in Rhodesia. In July, Shell/BP Nigeria was nationalised in protest against the sale of Nigerian petroleum to South Africa. The Nigerian Government then dumped £500 million sterling on the international currency exchanges in order first to destabilise sterling and secondly to dispel any doubts about Nigeria's determination and regional economic clout.[3]

Jimmy Carter, meanwhile, made his decision, and announced that the US Government would not be lifting sanctions against Rhodesia. If Thatcher had been sitting on the fence, then this helped tilt her towards the inevitable.

Her next challenge came with her first Commonwealth Heads of Government meeting, to be held in Lusaka in August of that year. It was there in the heartland of the liberation struggle that the Frontline presidents were preparing to do bloody battle with the British. Thatcher was naturally forewarned and arrived at the venue cautioning all that she intended to stand her ground. Many supposed that this presaged a spirited defence of white Rhodesia. Smith held the same hope, but he was out of power and the debris of many past failures had been flushed away with him. Thatcher may have been the Iron Lady but she was no fool. The defence of white hegemony in southern Africa was indefensible in the context of modern politics, and she of all people knew it. Just as she had no tolerance for being pushed around by blacks, she was not going to be prevailed upon by a population of deluded expatriates, even if they were her kith and kin.

Sally Mugabe, as First Lady of ZANU — and no doubt of Zimbabwe in waiting — offered a thoughtful opinion on what was expected from Thatcher. 'What does Lady Thatcher want to prove, that she is racist? I suspect she is…it would only be a racist who would underscore the Smith/Muzorewa regime.'[4]

Even this pejorative tone was too soft for some. Edgar Tekere was chosen to represent ZANU at the Lusaka meeting and for this he was armed with some very strong language indeed.

> Mrs. Thatcher will be fighting to have the conference totally ignore the vitally important question of the need to get rid of the evil settler racist armed forces and have them replaced by the peoples patriotic force…because her racist mind deeply appreciates that the minority racist settler interest will remain securely entrenched by the racist settler forces on whose back treacherous Muzorewa rides.[5]

If Margaret Thatcher shuddered a little at this salvo of Stalinist invective, it at least primed her to understand what sort of people she would be dealing with. She said nothing at the time, but in her later memoirs she had much to get off her chest.

> …their forces [The Patriotic Front] had carried out atrocities which disgusted everyone and I was as keen to avoid dealing with terrorists as I would be at home.[6]

The world had changed a lot since the days of Federation and the early months and years of UDI. There was no longer any question of compromise, of easing in the black majority or devising complex formulas for power sharing. The white stand in Rhodesia had now become a bitter rearguard action and, for those unwilling to live under black rule, there would be no future anywhere in Africa. Thatcher was faced with certain unpalatable facts, but she was nonetheless unafraid to confront them.

> Our strategy was to take full responsibility ourselves for reaching a settlement…to obtain that result we had to make it clear that Britain would be ready to resume authority in Rhodesia and to hold fresh elections. We knew also that there would have to be significant changes to the present constitution of Rhodesia if, after elections, the new government was to receive international recognition and acceptance.[7]

The hot war in the meantime continued to be bloody and bitter. To illustrate the fact that the Rhodesians still had plenty of fight left in them, the 1979 Commonwealth Heads of Government meeting opened with the Rhodesians raising smoke and dust all over Lusaka. Two raids in quick succession destroyed ZIPRA's intelligence HQ in the Roma suburb and a huge ZIPRA arms dump a few miles west of the capital. There was much talk at ComOps about aiming some action directly at the conference itself— which might help to remind the Frontline leaders that it was Rhodesia that still called the shots north of the Limpopo.

In the end it was humour that dug most deeply into the spleen of the black worthies present. Their dignity was fragile as they assembled rather nervously in the Zambian capital. The time had come to parade their sovereignty to the world and to wring from Margaret Thatcher the last drop of colonial blood. A cartoon appeared in the Rhodesian *Sunday Mail* depicting the fabled Green Leader circling Lusaka Airport in his Canberra jet with the pilot giving the thumbs up to Her Majesty's aircraft to land. To Kenneth Kaunda's inexpressible relief, the shots fired at the 1979 Commonwealth Heads of Government Meeting remained oratorical and no one was killed.

* * *

In every respect these exchanges proved to be more damaging to white Rhodesia than any action so far seen in the shooting war. Guyanan Director General of the Commonwealth Sonny Ramphal, was clearly among the Afro-Asian majority. He kept the Rhodesia issue off the agenda for three vital days, allowing others of the bloc ample time to petition Thatcher on the sidelines and to ensure that she clearly understood which road to take.

Thatcher would have preferred ambiguity — in the time-honoured Whitehall tradition — in order to leave some room for manoeuvre later. But Sir Anthony Duff, future head of MI5 and current Under Secretary of State for the Foreign Office, lent the Prime Minister and Foreign Secretary, Lord Peter Carrington, the benefit of his experience. In this instance, ambiguity would serve no purpose. Clarity was essential. It was finally an all black show and Ian Smith, who for 15 years had rubbed British noses in the dirt, was now out of the picture.[8] It was time for past failures of British diplomacy in Africa to be expunged. Thatcher agreed and, leaving the details of her statement on Zimbabwe-Rhodesia to Duff and Carrington to prepare, she retired early to prepare for the conference.

The following day she delivered her address to the assembled Commonwealth leaders with less tight-lipped resentment than might have been expected. She assured her audience that Britain had every intention of recognising Rhodesian independence, but not under the current Constitution and not within the terms of the internal settlement as it stood. The power that the white minority enjoyed to block any undesirable amendment to the Constitution, was disproportionate to their demographic representation. This rendered the internal settlement defective in the view of the British Government.

Such had been the negative expectation, that this moderate change of British direction was seen by the black delegates as a major coup. It won Margaret Thatcher rapturous and sustained applause. Ian Smith must have seen the life of Rhodesia flashing before his eyes as he heard the news.

The Commonwealth leaders deluged Thatcher with petitions to push the envelope further, while the momentum was still there. The first to reach her as the glow of victory passed were Kenneth Kaunda, Michael Manley of Jamaica and Malcolm Fraser of Australia. All three urged her to convene another constitutional conference where the internal settlement could be reworked. It would be fine if it was expanded to include the Patriotic Front, for clearly Muzorewa's government lacked the authenticity of genuine black power. White abhorrence towards dealing with Mugabe and Nkomo would have to be overcome. In any case, theoretically it was no longer a white decision.

The British Prime Minister agreed to follow this route, although no one knew how easily Nkomo, Mugabe or Muzorewa could be persuaded to comply. What could be taken reasonably for granted, would be that the enthusiastic endorsement of the Frontline States would give the Patriotic Front very little space to deviate from the general consensus.

Abel Muzorewa's commitment to the scheme was neither immediate nor enthusiastic. He knew with a deep certainty that his short and largely ineffective reign would not be able to survive a head-to-head encounter with Robert Mugabe. From the right wing of his coalition, the voices of Smith and others counselled against accepting any invitation to re-negotiate. However, on his left, the voices of the two chiefs were equally insistent that he should. The reasons for this were important, and close to the heart of all good and Christian men. And if nothing else, the Bishop was a man of deep moral rectitude.

Neither Jeremiah Chirau nor Kayisa Ndweni stood any chance whatsoever of winning overall power, so they could apply their thoughts to practical matters like the suffering of the people, rather than to politics. The Security Forces had realised by then that the war within Rhodesia itself was, if not lost, then at least unwinnable. Besides protecting vital transport and economic interests, the Army had more or less abandoned the countryside. The policy now was to concentrate resources on destroying the enemy outside and to batter the neighbouring infrastructure as much as possible in order to effect a change of heart among the Frontline leaders. The net result of this was to give the guerrilla factions — already deployed — a virtual free run of the tribal areas. The nationalist presence there soon degenerated into a reign of terror. Desensitised, swaggering, power-drunk youth without moral compass, behaved with abominable cruelty and inhumanity. Their job was to ensure the political eminence of their party and this more than anything catalysed a ferocious cycle of horror and counter horror that persisted until the end of the colonial period, and beyond.

The people could barely tell one faction from the other and it was a simple choice of who they feared the most. The police documented daily reports of horrific killings, torture, burnings, maiming and rape. These atrocities might have been merely a symptom of Africa to many whites, but to the two chiefs and to Muzorewa, the human cost was simply too high. In due course, and to his credit, Muzorewa grasped the nettle. On 22 August he announced to Parliament that he had accepted an invitation from the British Government to attend a constitutional conference to be held in London the following month.

Operation Uric (Rhodesian operation) Operation Bootlace (South African operation)
The conference opened in London on 10 September 1979 amid huge fanfare and anticipation. Politicians of all hues and opinions gathered at the magnificent Lancaster House, amid the autumnal groves of plane trees and oaks, in the peace and gentility of predictable laws and rational actions. But the chapter of blood and iron in southern Africa had not quite run its course.

The seeds of *Operation Uric* were sown in April 1979, as Lusaka was feeling the weight of *Operation Bastille*. A new and disturbing dimension to the war was revealed when a single FRELIMO soldier was captured some 200 kilometres inside Rhodesia. Under interrogation the cadre revealed that he was part of a much larger combined FRELIMO and ZANLA operation. This finally exposed the consummation of the marriage between Robert Mugabe and Samora Machel, the vows of which had been spoken in Quelimane. The objective of this alliance was to penetrate Rhodesia far enough to destroy the vital rail links to South Africa, which — together with some associated disruption of road transport — would bring about a rapid economic collapse and an end to the war.

Rhodesia's rail link to the south was a single artery that, once severed, would effectively cut off sustenance to the nation. ZANLA's first attempt was felt in January 1979, when Romanian-trained explosives handlers rigged a boosted Soviet TMH anti-tank mine beneath the line linking Rutenga to Shabani. A locomotive detonated the charge and blasted out a metre of rail but failed to derail the rolling stock. Later that month another section of line was blown not far from the first, and more sabotage attempts followed.

A clever means to counter these attacks was devised by the Rhodesian Engineer Squadron. A light electrical charge was sent up the line that was not sufficient to cause a shock but enough to trigger any electrical detonators that were handled while touching the rail. A good many ZANLA sappers were killed in this way without their comrades being any the wiser.[9]

At this time it was estimated that at least 500 FRELIMO troops were operating in the country alongside ZANLA. ZANLA had also gained more or less free use of the entire FRELIMO logistics, transport and communications structure, which effectively brought FRELIMO and Mozambique into the internal war. Part of the combined FRELIMO/ZANLA strategy, not unlike Nkomo's conventional plan, was to try and gain control of apiece of territory, in order to improve its standing at any future power negotiations.

Of course this could not be allowed to happen, and Rhodesia had its own strategy to counter it. Under PW Botha, the South Africans were vastly more liberal in dispensing their military favours, and while that particular iron was hot, the Rhodesians intended to strike. Assistance in the form of Special Forces and SAAF aircraft was provided under the code name *Operation Bootlace*. Thed operation was planned to smash Mozambique's ability to transport guerrillas to Rhodesia while at the same time illustrating the high price of picking a fight with white Rhodesia.

Arguably the most important access route for ZANLA guerrillas into Rhodesia was through the Gaza province, where road and rail links ran from Maputo to Rutenga. This conduit brought ZANLA men and equipment west, through a FRELIMO forward base at Mapai. Both the road and the railway line followed the Limpopo River on its north bank, with a vital bridge at the small town of Chokwe and any number of secondary bridges and culverts thereafter. The main thrust was to take out as many of those bridges as possible, and in particular the main bridge over the Limpopo. The purpose was twofold: to cripple the local Mozambican transport network, and to isolate the large FRELIMO/ZANLA forward base at Mapai prior to an attack.

The operation began on Saturday 1 September 1979 and continued for most of the following week. It combined waves of air and ground assaults on selected targets up the length of the Limpopo Valley that severely disrupted communications between Maputo and the FRELIMO and ZANLA forward bases near the Rhodesian border. On 6 September, an assault on the main base at Mapai quickly deteriorated into intense and bloody trench fighting. As the day wore on, RLI units were forced to swallow the unprecedented humiliation of having their attack beaten off by an inferior enemy. A South African Puma helicopter carrying 14 Rhodesian soldiers took a direct hit from an RPG7 rocket that crashed killing all on board. Army units despatched to investigate found the wreckage and the bodies and assumed that they would be recovered once Mapai had been taken. Mapai remained untaken, however, and the bodies remained unrecovered.

In Durban, 700 kilometres to the south, the Rhodesian national rugby squad prepared to challenge Natal. The match was the epilogue to an otherwise disastrous 1979 Currie Cup season. News came through that Rhodesian full back Leroy Duberly, excused from the match due to prior military commitments, had been one of those travelling in the downed Puma. A shocked crowd at Kingsmead Stadium stood and observed a minute of silence, after which a lone bugler played the last post. The two teams took the field in what would be one of the last games Rhodesia would play as an honorary province of South Africa.

Lancaster House

Robert Mugabe arrived in London angry and frustrated. He felt for the umpteenth time that he was being forced to divert his attention from war, when war was clearly the only strategy achieving results. It was obvious that the more frantic and ferocious the Rhodesian attacks became, the closer she was to collapse. It surprised him that neither Machel nor Kaunda seemed able to accept this fact.

Immediately prior to his arrival in London, Mugabe attended a meeting of non-aligned states held in Havana, Cuba. There he and Nkomo lobbied extensively for a resolution to be framed repudiating the Lusaka Accord. Instead, the two were summoned to a meeting on the sidelines with Nyerere, Kaunda and Machel. It was made clear to both that the war was proving too costly, and if the Patriotic Front boycotted the conference, their bases in Zambia and Mozambique would be closed and white Rhodesia would walk away with the spoils of war.

Thus the two put in a reluctant appearance in London, with Mugabe in particular in a sullen and combative mood. The British had tended to be remote from the process over most of James Callaghan's term, and this time Mugabe sensed that the Conservative Government had returned with some of the old flame of kith and kin restored. His nose was attuned to a conspiracy and the place was crawling with rats. No one liked him and every faction other than his own would have gladly paid to see him dead. He distrusted whites in general and the British in particular, and while he was not above theatrics, his initial concerns for his own security were both sound and genuine. He accepted a two-member security detail from the British Special Branch as a necessary evil, but preferred to rely on his own ZANLA 'protocol' unit.

Mugabe had good reason to fear for his safety in London. The recent attempt on Joshua Nkomo's life in Lusaka was fresh in his memory, as were the deaths of Chitepo and Jason Moyo as well as the still unexplained disappearance of Edson Sithole. While Smith had been compromised and his governing establishment cast into disarray, the Rhodesian security services were still lean, active and very dangerous. At this, the 11th hour, Mugabe had finally been accorded the status of Rhodesian Public Enemy Number 1 and that meant that if at all possible he had to be disposed of. On 31 August 1979 Alan Brice — until recently known only by the nom de guerre of 'Taffy' — was given his most important mission.

Mugabe had been well protected in Mozambique. Unlike Lusaka, Maputo had few resident whites among whom a Rhodesian assassin could mingle. It was therefore decided that the assassination would take place in London where, as a Welshman, Brice could merge without difficulty. However, the Lancaster House conference was due to commence on 10 September which gave him little time to prepare.

Brice had proved himself, by his British SAS training and experience, to be a cunning, remorseless and dangerous operative. He experimented in advance with a variety of strategies including using a ricin-smeared air rifle pellet, a sniper attack and a claymore explosive device in a briefcase. After much experimentation and consideration he opted for a form of the latter. Plastic explosives would be sealed into fruit cans labelled guavas to enable him to smuggle them through UK's border security. Once there the cans would be packed into a briefcase with ball bearing glued inside and with reinforcing on one side to turn it into a directional claymore. Brice conducted close-in reconnaissances of the Royal Gardens Hotel, Kensington where Mugabe was staying. He watched his daily comings and goings through the lobby until he had established precisely where and when the bomb could be planted and most effectively detonated.

The code word for the operation was 'See you in November'. When the ground had been minutely studied, Mugabe's movements to and from Lancaster House mapped and the bomb prepared, Brice telephoned his contact in Johannesburg.

'Will I be seeing you in November?' he asked

'No', came the reply, 'we will not be seeing you in November'.

The mission had been aborted by persons unknown and for reasons that remain obscure to this very day. Was it the jitters? Was it the old Rhodesian 'let's wait and see'? Brice suspected an MI6 mole in Rhodesian intelligence — perhaps even Ken Flower. An innocent ex-SAS man on a hiking trip to Europe had been detained and questioned thoroughly as he re-entered Britain, which was a clear indication that British intelligence had been tipped off. Someone at a very senior level in Britain was protecting Mugabe.

Had Brice been given the signal to go ahead and kill Mugabe, he would undoubtedly have succeeded and the history of Rhodesia/Zimbabwe would have been very different. Meantime on a political front, Mugabe was also the subject of a conspiracy that in his eyes at least was probably no less sinister. Without question, Thatcher and her Cabinet wanted to recognise Zimbabwe-Rhodesia, and in this they were probably supported by most of the centrists and Conservatives in the British establishment. While they could not openly do so, Mugabe suspected that they would try to do so on any pretext. If they succeeded it would mean an end to sanctions and, effectively an end to the war. It would also most certainly be the end of Mugabe's personal bid for power.

Mugabe might well have been paranoid, but it was a paranoia that was justified. From his vantage point on the fringes of the conference, Ken Flower also thought he caught a sniff of conspiracy. Occasional rumours and hints suggested that the British intended to try and nudge the Patriotic Front into staging a walk-out. If this could be achieved, then the conference could go on ratify a solution that would avoid taking into account the input of the extremist elements.

A walk-out was precisely what Mugabe had in mind, but it had to be planned in such a way that he could not be held personally responsible. He needed to expose the conference as a sham, while at the same time giving Samora Machel no possible excuse to withdraw his sponsorship of the war. To achieve this, Mugabe needed to play his game very diligently, which he cert6ainly did.

But for better or for worse, the chairman of the conference was in every respect as cunning and Machiavellian as Robert Mugabe. Lord Peter Carrington had his eye on Mugabe, but he was not as determined to exclude him from the deal as Mugabe supposed. Carrington had cut his political teeth during the Winds of Change period, and his cue with regard to colonial disengagement was taken largely from Macmillan. But it was not Mugabe who was languishing in the crosshairs of Carrington's sights, but Ian Douglas Smith.

Smith was a much easier man for a fellow warrior like Carrington to like, and of course he was more culturally in tune with the British than Mugabe could ever be. It also helped Carrington in no small way that Smith had the most lamentable understanding of constitutional law. Smith had arrived in London believing that any new constitution arrived at would be subject to the approval of the parliament of Zimbabwe-Rhodesia, and as a consequence he thought that he would still be able to engineer the blocking of its adoption. That was his secret weapon. He was therefore dismayed and enraged when Chief Justice Hector Macdonald arrived in London and briefed the Muzorewa delegation on the true constitutional position. In his memoirs, Smith went as far as accusing Macdonald of treason. Despite this, the message was simple,: Britain did not recognise the Muzorewa government or the Zimbabwe-Rhodesia Constitution.

Thus Smith lost control of events and was effectively shunted aside as an anachronism. His very existence was a brake on the sad but inevitable business at hand. Nevertheless, the British knew they had a fight on their hands, and Margaret Thatcher, who played no direct role, was monitoring events very carefully.

> I had no illusions about the scale of the task ahead: it was never going to be easy to steer
> Rhodesia to independence, legitimacy and stability.[1]

How seriously she took the matter was evidenced by the fact that Lord Carrington had been chosen to chair the conference. The lowly Ivor Richard had hosted Geneva, but the Foreign Secretary himself chaired Lancaster House. If this was not enough, it is arguable that Carrington was the most accomplished and determined Foreign Secretary that the office had seen for almost 30 years. He was no experimental newcomer like David Owen. He was an Eton and Sandhurst graduate who had succeeded his father as the 6th Baron Carrington in 1938, and had taken up his seat in the House of Lords at the tender age of 21. He rose to the rank of major in the Grenadier Guards during World War-II, and from there served a number of British Prime Ministers including Churchill and Anthony Eden. He was later appointed High Commissioner to Australia, and by the time he joined Margaret Thatcher's Cabinet he had been in public office for 34 years. He was more than ready to deal with a problem that had vexed Whitehall almost from the moment that the Union Jack first felt the buffet of a Mashonaland wind.

Carrington and Mugabe both had secret weapons. Carrington's was his stooped and vaguely owlish appearance, which along with a sometimes detached demeanour, made him appear bungling and obtuse. Smith swallowed the ruse and made the mistake of treating Carrington accordingly. Mugabe on the other hand, although to a degree uncertain about Carrington's ultimate purpose, at no time mistook him for a fool. Mugabe's secret weapon was infinitely less subtle but no less effective. He introduced as his press secretary the theatrical and acerbic Edson Zvobgo, who was to act as his cruder alter ego as well as to ensure that no opportunity was lost to exploit the power of the press. Zvobgo was an interesting character. He had batted at one time or another for all the main nationalist teams and had all the relevant credentials of detention, self-education and membership of the Rhodesian bar. He had a viciously caustic turn of phrase that was perfectly adapted to represent Mugabe's mood of the moment.

It was Zvobgo's job to regurgitate the events of the Lancaster House Conference into suitable vignettes for the consumption of the press. Apart from this, he was permitted to entertain himself in any way he chose. He commonly drank himself into insensibility and deployed such verbal flourishes as telling Margaret Thatcher she could jump in the Thames. Thatcher could quite easily have shredded Zvobgo's back with a thorough lashing of her own tongue, but she never did.

Zvobgo gave a public face to ZANU's position that was a notable evolution in the use of the media. The Foreign Office would occasionally strike back with a luke-warm poke in the ribs such as suggesting that Zvobgo was a drunkard — to which the accused would usually agree. The most important result of his monopoly of Patriotic Front press statements, however, was that Joshua Nkomo was given almost no opportunity to make any of his own. Zvobgo was, and remained for many years, Robert Mugabe's man.

Carrington perceived very quickly that the only way the Conference could be brought to a satisfactory finale was to settle matters in such a way that Robert Mugabe was guaranteed victory. If things did not go the way of the ZANU leader, he would extricate himself from the Conference and move in some way to destroy its credibility. Carrington therefore pondered two possible strategies. The easiest — and in the short term that most likely to succeed — would be a second-class solution that came to be known euphemistically as the 'low road'. The 'low road' was Mugabe's darkest fear. It required that the Patriotic Front be pushed to walk out, allowing the delegates to pursue a settlement with Muzorewa. This would be legitimised by the fact that Nkomo would be likely to be drawn in to include himself in some capacity. The 'high road', or the all-party route, would be infinitely more difficult to achieve, although it would do no more than ameliorate losses to the other parties. But it was the route that Carrington preferred and the one that he doggedly pursued. He used the 'low road' only as a threat from time to time to anchor Mugabe to reasonable commitments.

On a practical level, Carrington's strategy was to break the process up into units and deal with each conclusively before moving on to the next. On this basis he dealt with and disposed of the constitutional issue first. This was achieved with deceptive ease. One minor difficulty was deciding the number of seats to be reserved for whites. The 28 agreed under the Zimbabwe-Rhodesia Constitution were reduced to 20. Also removed was the constitutional blocking mechanism that had been attached to those seats. To compensate, minority rights — including civil service jobs, pensions, homeowners and land rights — were protected by a Bill of Rights that was guaranteed against amendment for ten years. The Civil Service lost the general protection it enjoyed under the Zimbabwe-Rhodesia Constitution. A clause labelled 'the Presidential Directive' allowed the President, on the advice of the Prime Minister, to appoint personnel to key administrative positions that made the Constitution a great deal more acceptable to the black intelligentsia. The requirement that the Cabinet be based on proportional representation was omitted, which meant that ministerial selection was entirely the prerogative of the Prime Minister.

The only moments of real crisis during this phase of the discussions, came over the question of land. Current ownership rights would be entrenched, forcing the incoming government to acquire land for resettlement via the willing buyer/willing seller principle. Mugabe almost threw in the towel at this point. Not only was this historically skewed but it would place an intolerable burden on the fiscus. The war, after all, had been fought primarily over the question of stolen lands. It seemed to be a fair point and was smoothed over only by assurances that the money for land purchases would be made available by Whitehall.

With this out of the way, Mugabe provisionally accepted the terms. It was Bishop Muzorewa who unexpectedly dithered. His difficulty was finding a consensus in a delegation made up of the disparate elements of his UANC, Ndabaningi Sithole and members of his chapter of ZANU, Chief Kayisa Ndweni's United Federal Party and, of course, the Rhodesian Front.

Muzorewa might have achieved more if he had not been so obviously overawed by Mugabe. He was also unable to make effective use of the experience of either Ian Smith or Ndabaningi Sithole since both were politically suspect. Much of the time he had no choice but to depend on Carrington to ensure fair play. However, what Muzorewa was most guilty of — and in this he was joined by a good many influential whites — was being too willing to fall in with British assurances that he and they were both on the same side. Neither side wanted a Marxist government in control and it was perceived, and hoped, that the British would push things in the right direction. Dissension came mainly from the white members of Muzorewa's coalition who voiced concern about the white protection clauses. Driven to despair, Muzorewa issued an ultimatum and amid much grumbling, seat shifting and threats, he managed to muster an unwilling but broad consensus.

On 3 October, details of the new constitution were published. At this point Carrington was introduced to Mugabe's favourite tactic, and in a complete volte-face, the Patriotic Front rejected the constitution in its entirety and demanded a renegotiation from scratch. Carrington was ready, however, and immediately announced that he would proceed to discuss the transitional arrangements with Muzorewa with or without the Patriotic Front. The existence of the 'low road' strategy was leaked and Carrington hinted that he had the full support of the Prime Minister. After some tense moments the ploy worked and a fortnight later the Patriotic Front gave in and accepted the proposals.

The transitional arrangements always promised to be difficult, and indeed they were. Muzorewa's decision to step down in favour of a British governor, was perhaps the moment of highest drama in the Rhodesian camp. Such an event was unprecedented anywhere in Africa and it cut to the core of the Rhodesian dilemma. Once power had been removed, it could not be reclaimed without renewed process. If the British retook control they could then impose their own solution and no one could move forward without a return to legality. Of course the Patriotic Front rejected outright any suggestion that the current unrecognised government should oversee any transition period.

The answer was obvious. The weakest link was Muzorewa, and Carrington immediately went to work on him. The interim Prime Minister was immediately plunged into an awful quandary. His Government had been in office for nine months and had been able to survive only because of white support. If he willingly handed over power, how could he return to the people as a strong man? Mugabe was getting his way…he was the strong man, and it was against him that an election would have to be fought. And yet for the greater good, Muzorewa had no choice. Ken flower put this fact to him, and pointed out that the wages of his sin would be ignominy, when the day inevitably came that the British would betray him. By then it would be too late to speak for himself. He would go down in history as the yes-man that Smith had known all along that he was, even when Smith for once would have preferred that he was not.

With all this weighing on his mind, Muzorewa therefore allowed himself to be lied to. Carrington warmly assured him that he would be back in Government House in no time. This and similar assurances were too easily made and were underlined by feverish shuttling between the delegations as the British tried to keep the Conference afloat. Threats, double dealing and unrecorded commitments were the pontoons. A top British official admitted that keeping things together so far had been an enormous con job.[2] 'Of course everyone knows that you are going to be the incoming Prime Minister', Carrington assured a morbid Bishop, 'so you may leave your slippers behind in your office to await your return.'[3]

Smith was more realistic and complained bitterly to Carrington that once Muzorewa had given up office, the chances of him ever retrieving it were almost zero. There was no possibility that he could win an election that included Mugabe and Nkomo. This was not, he was quick to add, because of questions of popularity, but simply because of the violence and intimidation already taking place in the countryside.

Carrington disagreed. 'My dear Mr Smith', he replied in typical Foreign Office language, 'I want to assure you that our whole strategy has been formulated to ensure that your prognosis will not eventuate. Quite the reverse. We have no doubt that your next government will be formed by a combination of Muzorewa, Nkomo and Smith. Moreover, should your worst fears materialise with a victory for the external factions, the leader will be Nkomo and not Mugabe.'[4]

Once again Smith might have had something to say about a metropolitan Englishman telling him how things worked in Africa. He looked to the blacks in his delegation for support but found them mentally falling in behind Muzorewa. Their weariness in the face of an almost unstoppable Patriotic Front momentum deeply saddened Smith. Without authority, though, he could do nothing but watch with dismay.

Whites wondering what was going on were calmed somewhat by a pledge from Carrington, that a kind of promissory note would be drafted that would secretly give the Muzorewa government full authority over the election process, and that the Governor would be answerable to this understanding. If the Patriotic Front broke the terms of the ceasefire — and in some quarters this was seen as almost inevitable — Carrington undertook to immediately proscribe the Party. Muzorewa and his white cabal would then be back in the driving seat and they could drive wherever they wanted. When written confirmation of this commitment did not appear, Muzorewa made inquiries, in response to which the British tittered and prevaricated in expected fashion. Of course it could never actually be put in writing. It would be simply too explosive! The Rhodesians would have to rely on a 'gentleman's agreement'.

On 27 October Lieutenant-General Peter Walls appeared at the Conference in order to lend his weight. While the arrival of Rhodesia's top soldier threatened hellfire on any dissidents to the process, Walls privately absorbed the ritual of British trench diplomacy like a sponge. Carrington invited him to his apartment where in the personable atmosphere of his parlour he delivered a vital assurance. If Muzorewa was to step down and power returned to the British, then Walls could take Carrington's word that he would remain in charge of the Army, would not be answerable to the Governor and could continue his cross-border operations during the transition period. If any problems occurred with this arrangement, Carrington promised Walls that he would have direct access to Margaret Thatcher. Nothing in writing again, and Walls could make of it what he would.

By then dialogue was moving on to the question of cease-fire arrangements. Walls took strength from his interview with Carrington and presented to the Conference the largely unsubdued face of militant white Rhodesia. If Smith was shackled by irrelevance, then Walls was next in line as the white man most to be feared.

While he had latterly been forced to admit that without a political settlement Salisbury would soon be threatened, Walls was suddenly offering himself as a coup master in the event of white Rhodesia's future being too severely compromised. When pressed he agreed that a political solution was vital, but reminded his audience that without military might, a political solution was apt to resemble a rout. He also warned that if the Patriotic Front did not toe the line more visibly and negotiate in a spirit of co-operation, it would be crushed as an outsider once political and economic normality had returned under Muzorewa.

Until that moment Carrington had almost succeeded in persuading Mugabe to accept that the British Governor would base his transitional government on the existing white-dominated civil and security service. Mugabe, however, was starting to feel insecure and was not about to be outmanoeuvred. He pointed the finger at Carrington and accused him of trying to usher in Muzorewa on the back of an administration biased in his favour. Mugabe demanded that the United Nations be mandated to bring in a peacekeeping force and that the Rhodesian Army be demobilised. To this Carrington simply shook his head. Mugabe's voice then rose an octave. 'Unless Lord Carrington relents', he cried, 'we will pack our bags and go back to war!'[5] The conference was immediately frozen in breathless anticipation as Walls, Smith and Muzorewa waited in silence. Prayers were spoken that for once Mugabe would be as good as his word.

Balancing on a knife-edge, Mugabe played a doubtful hand that had no great chance of success. He returned to his weary allies in the Frontline States and called for some statement of unequivocal support for the continuation of the war. Both Nyerere and Machel rallied to his side and the necessary verbiage flowed back to Lancaster House. Mugabe could then stand with his allies behind him and metaphorically raise his fist to the continuation of the war.

Obviously the question was not one of who could shout the loudest — for the shouting war had often been louder than the shooting war — but who would blink first. Neither Carrington nor Mugabe gave any ground until Kenneth Kaunda put in a personal appearance and showed for the first time a crack in the façade of Frontline support. He sat down with Nkomo and Mugabe and listened to a litany of complaints while he waited for his moment to issue a simple message of warning. In both Mozambique and Zambia tolerance for the war had reached its limits. Although this did not mean peace at any price, it also did not mean war at any price.

While this meeting sobered Mugabe, it did not entirely divert him. Kaunda was Nkomo's man, not his. Mugabe saw him as a weak character — a weeping humanitarian who was not a fit soul to lead an African nation. Mugabe did accept, however, that this was not the right moment to precipitate a split and compromised sufficiently to see the process moving forward. While he was unable to oust the Rhodesian Security Forces entirely from their proposed role in the transition process, Mugabe at least was able to gain legal recognition for his own ZANLA army. It was duly inserted in paragraph 13 of the interim proposals that 'The Patriotic Forces will be required to comply with the directives of the Governor'.

General Walls' gruff comment on this concession was: 'If anybody shoots at us we will stop them shooting anymore.'[6] If that 'anybody' entertained lingering doubts about the General's earnestness, they would have been disabused by intelligence coming in from Zambia. A series of dramatic SAS penetrations into that country echoed *Operation Uric* in another codenamed Operation Dice. Dice completely crippled Zambia's transport network by blowing up a series of bridges on the roads from Lusaka to Livingstone, Chirundu and Tanzania. Operations Cheese and Tepid destroyed bridges north of Lusaka and effectively severed Zambia's rail and road links with Tanzania. The objective of these attacks was threefold: firstly to send the same stark message to Kaunda as had recently been delivered to Machel; secondly to frustrate preparations for a Russian/Cuban-backed conventional assault on Rhodesia; and thirdly to deliver a killing blow to the Zambian economy. On 18 September, the SAS — again with the help of the South African navy and Recces — launched another seaborne raid on Beira, this time with the intention of scuttling the dredger fleet in the harbour mouth. Beira's deep-water harbour depended on working dredgers, because without them the harbour would silt up rapidly. Two out of three were sunk, after which normal operations did not recommence for six months. In fact, it is arguable whether they ever did.[7]

Now that an all-party election seemed imminent, Nkomo became anxious to ensure that as many ZIPRA units as possible were infiltrated into Rhodesia. It was vital that he had the capacity to match Mugabe in proving his axiom that 'one man with a gun is worth a thousand votes'. But Nkomo's ability to mobilise was dramatically arrested by the SAS raids and he found himself at something of a tactical disadvantage. A month or two later, white Rhodesians realised they hated Mugabe more than they hated Nkomo, whereupon they had cause to regret the latter's failure to muster his forces effectively.

The next bone that Mugabe began to chew was the issue of practical cease-fire arrangements. Justifiably, he was outraged at proposals that his forces be maintained in assembly points dotted around the country. Even an amateur military strategist would concede that this placed them at the mercy of the Rhodesian Security Forces which would still have effective control of the country. An emergency meeting of the Frontline Presidents was convened in Dar-es-Salaam, and attended by both Machel and Nyerere. Kaunda, however, stayed away to attend to the ongoing military punishment of his national infrastructure.

Mugabe and Nkomo flew to Dar-es-Salaam to once again put their case to their allies. Again they were sternly warned that while they were not expected to capitulate, it was to be borne in mind that the Frontline leaders wanted an end to the war. Mugabe was marched back to Lancaster House glumly muttering: 'We will be going back to London to negotiate.'[8]

He and Nkomo returned to the Conference insisting that the Rhodesian Army be confined to its bases before his men would come in from the countryside. Mugabe's obsession with a conspiracy between Muzorewa and Carrington had been replaced by another — that the South Africans were poised to bomb the assembly points in the event that a solution was not to their taste. He now demanded the public neutering of any possibility of South African interference, but this was obviously beyond the powers of the British to achieve. A ripple of dismay spread through the Foreign Office and for the first time Carrington found himself seriously pondering the 'low road' option.

Commonwealth Secretary General Sonny Ramphal partially diffused the crisis by drafting a declaration that Mugabe grudgingly accepted. It stated that under a British Governor there would be no external interference, and that the Rhodesian Security Forces would be placed under exactly the same restrictions as the guerrilla forces. During the transition phase law and order would instead be attended to by a 1 200-man Commonwealth Monitoring Force. Mugabe initially accepted this, but then insisted that the statement prohibiting outside involvement specifically mention South Africa. Carrington was unable to implement this and the situation reached another impasse.

Carrington let it be known that he was of a mind to continue the Conference without the Patriotic Front. Mugabe, of course, dug in his heels. Carrington conceded and a dangerous precedent was set. It began to look as though Mugabe was gradually forcing the tide. The cease-fire question was put away but that was not the end of it. The South African question, in terms of wording a declaration, was simply a rhetorical point. Mugabe now moved to push for more substantive gains.

In the meantime a Governor had been selected, in the form of Lord Christopher Soames. Much of Soames will be heard later, but for the present he was sent to take up office in Salisbury on 11 December 1979, some time before negotiations in London were completed. To send out a Governor with little or no constitutional, military or executive control was a bold if desperate move on Carrington's part, to try and force the pace of the conference. Edson Zvobgo put the issue in perspective by musing in public that it appeared the Patriotic Front was now at war with Britain. This certainly was the risk if things fell apart after the date of Soames' occupation of Government House.

This did not stop Carrington from continuing to heap on the pressure. He unveiled plans for a ceasefire which decreed that the Rhodesian Army was to have 47 operational bases and the Patriotic Front just 14. This in itself did not produce the outcry. That came from the fact that neither ZIPRA nor ZANLA were to be given an assembly point within the white farming areas of the central watershed, or in the economic heartland of the country. Therein lay the seeds of the biggest crisis of the negotiations so far.

For Mugabe, the moment had at last arrived when he could seize the moral high ground and retreat from the Conference with a justifiable grievance. He insisted that this dispensation would have a crucially negative psychological effect on his men. Fighters moving towards the assembly points situated on the fringes would be seen as evacuating the vital strategic zone, which would give the impression of defeat. This he could not accept. It was also probably fair to say that neither he nor his military command could realistically have persuaded ZANLA to leave an area they had fought for, and held for so long. Unspoken was the fact that isolated assembly points would limit guerrilla access to the population, and that would limit their ability to intimidate. There was no conceivable way that the Rhodesians and Mugabe were going to see eye-to-eye on this.

The impression that Carrington might have lost his grip, was then abruptly stripped away. He allowed the uproar to wash over him and proceeded to name Saturday 15 December as the deadline for acceptance of the terms of the cease-fire. Thereafter the Conference would wrap up with or without the Patriotic Front. Thus the stage was set for another round of brinkmanship. On the Friday before the deadline, Zvobgo called a press conference at which he declared in the most animated terms that Carrington could go to hell.

> The answer is a clear and eloquent "No" to Carrington: the answer is "No" and he and his Governor can go hang.[9]

As the deadline arrived, Mugabe apologised for his press secretary's excesses but reiterated that the answer was 'No'. Carrington sighed and flew to Washington with Margaret Thatcher for an official visit, leaving the situation temporarily in hiatus. He was confident, however, that on his return he would find Mugabe in agreement.

Carrington sensed that the moment was almost ripe to reveal his hand. For 15 weeks he had sat and endured the boorish behaviour of Zvobgo, the simpering coercion of Nkomo, the hand rubbing and indecisive pleas from a tearful and overwrought Muzorewa, the angry exhortations of Smith and the cold and devious manipulations of Mugabe. Carrington, however, knew one man at least who had the courage and honesty to go so far and no further. Before he left for Washington he put a telephone call through to Maputo and through an interpreter warned Samora Machel that his protégé had just packed up and was leaving town. It was his intention to fly to the United States and gain support for a continuation of the war. That, for all intents and purposes, would be the end of the Lancaster House Conference.[10] Carrington may or may not have also made the point to Machel that since a British Governor was resident in Salisbury, if Mugabe went back to war he would in turn drag Mozambique into a war with Britain. In the light of modern entente, how did this sound in Maputo?

Samora Machel was appalled. Mugabe had gambled that a fait accompli based on such unbearable provocation would force the Mozambican President to grasp the nettle. No such thing. Machel immediately dispatched his London Ambassador to Heathrow where Mugabe was narrowly intercepted. It was made absolutely clear to the ZANU leader that if he left the Conference at this point he could expect a comfortable villa in Mozambique but no more. Seeing the light, Mugabe cancelled his flight and returned in a state of utter abjection to his London hotel. A few days later, on 21 December — after a total of 47 plenary sessions — the Lancaster House Agreement was signed.

See! — We Told You So

Although Smith did not attend the signing ceremony, the Rhodesian Front held a caucus meeting and made the rather academic decision to accept the terms of the Lancaster House Agreement. Most whites, although it was a less than perfect solution, felt a significant weight of anxiety lift from their hearts. Most adopted a wait and see attitude and got on with their day-to-day lives. A general understanding prevailed, fuelled by rumour, hope, denial and all the other human traits of survival, that Mugabe was unlikely to win an outright majority, and even if he did there was still the army to take care of any unpleasant surprises.

There was also a tendency to believe British assurances that even the merest hint of foul play would result in the banning of the guilty party. Terrorists would be confined to assembly points and could do no damage, besides which white Rhodesians were tending now to look upon Nkomo in a more friendly light. Even if the Bishop failed to achieve his expected majority, a coalition government would be formed with Nkomo that would at all costs exclude Mugabe.

Mugabe of course had other plans. Before the ink on the agreement was dry, hundreds —indeed thousands of ZANLA guerrillas were channelled into the country in contravention of the cease-fire agreement. Nkomo was trying to do the same, but he had been hampered by Rhodesian military action along the Zambezi River. Besides this, Nkomo had tended to follow the advice of his ubiquitous Russian military advisors in allowing his forces to build up their conventional capacity outside Rhodesia. He had therefore limited the number of his military personnel actually deployed into Rhodesia that now left him at a distinct disadvantage.

Mugabe as usual was prepared to gamble. This time he was gambling that the British would not provoke a political incident by appearing to be too eager to ban his party. Although Carrington had scored a coup at Lancaster House, he had in doing so learned that Mugabe was a dangerous man. Proscribing ZANU would not be easy. Categorical proof of impropriety was almost impossible to obtain from behind a screen of black silence. Two other factors also tended to work in Mugabe's favour. The first of these was the removal from the scene of a very unlikely moderate in the form of Josiah Tongogara.

Tongogara had been a perennial in the political process since the early 1970s. While his fortunes had ebbed and flowed he remained a dark horse in the eyes of Rhodesian whites. It came as a pleasant surprise then, to among others General Walls and Ian Smith, when at Lancaster House a moderate side to Tongogara's nature was revealed. The three at different times held a series of pleasant conversations which were in fact the only instances of social intercourse that were attempted across the ideological divide. Smith was reminded of old times, when Tongogara enquired after the health of his mother, Agnes. Agnes Smith had employed a young Josiah Tongogara as a garden hand when the guerrilla leader was still a boy. Tongogara remembered the kind treatment he had received at the hands of the old lady, that naturally softened considerably Smith's natural suspicion of one of Rhodesia's primary enemies. As an aside to this story, and after Tongogara's death, Smith received a curious message from 'some Portuguese chap' in Maputo wondering how he could ship a parcel of prawns to Smith's mother. This was from Tongogara who had ordered the consignment of prawns as a gift to Agnes Smith. Carrington also found Tongogara a crucial moderating force.

Tongogara's position on the future was that unity between ZANU and ZAPU was essential for post independence reconstruction. Without a strong and united nationalist front, Zimbabwe would immediately split along tribal lines. An expensive and bloody equalization would then be needed before the new nation could grow. To Mugabe such sentimentality was irrelevant, and he had no such thing in mind. He suffered no particular fear of equalisation, besides which the Patriotic Front was largely a spent force, and Nkomo no man to share power with. Mugabe wanted sole authority, and he wanted a one party state. In Africa, men had always deferred to the 'big man' and big men do not share power. Most worrying about Tongogara, was that he took the whole Lancaster House business far too seriously. Left to him, ZANLA forces would have complied with the cease-fire terms and reported to their respective assembly points. Violence and political intimidation would then have been checked. This would of course have seriously inconvenienced Mugabe's plans.

Tongogara died in a car accident while travelling up the road from Maputo to Beira late on Christmas Eve. He was on his way north to brief the various camp commanders on the new rules of play. Rex Nhongo later claimed in an election speech that Tongogara had been murdered because he favoured the cease-fire and opposed Mugabe. The truth of this assertion has never been proven but it is a belief held by many. Officially Tongogara's death was ruled an accident. Edgar Tekere, who in later years was no particular friend of Mugabe's and who exposed many other controversial claims, stated categorically that Mugabe was not involved.

The official version states that Tongogara was driving a Land Rover north on a moonless night when he attempted to overtake a lorry. While surging forward on the right hand side of Mozambique's main trunk road, his vehicle hit the back of a second lorry that was displaying no rear lights. Gauging the condition of Mozambique's roads and the general standards of vehicle maintenance at this time, there is nothing implausible in this story. ZANU, however, set alarm bells ringing when it released an undertakers report without autopsy results or any supporting pictures, that stated Tongogara's injuries were consistent with a car accident. In the meantime, an eye–witness claimed to have seen Tongogara shot three times, and then bludgeoned with an axe in order that his injuries might seem consistent with a car accident.[1] An ex-member of the law and order section of the BSAP, was later able to see a photograph of the body and claimed to be able to identify three bullet holes.[2] Both the Soviet and US Ambassadors to Zambia declared the death to be an inside job.[3] Why the British, in particular Governor Soames, did not insist on a proper autopsy being conducted probably had much to do with their unwillingness to provoke any histrionics from ZANU, and not to interfere in any way with the nominally smooth progress of the elections.

Whatever might have been the truth, Tongogara's death opened the way for Rex Nhongo, a far less scrupulous man than he, to assume the military leadership of ZANLA. This in turn opened the way to the misuse of the armed forces, that in the end influenced to no small degree the outcome of the election.

The second thing that worked in Mugabe's favour, was that the Englishman he was now in direct conflict with was not the shrewd and manipulative Lord Carrington, but a much more avuncular character in the form of Governor Lord Christopher Soames. Soames was a corpulent and amiable member of the British Parliament, and one time War Secretary when no war existed. He had otherwise served in such government portfolios as Agriculture, Fisheries and Food, and more congenially as British Ambassador to France. He had never served in any school that could teach him how to grapple with Africa's fiercest intellectual warrior.

It can be said of Soames, however, that he was at least pragmatic. From the moment that he arrived in the country he was assailed by complaints from all the moderate parties that the extremists, and

ZANU in particular, had already begun the process of black politicisation with customary brutality. Soames shrugged his shoulders when asked by the press what he intended to do about it: 'I want to see the freest, fairest elections possible in this country,' he said, 'but intimidation is rife, and I've got to do everything I can to minimise this.' The Governor then went on to illustrate his predicament with perhaps the most memorable quote of the entire Rhodesian saga. 'You must remember,' he said, 'this is Africa. This isn't Little Puddleton-in-the-Marsh, and they behave differently here. They think nothing of sticking tent poles up each other's whatnot, and doing filthy, beastly things to each other. It does happen, I'm afraid. It's a very wild thing, an election.'[4]

Wild indeed. Soames was forced into breaking the terms of the cease-fire agreement himself when he agreed to the redeployment of the Rhodesian Security Forces along the eastern border, in a forlorn attempt to try and stem the inflow of ZANLA combatants. This was undeniably forlorn since, in eight years of war the Rhodesian Army had failed to achieve just that. Meanwhile, as hundreds of guerrillas slipped in through the back door, others came in through the front. On Boxing Day 1980, the first of the bona fide returnees began to make their way home. Thousands of cheering blacks gathered at Salisbury Airport to welcome home 82 ZANLA and ZIPRA military commanders. Rex Nhongo stepped onto the tarmac and walked towards the terminal hand in hand with senior ZIPRA Commander Lookout Msuku, and a fortnight later Simon Muzenda, Mugabe's Deputy in the newly named ZANU Patriotic Front, or ZANU-PF, arrived at the airport at the head of a group of 108 party officials. These, of course, included a grinning and slightly inebriated Edison Zvobgo.

A few days later Joshua Nkomo landed in the company of a girl's choir and was promptly airlifted from the tarmac to a welcoming rally in Highfields. There, a huge crowd, including thousands of ZAPU supporters, specially bussed in from Bulawayo, greeted him. The elephantine ZAPU leader then launched into an attack on Mugabe and ZANU for failing to agree to run with him in the election. He triumphantly claimed the name Patriotic Front for himself. ZAPU was now PF ZAPU. Nkomo also made a point of calling on Ian Smith, with whom he discussed the possibility of a coalition government.

Smith had by then been fully briefed on the intimidation underway in the countryside, and was more or less resigned to the fact that Mugabe was heading towards an outright majority. As he wrote later in his biography: '…those poor, defenceless, confused people had got the message — did they want to remain alive or not?'[5] Smith did approach General Walls in order to press him to reveal exactly what plans he had in the event of a whitewash. Walls was reluctant to reveal much but was prepared to concede, truthfully or otherwise, that in the final event he did not intend to allow Mugabe to win.[6]

In those final days, it became the turn of Salisbury's whites to gather in numbers at the airport to witness the novel sight of RAF Hercules transporters and American Lockheed C141 Starlifters, arriving with the 1 200 men of the Commonwealth Cease-fire Monitoring Force. Rhodesian whites were then treated to the even more novel sight of a flood of foreign troops in their country. These were mainly from the United Kingdom and the dominions, and were welcomed into the country without reservation. Welcome also was the handful of black Englishmen, many of whom were invited to private homes just for the novelty of hearing them speak Brummy, Geordie or Cockney. It was uniquely amusing for whites to observe the astonishment on the faces of the black cooks and houseboys, who served up meals to other black men sitting in the living room, sharing a beer and chatting about England with the *Baas*.

As these brief and cordial exchanges took place, the Monitoring process itself slipped into gear. Roughly 500 of the CFMF troops were deployed into the countryside to take up positions at the various assembly points. The remainder, acting in staff and liaison capacities, settled into hotels and motels, in the various smaller centres around the country. ZANLA and ZIPRA in the meantime, established their operational headquarters at the Teacher Training College Hostel attached to the

University in Mount Pleasant. The Commonwealth Monitoring Force Commander, Major-General John Acland, set up his Salisbury headquarter at Morgan High School in Arcadia.

Guerrilla entry into the assembly points was initially slow, due to the obvious and not unjustified suspicion of attack. Rhodesian territorial units were temporarily suspended while the RLI and other regular units were confined to their operational bases. From there they pondered the gathering of their once elusive enemies into easily containable groups, and do doubt there were many who would have taken no persuasion at all to gather their weapons and move in to finish the job.

In the end, the Governor gave the guerrillas a deadline of 2 January to assemble. By that date only about 12 000 had actually done so, meaning that the majority were still at large. Soames was himself conscious that the temptation to strike might overwhelm the middle level command of the Rhodesian Army. It would be relatively easy to mobilise the old formations of Fireforce and move in rapidly to obliterate the assembly points. While officially Soames declined to extend the deadline, it was reasonably decided that the assembly points should remain open to accept incoming guerrillas for a further two days. By that time an estimated 18 000 were held in camps, which, according to the two guerrilla Commanders, Rex Nhongo and Lookout Masuku, accounted for the majority.

Rex Nhongo assiduously denied Rhodesian claims that the majority of assembly point arrivals were mujibas wielding out of service weaponry dug up from old arms caches. Edison Zvobgo was prepared years later to be more candid. He was interviewed for a Granada Television production dealing with the end of the British Empire in which he admitted:

> But when we were asked to declare how many guerrillas we had, we chose to declare 20000. If everybody thought we had 8 000, and we were willing to deliver 20 000, then clearly we didn't have anybody else left. In fact we had a very large army left, who remained as political commissars in the country simply to ensure that we would win the election.[7]

If Soames was prepared to overlook some of these more obvious breaches of the cease-fire agreement, he left it to his spokesman Nicholas Fenn to express official Government House dismay. Fenn concluded that there had been: '…substitution by young thugs and others of guerrillas for the purpose of intimidating the rural population.'[8] In this, Fenn was absolutely correct, for Commonwealth monitoring personnel had been given instructions to classify anybody, regardless of age or sex, who was carrying a weapon of any sort, as a combatant. Local youth and mujibas were without doubt given oddments of weaponry and sent into the camps posing as trained terrorists. This left thousands of fighters at liberty in the countryside to politicise and campaign for ZANU.

As far as methods of intimidation went in fact, much of the trench work had already been done. Many tribesmen had by then died horrible deaths in the name of unity and the fact that this fate awaited sell-outs did not need to be reinforced. Weapons were cashed in plain sight of local tribesmen, who needed no reminder of how bad it could get if the line was not towed. The most persuasive threat was that if ZANU did not win the election it would take the country back to war. Unsophisticated peasants could not be expected to read the wider dynamics and see this as a lie. What they saw was what they believed, and what they saw was evidence of ZANLA force. There was no longer any sign of the Rhodesian Army in the countryside, which implied nationalist victory, as indeed it probably was.

In the face of this, there was very little that either Soames or Nicholas Fenn could do in practical terms. Soames had no choice but to rely on the Rhodesian Security Forces to maintain order in the country, which he did with no direct control over their deployment. The only force that he had under his direct control was the Commonwealth Cease-fire Monitoring Force, which numbered only 1 200 men. Being lightly armed it had little chance of imposing any authority on a hostile situation in a tempered war zone. It was, as its name implied, a force conceived not to enforce the cease-fire but merely to monitor it.

Soames was also aware that politically it would be almost impossible to completely proscribe ZANU-PF. He was prepared to censure the party symbolically, but could see that there was little he could do beyond that. ZANU was not permitted to import its vehicles or its more militant campaign literature, while permission was withheld briefly for Mugabe to return to Rhodesia. The ostensible reason for this fluctuated between Mugabe's refusal to release many of his political prisoners still held without trial in Mozambique, and the fact that his dates would clash with other political rallies already being held in the townships.

Mugabe could see this all for what it was, and took comfort from the implications of immunity. However he narrowly avoided an assassination attempt devised by Special Branch Selous Scouts when he finally left Maputo on the morning of 27 January 1980.

A car packed with P4 plastic explosives had been rigged in South Africa by South African Special Forces engineers and driven north, where it was parked along the main road to Maputo airport. A short distance away was parked a second vehicle with two Selous Scouts operators seated ready to detonate the charge as Mugabe's motorcade passed by. When it became clear that something had gone wrong, the vehicle was reclaimed by South African recce operators and driven back home. Mugabe had been tipped off and he and 100 ZANU-PF officials were smuggled to the airport by a different route. Mugabe, his wife Sally and his entourage left Maputo on time on a Mozambique nation carrier flight and a short while later landed at Salisbury Airport.[9]

Having abandoned his London bomb plot, Alan Brice needless to say was in the thick of things again. The moment that he returned to Salisbury from London he was charged with devising a back up plan in case the Maputo car bomb plot failed to eliminate Robert Mugabe. His idea was to rig up a series of Russian TM46 anti tank mines along Queensway, the road that Mugabe would take from the airport to Salisbury city centre. These would be command detonated by Brice himself who would hide in the bushes nearby. The plan was however again called off without explanation.[10]

Soames had, in the meantime, banned public demonstrations so, after suffering a certain amount of abuse and rough handling by junior airport officials, Mugabe immediately made his way to Highfields, where the first organised ZANU mass rally was held. This was by far the largest single gathering of human beings in the history of Rhodesia so far. The city's black population massed to meet the man most knew little about, but who claimed to be the only authentic liberator of Zimbabwe. Salisbury's whites remained largely oblivious to the phenomenon, until the following morning when an aerial photograph of the event was splashed across the front page of the Rhodesia Herald. It showed a sea of humanity over 250 000 strong, stronger than the entire white population of the country, overflowing the stadium and spilling out onto the streets of Highfield. This was to be the first of many such displays, but for a debut performance it was as impressive as it was sobering. It was a buoyant Mugabe who then made his way to Government House, to meet the Governor.

There, Mugabe was promptly confronted by a dossier of evidence detailing ZANU PF's ongoing breaches of the cease-fire code. Mugabe denied nothing, but instead attacked Soames for his redeployment of the Security Forces, equally in contravention of the cease-fire protocol, and the fact that Sithole and Muzorewa's Auxiliaries appeared to be able to move freely around the country while his men were contained.

To this, Soames responded as best he could within the rough parameters of African politics. On 5 February, he issued an ordinance that gave his office the power to ban political parties from campaigning in all or part of the country. He was also empowered to disenfranchise a whole district, if he judged political intimidation to have reached a level where a free and fair election was impossible.

Of course Soames had no chance whatsoever of effectively applying this authority. Mugabe threatened to send ZANLA back to war if any level of ban was applied to his party. Thatcher and Carrington had by then washed their hands of the future and Mugabe could indulge himself in these sorts of threats without any real fear. At the same time Mugabe loudly condemned Soames as being the 'chief violator', and harkening back to Lancaster House with withering accusations against the Governor of tilting the playing field in favour of his opponents. Soames, as might be expected, wilted under the sheer force of these exchanges, and although he made one or two cursory gestures, such as banning ZANU PF activity in the some areas of the southeast, he made no serious attempt to disenfranchise ZANU PF in any area. This left Mugabe confident that so long as a vote was permitted it would go to him. He allowed his men to continue the process of politicisation regardless of the persistent and sullen cries of foul from his competitors.

Lieutenent General Peter Walls and Ken Flower were in the meantime invited to visit Maputo by FRELIMO in order to discuss their 'new relationship'. It was a surreal moment for both men who had presided over a most destructive campaign of attacks against Mozambique for many years. Both wondered, not unreasonably, whether they were walking into a death trap. However both men were treated well, and while Walls discussed questions of military interest with his counterparts, Flower was urged by Joaquim Chissano, ex-transitional leader and current Mozambique Foreign Minister, to do what he could promote Mugabe as the heir apparent in Zimbabwe. Chissano urged Flower to avoid mistakes made in Mozambique where the whites had been lost to the immediate detriment of the economy. He also asked that CIO support for MNR be stopped. This occurred but Flower personally arranged for the handover of the organisation to the South Africans, who accepted the responsibility of supporting the organisation with notable enthusiasm.

Meanwhile, back in Salisbury, and as the election campaign was drawing to a close, Muzorewa recognised the likely course of events and sought counsel from Flower on the advisability of applying more pressure on Lord Soames to ban ZANU ahead of the ballot. Flower was resigned however. The election, he told the Bishop, had already taken on a life of its own, and besides that the Frontline States would never countenance any effort at this late stage to cut ZANU out of the process. Flower felt that the British would rather see the worst result than no result at all. Muzorewa then tried to put pressure on members of ComOps to petition the Governor to postpone the election, by force if necessary, but Walls, understandably, refused to sanction force. Like Flower, he believed that it was by then too late, and matters must now be allowed to take their own course.

In the end

A nger and heartbreak tended to find sustenance in alcohol and commiseration. In bars, clubs and messes all over Rhodesia, idle servicemen gathered to contemplate a sad future. Men could take pride in the fact that, although weakened, the Rhodesian Army stood undefeated. Maverick thoughts were aired. Schemes for coups and takeovers were pondered. But the fighting discipline drilled into the orthodox services precluded any such unauthorised action. These constraints did not, of course, limit the activities of individuals, and the Selous Scouts who were by then thoroughly accustomed to operating beyond recall.

On Sunday 3 February 1980, a vicious attack was staged against a bus carrying black wedding guests from Umtali to Salisbury. It had somehow been established that the passengers were UANC supporters. A Selous Scouts call-sign of seven operators mounted an attack on the bus, that was carefully planned to mimic a typical ZANLA operation. To complete the deception, various bits of ZANLA military equipment garnished the scene as well as the body of a recently killed ZANLA guerrilla suitably roughed up to appear as if he had accidentally caught the back blast of an RPG-7 rocket. A toothbrush and toothpaste and a box of matches of the sort issued by Australian elements of the Monitoring Force, were planted to implicate ZANLA cadres camped at a nearby assembly point. The attack was pressed home in the classic guerrilla ambush style, using RPG-7 rocket launchers and AK47s. The driver was killed in the opening fusillade, causing the bus to veer off the road and overturn. A further 16 passengers were killed and at least 25 were transported by ambulance to Rusape hospital. Others were shuttled by private vehicles.[1]

ComOps issued a prompt statement blaming ZANLA guerrillas for the attack. Lord Soames did not concur, commenting that there was insufficient evidence to determine who exactly was to blame. The commander of the Monitoring Force in the Thrasher area issued a suitably general, but none the less stinging attack, describing the assault as the worst violation since the cease-fire had been declared on 28 December. All others paled into insignificance. 'It raised the question of the mentality of people who do this sort of thing.'[2]

On Valentines Day 1980, a rash of unexplained bombings occurred in the capital. The incidents are best described in Assignment Selous Scouts, author Jim Parker's account of his days in the Selous Scouts Special Branch. Parker makes public the results of recent research into this and other incidents surrounding the last days of the regime. His personal knowledge combined with interviews with many who were directly or indirectly involved, sheds new light on an array of old mysteries.

Five bombs were manufactured to deliberately poor standards and placed at the doors of a selection of churches throughout the capital. This was no doubt done to deliver the impression that this was what could be expected in the future under a government of heathen communists. One of the bombs was designed not to detonate, in order that investigators could examine it and discover the Eastern Bloc origins of the explosives and other materiels. To limit any evidence of Security Force involvement, four teams were instructed to use their own private vehicles to conduct the operation.

A passer-by observed two blacks sitting in a Renault 12 sedan with the interior lights on. The pair appeared to be fiddling with something between them when the car was abruptly demolished in a major explosion.

By means of the vehicle's registration book and a chequebook found in the glove compartment, it was not difficult to trace the origin of the bomb. The occupants were exposed as Selous Scouts operators, which left ComOps in a quandary. The deaths were made public in a simple Security Force communiqué that offered just two paragraphs of bland disinformation. In 2003, Special Branch Selous Scouts Commander Mac McGuinness denied any ComOps involvement and, in an interview with Jim Parker, claimed that the attacks were carried out by 'out of step' Selous Scouts with their own agenda.[3]

These 'out of step' elements continued to be active throughout the election campaign. On 22 February a much more sophisticated operation was conducted. It involved the circulation of a counterfeit edition of the popular black newspaper *Moto*. The front page of the very authentic looking forgery contained a scurrilous personal attack on Robert Mugabe. 'Who is Robert Mugabe?' the opening sentence asked. 'Is he an enlightened, progressive Christian leader of a people seeking their destiny, or is he a ruthless, power hungry Marxist heathen?' It was a telling question, but was spoilt further on in the article by an obviously bogus 'Psychological Analyst', which took the form of a dubious personal attack.

A few days later a small group of Selous Scouts and a member of South African Special Forces, broke into the Gwelo premises of Mambo Press and rigged up a large explosive device beside the printing press. Various additions to the crime scene were made, to give the impression that it had been a ZANLA operation, presumably to avenge the published attack on their chief. Another recent ZANLA kill was signed out of the morgue, and planted on the scene with a Tokarev pistol slipped into his pocket. The facility was completely destroyed in the ensuing blast, and when a member of Gwelo CID arrived at 03:30 he found the remains of the planted corpse. But to his astonishment he also found the dismembered remains of a white man who — even more curiously — had South African notes and coins in his pocket.

In the meantime, Robert Mugabe suffered such a barrage of direct or proposed attempts on his life during those tense weeks, that a fake edition of *Moto* with a colourful psychological analysis must have seemed quite trivial, and it was. Many people had an interest in seeing Mugabe dead, and between the time he left Maputo for a triumphant arrival in Salisbury, and receiving the laurels of Zimbabwe's first Prime Minister, he experienced quite a few narrow escapes.

Alan Brice was still feverishly working for Mugabe's demise, and his next plan had all the hallmarks of his unique resourcefulness. Mugabe had acquired a property on Quorn Avenue in the upmarket suburb of Mount Pleasant where he took up residence on his return to Rhodesia. An underground storm drain running along the front of the property could be entered through a manhole. Here Brice conspired to plant 50 kilograms of high explosive, that he intended to detonate by remote means as Mugabe made for his front door. Again the plan was inexplicably cancelled and, for the third time, Mugabe narrowly escaped a mortal brush with the deadly CIO assassin.

In the early hours of 7 February, a hand grenade was tossed over the wall and into Mugabe's property but no one was injured. A little earlier two RPG-7 rockets had been more successfully fired into the bedroom of Kumbirai Kangayi, ZANU-PF's Secretary for Welfare and Transport, seriously injuring him. There was no indication of who was behind either of these two attacks.

Another scheme of a much more ambitious nature was germinating in Bulawayo. This was a combined SAS/Selous Scouts operation focused on a ZANU-PF rally that Mugabe was scheduled to address on 9 February. The plan had two fall-back phases in case the initial attack didn't succeed. The opening gambit was to position a former Selous Scouts captain in an ambulance at the Bulawayo airport. Armed with a Soviet surface-to-air missile, he would easily be able to bring down the aircraft carrying Mugabe and his entourage. Should this fail, phase two would involve positioning a ten-man SAS team to ambush Mugabe's motorcade as it left the airport. If this also failed, phase three would then be activated. This required a black Scouts operator, with forged Drum magazine press credentials, to place a microphone packed with ball bearings and explosives on the podium where Mugabe would speak. Mugabe was again tipped off that something was afoot and cancelled the rally. As he explained to Soames, he had become aware that Nkomo and his minions were planning to assassinate him.[4]

The following day, Mugabe addressed a rally in the Mucheke Township of Fort Victoria. At 13:55 he left the venue and joined a three-vehicle convoy heading for the local airport, from where he was to fly back to Salisbury. A small SAS team had planted an explosive charge under a culvert on the access road leading to the airport. The charge was, however, detonated under the wrong vehicle.[5]

These attacks were loosely related to a more complex Security Force operation, that had been formulated to counter the possibility of Mugabe gaining an outright majority. The plan was in two parts — codenamed *Operation Hectic* and *Operation Quartz*. The former was the direct attempt to remove Mugabe by assassination, the latter to neutralise his power, in the event of his gaining a significant electoral majority. While this was not thought to be particularly likely, it was nonetheless tacitly agreed between the British and the Rhodesians that such a result was undesirable. Far more acceptable to all would be a moderate coalition of Muzorewa, Sithole and Nkomo. Senior British Foreign Office and MI6 representatives assured Superintendent Mac McGuinness that, if by happenstance Mugabe did emerge with an outright majority, Soames would be primed in advance to declare voting in certain areas null and void.

Meetings to establish all this were held in Rhodesia as the Constitutional Conference in Lancaster House was under way. It was correctly assumed by everybody that a settlement was imminent, and that all-party elections would follow. It was also taken for granted that electioneering would become violent, and that both the warring nationalist parties would make use of voter intimidation to influence the poll. A senior MI6 operator suggested that a complete dossier of all reports on intimidation should be compiled to assist the Governor, and should he be required to ban one or other of the political parties. To jump-start the process, Selous Scouts were ordered to commence pseudo operations, to make it appear that guerrilla groups had already begun to harass the rural population. Although it never happened, the Scouts were authorised to kill members of the Commonwealth Monitoring Force if it could be established that this would advance the deception.

If it became necessary to ban Mugabe from the election or if he lost the poll to one of his rivals, there seemed little doubt that he would pull his forces out of their camps and send them back to war. Since he was most likely to issue the necessary commands on publication of the election result, the ZANLA assembly points were to be annihilated prior to this. Since Nkomo would be a coalition partner, ZIPRA camps were to be spared as far as possible.

The SAS and the RLI would share the burden of destroying ten ZANLA assembly points scattered around the country. They would be supported by the usual Air Force arsenal, that would itself be backed up by the possible deployment of South African Air Force Mirages and Canberras. At the same time, the SAS, supported by the Armoured Car Regiment, would attack ZANLA's Salisbury headquarters as well as the homes of all the main ZANU-PF officials. Naturally Mugabe's Mount Pleasant Home and Simon Muzenda's home in Highlands were on the list. A second strike force would move against the Patriotic Front's Military HQ contained within the grounds of the University of Rhodesia. Troops would also be positioned to strike the main ZANU-PF administrative HQ at the Medical Arts Centre in Highlands. The code word for the operation was *Quartz*.

As polling for the common roll got under way on 27 February, the SAS teams positioned around the capital waited for the signal to launch their attacks. Across the country an astounding 2 702 275 people — 93% of those eligible — queued up to cast their votes. Throughout the capital — and indeed everywhere in the country — voting was conducted in an atmosphere of orderly calm. At each polling booth, a pair of British policemen stood in the sunshine and kept an eye on the crowd. They were an incongruous sight in their shirtsleeves and distinctive service helmets, and benignly ignorant of the dark undertow of symbolism and intimidation that followed the voters even to the polls.

As the supernatural had been the early glue of the fighter/civilian bond, it also reared its head in the election campaign. ZANLA fighters claimed that ZANU-PF had an evil eye that would betray traitors when the day came to vote — and everybody knew what a traitor could expect. The Party's campaigners also claimed to have a 'black box', supplied by the Romanians, that could identify whose cross had been placed where. Credulous tribesmen believed what they were told, and even if they did not, they gave the stories the benefit of the doubt, since no threats of any consequence were coming from any other quarter.

On 2 March, two days before the results were due to start being announced, Robert Mugabe and 28 members of his Central Committee, flew to Maputo for a weekend visit. The SAS's Kabrit Barracks were located adjacent to Salisbury Airport and it was planned that a surface-to-air missile would be fired from there to bring down Mugabe's aircraft. The plan floundered on the unwillingness of the gunner to be responsible for the deaths of crew and civilians on the flight.

On 4 March, military units waiting at various points around the country gathered around transistor radios and listened as Registrar-General Eric Pope-Symonds began to read out the preliminary election results. The news was bad. Out of the 80 African seats, Mugabe had won 57, Nkomo 20 and Muzorewa three. Sithole, Chirau and Ndweni didn't win a seat. 20 seats were reserved for whites. Mugabe had won his outright majority. Knuckles turned white as men closed their eyes and prayed for one word: *Quartz*. Even at that stage it was not too late. As the news began to sink in, however, most came to accept that the order would not be coming. It soon became clear that, all things being equal, Mugabe would form the next government.

Several theories exist regarding the demise of *Operation Quartz*. It has been suggested that Walls refused to give the order upon realising that Mugabe's electoral victory was simply too great. Perhaps it was never planned to implement *Quartz* in the first place. Uniting the entire military in a single plot to subvert the process, might simply have been intended to prevent individuals or middle ranking officers from taking matters into their own hands. If that had happened, her Majesty would have been at war in Rhodesia before the Governor had a chance to leap into a homeward-bound British aircraft.

It was not long after this that General Walls and almost the entire membership of ComOps visited Robert Mugabe and offered their allegiance to the new government. In due course, Walls accepted the position of Commander of the new Zimbabwe National Army. In a later interview with Jim Parker, Chief Superintendent Mac McGuinness denied any knowledge of the planning and arrangements for *Operation Quartz*. This would appear to vindicate ComOps, and indicate that rogue elements within the security services and the Selous Scouts Special Branch were alone responsible. As far as McGuinness was aware, Special Branch Selous Scouts were only involved in ballot box stuffing to swell the Muzorewa vote. The said rogue elements, assisted by some South African Special Forces personnel operating in Rhodesia, carried out all the other dirty tricks during the campaign.[6]

* * *

Lord Soames, in his usual pragmatic way, was now able to air the thought that even though there had been massive and widespread intimidation, the probable truth was that it had not materially affected the outcome of the election. In the hours that followed the result, the clearest indication of the broad white response was the fact that thousands of homes went on the market and an exodus gathered momentum. In a combined broadcast to the nation, Soames was the first to have his say.

'This is a solemn hour for Zimbabwe', he intoned, airing that loved and hated name for the first time in a public forum. 'There must be no violent action or reaction of any kind…my purpose is to bring about an orderly transfer of power to a stable government.'

Walls, it appeared, had the same purpose. He spoke in a voice crisp and businesslike, containing no hint of bitterness. 'I appeal to you all for calm, for peace', he said.

And then it was Mugabe's turn and — as he spoke — the nation held its breath. 'Let us join together', he began. 'Let us show respect for the winners and losers.' He paused for a moment, perhaps swallowing a lump in his throat. 'There is no intention on our part to victimise the minority. We will ensure that there is a place for everyone in this country. I want a broadly based government to include whites and Nkomo.'[7]

With that said, the Prime Minister-elect went on to allay white fears. He promised the business community that there would be no sweeping nationalisation. He promised civil servants that their pensions and jobs would be guaranteed. He assured homeowners and farmers that their property rights would be respected. Mugabe's speech left a deep impression on his white listeners. As it began to appear that he was intent on keeping his promises — such as maintaining certain white ministers and asking Peter Walls to oversee the integration of the army — whites began to allow a residue of hope to slip into their view of the future. A significant number of white homes were taken off the market, resignations were reconsidered and the time-honoured 'wait and see' attitude was re-adopted.

As this was going on, Ian Smith received an unexpected invitation to visit the ZANU-PF leader and Prime Minister designate at his Mount Pleasant home. Smith was naturally apprehensive as he was driven to the meeting, but was pleasantly surprised at how cordially he was received by his enemy. Perhaps Smith was reminded then of his rugby analogy: that according to the rules, one tackles not only friends but enemies too, and then shakes their hands at the end of the game.

Mugabe was businesslike and came straight to the point. He was quick to acknowledge that he and his people were extremely fortunate to inherit the Jewel of Africa, with its sophisticated infrastructure and its status as the breadbasket of the region. Smith listened politely as Mugabe went on to stress that in order to maintain this position, a lesson ought to be learned from Mozambique: namely that it was vital that the skills base –whites in other words — be encouraged to stay and participate in the new nation. He further stressed that although changes would have to be made, he and his people were sufficiently pragmatic to accept that the economic structure of Rhodesia was capitalist, and that those changes would be gradual. When asked for his comments, all Smith could muster was to advise Mugabe to moderate his image as a Marxist, in the interest of soothing not only the fears of the local whites, but also those of Western investors. Mugabe agreed, and the two parted, Smith probably wondering whether he had been the victim of some waking hallucination.

In the days that followed, Ian Smith was able to indulge himself in some hollow humour as, at various times, all the other black leaders visited him and pleaded with him to lead the way in somehow overturning the result. Smith shrugged. It was their party now, he told them, but if they could approach the military and gain some support from that quarter, action might be possible. He did not believe it, though, and nor did anybody else. The game was over and Mugabe had won. Blacks were in substantive control for the first time in almost a century — and for the Mashona coalition, even longer. Smith called on Mugabe one more time, when such banalities as Cabinet positions and future government structures regarding whites were discussed. A general agreement was reached to let bygones be bygones and for both races to unite as best they could. Upon this rather unlikely notion, the two parted on apparently reasonable terms.

Somewhat late in the day, many South Africans suddenly woke up to the unpalatable truth that they were now strangers in a Marxist neighbourhood. As the Prime Minister elect waited for the moment of his ceremonial inauguration, the well of dirty tricks did not run dry, but was simply shifted south by hardline Rhodesian Security Force operators. There it fell under the aegis of South African Special Forces — at which point things became more desperate and dirtier still. Immediately after the election results were announced, a meeting of the State Security Council declared Messina an SADF operational area. A powerful Battle Group was assembled and code named and sent in dribs and drabs to Messina. Charlie comprised 102 Eland Armoured cars, Ratel armoured troop carriers, five batteries of artillery and six battalions of infantry and support troops.

Central to every plan — to maintain the old order as far as possible — was the killing of Robert Mugabe. The latest plan, however, was breathtakingly audacious and went far beyond the removal of Mugabe alone. The nefarious scheme also called for the assassination of the heir to the British throne, Prince Charles — who was to represent the Crown at the handover — the Governor Lord Soames and his wife, Lord Peter Carrington and others. The plan was to intercept the dignitaries' official motorcade when it was travelling between Government House and Meikles Hotel, where a ZANU reception was planned just hours before the ceremony, marking the inauguration of the new state on 17 April.

In terms of the practicalities of the scheme, a series of powerful explosive charges would be secreted in containers manufactured to resemble traffic control boxes and linked together. These were to be positioned by the roadside over a short distance in Jameson Avenue where the motorcade would have to slow down before turning left into Second Street. The execution of the plan would be carried out by a team of erstwhile Selous Scout operators who had been recruited into South Africa's Special Forces. One would be positioned on an adjacent rooftop from where he would command-detonate the massive explosive device.

Clearly the ramifications of such a plan succeeding would have been very severe. It was predicted that the massive euphoria created amongst the celebrating black Zimbabweans would be converted into mass rage when the life of their hero was snatched from them at the eleventh hour. It was expected that a feeling would permeate the crowd that somehow the whites had been involved. No doubt Rufaro Stadium would empty and it was anticipated that a huge mob would head for the nearby European residential areas. There, it was predicted, bloody revenge would be wreaked on the whites resulting in wholesale arson, rapes and murders.

Of course, a deafening international outcry would be raised against the high profile assassinations and the consequent civilian carnage. With the Rhodesian security machine disassembled, the guerrilla armies complicit and the Monitoring Force spread around the country and in any case, too weak to intervene, no objections would be raised after South Africa launched Battle Group Charlie across the border to 'restore order'. Pretoria would take direct control of the country and form an interim government comprised of Joshua Nkomo and other losing parties in the election .ZANU-PF, being absolutely discredited because of the atrocities and with its leader dead, it would be left out of any political arrangements with no one raising any objections.

Chief Superintendent Mac McGuinness, however, got wind of the assassination plans. He passed the information to the CIO who went into action. Word quickly got back to the South African team who promptly cleared their safe house of incriminating evidence. A small arsenal was loaded onto a bakkie, which was driven out of town and abandoned in the bush off the side of the Salisbury-Bulawayo road. The plotters were probably picked up there by a light aircraft and flown to South Africa. No arrests were made.[8]

Independence

By then Mugabe was reaching the end of his tether, and needless to say stringent security precautions were put in place. The handover of Rhodesia to the new ZANU-PF government proved to be something of an international jamboree, with dignitaries arriving from all over the world. This was Mugabe's coming out, and these were the most important days of his life. Truly a Moses he was about to receive the Promised Land. It was his intention to live to savour the moment.

One of the first to arrive in the country was Jamaican reggae legend Bob Marley. Marley and his band, The Wailers, had been invited by the organisers to entertain the crowd at Rufaro Stadium. He was met at the airport by an army of press photographers and television cameras. Few in conservative white Rhodesia had ever heard of Marley, let alone hummed his liberation anthem 'Zimbabwe'. Things had really gone to the dogs when a scruffy little bugger wearing a tea cosy on his head, was treated like royalty and featured as the headline story on the evening news. *Africans a-liberate Zimbabwe!* Indeed. 'Bob Marley and the Wailers' had a catchy ring however, and it was not long before it was adapted and adopted to express white distaste at Mugabe's ostentatious motorcade, with its robust security detail and at least a dozen screaming police sirens. For years afterwards the number was met with a chuckle and a reference to 'Bob Mugabe and the Wailers'.

On 17 April, Salisbury airport became a hub of unprecedented international air traffic. The first to step onto the tarmac was UN Secretary General Kurt Waldheim, who was followed by the heads of state and representatives of 96 nations. Botswanan President Sir Seretse Khama was the first of the Frontline leaders to land, his chartered jet being escorted in by an Air Force guard of honour. He was met by both Mugabe and president-in-waiting Canaan Banana. Kenneth Kaunda was the next to arrive and there was a predictable sternness in Mugabe's greeting of his old antagonist.

Kaunda would not be favoured with a great deal of attention during the proceedings, and his name would not be conspicuously honoured by the revolution. When the day came, that the major thoroughfares of Queensway and Jameson Avenue in Salisbury were renamed Julius Nyerere Way and Samora Machel Avenue respectively , Kaunda was thrown the sop of a having the distinctly seedy Railway Avenue named after him.

A busy day of junketing and diplomatic flourishes was finished off, when the principal guest, HRH Prince Charles, flew into the country. He joined the Governor and his wife on the lawns of Government House to witness the final beating of the retreat and the lowering of the Union Jack, before a brief Governor's reception. Neither Smith nor Mugabe attended. Senior members of the African National Congress and the Pan Africanist Congress represented South Africa, but no official representative of the South African Government was invited.

By 19:30, the grounds of Government House had emptied, as invited guests made their way to Meikles Hotel for the state banquet to be hosted by the Rev Canaan Banana. Mugabe attended but he was in sober mood. He had been driven to the hotel by a secret route and left early, equally secretively, to return to his Quorn Avenue residence. There he dressed and prepared himself for what would arguably be the climax of his life.

Senior party official Emerson Mnangagwa and CIO officer Danny Stannard were jointly charged with the sensitive details of Mugabe's security. It was decided that the ZANU chief's motorcade would make its way to Rufaro Stadium without him, while Mugabe himself would travel in a small police convoy, by a circuitous route, and meet up with the motorcade at the gates of the venue. Crowds had been closing in on Rufaro Stadium for most of the day. With seating capacity limited to 30 000, many more than this milled around in the streets outside and agitated for access. A tense situation was inflamed when the hushed mood of expectation was suddenly shattered, as Bob Marley launched into his pop anthem 'Positive Vibration'.

Among whites the sound stirred no particular emotions, but to blacks the tempo struck a note of such pure liberty that violence was the only outlet. The thousands of would-be spectators who were locked out, began to beat on the doors and the mood got uglier. A quarter of an hour into the concert, the band was silenced as riot police moved in and tear gas and dogs were used to disperse the mob. Order inside the stadium was restored by a ZANLA formation marching across the field with raised fists.[1] A moment later, Marley retook the stage and greeted the ZANLA men with a raised fist of his own, and a cry of Freedom! The crowd roared. The band struck up again and the sounds of Marley's War echoed across Salisbury.

Then, at precisely 23:00, the official motorcade pulled up at the stadium doors. Mugabe was quickly ushered from the unmarked police car into his official vehicle. Behind the pilot car rode Prince Charles in an open-top Rolls Royce, until then the official vehicle of the Governor. The entourage was joined by a mounted escort of the BSAP, in full dress with whitened helmets and bearing lances. A combined ZIPRA, ZANLA and Air Force choir took up the haunting strains of *Nkosi Sikelela Africa*, the unofficial anthem of southern African liberation movements. Already thoroughly warmed up by Bob Marley, the crowd was euphoric. Lined up in ranks on the field was the guard of honour made up of the 1st Battalion Rhodesian African Rifles under the command of Lieutenant-Colonel Mick McKenna.

Prince Charles, in his Royal Navy uniform, was led up to the podium, where he delivered a message of goodwill from his mother, Queen Elizabeth. Charles bade a warm valediction to the colony of Rhodesia and welcomed Zimbabwe as the 43rd member of the Commonwealth. The Reverend Canaan Banana was sworn in as the first president, and he in turn took Robert Mugabe's oath, as the nation's first prime minister. Banana was then handed the constitutional instruments of a free Zimbabwe. 'We now enter a new era of international acceptability', he said, 'following our long hard-fought battle for freedom and independence.'[2]

At midnight on 18 April 1980, a lone bugler sounded the last post. The Union Jack was lowered for the last time in southern Africa, to be replaced by the revolutionary colours of the 50th free state of Africa. Then, to thunderous applause, Mugabe stepped forward to light an eternal flame in honour of the fallen heroes. Lord Carrington read a warm and fraternal message to the nation, welcoming Robert Mugabe into the exclusive club of international statesmen. With tongue in cheek, Mugabe thanked Margaret Thatcher for the decisive role she had played in the vital final quarter. He then read his address to the nation.

> The people of Zimbabwe must strive to unite themselves … intellectually and spiritually, to the reality of political change and relate to each other as brothers bound to one another by a bond of national comradeship…if yesterday I fought you as an enemy, today you have become a friend and an ally with the same national interests, loyalty, rights and duties as myself. If yesterday you hated me, today you cannot avoid the love that binds me to you and you to me.[3]

Before disappearing into history, Rhodesia reserved the last word for herself. It was a bitter little jibe, but cuttingly to the point and aptly delivered. A flyover of a single Canberra bomber concluded the official ceremony. A white Rhodesian pilot was at the controls and as he approached the stadium he opened the bomb bay. The Canberra was configured so that the slipstream created by the open bomb doors caused an otherworldly howl that was all too familiar to those who had been bombed by the old warhorse. The RAR, who never had, kept their ranks, but the ZIPRA and ZANLA men on the field and in the stands dived for cover.

In bars and private homes throughout the country, whites watched the unfolding events on television or listened to the ceremony on radio. The voice of the apparently humble ex-schoolteacher rang across the nation and declared a new era of hope. Many young white men of fighting age drowned their sorrows, and remembered friends and comrades who had fallen along the way. There was certainly no glory in this defeat ... no sympathy and no refuge. The war had been discredited and the losers had received their just deserts. While many stayed to give Mugabe and the new order the benefit of the doubt, many more packed up and left.

Immediately after the elections, all members of the various territorial units were disarmed and sent home. This included all nine battalions of the Rhodesia Regiment, the territorial members of the Selous Scouts and the Rhodesia Defence Regiment. Likewise, the National Service independent companies were disarmed and disbanded, as was the Guard Force and the full spectrum of Security Force Auxiliaries. All the aircraft of the Rhodesian Air Force were recalled to the main bases of Thornhill in Gwelo and New Sarum in Salisbury, to await the pleasure of the new military command.

On 1 November 1980, the Rhodesia Light Infantry was disbanded as a unit. This last cut came long after the cream of its personnel had left the country. The few remaining officers and troops would assist in the formation and training of the new Zimbabwe National Army (ZNA). The famous RLI 'Troopie' statue was smuggled out of the country, along with other treasures of the regiment, while the regimental colours were hung in the Anglican Cathedral in Salisbury.[4] The Rhodesia African Rifles was disbanded soon after independence and — with somewhat less trauma — integrated into 1, 3 and 4 Brigades of the ZNA.[5]

The SAS was withdrawn from the field and confined to barracks at the Kabrit Base, although by April 1980, the majority had followed Lieutenant Colonel Garth Barrett to South Africa where they reformed as 6-Recce Commando. On 31 December 1980 the remains of the unit was disbanded entirely. It died cleanly and completely, without the indignity of integration. At a ceremony on 13 December the unit was addressed by its Commanding Officer, Major Grahame Wilson — the most highly decorated member of the Rhodesian Security Forces — who spoke to the remainder of his troops for the last time. 'We will leave here not only in sorrow but filled with pride, dignity and honour in ourselves and in 1-SAS. We have much to be grateful for.'[6]

The Selous Scouts — Cain to the SAS's Abel — did not so much disband as simply fade away. As the news filtered out that Mugabe had won the election, the regiment imploded with the exodus of all the irregulars. As Lieutenant Colonel Reid Daly lamented, the mud that had continually been thrown at the regiment had begun to stick. There were few in the establishment who wanted any more to do with it. Those in the field were brought in, the peripheral bases were shut down and the regulars confined to the fort at Inkomo Barracks. 'Turned' guerrillas were now largely stranded and of course had much to fear. Many white operatives followed the surviving SAS members to South Africa where they were absorbed into the Recce Commandos.

As the dust settled and the fanfare subsided ... as dignitaries wound up their visits and trooped back to the airport ... as Mugabe named his new Cabinet and took up occupation of Government House ... as whites prepared to give it a chance settled in ... and those who had sworn they would never leave, did ... as blacks basked in the afterglow of black rule — the curtain finally fell on 90 years of white rule. Rhodesia was no more.

Epilogue

Our votes must go together with our guns. After all, any vote we shall have, shall have been the product of the gun. The gun which produces the vote should remain its security officer – its guarantor. The people's votes and the people's guns are always inseparable twins.

Robert Mugabe

On a bright autumn morning a dishevelled black man stepped out of a police vehicle and walked through a crowd of onlookers towards his court arraignment. He was short and overweight, his clothes were torn and disarrayed and his usually avuncular appearance was now solemn and disturbed. One side of his head was shaved, revealing an ugly wound that had recently been stitched. His right eye was bloody and his face bloated and bruised. The man was Morgan Tsvangirai, leader of the opposition in the democracy of Zimbabwe, and this was what he looked like after two days in police custody. Robert Mugabe, backed into a tight corner by 27 years of increasing misrule, brooked no opposition, and this was one way he made that fact clear to the nation.

Tsvangirai, modestly educated and cut largely from the same cloth as Roy Welensky — or perhaps Polish trade unionist Lech Walesa — was the ex-teamster and labour leader, the plucky little man who was taking on a monolithic ZANU-PF.

'I told SADC that yes, he was beaten and bashed', Mugabe unashamedly admitted, '… and I told them that this was done by the police. I did not hide anything … and he went to cry to tell [Christopher] Dell [US ambassador to Zimbabwe] that he had been beaten.'[1]

Robert Mugabe, then-83-years old, viewed himself less as a democratic leader than as a monarch with the institutions of the nation his own to use and abuse at will. The monarch had been responsible for many crimes over the years. His use of violence and genocide against his perceived opponents tended to slip under the international radar during the Cold War of the 1980s. Not long after he acceded to power, he caused tens of thousands of Ndebele to be slaughtered by his brutal North Korean trained 5th Brigade. When news of these atrocities eventually filtered out, the world merely shrugged — it was just another of those little problems in Africa. However, by the advent of the liberated 1990s, things had changed somewhat, and crimes against his own people re-emerged to threaten both his reputation and his liberty. Not wishing to follow the likes of a pseudo-palsied Augusto Pinochet into a wheelchair, or Slobodan Milosovic to the International Court of Justice, his only protection was to remain in office, and he resolved to stay there until he died, no matter what it took.

This, then, was the state of the revolution by mid-2009. The evolution of national affairs from independence had been rapid, and in many ways a vindication of the white old guard who swore on handing over power, that the country would be reduced to ashes in a single political generation. For the common black proletarian — the povo or the man in the street — the revolution was sacred and remained so for many years. Then, as conditions worsened, an almost verbatim re-enactment of George Orwell's Animal Farm began to play out. The revolution was hijacked and narrowed down, to represent only those in power — senior members of ZANU-PF who had been bonded by involvement in the Liberation Struggle.

511

This sad parody of African independence had its roots in genuine optimism. Whatever may have been the end result, the genesis of ZANU rule was characterised by integrity, and the apparent determination of Mugabe and his people to do the right thing. On the eve of independence, all the white power brokers swore their allegiance to the new government. Ken Flower, Peter Walls and most other heads of services, including even Ian Smith to a degree, fell into line, hoping against hope — and indeed believing — that everything was going to be all right. Notwithstanding the joy and expectation surging through the black community, it was recognised at all levels that Zimbabwe's was a capitalist economy, dependent on white skills, productivity and expertise. White business and agricultural interests were warned to expect changes, but it was promised that these would be gradual and applied in a manner beneficial to all. Whites, and a lot of blacks, probably misinterpreted the signals of tolerance and reconciliation to mean that they had licence to speak out freely and organise as they chose. This was not so. The friendly overtures from Government House were issued on behalf of ZANU-PF and not the recently elected majority rule government, and were based entirely on an expectation of support for the ruling party.

Soon after independence Mugabe began making it plain that his objective for Zimbabwe was a centralised economy under a single, omnipotent political party. The identity of the party and its supreme leader were never in doubt. Neither ZANU-PF nor Mugabe planned a career of parliamentary jostling, but saw themselves as a vast umbrella organisation under which everyone was expected to take shelter whether they liked it or not. In the grand tradition, it was to be one-man-one-vote once, and elections or not, Mugabe had every intention of remaining president for life.

Under the long afterglow of independence, no challenge existed to Mugabe's authority anyway, so he was generous in his attentions to the nation. Flush with foreign aid and buoyed by the acclaim he had been greeted with in the halls of international power, he initiated a series of programmes to widen the reach of health, education and land redistribution. With the weight of sanctions lifted and the threat of sweeping nationalisation limited, economic growth was steady and consumer satisfaction was general.

Land reform was seen to be the most pressing as well as the most politically charged issue of the times. Since the passing of the Land Husbandry Act in the 1950s, war had paralysed any serious agricultural extension work and the 'native reserves' existed much as they had in Huggins' day. By 1980, four million people lived on tribal trust land that was now renamed Communal Areas, but it was no less dry, overcrowded, eroded and destitute. Each year these Communal Areas contributed 40 000 individuals to the population, with no concurrent growth in wealth or resources.[2] Politically, land was at the root of the *Chimurenga*, just as it had been in 1896, and this potent issue had never been off the agenda since. The imbalance of land distribution — despite Mugabe's rhetorical nurturing of the golden goose — would keep the revolution alive and the enemy more or less unchanged. The President filed away the explosive perennial issue in his armoury against the day he needed to bring it out as political ammunition.

In the meantime, property rights were protected by the Lancaster House Constitution and there was nothing revolutionary that could be achieved within the first decade of independence. For the time being Mugabe focussed his attention on two matters of abiding personal interest. The first was his quest for a one-party state. The second was the desire to take an ideological stab at an ancient enemy in the form of the Ndebele. This group largely fell under the PF-ZAPU banner, and were indisputably led by Joshua Nkomo.

To show willingness, Mugabe initially agreed to a coalition government that included Nkomo and other members of ZAPU. Nkomo resisted efforts to marginalise him with an impotent presidency, and instead fought for and won the Home Affairs portfolio. This put him in charge of the regular police, but not the security police or the CIO, for which Mugabe assumed personal responsibility. The two armies of ZIPRA and ZANLA were in technical co-operation in an integrated army, but in reality ZIPRA personnel were generally left in no doubt that they were not welcome in the Zimbabwe National Army.

One of Joshua Nkomo's most implacable enemies, Enos Nkala, who had been humiliated during the Cold Comfort conference of the 1960s, led the charge against him with inflammatory and divisive invective. Nkala spoke openly of the need to 'crush' ZAPU, but Edgar Tekere was even more provocative. 'Nkomo and his guerrillas are germs in the country's wounds', he declaimed, 'and they will have to be cleaned with iodine. The patient will have to scream a bit.'[3] The iodine was already being formulated behind the scenes. In October 1980 Mugabe signed an agreement with North Korea whereby the secretive Stalinist state would train a separate army brigade for the specific function of dealing with internal dissidents. This unit came to be known as The Fifth Brigade. It was an exclusively Mashona division, that trained separately from other branches of the military and was answerable directly to Mugabe.

By early in 1981, Mugabe felt confident enough to provoke a breach with Nkomo. A number of arms caches were discovered on farms belonging to Nkomo and other high ranking ZAPU members. Nkomo was accused of plotting a coup and was fired from government. This triggered the seizure of most of ZAPU's property and businesses, and the open persecution of ZIPRA members serving in the armed forces. In response to this, hundreds fled into the bush taking their arms with them. They reformulated as dissident groups with no particular objective in the short term other than survival. Banditry with vaguely political overtones flourished and found an outlet in attacks on isolated villages and white farms.

These events gave South Africa — already pursuing a destabilisation policy towards her northern neighbours — the opportunity to stir the pot, using ex-Rhodesian operatives and providing financial and logistical support to dissident groups. All this played into Mugabe's hands, and he ratcheted up the tension with the help of a handful of loquacious ministers. It was an emergency situation and Mugabe warned parliament in 1982 that some measures that might be used by his government against its enemies would be 'extra legal'.[4]

Between January and February 1981 tensions between ZIPRA and ZANLA, and ZANU and ZAPU, and of course Ndebele and Mashona, erupted into fighting that almost overwhelmed the Matabeleland capital of Bulawayo. An irony of what became known as the Battle for Bulawayo was that Mugabe deployed the remnants of the Rhodesian Army to put down the rebellion, and owed the continuation of his rule to Colonel Mick McKenna and the Rhodesian African Rifles, and to an Armoured Car Regiment troop commanded by a plucky ex-Australian Sergeant Stephen 'Skippy' Devine.

At the beginning of 1983, 5-Brigade, nicknamed *Gukurahundi* in idiomatic chiShona was deployed into Matabeleland. *Gukurahundi* was a flexible term that Mugabe had used to name 1979 The 'Year of the People's Storm'. In its recycled form it was intended to mean 'the spring rains that disperse the chaff', or more directly 'the sweeping away of rubbish'. It summed up what Mugabe intended to do to the Ndebele. From the onset it was clear that 5-Brigade was not a conventionally oriented fighting unit, but a finely tuned and violent enforcement tool of Mugabe's political policy.

History was used to remind the Mashona of the Ndebele's long and bloody record of bloodshed that was finally to be rewarded in kind. 5-Brigade fell on Matabeleland with the fury of the first rains of the season, in a genocidal campaign of retribution aimed at crushing any and all Ndebele political organisation and opinion. By the end of the campaign between 15 000 and 30 000 civilians had been massacred, often as a consequence of torture. Tens of thousands were injured, intimidated or displaced and hundreds of villages and homesteads destroyed. 'Where men and women provide food for the dissidents, when we get there we eradicate them. We do not differentiate who we fight because we can't tell who is a dissident and who is not.' How history repeats itself.

An even more sinister tool of social engineering emerged that would henceforth be used against opposition — real or perceived — for many years to come. In its third year of drought and lack of development, Matabeleland had become dependent on food aid and the purchase of food from local stores. The government closed all stores and barred the distribution of drought relief and food aid. Of course this quickly translated into widespread hunger, and then starvation. The policy was explained as a means to starve out the dissidents, or as a 5-Brigade officer put it at a public briefing: 'First you will eat your chickens, then your goats, then your cattle, then your donkeys. Then you will eat your children and finally you will eat the dissidents.'[5]

In the run up to the first parliamentary elections to be held in 1985, the level of government sponsored brutality in Matabeleland intensified. The familiar youth brigades, now organised on national lines, uniformed and paid, were set loose on the population to repeat the established routine of violent politicisation. Mugabe spoke to the enemies of his regime when he asked: 'Is it war or peace tomorrow? Let the people of Matabeleland answer this question.'[6]

The question was duly answered when ZAPU, despite withering intimidation, won all 15 Matabeleland parliamentary seats. In due course, Nkomo's home was raided and his aides and bodyguards arrested. The police raids continued until five ZAPU MPs, eleven Bulawayo City councillors and some 200 council employees were locked up. ZAPU political meetings were banned, its offices closed and rural councils run by ZAPU dissolved. Clearly Mugabe was bearing down on his long-held objective of crushing Nkomo and ZAPU.

This campaign culminated on 27 December 1987, when ZAPU and ZANU-PF officially merged. In fact, ZAPU was simply absorbed by ZANU. It was a complete capitulation on the part of Nkomo who was accepted into the government as second vice-president alongside Simon Muzenda. Muzenda was Mugabe's substantive deputy for the usual reasons of slavish loyalty and lack of intellectual gifts. Nkomo, on the other hand, settled into an honorary and largely powerless adjunction.

* * *

Independence brought about the reopening of the old Mozambique transport corridors, which had been closed since 1976. These old trade routes, utilising the three strategic conduits of Tete, Beira and the Limpopo, became vital once again. This was thanks largely to South Africa, applying the same tactics to try and draw political concessions from Zimbabwe, that had been so successfully used against Rhodesia. By November 1980, 50 000 tons of Zimbabwean goods were held back at South African ports, and the following year this rose to 300 000. In April 1981, South African Railways announced the end of its trade agreement with Zimbabwe and demanded the return of 24 diesel locomotives that were on loan.

In addition to this, large-scale freight traffic routed via the Beira Corridor, was immediately targeted by Renamo, now enjoying the patronage and support of South Africa. On 29 October 1981, the road and railway bridges over the Pungwe River were blown up — also severing Zimbabwe's oil pipeline. In December 1982, the oil storage depot at Maforga was also blown up, resulting in such a chronic fuel shortage in Zimbabwe, that road traffic was brought to a virtual standstill. Only the clandestine movement of fuel along the old sanctions-busting route saved the country from disaster.

The first Zimbabwean mechanised units appeared in Mozambique towards the middle of 1984, a year before Samora Machel formally requested Zimbabwean and Tanzanian troops to help restore law and order in his country. Apart from having much Mozambican support to repay, Zimbabwe needed to maintain the vital road and rail links between itself, the coast and the lakes region. Apart from protecting these routes, Zimbabwean forces launched several major operations against RENAMO from there.

In November 1990 a partial cease-fire was signed between RENAMO and FRELIMO, both by then exhausted by war. This paved the way for the withdrawal of Zimbabwean troops, which was completed after a total cease-fire was signed in Rome in October 1992. Multi-party elections took place in Mozambique in 1994, in which RENAMO took part as an opposition party. Since then the country has been peaceful and its devastated economy is slowly being restored.[7]

* * *

The cordiality that existed between Ian Smith and Robert Mugabe, for over a year after their initial meeting, came to an abrupt halt in July 1981. Smith, as leader of the Conservative Alliance of Zimbabwe — or the reformed RF — met Mugabe to query his public utterances regarding his intention of creating a one-party state. Was Mugabe aware, Smith asked, how such statements eroded investor confidence and drove vital skills and expertise — in effect, whites — out of the country? Smith also asked why Mugabe had chosen that moment to make such unnecessarily divisive comments, since no constitutional changes could be made for seven years.

It seems that Mugabe had indulged Smith up until then, be it for cosmetic reasons or a desire for genuine rapprochement, but he appeared in the end to have taken none of the advice of his predecessor particularly seriously. Certainly the constant recommendation that Mugabe should tone down the anti-white rhetoric of his ministers was a naive expectation on Smith's part. Mugabe was an established anti-white racist by then and he had every intention of augmenting the ongoing vitriol of his cabinet with some choice sentiments of his own. The two men parted company and Smith observed: 'He [Mugabe] was obviously displeased, and our parting, unlike on previous occasions, was cool. He stood his distance. From that day onwards, he has refused to meet me.'[8]

Mugabe's speeches from then on began increasingly to reflect the anti-white movement in government that was gradually but noticeably building momentum. The President was quoted on the BBC on 8 August 1981 condemning whites for not supporting his party. He let it be known that blacks would be within their rights to seek retribution, and to 'hit the whites in return!'[9] When receiving the freedom of the City of Gweru (formerly Gwelo), he dedicated his speech to the 'evils of the previous racist colonial regime'.

Whenever Mugabe made such a speech, it usually followed that the security situation for white farmers deteriorated. In November 1981 he made such a speech in Lomagundi that resulted in the death of two whites and assaults on several others. By the end of that year, according to Smith, the exodus of whites was running at 10 000 a month, and no one in central government was even slightly concerned. Within three years, more than half the whites present at independence had fled the country, leaving a core of about 100 000 who were either too financially straitened to leave or were reluctant to abandon the generally comfortable life still available to them in Zimbabwe.

As the government conducted a war against its own citizens, the exterior threat remained. The South Africans conducted a series of attacks using a number of former soldiers of the Rhodesian Security Forces. Among the most serious was an effort to destroy much of the ZNA's motorised ordinance stockpiled at King George VI Barracks, less than a kilometre from State House in Harare. Explosive devices slipped into fuel tanks were discovered only after a few parked vehicles had blown up. This incident was followed by the assassination of the South African ANC's representative in Harare. On 16 August 1981, a devastating explosion shook the old Selous Scouts base of Inkomo Barracks. The barracks again housed weapons and ammunition that had accumulated since the end of the war. A carefully planned sabotage operation set a match to the gunpowder, and caused massive destruction. In December 1981, an explosion that killed seven and injured 124 people destroyed ZANU-PF headquarters in Manica Road, Harare.

In August 1982 a sabotage team mounted a raid on the Zimbabwe Air Force's main base of Thornhill just outside Gweru, destroying much of Zimbabwe's rather theoretical air strike capability. This stirred up a surge of anger, directed at the unendingly troublesome white malcontents operating from South Africa. Nothing could be done about them, but a political reprisal against local whites was a satisfying substitute, and its effects were felt very quickly. Several senior white Air Force officers were arrested in the aftermath and tortured into making signed confessions which were then used in court. The confessions were disallowed and the men acquitted. But all were immediately rearrested, and released only after British intervention and undertakings that they would leave the country forthwith.

At that point Mugabe declared that the honeymoon was over. He expressed bewilderment at how the whites of the country had so consistently scorned the hand of friendship — even those who by right should have faced a firing squad but were instead forgiven. All whites, it seemed to him, had maintained a rigid and counter-revolutionary stance. The privileges they had enjoyed would be removed, he promised, and their economic monopolies dismantled. In 1985 when whites went to the polls to elect their own representatives for the last time, Smith and his Conservative Alliance triumphed. Where was the repentance in this? Mugabe asked. When he had opened the doors to his Party by appointing two white ministers, why had he been scorned?

* * *

Corruption had become endemic in Zimbabwe, Mugabe's own brand of it being more in pursuit of power than wealth — although wealth remains necessary in a functioning plutocracy, for the accumulation of power and the corruption of ministers. All these old heroes of the struggle had applied to themselves the title of 'Comrade', but had nonetheless since independence cast their eyes greedily over the newly liberated landscape for opportunities for personal enrichment.

On 30 December 1987, Mugabe was declared by Parliament to be Executive President of the nation with huge personal power. His position combined the roles of Head of State, Leader of the Government and Commander-in-Chief of the armed forces. He had powers to dissolve Parliament and declare martial law. He had an open-ended ticket with no limitation on his term of office. With skill, both innate and acquired, he consolidated his rule at every level, using patronage and awarding high-level political, military, civil and judicial appointments to ensure loyalty. Intertwined with this was money and business, for an appointment to any senior position carried with it an appropriate degree of access to the economic trough.

An example of this was the so-called Willowgate Scandal. The Willowvale car plant assembled Japanese cars, imported in kit form to supply the local market. A precipitous economic decline, brought about by government extravagance and general mismanagement — at that time Zimbabwe had the largest government per capita in the world — resulted in a severe shortage of foreign currency. The Willowvale vehicles were consequently in short supply, and were theoretically available only on the basis of a waiting list. Prices were controlled by the government, and senior members used their positions to jump the queue, buy the vehicles at the regulated price and promptly resell them on the open market for twice — sometimes three times –what they had paid.

An independent newspaper illuminated the grubby activities of many of the high-ranking scamsters. Most notable among these was Maurice Nyagumbo, the revolutionary fist fighter and lately Minister of Mines. Nyagumbo, who had at one time been a principled man, was mortified by his exposure. Perhaps his conscience urged him to clean house, for he muttered often that he was not alone, and that others similarly needed to be exposed and punished. Nyagumbo committed suicide over the issue, failing to point the finger at many who had no interest in making peace with either their god or the voting public.

A second public scandal broke out when it came to light that government ministers and their cronies had systematically looted a fund set up to compensate war victims. Here was the rather sickening spectacle of senior officials and their family members, claiming ridiculous degrees of disability for which they were awarded astonishing sums in compensation. The genuine war veterans were either forgotten or ignored.

Mugabe, meanwhile, began to cultivate airs reminiscent of his heroes in the Eastern Bloc. Common knowledge was his respect for and friendship with Nicolae Ceausescu, whom he publicly feted, a day before the Romanian dictator was detained, tried and shot. How much the fate of his friend affected him it is hard to say, but the external signs of Mugabe's paranoia were becoming difficult to ignore. Government House was fortified in a way never deemed necessary by the former white government. Razor wire looped the length of a city block while each corner was guarded by a helmeted sentry of the presidential guard, each cradling an AK-47 with a nasty-looking 'pig sticker' bayonet affixed.

Mugabe invariably travelled in an extensive motorcade, his navy blue Mercedes Benz presidential limousine accompanied by jeeps packed with heavily armed men, several support vehicles and a number of police outriders who cleared traffic some distance in advance of the convoy. There was an aggressive and sinister air to 'Bob Mugabe's Wailers', and it was not uncommon for a dithering motorist to be pulled over and violently punished, for tardy respect to the President. Admittedly, this was benign by African standards, but it still presented a degree of imperium and moral decay that was becoming very difficult to ignore.

Symptomatic of a creeping remoteness from day-to-day political realities, Mugabe was frequently heard speaking on the merits of Marxism even as the Eastern Bloc was teetering on its foundations. Thereafter he would hang up the coat of a Marxist revolutionary and don instead one of his many Saville Row suits, clip on one of his gold Rolex watches and depart the country with his entourage for regular bouts of foreign junketing.

Mugabe's status on the international stage was inflated significantly by his assumption of the leadership of the Frontline States. It was enhanced too by his personal crusade against South Africa. Although this never resulted in border closures or any overt hostility, the antipathy simmered beneath the surface, and was vented often by bitter and implacable rhetoric.

Through all this, the nuts and bolts of government began to slip through his fingers, and the outrageous style of living of most of those around him rendered his talk of socialism nothing less than preposterous. Grandiose development schemes supported by foreign aid, began to wither as donors, wary of feeding numbered Swiss bank accounts, tended more and more to keep their hands in their pockets. Industry was contracting at an accelerating pace until, by 1989, the value of the Zimbabwe dollar had declined by 65%. Annually, tens of thousands of school leavers entered the job market with a high level of education but a decreasing availability of employment. As inflation crept up steadily, the diminishing numbers of employed found the gains made in the first years of independence, whittled away by corruption and maladministration.

The process of land redistribution was predictably hampered by inefficiency and corruption. After the first decade of independence, 52 000 families had been resettled on 6.5 million acres of land, which had either been acquired on a willing-seller-willing-buyer basis or had been abandoned. This was a commendable achievement for a new government, but more sobering when viewed against the quiet accumulation of land by ministers, MPs, the heads of services and senior civil servants. There is a no doubt that a great deal more official energy was applied to this agenda than to the resettlement of peasant farmers — or indeed the many war veterans who were waiting patiently on the sidelines for some of the promised rewards of emancipation.

Many of the veterans had sacrificed much more for the revolution, than any members of the ruling elite. Most had signed up as youth and thus sacrificed their education, which meant that they re-entered society equipped with neither skills nor experience. As a body they were awarded stipends for the first two years of independence, but nothing thereafter. Many joined co-operative ventures in home industry or farming in compliance with the popular creed of collectivisation. However, the majority of these schemes failed and the veterans drifted into the cities for menial work or repaired to the communal areas where they struggled to scratch a living from the soil. By the end of the first decade of independence, an estimated 30 000 claimants for war veteran status were unemployed.

As the decade ended, and another visit to the polls became due, Mugabe slipped the land card out of his sleeve and, although at this stage he did not play it, he made it the focus of his re-election campaign. Highlighting the absurdity of the situation, whereby the nation's erstwhile colonisers owned most of the nation's arable and ranch land, Mugabe abruptly declared that he planned to redistribute some 13 million acres of land to peasant farmers. The news was greeted at home and abroad with disbelief. In a frenzy of debate, a constitutional amendment was passed that allowed for the seizure of land by government at its own price, and with no right of appeal to the courts. Pleas for him to reconsider came not only from farmers themselves but from foreign lenders and donors too. Mugabe couched the whole issue in terms of history and the righting of skewed racial imbalances. He was widely counselled to avoid cutting so deeply and so suddenly into the productive sector. But as had always been the case, revolutionary symbolism closely stitched together with practical vote-winning policy, overrode more prudent economic concerns.

White farmers sought the protection of a judiciary that had not yet been wholly subverted. Most farmers had bought their land since the days of Jameson's decree and the Carter Commission, and indeed, many since independence with the blessing of the government. Those days were gone. Mugabe made his point painfully clear. 'I, Robert Mugabe...' he declared, 'cannot be dragged to court by a settler.'[10]

In due course Mugabe partially relented, and allowed for the intervention of the courts to fix a fair price for land. Seizures went ahead, however, although in such an ad hoc way that out of 13 farms initially expropriated, seven were soon 'undesignated' upon the realisation that they were too productive to destroy. As ludicrous as it all was, it — together with the usual diet of violence and ballot gerrymandering — won Mugabe the election, opposed only by a flighty Zimbabwe Unity Movement briefly convened by his erstwhile friend Edgar Tekere.

In April 1994, when it was discovered that a 3 000 acre farm forcibly acquired against the objections of the owners had been awarded to the Minister of Agriculture, Witness Mangwende, suspicions about the integrity of the land reform process began to reach the ears of the British Government. The British were, of course, bound by an unconventional convention to pay for the whole process. It was further revealed that 300 farms, intended for redistribution to peasants, were in the hands of various ZANU-PF luminaries. Bowing to foreign pressure, Mugabe cancelled a handful of these questionable leases. As soon as the lights were out again, however, the cockroaches re-emerged and again Mugabe's cronies and political allies gorged themselves on state largesse.

* * *

On 11 February 1990, Nelson Mandela walked out of Victor Verster Prison in Paarl near Cape Town, and the world celebrated. With the exception of many South African whites and a few blacks, this precursor to South African independence was greeted with universal joy. Alone in the depths of gloom, through which he contemplated the event, however, was Robert Mugabe. Gone in an instant was his raison d'être for international statesmanship, gone was the frontline and the Frontline States, and gone was his leadership of the great black anti-imperialist struggle. He could replace none of this with the status of Elder African Statesman, since Nelson Mandela again immediately eclipsed him in that regard.

Another major concern was that an increasing amount of the dirt he had lately wallowed in was beginning to stick. He needed something to divert attention from his indiscretions, and it was not long in coming. The British, having already spent upwards of £44 million on land acquisition,

518

recognised that their tax revenues were being spent on the enrichment of Zimbabwean politicians and civil servants, and so immediately cut off funds. This was clearly acceptable — if not obligatory — public policy, but it played perfectly into Mugabe's hands. Thereafter he would cry long and shrill that the British had reneged on their Lancaster House commitments, so why, therefore, shouldn't he? It was the perfect shield for a multitude of sins.

It is worth making the observation that Mugabe's placing of the land reform programme on an extra-legal basis was, like the Land Husbandry Act before it, the only way in which it could be successfully implemented. Until he was in a position to deny the constitutional rights of the current landholders, he could never separate them from their property. This is in the nature of revolution, and for Mugabe — and indeed many blacks — the revolution was ongoing.

* * *

Such greed and open corruption could not but ferment a groundswell of discontent that, as the 1990s commenced, began to attract increasing attention. So isolated had Mugabe become that it is doubtful he was even aware that this was the sad state the revolution had reached. Never known for his sensitivity to the common man, and often accused of neglecting the warriors in favour of the war, Mugabe was genuinely surprised when his fiercely loyal war veterans came out against him. In a series of noisy demonstrations in the capital, the veterans finally pitched their demand for a slice of the pie. Unnerved perhaps, Mugabe at first chose to ignore them. When the government-supporting press took sides with the demonstrators, the signs of a general mutiny became unmistakable. After weeks of indecision, the President capitulated and agreed to a package of benefits.

Analysts nowadays point to this moment as the beginning of the end for Mugabe's Zimbabwe. The ranks of the war veterans had swollen appreciably since independence, as others who had either been mujibas or had not been involved in the war at all replaced those who died. It was a potential windfall for which many held out their hands. The cost of paying off the veterans capped an already top-heavy fiscus with an unbudgeted weight that threatened to topple it. Mugabe received a gale of cautionary advice from abroad, all of which he ignored, and instead announced in November that the new benefits would be paid by Christmas. As the value of the Zimbabwe dollar plunged, the World Bank suspended benefits, as did most other foreign lending programmes.

The land issue leapt to the fore again as Mugabe began to ponder considerations other than cash. He plunged into the usual volley of anti-white rhetoric before revealing that he intended to seize all 'white' land, and pay not a penny for it. Compensation might be paid at some point for infrastructural improvements such as dams, buildings and roads, but not for the land itself. This statement was backed up by a list of 1 503 farms to be seized, totalling 12 million acres.

The warnings grew louder as Britain rebuffed claims for renewed funding. The economy began to pitch more steeply downwards and threatened to slip into a tailspin. Mugabe faced the real possibility of mass opposition, particularly after proposing that the war veterans' compensation be paid for by increased taxes and levies. A general strike in early 1998 was followed by food riots that brought the army onto the streets of the capital for the first time since independence.

Starved of money and desperate for loans, Mugabe eventually swallowed his pride, and agreed to shelve plans for the immediate seizure of 'white' land. He also permitted the convening of a major conference in Harare, that brought together experts from the UN, the World Bank, the IMF, the EU and 23 foreign governments, to find a workable solution to the land crisis. Never losing sight of the political value of land, Mugabe saw no purpose in having the matter resolved in this context. The delegates devised a workable strategy that Mugabe accepted. He then bade farewell to the conference and shelved the matter entirely. Instead he cast his eyes further afield for money and a political distraction.

With 60% inflation, 50% unemployment and a population poorer than it had been in the 1970s, Mugabe bypassed Parliament and the Cabinet and sent a military expedition north to the Democratic Republic of Congo, to prop up the non-elected President Laurent Kabila. He staged the military intervention as a Southern African Development Community (SADC) response, but the affair was widely rejected by the membership. Deals were made to exploit mining and timber as a means of offsetting the cost of the adventure. In practice though, the spoils remained in the hands of politicians and military commanders and the fiscus did not benefit at all. Therefore the country itself carried the cost of an unnecessary war on top of an already crippled economy.

As the old style of African despot was being weeded out across the continent, Mugabe loomed large as a significant blot on the landscape His electorate was fast losing confidence in him. Out of increasing hardship on the streets of Zimbabwe's industrial centres, a genuinely popular opposition began to take shape. Leading it was the tough and charismatic union boss, Morgan Tsvangirai. The Movement for Democratic Change was in fact an alliance of trade unions, lawyers, academics and civic organisations gathered for the purpose of mounting a challenge to Mugabe and ZANU-PF at the upcoming 2000 general election.

Constitutional reform became an opposition clarion call, and in view of the fact that the Lancaster House Constitution was more than a decade old and a source of limitation to the government, Mugabe agreed. However the constitutional commission was packed with Mugabe supporters and was more or less directed to entrench the powers of the president — which is what it tried to do. Mugabe inserted his own clause after the draft was complete, allowing for the expropriation of land without compensation. Responsibility for compensating the dispossessed whites, was placed at the feet of the British, who could pay or default as they chose. It made no difference to Mugabe.

The draft constitution was revealed to the nation and, in early 2000, it was narrowly defeated in a national referendum. Coming at a time of mass disaffection, poverty and unemployment, the victory of the 'No' campaign had an urban flavour and was less a rejection of the Constitution than of Mugabe himself. The President recognised this fact immediately, and while solemn and thoughtful during a television appearance, he acknowledged the result of the referendum and undertook to respect it.

Behind the scenes, however, the Government saw the loss as the catastrophe it was. Suddenly the vast network of patronage — the roots that sustained the tree itself –was in danger of being overrun by political opposition. The one-party state had so far been de facto but never de jure. In theory, a political opposition could still win an election, and as a matter of urgency that loophole in the law needed to be plugged.

Convinced that whites had orchestrated the electoral defeat, Mugabe decided it was high time to show them who was boss. Suddenly white farmers in their isolated homesteads found themselves threatened by chanting blacks demanding their land. The invasions began in ones and twos in a few select areas, but very quickly they became general as whites in the countryside found themselves besieged. Most disturbing of all was that, as the tension grew and violence escalated, the police watched and did nothing. Even in the bad old days, whites had the agric-alert system that put the cavalry on the doorstep in minutes. This time they were isolated and any response in kind to violence, would be decried as racism and would bring swift retribution.

The amorphous body of war veterans, who co-ordinated these attacks, were often less veterans than unemployed rural and urban youth, for whom the doors to the banquet had been thrown wide. An appreciable portion of the electorate were the 400 000 or so agricultural workers who existed in close commerce with the baas and his interests. Their loyalty was suspect and as a consequence they were savaged with no less vigour than the whites. Many of them were expatriates of old from northern Mozambique or Malawi and in the tightly tuned racial atmosphere of the moment, this too made them fair game.

Embattled farmers flocked to the high court where they usually found legal relief. Mugabe responded with indifference to the judgements and belligerence towards the petitioners. If whites wanted a fight, then as far as he was concerned the battle was on. Police were instructed to ignore the court orders and the farm invasions continued. Newsreel images of whites with their pickups loaded to the gunwales with dogs, kids and furniture, fleeing their farms in the wake of fist-waving blacks, were flashed across the globe. There were gasps from many quarters. In the long history of the Anglo-Saxon union this was the first time that the black man had severely kicked the white man's arse and got away with it. Whites in the diaspora were dismayed while blacks everywhere were delighted.

In practical terms, the strategy was catastrophic. As Mugabe girded his loins for an election battle against the rapidly swelling ranks of the MDC, he had behind him the rural Mashona, the veterans, the neighbouring state presidents and every black academic, philosopher and homeboy in the world. But with the army siphoning vast amounts of the fiscus into the DRC, social systems collapsing, foreign donors and lenders retreating and the economy in freefall, the destruction of Zimbabwe's only economic support pillar pitched the nation and its leaders utterly beyond the pale.

Politically, however, the strategy saved Mugabe's skin, and the results of the 2000 parliamentary elections revealed a clean urban/rural split. The MDC, after nine months of existence, seized 47 per cent of the vote and 57 parliamentary seats. ZANU-PF returned 62 seats that, along with the President's own appointments, secured a less than comfortable majority in the House. The MDC won all the seats in Bulawayo and Harare and ten of the 12 Matabeleland constituencies, as well as achieving a strong showing in most other urban centres. ZANU-PF retained the rural Mashona vote and little else.

The moment was a defining one for Mugabe. Global precedents were stacking up for the old dogs of the cold war to be dragged to The Hague for trial. Milosovic, of course, was an obvious example, as was Pinochet, but closer to home the prosecution of Frederick Chiluba in Zambia and the arrest and internment of Charles Taylor — former strongman of Liberia — all conspired to convince Mugabe that for the *Gukurahundi* at least, he could be facing possible charges in the International Court. His personal survival was dependent on his political survival, and so far into obloquy had he now descended that he had little to lose by tossing out all the remaining rules of fair play.

To run through the entire gamut of abuses that Mugabe and his close inner circle have so far inflicted on the nation would be tedious, and beyond the scope of this narrative. However, since a presidential election in the order of things followed the parliamentary, Mugabe was to add massive election fraud to a growing list of excesses. In his personal tournament against Morgan Tsvangirai, he could not possibly allow himself to lose. He was simply unable to picture himself, a great man, the saviour of Africa, being toppled by a gnomish nobody who lived in a cinderblock bungalow in an unremarkable suburb.

As the land invasion took root and grew more organised and systematic, Mugabe unleashed his war veterans on white business. In a rash of crude and disturbing attacks on the captains of commerce and industry — and many smaller operators too — business owners were subject to invasions, kangaroo courts, massive staff payouts and extortion at the hands of empowered thugs vaguely reputed to be war veterans. As all this was under way Mugabe sent out his youth brigades and political enforcers, to remind the people that the old man was still alive, still in power and still as hard as rock. Using the rules of idiomatic Shona, he told an assembly of delegates at the 2001 Party conference that they were soldiers of ZANU-PF and 'when the time comes to fire the bullet, the ballot, the trajectory must be true.'

Indeed the old fire of Chimurenga was alive and well, and the beatings, murders, burning and rapine raged across the countryside. In the meantime, a delineation committee rearranged constituencies to magnify the rural vote, while urban voters were harassed by registration restrictions, rules demanding that they register and vote in their home constituencies and finally a massive reduction of the number of polling stations in urban areas that, along with foot dragging and officiousness on the part of staff, robbed many urban voters of a chance to cast their ballots. Besides this, the military in the DRC were allowed mail votes, which were universally tampered with, to reflect a vote for the ruling partly, while the millions who had fled the country and who could be relied upon to vote MDC, were disenfranchised. As the foreign observers flew in, the violence in the countryside was quelled, and voting went ahead in a relatively orderly fashion. Tsvangirai was narrowly beaten, foreign disquiet ignored and the whole charade roundly endorsed by African observers — most notably South African — as being substantially free and fair.

South African president Thabo Mbeki was at the fore of those African leaders who scrambled to give a clean bill of health to the charade which was as disturbing a development as had yet occurred in Zimbabwe. Much hope had been placed on South Africa repeating history from the apartheid days by pressuring Zimbabwe to recognise the will of the Zimbabwean people. But it was not to be, Mbeki the most powerful of sub-Saharan leaders proved himself to be supine in the face of Mugabe's personality. Hope seemed to be a very scarce commodity indeed.

Mbeki's posture towards Mugabe was extraordinary throughout his presidency. From 2000 on he pressed his idea of 'Quiet Diplomacy' towards Zimbabwe which seemed to be merely an excuse to continue exercising South African support for the despot. Brushing aside the fact that while he did so Zimbabwe was progressively sinking deeper into poverty and government-sponsored lawlessness.

There had been some oblique criticism of Mbeki's policy by Deputy President Jacob Zuma when speaking in Cape Town after the signing of a binational commission with Nigeria in May 2000. He had called for a review of the principle of non-interference in the domestic political affairs of neighbouring countries. Obviously referring to Mugabe, he said:

> African had failed to campaign vigorously against the manipulation by African leaders of their country's constitutions — which they had participated in drafting, accepting and promulgating. Africa, he said, should act against unconstitutional leaders who undermine efforts to build a culture of good governance on the continent. 'We can no longer afford to be tolerant, as they undermine all our efforts to create conditions for economic growth and development. [11]

Former President Nelson Mandela also had his say when speaking before an audience of children adolescents and development workers on 6 May 2000. He departed from his prepared speech and launched a thinly veiled attack on Mugabe and by inference Mbeki's policy of 'quiet diplomacy':

> The tyrants of today can be destroyed by you [the people] and I am confident you have the capacity to do so. There are leaders in Africa, here and elsewhere who have made enormous wealth ... leaders who once commanded liberation armies ... and when they won they tried to better the lives of their people. But rubbing shoulders with the rich, the powerful, the wealthy has made some leaders despise the very people who put them in power and they think it is a privilege to be there for eternity.
>
> Some have reasons for not wanting to step down because in the course of their presidency they have committed crimes for which they can be investigated and charged. They do not want to step down because to step down will be to expose them. They want to die in power so that there should be no investigations while they are alive.
>
> We have to be ruthless in denouncing such leaders. But the attitude adopted by our president of saying we have diplomatic relations with certain countries and we will use diplomatic channels to settle specific issues in a particular country is the best way of doing

so. But the masses of the people themselves, have no reason to follow the president of this country or me. They can speak out because unless you speak out about these subjects these tyrants are going to continue exploiting poor people and mobilising children to go and die so they can be personally enriched. That is something we must put an end to and I am confident that it is the masses of the people who can do that

Referring to tyrants in history like Alexander the Great, Julius Caesar, Napoleon and Hitler he said:

But where are they today? They were destroyed by the ordinary masses of the people, not by generals but by you and I picking up the rifle and fighting for liberation. That is the lesson of history.

When asked directly if he was referring to Mugabe, he said:

Everybody knows very well whom I am talking about. If you don't know who I am talking about, there is no point in telling you.[12]

No further criticisms by Nelson Mandela of Mugabe, and indirectly of Mbeki, have been recorded In the years that followed the 2002 presidential election, Mugabe set about completing the work of entrenching the party and purging from its ranks any hint of disloyalty. Work on any level of the police, the civil service and the judiciary, was contingent on party membership and loyalty. Corruption that had once been conducted under a veneer of denial flowered, and in due course became a standing joke in many quarters. No police roadblock could be passed without a request for 'drinks'. No official document or licence could be acquired without graft. The police gave up any pretence of impartiality. A large part of its criminal investigation and law enforcement responsibilities, were ignored and the service slipped into the role of enforcement agency for the ruling party.

The economic collapse passed the point of no return, and the Treasury shrunk to the level of protecting and supporting the governing structures and the ruling clique alone. Urban infrastructure began to collapse and crime became epidemic. The cities of Harare, Bulawayo and Mutare, that had once attracted praise for their orderliness and cleanliness, became better known for pot holes, accumulated refuse, beggars, broken traffic and street lights and empty shop shelves.

With the loss of the farming community came also the loss of many private and co-operative game conservancies, particularly in the southeast. Protected areas and national parks experienced a massive increase in poaching, as starving people sought any means of survival. The tourist industry collapsed, and since this had been an industry dominated by whites, another wave packed up and left.

The value of the Zimbabwe dollar, that had begun its decline thanks to the war veteran payouts, was by then in unashamed freefall. A government determination to control the value saw a huge dichotomy between the official and the black market values of a greenback. This in turn opened vast and lucrative opportunities for connected people to source foreign exchange from the reserve bank at the official rate and sell it at anything up to 1000% profit on the black market, and in fact towards the end of the crisis much more even than this.

Even this was nothing compared to what came later. Rampant inflation became hyperinflation, perhaps beyond anything the world has previously seen. The official inflation figure in July 2008 was 231 million per cent and rising. Soon after, the rate became unmeasurable, but was generally believed to be at least in the quadrillions, if not sextillions (a number with 21 zeroes). In February 2009 US$1 bought $Z30 trillion and banknotes in denominations of up to $100 trillion were in circulation. Before the currency was replaced in April 2009 by South African rands and US dollars,

25 zeroes had been knocked off its value.

Politically there was certain liberty to be found in being outlawed. Mugabe, ever the consummate gamesman, found it easy to mould African weariness of white carping into unwillingness on the part of the African Union to be seen criticising him in response to white demands. This, and the fact that under the surface — and sometimes not that far under — black leaders were supportive of Mugabe in the light of his land redistribution programme, and the fact that he was willing to stand up to the imperialism and bullying tactics of the west. So long as he could claim the support of his black brethren, the old kith and kin no less, Mugabe could thumb his nose at the West, and he did.

* * *

2008 proved to be a watershed year for the revolution. By then tattered and abused, moulded by varied personal interests and perverted to reflect only the legitimacy of one party, efforts intensified to seize back what once had been of and for the people. This was to be an election year, and with so many lessons learned, it seemed unlikely that somehow this would not be the year of change.

In April 2007, South African President Thabo Mbeki was mandated by the Southern African Development Community (SADC) to mediate in the Zimbabwe crisis between ZANU-PF and the MDC. To the disappointment of many, the MDC — succumbing perhaps to the tremendous pressures heaped upon it — split into two rival factions, ostensibly over a disagreement whether to support or reject government efforts to institute a bi-cameral parliamentary system. The main MDC faction remained loyal to Morgan Tsvangirai, while a much smaller faction departed, taking with it some of the leading lights of the original party and falling in behind academic Arthur Mutambara.

This naturally weakened the MDC as an opposition movement and strengthened ZANU-PF. It also made things more difficult for Mbeki who was generally believed to be ideologically and personally allied to Mugabe, or at the very least subservient. Despite repeated public assurances, the South African leader had in the end confirmed the assessments of his critics and notably failed to advance the democratic order in Zimbabwe. The essence of his mediation on this occasion — a desperate hope it would seem — was to try and create the appearance of an election environment that could be judged clean and internationally acceptable. The intervention would not only tend to sweep Mbeki's many previous failures under the carpet, but if it also kept Mugabe — or at least ZANU-PF — in power, then so much the better.

Mbeki's whimsical — and at times disengaged — style caused many to suspect that he possessed neither the will nor the means to browbeat Mugabe into any meaningful change. Rumours frequently claimed that Mbeki's hand had somehow been in the dirty dealings during the DRC war, that had left him in fear of Mugabe who could at any time reveal the fact to the world. This view tended to be validated as Mugabe, displaying his usual truculence and inflexibility, appeared always to get the better of Mbeki in negotiations. In fact, while these talks were taking place, Mugabe unilaterally announced that a 'harmonised' election — meaning the co-ordination of the senate, local government, parliamentary and presidential ballots — would be held at the end of March 2008. Totally ignoring loud protests from opposition parties — in particular Tsvangirai's MDC — the date was gazetted and became a fait accompli. Mbeki seemed to do little but thoughtfully concur.

Thereafter, and despite lavish undertakings to permit unencumbered campaigning and absolute freedom of access to the state media, the usual routine of muffled reporting and state-sponsored violence barred the opposition from effective electioneering. Violence against the MDC and other anti-government elements was not quite as overt as in previous elections, but clearly the message had already been delivered. Under such severe scrutiny from the outside world, it seemed unnecessary to endlessly reinforce the point that Zimbabwe could expect very hard times if Robert Mugabe failed to renew his mandate to govern.

Meanwhile, all was not well within ZANU-PF itself. Indeed, the gravy train remained very lucrative and opportunities such as the evergreen foreign currency market, the appropriation of farming land and such sidelines as commercial trophy hunting in national parks, continued to net excellent returns. However, there were many on the fringes of business and the civil service — in particular the rank and file of the police and army — who were feeling the pinch, along with the vast bulk of the population. Combined with this, factions were forming within the Party. Alliances of old that had held firm throughout the liberation struggle and the golden years of independence, were beginning to show strain.

Robert Mugabe was now well into his 80s and the question of succession had been brewing for some time. Rumours suggested that Mugabe was keen to retire. But it was imperative for him first to be certain of the loyalty of any succeeding president or government, for the risk of prosecution hung like the Sword of Damocles over his head, and unless that risk could be neutralised he would never willingly give up office.

At that time, Mugabe's plan appeared to be to win a two-thirds legislative majority in the upcoming election, in order that he might amend the Constitution to allow for his successor to be selected by a parliamentary majority. He would then lead the party to a final victory, retiring shortly afterwards with significant behind-the-scenes authority, a handpicked successor and a rubberstamp parliament. The estrangement of Solomon Mujuru (nom de guerre Rex Nhongo) and a significant faction of the upper echelons of the Party, weakened the command structure but did not fatally compromise it. Charismatic former finance minister Simba Makoni was another disappointing defector. Makoni had been touted as both a potential compromise leader and Thabo Mbeki's personal preference, to give ZANU-PF an acceptable face on the international scene. Makoni announced his candidature as an independent and was quickly followed by ex-ZIPRA Intelligence supremo and ex-Cabinet Minister Dumiso Dabengwa, who threw his weight behind Makoni, promising that many other Party heavyweights would follow.

This was a very shaky moment for both ZANU-PF and Tsvangirai's MDC, for Arthur Mutambara had also joined Makoni in a high profile alliance. Many felt that Tsvangirai should also put aside personal ambition and support the person widely seen as the only compromise candidate who had a chance of breaking Mugabe's stranglehold.

In the event, the election held on 29 May 2008 proved that Tsvangirai had been wise to maintain his own independence. Despite the full weight of state machinery, massive election fraud and visible intimidation, Tsvangirai achieved a narrow parliamentary majority and an apparently clean sweep of the presidential vote.

Proof of the latter seemed to be the initial reluctance of the electoral commission to release the results of the presidential election. Suspicion turned to certainty as weeks followed days and nothing but deflections emanated from the information department. Behind the scenes it appeared that frantic consultations were taking place between Mugabe and his service chiefs. Information circulating immediately after the election suggested that the incumbent had briefly been willing to concede defeat, but his panicked security commanders would have none of it.

When results were eventually released several weeks later, the count — as expected –indicated a narrow defeat for Mugabe, but an insufficient margin for Tsvangirai to claim outright victory without a deciding run-off. It is highly probable that in the intervening period the results had been massaged and manipulated as far as was possible without instigating a national uprising.

Nevertheless, this was the signal for the bad old ZANU-PF to shake off its cloak of compromise and get back to the business of murdering, raping, burning and beating the general voting public into line. The runoff date was set, the ballots were cast, and as the nation reeled under a ferocious campaign of violence, Mugabe inevitably slipped through to a narrow presidential victory.

All that the run-off achieved, was to set the tone for a negotiation process that by one means or another Mugabe hoped to pervert as usual. The advantages that he enjoyed were the informal patronage of the South African presidency, the status of having little to lose, and considerable experience of scuttling agreements and breaking his word. The angst apparent in SADC — a body populated largely by progressive African leaders, trying to debunk negative African stereotypes — resulted in measured public criticism but strong behind the scenes pressure for either a transitional government — the MDC preference — or a government of national unity — the ZANU-PF preference.

After exhaustive negotiations under the careful tutelage of Thabo Mbeki, Mugabe predictably emerged as the ostensible victor, with an agreement wrung for a government of national unity. The agreement provided for a reasonably even power split, that would leave Mugabe in his accustomed role of Executive President, Tsvangirai as Prime Minister, and Mutambara claiming the 10% kingmaker's role. Amid great ceremony and an audible outpouring of relief, the irreconcilable foes shook hands and committed to the future.

Within weeks, however, the agreement was mired in disagreement and recrimination. The vital portfolios of Defence, Home Affairs — including Police, Finance and Agriculture, remained unresolved, and as if Tsvangirai could not have guessed, this was just the manna that Mugabe loved with his passion for mendacity and the exploitation of grey areas. His scope for confusion was increased when Thabo Mbeki's presidency abruptly collapsed and an interim president was appointed, before Jacob Zuma took his place at the helm of South African politics.

For all this, Mugabe should have been jubilant, and there's no doubt that, on a certain level, he was. But behind him, hovering like a malevolent shadow, were the service chiefs and other powerful backers who, over the years, had washed their hands in blood on his behalf. Clearly Mugabe was now less the architect of his own destiny than he had once been. The threat of international law hung over him and all those who, like him, had crossed the moral Rubicon — time and again — to maintain a grip on power from which none could now escape. With this diminishing clique, Mugabe was now locked into a tryst of mutual dependence. He was an elderly man condemned, like the mythical Sisyphus, to roll a boulder up a hill into perpetuity. His hubristic belief in his own genius was his crime, and his inability to leave office alive is his punishment.

As the close of the first decade of the new millennium fades this unresolved danse macabre enacted between Mugabe and Tsvangirai continues. For Mugabe the moral release that he so clearly desires remains elusive as does the inheritance of authentic power for Tsvangirai. Thus the future remains uncertain, with the predictable voices of optimism within the SADC community expressing it, and the usual portenders of despondency elsewhere doing likewise. The population of Zimbabwe has begun to enjoy a few fresh shoots of economic revival, but a very few indeed, while political liberty, press freedom and independent thought and activity remain tightly controlled.

However the inevitability of change remains a factor in this uncertain mix. That Mugabe — by now an octogenarian — must die or be rendered incapable at some point is in itself a source of hope. That he alone seems to be the glue binding the aging party together also gives hope that upon his demise the edifice will crumble. Most within and without Zimbabwe seem by 2010 to have succumbed to the inevitable. If the old man has a few good years left in him no amount of leverage will remove him. So long as he retains the power to manipulate any constitutional review and muster the forces of law and order to his bidding any quest for true democracy is hopeless. Thus the situation appears — temporarily at least — to be frozen.

Bibliography.

Ainslie, Rosalynde, Hoskyns, Catherine, Segal, Ronald. *Political Africa: A Who's Who of Personalities and Parties,* (Frederick A. Praeger, New York, 1961); **Anderson, David.** *Histories of the Hanged: The Dirty War in Kenya and the End of Empire,* (Norton, New York, 2005);**Arnold, Guy.** *Africa: A Modern History,* (Atlantic Books, London, 2005); **Arnold, W.E.** *The Goldbergs of Leigh Ranch,* (Books of Zimbabwe, Bulawayo, 1980.); **Atkinson, N.D.** *Teaching Rhodesians,* (Longmans, London, 1972); **Beach, David.** *The Shona And Their Neighbours,* (Blackwell, Oxford, 1994); **Becker, Peter.** *Path of Blood,* (Longmans, London, 1962); **Black, Colin.** *The Story of the Salisbury Club,* (Colin Black, Harare, 1980.); **Bhebe & Ranger.** *Soldiers in Zimbabwe's Liberation War, Vol. 1,* (University of Zimbabwe Publications, Harare, 1995); **Bhebe, Ngwabi.** *Simon Muzenda,* (Mambo Press, Gweru, 2004); **Blake, Robert.** *A History of Rhodesia,* (Alfred A. Knopf, New York, 1978); **Bond, G.** *The Incredibles: The Story of the First Battalion RLI,* (Sarum Imprint, 1977); **Bourdillon, M.F.C.** *The Shona Peoples,* (Mambo Press, Gwelo, 1976); **Bradley, Kenneth.** *Once a District Officer,* (Macmillan, London, 1966); **Cann, John P.** *Counterinsurgency in Africa: The Portuguese Way of War, 1961/1974,* (Greenwood Press, Westport, 1997); **Caute, David.** *Under the Skin,* (Penguin, UK, 1983); **Cary, Robert.** *A Time To Die,* (Howard Timmins, RSA, 1968); **Cary, Robert.** *The Story of Reps,* (Galaxie Press, Salisbury, 1975); **Cary, Robert & Mitchell, Diana.** *African Nationalist Leaders in Rhodesia Who's Who,* (Books of Rhodesia, Bulawayo, 1977); **Chigwedere, Aeneas.** *The Karanga Empire,* (Books for Africa, Harare); **Clements, Frank & Harben, Edward.** *Leaf of Gold,* (Methuen & Co, London, 1962); **Cole, Barbara.** *The Elite: The Rhodesian Special Air Services,* (Three Knights Publishing, Transkei, 1985); **Colquhoun, Archibald.** *From Dan to Beersheba,* (Kessinger, USA, 1908); **Danaher, Kevin.** *The Political Economy of U.S. Policy toward South Africa,* (Westview Press, Boulder Co., 1985); **Davidson, Appolon.** *Rhodes & His Time,* (Progress Publishers, Moscow, 1984); **Douglass, Frederick.** *Life and Times of Frederick Douglass,* (Collier Books, New York, 1962); **Dove, Father John.** *Strange Vagabond of God,* (Gracewing, UK, 1983); **Duffy, James.** *Portugal in Africa,* (Harvard University Press, Cambridge, MA., 1962); **Dupont, Clifford W.** *The Reluctant President,* (Books of Rhodesia, Bulawayo, 1978); **Ellert, Henrik.** *The Rhodesian Front War,* (Mambo Press, Gweru, 1993);**Fairbridge, Kingsley.** *Kingsley Fairbridge: His Life and Verse,* (Books of Rhodesia Publishing Co. Bulawayo, 1974); **Flower,Ken.** *Serving Secretly,* (Galago, Alberton, 1987); **Franck, Thomas M.** *Race and Nationalism,* (Fordham University Press, New York, 1960); **Gale, W.D.** *The Rhodesian Press,* (Rhodesian Printing & Publishing Company, Salisbury, 1962); **Gann, L.H. & Gelfand, M.** *Huggins of Rhodesia,* (George Allen & Unwin, London, 1964); **Gikandi, Simon.** *Encyclopaedia of African Literature,* (Routledge, New York, 2002); **Godwin, Peter and Hancock, Ian.** *Rhodesians Never Die,* (Baobab, Harare, 1999); **Gray, Richard.** *The Two Nations,* (Oxford University Press, London, 1960);**Hanhimäki, Jussi.** *The Flawed Architect: Henry Kissinger and American Foreign Policy,* (Oxford University Press, New York, 2004); **Hanna, A. J.** *The Story of the Rhodesias and Nyasaland,* (Faber and Faber, New York, 1960); **Hargreaves, John D.** *Decolonisation in Africa,* (Longman, London, 1996); **Holderness, Hardwicke.** *Lost Chance: Southern Rhodesia 1945-1958,* (Zimbabwe Publishing House, Harare, 1985); **Howarth, David.** *In the Shadow of the Dam,* (Collins, London, 1961); **James, Lawrence.** *The Rise and Fall of the British Empire,* (Little, Brown & Company, London, 1994); **Jardim, Jorge.** *Sanctions Double Cross,* (Books of Rhodesia, Bulawayo, 1979); **Johnson, Lt. Col. Frank.** *Great Days,* (Books of Rhodesia, Bulawayo, 1940); **Johnson, R.W.** *South Africa: First Man Last Nation,* (Jonathan Ball, Johannesburg, 2004.); **Kaunda, Kenneth David.** *Kaunda on Violence,* (Sphere, London, 1982); **Keatley, Patrick.** *The Politics of Partnership,* (Penguin Books, Baltimore, 1963); **Keyworth**

Davies, Dorothy. *Race relations in Rhodesia 1972-73*, (Rex Collings, London, 1975); **Knight Bruce, Bishop.** *Memories of Mashonaland*, (Rhodesia Reprint Library, Bulawayo, 1970); **Kriger, Norma J.** *Zimbabwe's Guerrilla War*, (Baobab, Harare, 1992); **Lan, David.** *Guns & Rain*, (University of California Press, Berkley, 1985); **Lardner-Burke, Desmond.** *Rhodesia*, (Oldbourne, London, 1966); **Lea, David.** *A Political Chronology of Africa*, (Europa Publications, London, 2001); **Lefever, Ernest W.** *Crisis in the Congo: A United Nations Force in Action*, (Brookings Institution, Washington DC, 1965); **Lewis, Arthur R.** *Too Bright the Vision*, (The Covenant Publishing Company, London, 1992); *Livingstone 1873 – 1973*, edited by **Lloyd, B.W.** (C. Struick (Pvt) Ltd, Cape Town.); **Lockhart, J.G. and Woodhouse, The Hon. C.M.** *Rhodes*, (Hodder & Stoughton, London, 1963); **MacBruce, James.** *When the Going was Rough*, (Femina Publishers, Pretoria, 1983); **Mackenzie, Rob.** *Livingstone*, (Fig Tree Publications, Chinoyi, 1993); **Mao Tse Tung**: *Selected Works, 1934, Vol. I*; **Martin, David & Johnson, Phyllis.** *The Chitepo Assassination*, (Zimbabwe Publishing House, Harare, 1985); **Martin, David & Johnson, Phyllis.** *The Struggle for Zimbabwe*, (Zimbabwe Publishing House, Harare, 1981); **McCulloch, Jock.** *Black Peril, White Virtue: Sexual Crime in Southern Rhodesia*, (Indiana University Press, Bloomington IN., 2000); **McDonald, J.G.** *Rhodes: A Life*, (Geoffrey Bles, London, 1927); **McIntyre, David W.** *A Guide to the Contemporary Commonwealth*, (Palgrave, New York, 2001); **McLaughlin, Janice.** *On the Frontline*, (Baobab, Harare, 1998); **McLaughlin, Peter.** *Ragtime Soldiers*, (Books of Zimbabwe, Bulawayo, 1980); **Meadows, Keith.** *Rupert Fothergill*, (Thorntree Press, Bulawayo, 1996); **Megahey, Allen.** *Humphrey Gibbs, Beleaguered Governor*, (Macmillan, London, 1998.); **Meredith, Martin.** *The State of Africa,* (Jonathan Ball, Johannesburg, 2005); **Millin, Sarah Gertrude.** *Rhodes*, (Chatto & Windus, London, 1934.); **Moorcraft, Paul L.** *A Short Thousand Years*, (Galaxie Press, Salisbury, 1980.); **Mugabe, Robert.** *Our War of Liberation: Speeches, Articles, interviews 1976-1979*, (Unknown Binding, 1983.); **Murray, D.J.** *Government Systems in Southern Rhodesia,* (Oxford Press, London, 1970); **Mutasa, Didymus.** *Rhodesian Black Behind Bars*, (Mowbray's, Oxford, 1974.); **Nutting, Anthony.** *Scramble for Africa: The Great Trek to the Boer War*, (Constable & Co, UK, 1994); **Nkomo, Joshua.** *The Story of My Life*, (Methuen, London, 1984); **Nyagumbo, Maurice.** *With The People*, (Graham Publishing, Salisbury, 1980); **Nyangoni, Wellington W.** *Africa in the United Nations System*, (Associated University Presses, Rutherford NJ., 1985); **O'Reilly, John.** *Pursuit of the King*, (Books of Rhodesia, Bulawayo, 1970); **Orde-Brown, Sir Grenville,** *The African Labourer,* (Frank Cass & Co, London 1967), **Irvin Painter, Nell.** *Creating Black Americans.* (Oxford University Press, New York, 2006); **Pakenham, Thomas.** *The Boer War*, (Jonathan Ball, Johannesburg, 1979); **Pakenham, Thomas.** *The Scramble for Africa*, (Jonathan Ball, Johannesburg 1991); **Parker, Jim.** *Assignment Selous Scouts*, (Galago Press, Alberton RSA, 2006); **Peck, A.J.A.** *Rhodesia Condemns*, (Three sisters books, Salisbury, 1967); **Pétré-Grenouilleau, Olivier.** *From Slave Trade to Empire: European Colonisation of Black Africa, 1780s-1880s*, (Routledge, New York, 2004); **Raeburn, Michael.** *Black Fire: Accounts of the Guerrilla War in Rhodesia*, (Julian Friedmann, London, 1978); **Ranger, Terence.** *Are We Not Also Men?* (Baobab Books, Harare, 1995); **Ransford, Oliver.** *Livingstone's Lake,* (John Murray, London 1966); **Ransford, Oliver.** *Rulers of Rhodesia*, (John Murray, London, 1968); **Richards, Hylda.** *Next year Will be Better*, (Howard B. Timmins, Cape Town, 1952); **Ritter, E.A.** *Shaka Zulu*, (Panther Books, London, 1958.); **Samkange, Stanlake.** *The Mourned One,* (Heinemann, London, 1975); **Saunders, Colin.** *Murray Macdougall and the story of Triangle*, (Triangle Ltd. 1989); **Schreiner, Olive.** *Trooper Peter Halket of Mashonaland*, (A.D. Donker, Johannesburg, 1897); **Shay, Reg & Vermaak, Chris.** *The Silent War*, (Galaxie Press, Salisbury, 1971); **Sherington, Geoffrey & Jeffery, Chris.** *Fairbridge: Empire & Child Migration*, (UWA Press, Nedlands, Western Australia, 1998.); **Sithole, Masipula.** *Zimbabwe: Struggles within the Struggle*, (Rujeko Publishers, Harare, 1999); **Sithole, Ndabaningi.** *African Nationalism*, (Oxford University Press, London, 1959);

Skinner, Elliot. *African Americans and U.S. Policy Towards Africa, 1850 – 1924*, (Howard University Press, Washington DC, 1992); **Smith, David & Simpson, Colin with Davis, Ian.** *Mugabe,* (Pioneer Head, Harare, 1981); **Smith, Ian Douglas.** *The Great Betrayal*, (Blake, London, 1997); **Smuts, Jan.** *Jan Christian Smuts*, (Cassell & Co. Ltd, Cape Town, 1952.); **Solzhenitsyn, Aleksandr.** *One Day in the Life of Ivan Denisovich*, (Penguin, London, 1975); **Stent, Vere.** *A personal Record of some Incidents in the Life of Cecil Rhodes,* (Unknown binding, 1924); **Storry, J.G.** *The Shattered Nation*, (Howard Timmins, Cape Town, 1974); **Stiff, Peter.** *Cry Zimbabwe*, (Galago Publishing, Alberton RSA, 2000); **Stiff, Peter.** *The Silent War*, (Galago Publishing, 1999.); **Stiff, Peter.** See *You In November*, (Galago Publishing, Alberton RSA, 1985); **Stiff, Peter.** *Selous Scouts: Top Secret War*, (Galago Publishing, Alberton RSA, 1982); **Sutton Pryce, Ted.** *Zimbabwe: A Model for Namibia*, (Academica, Pretoria, 1989); **Sykes, Frank W.** *With Plumer in Matabeleland*, (Books of Rhodesia, Bulawayo, 1972); **Tawse Jollie, Ethel.** *The Real Rhodesia,* (Books of Rhodesia, Bulawayo, 1971); **Thompson, Carol B.** *Challenge to Imperialism: The Frontline States in the Liberation of Zimbabwe*, (Westview Press, Boulder CO., 1986) **Tredgold, Sir Robert.** *The Rhodesia that was my Life*, (Allen & Unwin, London, 1968); **Twain, Mark.** *Following the Equator*, (Project Gutenberg 2006); **Washington, Booker T.** *Up From Slavery.* (A.L. Burt, New York, 1901):**Welensky, Sir Roy.** *4000 Days,* (Collins, London, 1964.); **Young, Kenneth.** *Rhodesia and Independence*, (Eyre & Spottiswoode, London, 1967); *Zimbabwe: Search for Common Ground.* From the Pages of *Drum Magazine.* (Bailey African Photos Archive Production, 1992.)

Reports

Corfield, F.D. *The Origins and Growth of Mau Mau: A Historical Survey*, (1960); **McNamee, J. P.** *Report on Native Urban Administration in Bulawayo* 2 December 1948

Newspapers and Magazines

Kanengoni, Alexander. *Memories of Sobbing Shadows at Nyadzonia*, Sunday Mail, 08 August (2004.); *Heritage of Zimbabwe* (Nos. 1 to 12.)

Web Sources

Wikimedia Foundation, Inc; www.*rhodesia.net*

Notes

Chapter 1
1 Ransford, Oliver. *Livingstone's Lake*, p95.
2 Mayr, Hans. *Modern History Sourcebook: The Voyage and Acts of Dom Francisco*. Taken from http:www.fordham.edu//halsa/mod/1505mayr.html
3 Ransford, Oliver. *Rulers of Rhodesia*, p31.
4 Wikipedia Foundation.

Chapter 3
1 Quoted: Pakenham, Thomas. *The Scramble for Africa*, p46.
2 McDonald, J.G. *Rhodes: A Life,* p29.
3 Quoted: Millin, Sarah Gertrude. *Rhodes*, p29.
4 *Ibid.* p32.

Chapter 4
1 Godwin, Peter. *Rhodes to Hell*, (Slate Magazine, January 1998)
2 McDonald, J.G. *Rhodes: A Life,* p83.

Chapter 5
1 Quoted: Davidson, Appolon. *Rhodes & His Time*, p169.
2 Blake, Robert. *A History of Rhodesia*, p50.
3 Quoted: Davidson, Appolon. *Rhodes & His Time*, p163.

Chapter 6
1 Blake, Robert. *A History of Rhodesia*, p61.

Chapter 7
1 Hensman, Howard. *A History of Rhodesia*: www.rhodesia.nl/hensman.pdf

2 Blake, Robert. *A History of Rhodesia*, p72.

Chapter 8
1 Quoted: Davidson, Appolon. *Rhodes & his Time*, p195.
2 *Ibid.* p195.
3 Hensman, Howard. *A History of Rhodesia*.
4 Johnson, Lt. Col. Frank. *Great Days,*.
5 Hensman, Howard. *A History of Rhodesia*.
6 Hillegas, Howard C. *Portuguese East Africa As a Hunting Field.* www.aafla.org
7 Colvin, Ian. *The Life of Jameson*, p156.
8 Ransford, Oliver. *Rulers of Rhodesia*, p223.

Chapter 9
1 Clements, Frank & Harben, Edward. *Leaf of Gold*, p37.
2 Blake, Robert. *A History or Rhodesia*, p114.
3 *Ibid.* p96.
4 Gale, W.D. *The Rhodesian Press*, p11.
5 Lockhart, J.G. & Woodhouse, The Hon. C.M. *Rhodes*, p248.
6 Gale, W.D. *The Rhodesian Press*, p13/14.
7 *Solomon M. Mtswairo. Cecil Rhodes & his Time*, p196.

Chapter 10
1 Quoted: Davidson, Appolon. *Cecil Rhodes & His Time*, p209.
2 Plaque attached to oil painting by Allen Stewart, *To the Memory of Brave men.*
3 The *Wikipedia* Foundation
4 Blake, Robert. *A History of Rhodesia*, p108.
5 Ransford, Oliver. *The Rulers Of Rhodesia*, p250.

6 O'Reilly, John. *Pursuit of the King*, (Books of Rhodesia, Bulawayo, 1970), p90.
7 *Ibid.* p88.
8 *Ibid.* p91.

Chapter 11
1 Sykes, Frank W. *With Plumer in Matabeleland*, (Books of Rhodesia), Bulawayo, 1972), p11.

Chapter 12
1 Twain, Mark. *Following the Equator*, p687.
2 Smuts, Jan. *Jan Christian Smuts*, p33.
3 Millin, Sarah Gertrude. *Rhodes*, p277.
4 *Ibid.* p281.
5 Pakenham, Thomas. *The Boer War*, p4.

Chapter 13
1 Sykes, Frank W. *With Plumer in Matabeleland*, p14.
2 Sykes, Frank W. *With Plumer in Matabeleland*, p263
3 Stent, Vere. *A personal Record of some Incidents in the Life of Cecil Rhodes,* p27/62.
4 *Ibid.* p27-62.
5 *Ibid.*

Chapter 14
1 Millin, Sarah Gertrude. *Rhodes*, p335.
2 Fairbridge, Kingsley. *Kingsley Fairbridge: His Life and Verse,* p17.
3 Skinner, Elliot P. *African Americans and US Policy towards Africa, 1850 – 1924*, p156.
4 Tanser, GH. *A Scantling of Time*, p.179.
5 Hensman, Howard. *A History of Rhodesia*, p45

6   Fairbridge, Kingsley. *Kingsley Fairbridge: His Life and Verse*, p21. Dumblain', corruption of *'down below'* in the mine.

7   Fairbridge, Kingsley. *Kingsley Fairbridge: His Life and Verse*, p42.

8   Millin, Sarah Gertrude. *Rhodes*, p349.

Chapter 16

1   Tawse Jollie. Ethel, *The Real Rhodesia*, p34.

2   W.D. Gale, *The Rhodesian Press*, p80.

3   *Ibid.* p82.

4   *Ibid.* p83.

5   Tawse Jollie, Ethel. *The Real Rhodesia*, p61.

Chapter 17

1   McLaughlin, Peter. *Ragtime Soldiers*, p2.

2   James, Lawrence. *The Rise and Fall of the British Empire*, p353.

3   Smuts, J.C. *Jan Christian Smuts*, p155.

4   *Ibid.* p169.

5   McLaughlin, Peter. *Ragtime Soldiers*, p75.

Chapter 18

1   Tawse Jollie, Ethel. *The Real Rhodesia*, p75.

2   Gale, W.D. *The Rhodesian Press*, p117.

Chapter 19

1   Murray, D.J. *Government Systems in Southern Rhodesia*, p16.

2   Clements, Frank & Harben, Edward. *Leaf of Gold*, p92.

Chapter 20

1   Murray, D.J. *Government Systems in Southern Rhodesia*

2   Samkange *Archives*, quoted: Ranger, Terence.

Are we not also Men? p15.

3   Elliot, W.A. to L.M.S. Board, 19th February 1890.

4   Quoted: Ransford, Oliver. *The Rulers of Rhodesia*, p107.

5   Bishop Knight-Bruce to the S.P.G. Boards 19/11/1893. Quoted Atkinson, N.D. *Teaching Rhodesians*, p27.

6   Samkange, Stanlake. *The Mourned One,* p53.

7   *Graham Committee Report*, 1911. *para* 88. Quoted: Atkinson, N.D. *Teaching Rhodesians*, p94.

8   Keyworth Davies, Dorothy. *Race relations in Rhodesia 1972-73*, p262.

9   *Samkange Archives*, quoted Terence Ranger, *Are we not also Men?* p7/8.

10 Samkange, Stanlake. *The Mourned One*, p119.

Chapter 21

1   Tredgold, Sir Robert. *The Rhodesia that was my Life*, p 154/5.

2   Quoted: Blake, Robert. *A History of Rhodesia*, p215.

Chapter 22

1   Clements, Frank & Harben, Edward. *Leaf of Gold*, p91.

2   Bradley, Kenneth. *Once a District Officer*, p150.

3   John D. Hargreaves, *Decolonisation in Africa*, p6.

4   Gray, Richard. *The two Nations*, p5.

5   Douglass, Frederick. *Life and Times of Frederick Douglass*, p337.

6   Gray, Richard. *The two Nations*, p7.

7   *Ibid.* p41.

8   *Memorandum on Native Policy in East Africa* (Cmd. 3573, 1930).

9   Central African Archives, ZAH 1/1/3, pp. 1625-8.

Chapter 23

1   McCulloch, Jock. *Black Peril, White Virtue: Sexual Crime in Southern Rhodesia*, p176.

2   Gray, Richard. *The Two Nations,* p20.

Chapter 24

1   Richards, Hylda. *Next year Will be Better*, p15.

2   *Ibid.* p16.

3   *Ibid.* p17.

4   The African Labourer, p87.

5   Richards, Hylda. *Next year Will be Better*, p190.

6   Holderness, Hardwicke. *Lost Chance: Southern Rhodesia 1945-1958,* p12.

7   Fairbridge, Kingsley. *Kingsley Fairbridge: His life and verse*, p12.

Chapter 25

1   Gann, L.H. & Gelfand, M. *Huggins of Rhodesia*, p96.

Chapter 26

1   Sithole, Ndabaningi. *African Nationalism*, p23.

2   *The Younger Church in South Africa. A Contribution to Missionary work in South Africa and to the International Missionary Council at Madras,* 1938.

Chapter 27

1   Blake, Robert. *A History of Rhodesia*, p233.

2   Gann, L.H. & Gelfand, M. *Huggins of Rhodesia*, p166.

Chapter 28

1   Washington, Booker T. *His Educational Philosophy.* Atlanta Compromise Address.

2   Sithole, Ndabaningi. *African Nationalism*, p37.

3   Nell, Irvin Painter. *Creating Black Americans*, p11.

4   Gray, Richard. *The Two Nations*, p29

5   *S.R. Debates*, 2-3 November 1944, cols. 2499-2506.

6   Sithole, Ndabaningi. *African Nationalism*, p39.

7   Quoted: Gray, Richard. *The Two Nations*, p254.

8   McNamee, J.P *Report on Native Urban Administration in Bulawayo* 2/12/48.

9   Quoted: Ranger, Terence, *Are We Not Also Men*, p91.

10   Peter Gibbs, *Stronger than Armies*.

11   *S.R. Debates*, 5 May 1948, col. 19.

12   Holderness, Hardwicke. *Lost Chance: Southern Rhodesia 1945 – 1958*, p67.

Chapter 30

1   *Reformed Industrial and Commercial Workers Union of Africa*. Quoted: Holderness, Hardwick. *Lost Chance*, p74.

2   Holderness, Hardwick. *Lost Chance: Southern Rhodesia 1845 - 1958*, p76.

3   *Ibid*. p77.

Chapter 31

1   *Time Magazine,* 27/4/62

2   Welensky, Sir Roy. *4000 Days,* p15.

3   Hanna, A. J. *The Story of the Rhodesias and Nyasaland*, p248.

4   Welensky, Sir Roy. *4000 Days,* p33.

5   *Ibid, p34/35.*

6   Hanna, A. J. *The Story of the Rhodesias and Nyasaland*, p252.

7   Kaunda, Kenneth David. *Kaunda on Violence*, p25.

8   Corfield, F.D. *The Origins and Growth of Mau Mau: A Historical Survey*, 1960, p136.

9   Anderson, David. *Histories of the Hanged: The Dirty War in Kenya and the End of Empire,* p224/5.

10   *Zimbabwe: Search for Common Ground.* From the Pages of *Drum* Magazine. 1992. p43.

Chapter 33

1   Quoted: Ainslie, Hoskyns, Segal. *Political Africa: A Who's Who of Personalities and Parties.* p260.

2   Franck, Thomas M. *Race and Nationalism,* (Fordham University Press, New York, 1960), p65.

3   *Ibid*. p66.

4   *Report of the Chief Native Commissioner* for 1913 (A8-1914).

5   *Southern Rhodesia Legislative Assembly Debates,* vol. 29 Nov. 1948.

6   Gray, Richard. *The Two Nations,* p61.

7   Alvord, e.d. *National Affairs Association Lecture*, 1948.

8   Holderness, Hardwicke. *Lost Chance*, p110.

9   *Ibid*. p114.

10   Keatley, Patrick. *The Politics of Partnership*, p22.

11   Smith, David & Simpson, Colin with Davis, Ian. *Mugabe*, p19.

Chapter 34

1   Tredgold Report, *supra* note 40, at 1. Quoted: Franck, Thomas M. *Race and Nationalism*, p183.

2   Franck, Thomas M. *Race and Nationalism*, p182.

3   *Tredgold Report, supra* note 40, at 6. Quoted: Franck, Thomas M. *Race and Nationalism*, p183.

4   *Zimbabwe: The Search for Common Ground*, 1992, p70.

5   *Time Magazine*, Feb 22/2/54

6   *The World Federation of Trade Unions*, United Kingdom (Case No. 103) Report No 15. Vol XXXVIII 1955, No. 1.

7   *Time Magazine*, 22/2/54.

8   Smith, Ian Douglas. *The Great Betrayal*, p35.

Chapter 35

1   Welensky, Sir Roy. *4000 Days*, p68.

2   Quoted: Keatley, Patrick. *The Politics of Partnership*, p433.

3   Welensky, Sir Roy. *4000 Days*, p85.

4   Sithole, Ndabaningi. *African Nationalism*, p36.

5   Flower, Ken. *Serving Secretly*, p9.

Chapter 36

1   Blake, Robert. *A History of Rhodesia,* p326.

2   Lefever, Ernest W. *Crisis in the Congo: A UN Force in Action*, p3.

3   *Zimbabwe: Search for Common Ground*, 1992, p73.

4   Keatley, Patrick. *The Politics of Partnership*, p219.

5   Kaunda, Kenneth. *Kaunda on Violence*, p41.

6   *Zimbabwe: Search for Common Ground*, 1992, p72.

Chapter 37

1 Dupont, Clifford W. *The Reluctant President*, p110.
2 *Ibid*. p110.

Chapter 38

1 Smith, Ian Douglas. *The Great Betrayal*, p35.
2 Quoted: Megahey, Alan. *Humphrey Gibbs: Beleaguered Governor*, p56.
3 Blake, Robert. *A History of Rhodesia*, p320.
4 Holderness, Hardwicke. *Lost Chance*, p223.
5 Blake, Robert. *A History of Rhodesia*, p320.
6 Quoted: Smith, Ian Douglas. *The Great Betrayal*, p35.
7 Holderness, Hardwicke. *Lost Chance*, p227.

Chapter 39

1 Nkomo, Joshua. *The Story of My Life*, p82.
2 *Zimbabwe: Search for Common Ground*, 1992, p65.
3 Johnson, R.W. *South Africa: First Man Last Nation*, p151/2
4 *Zimbabwe: Search for Common Ground*, 1992, p65.
5 Keyworth Davis, Dorothy. *Race Relations in Rhodesia 1972-1973*, p194.
6 Smith & Simpson with Davis. *Mugabe*, p28.
7 Cary, Robert & Mitchell, Diana. *African Nationalist Leaders in Rhodesia Who's Who*, p165.
8 Smith & Simpson with Davis, *Mugabe*, p18.
9 *Zimbabwe: The Search For Common Ground*, 1992, page 85.
10 *Ibid*. p79.

11 *Ibid*. p89.

Chapter 40

1 *Zimbabwe: The Search For Common Ground*, 1992, p92.
2 Bhebe, Ngwabi. *Simon Muzenda*, p109.
3 Nkomo, Joshua. *The Story of My Life*, p98.
4 Gikandi, Simon. *Encyclopaedia of African Literature*, p495.
5 Bhebe, Ngwabi. *Simon Muzenda*, p129.
6 Smith & Simpson with Davis, *Mugabe*, p41.
7 Young, Kenneth. *Rhodesia and Independence*, p63.
8 Shay & Vermaak. *The Silent War*, p11.
9 *Zimbabwe: The Search For Common Ground*, 1992, page 80.
10 *Ibid*. p81.
11 *Ibid*. p160.
12 *Ibid*. p128.
13 Sithole, Masipula. *Zimbabwe: Struggles within the Struggle*, p15/16.
14 *Hansard/Commons*, Vol. 737, 7 December 1966.
15 Ellert, Henrik. *Rhodesian Front War*, p2.
16 Young, Kenneth. *Rhodesia and Independence*, p61.
17 *Ibid*. p53.
18 Nyangoni, Wellington W. *Africa in the United Nations System*, p111.

Chapter 41

1 Megahey, Alan. *Humphrey Gibbs: Beleaguered Governor*, p80.

Chapter 42

1 Sithole, Masipula. *Zimbabwe: Struggles within the Struggle*, p40.
2 *Ibid*. p41.

3 Bhebe & Ranger. *Soldiers in Zimbabwe's Liberation War, Vol. 1*, p26
4 Sithole, Masipula. *Zimbabwe: Struggles within the Struggle*, p40.
5 *Ibid*. p38.
6 Quoted: Sithole, Masipula. *Zimbabwe: Struggles within the Struggle*, p39.
7 *Zimbabwe: The Search for Common Ground*, 1992, p210.
8 *Ibid*. p218.
9 Raeburn, Michael. *Black Fire: Accounts of the Guerrilla War in Rhodesia*, p63.
10 Stiff, Peter. *See You In November*, p126.

Chapter 43

1 Welensky, Sir Roy. *4000 Days*, p359.
2 Smith, Ian Douglas. *The Great Betrayal*, p50.
3 *Ibid*. p51.
4 Young, Kenneth. *Rhodesia and Independence*, p75.
5 Smith, Ian Douglas. *The Great Betrayal*, p51.
6 *Ibid*. p53
7 *Ibid* p54.
8 Flower, Ken. *Serving Secretly*, p24.

Chapter 44

1 Flower, Ken. *Serving Secretly*, p32.
2 Quoted: Young, Kenneth. *Rhodesia and Independence*, p171.
3 Smith, Ian Douglas. *The Great Betrayal*, p84.
4 Quoted: Megahey, Alan. *Humphrey Gibbs: Beleaguered Governor*, p93.
5 Blake, Robert. *A History of Rhodesia*, p371.
6 Quoted: Blake, Robert. *A*

History of Rhodesia, p371.

7   Megahey, Alan. *Humphrey Gibbs: Beleaguered Governor*, p95.
8   Smith, Ian Douglas. *The Great Betrayal*, p92.
9   *Ibid*. p94.
10 Rhodesia Christian Group, *Occasional Newsletter*, June 1999.
11 Quoted: Megahey, Alan. *Humphrey Gibbs: Beleaguered Governor*, p104.

Chapter 45
1   Flower, Ken. *Serving Secretly*, p50.
2   Nyangoni, Wellington W. *Africa in the United Nations System*, p115.
3   Megahey, Alan. *Humphrey Gibbs: Beleaguered Governor*, p98.

Chapter 46
1   Flower, Ken. *Serving Secretly*, p77.
2   Dupont, Clifford. *The Reluctant President*, p165.
3   *Ibid*. p165.
4   Quoted: Flower, Ken. *Serving Secretly*, p79.
5   Wikipedia Foundation.
6   Macdonald, Judge Hector N. QC. *A Critical Survey of UDI*, 1997, p14.
7   Smith, Ian Douglas. *The Great Betrayal*, p109.
8   *Prime Minister Harold Wilson's speech to the House of Commons on November 11, 1965*. Quoted: Nyangoni, Wellington W. *Africa in the United Nations System*, p115.
9   Moorcraft, Paul L. *A Short Thousand Years*, p19.
10 Arnold, Guy. *Africa: a Modern History*, p291.

11 Smith, Ian Douglas. *The Great Betrayal*, p115.
12 *Ibid*. p114.
13 *News of the World*, 10/9/78. Quoted: Nyangoni, Wellington W. *Africa in the United Nations System*, p125.
14 Wellington W. Nyangoni, *Africa in the United Nations System*, p128.
15 Stiff, Peter. The *Silent War*, p26.
16 Ellert, Henrik. *The Rhodesian Front War*, p11.
17 Flower, Ken. *Serving Secretly*, p106.
18 *Ibid*. p106/7.

Chapter 47
1   Arnold, Guy. *Africa: a Modern History*, p292.

Chapter 48
1   Nyangoni, Wellington W. *Africa in the United Nations System*, p120.
2   *Sunday Independent* (SA) 20/1/08.
3   Smith & Simpson with Davis, *Mugabe*, p57.
4   Eddison Zvobgo, Quoted: Bhebe, Ngwabi. *Simon Vengai Muzenda & The Struggle for and Liberation of Zimbabwe*, p149/150.
5   *Zimbabwe: Search for Common Ground*, 1992, p240.
6   *Ibid*. p242.
7   *Ibid*. p245.

Chapter 49
1   Flower, Ken. *Serving Secretly*, p85.
2   Megahey, Alan. *Humphrey Gibbs: Beleaguered Governor*, p138.
3   Ellert, Henrik. *The Rhodesian Front War*, p27.
4   Moorcraft, Paul L. *A Short*

Thousand Years, p34.
5   *Ibid*. p18.
6   Solzhenitsyn, Aleksandr. *One Day in the Life of Ivan Denisovich*, p36.
7   Bhebe, Ngwabi. *Simon Vengai Muzenda & The Struggle for and Liberation of Zimbabwe*, p153.
8   Nyagumbo, Maurice. *With The People*, p204.
9   *Ibid*. p206.
10 Smith & Simpson with Davis, *Mugabe*, p67.

Chapter 50
1   Smith, Ian Douglas. *The Great Betrayal*, p153.
2   Flower, Ken. *Serving Secretly*, p100.
3   Arnold, Guy. *Africa: a Modern History*, p505.
4   Mutasa, Didymus. *Rhodesian Black Behind Bars*, p92/93

Chapter 51
1   Cann, John P. *Counterinsurgency in Africa: The Portuguese Way of War*, p1.
2   Stiff, Peter, as told to by R Reid Daly. *Selous Scouts Top Secret War*, p24.
3   Flower, Ken. *Serving Secretly*, p135.
4   *Ibid*. p121.
5   Josiah Tungamirai. Quoted: Lan, David. *Guns & Rain*, p77/78.
6   Lan, David. *Guns & Rain*, p157.
7   Godwin, Peter & Hancock, Ian. *Rhodesians Never Die*, p101/2
8   Ellert, Hendrik. *The Rhodesian Front War*, p117/8
9   Quoted: Flower, Ken. *Serving Secretly*, p113
10 *Ibid*. p121.

11   Godwin and Hancock, *Rhodesians Never Die*, p88

Chapter 52

1   Press Release 7 October 1971. Quoted: Sithole, Masipula. *Zimbabwe: Struggles-Within-The Struggle*, p120.
2   *Ibid.* p120.
3   *Ibid.* p122.
4   Martin, David & Johnson, Phyllis. *The Struggle for Zimbabwe*, p99
5   *Ibid.* p100
6   Smith, Ian Douglas. *The Great Betrayal*, p157/8.
7   Sithole, Masipula. *Zimbabwe: Struggles-Within-the Struggle*, p141.

Chapter 53

1   Flower, Ken. *Serving Secretly*, p138.
2   *Ibid.* p138
3   *Ibid.* p139.
4   Parker, Jim. *Assignment Selous Scouts*, p74.

Chapter 54

1   Stiff, Peter. *The Silent War*, p152.
2   Parker, Jim. *Assignment Selous Scouts,* p159
3   *Ibid.*
4   *Ibid.*
5   *Ibid.*
6   *Ibid.*

Chapter 55

1   *Wikimedia Foundation, Inc.*
2   *Ibid.*
3   *Pieter van de Byl, Pieter Rich, white aristocrat behind Rhodesia's bid to stop black rule, The Guardian*, 30/11/99.
4   Parker, Jim. *Assignment Selous Scouts*, p43.
5   Nyagumbo, Maurice. *With the People*, p217.
6   Martin & Johnson, *The Struggle for Zimbabwe*, p151.
7   Ellert, Hendrik. *The Rhodesian Front War*, p62.

Chapter 56

1   Martin & Johnson. *The Struggle for Zimbabwe*, p160.
2   Stiff, Peter. *See You In November*, p109.
3   Sithole, Masipula. *Zimbabwe: Struggles-within-the-struggle*, p75.
4   *Ibid.* p75.
5   Parker, Jim. *Assignment Selous Scouts,* p43.
6   Stiff, Peter. See *You In November*, p110.
7   Milius, John and Ford Coppola, Francis. *Apocalypse Now,* original screenplay.
8   Stiff, Peter. See *You In November*, p118.
9   Smith & Simpson with Davis, *Mugabe*, p82.

Chapter 58

1   Mgagao Declaration. Quoted: Martin & Johnson, *The Struggle for Zimbabwe*, p201.
2   *Ibid.* p202.
3   Quoted: Smith & Simpson with Davis. *Mugabe*, p86.
4   Martin & Johnson. *The Struggle for Zimbabwe*, p223.
5   Parker, Jim. *Assignment Selous Scouts*, p46.
6   *Ibid.*
7   *Ibid.*
8   *Ibid.* p55.
9   Godwin & Hancock, *Rhodesian Never Die*, p148/9.
10   *www.rhodesia.nl*

Chapter 59

1   Lea, David. *A Political Chronology of Africa*, p327.
2   Cole, Barbara. *The Elite*, p245.
3   *Sunday Independent* (SA), 20/1/08.
4   Moorcraft, Paul. *A short Thousand Years*, p35.
5   Kanengoni, Alexander. *Memories of Sobbing Shadows at Nyadzonia, Sunday Mail*, 08/08/2004 August 2004
6   Parker, Jim. *Assignment Selous Scouts*, p77.

Chapter 60

1   Hanhimäki, Jussi. *The Flawed Architect: Henry Kissinger and American Foreign Policy*, p425.
2   Stiff, Peter. *The Silent War*, p242.
3   Wikipedia Foundation
4   Danaher, Kevin. *The Political Economy of U.S. Policy toward South Africa*, p124.
5   Flower, Ken. *Serving Secretly*, p165.
6   Smith, Ian Douglas. *The Great Betrayal*, p202.
7   Caute, David. *Under the Skin*, (Penguin, 1983), p113.
8   Smith, Ian Douglas. *The Great Betrayal*, p201.
9   Rhodesian Christian Group, *Occasional Newsletter*, June 1999.
10   *Ibid.*
11   *Ibid.*
12   Martin & Johnson. *The Struggle for Zimbabwe*, p252.
13   Smith & Simpson with Davis. *Mugabe*, p92.

14   Bhebe, Ngwabi. *Simon Vengai Muzenda & The Struggle for and Liberation of Zimbabwe*, p199.

Chapter 61
1   Smith & Simpson with Davis. *Mugabe*, p95.
2   Flower, Ken. *Serving Secretly*, p173.
3   Caute, David. *Under the Skin*, p69.
4   Smith & Simpson with Davis, *Mugabe*, p95
5   Caute, David. *Under the Skin*, p68.
6   *Ibid*. p78.
7   Smith, Ian Douglas. *The Great Betrayal*, p222.

Chapter 62
1   Smith & Simpson with Davis, *Mugabe*, p98.
2   Ellert, Hendrik. *The Rhodesian Front War*, p67
3   *Ibid*. p68.
4   *Ibid*. p72.

Chapter 63
1   McLaughlin, Janice. *On the Frontline*, p150.
2   *rhodesia.net*
3   Nyangoni, Wellington W. *Africa in the United Nations System*, p131.
4   Smith, Ian Douglas. *The Great Betrayal*, p223.
5   *Ibid*. p260.
6   Stiff, Peter. *The Silent War*, p257.
7   Caute, David. *Under the Skin*, p136.
8   Smith, Ian Douglas. *The Great Betrayal*, p233.
9   Caute, David. *Under the Skin*, p100/1
10   Parker, Jim. *Assignment Selous Scouts*, p121.
11   *Ibid*. p 121

Chapter 64
1   Caute, David. *Under the Skin*, p109.
2   Smith, Ian Douglas. *The Great Betrayal*, p230.
3   Flower, Ken. *Serving Secretly*, p182.
4   *The Zimbabwe Patriotic Front on British 'Proposals for a Settlement' in Rhodesia*. Quoted: Martin & Johnson, *The Struggle for Zimbabwe*, 1981, p273.
5   Mugabe, Robert. *Our War of Liberation: Speeches, Articles, interviews 1976-1979*, p6.
6   Flower, Ken. *Serving Secretly*, p193.
7   Smith, Ian Douglas. *The Great Betrayal*, p241/2.
8   Smith & Simpson with Davis, *Mugabe*, p107.
9   Nyangoni, Wellington W. *Africa in the United Nations System*, p152.
10   Smith, Ian Douglas. *The Great Betrayal*, p247.

Chapter 65
1   Godwin and Hancock, *Rhodesians Never Die*, p210.
2   *Rhodesia Herald*, 27/6/77
3   Caute, David. *Under the Skin*, p257.

Chapter 66
1   Nyangoni, Wellington W. *Africa in the United Nations System*, p152.
2   *The Times*, 26/4/7. Quoted: Flower, Ken. *Serving Secretly*, p198.
3   Flower, Ken. *Serving Secretly*, p197.
4   *Ibid*. p201
5   Mugabe, Robert. *Our War of Liberation*.
6   Stiff, Peter. *See You In November*, p187.
7   Stiff, Peter. *See You In November*, p193.
8   Mugabe, Robert. *Our War of Liberation*.
9   Godwin and Hancock, *Rhodesians Never Die*, p209.
10   Ellert, Hendrik. *The Rhodesian Front War*, p77.
11   Caute, David. *Under the Skin*, p346.

Chapter 67
1   *Rhodesia Herald,* 03/05/78
2   Caute, David. *Under the Skin*, p299.

Chapter 68
1   Smith & Simpson with Davis, *Mugabe*, p113.
2   Cole, Barbara. *The Elite*, p271.
3   *Ibid*. p260.
4   Wikipedia Foundation.
5   Cole, Barbara. *The Elite*, 1985, p272.
6   *Ibid*. p274.
7   Flower, Ken. *Serving Secretly*, p222.
8   *Ibid*. p223.
9   *Ibid*. p222/3.
10   Smith, Ian Douglas. *The Great Betrayal*, p309.
11   Caute, David. *Under the Skin*, p361.
12   Sutton-Pryce, Ted. *Zimbabwe: A Model for Namibia*, p4/5.

Chapter 69
1   *Rhodesia Herald*, May 1979.
2   Thompson, Carol B. *Challenge to Imperialism: The Frontline States in the Liberation of Zimbabwe*, p66.
3   *Ibid*.
4   Smith & Simpson with Davis, *Mugabe*, p118.
5   *Ibid*. p119.

6   Quoted: Macdonald, Judge
    Hector N. QC, *A Critical
    Survey of UDI,* 1997, p12.
7   *Ibid.* p20.
8   *Foreign Office Briefing
    Notes release under 30 year
    rules.* Quoted Peter Stiff.
9   Parker, Jim. *Assignment
    Selous Scouts*, p246.

Chapter 70
1   Quoted: Macdonald, Judge
    Hector N. QC, *A Critical
    Survey of UDI,* 1997, p20.
2   Sutton Pryce, Ted.
    *Zimbabwe: A Model for
    Namibia*, p10.
3   Smith, Ian Douglas. *The
    Great Betrayal*, p319.
4   *Ibid.* p316.
5   Smith & Simpson with
    Davis, *Mugabe*, p130.
6   *Ibid.* p137.
7   Stiff, Peter. *The Silent War*,
    p273.
8   Smith & Simpson with
    Davis, *Mugabe*, p140.
9   Flower, Ken. *Serving
    Secretly*, p247.
10 Sutton Pryce, Ted.
    *Zimbabwe: A Model for
    Namibia*, p13.

Chapter 71
1   Sutton Pryce, Ted.
    *Zimbabwe: A Model for
    Namibia*, p21.
2   *Wikimedia* Foundation.
3   *Ibid.*
4   Quoted: Flower, Ken.
    Serving Secretly, p256.
5   Smith, Ian Douglas. *The
    Great Betrayal*, p332.
6   *Ibid.* p339.
7   Quoted: Flower, Ken.
    Serving Secretly, p255.
8   Sutton Pryce, Ted.
    *Zimbabwe: A Model for
    Namibia*, p20.
9   Parker, Jim. *Assignment
    Selous Scouts*, p274.

10 *Ibid.* p274.

Chapter 72
1   Parker, Jim. *Assignment
    Selous Scouts*, p276.
2   *Ibid.* p277
3   *Ibid*, p283.
4   *Ibid.* p279
5   *Ibid.* p279.
6   *Ibid.*
7   Flower, Ken. *Serving
    Secretly*, p267/8.
8   Parker, Jim. *Assignment
    Selous Scouts,* p318.

Chapter 73
1   *www.manikus.com*
2   Quoted: Parker, Jim.
    Assignment Selous Scouts,
    p321.
3   *Drum Magazine*: May 1980
4   *Wikipedia* Foundation
5   *Ibid.*
6   Cole, Barbara. *The Elite,*
    p431.

Epilogue
1   Zimbabwe Independent 11
    April 2007.
2   Martin Meredith, *The State
    of Africa*, p619.
3   *Ibid.* p620
4   Stiff, Peter. *Cry Zimbabwe,*
    p93
5   Martin Meredith, *The State
    of Africa Ibid.* p623.
6   *Ibid.* p624.
7   Raids on Gorongoza:
    Zimbabwe's Military
    Involvement in
    Mozambique1982 — 1992
    by Norman Mlambo.
8   Smith, Ian. *The Great
    Betrayal*, p372.
9   *Ibid.* p373.
10 Martin Meredith, *The State
    of Africa*, p630
11 Stiff, Peter, *Cry Zimbabwe,*
    p425
12 Stiff, Peter, *Cry Zimbabwe,*
    p429

Index